READING TO LEARN
IN THE
CONTENT AREAS

SECOND EDITION

READING TO LEARN IN THE CONTENT AREAS

JUDY S. RICHARDSON

Virginia Commonwealth University

RAYMOND F. MORGAN

Old Dominion University

WADSWORTH PUBLISHING COMPANY

Belmont, California

A Division of Wadsworth, Inc.

Editorial Assistant: Kate Peltier
Production: Cecile Joyner/The Cooper Company
Production Service Coordinator: Debby Kramer
Print Buyer: Karen Hunt
Permissions Editor: Peggy Meehan
Designer: Janet Bollow
Copy Editor: Margaret C. Tropp
Illustrators: John and Judy Waller
Cover: Rob Hugel
Compositor: Thompson Type
Cover Printer: Phoenix Color Corporation
Printer: Arcata Graphics/Fairfield

 This book is printed on acid-free recycled paper.

International Thomson Publishing
The trademark ITP is used under license.

1 2 3 4 5 6 7 8 9 10 — 98 97 96 95 94

LIBRARY OF CONGRESS CATALOGING-IN-PUBLICATION DATA

Richardson, Judy, 1945–
    Reading to learn in the content areas / Judy Richardson, Raymond F. Morgan. — 2nd ed.
      p. cm.
    Includes bibliographical references and index.
    ISBN 0–534–20328–0
    1.   Content area reading — United States.   I.   Morgan, Raymond F.
II. Title.
    LB1050.455.R53   1994   93-24218
    428.4'0712 — dc20

To my husband, Terry, who has always loved me, no matter how impossible I have been to live with, and to my three sons — Kevin, Darren, and Andrew — who have kept me grounded in reality when I tended to wander too far into the ivory tower.

JUDY S. RICHARDSON

To my wife, Sue, and sons, Jon and Chris, who have made the difference in my life.

RAYMOND F. MORGAN

CONTENTS

Part Three   Assistance and Reflection   151

CHAPTER 5

Assisting Reading Comprehension   152

Part Four   How PAR Works   247

CHAPTER 8

**Writing
and Reading
to Learn 287**

CHAPTER 9

**Study Strategies
and Systems
of Study 329**

CHAPTER 10

Cooperative Study for Reflection and Retention   371

Part Five   Special Applications   399

Who Should Read This Book?

This textbook concerns using reading to learn in content areas. It is designed for anyone who wants to know how to excite students to learn by using reading and the other language arts as tools for acquiring that knowledge. We are not writing about learning to read; that is for other authors, other courses. This book is for readers who have never studied about reading, as well as for those who have studied reading methodology but not ways to apply that information to subject area learning.

Why Did We Write This Book?

We love to read in order to learn about new things and to augment our knowledge. We always have, which is why we both have been teachers and college professors for 25 years. We believe in what we teach. We have a sense of humor, realizing that all serious learning must be put in perspective. We have ideas about how to share the joy of reading, thinking, and learning with students of all ages. We have ideas to share with you.

These are changing times; these are troubling times for educators. Education in the United States is being scrutinized and found wanting. Students are losing out because they are unable to think critically. Their reading seems to be superficial. Many students today can complete basic reading tasks, but not the complex tasks required for professional and personal advancement.

Teacher preparation has been criticized. Some say teachers learn too much content and not enough methodology; some say just the opposite. Some teachers have learned to teach content rather than to teach students the content.

We think we have some solutions to these problems. We believe that, if teachers learn to follow a simple instructional framework and teach strategically by using activities that demonstrate how reading can be a tool for learning, many of our classroom problems can be alleviated.

Special Features of This Textbook

1. Reader involvement is important in this textbook. We practice what we preach. We believe that readers need to be prepared to read, need some assistance to understand, and need to be guided to reflect on their reading. So we ask readers to engage in all three stages as they read each chapter of this textbook. We are also reader-friendly: We introduce new terms first with a checklist, then in boldface with explanation; we also maintain informality to keep our readers comfortable and interested.

2. We take a balanced approach, providing a realistic and practical treatment of reading and methodology issues, theory, research, and historical perspective. We emphasize the effect of the past on the present; we keep the baby and pour in new bath water.

3. We address teachers of primary through secondary grades. We look at reading in the classroom as a natural tool for learning, no matter what grade level or content area. We provide examples that show how an activity can work at different levels and in different contents.

4. We use one instructional framework, which reflects current thought but is uniquely ours: PAR (Preparation/Assistance/Reflection). We explain it, compare it, and stick to it throughout the book. Readers will appreciate this consistency and our constant reference to the framework.

5. Our organization is considerate of our readers. You can expect to find a graphic organizer at the beginning and end of each chapter; the Prepare to Read section that starts each chapter builds reader background and provides objectives; a one-minute summary (for the streamlined reader) is always provided; and Assisting as well as Reflecting activities provide chapter closure.

6. Visual literacy is emphasized in this textbook. We use plenty of visuals because visual literacy is the first literacy. One important visual is the Activity Chart on pages 548–549, which identifies specific activities for different content areas and grade levels.

7. Our philosophy is that reading and the other language arts work together. Just as students listen and discuss to learn, so do they read and write to learn. We integrate the communicative arts. When an activity is presented, we explore with the reader how that activity facilitates/encourages discussion, reading, and writing. We present information on writing to learn, an exciting area of current study, in Chapter 8.

8. Ours is a strategy-based approach. When readers learn about a new activity, they should understand that activity as a strategic means to aid learning. We present the activity as a way to enhance instruction and help teachers see how this activity can be both an instructional strategy and a learner strategy.

9. We include several unique chapters. Chapter 2 discusses the role of affect in reading to learn—a topic crucial to learning but so often neglected. Chapters 9 and 10 provide more attention to study skills than many content textbooks do. Chapter 11 presents ways to help the at-risk reader in the content classroom. These chapters cover information that is on the cutting edge of content area instruction.

What Is New to the Second Edition?

The Preparation chapters have been substantially rewritten to emphasize text coherence and structure as significant contributors to the readability of textbooks, with the role of readability formulas viewed within this larger context. At the same time, what the reader brings to the text continues to be important.

Chapters on comprehension have been revised to more clearly demonstrate the roles of Assistance (Chapter 5) and Reflection (Chapter 6). Chapter 11, Reading for At-Risk Students, now discusses the topics of students with limited English proficiency, students with low socioeconomic environments as well as low self-esteem, and students who are poor readers. Linda Gambrell, a noted expert in the field, contributed to this revised chapter.

Two new chapters have been added. Chapter 8, Writing and Reading to Learn, discusses the integral relationship of these two communicative arts and suggests several ways to incorporate writing into content subjects. Chapter 12, Supporting the Textbook with Literature, shows teachers how literature enhances content instruction and gives specific examples for such integration.

Current research and professional resources have been incorporated into the revision. Even more teacher-tried examples of activities — over 190 — are included in this edition than in the last, with the examples drawn from primary to secondary levels and from the major content areas, including vocational education examples.

We have endeavored to maintain a theory-to-practice balance. Visuals continue to play an important part in expressing our ideas; cartoons, diagrams, and examples are provided throughout.

Organization of This Book

The first two chapters are foundational. Chapter 1 discusses research and principles of content area instruction. In it you will discover our philosophy of teaching. Also, a capsule view of the PAR framework for instruction and how it works in two very different types of classrooms is given. Chapter 2 explains how to provide an affective focus for reading to learn.

Chapters 3 through 6 are PAR Framework chapters. Chapters 3 and 4 are the *Preparation* chapters. In them we present text and reader-based considerations for building reader background. Chapter 5 is an *Assistance* chapter; here we show why and how to provide an appropriate instructional context to develop comprehension. Chapter 6 is a *Reflection* chapter because it focuses on why and how to help readers think critically about their reading, extend their reading, and demonstrate their knowledge of their reading.

Chapters 7 through 10 demonstrate how PAR works. We show how vocabulary, writing, and study skills can be used at all phases of the PAR framework.

Chapters 11 and 12 are special-application chapters. Chapter 11 pertains to the challenge of working with students who are at risk of failure, and in Chapter 12 we explore the excitement of integrating literature in the content areas.

Instructor's Manual

The *Instructor's Manual* is designed to help instructors teach the class. It summarizes each chapter's main points, theories, and strategies and also provides test questions. With it, instructors will be able to: assign group activities for their classes; assign individual activities for homework; guide their students in analyzing content area reading material; select test items for multiple-choice, true/false, and essay tests; give out assignment sheets to their classes; and display the authors' Graphic Organizers and Vocabulary Inventories for each chapter.

Section I explains the features of the *Instructor's Manual*. Section II contains recommendations about Grouping. Section III contains Preparation, Assistance, and Reflection activities; teaching tips on how to use the activities; and other resources that may be used in class, such as quotes, suggestions for further reading, book lists, graphic organizers, vocabulary inventories for each chapter, and test items. In Section IV the authors provide possible assignments for the course, such as guides to analyze a chapter in a content area textbook.

Acknowledgments

We extend our thanks to our colleagues who encouraged us and aided and abetted us in this endeavor. We appreciate the comments of our students who used the first edition of the textbook and provided useful suggestions. We also gratefully acknowledge the contributions of the reviewers of this edition, who gave us such excellent suggestions throughout the writing of this textbook: Ernest Balajthy of the State University of New York at Geneseo, Shirley A. Biggs of the University of Pittsburgh, John A. Diehl of Georgia State University, Lisbeth Dixon-Krauss of the University of West Florida, Barbara Guzzetti of Arizona State University, James E. McGlinn of the University of North Carolina at Asheville, Daniel L. Pearce of Texas A&M at Corpus Christi, Elaine C. Stephens of Saginaw Valley State University, and Roger Stewart of the University of Wyoming.

Our writing was a more pleasant experience because of the support and kind assistance of our former editor, Suzanna Brabant, our production editor, Cecile Joyner, and our editorial assistant, Kate Peltier.

Judy S. Richardson
Raymond F. Morgan

PART ONE

FOUNDATIONS

CHAPTER 1

Content Reading Instruction

A PRINCIPLED VIEW AND A FRAMEWORK FOR INSTRUCTION

"We have this notion that teaching is standing up in front of a group of young people and delivering material, and either they get it or they don't. That just won't work anymore. The kids aren't getting it. We know that, and we have to make changes."

Frances Bolin, in Emily Sachar, *Shut Up and Let the Lady Teach*

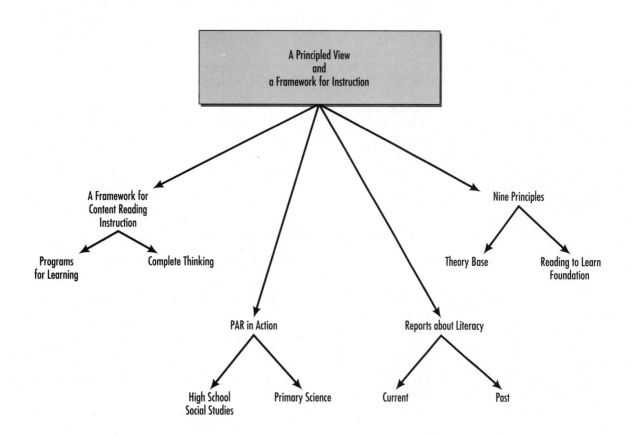

Prepare to Read

1. Following are five recommendations from the report entitled *Becoming a Nation of Readers*. Check those with which you agree. Be ready to explain your choices. After you have read this chapter, you will be asked to reconsider your selections.

    ___ Teachers should devote more time to comprehension instruction.

    ___ Children should spend more time in independent reading.

    ___ Children should spend more time writing.

    ___ Textbooks should contain more adequate explanations of important concepts.

    ___ Schools should cultivate an ethos that supports reading.

2. Following is a list of terms used in this chapter. Some of them may be familiar to you in a general context, but in this chapter they may be used in a different way than you are used to. Rate your knowledge by placing a + in front of those you are sure that you know, a √ in front of those you have some knowledge about, and a 0 in front of those you don't know. Be ready to locate and pay special attention to their meanings when they are presented in the chapter.

    ___ programs

    ___ two-finger thinking

    ___ framework

    ___ PAR

    ___ culturally illiterate

    ___ overlap factor

    ___ real reading

    ___ primary

    ___ visual literacy

    ___ assumptive teaching

    ___ fading

Objectives

As you read this chapter, focus your attention on the following objectives. You will:

1. be able to describe the reading framework PAR.

2. be able to apply PAR to two classroom examples.

3. become familiar with several recent reports about schooling and how these reports relate information about reading, thinking, and learning to content teaching.

4. become familiar with past recommendations about reading instruction and their relevance for current application in content classrooms.

5. become acquainted with nine principles for content reading instruction and understand the importance of each.

A Framework for Content Reading Instruction

"What do I do when I read? First, I open the book and remember where I left off last
time. Then I look ahead to see how long the next chapter is. Then I plan whether I
have time to finish a whole chapter in the time I have to read right now. Then I go
back and really start reading. I try to concentrate. Sometimes I get so involved that I
forget I have to stop!"

Interview with a reader

Programs for Learning

Most of us have a system for completing activities. The reader in our interview describes a set of steps she uses when beginning a reading activity. Hart (1983) believes that humans acquire and activate **programs** to learn. He defines a program as "a fairly fixed sequence of steps to achieve some goal" (p. 6). Programs are used consistently as a reliable way for a person to accomplish an objective. A person usually follows a sequence of steps in starting a car; another person might reorder the steps, but still performs the same actions to start the car. Using a word processing program is another example. Although Microsoft Word is complex while Bank Street Writer is simpler, the basic features and steps for use are similar: both programs will allow the user to record data, revise data, and save and print the product.

Any program becomes fairly automatic with practice. As the steps are learned and applied with facility, concentration on the final goal becomes more important. After a person learns to start a car, for example, the act of starting it is relegated to a position of lesser importance than driving to a destination. After a person learns a word processing program, writing the material is what becomes important, not the steps that facilitate the writing. Knowing the program allows the focus to shift to accomplishing the goal in the most efficient manner.

Similarly, students read to learn by using programs. For example, a student may develop a program to identify the characteristics of a story. Once the program is learned and applied to the reading of new stories, the learner can focus on the theme, plot, and characters in stories. Knowing these characteristics facilitates the learner's appreciation of the story. Mathematical word problems are easier to solve if students learn a consistent set of steps to follow; these steps will help them identify the problem to be solved and the clues to its solution. To help students realize the steps they should follow to learn the content information, teachers can introduce programs for learning. As a result, students learn strategies that can be used independently of the teacher.

Complete versus Incomplete Thinking

Optimal programs include enough steps to accomplish the goal. Many students try to manage with fewer steps than they should, which ultimately causes them confusion. As long as the learning task is simple, skipping steps may work. But when the task becomes more complicated, the student who has trouble identifying all of the steps will have to slow down and rediscover those steps, or grind to a halt. This short-cutting of steps has been called **two-finger thinking** (de Bono, 1976), akin to the two-finger typing of someone who has never learned the proper positioning of fingers on the keyboard. Typing with two fingers may be adequate as long as the typist has a lot of time and needs to type only a few pages. Since the purpose of typing is usually to save time, however, it is preferable to take the time initially to learn to type well, thereby saving much more time later.

Two-finger thinking is incomplete. The learner is missing steps crucial to achieving the learning goal; it is like thinking with only part of the brain. Many readers may be victims of such incomplete thinking if they try to use an incomplete program: just turning pages is a way of seeing material, but it is not necessarily a way of comprehending.

Similarly, teachers who have learned to rely only on the teacher's manual for their instructional resources are victims of incomplete thinking. Houseman (1987) experienced great difficulty in trying to teach social studies to fourth-graders until she completed a content reading course and discovered new ideas. What Houseman learned enabled her to expand her program for teaching social studies. She reports a very positive change in her own and her students' receptiveness to social studies after using her newfound knowledge.

Characteristics of a Framework

A **framework** is the arrangement of the basic parts of something. It is an organized plan condensed to a series of steps, usually represented by key words. A framework represents a program because it suggests how to do something. Because a framework is a model for completing a task, it must be complete. All pertinent steps must be identified. Hence, a framework for instruction should be an aid to thinking and learning and a way to activate student programs for learning. An instructional framework that identifies successful components of a content lesson facilitates the relationship among reading, thinking, and learning.

Frameworks for content reading instruction are becoming increasingly popular (Herber, 1978; Singer & Donlan, 1985; Vaughan & Estes, 1986). This is so because frameworks represent programs that are complete and flexible as well as easily implemented by teachers. They are explanations or "how-tos" of the instructional process; they guide the learning process. The most popular content reading frameworks include the same three basic assumptions: (1) The learner must be ready to learn; thus, the teacher must prepare the learner beforehand. (2) The learner must be guided through the learning; that is, the teacher must develop comprehension during the lesson. (3) The learner should review what was learned; to this end, the teacher must provide after-reading opportunities, such as comprehension checks. If these basic steps are repeated consistently in the instructional sequence, the learner begins to use them independently of the teacher, in a self-instructional manner.

It does not matter what key words are used in a framework, as long as they stimulate recall of the program represented by the framework. Table 1.1 shows a

TABLE 1.1

A Comparison of Content-Area Reading (CAR) Frameworks

IF	DRA	ARC	PAR
Herber 1978	Singer & Donlan 1985	Vaughan & Estes 1986	Richardson & Morgan 1990; 1994

Preparation
  Motivate
  Provide
    background
  Develop purposes, anticipation
  Provide direction
  Develop language
	Determine background
	
	Build background
	
	Prequestion and read
		Anticipation
		
		Realization
			Preparation
			  Text-based solutions
			  Reader-based solutions
			
			Assistance
			  Text coherence
			  Instructional context

Guidance
  Develop reading guides
  Develop reasoning guides
Independence
	Review actively
	
	Provide extension
		
		Contemplation
			
			Reflection
			  Critical thinking
			  Extending the reading experience
			  Demonstrating learning

comparison of four content-area reading (CAR) frameworks, including ours: Preparation, Assistance, Reflection (PAR). Herber's instructional framework (IF) is considered to be the first CAR framework. Singer and Donlan's modification of the directed reading activity (DRA) for content instruction has components similar to Vaughan and Estes' ARC (anticipation, realization, contemplation) and to PAR. All four frameworks have similar steps. Rosenshine and Stevens (1984) also found these same basic steps in the instructional sequences they studied.

PAR – A Framework for Instruction

PAR, which stands for Preparation, Assistance, and Reflection, is a framework for content reading instruction. In the Preparation step, teachers need to consider text problems and student background. In the Assistance step, teachers need to provide an instructional context for text. In the Reflection step, teachers use the material that was read to provide extension, enrichment, and critical thinking opportunities. Only at this step can teachers determine whether students have comprehended the material. After teachers have consistently modeled the PAR steps, students will begin to adopt the steps as they read on their own. Each step will be discussed in greater depth, with suggested activities and examples, in subsequent chapters of this book. Two examples of content lesson units that apply a PAR framework are presented in this first chapter to provide the reader with an overview of PAR.

Special Features of PAR

PAR is a new acronym, but it represents the basic sequence of steps included in other content instructional frameworks. We coined the acronym PAR deliberately to develop an association with the golf term *par*, which means to complete a hole of golf taking only an allotted number of strokes but not exceeding the limit. Golfers usually feel very pleased that they've played a good game if they achieve *par for the course*. By achieving par, they have reduced their *handicap*, or overcome any disadvantages so they can equalize their chances of winning. In the same way, we want teachers to be satisfied with their instructional performance in *their* courses. In the words of one teacher we know: "The purpose of PAR is to cut down on your students' handicaps!"

PAR's three basic steps are applicable in any content area and at any grade level, for both narrative and expository material. Following these instructional steps ensures maximum thinking and learning from the reading experience. The basic terms — Preparation, Assistance, Reflection — are already part of the professional language of teachers. But the terms are combined in a new way to create an acronym that we hope will form a special association for content teachers. Just as achieving par is an aspiration of many golfers, we hope that PAR will inspire teachers to follow the three steps of Preparation, Assistance, and Reflection that promote solid instruction and learning.

PAR in Action: Two Examples

Following are two illustrations of how PAR might be applied by teachers at different grade levels and in different content areas. These are "big picture" examples that show how teachers might use PAR in their content instruction. In each situation, the same basic program, or framework — PAR — was used. The specific activities described worked for the teachers who selected them; others might work better for you. However, both teachers were able to use the same framework and lead their learners strategically before, during, and after reading about the subject. Because these examples are meant only to provide an overview, directions for constructing the activities will be found in succeeding chapters, where they are presented in a larger context.

EXAMPLE 1: PAR FOR A TENTH-GRADE SOCIAL STUDIES TEACHER

Mr. Smith, a tenth-grade social studies teacher, wanted to introduce some value thinking using the topic of capital punishment. Fortunately, he was able to locate an abundance of material on this topic. He selected a letter written in February 1960 by Caryl Chessman (Gervitz, 1963), a San Quentin death-row inmate, to California's governor, Edmund Brown. This short, charged reading, he thought,

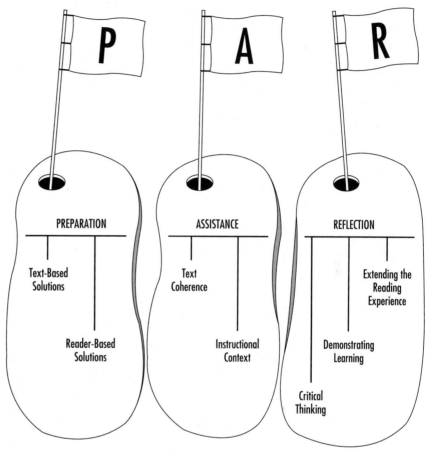

PREPARATION

Text-Based
Solutions

Reader-Based
Solutions

ASSISTANCE

Text
Coherence

Instructional
Context

REFLECTION

Extending the
Reading
Experience

Demonstrating
Learning

Critical
Thinking

Developed by Dawn Watson and Walter Richards.

would entice his students with its personal element more effectively than a textbook entry.

Chessman's letter is challenging material, stylistically sophisticated and enriched with vocabulary usually beyond the reading experiences of tenth-grade students. Mr. Smith considered its match for his students by using a checklist (see Chapter 3). He decided that, although the letter would be challenging for his students to read, it would nevertheless be very useful for his and his students' purposes.

How would he instruct using this material? What was important to teach? Keeping the content subject foremost is a content teacher's job. So he studied the selected letter to identify major concepts he wanted to teach. He saw that the letter was very well written and so might serve as a model for writing persuasive letters. He saw that Chessman's rich vocabulary might serve as a model for teaching word meanings and associations. He saw that he could teach a history lesson as well, since this letter was written in 1960 and might illustrate how the same issue has been debated and regulated over a long period of time. Chessman's references to the interdependence of the three branches of government in making decisions about capital punishment could also help Mr. Smith explain the American system of government. A lesson on social systems in the United States was also possible.

However, he probably could not teach all of this to his students unless he used this material for far longer than he originally intended. He considered what he knew about his students. They would read challenging material thoughtfully and eagerly if they enjoyed it and saw a need for the lesson. But he had noticed that they seemed rather vague about the three branches of government. Because value thinking about capital punishment was his primary reason for using this letter, he decided on the following major goals:

1. To present the topic of capital punishment by providing one very compelling viewpoint and provoking discussion.
2. To introduce the three branches of government by considering how laws about capital punishment can be made and changed within that organizational system.

Although we cannot provide his entire lesson, we can show how the reading activities he selected enhanced this lesson.

The first step in PAR is Preparation, which includes studying what the text offers and what the reader brings to the text in order to prepare relevant learning opportunities. Mr. Smith had already determined some background as he considered what he knew about his students' reading habits and understanding of government. Next, he determined and built background using PreP (Langer, 1981, p. 154), which will be explained in Chapter 4. Part one of PreP is "initial associations" with concepts. Thus, Mr. Smith asked his students to tell him all the facts they knew about capital punishment and the associations the term brought to mind. He was pleasantly surprised to discover that his students already knew a great deal, as the list he compiled illustrates.

controversial	crime	death row
execution	electric chair	Mecklenburg boys
pain	fried	Briley brothers
murder	appeal	stay of execution
jail	protest	

Part two of PreP calls for reflecting on the initial associations, so he asked students what made them think of particular responses. In part three of PreP, which calls for reformulation of knowledge, he asked whether they had gained any new ideas about capital punishment. By using these steps, he helped students build their own background of information. As a result, they felt more confident that they would understand the material about to be studied and were more receptive to learning.

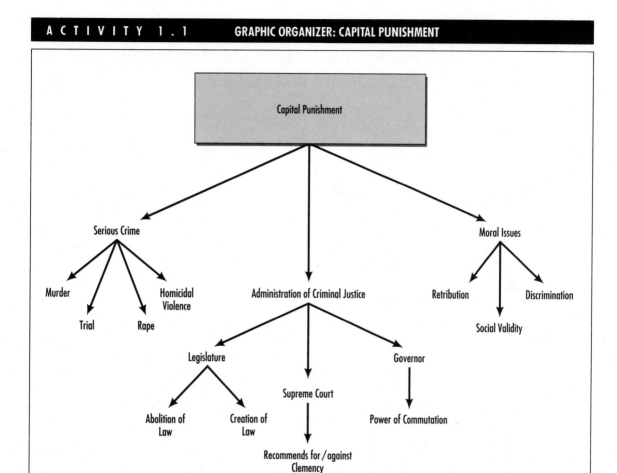

In considering their responses, Mr. Smith could see that his students had at least a partial understanding of the information presented in the Chessman letter. Since the only word association they gave that related at all to administrative structure was *appeal*, he was reassured that his goal of teaching in this area was important. Using some of the responses his students gave and relying on vocabulary in Chessman's letter that illustrated his goals, he then designed a "graphic organizer" (see Activity 1.1). This technique, described in Chapter 3, is a visual means of providing further background for the reading assignment. He presented it to the class by showing and explaining each of the three major categories one at a time. He did not define unknown words, but asked his students to notice how those words were used in the letter.

The second step in PAR is Assistance. To assist his students' reading, Mr. Smith first explained that Chessman was a death-row prisoner when he wrote his letter about capital punishment to Governor Brown. He said that when he read the letter, he was emotionally swayed and found himself reacting to capital punishment in a new way. He hoped that the letter would have an impact on them, too. To establish a purpose for reading, he suggested that, as they read, they refer to the list of terms they had generated earlier and compare it to terms Chessman used. He also encouraged them to refer often to the graphic organizer as they read what Chessman wrote about the three branches of government. He made sure that copies of their terms and the organizer were available.

When students finished reading, he developed comprehension with a discussion in which they compared their list of terms to Chessman's terms. They then made a second, expanded list of terms about capital punishment. Mr. Smith asked them to explain why they thought he had constructed the graphic organizer as he did. To further develop their comprehension, he "mapped" their responses to this question: What might Governor Brown do now? The resulting map is shown in Activity 1.2. (For more information about mapping, see Chapter 5.)

The third step in PAR is Reflection. To enrich and extend his students' thinking, Mr. Smith invited a judge to speak to the class. He also asked them to be on the lookout during the following week for any information on capital punishment and on the administrative procedures related to it. Next, as a critical thinking activity, he asked students to form small groups and map responses to these questions: How are decisions made about capital punishment? Is capital punishment justified?

As a final Reflection activity, Mr. Smith asked students to demonstrate their comprehension. If they could demonstrate what they had learned, he would know that he could continue to the next topic. He chose a nontraditional test format. (For more information about designing tests, see Chapter 7.) Capitalizing on his activities, he presented the same graphic organizer, but with some gaps (see Activity 1.3).

He asked students to fill in the gaps and explain their choices. Then he asked them to answer a question they had previously mapped: How are decisions made about capital punishment? Using their maps as references, they were to write an essay that included at least three ways decisions are made. Each paragraph was to discuss one way, with supporting information. In a fourth paragraph, they were to argue two points of view about capital punishment.

EXAMPLE 2: PAR IN A PRIMARY SCIENCE LESSON

Mrs. Jones, a primary teacher, wished to set up an aquarium in her classroom so the children could observe goldfish and begin to realize how an ecosystem operates. She wanted the children to help select the type of goldfish for the aquarium and to learn how to take care of them. Rather than tell them what to do, she preferred to use written materials as the source of information, because she believed that her students needed practice reading to learn and would find discovery more interesting and appropriate than lecture.

A C T I V I T Y   1 . 2   **MAPPING**

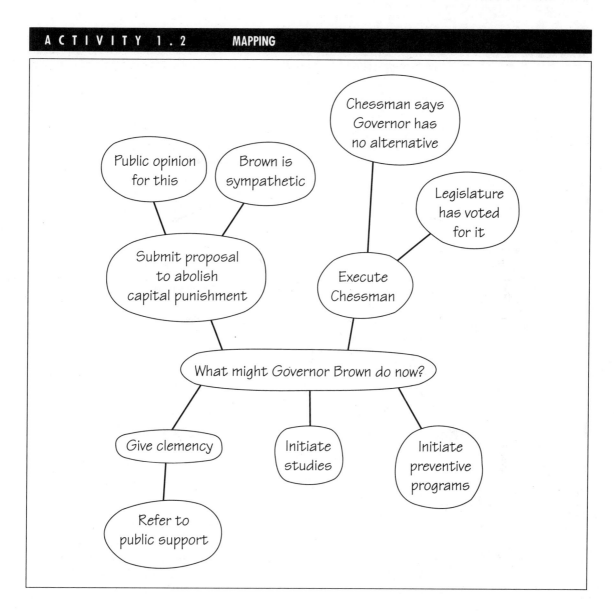

To find appropriate materials, she consulted the school media specialist, who suggested several informational books written for young audiences. Mrs. Jones prepared her readers by selecting several books that matched their reading and interest levels and allowing them to browse in these books to gather ideas before any instruction began. She placed all of the books on classroom shelves and selected *All About Goldfish as Pets*, by Kay Cooper, to read aloud to the class. She decided on Cooper's book because it provides a lot of information about goldfish and is divided into short sections, each of which she could read in a time

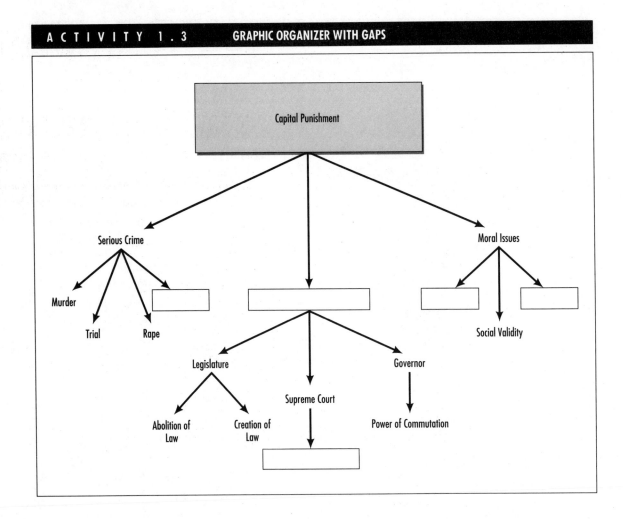

frame that matched her students' attention span. By using the checklist discussed in Chapter 3, she was satisfied that *All About Goldfish* was a suitable resource.

Next, she formulated her goals and objectives. The following were her overall goals:

1. Children will learn about an ecosystem.
2. Based on reading about goldfish, children will make informed choices about providing the best environment for them.

Her specific objectives were as follows:

1. Children will select from many kinds of goldfish the kind they want to raise.
2. Children will identify the materials needed to equip the aquarium.
3. Children will learn what goldfish need to live and will monitor their goldfish for several months.

Parts of

eye

gill

mouth

fins

fins

The Goldfish

Care of

food

aquarium

disease

small amount

plants

filter

fungus

dry

treated water

fin rot

Koi

whiskers

big tail

fingertail

Types

big eye

celestial

black

moor
telescope

The first step in PAR is Preparation. To determine what the children already knew, Mrs. Jones asked them to tell her about goldfish. As they answered, she wrote their responses on the board. They said:

They are gold.   They are good pets.   They have to live in water.
They swim.   Sometimes they die.   They have fins.

Mrs. Jones was satisfied that her class already had some knowledge and even firsthand experience with goldfish, so she did not have to "start from scratch" in her instruction. She began to build background by using their responses to construct a graphic organizer, shown in Activity 1.4. This graphic organizer, which is very different from the one shown for tenth-graders, is suitable for primary children.

When she showed the graphic organizer to the children, she used their list of sentences as a base for her explanation. "You said that goldfish are gold, but there are fish in the goldfish family of a different color. You said that goldfish have fins; different goldfish have differently shaped fins."

Next, Mrs. Jones assisted her students in their learning by guiding their listening behavior. (Chapter 10 describes such listening guidelines.) She told them to listen carefully for all of the new information they heard about goldfish as she read one section of *All About Goldfish* to them. Such a statement sets a purpose for listening. After reading the section, she asked the children to tell her the new information they had heard. She wrote their responses on the board. Then she read the list, told them to listen again, and reread the section of the book. The children then revised their list. Such an activity develops comprehension, as well as demonstrating the first steps of note taking. Now the students were ready to decide what type of goldfish to purchase (they selected black moor telescopes). Then they planned what would go into the aquarium and prepared it 24 hours in advance so the environment would be right for the goldfish.

For Reflection, Mrs. Jones encouraged her students to leaf through the many books on goldfish and add to their knowledge. They collected information, writing it down or asking another student or the teacher to record facts. The children then used these notes to organize and write a group report entitled "An Ecosystem for Fish." She guided their writing by encouraging students to plan, draft, and revise their report.

Mrs. Jones did not assess comprehension by testing. The best evidence of learning came when the children discovered that their fish had white spots on their fins. They researched this problem to find out about fin rot and its treatment. When they cured their fish, Mrs. Jones knew that they had learned.

Special Note: Even though many primary children have not yet learned to read with proficiency, PAR is applicable when reading is viewed in a total communicative arts perspective. The teacher may be the main reader; for the students, listening, discussion, and comprehension will take the place of actual reading. Even at the high-school level, reading should not be isolated from the other communicative arts. Listening activities are often a welcome change for all students.

Literacy in the Schools

An Overview of Recent Reports

Education in the United States has received a great deal of attention in the past several years. Miklos (1982) provides a synopsis of the National Assessment of Educational Progress (NAEP) data through 1981, which indicate that elementary students were doing well in the reading basics but that older students showed declining inferential comprehension skills. The consensus of several NAEP reports published in the mid- to late 1980s is that schools are performing well in teaching the fundamentals of language arts, but not in teaching advanced reading and expressive skills.

The Reading Report Card: Progress Toward Excellence in Our Schools (1985) describes trends in reading achievement over a 14-year period for students at ages 9, 13, and 17, using data from four national assessments. Although young readers seem to be achieving better in this decade than in the last, students still seem to have the most difficulty with higher levels of comprehension. *The Writing Report Card: Writing Achievement in American Schools* (1987) indicates that students, as measured in 4th, 8th, and 11th grades, can write to communicate only at a minimal level and have difficulty using critical thinking and organizational skills to express themselves.

Kirsch and Jungeblut (1986) sampled the U.S. population at ages 21 to 25. In *Literacy: Profiles of America's Young Adults*, they portray this group as able to read simple material with facility but unable to understand complex material nearly so well. They conclude that although the United States may not have a major *illiteracy* problem, we do have a *literacy* problem. Applebee, Langer, and Mullis, in *Learning to Be Literate in America* (1987), summarize several NAEP surveys and caution that schools need to help students learn to learn.

All of these reports, published within a few years of each other, indicate that students experience difficulty with higher-level reading and writing skills such as critical thinking, drawing inferences, and applying what is read.

Caution is necessary in embracing these conclusions. Many of the reports seem "fraught with design and interpretation problems" (Kaestle, Damon-Moore, Stedman, Tinsley, & Tollinger, 1991) and may imply a worse scenario than actually exists. Test scores for children who experience a strong literacy climate at home have remained stable. Schools really are doing a better job than some interpretations of national test results may indicate. Students are learning what they are taught (Westbury, 1992). Bracey (1992) suggests that we take a positive approach. Instead of bashing schools, we need to get to work on the problems of those schools truly in crisis and recognize that the educational system reflects societal values.

Even if the national test scores are not so grim, the conditions for learning in classrooms leave much to be desired. Goodlad, in *A Place Called School* (1984), comments on the "sameness and emotional flatness" (p. 100) of American classrooms. He observed students completing exercise after exercise without active involvement. He saw little opportunity for students to use knowledge in an active thinking environment. In his best-seller *Cultural Literacy* (1987), Hirsch describes the problem of persons who can "read" but don't understand. He attributes this problem to students' general lack of exposure to "essential" knowledge. Such students, writes Allan Bloom in *The Closing of the American Mind* (1987), are **culturally illiterate**: "To put the matter at its baldest, we live in a thought-world, and the thinking has gone very bad indeed" (p. 17). Bloom further asserts that "our students have lost the practice of and the taste for reading" (p. 62).

Fredericks (1992) contends that the solution Hirsch and Bloom propose — ensuring that students gain "essential knowledge" — is less effective than teaching students to *think* about what they read. In *Becoming a Nation of Readers*, Anderson, Hiebert, Scott, and Wilkinson (1984), after reviewing a large amount of the professional literature on reading, have drawn several conclusions and have recommended ways to improve the reading performance of American students. They advocate a greater emphasis on literacy education, particularly in the area of reading for meaning. Five of their recommendations were presented for your consideration at the beginning of this chapter.

Students are not the only ones who need more effective education, according to recent reports. In *A Nation Prepared* (1986), Branscomb et al. recommend better training of prospective and practicing teachers, including a broader background in the content areas and the liberal arts, as well as instruction in methodology. Goodlad (Callan, 1990) encourages universities to educate teachers who can pay attention to the "educational health of school, education and community." The consensus is that teachers need more exposure to information that will enable them to attain — and then teach — higher levels of literacy in a positive environment.

The implications of all these reports are disturbing but relevant to content-area teachers as they plan their instruction. It would seem that students are *not* learning what content teachers would like them to learn. Many current reports indicate that American students

1. are unable to express themselves effectively, in either oral or written form.
2. are unable to make inferences from their reading.
3. are unable to think critically about what they read.
4. cannot process complex written material with facility.
5. do not recognize a large body of content knowledge that experts consider essential for informed readers.
6. do not prefer reading as a way to learn.

But content teachers depend on written materials as a primary instructional source. They expect that students in their classes will be able to process that material with facility, inferring and reading critically. They assume that students will be able to express their understanding of the material orally and on tests. They expect that students possess a certain amount of knowledge and have a desire to read to learn. The mismatch between what many research reports indicate about students' literacy profile and what most content teachers assume creates a grave instructional dilemma. Even acknowledging that the schools are doing better than some interpretations of reports would indicate, most educators think that schools should improve a great deal. A recent Delta Kappa Gamma poll (Day & Anderson, 1992) identified confronting "at-risk" issues and advancing literacy as two of the leading educational concerns for the 1990s.

What are the answers? Some can be found in past research and writing about literacy, others in current research. In the sections that follow, we will present some suggestions from the past and a set of principles to guide the future of reading to learn.

Does Anyone Here Hear Huey?

Professional concern with the problem of underprepared readers is not new. Although most of the reports cited so far were written within the past decade, their findings are less startling when we realize that others have written about these problems and offered suggestions over a span of many years. Here, for example, are some of the tenets advocated by Edmund Burke Huey in 1908:

> The home is the natural place for learning to read.
>
> Reading should always be accomplished with a purpose in mind that is known by the student.
>
> Reading should not be an "exercise," done as a formal process or end in itself. Rather it should be meaningful, with intrinsic interest and value. Children should learn to read "real literature" — books, papers, records, letters, children's own experiences or thoughts. These should be read as the need arises in a child's life.
>
> Reading matter should be sufficiently interesting to challenge children and thereby discipline their minds for lifelong learning.
>
> Children should be taught to group essential meanings, select and gather books for their own purposes, ignore the irrelevant, and contemplate the value of what is read.
>
> Study skills such as library skills and note taking should be taught as early as possible in the elementary grades.
>
> Real reading should increase rather than decrease in importance among school studies.
>
> We should read the classics for the same reason we read in the sciences: for information, for control of nature, and for disciplining the mind.

If readers did not know that Huey's *Psychology and Pedagogy of Reading* was published in 1908, they might well think that these tenets were "modern" in origin. Huey's book was recently reprinted because, according to Robinson (1977), the ideas discussed are as relevant, or more so, today than they were in 1908. Bloom and Hirsch would probably agree with Huey about the need for wide reading. Some of Huey's tenets are almost identical to the first several recommendations in *Becoming a Nation of Readers*. His views also seem to support the recommendations of the NAEP studies.

Of similar interest to modern educators is *The Twenty-Fourth Yearbook of the National Society for the Study of Education* (1925), whose objectives were to enable the reader (1) to react intelligently to the world and appreciate it, (2) to develop strong reasons to read and a permanent interest in reading, and (3) to form attitudes, skills, and habits for the many different reading activities that readers might encounter. These objectives are still viable for teachers in content-area subjects today, and they still drive the research and writing of professionals in the reading field.

Robinson (1977) calls this contribution of information from the past to current literature the **overlap factor**. Herber (1987) also refers to the concept of overlap in the use of past reports to influence current knowledge. By considering the past as well as the present, content teachers can find much that is relevant to help them plan the best instruction for their students.

Nine Principles for Content Reading Instruction

Did you laugh when you saw the cartoon about the one-meter fun run? We hope so. The trouble is, too many students don't laugh when they encounter a joke like this. Why? Don't they have a sense of humor? Or is it that they don't understand the joke? For most students, the latter is probably true. Clues to the joke are available: a mouse on a treadmill; "fun run"; metric terminology. But if students don't know that a meter is only a yard, then seeing the mouse on the "fun run" may not make much impact. The clues for this cartoon illustrate some of the basic problems in content reading instruction today: the communicative arts, including visual literacy, are not stressed enough in instruction and are not used by students as they read; students often lack a personal store of experiences and do not see that they must insert themselves into the act of reading; reading words without meaning sabotages critical thinking in the content areas; teachers make undue assumptions about what students know. In short, students are not engaged in enough **real reading**! The nine principles presented here are designed to deal with these problems.

Teachers who, as a result of professional study, are able to articulate their beliefs about teaching are in a good position to improve their instruction. Like all learners, teachers will alter their approaches if they see a need to do so. We, the authors of this textbook, have altered our own instruction based on current research. To help us consistently practice what we believe, we have encapsulated our approach in nine principles. By sharing these principles with teachers and demonstrating how they relate to content-area teaching, we hope to influence teachers to consider instructional changes in their own classrooms.

These principles are grounded in theory. As Wassermann (1987) notes, "the word *theory* has a bad reputation among educational practitioners" (p. 462). Many teachers think that theory has nothing to do with the classroom, perhaps because theory has been presented to them in isolation from its application. But we think that when teachers ask for "what works," they are also asking for the reasons why a particular technique works so that they can replicate it in optimal circumstances. We believe that teachers want more than "a bag of tricks." They know that superimposing an activity on students in the wrong circumstances can be a teaching disaster. No activity has much merit aside from the construct underlying it (Hayes, Stahl, & Simpson, 1991). However, when teachers present

1-METER FUN RUN

Developed by Robert Davis. Reprinted with permission.

a strategy—such as helping students prepare to read by eliciting prior knowledge—through appropriate activities, students learn. Teachers want theory that makes sense because it explains why some activities work well at a particular time in the instruction.

Just as there is really "nothing new under the sun," the principles we present are not necessarily new. They are distinct expressions of what we believe, based on our own study and the study of others. As we present each principle, we recognize the overlap factor by introducing some of the history, as well as recent insights, underlying the principle. After introducing them here, we will return to these principles throughout the textbook.

1. The communicative arts are tools for thinking and learning in content subjects.

The traditional communicative arts (sometimes called language arts) are listening, speaking, reading, and writing. In natural circumstances, listening and speaking are almost inseparable. Someone talks, someone listens, response and interaction occur. Writers express thoughts as a result of listening, speaking, and reading. Readers read writers' thoughts. Kellogg (1972) describes the communicative arts as blocks that build on one another. From a base of experience, a child begins to listen, then speak. Lubarsky (1987) notes that talking is pivotal in enriching the other language arts. Huey seems to have agreed that listening and speaking are the foundation for reading and writing. One cannot use one communicative art without also using another. This integration occurs with greater facility as children practice each literacy.

Yet school environments are often artificial rather than natural in their application of informative communication. Usually, teachers talk and students listen so much of the time that little response and interaction can take place. Gagne (1965) noted that learners remember about 10 percent of what they read, 20 percent of what they hear, 30 percent of what they see, and 70 percent of what they say. Who *says* the most in schools? Teachers! We might conclude, then, that those learning the most in classrooms may be the teachers. When Armbruster (1992) reviewed the 51 articles on content reading published in *The Reading Teacher* from 1969 to 1991, one trend she noted was the "emphasis on the importance of integrating writing and reading in content instruction." It is our premise that students can learn more if they spend more time practicing all of the language arts in their content subjects.

Subject matter and language are inextricably bound. But the main concern for the subject-matter teacher is teaching the content. Nila Banton Smith (1965) reminds readers that the term *primer* did not originally mean "first book to read," as it does today, but referred to the contents of a book as being **primary**, or foremost. Today, the content of a subject is still primary for the teacher, as it should be. But using the communicative arts as a major learning tool creates a very positive combination for enhancing critical thinking and learning. For example, Feathers and Smith (1987) report an observational study of content instruction in elementary and secondary classrooms. Although content predominated in instruction at both levels, content was presented differently in the different grades. Secondary teachers transmitted content mainly through lectures or text reading, whereas elementary teachers infused content with more of the communicative arts. The latter method was seen to be more effective.

Kane, a social studies teacher, puts it this way: "Education is premised upon language. . . . You cannot separate language from education. Language not only conveys, it shapes. If you increase or refine the ability of a human being to use language, you literally affect his mind. You cannot deal with any subject on any level without language. Indeed, how you use language affects the subject matter" (1984). In short, listening, speaking, reading, and writing are integral to learning; they are tools for thinking and learning. They enable learning to occur by providing a form in which signals can be transmitted to and from the brain. They are demonstrations of learning. Thus, the communicative arts are *essential* to teaching content-area subjects, and teachers will want to encourage students' use of all the communicative arts as effective thinking and learning tools. As we present activities in this book, we will often identify how they facilitate the use of language to enhance content learning. The role of writing, in particular, will be discussed in Chapter 8.

FIGURE 1.1

Stage three of literacy development: visual literacy and its interactive relationship with the oral and written languages

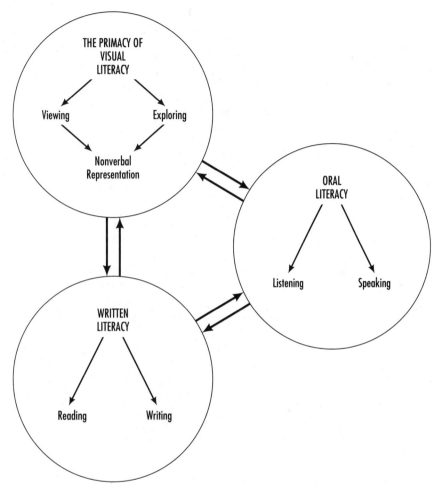

From R. Sinatra, *Visual Literacy Connections to Thinking, Reading and Writing*, 1986. Courtesy of Charles C Thomas, Publisher, Springfield, Illinois.

2. Literacy includes not only the traditional communicative arts but also visual literacy.

Sometimes communication occurs most easily through nonverbal, **visual literacy**. For instance, a picture of a pie divided into pieces may convey the concept of fractions more effectively than a page of explanation. Sinatra (1986) calls visual literacy the first and most pervasive literacy. Sinatra's model of literacy development suggests the interactive relationship of visual literacy with the oral and written literacies (see Figure 1.1).

Visual literacy, which conveys emotion through such means as illustration, art, and music, precedes listening and builds experiences necessary to thinking and learning. Visual literacy is impressionistic and action-oriented; the scribbles that young children call writing are a manifestation of visual literacy. Teachers discover that when they make use of visual aids such as graphs and pictures, they ensure a concomitant and reinforcing approach for many students and an alternative for those who excel in visual but not traditional literacy. Because visual literacy has implications for the affective aspects of instruction, it will be discussed further in Chapter 2. In addition, several activities presented in this book capitalize on visual literacy.

3. Reading for meaning is a highly individualized process influenced by the reader's personal store of experiences and knowledge.

Even though many people may share the same experience, read the same book, or hear the same lecture, the thinking and learning that occur will differ from individual to individual because of what each brings to the experience. Persons relate to a common body of knowledge in different ways because of what they already know — or don't know. Thus, for example, converting to the metric system will probably be more difficult for those learners who were taught measurements in terms of inches, feet, and miles instead of centimeters, meters, and kilometers. Readers unfamiliar with Tennyson's poem "The Charge of the Light Brigade" would probably think the phrase *Charge of the Right Frigate* a strange choice of words for a headline accompanying an article on naval buildup; they would not see the headline as a play on words. If learners cannot find relevance in a subject, they are likely to ignore it. Teachers, then, must become aware of what previous knowledge and experiences their students possess about a particular concept in content subjects. They can then use this information to generate assisted reading that is directed, meaningful, and highly personalized.

4. The most effective thinking and learning occur when critical reading is encouraged.

The act of reading should provoke thought. Real reading is an active, thinking-related process. As soon as readers can pay more attention to the meaning of words than to their recognition, they can begin to think and learn about the material itself rather than about reading the material. One of the messages of the reports mentioned earlier in this chapter is that students lack critical thinking skills. It is not that students are incapable of critical thinking; they just have not had the practice. By using the tools of literacy and being immersed in a thinking climate, students can practice these skills. Raths, Wassermann, Jones, and Rothstein (1986) believe that teachers who provide students with extensive practice in thinking will train thinkers. Readers must be challenged to think critically about what they read. Where only "lower-order" exercises are provided, thinking deficits will occur (Wassermann, 1987).

The concern for teaching critical reading is not new. Robinson (1977) cites Keagy, a key reading figure in the late 1700s, who emphasized that thinking during reading is the crucial element in the act of reading. Following Keagy in the late 1800s, Horace Mann and others advocated a thinking approach to reading instruction. This emphasis has remained fairly consistent in the literature, with proponents such as Nila Banton Smith, Russell Stauffer (1969b), and more recently, Frank Smith. Most authorities agree, and have for a long time, that critical reading leads to effective thinking and learning. The problem seems to be "that most teachers do not teach these skills" (Beyer, 1984). We speculate that teachers feel constrained by an overload of prescribed curriculum goals that seem to stress lower-level reading comprehension. Hence students are being taught to be regurgitators of information rather than thinkers, reasoners, and problem solvers.

Special Note: Literal reading is often a necessary first step toward critical reading. While we emphasize critical reading, we are not disregarding the importance of factual reading. A reader who already understands material at a factual level and is able to interpret what is read can respond critically with greater success. However, many students who are unable to recall names or dates can predict and infer. It is probably because teachers realize the necessity of literal reading that so much classroom time is spent on literal recall of reading material, to the detriment of higher-level thinking and reading comprehension. What we must realize is that only literal knowledge relevant to higher-order thinking should be stressed. By being discriminating, we can guide readers to discriminate.

Piaget (1952) observed that children need to form concrete associations before they can form concepts. Descriptions of comprehension levels include a literal or factual level that precedes the critical level. Our principle 3 assumes a store of experience *and* knowledge that a reader must have before reading for learning and thinking can begin. Persons cannot think about nothing; there must be a base for thinking and learning. However, we do think that too much emphasis is placed on knowing facts and not enough on knowing when and how to use them to learn. Teachers need to design content lessons in which the facts have a place in the larger scheme of thinking and learning.

5. Meaningful reading about content subjects is a lifetime experience that should start early and continue throughout life.

Learning content material is part of most school curricula from first grade on. Some schools even introduce science, math, and social studies material in kindergarten. *The Weekly Reader*, that ubiquitous early-grades newspaper, contains content material. Because most children are still learning to read in the early grades, reading to learn may not be employed as often as visualizing, listening, and speaking to learn. However, as a result of current studies on how literacy emerges, reading and writing to learn are being advocated more frequently for children in early grades.

There is really nothing new about this principle. Just as Huey stressed "real reading," so Bloom (1987) wishes that the classics were introduced much earlier in children's lives. Hirsch (1987) says that "the single most effective step would be to shift the reading materials used in kindergarten through eighth grade to a much stronger base in factual information and traditional lore" (p. 140). Teachers need only peruse their curriculum guides to see objectives for content instruction at every grade level. No matter what the communicative arts medium, we must begin early to teach thinking and learning in content-area subjects.

By the same reasoning, learning about content subjects continues far beyond high school. The need to think about and apply content information faces learners daily as they listen to and watch television, read the newspaper, and write to communicate. The basic difference in this learning is that the learner can structure the environment and choose what to learn and what to avoid. The adults whom teachers meet daily will attest that they continue to enjoy and learn about topics that interested them in school. The topics that remain interesting are most often those that they understood best and with which they were most successful. And so the cycle continues. Teachers want students to learn their content subjects, and students are stimulated to learn more when they are successful in their learning. We develop lifelong learners by introducing them to reading for learning's sake at an early age.

6. Reading should be a rewarding experience.

Reading in content subjects should be satisfying. People avoid doing what is not interesting or rewarding in some personal way. Students avoid reading in content subjects if they find it uninteresting and unrewarding. The authors believe that there should be a natural flow between students' attitudes and reading habits. Sinatra (1986, p. 142) expresses it this way: "The climate should be based on a meaningful need to know in which the learning of the 'three Rs' is bound to the learning of the natural and artistic world and in which eagerness to know forms the emotional basis of the classroom learning atmosphere." Huey, too, believed that interest generates reading rewards. Students, like everyone else, want to satisfy a need for feeling good. When left to their own devices, children will often select content (nonfiction) books to read just as readily as fiction. We have noted that younger children are even more likely to read for information than are older ones. If teachers can help by providing a beneficial reading environment in content subjects, learning will improve. Because we think and feel that this principle is so important, we have devoted an entire chapter — Chapter 2 — to the affective dimension of reading in the content areas.

Pleasurable feelings about reading will lead to successful reading, and to more reading. After listing "twelve easy ways to make learning to read difficult," Frank Smith (1973) provides one difficult way to make reading easy: provide students with *a lot of reading*. Taylor, Frye, and Maruyama (1990) have documented that the amount of time students spend reading at school contributes significantly to their level of achievement. The more students observe teachers and parents reading, the more they will want to try it. The more students hear parents and teachers read to them, the more they will want to try it. In his introduction to *The Princess Bride*, William Goldman (1973) tells how he hated to read until the age of ten. Then, while he was recuperating from pneumonia, his father read him *The Princess Bride*. As a result, Goldman became a voracious reader.

Teachers would like to teach students who possess good reading habits. This cannot happen simply because teachers tell, or even implore, students to read. However, it will happen through modeling. Modeling takes place when teachers share a newspaper article on the content subject or a book they've read that relates to the topic at hand. Modeling is a form of visual literacy. When teachers model reading visually, they are using one communicative art to promote another. The double whammy really works!

Good readers tend to read because it gives them pleasure and because they do it well; consequently, they get practice in reading and thus get better at it. Poor readers tend to avoid reading because it is not easy, pleasurable, or satisfying. In a series of questionnaires administered over a four-year period to incoming college students, one of the authors found a consistent correlation between those who chose not to read and those who perceived that they had poor reading and study habits. Teachers need to provide many opportunities for successful reading in their content classrooms.

7. Content-area reading requires interaction among the reader, the text, the teacher, and the environment.

Successful reading depends on numerous factors. The reader's store of knowledge and experience will certainly contribute, as well as the reader's attitude toward reading. The appeal of the reading material and the enthusiasm of the teacher also play a role. Novak and Gowin (1984) describe this interaction in the following way: "It is the teacher's obligation to set the agenda and decide what knowledge might be considered and in what sequence. . . . The learner must choose to learn; learning is a responsibility that cannot be shared. The curriculum comprises the knowledge, skills, and values of the educative process" (p. 6).

A text that is optimal for one student or set of students will not be optimal for another. Although there are some factors that make a text very readable, that does not mean that all readers will be equally willing and able to read it.

The environment is also a crucial factor. Bracey (1991) encourages us to realize that students need to understand how literacy complements the social skills necessary in the work world. Literacy is a social skill and thrives in a social context. As Frank Smith (1989) states, students achieve literacy as much from the people they read and write with as from formal instruction.

8. Assumptive teaching is "unclear" teaching.

Herber (1978) has used the term **assumptive teaching** to describe what teachers do when they unconsciously take for granted that students know something that the students really don't know. Teachers do make assumptions about students. They may assume that students will appreciate poetry and enjoy mathematics. They may assume that students understand what war is. Teachers often assume that students know how to read, that they will use reading to learn, and that they have the motivation and interest to do so. Teachers may picture all students as having plenty of reading resources and supportive home environments. Unfortunately, these assumptions are not always true.

Some assumptive teaching is necessary. Teachers cannot "start all over again" every year in a content subject. They may need to assume that a particular skill or concept was covered the year before. And yet, if a teacher assumes too much about a student's knowledge or frame of mind, that "teacher often behaves as though the persons being taught already know what is being taught" (Herber, 1978). Finding the point of familiarity with a concept and guiding the students forward is crucial. Content-area teachers should be very clear about what they are assuming their students already know. Further, they should be sure that their assumptions are fair. By learning to determine and build student background, teachers can avoid unfair assumptive teaching.

9. Content reading instruction should enable students to become responsible and independent readers.

Dependent readers wait for the teacher to tell them what the word is, what the right answer is, and what to do next. Such readers are crippled. When they need to function independently, they will not know how. Teachers who abandon the textbook because it seems too hard for their students do their students no favor. Teachers who give students all the answers or hand out the notes already organized in the teacher's style have bypassed opportunities for the students to learn how to find answers or to take notes. Kane, the high school social studies teacher quoted earlier, is concerned that high school is a place where students avoid responsibility. He thinks that schools perpetuate an environment in which students are excused from learning. (His essay appears as Appendix A.) There is an old saying that applies here: Give a man a fish, and you feed him one meal; teach a man to fish, and he can feed himself forever.

Herber and Nelson-Herber (1987) agree that many students are dependent learners but stress that they do not have to remain so. However, "students should not be expected to become independent learners independently" (p. 584). It is not fair to expect that students can use communicative arts to think and learn without the benefit of instruction. No matter what the grade level or content subject, teachers can assist students in the transfer to responsibility when they balance the students' level of proficiency and the content to be studied. **Fading** describes this change from dependence to independence (Moore, Moore, Cunningham, and Cunningham, 1986). Singer and Donlan (1985) have called it "phasing out the teacher and phasing in the student." Armbruster (1992) identified as a trend in content reading the "need to foster independent learners" (p. 166). Early elementary-level children can become responsible just as high-schoolers can. However, before they can be responsible for their own thinking and learning, students need to be taught a system that makes sense and that they can readily apply by themselves. PAR, explained in this chapter and used as the basis for this textbook, is such a system. PAR enables the teacher to show students how to become responsible learners. The teacher first models PAR, then gradually weans students to independent use of PAR. The two examples described at the start of this chapter illustrate such independent learning.

What's Next? The Organization of This Textbook

The themes underlying the nine principles presented in this chapter will surface in every chapter. Chapters 1 and 2 are foundation chapters; they present the basic theory and rationale for the approach used in this text. Chapters 3 and 4 focus on the Preparation step, Chapter 5 on the Assistance step, and Chapter 6 on the Reflection step. Applications for teachers are provided, as well as examples from several content areas and grade levels. Chapters 7 through 10 discuss how PAR works with vocabulary, writing, and study skills. Chapters 11 and 12 are specialized chapters about at-risk learners and literature across the curriculum. Specific strategies and activities are provided. The principles are an integral part of the discussion in all of these chapters.

In each of these chapters, we employ the PAR steps by asking readers to *prepare* themselves to read and then to *assist* as well as *reflect* on their comprehension. To aid you in applying information, we recommend that you now select a subject textbook, one that you are currently using or may use in the future as you teach students. The book you select will be a resource for completing some of the assignments given at the end of each chapter. Upon completion of this textbook, you should be able to pick up a textbook in a selected subject area and analyze it for its suitability for learners, its affective qualities, its attention to PAR, its study skills and vocabulary aids, and its attention to different learners. In addition, you should be able to construct activities that help teach content through a reading-to-learn approach.

One-Minute Summary

In this chapter, we have demonstrated the need for an instructional framework in content reading instruction. We have explained our framework, PAR, and have provided two examples, one from secondary social studies and one from primary science, to assist our readers in their understanding of how PAR works. We have introduced you to some major reports and recommendations, both current and past, that demonstrate the importance of a reading-to-learn approach in content classrooms. We have summarized our beliefs about reading to learn and have laid the foundation for this textbook in the form of nine principles for content reading instruction. Finally, we have discussed how our nine principles and the PAR framework will be applied throughout this textbook, as well as how the textbook is organized.

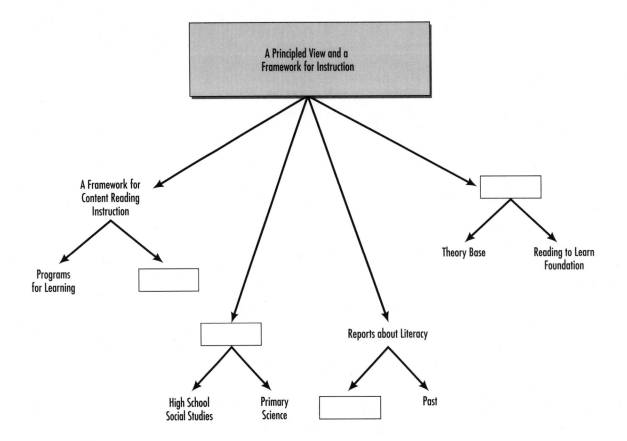

End-of-Chapter Activities

Assisting Comprehension

1. Study the graphic organizer shown here, and fill in the blanks with words that convey key concepts taught in this chapter. You may scan back through the chapter text. What does each term mean, and what is its relationship to reading, thinking, and learning?

2. Return to the terms presented at the beginning of this chapter. Has your understanding of these terms altered? In what ways?

Reflecting on Your Reading

If you'd like to read a book about one teacher's struggles to teach content, please try Eliot Wigginton's *Sometimes a Shining Moment*. It's enjoyable, inspiring, and informative! If you'd like to see how reading can inspire a child, read the preface to Goldman's "good parts version" of *The Princess Bride*.

CHAPTER 2

Affective Teaching in Content Areas

"The desire to know, when you realize you do not know, is universal and probably irresistible. . . . it is a desire, as Shakespeare said, that grows by what it feeds on. It is impossible to slake the thirst for knowledge. And the more intelligent you are, the more this is so."

Charles Van Doren, *A History of Knowledge: Past Present and Future*

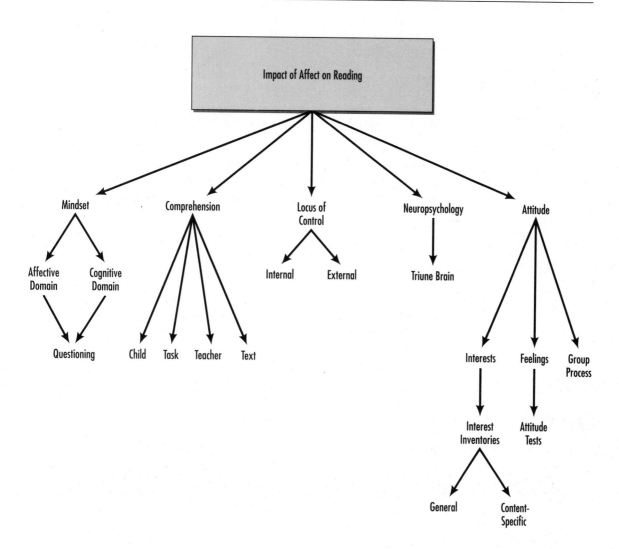

Prepare to Read

1. One of the authors was admonishing his three-year-old not to play with an older child who was being particularly hard on the younger child. The toddler was told not to play with such a "bad boy." The three-year-old's retort was, "No, he's a good boy. He just does bad things to me." This statement dramatically illustrates an important point adults need to keep in mind: Good children do bad things, but we must not equate the things they do with the spirit within. This point is especially important to teachers. When children behave poorly in classrooms, there are reasons. We need to discover why some students are discipline problems and others are not.

   This chapter is devoted to affective teaching and its importance in every classroom. Affective teaching is that which brings about an emotional response or change in the learner. The following questions are designed to test your "affective quotient" (AQ as opposed to IQ) and to help you discover how much you know about this important area of teaching.

   a. What is your definition of affective teaching?
   b. How can teaching to the affective domain influence comprehension and achievement?
   c. What is the locus of control? What role does it play in teaching?
   d. How can students' actions be tied to the way they feel? How can students' actions be tied to brain function?

2. Following is a list of terms used in this chapter. Some of them may be familiar to you in a general context, but in this chapter they may be used in a different way than you are used to. Rate your knowledge by placing a + in front of those you are sure that you know, a √ in front of those you have some knowledge about, and a 0 in front of those you don't know. Be ready to locate and pay special attention to their meanings when they are presented in the chapter.

   ___ affective   ___ attitude
   ___ neuropsychology   ___ commitment
   ___ triune brain   ___ consensus
   ___ old mammalian brain   ___ arbitration
   ___ reptilian brain   ___ locus of control
   ___ downshifting   ___ GATOR

Objectives

As you read this chapter, focus your attention on the following objectives. You will:

1. be able to define what is meant by the affective domain.

2. understand why affect is important to reading.

3. understand what part neuropsychology plays in affective teaching.

4. understand how to improve student attitudes through reading.

"SOON AS YOU LEARN TO READ, JOEY, THE WHOLE WORLD'S AGAINST YOU."

Dennis the Menace. Used with permission of Hank Ketcham and © by North America Syndicate.

5. be able to incorporate affective strategies into the content-area curriculum.

6. better understand the construct of locus of control and its importance for content-area instruction.

Principle 6 stated that reading should be a rewarding experience. In this chapter and throughout the book, we will be describing strategies that students will enjoy and find pleasure in. When reading is pleasurable, students will tend to read more. This principle, then, speaks to the importance of the affective domain of teaching. Here are two examples of what we mean.

The Importance of Affect to Reading

Chris, 16, is happy in his vocational-education class in carpentry. The beginning of class often finds the teacher at the door greeting the students by name. The classroom is relaxed, and Chris and others are always allowed to express their opinions on important subjects. The students often work in small groups in problem solving, both in reading the chapters and in constructing carpentry projects. The teacher always begins a new chapter by asking the students what they know about the topic. Often there are lively discussions, and the teacher always seems interested in the views of the students. Chris always knows what he has to do to get a good grade; directions and assignments are always clear. The teacher is different from other teachers, according to Chris. This one doesn't emphasize simply getting the right answer, but how students arrived at the answer and the thinking that was undertaken. Problems are posed in carpentry for the students to solve in small groups, and support is always given if they work through their attempts to solve the problem. Chris looks forward to coming to the class and sometimes thinks about becoming a carpenter when he finishes school.

Jon dreads going to his tenth-grade history class. He describes the teacher as mean and one who doesn't trust the class or care much for students' opinions. No talking is allowed in the class, and the teacher often yells at students who whisper or otherwise misbehave. The teacher mostly lectures and tells the students what they need to know to be successful in class. Jon is afraid to speak up even when he might know an answer for fear that, if wrong, he will be ridiculed or given a lower grade. The teacher is tough in grading, according to Jon, and most students get grades of C or lower. Jon says the class is not much fun and he wishes he didn't have to take it. He often tries to make up excuses to be absent from class. Jon has decided that his least favorite subject is history.

These two classroom descriptions illustrate the importance of the affective domain to student satisfaction with the learning process. Even if no more facts and concepts are learned in classroom 1 than in classroom 2, students such as Chris are finding that learning can be enjoyable—a necessary prerequisite for the study that Chris must do throughout his life.

Any response to a stimulus that evokes feelings or emotions is said to be a part of the **affective** domain of learning. Students in kindergarten through 12th grade dwell in the affective domain; that is, feelings, emotions, and strong attitudes are very much a part of almost every waking hour. Conversely, teachers dwell mainly in the cognitive domain, where student achievement is perceived to be the single most important *raison d'être* of schooling. It is our contention that because of this perceptual mismatch, teachers and students often don't "meet" intellectually in the classroom. (See Figure 2.1.) Put another way, their needs are so different— teachers driven to impart knowledge, students to discover the range of emotions inherent in each new day—that real communication sometimes does not occur in classrooms where the focus of instruction is only on content.

Of course the importance of affect has been known to educators for a long time, even before the term *affect* was widely used. Notice this gem of a passage by Emerson White, written in 1886:

> It seems important to note in this connection that the development of the intellectual faculties is conditioned upon the corresponding development of the sensibility and the will. The activity of the mind in knowing depends, among other things, on the acuteness and energy of the senses, the intensity of the emotions and desires, and the energy and constancy of the will. (p. 92)

FIGURE 2.1

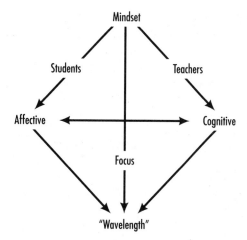

Almost 100 years later, Paris, Lipson, and Wixson (1983) note the importance of motivation and affect in a student's ability to become an independent learner. They note that developing independence requires both the skills of reading and the will to learn in increasingly more complex environments.

More than six decades ago, Adler (1931) wrote of the importance of self-concept and of children who can learn but won't (p. 159). More recently, Dechant (1970) concluded that

> learning may be motivated not so much by what the teacher does or by the after-the-learning events such as rewards and punishments, as by what the learner wants, is interested in, or by what he feels will enhance his self-esteem and personal worth. The motivating condition begins within and is more psychological than physiological. (p. 537)

As was noted in Chapter 1, many reports have indicated that our students are not reading well. Glasser (1986), in his book *Control Theory in the Classroom*, states that more than half of all students are making little or no effort to learn, mainly because they don't believe that school provides any satisfaction. In a spirited repudiation of stimulus–response theory, Glasser maintains that human behavior is generated by what goes on inside the person. In an interview (Gough, 1987), Glasser spoke eloquently of the importance of affect:

> Except for those who live in deepest poverty, the psychological needs — love, power, freedom, and fun — take precedence over the survival needs, which most of us are able to satisfy. All our lives, we search for ways to satisfy our needs for love, belonging, caring, sharing, and cooperation. If a student feels no sense of belonging in school, no sense of being involved in caring and concern, that child will pay little attention to academic subjects. (p. 657)

It has long been known that student attitude is an important variable in reading achievement (Purves & Bech, 1972; Walberg & Tsai, 1985). Frank Smith

(1988) notes that the emotional response to reading "is the primary reason most readers read, and probably the primary reason most nonreaders do not read" (p. 177). M. Cecil Smith (1990) has found, in a longitudinal study, that reading attitudes tend to be stable over time from childhood through adulthood. It may be true that poor attitudes toward reading (or good attitudes) inculcated early in schooling tend to remain stable throughout one's life.

What Teachers Can Do to Improve Student Attitudes

Research by Heathington and Alexander (1984) indicates that although teachers see attitudes as important, they spend little time trying to change students' poor attitudes. The keys to promoting positive attitudes in all classes are caring, empathy, feeling, high expectations, sensitivity, vulnerability, honesty, firmness, support, respect, and humanness. A number of activities for promoting favorable attitudes toward reading have been described by Readance and Baldwin (1979), Cooter and Alexander (1984), and Rieck (1977). To change student attitudes in general, these researchers note that the teacher should

accept students as they are

assume students want to learn

expect considerable achievement

praise whenever appropriate

be critical in a constructive manner

be honest with students

accentuate the positive — that is, build on strengths

talk *with* students, not *at* students

have a sense of humor

learn some interesting characteristics of each student

trust students and exude warmth

be enthusiastic

call students by first name or preferred name

To change student attitudes about reading, the teacher should

actively listen to student comments and discussions

make reading fun and rewarding

encourage students to read on their own

make reading assignments shorter for poor readers

have frequent group and sharing experiences

speak well of reading and share the books he or she is reading

use the PAR system described in Chapter 1

Teachers need to realize the importance of creating a positive classroom climate in the learning process (Brophy, 1982; Fisher & Berliner, 1985). Teachers are very important in the lives of students and should provide the type of climate that says "I am never going to give up on you; I believe in you." Many famous people did poorly in school, including Albert Einstein, Woodrow Wilson, Thomas Edison, George Bernard Shaw, Pablo Picasso, William Butler Yeats, Henry Ford, and Benjamin Franklin. If we emphasize the positive, each of us might someday play a central role in helping a future genius realize his or her potential. Most important of all, the teacher must value—and we mean truly value—inquiry, problem solving, and reasoning. By keeping an open mind and letting students take part in open-ended discussions, the teacher will be making a statement about the true art of teaching that cannot be ignored or misinterpreted by even the most limited students.

Any discussion of attitudinal teaching would be incomplete without some mention of teacher discouragement, otherwise known as burnout. Dreikurs, Grunwald, and Pepper (1971) described succinctly the discouragement a teacher faces when teaching students who can learn, but won't. The progression from frustration to discouragement and finally to burnout is as much a fact of life today as it was two decades ago. More recently, Wigginton, in *Sometimes a Shining Moment* (1986), has documented through teacher questionnaires the depths of discouragement teachers, especially career teachers with much experience, can encounter. To combat these real feelings of frustration at not getting through to problem children, according to Wigginton, teachers need to develop the following three attributes:

flexibility—keeping a positive attitude by ignoring all negative thoughts and by being open and receptive

willingness—being willing to try new ways of reaching problem students without sacrificing tried and true methods

ability—working and struggling to be the best teacher one can be in order to inspire students

Teachers must remember that they can and do exert a significant influence on children. By being flexible, willing, and able, they can influence even the hard-to-reach child. In Chapter 11, we discuss strategies for reaching these students.

Teachers must realize that they may not have the same degree of success with every student. But there is always the possibility that with the next teaching experience, the reluctant student will experience an attitudinal change. Teachers must balance the real and the ideal in their role as teachers of cognition and affect.

Neuropsychology and Affect

The relatively new science of **neuropsychology** is the study of the relationship between brain function and behavior (Kolb & Whishaw, 1985). Researchers are beginning to understand the importance of feelings and emotions in language development and brain development (Grady, 1990). Sinatra (1986) has theorized that feelings, like language, are linked to brain activity. Debunking the simplistic "left brain/right brain" literature, Sinatra cites a wealth of new research to show that most learning tasks require both left-hemisphere and right-hemisphere processing. He cites Restak's (1982, 1984) research indicating that cooperation rather than competition between the two brain hemispheres is the prevailing mode in most learning. Moreover, Sinatra proposes the importance of the two subcortical brains in the emotional and motivational aspects of learning. He states that "since the neural pathways between the cortex and the reticular and limbic systems function all the time without our conscious awareness, educators must realize that curriculum content cannot be approached solely by intellectual reasoning. The systems regulating feeling, emotions, and attentiveness are tied to the very learning of information" (p. 143). He further states that the teacher's attitude toward the reason for learning information, and toward the learners themselves, may be a more important factor in how well something is learned than the specific content. In making learning interesting and challenging, teachers are, in reality, activating brain subsystems responsible for alertness and emotional tone (p. 143). Sinatra criticizes dull worksheet drills as decoding exercises that negate students' eagerness to learn. Berry (1969) agrees that motivation, attention, and memory all operate in an interlocking fashion to enhance learning.

Sinatra's work is compatible with the **triune brain** theory described by MacLean (1978). This model clarifies how the brain works in general and precisely why affect is so important in reading. The middle section of the brain—which MacLean calls the **old mammalian brain**—is the seat of the limbic system. Sometimes called the "emotional mind" (Clark, 1983), it contributes significantly to the learning process. Students who feel positive and happy about a learning experience will be better able to process and retain information. Students who are uncertain and unhappy in a learning situation, either at school or at home, will become, in a real sense, emotionally unable to attend to a task for any length of time. Medical researchers know that, through the release of limbic system neurotransmitters, cells of the neocortex are either helped or hindered in their functioning. The limbic system actually secretes different chemicals when one is experiencing a negative emotional event, thereby impeding learning and retention. Research has also shown that brain functioning increases significantly when novelty is present (Restak, 1979) and when subjects experience feelings of pleasure and joy (Sagan, 1977). Conversely, researchers have found that removing touch and movement has resulted in increases in violent behavior (Penfield, 1975). All of this gives credence to the importance of attitudes, feelings, emotions, and motivation in thinking, reading, and learning.

To take an analogous example, a small boy fell into Lake Michigan's 32-degree water in the dead of winter. When he was rescued after 20 minutes, no heartbeat or pulse was detectable. And yet, a year later, he had recovered almost fully. How could this be? The explanation scientists think most likely is that a biological phenomenon called "mammalian diving reflex" enables humans to live without breathing for long periods of time (*Richmond Times-Dispatch*, 13 January 1985).

If a human is in a life-threatening situation, with no time for reflection, an instinctive action is called for. The **reptilian brain** "kicks in" at the message of panic from the old mammalian brain and overrides reason. This scenario probably applies to the case of Jimmy Tontlewicz, the boy in the lake. When his body was first recovered, the prognosis was very grim. However, Jimmy is now functioning at much the same level as other children his age. Doctors speculate that his brain "shut his body down" to minimal performance in order to save his life. Jimmy did not will his brain to do this; the brain reacted automatically. Hart (1983) describes this process, in which messages are sent from the old mammalian to the reptilian brain, as **downshifting**.

How does this theory of the triune brain apply to reading and thinking about content material? Suppose that Jon—the boy who dreads tenth-grade history—has not read the assignment and is confronted with a pop quiz. The old mammalian brain may be activated; a sense of frustration, even panic, may occur. Since the new mammalian brain (neocortex) has little information to contribute, and since hormones associated with anxiety are being generated by the old mammalian brain, the message gets routed or rerouted from the new mammalian brain to the reptilian brain: Shut down and save me! When students say "My mind went blank," they have provided an apt description of what literally happened. Similarly, consider the teacher who is struggling to find a way to present content material but cannot seem to get it across to her students. She is using the chapter information, but it just isn't working. She becomes more and more frustrated and less and less effective. Again, a sort of downshifting may be occurring.

Focusing on the brain and how students learn, Hart (1975) proposes that the following are important in teaching:

1. making learning immediately important to students in order for them to make sense of the situation
2. giving students opportunities to talk about what they are learning to allow heightening of brain activity
3. providing a free environment in which students can move around and talk about the projects they are doing
4. allowing students time to build elaborate "programs" of thinking for storage and memory retrieval by the brain
5. limiting threats and pressures, which cause the neocortex (newest and highest level of the brain) to function poorly
6. stressing intuitive learning as much as step-by-step logic to allow creative thinking to emerge

A Model of Affective Comprehension

McDermott (1978) suggests that a child's progress in reading is influenced less by the nature of the reading activity than by the personal relationship the child has developed with the teacher. The argument is that children respond more

FIGURE 2.2

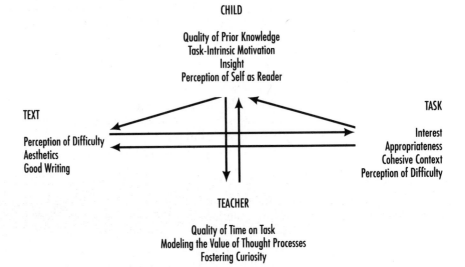

often to the feelings the teacher displays when asking them to complete an assignment than to the activity itself. Implied in McDermott's theory is that reading is as much a social event or transaction as it is an intellectual one. Building on McDermott's and Dechant's work, Meeks (1987) has proposed a model of "affective metacognition," postulating that affect and metacognition (students thinking about what they do and do not know) are so interwoven that they cannot be artificially separated. Figure 2.2 represents the four key elements of the model and the subelements inherent in each. Following is a brief description of each of the components of the model:

THE CHILD

Quality of prior knowledge. The learner's prior knowledge may be clear and factual or unclear and represent false knowledge.

Task-intrinsic motivation. This refers to a child's readiness to perform an activity as a goal in itself.

Insight. This is reflective awareness that comes through cooperative interchange among students.

Perception of self as a reader. This perception is important for children because they must see themselves as generators of information, not passive receptors of knowledge.

THE TEACHER

Quality of time on task. Teachers must develop caring relationships with children in completing the task.

Modeling the value of thought processes. Teachers must value thinking and discussion as tools to develop the thought processes of children.

Fostering curiosity. Teachers must believe inquisitiveness and curiosity are most important in the learning process.

THE TEXT

Perception of difficulty. Students cannot perceive the book in a negative way, as being too difficult to comprehend.

Aesthetics. The text must be appropriate for the audience, with a pleasing format.

Good writing. The subject must come alive through the author's use of good writing.

THE TASK

Interest. The task must be interesting to the student.

Appropriateness. The task must be appropriate to the intellectual, psychological, social, and moral development of the student.

Cohesive context. The student must perceive that the task assigned makes sense in relation to what is read.

Perception of difficulty. Students cannot perceive the task in a negative way, as being too difficult to perform.

In this model, Meeks sees the thinking process and its expression in class discussion and group process as legitimate and important ends in their own right. Thought emerges as a social process; material is internalized only after it has been expressed socially. According to this interactive model, teachers who stress affect show that they value inquiry, sharing, and curiosity about learning. This model is important for content-area teachers because it suggests that all four elements of the model must be included in a lesson plan. To treat the affective domain adequately, the teacher must assess how these four variables are operating at any one time in the content lesson. Is the teacher modeling reasoning and thinking strategies during the lesson? Do students have enough background knowledge of the subject? Is the text "user friendly"—that is, readable and enjoyable? Is the task reasonable, or is it too difficult? Students probably will not enjoy what they are doing and will not be successful at it unless the teacher pays close attention to the four aspects of teaching described in the model. According to Meeks, overemphasis on any one element in a lesson will weaken learning and retention.

Assessing Attitudes of Teachers and Students

One factor that has been found to be positively correlated with both teacher effectiveness and attitudinal changes in students is teacher enthusiasm (Rosenshine & Furst, 1971; Gage, 1979; Hamachek, 1975; Rosenshine, 1968; Streeter, 1986). According to Collins (1977), teacher enthusiasm affects vocal delivery, eyes, gestures, body movements, facial expressions, word selection, acceptance of ideas and feelings, and overall energy. Sometimes it is necessary for teachers to look inward to make certain they are exhibiting a positive attitude toward students. **Attitude** can be defined as the mental disposition one exhibits toward others. The teacher attitude survey provided here (Activity 2.1) will help teachers assess whether they are exhibiting an enthusiastic and positive attitude about reading in their classroom. This survey can be used for self-assessment by any K–12 teacher.

Besides assessing how well we teach and model affect, we should also assess students to determine positive and negative attitudes toward reading. The Mikulecky Behavioral Reading Attitude Measure (Mikulecky, Shanklin, & Caverly, 1979) for older students (Activity 2.2) and the Elementary Reading Attitude Survey (McKenna & Kear, 1990) for early elementary-grade students (Activity 2.3) were designed to cover a broad range of affective interest and developmental stages. Keys for interpreting these two surveys are provided in Appendix B, along with more technical information on their construction and validation. These tests can be given as pretests and again after 12 weeks as posttests to determine whether students' attitudes have improved significantly over the period.

Strengthening Affective Bonds through Group Process and Decision Making

One of the main goals in teaching is to help students become self-managing learners. Recent research has shown that students may not exhibit independent learning habits even when they know and use certain cognitive strategies (Borkowski, Carr, Rellinger, & Pressley, 1990; Paris & Winograd, 1990). Teachers need to help students become independent by encouraging group decision making and having students work in teams or small groups whenever possible. Learning is enhanced when such cooperative learning teams are emphasized in content teaching (Meloth & Deering, 1992; Johnson & Johnson, 1989; Abrami, Chambers, d'Apollonia, Farrell, & DeSimone, 1992).

In having students work in groups, we recommend a stylized three-step process analogous to the steps in the PAR lesson framework described in Chapter 1. In the preparation phase, it is important for individual students to commit to something, usually written, to be shared later with the group. In this individual phase, the teacher is attempting to get a **commitment** from the student. This can be difficult because students today often do not wish to commit to anything; their "cop-out" is not to get involved in classroom activities. This sense of involvement is crucial to successful group interaction, however. Lack of commitment is the reason so much group work "degenerates," with students getting away from the subject to be discussed or the problem to be solved.

The second phase is the actual work to be done in groups. The key word in the group phase in **consensus**. Here the students should share what they have done individually and arrive at a consensus, whenever possible, on the best possible answer. The teacher provides much assistance in this phase by floating from group to group to help students with areas of difficulty and to make certain groups are staying on the topic.

In the third phase, involving reflection, the teacher may lead a discussion with the groups, an exercise in **arbitration**. Here the teacher acts as an arbiter to

Directions: Please read each of the following questions and then circle *often, sometimes, seldom,* or *never* after each question.

1. Do you have patience with those who are having difficulty reading?	often	sometimes	seldom	never
2. When you finish explaining the reading assignment, do your students want to find out more about the assignment?	often	sometimes	seldom	never
3. Do your students ever get so interested in your reading assignment that they talk about the assignment after it is completed?	often	sometimes	seldom	never
4. Do you ask thought-provoking questions about the reading assignments?	often	sometimes	seldom	never
5. Do you discuss with your students concepts they might look for before reading their assignment?	often	sometimes	seldom	never
6. Do you make difficult material seem easier to read?	often	sometimes	seldom	never
7. Do you give students aid in finding resource books for assignments?	often	sometimes	seldom	never
8. Do you refrain from giving reading assignments from materials that are too difficult for students to understand?	often	sometimes	seldom	never
9. Do you explain or define the new concepts in reading assignments?	often	sometimes	seldom	never
10. Do you tell students when they have done a creditable job on a reading assignment?	often	sometimes	seldom	never
11. Do you give reading assignments of appropriate length?	often	sometimes	seldom	never

(continued on page 44)

A C T I V I T Y   2 . 1   **CONTINUED**

12. When students are reading silently, do you monitor the classroom to make certain the environment is conducive to quiet study?	often	sometimes	seldom	never
13. Do you talk to students about the value of reading well in today's society?	often	sometimes	seldom	never
14. Do you enlist the help of students in deciding how much reading is needed to complete assignments?	often	sometimes	seldom	never
15. After an assignment, do you ask students what they would like to read for further study?	often	sometimes	seldom	never
16. Do you know how interested your students are in reading?	often	sometimes	seldom	never
17. Are you interested in reading in your daily life?	often	sometimes	seldom	never
18. Do you read books for pleasure?	often	sometimes	seldom	never
19. Are you flexible in your reading — i.e., do you read at different rates for different purposes?	often	sometimes	seldom	never
20. Do you find yourself exhibiting more enthusiasm than normal when discussing a certain book?	often	sometimes	seldom	never

All 20 items should be answered *often* or *sometimes*.

Scoring key:

15–20	*often*	or	*sometimes*	responses		Very effective
12–14	"	"	"	"		Reasonably effective; fair in the affective areas
8–11	"	"	"	"		OK; need some improvement
0–7	"	"	"	"		Poor; do some rethinking!

Adapted from a questionnaire developed by James Laffey in *Successful Interactions in Reading and Language: A Practical Handbook for Subject Matter Teachers* by J. Laffey and R. Morgan, 1983, Harrisonburg, VA: Feygan.

A C T I V I T Y 2 . 2 MIKULECKY BEHAVIORAL READING ATTITUDE MEASURE

On the following pages are 20 descriptions. You are to respond by indicating how much these descriptions are either unlike you or like you. For *very unlike* you, circle the number 1. For *very like* you, circle the number 5. If you fall somewhere between, circle the appropriate number. Example:

You receive a book for a Christmas present. You start the book, but decide to stop half-way through.

Very   1   2   3   4   5   Very
Unlike Me   Like Me

1. You walk into the office of a doctor or dentist and notice that there are magazines set out.

   Very   1   2   3   4   5   Very
   Unlike Me   Like Me

2. People have made jokes about your reading in unusual circumstances or situations.

   Very   1   2   3   4   5   Very
   Unlike Me   Like Me

3. You are in a shopping center you've been to several times when someone asks where books and magazines are sold. You are able to tell the person.

   Very   1   2   3   4   5   Very
   Unlike Me   Like Me

4. You feel very uncomfortable because emergencies have kept you away from reading for a couple of days.

   Very   1   2   3   4   5   Very
   Unlike Me   Like Me

5. You are waiting for a friend in an airport or supermarket and find yourself leafing through the magazines and paperback books.

   Very   1   2   3   4   5   Very
   Unlike Me   Like Me

6. If a group of acquaintances would laugh at you for always being buried in a book, you'd know it's true and wouldn't mind much at all.

   Very   1   2   3   4   5   Very
   Unlike Me   Like Me

7. You are tired of waiting for the dentist, so you start to page through a magazine.

   Very   1   2   3   4   5   Very
   Unlike Me   Like Me

8. People who are regular readers often ask your opinion about new books.

   Very   1   2   3   4   5   Very
   Unlike Me   Like Me

(continued on page 46)

9. One of your first impulses is to "look it up" whenever there is something you don't know or whenever you are going to start something new.

    Very   1   2   3   4   5   Very
    Unlike Me   Like Me

10. Even though you are a very busy person, there is somehow always time for reading.

    Very   1   2   3   4   5   Very
    Unlike Me   Like Me

11. You've finally got some time alone in your favorite chair on a Sunday afternoon. You see something to read and decide to spend a few minutes reading just because you feel like it.

    Very   1   2   3   4   5   Very
    Unlike Me   Like Me

12. You tend to disbelieve and be a little disgusted by people who repeatedly say they don't have time to read.

    Very   1   2   3   4   5   Very
    Unlike Me   Like Me

13. You find yourself giving special books to friends or relatives as gifts.

    Very   1   2   3   4   5   Very
    Unlike Me   Like Me

14. At Christmas time, you look in the display window of a bookstore and find yourself interested in some books and uninterested in others.

    Very   1   2   3   4   5   Very
    Unlike Me   Like Me

15. Sometimes you find yourself so excited by a book you try to get friends to read it.

    Very   1   2   3   4   5   Very
    Unlike Me   Like Me

16. You've just finished reading a story and settle back for a moment to sort of enjoy and remember what you've just read.

    Very   1   2   3   4   5   Very
    Unlike Me   Like Me

17. You *choose* to read nonrequired books and articles fairly regularly (a few times a week).

    Very   1   2   3   4   5   Very
    Unlike Me   Like Me

(continued on page 47)

18. Your friends would not be at all surprised to see you buying or borrowing a book.

    Very   1   2   3   4   5   Very
    Unlike Me   Like Me

19. You have just gotten comfortably settled in a new city. Among the things you plan to do are check out the library and bookstores.

    Very   1   2   3   4   5   Very
    Unlike Me   Like Me

20. You've just heard about a good book but haven't been able to find it. Even though you're tired, you look for it in one more bookstore.

    Very   1   2   3   4   5   Very
    Unlike Me   Like Me

Reprinted with permission of Larry Mikulecky. Data regarding the construction, validation, and interpretation of this test are contained in Appendix B.

resolve difficult points of the lesson where students could not come to consensus. Also in this phase, groups may give reports to the whole class on their group findings.

To recap, here are the three phases of good group process:

Phase I	Individual	Key concept: commitment
Phase II	Group work	Key concept: consensus
Phase III	Teacher-led discussion	Key concept: arbitration

Interests and Interest Inventories

When teachers show students that they are interested in them as persons, great changes can occur in student behavior. Sometimes by simply finding out what students like to do in their spare time, by being aware of their goals and perceived needs, teachers can ensure a more positive atmosphere in the classroom. To this end, teachers can create general interest inventories such as the one shown in Activity 2.4.

Teachers can also construct interest inventories specific to a content-area subject, such as the one shown in Activity 2.5. Whichever type of interest inventory is used — general, content-specific, or a combination of the two — such an inventory can be a powerful tool in teaching to the affective domain. For instance, if students express a preference for physical content, teachers can modify their lessons accordingly.

A C T I V I T Y   2 . 3   **ELEMENTARY READING ATTITUDE SURVEY**

School _____   Grade _____   Name _____

GARFIELD: © 1978 United Feature Syndicate, Inc.

1. How do you feel when you read a book on a rainy Saturday?

JIM DAVIS

2. How do you feel when you read a book in school during free time?

3. How do you feel about reading for fun at home?

4. How do you feel about getting a book for a present?

(continued on page 49)

A C T I V I T Y   2 . 3   CONTINUED

5. How do you feel about spending free time reading?

6. How do you feel about starting a new book?

7. How do you feel about reading during summer vacation?

8. How do you feel about reading instead of playing?

(continued on page 50)

A C T I V I T Y   2 . 3   **CONTINUED**

GARFIELD: © 1978 United Feature Syndicate, Inc.

9. How do you feel about going to a bookstore?

10. How do you feel about reading different kinds of books?

11. How do you feel when the teacher asks you questions about what you read?

12. How do you feel about doing reading workbook pages and worksheets?

(continued on page 51)

A C T I V I T Y   2 . 3   CONTINUED

GARFIELD: © 1978 United Feature Syndicate, Inc.

13. How do you feel about reading in school?

14. How do you feel about reading your school books?

15. How do you feel about learning from a book?

16. How do you feel when it's time for reading class?

(continued on page 52)

17. How do you feel about the stories you read in reading class?

18. How do you feel when you read out loud in class?

19. How do you feel about using a dictionary?

20. How do you feel about taking a reading test?

GARFIELD: © 1978 United Feature Syndicate, Inc.

A C T I V I T Y   2 . 4   **INTEREST/ATTITUDE INVENTORY: ENGLISH**

Date _____

Bell _____

My name is _____ You can call me _____

My phone number is _____

My career goal is _____

_____

My educational goal is (how much schooling do you want to pursue?)

_____

I feel computers are _____

_____

English class makes me feel _____

_____

I think writing is _____

_____

When I work in a small group in class, I tend to _____

_____

In my spare time, I (hobbies) _____

_____

I do/do not (circle one) hold a job after school. If I have a job, it is _____

_____

My secret ambition is _____

_____

_____

Not many people know that I _____

_____

_____

My special need is _____

_____

ACTIVITY 2.5   **INTEREST INVENTORY: BIOLOGY**

HOW INTERESTED IN BIOLOGY AM I?

This is a preference inventory to determine your level of interest in biology. Answer each set of questions with a (1) for your first choice, (2) for your second choice, and (3) for your third choice.

1. I would rather read about:
   _____ how the body works.
   _____ how electricity works.
   _____ the earth's atmosphere.

2. I'd prefer to:
   _____ determine the content in aspirin.
   _____ dissect an animal.
   _____ determine the effects of friction.

3. I would rather take a field trip to:
   _____ an island conservatory.
   _____ NASA.
   _____ a hospital lab.

4. I would rather receive as a gift:
   _____ an animal (puppy, kitten, hamster).
   _____ a chemistry kit.
   _____ a model airplane.

5. I learn best by:
   _____ hearing about it.
   _____ watching someone do it.
   _____ doing it myself.

Answer the following questions with a yes or no.

1. _____ I have plants at home that I take care of.

2. _____ I would like to learn how to propagate plants (take one plant and make others from it).

3. _____ Science has always been my favorite subject and one in which I make my best grades.

4. _____ Science has always been hard for me to understand.

5. _____ I think all animals function in similar ways.

6. _____ I am taking biology because I am required to for graduation and it is easier than chemistry or physics.

7. _____ I am taking biology because I want to.

8. _____ Dissection sounds interesting to me.

9. _____ I am a visual learner.

10. _____ I like to work with others (in pairs or groups).

Developed by Terri Kilmer.

Locus of Control and the Affective Teaching of Reading

The **locus of control** construct is said to have originated with Rotter's (1966) social learning theory, which suggested that individuals attributed their successes and failures to different sources. People with an "internal" locus of control accept responsibility for the consequences of their behavior. They also perceive the relationship between their conduct and its outcomes. Those with an "external" locus of control, in contrast, blame fate, chance, other individuals, or task difficulty for their successes and failures (Chandler, 1975). The concept of locus of control is a promising diagnostic tool for affective teaching because it helps teachers understand and predict affective behaviors in the classroom.

Several studies have specifically tested locus of control and reading achievement (Lefcourt, Gronnerud, & MacDonald, 1972; Drummond, Smith, & Pinette, 1975; Culver & Morgan, 1977). These studies support the notion that internally controlled students make greater gains in achievement in general, in reading achievement, and in classroom adjustment. More recent studies have found internally controlled individuals to be more cognitively active in search and learning activities involved in reading (Creek, et al., 1991; DeSanti & Alexander, 1986; Curry, 1990). Earlier, Coleman et al. (1969) found that the largest deficiency in ghetto children was their acceptance of their inability to control their environment. Coleman concluded that passivity caused these children to accept control by others as their fate; often, this perceived control became reality.

Morgan and Culver (1978) have proposed certain guidelines for teachers to help them select activities that reinforce internal behaviors. Table 2.1 summarizes these guidelines, contrasting activities that reinforce internally controlled behaviors with those that reinforce externally controlled behaviors.

First, teachers need to minimize anxiety over possible failure by building patterns of success for each student in the class. This can be accomplished in

TABLE 2.1

REINFORCING EXTERNALLY CONTROLLED BEHAVIORS	REINFORCING INTERNALLY CONTROLLED BEHAVIORS
1. Arbitrary grading	1. Using concept of mastery in grading
2. Setting time limits for tasks, which makes students constantly aware of time (compulsiveness)	2. Allowing students enough time to complete and master a task
3. Building anxiety over possible failure	3. Building patterns of success
4. Neglecting to offer rewards for efforts	4. Rewarding student in a controlled manner for effort (praise)
5. No graduated sequencing in learning tasks	5. Developing graduated sequences for the learning tasks
6. Neglecting students' needs for counseling and guidance; students do not develop goals	6. Counseling student toward realistic academic and life goals

several ways. To begin with, teachers need to develop a realistic reward system of praise for work completed. A system of rewards can be made simpler if the teacher uses a contractual type of arrangement that specifies a sequence of graduated tasks, each of which is attainable. The teacher should stress the concept of mastery of the task in grading students, thereby eliminating arbitrary grading, which serves as a source of agitation for those students who are external in their thinking. Also, the teacher can deemphasize the concept of time and thus lessen compulsiveness by allowing students unlimited time to complete and master certain tasks. In addition, teachers should aid school guidance staff in counseling students toward realistic life goals, since externally controlled persons often have unrealistic aspirations, or no aspirations at all.

Teachers can also adopt strategies that foster self-direction and internal motivation in the learning process. For instance, teachers can let students make a set of rules of conduct for the class and start their own class or group traditions, to reinforce the importance of both the group and the individuals in the group. Such an activity, which relies on listening and speaking, can be implemented even in the early grades. Another excellent activity for older students is the "internal–external" journal. Students keep a record of recent events that have happened to them. In the journal, they can explain whether the events were orchestrated and controlled by someone other than themselves and, if so, whether these externally controlled events frustrated them. As a variant on the journal idea, students can make a "blame list" to identify whether positive and negative events that happen to them are their own fault or the fault of others. These activities rely on the use of writing, thus integrating another communicative art into affective education.

One of the most important classroom strategies for helping students develop an internal locus of control is to have them practice decision making whenever possible. Study guides and worksheets described later in this text can be constructed in such a manner that individuals and groups are asked to reason and react to hypothetical situations in which decisions need to be made. Group consensus in decision making about a possible conclusion to a story can be a powerful way to teach self-awareness and self-worth and to teach about relationships with others. The Directed Reading/Thinking Activity (Stauffer, 1969a) is another excellent strategy for teaching group decision making through hypothesizing the outcome of a story. This activity, explained in Chapter 5, enables students to believe in themselves by feeling that what they have to say and predict has dignity and worth.

Questioning in the Affective Domain

Questions in the affective domain provide linkage among emotions, attitudes, and thought or knowledge (Jones, Morgan, & Tonelson, 1992). For example, when students examining the problems faced by Richard Nixon as president of the United States are asked to consider their feelings about these problems, they are connecting knowledge and feelings.

A scheme developed by Krathwohl, Bloom, and Masia (1964) seeks to order and relate the different kinds of affective behavior, using the concept of internalization — the process of incorporating something into one's behavior as one's own. Internalization can be viewed as movement not only from the external to the internal, but also from the simple to the complex and from the concrete to the abstract. The scheme is reproduced in part here:

1.0 Receiving (attending)
- 1.1 Awareness — the person is aware of the feelings of others whose activities may be of little interest to him.
- 1.2 Willingness to receive — the person listens to others with respect.
- 1.3 Controlled or selected attention — the person is alert toward human values and judgments of life as they are recorded in history.

2.0 Responding
- 2.1 Acquiescence in responding — the person obeys job regulations.
- 2.2 Willingness to respond — the person practices the rules of safety on the job.
- 2.3 Satisfaction in response — the person enjoys participation in activities and plays according to the rules.

3.0 Valuing
- 3.1 Acceptance of a value — the person accepts the importance of social goals in a free society.
- 3.2 Preference for a value — the person assumes an active role in clarifying the social goals in a free society.
- 3.3 Commitment — the person is loyal to the social goals of a free society.

4.0 Organizing
- 4.1 Conceptualization of a value — the person judges the responsibility of society for conserving natural resources.
- 4.2 Organization of a value system — the person develops a plan for conserving natural resources.

5.0 Characterization of a value or value complex
- 5.1 Generalized set — the person faces facts and conclusions that can be logically drawn with consistent values orientation.
- 5.2 Characterization — the person develops a philosophy of life.

The extent to which teachers stress affective teaching depends, of course, on the objective of the lesson, but certainly teachers can try to elicit emotional responses during selected lessons in all content-area subjects. For example, following Krathwohl's taxonomy, teachers can do the following:

1. *Receiving.* Questions can be formulated to determine whether students are actively involved — that is, whether they are receiving from the text, lecture, or other source. Teachers can ask students to explain what they think about a subject at any time during the lesson. Through these techniques, teachers can assess the degree of student involvement.

2. *Responding.* Teachers should periodically call upon students to respond to emotions and feelings inherent in a given lesson. A teacher might say, "Tell me how you feel now that you have answered that question." Students need to feel good about their responses to questions.

3. *Valuing.* This is usually the highest level of attainment reached in the classroom situation. Here, students show that they appreciate and value reading. Teachers can ask students why they value a certain literature selection, a chapter in social studies ("because it teaches me about other cultures"), or a particular application to a mathematics problem. Teachers stress valuing anytime they ask students why they enjoyed a reading selection.

4. *Organizing.* At this level, students conceptualize their values over a period of time, internalizing the concept valued and making it a part of their belief structure. Teachers can emphasize this affective level by asking students to write about their beliefs regarding particular national, state, or local issues. Anytime a teacher asks "What do you believe?" she or he is helping in the creation of a value system.

5. *Characterization.* This level represents a continuation of level 4, in that the student recognizes that a value has been internalized. At this level, the student is committed to the value. Teachers can determine whether students are on this level by asking if students believe strongly in a certain concept.

The **GATOR** (Gaining Acceptance Toward Reading) system can assist teachers in asking more affective questions. To help gain student acceptance of reading, the teacher announces that all questions asked about a lesson, either by the teacher or students, must be based on "feelings," as must all the responses. The entire lesson is taught with questions such as

How did that make you feel?

Why is this lesson important to you?

How did you feel about the main character? Why would you have done or not done what the main character did?

Why is this chapter important?

Tell us why you like what you just read.

GATOR can also be played as a game — the feelings game — in which students in small groups are allowed to discuss only emotion-laden questions. In this way, the teacher stresses what we call "meta-affection" — the act of thinking about how one feels directly after a reading. No matter what variation is used, the most important aspect of GATOR is that no factual comprehension questions can be asked by anyone, students or teachers. There are no "What happened here?" or "What happened there?" questions. We recommend GATOR as an excellent affective teaching strategy — one that will not "snap back" on you!

The following affective questions were generated by teachers and students during a brainstorming session after reading *Goodbye, Grandma* by Ray Bradbury:

If you knew that a close relative of yours was about to die, would you treat him or her differently?

How do you think Grandma felt about the beginning and ending of her life?

What if you were given three years to live; how would you do things differently?

There is humor in this story. How do you feel about having humor in a story about death?

Do you feel Grandma is like anyone you know?

What lasting feeling were you left with at the end of the story?

During what parts of this story did you have a warm, happy feeling? Read these parts aloud to the class.

How do you think it will feel to be old?

Do we treat people differently when we know they are dying? Should we?

Using expository materials in a middle-school lesson about seasons and climate from an earth science textbook, a teacher could ask the following affective questions:

How do you feel about today's weather?

Can weather affect your mood and how you feel? Give examples.

How do you feel about the seasons?

What if there were never any change of seasons? Describe your feelings.

One-Minute Summary

Probably no area is so misunderstood and neglected as the area of affect in teaching. In this chapter, we have maintained that students rarely, if ever, achieve without having certain concomitant feelings, including a positive attitude and strong emotions of belonging and caring for other students, the subject, and the teacher. Teachers in every content area must be aware of the importance of the smile, the gesture, the kind remark. They should try to structure positive experiences as an integral part of daily instruction. In addition, teachers need to plan how to deliver a lesson so that students enjoy what they are learning and see purpose in the material to be studied. The classroom atmosphere should be warm and supportive, so that students feel good about both what they know and how much they can learn. Students need to explore and take part in discovery types of learning activities, which lead to a more internal locus of control. Most important of all, to bring about lasting achievement, teachers must pay attention to both the cognitive and affective domains of learning. Classroom teachers who use affective strategies, such as those described in this chapter, to teach the cognitive skills of reading will be considerably more successful than those who omit such strategies from their reading program.

End-of-Chapter Activities

Assisting Comprehension   Study the graphic organizer shown here, and see if you can incorporate the listed terms in a way that makes sense to you. If asked by the instructor, be prepared to justify your choices in a small group or to the class as a whole.

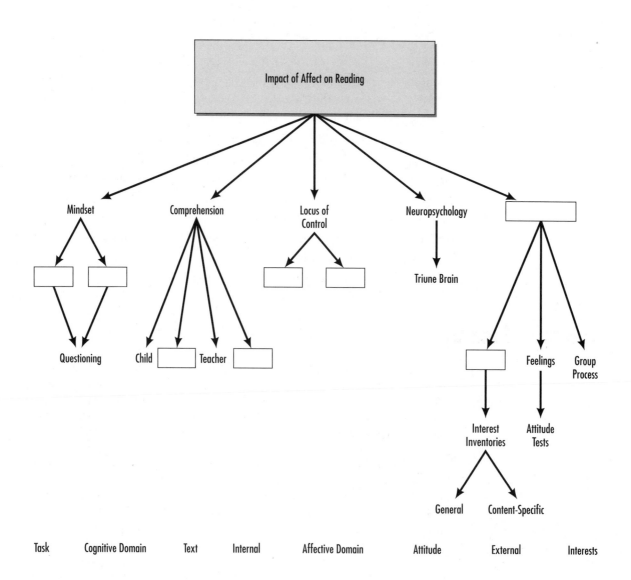

Task   Cognitive Domain   Text   Internal   Affective Domain   Attitude   External   Interests

Reflecting on Your Reading   A case has been presented in this chapter that no curriculum can be concerned solely with the cognitive domain of learning and that thinking and learning skills are actually interwoven with feelings, motivation, and attention. After reading the chapter, study the following diagram and write down your thoughts on how thinking through both domains of learning can be emphasized.

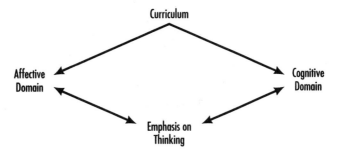

PART TWO

PREPARATION

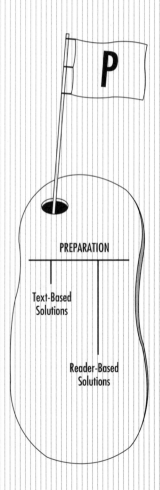

CHAPTER 3

PREPARATION

Text-Based
Solutions

Reader-Based
Solutions

Preparation

TEXT-BASED SOLUTIONS

"I do not like them, Sam-I-am. I do not like green eggs and ham."

Dr. Seuss

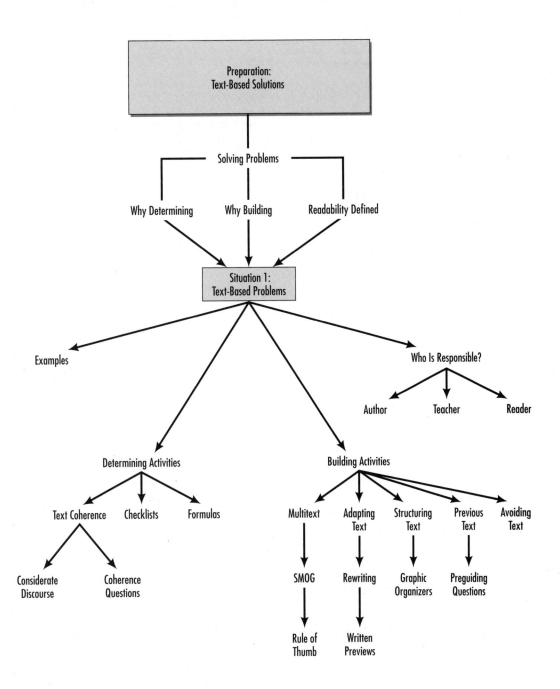

Prepare to Read

1. Have you read any material lately with which you just didn't "connect"? Perhaps you tried to read a software documentation guide or a technical report. Describe your experience. How did you react? How did you cope with this challenging material? What did you do to ensure your reading success?

2. Following is a list of terms used in this chapter. Some of them may be familiar to you in a general context, but in this chapter they may be used in a different way than you are used to. Rate your knowledge by placing a + in front of those you are sure that you know, a √ in front of those you have some knowledge about, and a 0 in front of those you don't know. Be ready to locate and pay special attention to their meanings when they are presented in the chapter.

___ readability   ___ readability formulas
___ inconsiderate discourse   ___ Fry graph
___ text coherence   ___ SMOG
___ dumbed-down text   ___ rule of thumb

Objectives

As you read this chapter, focus your attention on the following objectives. You will:

1. understand the importance of determining and building reader background.

2. define the term *readability*.

3. be able to make judgments about the readability of textbook material.

4. become acquainted with one of three basic situations that may cause readability problems and be able to use this information to determine if a readability problem exists.

5. become acquainted with several activities that can help build the match between a reader and the material to be read.

6. understand the responsibilities of author, teacher, and student in determining the reader's background for reading content material.

Spending Instructional Time Wisely: The Issue of Teacher Resistance

The need to prepare readers is often misunderstood by content teachers. Many teachers would like to believe that their "job" is to teach only content subjects; preparation for reading should be the responsibility of students, or of teachers at earlier grade levels. Teachers who hold such a view are mistaken on two counts. First, teachers teach *students* the content; they do not just teach content. Trying to teach only content without sensitivity to the students is like sending a message but having no receiver at the other end. Second, the time spent preparing students to read translates to efficient use of time. Teaching time may be wasted when students do not understand the relevance of the material to their needs.

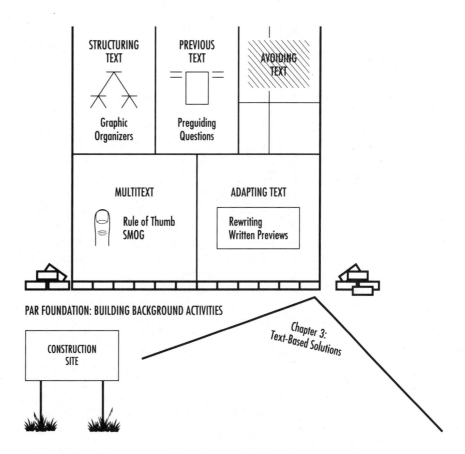

Preparation is like the foundation of a house. It takes time to build the foundation, but the house will be stable as a result. We are reminded of a local construction scandal. Houses were built on claylike soil without an appropriate foundation. Consequently, three years later, some houses are literally cracking up. The hurry to finish construction has resulted in expensive repairs and lost reputations.

The moral: The time spent in advance is more than recouped in the long term. When a teacher tells students, by words or actions, "Just read," students are cheated. They have not been guided to use arguably the most important reading strategy of all: preparation.

Why Is Determining a Match between Reader and Text So Important?

Most of us would like to feel comfortable with what we're about to read. Good readers usually explore material in advance to determine how much they already know about the topic, how interested they are in it, and why they ought to read the material. They will browse through the material to get "the gist" of it: Does it seem easy to follow? Is the content clear? They will also assess its relative difficulty: Is it easy for me to read, like a story (narrative style)? Is it somewhat more difficult, like a newspaper article (journalistic style)? Or is it challenging for me to read, like many textbooks (exposition with many new facts and concepts)? We all feel more confident when we know what lies ahead and can chart our course accordingly.

Expected Range in Classroom Reading Levels

For mature, proficient readers, this assessment may be almost automatic and unconscious. Until they reach this stage of proficiency, however, most students need the teacher's guidance to determine their background. How many students will need teacher guidance? Teachers can expect that few students will already be proficient at determining their own background. Singer and Bean (1988) suggest that "when a heterogeneous group of students progresses through the grades, we can expect its range of reading achievement (in reading age equivalents) to increase from four years at grade one to twelve years at grade twelve" (p. 162). To gauge the range of reading in a heterogeneous class, Singer and Bean advise multiplying the median age of the students by two-thirds. Thus, the range in a third-grade class (with a median age of eight) would be about five years; in a tenth-grade class (median age 15), the range would be about ten years. This indication of variation, though not a precise measure, does demonstrate how the same reading material can generate very different reactions from students.

It is crucial, then, that teachers carefully study their students' reading needs as well as the materials they use as teaching tools. By determining in advance as much as they can about what readers bring *to* the page and what readers will encounter *on* the page, teachers can help students think and read more effectively. If teachers and readers ignore this step, a crucial part of preparation for reading is neglected. Comprehension, not to mention the time spent on instruction, will ultimately be lost. Determining the background of the reader, so that an adequate match occurs between the reader and the text, makes good sense from every vantage point.

The Importance of Building Background

Green Eggs and Ham by Dr. Seuss is a favorite children's story. What a lot of time Sam-I-am spends arguing with his friend about trying this delectable concoction! The friend assumes that he won't like green eggs and ham, probably because green is not a color usually associated with eggs unless they're rotten. His background—limited to the color rather than the taste of green eggs—interferes. Poor Sam-I-am! His only strategy is to nag. Finally the friend does try the dish, and he likes it. He vows to eat it in any number of creative ways in the future. The ending of this delightful story is happy, and the nagging dialogue is fun for young readers.

In real life, convincing someone to try anything as seemingly revolting as green eggs and ham will require more than nagging. Teachers may often feel like Sam-I-am, nagging students to read the content material because it's really interesting if only they would try it. Unfortunately, sometimes students' backgrounds are as limited as that of Sam-I-am's reluctant friend. An unpleasant experience with any aspect of reading or with a subject can cause students to be just as stubborn about reading an assignment as about eating green eggs and ham. A teacher who assigns and nags doesn't have much impact. However, both research and practice confirm that strategies that build reader background do work. Such strategies entice students to try the reading and give them the connection point to understand what they read. For instance, a group of young students who had just completed a background-building activity remarked that it was fun and they wished that more teachers would "try this stuff." In this chapter, several strategies that convince readers to try a reading material will be discussed.

The process of reading in content areas can be compared to a basketball game. Actually *playing* the game really takes up the smallest amount of time; the greatest amount of time is spent in workouts, strategy sessions, and practice, all of which are intended to ensure success in the game itself. After the game, more time is spent analyzing what occurred on the court, and then the preparation for the next game begins. So it is with reading. A proficient reader spends time getting ready to read by determining and building background. Instead of plunging into the reading, this reader will prepare. Good comprehension is a natural result, just as playing a game successfully is the natural result of hard work in practice. Teachers who are aware of this phenomenon and aid students in the preparation stage of reading are like good coaches. Students who realize that preparation for reading is like court practice will reap benefits in higher achievement and better grades.

What Is Readability?

We prefer an encompassing definition for the often-used term **readability**. One such definition is suggested by Harris and Hodges in *A Dictionary of Reading* (1981). They equate the term with "ease of understanding or comprehension because of style of writing as well as many other variables including those inherent to the material *and* the reader" (p. 262). Dreyer (1984) has written that "the goal of readability research is to match reader and text" (p. 334). Simply stated, readability is that match. Readability is *not* a formula; it is an exploration of what characteristics within the reader and within the text will create a successful marriage. By considering readability, teachers are able to prepare readers appropriately to learn. Professional judgment is essential in determining readability; no score or formula can do more than help teachers understand the problems that may occur with the material. Too many factors are involved for teachers to settle for simple solutions.

To understand the complexity of readability, we would like you to participate in the following assignment.

Suppose you were assigned to read this passage on the pathology of viral hepatitis? Unless you were already highly interested in and knowledgeable about the topic, you might feel a little apprehensive. We are asking you to read the passage now, but we are telling you in advance that this is an experiment; you are not expected to learn the material. Instead, you will be asked to grade it according to the criteria that follow the passage.

> *The physical signs and symptoms that the person with hepatitis experiences are reflections of cellular damage in the liver. The hepatocyte has alterations in function resulting from damage caused by the virus and the resultant inflammatory response. The endoplasmic reticulum is the first organelle to undergo change. Since this organelle is responsible for protein and steroid synthesis, glucuronide conjugation, and detoxification, functions that depend on these processes will be altered. The degree of impairment depends on the amount of hepatocellular damage. The mitochondria sustain damage later than the endoplasmic reticulum. The Kupffer cells increase in size and number. The vascular and ductile tissues experience inflammatory changes. In most cases of uncomplicated hepatitis the reticulum framework is not in danger, and excellent healing of the hepatocytes occurs in three to four months.*

From Chapter 68, "Disorders of the Liver," in *Medical Surgical Nursing — A Psychophysiological Approach* by J. Luckmann and K. Sorensen, 1980, New York: D. B. Saunders Company.

Rate this reading material on each of the following criteria by circling a grade from A to F:

The language and vocabulary are clear to me.

A   B   C   D   F

The concepts are well developed.

A   B   C   D   F

The paragraph is organized.

A   B   C   D   F

The paragraph is well written.

A   B   C   D   F

The paragraph is interesting to me.

A   B   C   D   F

How did you rate this material? You might want to share reactions with your classmates. Now compare your impressions with those of 41 teachers, whose actual ratings were distributed as follows:

The language and vocabulary are clear to me.

A	B	C	D	F
2	0	7	16	16

The concepts are well developed.

A	B	C	D	F
2	3	19	8	9

The paragraph is organized.

A	B	C	D	E
6	12	14	3	6

The paragraph is well written.

A	B	C	D	F
2	9	14	12	4

The paragraph is interesting to me.

A	B	C	D	F
1	1	3	10	26

These 41 teachers represent a fairly homogeneous group: they have a common profession and a recognized level of competence. Therefore, we might expect their reactions to the passage to be fairly similar. Yet, these teachers rated the paragraph differently. Although all 41 teachers read the same material, the experiences and interests each brought to the material, the interaction each personally had with the material, and the skill of each reader greatly influenced their reactions.

The challenge of the classroom is even greater because of the heterogeneity of the students. The experiences, personal interactions, and reading skills of students will most likely be more varied than those of our 41 teachers.

Three Factors to Consider in Making the Match

Notice that the first and last ratings teachers made about the viral hepatitis passage relate to prior knowledge and interest; both are characteristics that reside within the reader. The 41 teachers in this group were generally not confident about the language and vocabulary of the material, nor were they particularly interested in it. The middle three ratings relate to the text itself—concept development, organization, and style. These characteristics reside within the text, not the reader. Notice that the teachers rated text characteristics higher. One can conclude that although the teachers did not bring the requisite vocabulary, knowledge, or interest to this material, they recognized that the text was well structured. Reading the complete chapter would be challenging for them because they would be constantly trying to fit new information into a limited background of knowledge, but the text would help them because the writer has presented the information well.

The higher ratings of the text itself illustrate the complexity of readability. Three basic factors influence readability: text structure, prior knowledge and interest, and reading skills. Each contributes to making text easier to read. Considering one without the other is incomplete thinking (see Chapter 1). To determine the match between the reader and the text, a teacher needs to consider all three factors. This total consideration is the first step in preparing the reader to read. In this chapter, we focus on the first factor, text structure. The other two factors will be examined in the following chapter.

Text-Based Problems That Affect Readability

The first factor that affects readability is text-related; that is, it pertains more to the material to be read than to the reader. Hill and Erwin (1984) found that more than half of the textbooks they studied were at least one level above their target grade. Social studies texts seemed to be the worst offenders. Some texts for middle-school students were found to be at college level! Other studies suggest that although textbooks are becoming less difficult for students to read, there is still a problem with material being too difficult for the target audience (Derby, 1987; Morgan, Otto, & Thompson, 1976).

Looking at readability level, text organization, and cohesion, Kinder, Bursuck, and Epstein (1992) found that social studies textbooks treating the same topic and intended for the same grade varied by as much as *six* grade levels. In short, although publishers have become more sensitive to producing materials that are both content-rich *and* readable by the intended audience, many materials that teachers are using today are difficult for their students.

When the 41 teachers rated the viral hepatitis passage for concepts, organization, and writing style, they were determining the suitability of the material based on the text itself. In text-based situations, all readers are likely to face similar problems because the material *is* the main problem. Even if students are interested in the material and have enough background to make that material easier to read, the text itself may prove too difficult. The energy required to "stick with it" may exceed the energy readers judge worth the expenditure (Stetson & Williams, 1992). What follows is a description of text-based problems and of activities that will help teachers determine if this type of problem exists in their materials.

INCONSIDERATE TEXT

"Your ring adjusters will shape to fit you right by following these simple steps."

Wait a minute! Are the *ring adjusters* going to follow some simple steps? Doesn't the author mean the *reader* is supposed to follow some simple steps? And will the ring adjusters change shape to fit the reader? or fit the ring? or help the ring fit the reader?

"Explain how are certain flowering times adaptive for plant species."

A sixth-grader brought his textbook to the science teacher, asking her to explain what this sentence meant. No wonder he had problems! By reviewing the chapter, the teacher was able to locate a subheading and text about "flowering times and survival." The question must have been drawn from the material under this subheading, but the wording of the question is unclear.

The reader will need to work extra hard to understand the meaning underlying text passages such as these. Is it worth it? When confronted with such inconsiderate text, the reader must make a decision. In content classrooms, readers make decisions all the time; too often, they decide that the text is simply not worth the energy.

How many readers have abandoned or postponed the mastery of a new software program because its documentation was poorly written or presented? The author of the manual may have "forgotten" whole sections of explicit instructions. How many parents have become exasperated with the poorly written instructions for assembling a toy? Similarly, some content material, particularly that found in textbooks, may be poorly written and therefore place unnecessary stress on a reader. If such is the case, then teachers must identify the difficulties in the material in order to help their readers expend the least energy for the greatest gain.

Anderson and Armbruster (1984) have examined several content textbooks and found them to be poorly written, primarily because the text material seemed to have no logical structure. Such texts may list facts or provide lengthy descriptions of events without reference to the underlying concepts which those descriptions are meant to support. Students are ill equipped to ferret out the theme or concept from such "wandering" exposition. This poorly written material is recognizable because of its loose organization, its lack of a discernible style, its incorrect syntax, or its incoherent passages. Armbruster and Anderson (1981) have assigned the label **inconsiderate discourse** to such material. When Olson and Gee (1991) surveyed 47 primary-grade classroom teachers about their impressions of expository content text for their students, 23% of them identified text characteristics such as "sentence length, page format, inadequate arrangement and unfamiliar presentation of topics, and lack of aids on how to read expository text" as the greatest problems, while another 69% cited unfamiliar words. College students indicated in a survey (D. Smith, 1992) that textbooks are generally boring because passages are too long, the writing style is hard to follow, graphics don't seem to relate to text, and information is either too detailed or repetitive. These factors all enter the mix that makes text considerate or inconsiderate, coherent or incoherent.

TEXT COHERENCE

For a text to be readable, it must exhibit **textual coherence** (Armbruster, 1984). Textual coherence—the clear presentation of material to facilitate comprehension—can be divided into two categories. *Global coherence* is the big picture. Text should contain major, superordinate ideas that span entire sections of the material. Readers should be aware of this globalness, and should be reminded of it frequently, so they can follow the ideas presented without becoming lost. The way the material is structured can ensure global coherence. Arrangement of ideas into logical organizational patterns, such as a clear sequence or cause-effect pattern, is a global aid. The type of text also aids a reader. A narrative style is usually easiest for readers, followed by a more journalistic style. Hardest to read is exposition. How clear that style is to the reader helps also. When an author is clearly telling a story, readers can follow this comfortably. It is confusing when a writer mixes exposition and story but doesn't cue the reader. "This is a story about. . ." or "The following description explains. . ." provide clear cues to the type of text to follow. If one type of text is used frequently, this also helps the reader understand and effectively use the structure of the text. Of course, the content of the material and how well the author matches it to the structure are also important for global coherence.

Local coherence involves the many kinds of aids that connect ideas at the more immediate, or local, level. These aids include cues within sentences — phrases or clauses, for example — between sentences, or within paragraphs. When the author clearly identifies the subject and then uses a pronoun to refer to that subject, coherence is much greater than when the pronoun referent is vague and the reader is forced to guess to whom or what the author may be referring. Clear connectors — *because, however, but* — help readers make the desired connections. When too many details are provided, readers tend to lose the major points. Questions interspersed frequently, rather than saved until the end of the material, also help readers stay tuned in to the content. The questions authors ask should be the ones that teachers think are important.

Readers should not have to work hard at understanding the *way* a text is presented; their work should be on the *content* presented. But, many times, text is written so inconsiderately that readers struggle too hard with the text and give up on the content. Consider, for instance, this passage:

> The lung is our great breathing machine. It draws in air and sends it out again. We call this breathing and take it for granted. But breathing is not as simple as it seems.

A reader will need to read extra carefully to determine that the first *it* refers to the lung, the second *it* refers to the air, the third *it* refers to the breathing process, and the fourth *it* refers to breathing. Many readers prefer not to work this hard.

Another type of poorly written text is that in which authors have tried to simplify content to an impossible degree. Former Secretary of Education Terrell Bell (Toch, 1984) expressed concern over such textbooks, calling them "dumbed down." In **dumbed-down text**, global coherence may be so simplified that the author really can't do justice to the content. Local coherence may be absent because there isn't enough complexity to the text. The important points and intricacies may both be lost. The reader loses content and cues.

Ways to Determine If Text-Based Problems Exist

There are several ways to determine the readability of text material, some preferable to others. The best ways may take the longest time, but net the best results in that they reveal specifically what problems make the text hard to read. When teachers know what's wrong, they can usually instruct accordingly. Just knowing that the material is too hard is probably not enough information on which to base sound instruction. Applying some of the following measures to determine readability will provide teachers with varying levels of insight. We try to indicate which we think are most valuable and why.

Questions for Teachers to Ask about Text Coherence

Text coherence is at the heart of most text-related problems (Armbruster, 1984). To determine if textual coherence is a text-related problem, students are really the best resource. Britton, Van Dusen, Gulgog, Glynn, and Sharp (1991) found that college students were able to select with 95% accuracy which of two texts on the same topic was easier to learn. Another way is to sample student and teacher opinion. Students and teachers might ask the following types of questions when reviewing text material:

1. Is the text narrative, journalistic, or expository?
2. How clear is this style to the reader? Has the author stated what the style is, or cued the reader in any way?
3. Can I identify a clear, major idea that pervades the text, chapter, section, lesson, paragraph?
4. Are the ideas arranged in a clear, logical organizational pattern? How clearly is this pattern revealed to the reader?
5. Does the content match the structure and organization?
6. Are aids available to help the reader, such as:

   a. headings and subheadings
   b. topic sentences
   c. lively presentation of information
   d. explicit statements to guide reader
   e. logical ordering
   f. consistency
   g. clarity of references, such as pronoun to subject
   h. questions asked often of the reader, not saved until the end
   i. enough, but not too many, details

Use of a Checklist

Another comprehensive way to determine whether material is difficult for a group of readers is to evaluate factors such as those suggested by Dreyer (1984): word frequency, clarity, and concept density. Linguistic features (Biber, 1991) should be identified and incorporated as well. Haas (1991) found that many concepts identified as crucial by teachers did not appear consistently in social studies texts. Teachers should pay close attention to concepts as they check their textbooks for text-based problems. Creating a checklist of such factors, which the teacher can then use as a guide, ensures both "readability and relevance" (Danielson, 1987, p. 185).

WALKER CHECKLIST

Walker (1985) has developed the following simple checklist and rating system. The items included on this list and the points per item will depend on teacher judgment.

Interest level 1–3

Appropriate vocabulary 1–2

Sentence length controlled 1–3

Suitable for use with study strategy 1–3

Locational skills suitability 1–2

Organizational patterns used 1–2

Graphics suited to extending skills 1–2

Vocabulary load (new) under 10% (depends on material) 1–5

Suited to research skills usage 1–2

Adjunct print aids for comprehension 1–3

Emphasis on higher-level comprehension 1–3

Rating: 26–30, Excellent; 21–25, Good; 15–20, Fair; 11–15, Poor

In using the rating system, teachers assign the higher numbers to the more desirable traits. For example, if the passage appears to be very interesting, then a rating of 3 would be given. "Sentence length controlled" refers to passages with no marked variation between very short and very long sentences. Passages "suitable for use with study strategy" would lend themselves to study techniques such as those described in Chapters 9 and 10. If information can be easily located in the passage, then "locational skills suitability" would rate a 2. If aids such as margin notes are provided, then "adjunct print aids" would rate a 3.

BADER TEXTBOOK ANALYSIS CHART

One fairly brief checklist to help teachers consider readability carefully and efficiently is Bader's (1987) textbook analysis chart (see Figure 3.1). The chart separates areas of concern in determining the readability of material and lists specific items for teachers to evaluate and comment on. The user is encouraged to summarize the textbook's strengths and weaknesses after completing the checklist and then to decide what this summary indicates for teaching the material presented. Charts completed by teachers of music and history are included in Appendix C.

The Bader analysis encourages teachers to consider several factors that contribute to readability. Under Linguistic Factors, for example, the items cover word difficulty more thoroughly than a word-length measure in a formula can do. The Writing Style category covers sentence length, but in a more direct and sensible manner than a formula could. Conceptual Factors and Organizational Factors include items that many authors have identified as crucial in determining text difficulty. In addition, the teacher is asked to think about Learning Aids for the students, because such aids will make otherwise difficult material easier to handle. The Teaching Aids category also gives teachers direction in how to guide reading of otherwise difficult material. As Sinatra (1986) points out, visual aids

FIGURE 3.1 Textbook analysis chart

+ Excellent/ Evident Throughout	√ Average/ Somewhat Evident	− Poor/ Not Evident		
			Book Title _____	
			Publisher _____	
			Grade Level _____	
			Content Area _____	

LINGUISTIC FACTORS:

				Comments
_____	_____	_____	Generally appropriate to intended grade level(s) according to _____ formula	_____
_____	_____	_____	Linguistic patterns suitable to most populations and fit intended level(s)	_____
_____	_____	_____	Vocabulary choice and control suitable	_____
_____	_____	_____	New vocabulary highlighted, italicized, in boldface, or underlined	_____
_____	_____	_____	New vocabulary defined in context	_____
_____	_____	_____	New vocabulary defined in margin guides, glossary, beginning or end of chapter	_____

CONCEPTUAL FACTORS:

_____	_____	_____	Conceptual level generally appropriate to intended grade level(s)	_____
_____	_____	_____	Concepts presented deductively	_____
_____	_____	_____	Concepts presented inductively	_____
_____	_____	_____	Major ideas are highlighted, italicized, in boldface type, or underlined	_____
_____	_____	_____	Appropriate assumptions made regarding prior level of concepts	_____
_____	_____	_____	Sufficient development of new concepts through examples, illustrations, analogies, redundancy	_____
_____	_____	_____	No evidence of sexual, racial, economic, cultural, or political bias	_____

ORGANIZATIONAL FACTORS:

_____	_____	_____	Units, chapters, table of contents, index present clear, logical development of subject	_____

(continued on page 78)

FIGURE 3.1 continued

+ Excellent/ Evident Throughout	√ Average/ Somewhat Evident	− Poor/ Not Evident		Comments
ORGANIZATIONAL FACTORS:				
_____	_____	_____	Chapters of instructional segments contain headings and subheadings that aid comprehension of subject	_____
_____	_____	_____	Introductory, definitional, illustrative, summary paragraphs/sections used as necessary	_____
_____	_____	_____	Topic sentences of paragraphs clearly identifiable or easily inferred	_____
_____	_____	_____	Each chapter/section/unit contains a well-written summary and/or overview	_____
WRITING STYLE:				
_____	_____	_____	Ideas are expressed clearly and directly	_____
_____	_____	_____	Word choice is appropriate	_____
_____	_____	_____	Tone and manner of expression are appealing to intended readers	_____
_____	_____	_____	Mechanics are correct	_____
LEARNING AIDS:				
_____	_____	_____	Questions/tasks appropriate to conceptual development of intended age/grade level(s)	_____
_____	_____	_____	Questions/tasks span levels of reasoning: literal, interpretive, critical, values clarification, problem-solving	_____
_____	_____	_____	Questions/tasks can be used as reading guides	_____
_____	_____	_____	Suitable supplementary readings suggested	_____

(continued on page 79)

FIGURE 3.1   continued

+ Excellent/ Evident Throughout	√ Average/ Somewhat Evident	− Poor/ Not Evident		Comments
TEACHING AIDS:				
_____	_____	_____	Clear, convenient to use	_____
_____	_____	_____	Helpful ideas for conceptual development	_____
_____	_____	_____	Alternative instructional suggestions given for poor readers, slow learning students, advanced students	_____
_____	_____	_____	Contains objectives, management plans, evaluation guidelines, tests of satisfactory quality	_____
_____	_____	_____	Supplementary aids available	_____
BINDING/PRINTING/FORMAT/ILLUSTRATIONS:				
_____	_____	_____	Size of book is appropriate	_____
_____	_____	_____	Cover, binding, and paper are appropriate	_____
_____	_____	_____	Typeface is appropriate	_____
_____	_____	_____	Format is appropriate	_____
_____	_____	_____	Pictures, charts, graphs are appealing	_____
_____	_____	_____	Illustrations aid comprehension of text	_____
_____	_____	_____	Illustrations are free of sexual, social, cultural bias	_____
SUMMARY:				
_____	_____	_____	Totals	_____

The strengths are:

The weaknesses are:

As a teacher, I will need to:

Original text analysis chart by Dr. Lois Bader, Michigan State University.
Used with permission of Lois Bader.

often make difficult material readable. Features such as typography, format, illustrations, and book appearance can enhance meaning in a text. Bader includes these items in her last category.

CAUTIONS ABOUT CHECKLISTS

The use of checklists to determine whether material is poorly written or difficult must be qualified. No one checklist can cover all factors important to teachers. Checklists must be general; only teachers can make them specific by adding their own items according to their own needs for the instructional material. Most checklists will cover instructional design, but not instructional content (Moore & Murphy, 1987). However, with such tools as those contained in this chapter and with a knowledge of why determining the difficulty factors of reading material is important, we believe that teachers can proceed wisely.

Special Note What makes math textbooks easier or harder to read? Here, the reading rules are a bit different. Examples often require bottom-to-top, circular, diagonal, or backwards reading rather than more conventional directionality. A math text should include specific explanations and directions for students (Georgia Department of Education, 1975). These directions should make clear to students that reading math materials may employ different rules.

Readability Formulas

Readability formulas have commonly been used as a major resource for determining the difficulty of material. Fry, a noted expert on readability formulas, quotes Farr as estimating that "over 40 percent of the state and local school districts in the United States use readability formulas as one criterion in textbook selection" (Fry, 1987, p. 339). Fry believes that "the reason educators use readability formulas is that if you match the learner's ability to the difficulty of the material, you can cut down on oral reading errors and increase silent reading comprehension" (p. 343). For content teachers, this reasoning is especially important because comprehension of the content material is very important. Readability formulas are *efficient* measures — if not always the most *effective* ones — to help make this match. A quick first look at material to screen anticipated problems with difficulty level can be accomplished using a readability formula.

What Readability Formulas Measure

Formulas most often report information about difficulty by reading-level scores. The assumption that it is possible to place material at a certain grade level of difficulty underlies most readability formulas. The use of a formula to determine reading level can be very helpful for decisions about content material when a prediction of difficulty is necessary. Such would be the case when a textbook adoption committee considers several texts but has no students on whom to "try out" the material. Similarly, a formula may be useful and efficient when a teacher wants to identify in advance of use several materials that students can read independently in the library. A readability formula gives a *bit* of information that predicts the difficulty of a material. It is a fairly quick measure, independent of student interaction. But we cannot rely on the grade level obtained as an exact measure; it is only a predictor.

How Readability Formulas Work

Klare (1974–75) reviewed the development and uses of readability formulas from 1960 to the mid-1970s and explained their basic components. Over the years, reading researchers have developed and statistically validated many readability formulas. Some are cumbersome in that they necessitate checking long lists of words. Both the Dale/Chall (1948) and the Spache (1953) measure "word familiarity"—that is, whether students should be expected to know a word within a given passage—by relying on a lengthy word list. Some formulas necessitate several computational steps (Bormouth, 1969). Such formulas require analysis of several factors relating to readability, but essentially, two measurements are used in the majority of formulas: one of sentence difficulty and one of word difficulty. The assumption is that the longer the sentences and the longer the words, the harder the material will be.

Usually, this assumption holds true; sometimes, however, it is questionable. For instance, in William Faulkner's *The Sound and the Fury*, several sentences are as much as one and a half pages long! Most readers would agree that the length of such sentences makes for challenging material. Yet, could one say that because Hemingway's style leans to short sentences, his material is easy to read? In either case, one will read to understand style and theme; sentence length will be of little import. To further illustrate the point, read these two sentences:

The children played on the playground with the elephant.

We reneged all prior briefs.

The first sentence would measure as more difficult on a readability formula, but would it be?

The syntactical structure of sentences probably deserves more attention than it receives in readability formulas (Hunt, 1965; Richardson, 1975). For example, sentences in the active voice may be easier to understand than those in the passive voice. Readability formulas do not measure with such sensitivity. However, teachers would probably agree that first-graders do need to read material with shorter sentences than sixth-graders can read. Teachers also recognize that first-graders can accommodate some variety in sentence patterns. So, if one is careful, longer sentences may be a fairly accurate measure of difficult material.

Just as short sentences seem to be easier to read, the assumption that short words are easier on a reader also seems generally true. First-graders do recognize a lot of one-syllable words with facility. Yet, wouldn't *elephant* be an easier word for young readers than *the*? *Elephant* may be longer than *the*, but it's a lot easier to see a picture of an elephant than a *the*! Since seeing the word in one's mind facilitates comprehension, the longer word is easier in this case. Few readers wish to encounter too many long words all at once, but they also would be very bored by too many short ones. Given these qualifiers, the way most readability formulas measure a material makes sense.

Many formulas are available for teachers to use in determining text difficulty; Klare (1974–75) describes several. A few formulas have remained popular over several years because they are easy to apply and seem reliable. In this text, we will present two: the Fry readability graph and the SMOG. Hill and Erwin (1984) found that most teachers in their study preferred the Fry formula to others. By presenting two formulas, we give teachers a choice according to their purposes for the measure. Both are simple to calculate and are accepted favorably by teachers.

THE FRY READABILITY GRAPH

The **Fry graph** was originally developed by Edward Fry in the 1960s for African teachers who taught English as a second language. In 1977, Fry revised his graph to include explanations, directions, and an extension to the 17th-grade level. The Fry graph offers a quantifiable, efficient way to measure the difficulty of material on which the teacher will provide instruction.

To use this graph, teachers select at least three 100-word passages from different parts of the material. (See Figure 3.2, direction 1.) For each 100-word passage, they make two counts: the number of syllables and the number of sentences (directions 2 and 3). The three counts of syllables are added, then averaged; the three counts of sentences are added, then averaged (direction 4). The teacher then locates the average for the number of syllables across the top of the graph and the average for the number of sentences along the side of the graph. The point at which these two averages intersect is the readability score. The point will fall within a fanlike, numbered segment on the graph; this number corresponds to the grade-level score. Teachers should note that Fry says to count all words, including proper nouns, initials, and numerals (direction 1) and that he defines *word* as well as *syllable* (directions 6 and 7). If a point falls in a gray area, it is an unreliable score and should be recalculated using additional 100-word passages. The worksheet (Figure 3.3) is designed to help the reader remember and apply the directions during readability calculations.

The Fry formula is more usable for upper-elementary and higher-level materials than at the younger grades because one must have at least 100 words for computation. One way to adapt the Fry for shorter materials was developed by Forgan and Mangrum (1985); their procedure is described and illustrated in Appendix D. Fry (1990) also suggests a formula for short passages, of 40–99 words. We have found it just as easy and efficient to think about the text coherence questions and Bader's checklist as to compute formulas, particularly for short passages.

THE SMOG

McLaughlin (1969) named his readability formula **SMOG** as a tribute to another formula—the FOG—and after his birthplace, London, where "smog first appeared" (p. 641). Some have said that SMOG stands for the Simple Measure Of

FIGURE 3.2 The Fry readability graph. From *Journal of Reading, 21,* 242–252.

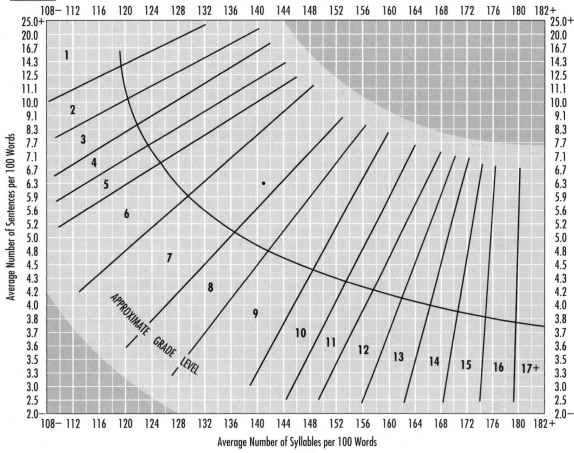

Average Number of Syllables per 100 Words

Expanded Directions for Working Fry Readability Graph

1. Randomly select three (3) sample passages and count out exactly 100 words each, beginning with the beginning of a sentence. Do count proper nouns, initializations, and numerals.
2. Count the number of sentences in the hundred words, estimating length of the fraction of the last sentence to the nearest one-tenth.
3. Count the total number of syllables in the 100-word passage. If you don't have a hand counter available, an easy way is to simply put a mark about every syllable over one in each word, then when you get to the end of the passage, count the number of marks and add 100. Small calculators can also be used as counters by pushing numeral 1, then push the + sign for each word or syllable when counting.
4. Enter graph with *average* sentence length and *average* number of syllables; plot dot where the two lines intersect. Area where dot is plotted will give you the approximate grade level.
5. If a great deal of variability is found in syllable count or sentence count, putting more samples into the average is desirable.

(*continued on page 84*)

FIGURE 3.2 continued

---

6. A word is defined as a group of symbols with a space on either side; thus, *Joe, IRA, 1945,* and *&* are each one word.
7. A syllable is defined as a phonetic syllable. Generally, there are as many syllables as vowel sounds. For example, *stopped* is one syllable and *wanted* is two syllables. When counting syllables for numerals and initializations, count one syllable for each symbol. For example, *1945* is four syllables, *IRA* is three syllables, and *&* is one syllable.

FIGURE 3.3 Fry Worksheet

Plot the averages found on the Fry graph.

	1st 100 Words	2nd 100 Words	3rd 100 Words	Average
Page #				
# Syllables				
# Sentences				

Gobbledygook! Although its name is very lighthearted, this formula is a serious solution to the problem of measuring the readability of material that students may have to read on their own.

The SMOG formula is very easy to compute. However, the teacher needs to use a calculator that computes square roots or have a table of square roots handy (see Table 3.1). To use the SMOG formula, follow these steps:

1. Count three sets of ten sentences (a total of 30 sentences).
2. Count all words of three or more syllables.
3. Take this number, and determine the nearest perfect square root.
4. Add 3 to this square root.
5. The final number is the readability level.

DIFFERENCES BETWEEN THE FRY GRAPH AND THE SMOG

Differences between the Fry graph and the SMOG are important to note. Since each formula is based on a different premise, the readability scores must be read differently. The Fry formula measures the readability of material used in an instructional setting. Since the difficult words and sentences will be explained by the teacher, the score is based on students' understanding 65 to 75 percent of the material at a given grade level. The SMOG formula is intended to measure the readability of material that a teacher will not be teaching. Perhaps it is material that the teacher has suggested a student use independently. Since the teacher will not be explaining the difficult words and sentences, the score is based on students' understanding 90 to 100 percent of the material. If a Fry and

TABLE 3.1

Perfect Square Roots

$\sqrt{1} = 1$	$\sqrt{16} = 4$	$\sqrt{49} = 7$	$\sqrt{100} = 10$
$\sqrt{4} = 2$	$\sqrt{25} = 5$	$\sqrt{64} = 8$	$\sqrt{121} = 11$
$\sqrt{9} = 3$	$\sqrt{36} = 6$	$\sqrt{81} = 9$	$\sqrt{144} = 12$

a SMOG were calculated on the same material, the Fry score would probably be lower. The chart in Table 3.2 illustrates the basic differences between these two popular measures of readability.

Some Cautions about Readability Formulas

In recent literature, professionals have warned teachers to be aware of the limitations of readability formulas. Walker (1985) even titles an article "Requiem for Readability" to emphasize the limitations. Readability formulas are not precise determiners of the difficulty of material; they are only predictors of how difficult the material might be for readers.

First, a readability formula gives a grade-level score, which is not a very specific measure of difficulty because grade level can be so ambiguous. Cadenhead (1987) describes this ambiguity as the "metaphor of reading level" and claims that it is a major problem of readability formulas. What does 17th-grade level mean when applied to "Pathology of Viral Hepatitis" without consideration of the reader's interests, background, and knowledge? A grade-level readability score gives teachers a start in their considerations of text difficulty, not a complete picture.

Second, although the lengths of sentences and words are convenient and credible indicators of readability and fit neatly into a formula, these measures are

TABLE 3.2   A Comparison of the Fry Graph and the SMOG Readability Formula

READABILITY MEASURE	PROVIDES READABILITY SCORE FOR	TEACHER WILL BE ASSISTING INSTRUCTION?	STUDENT IS EXPECTED TO COMPREHEND	READABILITY SCORE MAY BE	APPLY THIS FORMULA WHEN
Fry	instructional reading settings	yes	65–75% of material	lower°	teacher will instruct the group using the material being measured
SMOG	independent reading settings	no	90–100% of material	higher°	student will be reading the measured material on own, as in report-writing, homework, etc.

°as measured on the same passage

not comprehensive. Dreyer (1984), for one, suggests several other textual factors to consider, including word frequency, clarity of writing, and concept density. The various aspects of text coherence (Armbruster, 1984) are difficult to quantify. One cannot "compute" such factors in a simple readability formula.

Third, measures of word and sentence length are sometimes not the most accurate indicators of difficulty, as our references to Faulkner and Hemingway, *elephant* and *the*, and sample long and short sentences demonstrated. In one study (Carson, Chase, Gibson, & Hargrove, 1992), college students read texts measured by a formula as being at their level; however, the texts were not equally readable because of the conceptual difficulty of the material. To further illustrate this point, we refer readers to noted author E. B. White's essay "Calculating Machine," which recounts White's reaction when he received a "Reading-Ease Calculator" developed by General Motors and based on the Flesch Reading Ease Formula. "Communication by the written word," writes White, "is a subtler (and more beautiful) thing than Dr. Flesch and General Motors imagine" (p. 166). His point — that it is dangerous to reduce language to such simplistic evaluation — is well taken.

A fourth consideration involves questions of reliability and consistency. The fewer sections of material measured, the less consistent and reliable the resulting score is likely to be. Even three sections may be too few. This is why we chose not to feature the Fry Short Formula in this chapter, but to relegate it to an appendix. Because a readability formula is already a shortcut, a short formula is a shortcut for a shortcut! The Fry Short Formula should be used *only* when the material contains less than 100 words and the teacher cannot assess readability efficiently by relying on checklists and professional judgment. If three or fewer sections are measured, the teacher should be cautious about accepting the results.

Davison (1984) points out that readability formulas are a tool originally developed in the 1920s. We have conducted a great deal of research about text since that time; we know more and should be using our knowledge to move beyond rigid reliance on formulas. Although formulas can tell us some things — they yield levels based on the percentage of readers who have performed well at that level — they tell us a lot less than we need to know. Fry (1989) argues that some reading professionals may not like formulas because they are "so objective." When others argue that readability formulas are not comprehensive enough, his response is: "Readability formulas do not deny all this, they simply state that in general, on the average, the two inputs of sentence length and word difficulty accurately predict how easily a given passage will be understood by the average reader" (p. 295).

Rule of Thumb

A very quick and reader-centered way to determine readability is to teach students how to use a **rule of thumb** (Veatch, 1968). Younger students are told to select the book they want to read and to open to a middle page. If they spot an unknown word while reading that page, they press a thumb on the table. For each hard word, they press down another finger. If, when they have finished the page, they have pressed down five or more fingers, the book may be too hard. Three or fewer fingers indicates a more reasonable challenge. No fingers means the book is very easy. Of course, students should read the book even if it appears to be too easy or too hard, if they wish to. Older students can determine readability by using two hands and closing their fingers into fists. One closed fist indicates that the book is just right, two closed fists may indicate difficulty, and only one or two fingers in a fist indicates easy material. These activities are not very scientific, but they do ask the reader to be responsible for determining difficulty. This reader involvement promotes independence.

Activities to Overcome Text-Based Problems

So far in this chapter, we have described situations that cause a mismatch between reader and text, along with several ways to determine the mismatch. In this section, we present activities to overcome the mismatch. These activities are grouped in four categories: multitext strategies, adapting text, setting up text, and avoiding text.

Multitext Strategies

When material is poorly written and will require more energy than readers are likely to expend, a multitext strategy is a good idea. The teacher will need to locate other material that covers the same content as the text and offers easier reading. By enlisting the help of a media specialist, the teacher may discover several trade books that treat the topic to be studied. The teacher should then study the books to determine that they will match the reading levels and backgrounds of students. The match can be made with the help of checklists and formulas. The right book for the right student can then be assigned as a preparation for the content text, which will be introduced later. In Chapter 1, we described a multiple-text approach used by a primary teacher introducing a unit on goldfish. That teacher selected several trade books about fish and made them available to the children before starting the unit. The teacher prepared the children by encouraging them to browse and discover what they knew and might be learning about goldfish.

A multitext strategy is versatile, because different reading levels within a classroom can be accommodated when many books are used. The list of books can be expanded over the years with the help of the media specialist and through resources such as book reviews in professional journals. However, the multitext strategy requires additional time. Teachers must know thoroughly the content of the required material and then read each new book that might be included on the multiple-text list. In addition, most teachers will want to apply readability checks to each book for assurance of a good reading match.

If trade books are presented as a background builder before the required text is introduced, then their use represents a preparation strategy. We prefer multi-

A C T I V I T Y   3 . 1   MULTITEXT

BOOKS AND AUTHORS	SAMPLE 1 OF POLYSYLLABIC WORDS	SAMPLE 2 OF POLYSYLLABIC WORDS	SAMPLE 3 OF POLYSYLLABIC WORDS	TOTAL	NEAREST PERFECT SQUARE	SQUARE ROOT + 3	READING LEVEL
1. *Playing with Infinity* by Rózsa Péter	39	38	28	105	100	10 + 3	13
2. *A History of* π by Petr Beckman	33	37	47	117	100	10 + 3	13
3. *Realm of Measure* by Isaac Asimov	19	15	20	54	49	7 + 3	10
4. *Realm of Algebra* by Isaac Asimov	20	22	23	65	64	8 + 3	11
5. *Quick and Easy Math* by Isaac Asimov	13	19	13	45	36	6 + 3	9

Developed by Frances Reid.

text strategies at the preparation stage because we want our students to experience the required text also. We think that students need to encounter difficult, even poorly written text in order to develop their own strategies for dealing with such text. Over the years, all readers will be challenged by inconsiderate text, but they won't always have teachers around to guide them.

There are times, however, when the teacher will *substitute* multiple texts for the original textbook; in this case, the strategy can be classified as one to assist comprehension. Such an approach is often helpful to at-risk readers. Another popular way to use multiple texts is in a reflection activity. To enrich students' knowledge, teachers often give students a list of books from which to do independent reading.

An algebra teacher who worked with gifted students wanted to prepare a list of books that her gifted ninth-graders could read for assigned independent projects. She studied five books recently purchased by the school librarian. Using the SMOG, she determined a reading level for each book. As a result of this exercise, she identified three books by Isaac Asimov as best suited to her students' needs (see Activity 3.1). She also decided that she should become more involved in the selection process so that her library would stock trade books useful for her multiple-text approach.

The teacher can pull all books that might cover the content and make them available, but leave the responsibility of selection to the readers. Ammons (1987) demonstrates such a procedure with a class of fifth-graders preparing to learn about dinosaurs. First, the students pose questions to which they want to find answers. Next, Ammons introduces several trade books that might give them answers. Then the students select their own books and read to find answers. They can use the rule of thumb to help them in their selections. In this way, students build their background knowledge by using a multitext strategy.

Adapting Text

The obvious solution is to find easier and better-written material on the topic in question. This is sometimes easier said than done, however. Often the text provided to the teacher is all there is. The teacher has determined that text-based problems exist, but is limited to that material anyhow. In such a case, one solution is to adapt the text material.

One form of adaptation involves rewriting the material. Siedow and Hasselbring (1984) found that when eighth-grade social studies material was rewritten to a lower readability level, the comprehension of poor readers improved. In another study (Beck, McKeown, Omanson, & Pople, 1984) the researchers found that revising third-grade material significantly improved the children's comprehension. Currie (1990) also rewrote text by shortening sentences, replacing unfamiliar words, changing metaphors to more literal phrases, and clarifying. Teachers using these materials reported that students, whether high or low achievers, significantly improved their grades. Beck, McKeown, Sinatra, & Loxterman (1991) revised a fifth-grade social studies text to create a more causal and explanatory style, then compared students who read the original and revised versions. Students who read the revised version recalled and explained the events better, and answered more questions correctly.

Rewriting can be used to prepare students before introducing them to the original material. By using rewritten material as an introduction to the original text, teachers can simplify writing styles and make clearer those concepts that students may have difficulty understanding. However, by returning to the original material, teachers will still be using required materials, and students will receive the message that the text material is important.

The revision of Virginia Woolf's essay "Professions for Women" (Activity 3.2) illustrates rewriting. Rewriting this essay was a desperate move. One of the authors was teaching a freshman college English class and had assigned this required essay to stimulate the students' own writing. The students interpreted Woolf's metaphoric angel literally and thought that she had a ghost looking over her shoulder. They could not understand why Woolf would mention buying an expensive cat in this essay. Their backgrounds apparently did not include the metaphors or experiences that Woolf had selected, and they did not know how to relate to the allusions in the essay. The author chose to rewrite the essay because it was required reading for the course: no other could be substituted for it, even though it was clearly difficult for the readers. Students read the rewrite first, as an introduction, then read the original essay and compared the two versions. The results were very satisfactory. Students understood clearly the concepts Woolf was conveying, and, as an unexpected bonus, they realized how much better written was Woolf's essay than the author's! As a preparation strategy, rewriting in this case was very successful.

A C T I V I T Y   3 . 2   **A REWRITE OF "PROFESSIONS FOR WOMEN" (EXCERPT)**

I was asked to speak to you about women as professionals and tell you about what has happened to me. This is difficult because my experiences in my job as a writer may not be that outstanding. There have been many famous women writers before me who have learned and shown me the best way to succeed at writing. Because of their reputations, families today accept women who become writers. They know that they won't have to pay a lot of money for writing equipment or courses!

My story is this. I wrote regularly every day, then submitted an article to a newspaper. The article was accepted, I got paid; I became a journalist. However, I did not act like a struggling writer who spends her hard-earned money on household needs; I bought a Persian cat.

My article was a book review. I had trouble writing it and other reviews because something nagged at me. I felt that because I am a woman, I should be "feminine": have sympathy, be charming, unselfish, keep the family peaceful, sacrifice, and be very pure. When I began to write, this is what women were supposed to be like, and every family taught its girls to be this way. So when I started to write criticisms of a famous man's novel, all of the things I had learned about being a woman got in the way of my writing critically instead of writing just nice things. This problem was like a ghost whispering in my ear. I called this problem ghost "The Angel in the House" because it was always there, in my "house," telling me to be nice rather than truthful.

I got rid of this problem. I realized that being nice is not always the most important thing. Also, I had inherited some money, so I felt I didn't have to do what others expected of me in order to earn a living! I had to get rid of this obsession with being feminine rather than being truthful in order to write clearly. I killed my problem ghost before it could kill my true thoughts and reactions. This is really hard to do because "feminine" ideas creep up on you before you realize that what you're writing is not a true criticism but something you were raised to believe. It took a long time to realize what was my idea and what was society's idea about what I should write.

Readability as measured by Fry formula:
Original passage = 9th grade
Rewritten passage = 7th grade

Rewriting can reduce the readability level, as measured by a readability formula, sometimes to a significant degree. In the case of the Woolf essay, the original was found to be at ninth-grade level but the rewrite at seventh-grade level (according to the Fry graph). Sometimes a revision will not reduce readability level at all but will clarify difficult material. This was the case with the third-grade study reported earlier (Beck et al., 1984): researchers found that revision did improve comprehension, although a formula showed no change. The goal should be to present necessary material in a readable form, as a prelude to the original, not to show a change in a formula.

Like so many other activities, rewriting can be used at every step of PAR. If a rewrite is used in place of the original material, then it is no longer being used to prepare the reader; in that case, rewriting assists comprehension. One of the authors once rewrote portions of the Georgia Juvenile Court Code because the code was too hard for the students to understand in its legal form (measured at 14th-grade level). The rewrite, to seventh-grade level, enabled students to read with attention to the main points. Rewriting can also be used as a reflective reading technique. A teacher might ask students to think about the material and try to rewrite that material for younger students. In this way, students gain writing practice and demonstrate their learning. Thus, an integration of the communicative arts is taking place. Rewriting can also be a useful tool for the at-risk reader, who needs to learn the same content as classmates but has difficulty reading at the same level.

Rewriting takes time. For one rewrite of a 15-page social studies selection, one of the authors spent four hours. The Woolf rewrite consumed two hours. Since a teacher's time is precious, teachers will want to weigh their options carefully. In some situations, rewriting is the best option.

Craig (1977) suggests several steps for rewriting. The research studies cited previously also provide some useful models.

1. Read the passage; record the main ideas in your own words.
2. Identify the main ideas that are especially important for the students to know.
3. Do not attempt to rewrite a very lengthy passage; limit yourself to a portion of it.
4. Identify the most difficult words, especially those that represent difficult concepts. Try to use these words sparingly in your rewrite.
5. Follow some of these practical guidelines:

    a. Underline proper nouns and specialized vocabulary, which you can preteach.
    b. Limit sentence length, perhaps to five to ten words.
    c. Use terms familiar to students.
    d. Turn written numbers (five) into numerals (5).
    e. Use simple sentence construction and present tense.

Setting Up Text

WRITTEN PREVIEWS

Graves, Prenn, and Cooke (1985) suggest that teachers write brief previews of material to be read by students. These previews, which are especially valuable for difficult material, provide a reference point for the material and offer students a way to organize the new information. The preview should be fairly short and is usually read aloud to the class before silent reading of the original material is done. Students enjoy previews and demonstrate improved comprehension when they have used them. Teachers can use the information gained from their own previewing of the material to write a preview. In writing previews, a teacher can follow these steps:

1. Select a situation that students will know about and that relates to the topic. Describe the situation and pose a question that will lead to the topic.

A C T I V I T Y   3 . 3   PREVIEW OF "COUNTING SQUARES"

Have you ever built objects with plastic blocks? Before you began, did you have a plan for what your building would look like? It's important to make sure that you have the right number of blocks for the object you want to build. Otherwise, you might end up with a strange-looking building. Suppose you had a job and had to order the correct number of blocks to build a very large building. If you didn't order enough, you would have to order more later, which would waste time. If you ordered too many, you would be wasting money. Either way, your boss would be angry. What could you do to be sure that you were ordering the right number?

In this passage, you will read about Ahmose, a chief builder for an ancient Egyptian king. Ahmose had to order the right number of stone blocks for the king's home. If he made a mistake, the king would be angry. So he devised a counting table to help him figure correctly. This counting table was a lot like the multiplication table.

As you read this passage, see how a counting table and a multiplication table are alike. Discover how a multiplication table is more useful.

Based on pages 120–123 of *Mathemagic*, the 1978 *Childcraft Annual*.

2. If the material demands background knowledge that students do not have, write a brief section including this information.
3. Provide a synopsis of the material.
4. Provide directions for reading the material to facilitate comprehension.

After a teacher reads the first few sentences of the preview, he or she should allot time to discuss the questions posed in the first part of the preview. When the teacher has read the remainder of the preview, students should read the material right away. "Counting Squares" (Activity 3.3) is an example of a preview written for intermediate-level math; "Market Economy" is an example of a preview written for ninth-graders (Activity 3.4).

Written previews are less time-consuming than rewrites, and they accomplish similar purposes. They build reader background and help the reader organize the forthcoming material. If a teacher writes previews carefully, the structure of the text should be more apparent to readers.

STRUCTURING TEXT VIA GRAPHIC ORGANIZERS

Like written previews, graphic organizers help the reader prepare for reading by organizing the important concepts in the text. Particularly good when the teacher predicts that text will be difficult, graphic organizers present a road map of the text. As their name implies, they organize information graphically. The graphic organizer is a hierarchical overview that demonstrates how the important concepts, as represented by the vocabulary in a reading selection, fit together. A graphic organizer is effective because a teacher can prepare readers with a concise, comprehensive, and compact visual aid. Thus, the teacher can capitalize

| **A C T I V I T Y 3 . 4** | **WRITTEN PREVIEW: "THE PRINCIPLES OF OUR MARKET ECONOMY"** |

Several of you may have stopped at the corner convenience store on the way to school this morning. While there you may have bought several things. If so, you were playing the part of consumer in our economic system. Additionally, if you have a job, you are playing the part of a worker. The person you work for plays the part of the producer. Finally, as a consumer, you work together with the producer to determine the prices of the things that you bought this morning. How do you think that only three players — consumer, worker, and producer — can come together to make our economy work? } Step 1

In learning about how our economic system works, think back to the previous chapter, which described the various types of economic systems. You may recall that in a market economy private individuals own the factors of production, which are land, labor, and capital. These individuals are free to make choices about the things they produce. Our country is one of those identified as having a market economy. } Step 2

In this section, you will read about how the producer, the worker, and the consumer work together in making our economic system function. You will also read about what determines the price that producers charge and the amount you and I pay for their products. } Step 3

As you read this section, focus on the part you as the consumer play in our economic system. You will see that, as a consumer, you play a very important part. } Step 4

Developed by Carol Holmes.

on the visual literacy of the learner. Note that at the beginning of each chapter in this book, we present a form of graphic organizer to help readers see the relationships among the concepts and the key words and phrases in the chapter. This organizer is a visual representation of the content in each chapter.

Structured overview is another term for graphic organizer. A structured overview is generally a hierarchical diagram of words, whereas a graphic organizer may include a pictorial representation. The diagram in Chapter 1 for secondary social studies students (p. 11) might be called a structured overview; the diagram for primary students in studying goldfish (p. 15) might be more appropriately called a graphic organizer, because it contains an illustration as well as terms presented in an order. Structured overviews are generally associated with the preparation stage of content reading, whereas graphic organizers are often useful at all PAR stages. While most professionals agree that structured overviews are constructed by teachers, graphic organizers can be a postreading activity constructed by students. In the preparatory portions of the chapters in this textbook, we refer to the diagrams as graphic organizers because they are sometimes used for assistance and reflection also.

Earle and Barron (1973) comment that the research on prior knowledge supports the use of overviews or organizers. This finding makes sense because graphic organizers are designed to show relationships. When readers understand the relationships among concepts in a reading selection, they can begin to connect the new relationships to their previous knowledge. A graphic organizer is grounded in this theory.

Teachers usually find graphic organizers challenging to prepare but very much worth the effort. To construct one, a teacher should follow these steps:

1. Identify the superordinate, or major, concept and then identify all supporting concepts in the material.
2. List all key terms from the material that reflect the identified concepts.
3. Connect the terms to show the relationships among concepts.
4. Construct a diagram based on these connections, and use it to introduce the reading material.

It will not be necessary to use every word that might be new to readers in developing the graphic organizer. Some new words may not contribute to the diagram. It is useful to include words known to the students when these words represent key concepts, because the familiarity will aid understanding. We have found that when graphic organizers are pictorial, students enjoy and remember them better.

Teachers should explain to students why they prepared the graphic organizer as they did, noting the relationships. This presentation should include a discussion to which students can contribute what they know about the terms as well as what they predict they will be learning, based on the chart. Students should also have the organizer available for reference while they are reading, so that they can occasionally check back to see the relationships as they encounter the terms. After reading, students can use the graphic organizer as an aid for refocusing and reflecting on the learning. It can even be used as a check of comprehension. Thus, the graphic organizer is an activity that can be useful at all of the PAR steps and one that promotes integration of the communicative arts.

Activities 3.5 through 3.8 provide examples of graphic organizers prepared by teachers in several different content areas. The math and vocational-education organizers for secondary level follow a traditional format, much like the organizers that precede many chapters in this book. The organizer on nonfiction writing (middle-school level) is pictorial, and the organizer for primary science students uses circles, rectangles, and arrows to show relationships.

USING PREVIOUS TEXT: PREGUIDING QUESTIONS

Questions about previously read text can be used to set the stage for reading difficult new text. Preguiding questions are particularly useful when students have already read and reflected on some text material — for example, a chapter that builds the foundation for the next chapter — and will be required in the forthcoming chapter to relate new information to what is known. To design preguiding questions, the teacher should devise questions that can be answered from the prior text but will be answered more fully by the new text. The teacher should place the questions in a middle column, with space to the left for responses *before* reading and space to the right for responses *after* reading. In this

ACTIVITY 3.5   GEOMETRY OVERVIEW (KEY)

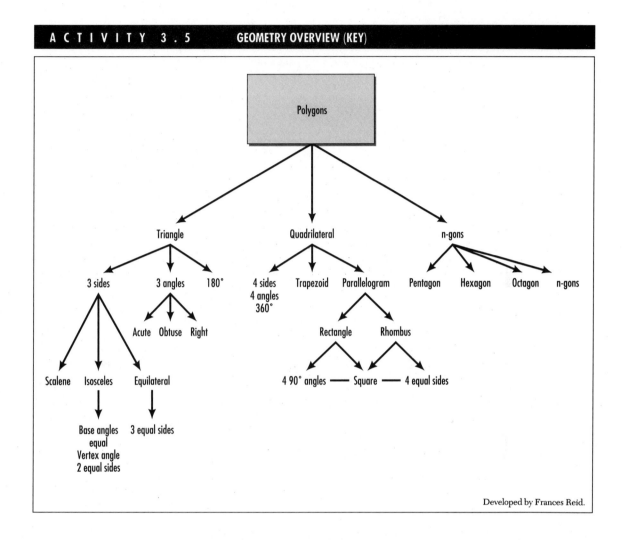

Developed by Frances Reid.

way, students will be able to see how the previous text applies and how it can help them understand the new text.

For example, a chemistry teacher devised a set of questions that related both to previous study about waves and to new information about light. He placed the questions in the middle of the page, with a prereading column on the left and a postreading column on the right (see Activity 3.9). Before the assigned reading, students wrote group responses to the questions in the prereading column, using their previous knowledge and predictions. After reading, they responded with the correct answers in the postreading column and compared their educated guesses to the facts. Group interaction promoted communication, and the activity spanned all PAR steps.

A C T I V I T Y   3 . 6   VOCATIONAL EDUCATION: MARKETING

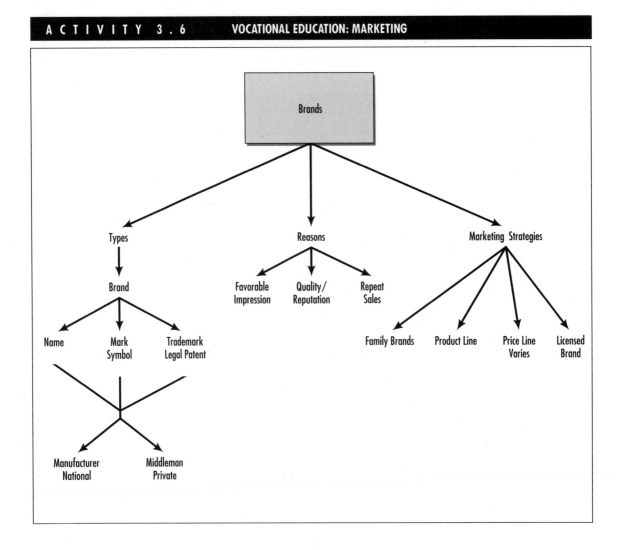

Avoiding Text

One response teachers use when they determine that text is difficult for readers is simply to avoid the text altogether. This response may occur because teachers are ambiguous about their use of textbooks (Hinchman, 1987). Teachers may not know what to do when they can tell that text is difficult for their students, and may resort to avoidance tactics in desperation. Some teachers read the text aloud to their students; others tell students the information and require no reading; still others have students take notes from the teacher's synopsis of the material. Some findings indicate that teachers do not rely on textbooks for much of their instruction because they realize that there is a mismatch between the text and the students. Davey (1988) found that several teachers used the textbook only as

ACTIVITY 3.7   **NONFICTION WRITING (MIDDLE SCHOOL)**

Developed by Rebecca McSweeney.

Decomposition / New Growth Cycle

exposed bark

termites

Healthy
Standing
Oak Tree

Decaying
Standing
Tree

rot

woodpecker holes

drops acorns

drops leaves in fall

New
Growth

fungus

beetles, grubs

Fallen
Tree

Soil
Fertilized

Developed by Kathryn Davis.

A C T I V I T Y   3 . 9   PREGUIDING QUESTIONS

Prereading

Postreading

1. What two ways can energy be transported?

2. What are the five general properties of waves?

3. We know that sound is transmitted through waves. Sound bends around corners, as evidenced by the fact that we can hear around corners. Light casts sharp shadows; we can not see around corners. Based on this knowledge about the behavior of light, would you classify light as a wave or particle? Explain your answer.

4. A beam of light strikes a smooth surface as pictured below; the angle of incidence (i) is found to be equal to the angle of reflection (r). Can a model of light based on waves be used to explain this behavior?

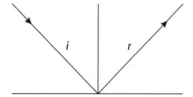

Developed by Tom Fleming.

a supplement to their instruction, not as a base for it. The teachers in this study indicated that they avoided textbooks because of differences among their students and because they lacked the time to cover the whole text.

We suspect that what Davey found is true in many classrooms. Teachers think that they cannot use a text because all of their students do not have the same ability, reading skills, or background knowledge. They think that it will take too much time to cover all of the text material, particularly if their students are heterogeneously grouped. When teachers use such reasoning, they have at least applied the first step in determining reader background. They are aware that they face a mismatch between students and text. But, as we have seen, this awareness is only a start.

We think that avoiding text is a poor response and sends students an undesirable message. Students may be learning that it is not necessary to read the text at all because teachers will tell them what they need to know. Teachers do students a definite disservice when they decide to avoid or skim the text material. Such messages to students are powerful deterrents to future reading for knowledge. First, important information in the text may be overlooked by the teacher and missed entirely by the students when teachers avoid the text material. Thus, students miss an opportunity to learn. Second, students need to read and see teachers valuing reading material if they are going to become informed and avid readers themselves. The less practice students receive in reading to learn, the weaker their reading will be. The more students receive the message that they can skip this material and just listen to the teacher, the more ambivalent they will be about reading to learn. Third, and most crucial, when teachers avoid the text material, they may be contributing to the literacy problem Kirsch and Jungeblut (1986) describe in their NAEP report. Students who have the basic skills to read but read little are ill equipped to live in a literate America.

A recently reported longitudinal study compared Asian — Taiwanese, Japanese, Chinese — to American students of comparable ages, school and city sizes, and socioeconomic backgrounds (Stevenson, 1992). Among the results were these findings:

1. Although reading abilities were comparable, American students spent less time reading for pleasure in grades K–12.
2. American children complete far less homework—one quarter as much as Taiwanese and one half as much as Japanese.
3. When asked to make a wish, 70% of Chinese students made a wish related to education, while less than 10% of Americans did so.
4. Asian systems stress effort. Parents, children, and teachers are expected to exert the effort needed to enable students to succeed. If a student is not learning, *more* effort is expected, not less!

From the study, Stevenson concludes that American students are passive learners. How has this happened? We think that by avoiding text material, teachers may be contributing to the very problem that their profession is supposed to be solving.

If, before assigning reading material, teachers take the time to build text background, all of the students in the classroom will have one common experience to aid their reading. Students will also begin to see the role that their personal store of experience and knowledge plays in reading for meaning. By building background, teachers ultimately give students the tools to become responsible and independent readers. This time spent up front enhances comprehension so greatly that using the text is much less time-consuming. In other words, an ounce of prevention is worth a pound of cure.

Who Is Responsible for Text-Based Solutions?

Of course, all parties involved have a responsibility. The interaction among textbook author, teacher, and reader is crucial. The particular responsibilities of each will be summarized briefly.

The Author's Responsibility

Some authors are inconsiderate of their readers. Authors should always keep their readers in mind as they write. If a passage includes many concepts, its organization should be very clear to readers and teachers. This clarity enables teachers to develop instructional activities that can help students learn those important concepts. Authors should include important terms in the material, but if the author suspects that these terms will be new to the reader, then meaning and pronunciation keys should be provided.

In his foreword to Allan Bloom's *The Closing of the American Mind*, Saul Bellow (1987), a noted novelist, admits that "it is never easy to take the mental measure of your readers." As he puts it: "A piece of writing is like an offering" (p. 15). Although textbook writers cannot know the individual literacy levels of prospective readers, nor their interests and attitudes, they can be sensitive to the general needs of a group of readers. Authors should take into account what readers should be expected to know and what they will need an author's help to learn. In this way, authors fulfill their responsibility to be considerate of their readers.

The Teacher's Responsibility

Teachers play a very important role in determining text-based problems and finding solutions, as this whole chapter has conveyed. Hittleman (1978) encourages teachers to think of readability as "ever changing. . . . We should never eliminate the reader and the act of reading from our concept of readability" (p. 121). Shanker (1984) discusses the importance of evaluating textbooks and lays the responsibility for doing so on the teacher. He calls for training in education courses to enable teachers to evaluate textbooks. Teachers must understand that text coherence comprises many factors. A formula is not enough information on which to base a judgment about text-based problems.

Teachers can determine a great deal about readability, but they also need help from other educational personnel. For example, Speigel and Wright (1983), reporting on a study of biology teachers' impressions of the readability of text materials they used, comment that teachers were aware of many readability factors. Teachers, they write, should be encouraged to apply this good, intuitive understanding in their selection of text materials. Such encouragement must come from administrators and textbook selection committees.

The Role of the Student

The ultimate consumer of the content material is the student. Students need to move toward independence in determining their own background for reading as soon as possible in their school careers. Students must begin to ask questions about their reading material by applying the factors discussed in this chapter: Is this material too difficult for me? Is it poorly written? What do I already know about this topic? What are the aids in this text I should find to make my reading easier? Questions such as these will not even occur to many students until teachers model their importance by helping students understand why they should be asked.

Many college textbooks on reading and study skills do encourage students to ask such questions. But we believe that, by then, it may be too late. Not all students attend college, and not all of those who do will take a reading and study skills course. If background for reading is discussed only in college textbooks, many students may be denied the opportunity to take a responsible role. Isn't a student's responsibility for determining background important throughout his or her school years? A first-grader is quite capable of determining the difficulty of a book by using the "rule of thumb." A fifth-grader can ask, "What do I know about fractions already?" A tenth-grader can assess whether poetry causes him difficulty. Perhaps students and teacher could construct a simple checklist of readability factors that students could then use on their own.

Ultimately, the "buck stops" with the students. But what a terrible burden to place on students as readers of content material if authors and teachers offer them little help as they try to assume responsibility for their own reading.

One-Minute Summary

In this chapter, we have explained the importance of determining and building background for reading textbook materials. We have presented the concept of readability and its importance for successful instruction in content areas. We have introduced three factors, both text-based and reader-based, and their impact on readability. We have shown how, through a series of activities, you can find out if text-based problems apply to your students. Finally, we have discussed how ensuring readability of content material rests not only with the student, but also with the textbook author and the teacher.

End-of-Chapter Activities

Assisting Comprehension

Practice assessing the readability of a text from which you will teach. Use the text coherence questions to start your assessment. Now apply the Bader analysis.

Next, select passages to rate, and then follow the formula procedures to obtain a Fry rating. What do you think about these ratings? Are they accurate and informative? Check Appendixes C and D for examples of how other teachers assessed their texts using the Bader and Fry.

Reflecting on Your Reading   Study Table 3.3. See how each activity compares with other text-based activities. We have rated each activity. Do you agree? Use the space provided to fill in your own ratings.

TABLE 3.3

Chapter 3 Activities Compared and Rated

ACTIVITY	PROBLEM/ SOLUTION	MATCH DERIVED BY	MATERIALS NEEDED	AUTHORS' RATING*	YOUR RATING?
Text coherence questions	Determines text-based problems	Teacher/student evaluation of text discourse	Student/ teacher, text	○○○○○	
Checklists	Determines text-based problems	Teacher evaluates text by specific criteria	Teacher, text	○○○○	
Fry formula	Determines text-based problems	Teacher computes sentence & word length	Teacher, text	○○	
SMOG formula	Determines text-based problems & builds solution	Teacher computes sentence & word length, selects books	Teacher, text	○○○	
Rule of thumb	Determines text-based problems & builds solution	Student assesses text by vocabulary, selects books	Student, text	○○○○	
Multitext	Builds background for difficult text	Teacher selects easier readings on the topic to precede the difficult material	Teacher, student, text	○○○○	
Rewriting	Builds background for difficult text	Teacher rewrites hard material by considering text coherence issues	Teacher, student, text	○○○	

(continued on page 104)

TABLE 3.3

continued

ACTIVITY	PROBLEM/ SOLUTION	MATCH DERIVED BY	MATERIALS NEEDED	AUTHORS' RATING*	YOUR RATING?
Written previews	Builds background for difficult text	Teacher writes preview to help students adapt to hard text	Teacher, student, text	ooooo	
Graphic organizer	Builds background for difficult text	Teacher constructs hierarchical overview to cue reader for text	Teacher, student, text	ooooo	
Preguiding questions	Builds background for difficult text	Teacher constructs questions that relate previous text to new text	Teacher, student, text	ooooo	
Avoiding text	Eliminates difficult text	Teacher ignores text on premise students cannot read it	Teacher, text	0	

*Up to five stars, based on value received for time spent.

Preparation

READER-BASED SOLUTIONS

"If I had to reduce all of educational psychology to just one principle, I would say this:
The most important single factor influencing learning is what the learner already knows.
Ascertain this and teach him accordingly."

David Ausubel, *Educational Psychology*

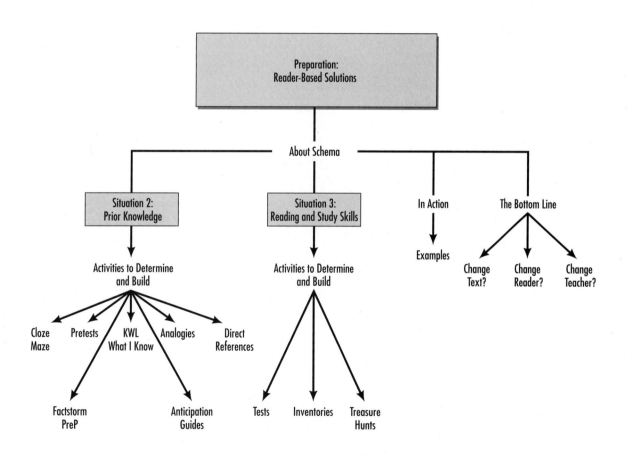

Prepare to Read

1. Following are three statements. Read and consider each one. If you agree with the statement, place a + beside it; if you disagree, place a − beside it. Be ready to explain your reasoning.

   _____ The more you know, the more you learn.

   _____ Hindsight is always better than foresight.

   _____ Readiness is a term associated with beginning reading instruction.

   As you read this chapter, each of these statements will be discussed in context. Compare your response with those in the chapter.

2. Following is a list of terms used in this chapter. Some of them may be familiar to you in a general context, but in this chapter they may be used in a different way than you are used to. Rate your knowledge by placing a + in front of those you are sure that you know, a √ in front of those you have some knowledge about, and a 0 in front of those you don't know. Be ready to locate and pay special attention to their meanings when they are presented in the chapter.

   ____ schema   ____ cognitive dissonance
   ____ chunk   ____ cloze
   ____ prior knowledge   ____ factstorming
   ____ readiness

Objectives

As you read this chapter, focus your attention on the following objectives. You will:

1. be able to identify pertinent research that supports the concepts of schema and prior knowledge.

2. become acquainted with two of three basic situations that cause readability problems and be able to use this information to determine if a readability problem exists for students.

3. become acquainted with several activities that help build the match between the reader and the material to be read.

4. understand how the teacher must consider all three situations to evaluate text material and guide readers appropriately.

The Importance of Reader Background

Two groups of college students were asked to read two passages about weddings. The groups were carefully matched, except for nationality: one group was American, the other was from India. The passages were carefully controlled, based on a consideration of many of the readability factors discussed in Chapter 3, except that one passage was about an Indian wedding and the other was about an

American wedding. When they tested the students' comprehension of the passages, the researchers (Steffenson, Joag-Des, & Anderson, 1979) found that the Indian students received higher comprehension scores on the passage about Indian weddings and the American students received higher scores on the passage about American weddings.

In a different study (Erwin, 1991), children ages 7 to 9 in two classrooms, one in Texas and one in England, listened to two texts involving British or Texan concepts. The children in England comprehended more of the British-concepts text, while the children in Texas comprehended more of the Texan-concepts text. With instruction, however, both groups improved their comprehension of each text.

These culture-specific results are not surprising: the more we know about something, the more we will understand about it. One who has grown up in a certain culture is familiar with the traditional ceremonies of that culture and can more easily read and understand material written about them. But those who have little experience in a culture cannot be expected to read and understand much about it until they have learned some background. In short, *the more you know, the more you learn.*

About Schemata

What Is a Schema?

A **schema** (plural, **schemata**) is a picture in one's mind of already-known information. Learning is much harder if we have no background—no schema—to relate the new information to. Psychologists have long studied the impact of past knowledge on present understanding. Ausubel, who was quoted at the beginning of this chapter, has been a chief advocate of the "conceptual starting place" (1968) of meaningful learning. Lange (1902) noted, at the turn of the century, that "we see and hear not only with the eye and ear, but quite as much with the help of our present knowledge, with the apperceiving content of the mind" (p. 21). More recently, Frank Smith (1971) has compared the reading activity that occurs between the page and the eye, and between the eye and the brain. He concluded that the eye-to-brain connection is far more complex than the mere intake of information. Learning occurs by a process of planning and building information in the brain. Just seeing words (page-to-eye) or even saying words (page-to-eye-to-mouth) is fairly superficial. Connecting the intent of the words to what is already stored in one's "mind diagram" (eye-to-brain) is real reading. Thus, what learners already know helps them to read more effectively.

Gestalt psychologists probably introduced the term *schema* in the 1930s (Anderson & Pearson, 1984). Bartlett (1932) used the term to explain how information that has been learned is stored in the brain and, with repeated use, becomes part of a system of integrated knowledge. Anderson and Pearson speculate that the term became popular because Piaget used it extensively. Piaget (1952) believed that children form a mental image of previous experiences, which in turn contributes to new experiences. Miller (1956) discussed the relationship of short-term to long-term memory in a similar way. Learners **chunk** knowledge in an organized fashion by connecting a new "chunk" to what is already known. Only by so doing can a learner move the new chunk of information from short-term memory to long-term memory.

Schemata, chunks, or **prior knowledge** is essential to new learning. According to psychologists Combs and Snygg (1959), learning takes place when the "perceptual field" is organized in a pattern. This perceptual field, which they define as a "more or less fluid organization of meanings existing for every individual at any instant" (p. 20), is the basis for a person's reactions to any new event.

Schema theory is a way of explaining how one's prior knowledge is stored in memory. The information a learner acquires about a topic is organized cognitively into a framework, which can be called a schema. The framework grows to include other topics, thus creating larger and larger schemata, with several schemata arranged in a hierarchy. Learners retrieve information by understanding how newly encountered material links to what they have already organized cognitively. Interrelationships among schemata aid understanding. Psychologists have stressed that learning new information depends on relating the new to something already known. Rumelhart (1980) stresses that schemata, which may be likened to diagrams or drawings stored in the brain, are fundamental to all processing of information. Often the diagrams are incomplete, but they create a fuller picture as more information is found to complete them.

Schemata and Content-Area Reading

The protagonist in our cartoon has read the first direction for making an angel food cake. But her cake is going to be mighty crunchy. She expects "separate" to mean only "to set or keep apart"; her schema for the word *separate* does not yet include a picture for "detached." Therefore, she is putting each egg in a different location, rather than detaching the whites from the yolks. A home economics teacher would need to realize what associations the cartoon character has made in order to help this "student" build a more sophisticated schema.

Anderson (1985) is credited with introducing schema theory to the field of reading, although the concept, if not the term, had been applied in reading

B.C. Reprinted with permission of Johnny Hart and Creators Syndicate, Inc.

research previously. When Chall (1947) tested sixth- and eighth-graders on their knowledge of tuberculosis and then tested their reading of a passage on the same topic, she found that those with the highest knowledge scores also had the highest reading comprehension scores. She concluded that previous knowledge heavily influences reading. Rumelhart (1980) has also written extensively about how learners comprehend by building "blocks of cognition" as they fill in a partially completed schema during reading. Hirsch (1987) writes that schemata are essential to literacy in two major ways: Information is stored so that it can be retrieved, and it is organized so that it can be used quickly and efficiently by the reader.

Reading professionals have defined schema as "a conceptual system for understanding something" (Harris & Hodges, 1981). Pearson and Spiro (1982) describe it this way:

> What is a schema? It's the little picture or associations you conjure up in your head when you hear or read a word or sentence. You can have a schema for an object (chair, boat, fan), an abstract idea or feeling (love, hate, hope), an action (dancing, swimming, buying) or an event (election, garage sale, concert). It's like a concept but broader. For example, you see the word *tree* and you conjure up the concept of a tree—trunk, branches, leaves, and so on. Your schema for a tree includes all this, plus anything else you associate with trees—walks down country lanes, Christmas trees, birds' nests, and so on. (pp. 46–47)

Content teachers will find schema theory useful as they prepare their students to read an assignment. For instance, suppose that fifth-graders in a rural community are about to study ballet in their music class. The teacher is sensitive to her students' misconceptions about ballet. She has determined that their schema for ballet includes such incorrect prior knowledge as "Ballet is sissy; it's something girls do, not strong men; it's boring." If the teacher ignores this schema, the students will likely reject any new information about ballet and hold fast to their previously formulated picture. Instead, a fifth-grade music teacher we know used the children's schema as a base for expanding knowledge. The music teacher used an anticipation guide, explained later in this chapter. By presenting the statements shown in Activity 4.1, she got students to verbalize their prior knowledge. Then she presented new experiences and information by showing a videotape of *The Nutcracker Suite*. The reader should note that these students reformulated their knowledge after discovering new information—they changed their opinions for all four statements! A different schema was created.

If learners cannot find relevance in a reading selection, they are likely to ignore it. Teachers, then, must become aware of their students' knowledge and experiences about a particular topic to be taught in the content subject. Discovering whether students have developed any schemata can help the teacher generate content reading lessons that are directed, meaningful, and highly personal.

As we noted in Chapter 1, Hart (1983) stresses the importance of building programs for learning that include as much information as possible. Readers should try to determine before they read new material what they do and don't know about the subject; this is part of a complete program for learning. Teachers

A C T I V I T Y 4 . 1	THE ANTICIPATION OF BALLET

Before we begin our lesson today, read each of the following statements carefully and circle Agree or Disagree to show what you think. Be ready to discuss your opinions with the class. Do not talk with anyone else *yet* about your answers. Remember . . . this is *your opinion* and it will not be graded!

Agree	Disagree	**1.** Ballet is only for girls.
Agree	Disagree	**2.** Ballet music is always slow and soft.
Agree	Disagree	**3.** Ballet dancers are strong, muscular, and in very good physical condition.
Agree	Disagree	**4.** The Soviet Union is one country that has produced many very good ballet dancers.

Developed by Todd Barnes.

will have to help their students by making this determination with them and, at the start of a student's reading-to-learn journey, for them.

The Role of Readiness

In the past, many teachers associate **readiness** with instruction for beginning readers. Thorndike (1932) proposed the term, in his "law of readiness," to mean a developmental stage at which new learning occurs. In its broadest sense, then, readiness means being ready to receive information. Reading readiness means being prepared for the material that is to be read. A young student does get ready to read, but all readers must achieve a state of readiness for any meaningful reading to occur. If a reader does not understand what separating eggs means, as it applies to baking a cake, that reader is not ready to read the instructions for baking a cake. Building background is readiness instruction. It means building the knowledge upon which learning is based. Look again at the third statement in Prepare to Read at the beginning of this chapter: "Readiness is a term associated with beginning reading instruction." We would want to rephrase that statement: Readiness is a term associated *not only* with beginning reading instruction.

Chall (1983) calls the background that readers possess "world knowledge," noting that it is "essential to the development of reading and writing skills" (p. 8). If readers have little world knowledge, they will have limited understanding. The examples cited previously—those who were Indian knew less about American weddings; those who lived in Texas knew fewer concepts about England—demonstrate how a lack of world knowledge can interfere with reading. We think that the best way to acquire world knowledge is through the thinking and learning that should occur in content classrooms every day. Acquiring world knowledge is a form of building *background*, which either equals or is closely associated with *readiness*. Readiness depends upon applying *prior knowledge*, which depends on activating *schemata*. All of these terms relate to the P in PAR, Preparation. In the case of preparation, then, hindsight is *not* better than foresight. Foresight is crucial. Furthermore, foresight is reader-based. No matter how well—or poorly—written the text, the reader must bring some knowledge to the page before the text can be unlocked. What does the reader already know about the content topic? What reading and study skills does the reader have to help him or her with the content material? For the remainder of this chapter, we will consider the two reader-based situations relevant to preparation.

Prior Knowledge and Interest

Prior knowledge and interest are reader-based: the possible problems they pose reside inherently in the reader and only secondarily in the material. As we saw in the teachers' ratings of the viral hepatitis passage in Chapter 3, the text is only one part of the necessary interaction. Even though the text was judged to be well written, the readers did not rate it highly in the categories relating to themselves as readers.

Drum (1985) found that fourth-grade science and social studies texts that were equal in vocabulary frequency, syntactic complexity, and overall structure were not equally easy for the fourth-graders in her study to read. Prior knowledge seemed to play a significant part in making the social studies texts easier for these students. In other words, no matter how well written material is, if readers do not possess background knowledge or interest in reading it, the material will be hard for them to read.

Lack of Prior Knowledge

It is conceivable that readers might have absolutely no background for a topic to be studied. Usually, this is not the case. More likely, readers will have some related experience, limited information, or even incorrect information. The teacher must find out what the students *do* know. Only then can relevant preparation be done.

The following dialogue illustrates how difficult it is to understand material when one has limited prior background.

"Do I deserve a mulligan?" asked Bob.

"No, but don't take a drop," said Al. "Use a hand-mashie, then fly the bogey high to the carpet and maybe you'll get a gimme within the leather."

"You're right," said Bob. "I'll cover the flag for a birdie and at least get a ginsberg if I'm not stymied." (Morgan, Meeks, Schollaert, & Paul, 1986, pp. 2–3)

If one is not a golfer, reading this dialogue would be an exercise in pronouncing the words. Answering the following questions would be very tough—in effect, a guessing game.

1. Does Bob deserve a mulligan?
   (a) yes (b) no (c) maybe
2. What does Al think Bob should do?
   (a) catch a gimme (b) take a drop (c) use a hand-mashie (d) fly a kite

3. What does Bob decide to do?
  (a) cover the flag (b) take a drop (c) birdie-up
4. How can Bob get a birdie?
  (a) by getting stymied (b) by getting a ginsberg (c) by covering the flag
5. If Bob is not stymied, what will he get?
  (a) a hickie (b) a birdie (c) a mulligan (d) a ginsberg

The problem lies in the reader's lack of prior knowledge. What is a mulligan? What is a birdie? Readers may try to create meaning for these words by calling on their store of information, but they don't really know the answers if they don't know golf! The following translation shows how providing a more familiar context makes the passage meaningful.

"Do I deserve a mulligan?" asked Bob.

Bob asks if he deserves a second shot without a penalty.

"No, but don't take a drop," said Al. "Use a hand-mashie, then fly the bogey high to the carpet and maybe you'll get a gimme within the leather."

Al says no, but warns him not to take the option of moving his ball from a difficult location and dropping it at a better spot. Although he could do this without a penalty, the better move is to kick the ball out of trouble with his foot (hand-mashie) and then hit the ball with a high trajectory to the green (where the hole is). If Bob gets the ball within 18 inches of the hole, or cup (leather), he can pick up his ball and give himself one stroke (gimme) rather than having to take several strokes (the more strokes or hits one has, the worse one's score in golf).

"You're right," said Bob. "I'll cover the flag for a birdie and at least get a ginsberg if I'm not stymied."

Bob agrees to hit the ball close to the hole so he has a chance for a birdie (one stroke under par). If he gets on the green, he can lay up his putt to the hole (ginsberg). In earlier days, golfers did not mark their balls, so you might get stymied by another ball—that is, have to shoot around the ball. Bob is being facetious here. One cannot get stymied on the green in modern golf.

Recall the nine principles introduced in Chapter 1. Principle 3 states: *Reading for meaning is a highly individualized process influenced by the reader's personal store of experiences and knowledge.* Textbook authors may write well but produce material that is difficult for some students if those students lack background in the subject. Children reading about coral reefs, for example, may have difficulty simply because they have never heard about or seen one. It is up to the teacher to determine if this is the case. Ausubel (1968) has stressed that what the learner already knows is the most important factor in future learning. Dechant (1970) has expressed a similar view: "Without the proper experience, the reader cannot respond with the proper meaning to the author's words" (p. 555). The situation will be dire if a reader has no background in the subject being taught. It is crucial that the teacher not assume that students know more than they do. Such assumptions lead to "fuzzy (unclear) teaching," which will most likely be wasted instructional time. Determining reader background is essential.

Preferably, readers will have some knowledge rather than no knowledge. Perhaps students know very little about the specific content to be read but do understand a related concept. For instance, fifth-graders may not know much about the Pilgrims, but they may know what it's like to be uprooted and have to relocate to a strange place. These students, then, would have some background the teacher could use in introducing the reading.

Incorrect Prior Knowledge

Sometimes, readers have incorrect knowledge about material to be studied. A teacher wrote this "telegram" to illustrate how incorrect knowledge can influence one's reading:

WON TRIP FOR TWO ST. MATTHEW'S ISLAND PACK SMALL BAG MEET AT AIRPORT 9 AM TOMORROW (by Grace Hamlin)

If readers "know" that islands are tropical, have a warm climate, are surrounded by beaches for swimming and sunbathing, they will pack a suitcase with sunglasses, shorts, bathing suits, and suntan lotion. However, St. Matthew's Island is off the coast of Alaska, where the average temperature is 37 degrees. Incorrect knowledge in this case will impede comprehension. Similarly, if readers "know" that the dinosaurs were destroyed by other animals, they will have difficulty reading and understanding a theory that proposed that dinosaurs were destroyed by the consequences of a giant meteor.

Maria and MacGinitie (1987) discuss the difference between having correct, if insufficient, prior knowledge and having incorrect prior knowledge. They conclude that students are less likely to overcome a problem of incorrect knowledge because the new information conflicts with their prior "knowledge." In this situation, determining students' background is very important because material will be most "unreadable" to students who refute the material.

The Role of Interest and Attitude

Even the most proficient reader will experience difficulty in understanding and thinking about a subject he or she is not interested in. Remember that a majority (26) of the 41 teachers who graded the paragraph in Chapter 3 gave it an F for interest! Yet these were good readers. We might speculate that their lack of interest in the subject negatively influenced a good match with this material. Some recent studies indicate that interest in a topic plays a very important role in students' comprehension (Schumm, Mangrum, Gordon, & Doucette, 1992; Wade & Adams, 1990).

If teachers recognize that their students bring little interest or negative attitudes to the content material, they can use many activities to stimulate greater interest, better attitudes, and more appreciation for the subject. But if a teacher simply assumes that students are interested in and positive toward the subject, it is likely that the teacher will be disappointed and the students will not understand the reading. This situation can be seen as a form of **cognitive dissonance**, which *A Dictionary of Reading* (Harris & Hodges, 1981) defines as "a perceived inconsistency between one's attitudes and one's behavior" (p. 54). In short, students' reading proficiency may conflict with their lack of interest to create a conflict that blocks learning.

We are reminded of an old story, told by one or our reading professors, about the little boy who goes to the library and asks for a book about penguins. The librarian, excited that this small child is requesting information, selects a large volume on penguins and offers it to him. The child takes the book, almost staggering under its weight, and trudges home. The next day he returns it. "How did you like that book about penguins?" the librarian eagerly asks him. "To tell you the truth," the boy replies, "this book tells more about penguins than I care to know." A similar situation occurs when teachers misinterpret a little interest as a lot and do not match the reader with a suitable text; that mismatch may lead to misdirected interest. Chapter 2 covers this situation in depth and offers the teacher several means to determine students' interests and attitudes, as well as activities to stimulate positive feelings. The activities offered in this chapter can also help determine interests and attitudes if teachers are sensitive to students' responses.

Some Activities for Determining Prior Knowledge

If readers have to build a base of understanding from scratch, reading will be harder work. If their "mind diagram" is incomplete at the start, readers may leave the material with pictures that are still incomplete. If they must reorient their thinking because they have incorrect information, their need to hold onto the familiar may prevail over their need for correct information. Unless the teacher determines such problems in advance and then helps students find ways to build background accordingly, reading comprehension may be in jeopardy. Following are some ways to determine if students possess prior knowledge.

The Cloze Procedure

The term **cloze**, first used by Wilson Taylor in 1953, reflects "the Gestalt principle of closure, the ability to complete an incomplete stimulus" (Harris & Hodges, 1981, p. 53). In the cloze procedure, a passage is cut up so that it can be filled in by the student. The premise is that readers will rely on prior knowledge and use of context as they close, or complete, the cut-up passage. This technique relies heavily on the Gestalt concept of perceiving the whole of things. Ebbinghaus, in the late 1800s, used a modified form of closure when he conducted his verbal learning and retention studies (described in Chapter 9).

When Taylor designed the cloze procedure, as we now use it, his purpose was to determine the readability of material. In its strict form, cloze is constructed by selecting a passage of 250 words or more and deleting words at regular intervals—every fifth, tenth, or nth (any predetermined number) word. The beginning and ending sentences remain intact. Blanks replace the deleted words, but no clues other than the context of the material are provided to the reader, who must refill those blanks.

In a review of the research, Jongsma (1980) found that the cloze procedure is useful at any grade level if the pattern of deletions is sensitive to the students' familiarity with language. We recommend that, generally, every tenth word be deleted for primary students because younger students are less proficient readers; they need more clues than older, more proficient readers because they have less reading experience. Every fifth word should be deleted for older students (fourth grade and above) because these older, more proficient readers should have had more experience with reading and using context.

HOW TO USE CLOZE

By using cloze, a teacher can find out if students have prior knowledge about upcoming material and if they can adapt to the author's style. The readers are able to demonstrate their prior knowledge because they have to apply it when determining the best word choices for a cut-up passage. Their background knowledge helps them fill in gaps; their prior knowledge of language also helps them make good choices.

If students complete the cloze with ease, they will achieve an independent-level score, indicating that they can read the material on their own. If they can adapt when instruction about the material is provided by the teacher, they will achieve an instructional-level score. A frustration-level score indicates that the material will be extremely difficult for readers to understand even with instruction.

Because the purpose of cloze is to help a teacher quickly determine if students have adequate background knowledge and understand the language clues used in the material in question, scoring should be as rapid and efficient as possible. Please note that, when cloze is used for the purpose of determining prior knowledge, students are not expected to see the cloze exercise again, nor will the teacher be using it as a teaching tool. When cloze is used to determine the match between reader and text, then, *exact word replacement* is the most efficient scoring procedure. In Taylor's presentation of cloze, only the exact word that was deleted was counted as a correct answer. Research (Bormouth, 1969) has indicated that the exact word score is the most valid. When synonyms are accepted, the scoring criteria change and the cloze must be modified, usually for instructional rather than readability purposes. Although scoring seems stringent, the criteria for achieving an instructional level of readability are quite relaxed to compensate. A score of only 40 to 60 percent correct is acceptable.

Here is a basic set of directions for constructing a cloze that will be used to determine reader background:

1. Select a passage of about 250–300 words.
2. Leave the first and last sentences intact to help the readers use context clues.
3. Delete *consistently* every nth (fifth, tenth, or other designated number) word, starting with the nth word in the second sentence and continuing until the next-to-last sentence.
4. Make a key of the exact words that have been deleted.

5. Write directions for your students. These directions should stress the purpose of the activity — to determine background, not to test them — and explain that they are to fill each blank with a word they think the author might have used. (*Note:* Even though the teacher will score as correct only the exact word, students might be anxious if their directions state that they must select the exact word.)

6. Count the number of correct responses, and express as a percentage. An easy way, if you have 50 blanks, is simply to double the number of correct responses. Otherwise, divide the number of correct responses by the total number of blanks and multiply by 100 to obtain a percentage.

7. Use these scores to determine the readiness level of each of your students. A score of 60% or higher indicates the independent level; these students will find the material easy. A score between 40% and 60% corresponds to the instructional level; the material is suitable for teaching these students. A score of less than 40% indicates the frustration level; the material may be too hard for these students. It may be helpful to list your students under each of these three levels, as follows:

Independent (scores above 60%) Material is easy	Instructional (scores 40% to 60%) Material is suitable	Frustration (scores below 40%) Material is too hard
(list students)	(list students)	(list students)

EXAMPLES OF CLOZE IN ACTION

An English teacher was faced with a textbook she had not previously taught from, and 11th-graders in a school new to her. She wondered how they might perform with the textbook, and what kinds of accommodations she might need to make. Although these students had been labeled "high ability," she knew that labels are often not indicative of true performance. So she developed a cloze on a 300-word passage from the introduction to the textbook. This passage compared the origins of early American literature to men landing on the moon — both were adventures and initial explorations of a new era. Would her students have sufficient background to understand this analogy? Would they have enough language skill to read this and ensuing passages with facility?

She administered the cloze during the first week of school, before issuing textbooks, so that she could anticipate difficulties before starting the year. Students were instructed to do their best to fill in words they thought would fit, as a way to help the teacher know them better; they would not be graded. The teacher never returned the cloze to the students; the exercise was for diagnosis, not instruction. She scored it using the exact word criterion. In this way, she was able to develop a quick profile of 55 students in two sections. Only one student scored at the independent level; two scored at the frustration level. The majority of students, then, did bring adequate background knowledge to this textbook, if she guided them well.

She made a note to watch the two students who scored poorly, as well as the high scorer. As the first weeks passed, she learned that one student came from an abusive home and simply could not concentrate on academics even though he was capable. The second student was very unhappy to have been placed in a high-ability class because all she wanted to do was play in the band and slide by in school. The teacher was able to find some appropriate help for each of them. The high scorer continued to perform almost flawlessly on the assignments during the beginning weeks of school. The teacher discovered that this student was new to the school but had been in advanced classes in her other school. However, this school had a policy that a student must obtain a teacher recommendation before being placed in advanced classes. Within the first three weeks, this teacher was able to recommend that the student proceed to the advanced level; the cloze results provided supporting documentation. The teacher might have missed an opportunity to help these students had she not administered that cloze. Very helpful diagnostic information was gleaned from an activity that took little time; it was administered to 55 students in one 15-minute period.

Activity 4.2 is a cloze constructed by an eighth-grade science teacher. She found that three of her students scored at the independent level, indicating to her that they were well matched to the material; that is, they seemed to possess prior background knowledge and language facility that made predicting the author's wording easy for them. These three students should have very little trouble reading the material assigned. Four students scored at the instructional level, indicating to her that they could read the assigned material fairly well if she provided background before making assignments. But two students scored at the frustrational level, indicating to her that these students had less background than they should have to do well with this material. The teacher realized that she would need to monitor them carefully and perhaps find easier material on the same topic.

A Cautionary Note A cloze procedure can reveal what students already know about a subject and can indicate if the material is appropriate. The better students do, the more they probably know about the topic. If most students fall in the frustrational level, the material is inappropriate for them because they may not bring enough background to it. Ashby-Davis (1985) cautions, however, that a cloze is not like the usual reading students do. Their reading speed, eye movements, and use of context are likely to be different when reading a cloze. Therefore, although a cloze may be a helpful indicator of the student's background in a particular topic, it should not be relied on to tell a teacher about a student's general reading skills.

CLOZE AS A TECHNIQUE FOR BUILDING BACKGROUND

When a cloze is used for instructional rather than diagnostic purposes, the range of possible cloze constructions is increased. Instead of exact replacement of

ACTIVITY 4.2   CLOZE FOR DETERMINING BACKGROUND

Purpose: Determining the individual levels of the students I teach is very important. Therefore, to determine background, I selected a passage from the text approximately 275 words long and have the students perform the cloze test on this passage.

Student Directions: Below is a passage taken from your science textbook. I have deleted some of the words the author wrote. Your job is to write in the blank a word that you *think* the author might have used in the same space. Your choices will help me get to know you as readers of this textbook. Do your best!

Energy, Reactions, and Catalysts

Energy is either gained or lost during a chemical change. In some reactions, ___1___ as burning, energy is ___2___. In other reactions, energy ___3___ be added for a ___4___ change to occur. If ___5___ is released, the reaction ___6___ called exothermic. If energy ___7___ be added during a ___8___, the reaction is called ___9___.

The burning of magnesium ___10___ an exothermic reaction. Though ___11___ heat is needed to ___12___ the reaction, the heat ___13___ off when magnesium bonds ___14___ oxygen is more than ___15___ to keep the reaction ___16___.

The reaction between ammonium ___17___ and barium hydroxide is ___18___ exothermic reaction. Energy is ___19___ as the two solids ___20___. The temperature of the ___21___ flask decreases. In fact, ___22___ may form on the ___23___ of the flask. A ___24___ amount of energy is ___25___ up as the products ___26___. However, much more energy ___27___ absorbed to keep the ___28___ going. Thus, the reaction ___29___ endothermic.

The time is ___30___ for a reaction to ___31___ can vary greatly. The ___32___ change that occurs when ___33___ tarnishes may take place ___34___ a few months. The ___35___ of silver chloride from ___36___ nitrate and sodium chloride ___37___ takes place in an ___38___. In some cases, a ___39___ may be too slow ___40___ be of use.

Recall ___41___ Activity on page 240 ___42___ the decomposition of hydrogen ___43___. Since the decomposition of ___44___ dilute solution of hydrogen ___45___ is a slow process, ___46___ dioxide is added. The ___47___ speeds the reaction so ___48___ oxygen is formed faster. ___49___, the MNO_2 is unchanged. ___50___ this case, MNO_2 acts as a catalyst. A catalyst changes the speed of a reaction without being permanently changed itself.

(continued on page 119)

A C T I V I T Y   4 . 2   **CONTINUED**

Answers:

1. such	**14.** with	**27.** is	**40.** to
2. released	**15.** enough	**28.** reaction	**41.** the
3. must	**16.** going	**29.** is	**42.** involving
4. chemical	**17.** thiocyanate	**30.** takes	**43.** peroxide
5. energy	**18.** an	**31.** occur	**44.** a
6. is	**19.** absorbed	**32.** chemical	**45.** peroxide
7. must	**20.** react	**33.** silver	**46.** manganese
8. reaction	**21.** reaction	**34.** over	**47.** MNO_2
9. endothermic	**22.** ice	**35.** formation	**48.** the
10. is	**23.** outside	**36.** silver	**49.** However
11. some	**24.** small	**37.** solutions	**50.** In
12. start	**25.** given	**38.** instant	
13. given	**26.** form	**39.** reaction	

Independent Level Material Easy Scores Above 60%	Instructional Level Material Suitable Scores of 40% to 60%	Frustrational Level Material Too Hard Scores Below 40%
Dawn (missed 16 = 68%) Charles (missed 15 = 70%) Elsie (missed 18 = 64%)	Walter (missed 20 = 60%) Chuck (missed 28 = 44%) Frances (missed 22 = 56%) Cyndi (missed 24 = 52%)	John (missed 32 = 36%) Bill (missed 34 = 32%)

Activity developed by Carole B. Forkey. Source of cloze material is *Focus on Physical Science* by Heimler & Price (1981). Charles E. Merrill. Reprinted by permission of the publisher.

vocabulary, synonyms can be considered. For instance, Beil's cloze, adapted from his article "The Emperor's New Cloze" (1977), uses a synonym key and much higher scoring criteria (see Activity 4.3). At the same time, the content of the cloze provides information about the many uses of this technique.

In constructing an instructional cloze, the teacher will still leave beginning and ending sentences intact, but deletions can serve different instructional purposes. For example, the teacher may delete all of the nouns and then ask students to predict what part of speech the words to replace deleted words must be. This cloze activity builds an awareness of nouns that helps readers to be proficient readers of their grammar book. An instructional cloze can also include clues. For example, the first letter of a word or all of its consonants may be left in. The number of letters in the word can also be indicated, or a list of words from which to select can be provided. Whatever the design, the instructional cloze can be

A C T I V I T Y   4 . 3   CLOZE FOR BUILDING BACKGROUND

Because no major publishing company has a cloze closet of its own, the catch is you have to make your own. There is a bundle to be made in new ___1___ , and there is no reason to wait for handy ___2___ or attractive boxes.

Now for the first step in ___3___ your new wardrobe, start with the next book you ___4___ to use in class. Select the *three* most meaningful ___5___ of 100–200 words each. Almost any source can be ___6___ : try classic literature, fantasy fiction (the clozed Hobbit is ___7___ treat!), Greek myths, or sci-fi and choose which passages ___8___ reflect the import and content of the story.

Some ___9___ in making new cloze is common. Basically, you uniformly ___10___ one word in every ten (some folks say every f ___11___ or every seventh word) throughout the passages and make ___12___ gaps ten spaces long. On some materials you may ___13___ to provide clues or cues to the cloze units, ___14___ blanks can have the same number of spaces as ___15___ missing words. Initial or ending consonants can also be ___16___ — as long as these aids help meet your need.

___17___ research or diagnostic purposes, keep the blanks and the ___18___ of the deletions internally consistent; for teaching grammar, vocabulary, ___19___ syntax, vary them as suits your purpose. Researchers often ___20___ the first and last sentences intact, but if the ___21___ chosen are interesting and meaningful enough, they will provide ___22___ the clues necessary for completion. *Good luck on furnishing your cloze closet!*

Answers:

1. cloze	**7.** a	**13.** want	**19.** or
2. kits	**8.** most	**14.** and	**20.** leave
3. designing	**9.** variety	**15.** the	**21.** passages
4. intend	**10.** delete	**16.** supplied	**22.** all
5. passages	**11.** fifth	**17.** for	
6. used	**12.** the	**18.** structure	

Scoring by Synonym Replacement:

Independent Level 91% or more 20 or more correct	Instructional Level 75%–90% 16–19 correct	Frustrational Level Less than 75% 15 or fewer correct

Adapted from "The Emperor's New Cloze" by Drake Beil, *Journal of Reading*, April 1977, pp. 601–604. Reprinted with permission of Drake Beil and the International Reading Association.

used to help teachers determine what their students already know and, by discussion of the choices made, build their knowledge of the material. Discussion should also whet the readers' appetites for the reading material that follows, thus giving students a purpose for reading and assisting their comprehension of the material.

Since discussing the students' choices is an obvious part of the activity when it is used for instruction, cloze also fosters listening and speaking opportunities. Although writing is limited to single-word entries, some writing is occurring as well. Some teachers find cloze useful as a technique for reflection. Such an activity, the interactive cloze procedure, will be explained in Chapter 7 on vocabulary.

Maze

A predeterminer similar to cloze but easier for students to respond to is a maze (Guthrie, Burnam, Caplan, & Seifert, 1974), which is especially useful for determining students' prior knowledge and understanding of a subject. The teacher selects a passage of 100 to 120 words from a representative part of the textbook and deletes every fifth or tenth word. The students are then given three choices: the correct word; a grammatically similar but incorrect word; and a "distractor," which is a grammatically different and incorrect word. Because a maze is easier for students to complete than a cloze, the scoring criteria are more stringent. Although a maze is a bit harder to construct than a cloze because the teacher must provide three choices, many teachers prefer it. Activity 4.4 shows how a maze for elementary (approximately fifth-grade) social studies material would look and be scored.

Like cloze, maze builds background as it determines it. Because three choices are given, students who lack prior knowledge have some material to react to. This interaction promotes the use of partial associations. In fact, many teachers prefer maze to cloze for building background because it is less threatening to students and promotes discussion successfully. From the maze, students can move right into reading the whole material, practicing the use of context clues.

Pretests of Knowledge

Pretests of knowledge are quick, sensible ways to measure background knowledge. Teachers construct these tests for students to take before they begin reading. These tests are not graded; the teacher and students use them to see what students already know and what they should learn. Pretests can be developed in any number of ways.

RECOGNITION PRETESTS

Recognition pretests are a good way to find out what students know about the content to be taught. Holmes and Roser (1987) recommend the recognition technique as an informal pretest. Teachers can use the subheadings in a chapter as stems for a multiple-choice format. Alternatives are derived from chapter content. The recognition pretest in Activity 4.5 was developed by a middle-school science teacher to determine background for a chapter on energy. For

A C T I V I T Y   4 . 4   A MAZE PREPARED ON AN EXCERPT FROM "THE BATTLE OF SEMPACH"

Purpose: To determine the background knowledge of students for the material.

Student Directions: Below is a passage for you to read. Notice that sometimes you will see three words where only one should be. Your job is to select which of these three words fits best in the sentence. This exercise will help me to know better how to help you read this material.

The Swiss knew that the enemy army was made up mostly of knights in armor, on

horseback. Knights usually fought only { one / a / get } way—they galloped straight

{ backwards / walk / ahead } in a charge, with { her / their / sword } long lances held straight { in / hurry. / out } They

would try to { smash / wander / enemy } into the Swiss and { straight / scatter / avoid } them.

But the Swiss { were / that / had } learned that the horses { would / will / night } not be able to

{ conquer / get / Swiss } past the wall of { horses / curly / pike } points. The charge would { come / go / but } to a stop in

{ side / front / with } of the square, with { knights / kings / gallop } and horses all jammed { fight / apart, / together } hardly able

to move. { Then / Charge / Before } those Swiss armed with { brief / long / wall } swords and axes would

{ up / wander / rush } out of the square { to / for / fight } hack and chop at { won / the / that } helpless knights. This

was how the Swiss had won their other battles.

(continued on page 123)

A C T I V I T Y   4 . 4   CONTINUED

Answers:

one	smash	would	come	together	rush
ahead	scatter	get	front	Then	to
their	had	pike	knights	long	the
out					

Independent Level Material Easy 90% and Above	Instructional Level Material Suitable 70%–90%	Frustrational Level Material Too Hard Below 70%

Pp. 110–111, *Stories of Freedom*, 1988, Childcraft Annual, World Book, Inc.

A C T I V I T Y   4 . 5   RECOGNITION: SOURCES OF ENERGY

Directions: Select the items which you think will complete each statement. You may select more than one item. This activity will help us realize what you already know about the topic and on what we need to concentrate the most during this lesson.

1. Energy can come in which of the following forms?
   a. electrical
   b. light
   c. magnetic
   d. heat
   e. chemical
   f. kinetic
   g. listening
2. Which of the following statements have the same meaning as the law of the conservation of energy? (Energy cannot be created or destroyed, but can be transformed.)
   a. energy can be changed from one form to another
   b. energy can be made from matter alone
   c. energy can be used up
   d. resources used to transform energy can be used up
3. Sources used in producing energy today include:
   a. fossil fuels (coal, gas, oil, water power, geothermal power)
   b. ocean tidal power
   c. nuclear power
   d. solar power
   e. lunar power

Source: Holmes, Betty C. and Nancy L. Roser. "Five Ways to Assess Readers' Prior Knowledge," *The Reading Teacher, 40*, March, 1987.
Developed for the classroom display by Holly Corbett.

ACTIVITY 4.6   RECOGNITION: WHAT I KNOW ABOUT KEYBOARDING

Directions: Circle the answers you think are correct.

1. Typewriters have which of the following types of prints?
   a. carbon and noncarbon
   b. pica and elite
   c. electrical and manual
2. Your body should be centered with which key?
   a. X
   b. O
   c. T
   d. P
   e. H
   f. M
3. The keyboarding home-row keys are
   a. ASDFJKL;
   b. ASDFGHJK
   c. ADFGJKL:
   d. QWERUIOP
4. Which finger is used on the space bar?
   a. pinkie
   b. middle finger
   c. thumb
   d. ring finger
5. On which side of the typewriter does the textbook belong?
   a. right
   b. left
6. To keyboard ALL CAPS items, which key needs to be pressed?
   a. return
   b. shift lock
   c. space bar
   d. tab
7. What is the center point for pica type?
   a. 41
   b. 50
   c. 51
   d. 42
8. What is the center point for elite type?
   a. 42
   b. 51
   c. 41
   d. 50

(continued on page 125)

A C T I V I T Y   4 . 6   CONTINUED

9. Pica type has how many letters per inch?
   a. 9
   b. 12
   c. 15
   d. 10
10. Elite type has how many letters per inch?
    a. 15
    b. 10
    c. 9
    d. 12

Answers:

1. pica and elite
2. H
3. ASDFJKL;
4. thumb
5. right
6. shift lock
7. 42
8. 51
9. 10
10. 12

Developed by Pam Lundy.

instance, she reworded the subheading "Energy Comes in Many Forms" as "Energy can come in which of the following forms?" Then she selected several of the energy forms mentioned in the section, as well as distractors, for the choices students could make. When students had completed her pretest, she could see how much students already knew about sources of energy.

Sometimes a teacher designs a pretest from the important points to be learned in a material. A seventh-grade vocational-educational teacher wrote questions for ten major ideas in a keyboarding chapter (Activity 4.6). Student answers helped her see what points needed the most emphasis in their lesson.

SELF-INVENTORIES

A discriminative self-inventory (Dale, O'Rourke, & Bamman, 1971) will help the teacher and students know which words in the text they do and don't know. The teacher identifies the important words and presents them along with a symbol system, such as checks for older students or faces for younger students. Students then react to each word. The self-inventory in Activity 4.7 was developed by a teacher to determine background for reading an eighth-grade mathematics text.

A C T I V I T Y   4 . 7   **SELF-INVENTORY: EIGHTH-GRADE MATH**

Below is a list of terms and symbols that we will use while working in Chapter 14. This exercise will not be graded; it will help you and me to know what you already know.

Place a + beside the ones you know; place a √ beside the ones you know something about; place a 0 beside the ones you don't know.

_____ range	_____ median
_____ mode	_____ mean
_____ outcomes	_____ favorable outcomes
_____ probability	_____ sample space
_____ compound probability	
_____ ∩	_____ ∪
_____ ⊂	_____ ⊃

Developed by Sherry Gott.

A C T I V I T Y   4 . 8   **SELF-INVENTORY: THIRD-GRADE HEALTH**

Use the following symbols to tell how well you know these words. Remember: you won't be graded and you aren't supposed to know all the words.

I know it!   So-so   I don't know it.

_____ **1.** FATS	_____ **5.** VITAMINS	_____ **9.** CARBON
_____ **2.** CAR-BO-HY-DRATES	_____ **6.** AMINO ACIDS	_____ **10.** HYDROGEN
_____ **3.** OXYGEN	_____ **7.** MINERALS	_____ **11.** FOOD
_____ **4.** WATER	_____ **8.** PROTEIN	_____ **12.** MARROW

Developed by Kathy Feltus.

The self-inventory in Activity 4.8 was developed by a teacher to determine background for reading a third-grade health text. Activity 4.9 was developed by a teacher who uses attention-getting symbols to capture her ninth-grade English students' interest in completing the activity.

After having students determine for themselves whether they know the words, by rating each one, the teacher and the students will be ready to focus attention

ACTIVITY 4.9   SELF-INVENTORY: NINTH-GRADE ENGLISH

The following words will be used in the selection you are about to read. In order to give me an idea of your vocabulary background, please check the appropriate category for each word. REMEMBER: This is not a test, and it will *not* be graded.

I know this word	Vaguely familiar	Don't know at all
____ **1.** persecuted	____ **5.** blunderbuss	____ **9.** puns
____ **2.** perpetuated	____ **6.** pillories	____ **10.** malapropisms
____ **3.** perilous	____ **7.** genealogy	____ **11.** parody
____ **4.** austere	____ **8.** idioms	____ **12.** allusions

Developed by Rebecca McSweeney.

better when they meet those words in the material to be read. Students appreciate such an activity because they feel more in charge of what they already know and better able to concentrate on finding out what they themselves have realized they don't know.

FACTSTORMING

Factstorming is another form of pretest that teachers can conduct very easily. Factstorming types of activities are very useful in determining reader background. A whole class can participate at once, informally, with no paperwork necessary. The activity proceeds from a single, generative question. Factstorming is similar to brainstorming but focuses on facts and associations pertinent to the topic, whereas brainstorming focuses on problem solving. The teacher asks students to tell anything they can think of about the topic to be read—for instance: "Tell anything you know about capital punishment." Responses are written on the chalkboard or a transparency and discussed as they are entered. An example of factstorming is given in Chapter 1 when the teacher asked her students to tell her about goldfish.

PreP A sophisticated version of factstorming is PreP, a prereading plan (Langer, 1981). An example of PreP was given in Chapter 1, where the secondary social

A C T I V I T Y   4 . 1 0   PreP (PREREADING PLAN)

The prereading plan will be used to estimate the level of background knowledge a fourth-grade class brings to the study of fractions. The plan will stimulate discussion and develop awareness of fractions in a class of six to twelve students. These students should be familiar with four of the major concepts to be developed in this unit; therefore, by listening and observing students, the teacher can tell whether the students have much, some, or little knowledge about fractions.

Phase 1: Initial associations with the concept
   Teacher: Tell me anything that comes to mind when you hear the word *fractions*.
As each student relates ideas that come to mind, the teacher writes the responses on the chalkboard. Students activate prior knowledge through the associations.

Phase 2: Reflections on initial associations
   Teacher: What made you think of *numerator*? (or *denominator, parts, equal parts, pies, regions, number lines, dividing, multiplying, sharing, whole*, etc.)
This phase helps students develop awareness of their networks of association and to interact with other ideas and change their own ideas about fractions.

Phase 3: Reformulation of knowledge
   Teacher: Based on our discussion, and before we study the chapter, have you any new ideas about fractions?
This allows students to verbalize associations, to probe their memories, and to refine responses.

Developed by Nancy Campbell.

studies teacher used this activity for preparation. PreP has three phases: (1) initial associations with the concept, as in factstorming; (2) reflections on the initial concept, when students are asked to explain why they thought of a particular response, thus building an awareness of their prior knowledge and associations; and (3) reformulation of knowledge, when new ideas learned during the first two phases are articulated.

PreP helps determine prior knowledge and also builds background. The steps encourage the reader to use whatever prior knowledge is available by listening carefully to the opinions of others. Misperceptions can be corrected in a non-threatening way, with whole group discussion as a supportive environment for expression. Listening, speaking, and reading are all taking place in a PreP activity. An example of PreP for fourth-grade mathematics is given in Activity 4.10.

Free Recall Free recall (Holmes & Roser, 1987) is similar to PreP. The teacher presents a situation and asks students to respond with ideas. The ideas give the teacher a picture of students' prior knowledge and a chance to begin the necessary building process. Holmes and Roser give this example of free recall: "Imagine that in this story is written everything there is to know about snakes. What do you think it will say?" (p. 647). They caution that free recall may work best with older students who have better organized knowledge than do younger students. We believe that younger students will benefit from the activity when it is used as a background builder rather than as a determiner.

KWL Yet another activity designed to find out what students already know about the content to be studied is KWL (Heller, 1986; Ogle, 1986, 1992; Carr & Ogle, 1987). The *K* stands for what students *know* before they begin to read. The teacher asks students to state facts they know in the first of three columns. The *W* stands for what the students *want* to know. When students tell the teacher this information, the teacher can determine what students think is important about the material. These responses are recorded in a second column. The *L* stands for what was *learned*. After reading, students consider the third column and match what they *knew* in advance and what they *wanted* to learn with what they did *learn*. This activity not only helps the teacher and students determine prior knowledge, it also models an appropriate reflection strategy after reading has occurred.

What I Already *Know*	What I *Want* to Know	What I *Learned*

What-I-Know (WIK) Sheet In our experience, teachers have felt limited with only the three KWL columns. They wanted to design an activity that better reflected the terminology and steps of PAR. In Activity 4.11, the columns are relabeled "What I Already Know" (to more clearly emphasize prior knowledge); "What I Know Now" (to more clearly emphasize what is known after reading); and "What I Still Don't Know" (to more clearly emphasize what students still need to find out after the reading has taken place). Students also fill in the topic and the purpose for reading. Before reading, students will factstorm on what they already know about this topic (column 1). After reading, they will list what they have learned and what else they should learn (columns 2 and 3). The What-I-Know sheet in Activity 4.11 was completed by a primary science class.

When students fill in the column labeled "What I Already Know," they are building their background as well as giving the teacher information about their prior knowledge. If students are encouraged to add to their own list after listening to and learning from class discussion, they are building background by using other students' knowledge. Reading to find out what else can be learned ("What I Know Now") and what wasn't learned ("What I Still Don't Know") will encourage development of comprehension and reflective thinking also. The class discussion and recording of associations integrate the communicative arts.

A second example, in Activity 4.12, shows how an English teacher makes clear the three steps in the reading-to-learn framework—before reading, during reading, and after reading—by incorporating these headings into a What-I-Know activity.

A C T I V I T Y   4 . 1 1   WHAT-I-KNOW SHEET

Topic: marine life
Purpose: to learn more about seashells

What I Already Know	What I Know Now	What I Still Don't Know
Some shells are round. Some of them are smooth. They come in different sizes. Some are in water. Some are pretty.	Some shells have points. They look different. They have different names.	What do shells come from?

Developed by Marcie Mansfield.

A C T I V I T Y   4 . 1 2   WHAT-I-KNOW SHEET

Name: Kia

Date: 11-25-91

TOPIC: Split Cherry Tree

PURPOSE:

BEFORE READING		DURING READING	AFTER READING	
What I Already Know:	What I'd Like to Know:	Interesting or Important Concepts from my Reading:	What I Know Now:	What I'd Still Like to Know:
It's about a cherry tree.	What happened in the story	When Mr. Sexton found out he has gems on his teeth, and he doesn't need a gun at school.	Split Cherry Tree was a very good story. ~~And some things need~~ you don't need a gun to settle things.	If they took their ma to school to see a gem and what she thinks about it too.

Developed by Leslie Tucker.

Anticipation Guides

Anticipation guides, also called reaction or prediction guides, prepare readers by asking them to react to a series of statements that are related to the content of the material. In reacting to these statements, students anticipate, or predict, what the content will be—hence the three different labels for this activity. An anticipation guide was used at the beginning of this chapter when readers were asked whether they agree or disagree with three statements and why. Each statement was reintroduced later in the chapter, in a discussion intended to focus the reader's attention.

Erickson, Huber, Bea, Smith, and McKenzie (1987) cite three reasons for the value of anticipation guides: (1) Students need to connect what they already know with new information and realize that they do already know something that will help them comprehend better. (2) Students tend to become interested and participate in lively discussion, which motivates reading. (3) Reading and writing instruction are easily integrated when anticipation guides are used. Anticipation guides, then, involve students in discussion and reading and can also include writing if students are asked to respond in writing to the statements. Many teachers also have students refer to the guide as they read, which enhances comprehension. If students return to the guide after reading, to clarify or rethink previous positions, then the guide is applied throughout PAR. Conley (1985) argues that such guides are also excellent tools for developing critical thinking and promoting cross-cultural understanding. For all of these reasons, anticipation guides are truly eclectic and very well received by both teachers and students.

Making an anticipation guide takes some thought, but it becomes easier with practice. The process has been described in several textbooks, including those by Herber (1978) and Readance, Bean, and Baldwin (1981). The basic steps for constructing an anticipation guide are as follows:

1. Read the content passage and identify the major concepts.
2. Decide which concepts are most important to stimulate student background and beliefs.
3. Write three to five statements based on the concepts. The statements should reflect the students' background and be thought-provoking. We have found that general statements, rather than statements that are too specific, work best. Famous quotations and idioms are successful.
4. Display the guide on the chalkboard, on an overhead projector, or on worksheets. Give clear directions. (These will vary depending on the age group and variations in the guide.) Leave space for responses.
5. Conduct class discussion with the statements as the basis. Students must support their responses; "yes" and "no" are not acceptable answers. Students should argue from their past experiences and explain their decisions. (After guides have been used a few times, small groups can conduct discussions simultaneously, or individuals can complete guides independently and then reconvene.)

A C T I V I T Y   4 . 1 3   **ANTICIPATION/PREDICTION GUIDE: SCIENCE**

Directions: Read these statements to yourself as I read them aloud. If you agree with a statement, be ready to explain why. We will check all statements we agree with in the prereading column. Then we will read to see if we should change our minds.

Prediction Guide for Mammals

Before   After

_____   🐦   are mammals.   _____

_____   🦋   are mammals.   _____

_____   All mammals have 4   🦵 .   _____

_____   🐳   are mammals.   _____

_____   Some mammals can   🐦 .   _____

6. It is best to return to the anticipation guide after the material has been read. In this way, students can compare their first responses to their new information.

An anticipation guide that was used with fifth-grade music students appeared earlier in this chapter (see Activity 4.1). Activities 4.13 through 4.16 provide examples of anticipation guides constructed by teachers of primary science, high school geography, vocational education, and middle-school art. One secondary teacher was so enchanted with anticipation guides that she wrote a tribute in the form of an acrostic (see Figure 4.1).

There is no "right" way to create an activity. Activities that reflect sound instructional principles and research are developed every day by enterprising

A C T I V I T Y   4 . 1 4   **ANTICIPATION/PREDICTION GUIDE: GEOGRAPHY**

Name _____ Date _____

PREDICTION GUIDE: CHAPTER 1, SECTION 2

Before reading pages 36–41, put a checkmark next to the statements you think will be true.

1. ____ English, Spanish, and French are all part of the same subfamily of languages.

2. ____ Institutions, such as the family and schools, are the means of passing a particular culture from one generation to the next.

3. ____ Religious beliefs are the most important building block of a culture.

4. ____ It takes at least two persons for language to exist.

5. ____ All language started in one central part of the world, and as it spread, local variations developed it into the different languages we have today.

6. ____ Ellen Semple found that isolated groups of people who have little contact with outsiders tend to develop new languages of their own.

7. ____ The more traffic an area has, in terms of trade and commerce, the more likely its language will change.

8. ____ The official language of Switzerland is Swiss.

9. ____ English is the official language of the country of India.

10. ____ African countries usually are made up of people of similar culture and language.

11. ____ American Indian tribes, such as the Powhatan, Apache, Navaho, and Iroquois, all speak languages from the same subfamily.

12. ____ German culture is similar to English culture.

Developed by Mark Forget.

teachers. In fact, we have discovered just how creative teachers can be when they like an activity and understand its benefits. One English teacher modified and merged factstorming and the anticipation guide format. He wrote three statements relevant to the short story "An Occurrence at Owl Creek Bridge." He presented these statements to the students and asked them to react to them with whatever thoughts came to mind. He listed their responses beside each statement and then asked for a consensus (see Activity 4.17).

Analogies

When a high school junior resisted reading a history chapter that explained the circumstances leading to the American Revolution, his parent (a reading specialist, of course!) tried this preparation strategy:

"Suppose," the parent suggested, "that your parents decided to go to Europe for six months, leaving you on your own at home. You would have the car and access to money; you would be able to make all of your own decisions. What would your reaction be?" As you might imagine, this high school junior thought this would be an excellent arrangement. "However," the parent continued, "we

ACTIVITY 4.15   ANTICIPATION/PREDICTION GUIDE: AUTO TECHNOLOGY

Directions: Read the statements below carefully. Put an X in the Agree column or in the Disagree column for each statement. Be ready to defend your choices.

Before Reading				After Reading	
Agree	Disagree			Agree	Disagree
___	___	1.	The user of oxygen-fuel equipment should know the hazards that could occur.	___	___
___	___	2.	Adding oxygen to a fire will reduce the temperature.	___	___
___	___	3.	A potential bomb exists wherever welding is going on.	___	___
___	___	4.	Safety plugs are not likely to leak.	___	___
___	___	5.	Stand directly in front of the regulator when opening cylinder valves.	___	___
___	___	6.	Oxygen and acetylene cylinders should be laid on their sides for storage.	___	___
___	___	7.	Oil and grease must never be allowed to come in contact with oxygen.	___	___
___	___	8.	Open cylinder valves slowly.	___	___

READING: Cooper, Paul D. "Safety Comes First in Oxygen-Fuel Welding," *Industrial Education*, May 1989, pp. 12–14.

Developed by Steve Boykin.

ACTIVITY 4.16   ANTICIPATION/PREDICTION GUIDE: ART

Directions: Read the statements below **before** and **after** you read Chapter 5. Put a check next to each statement to show your opinion. This is not a test.

Before Reading			After Reading	
Agree	Disagree		Agree	Disagree
___	___	The cave paintings in France and Spain are the earliest records man will ever have.	___	___
___	___	Early architects were concerned with religion, rituals, and self-preservation.	___	___
___	___	The largest and greatest pyramid was built for Cheops and covered thirteen acres.	___	___
___	___	The pyramids were built to honor the gods and as places of worship.	___	___
___	___	Egyptians used descriptive perspective in which the important figures are shown larger than the less important ones.	___	___

Developed by Joan Phipps.

FIGURE 4.1

Anticipation guide (developed by Linda R. Cobb).

A
N ecessary
T ool to use for
I nstruction in teaching
C ritical thinking and for getting students
I nvolved in
P redicting
A ctivities
T hat
I ntegrate the use
O f all of the communicative arts to comprehend
N ew material. The

G oal is to
U ltimately produce
I ndependent thinkers who use
D iscussion and reading to
E nhance comprehension.

A C T I V I T Y 4 . 1 7	MODIFIED ANTICIPATION/PREDICTION GUIDE

think scared worry overreact nervous cry How can we solve the problem?	confusion life flashes before eyes mad religion happy past thoughts	1. During a crisis, the mind works very rapidly.
pressure tired dentist, doctor, etc. illness death work school	practice, games accident pressure (extreme) movies family guys gals	2. Great stress can be provoked by everyday kinds of experiences.
escape pain family friends guilty or innocent	life/death future thoughts past thoughts Help! life is flashing before my eyes	3. The human mind undergoes many psychological reactions when a person is about to be hanged. Developed by Robert Witherow.

would arrive home again and take charge once more. We would want our car back, and you would have to ask for permission to use it. You would begin to receive an allowance again. You would have to ask permission to do the things you'd been doing freely. Now, how would you feel?" As you can imagine, this junior did not like the turn of events. "Would you still love us?" the parent inquired, assuming, of course, that teenagers *do* love their parents even though they have funny ways of showing it!

"Well, yes," the junior reluctantly agreed. "But I'd be insulted, and family life wouldn't be the same."

"Exactly," agreed the parent. "That's the way it was with the British and their American colony. The British had to attend to problems in Europe and in their own government. They let the American colonists have free rein for a while. Then they turned their attention back to the Americans. But the Americans didn't appreciate the intervention after this period of time. Many of them still 'loved' the British, but they resented the renewed control deeply. While you're reading this chapter, you might want to keep in mind your own reactions to this hypothetical situation and compare those feelings to the reactions of the colonists." Much later in the month, this junior grudgingly reported to his parent that the chapter had turned out to be "pretty easy to read" because he understood the circumstances better than with most of the chapters in the book.

This on-the-spot analogy was simple enough to construct. The teacher/parent understood several characteristics of 16-year-olds and applied them to building an analogy that would "hook" the reader to the content material. The informal analogy was a simple preparation strategy. It worked because the reading took on new meaning for the student. His comprehension was enhanced, enough so that he admitted it to a parent!

Analogies present comparisons between known and unknown concepts. In Chapter 3, we likened practicing for a basketball game to preparation for reading. That analogy relates a familiar concept to a less familiar one. Analogies are like previews in that both begin with a connection point to the reader's background. However, analogies carry out a comparison, whereas previews focus more directly on the material to be read. Analogies are excellent tools for content reading teachers because they are simple to create and so relevant for students. They can be presented in oral or written form, as an informal introduction to content material. They also promote listening and speaking, and if students are encouraged to write their own analogies after reading material, then analogies become useful reflection and writing activities as well. The lesson shown in Activity 4.18, on building background with an analogy as its base, was developed by a third-grade teacher.

To take another example, here is an analogy for primary children as they study about weight and volume (developed by Laura Allin):

Pretend that you are at home eating breakfast. There are two boxes of the same cereal on the table. Neither has been opened, but one has been sitting still and the other you have just shaken up. You open both boxes and find that the one that was shaken has

A C T I V I T Y   4 . 1 8   ANALOGY

Goal: To enable students to connect new knowledge with existing knowledge.
Directions: Read the following paragraphs as a primer for small-group discussion comparing cars with bodies.
Materials: Paper
           Pencils

Your body is very similar to a car in the way that it acts. You may have been told to "rev up your engine" one time. When a car revs up, it begins to go.

A car needs many different substances to keep it running well. It might need oil for the parts and air for the filters, as you would need oil for your joints or air for your lungs.

Actually, there are many other things that a car and your body have in common. A car needs gasoline to make it go. What do you need? (food)

Now divide the students into small groups and let them list on paper the ways that cars and bodies are similar. Some suggestions that you will be looking for are:

Fats/oil
Protein/gasoline
Carbohydrates/spark plugs
Vitamins/fuel additives, super power gasoline
Minerals/paint, rustproofers
Air/air conditioning
muscles/wheels
heart/engine

Return to the class in 15 or 20 minutes and share the group information. Write the analogies on the board. Ask for comments or changes.

Developed by Kathy Feltus.

cereal to the top of the box, but the other has several inches less. The reason for this is that you shook one box and the other cereal has had a chance to settle. They both have the same mass because both boxes of cereal weigh the same. They have different volumes because one of the boxes has cereal to the rim and the other doesn't; they take up different amounts of space. The matter would be the cereal in the boxes.

Direct References and Simple Discussions

Sometimes teachers find that students have incorrect knowledge. What is the best way to build background for readers with misconceptions? When Dole, Valencia, Greer, and Wardrop (1991) compared the use of interactive and teacher-directed strategies, they found that teacher direction increased students' comprehension of a passage. If none of the activities presented previously seems suitable, consider direct references and discussions.

Maria and MacGinitie (1987) conducted a study in which they asked students in fifth and sixth grades to read two types of materials. The first made specific reference to the misconceptions that the researchers had identified during a pretest and contrasted these misconceptions with correct information. The second was written with the correct information but no direct refutation of predetermined misconceptions. The researchers found that student recall was significantly better on the text that confronted the misconceptions.

In a research study, it makes sense to construct materials that will fit the particular questions being asked. In a classroom, teachers will not have enough time to alter text materials so that misperceptions can be countered. Yet, because making direct references to misconceptions appears to be such a good strategy for overcoming incorrect prior knowledge, teachers will want to incorporate it into lessons that build background. If some rewriting of portions of text can be done, the rewrite might include a specific confrontation. Another possibility is to use a simple discussion as a background-building activity. In such a discussion, the teacher who has determined that a misconception exists in students' prior knowledge can confront it with a written or oral statement. The misinformation can be compared with the correct information that will be read in the text. In this way, background can be built and the misconception cleared up. If students are assigned to write brief statements comparing a prior misconception to a revised understanding of the content, they will also be integrating writing with reading at the reflective step of PAR.

Guzzetti, Snyder, and Glass (1992) conducted a meta-analysis of studies about children's misconceptions. They found that some type of intervention "created in students' minds a degree of discomfort with their prior beliefs" (p. 648). Three types of strategies were found to be effective means of intervention. With refutational text, a teacher provided a passage that directly refuted the misconception; this is similar to the preview activity. Augmented activation activities used learners' prior knowledge to first activate and then supplement with the correct information; this is similar to what might occur with factstorming and PreP or anticipation guides. Also effective was the discussion web (Alvermann, 1991), which we explain in Chapter 6, because students must articulate and defend their positions by referring to text and discussing with peers. Guzzetti, Snyder, and Glass conclude that, regardless of which specific activity is used, dissatisfaction with incorrect prior knowledge must be created before the misconception will be altered.

Suppose that fourth-graders have a misconception about solving word problems. They think, based on prior—but incorrect—knowledge, that word problems are just stories that contain some number words. Such a misconception hinders their ability to read and solve word problems. They do not realize that they must identify the problem, the question, and then the clue words.

A group of teachers have developed an intervention activity they call "casting your line." As fishermen, students are to "catch" several stories and decide which is the real word problem. They are to keep only the "whale of a tale"—that is, the true word problem. Activity 4.19 shows the stories. As the children read, the teacher helps them identify pertinent attributes of a math problem:

Which one is the whale of a tale?

Read each of the three stories and choose the one that you think best fits your idea of what a math story problem is.

Cut out the one you chose. Use dotted lines as cutting guides.

Paste it on a whale.

Cut out the title in the box and paste it on the whale, too.

A Whale of a Tale:

A Math Story Problem

Casting your line for the first time:

Tammy got a new dress for her birthday. Her mother picked out a green silk dress that matched her shoes. That night her whole family went to a restaurant in New York City. For dessert the waiter brought a cake and a bouquet of flowers. How could Tammy ever forget her sixteenth birthday?

Casting your line for the second time:

Fourteen ships were from countries in Europe. Ten were from Africa and just two from China. That week there were a total of twenty-seven ships from foreign countries. The next week there was one from France and none from Africa. In 1990 there were twelve ships from China in the month of May. There were ten ships from France in June.

Casting your line for the third time:

David is strong. He did 5 push-ups. Then he did 3 more. How many push-ups did David do in all?

Developed by Janet Daingerfield, Sandra Davis, and Harriet Glass.

1. A story is told. Something happens to something or someone. Or the story character does something. Or, in time, other things happen.
2. The story contains numbers or number ideas. These numbers may be counted things, sizes, weights, or some other kinds of amounts.
3. The reader is given an unknown quantity (number) to figure out.

Afterward, the teacher uses a checklist to help students distinguish true word problems from other kinds of stories.

1. Is this a story? Yes _____ No _____ Maybe _____
2. If so, does this story involve numbers or amounts?
   Yes _____ No _____ Maybe _____
3. Does this item call for the reader to figure out an unknown?
   Yes _____ No _____ Maybe _____

This example demonstrates how incorrect prior knowledge can be altered by specific intervention.

Limited Reading and Study Skills

Reader-based problems can arise not only from insufficient prior knowledge or interest, but also from inadequate reading and study skills. The author of the material cannot be blamed for failing to predict this. For instance, if a text presents material through graphs but the students reading that text are not skilled at reading graphs, a readability problem exists. The author, of course, had to assume that the readers would have this skill.

It is also possible that students will have in mind one definition for a word, perhaps a general meaning, but the text is using that word in a very specific, content-oriented way. *Bank* is such a word. Does it mean the slope of a riverside? a place where money is kept? to count on something? Realizing that words have multiple meanings and are dependent on context and content is a reading skill that some readers do not possess fully, and some do not possess at all.

When students assure the teacher that they "studied," but in fact their definition of study is to read over the material for the first time, they have incorrect knowledge of a study skill. Many studies conducted in the past few years indicate that some children, particularly those tested in grades three through nine, do not understand the difference between a major idea and supporting ideas; they have difficulty distinguishing a main idea from its details (Garner, Alexander, Slater, Hare, Smith, & Reis, 1986; Meyer, Brandt, & Bluth, 1980; Williams, Taylor, & Ganger, 1981).

Teachers need to make sure that students do have the skills required to read and study the material. If students don't possess the appropriate skills, the teacher will simply be wasting time teaching content material unless the skill can be taught along with the content.

Some Methods for Determining Reading and Study Skill Levels

Because comprehension, vocabulary, and study skills for content reading are addressed in other chapters of this book, they will not be discussed in depth here. However, teachers should be aware that they need to determine how reading skills affect the match between the reader and content material. They should also realize that if the problems they discover are severe, a reading specialist needs to be called on for help. Content and regular classroom teachers should not be expected to diagnose and remediate severe reading difficulties. Nor should the regular teacher be responsible for special testing to determine such difficulties. However, if the teacher suspects that basic reading or study skills are the problem, the activities described here may be helpful in confirming those suspicions.

If lack of study skills is a problem, the content teacher is in a good position to teach the study skill while teaching the content. Such instruction makes the best kind of sense for reading to learn because it integrates content and skill. All learners do better when they see the immediate need for a skill in relation to what is to be learned. If, however, lack of basic reading skills is the problem, the best option is to depend on the school reading specialist. Classroom teachers cannot be expected to teach beginning or remedial reading. Their job is to teach reading as it relates to the content, in a developmental sense.

Standardized Tests

Sometimes the results of standardized achievement tests—those given to students to determine the general progress of a school system—can be used by classroom teachers. If the test results report subscores for areas of reading achievement such as word knowledge and comprehension, they will provide at least an indicator of students' levels of achievement. Teachers who suspect that their students have poor reading skills might start their process of determining students' background by reviewing these already-available scores.

If a teacher discerns a pattern—the vocabulary scores for a majority of the class are below grade level, for example—it is a clear indicator for adapted instruction. The key here is discerning a pattern or trend within the class. Rather than using standardized tests as a measure of a student's individual achievement, teachers will find that standardized tests provide an overview of the performance they can expect from the whole class. Group standardized tests are designed to compare groups, not to diagnose individuals. Standardized tests are described further in Chapter 6, which discusses reflection and comprehension.

Already-Constructed Informal Inventories

A content teacher who decides to test students' reading and study skills needs adequate time to administer, score, and interpret the results. Although creating informal measures is time-consuming, the effort can be useful over a long period of time and reveal much information to teachers. Informal ways to measure students' general study skills will be discussed in Chapters 9 and 10. Informal

ACTIVITY 4.20   SAMPLE ITEMS FROM WIEBE-COX INVENTORY

Part 1 Circle the word I say:

once   ones   won   no   none

Part 2 Which picture tells about the word?

Minute

   34

Part 3 Which word tells about the underlined word?

<u>pair</u>

part of   quail   paid   two   three

Part 4 Which word fills in the blank best?

A triangle is a _____.

numeral   multiply   shape   shame   measure

From J. Cox and J. H. Wiebe, "Measuring Reading Vocabulary and Concepts in Mathematics in the Primary Grades," *The Reading Teacher*, January 1984. Reprinted with permission of Juanita Cox and the International Reading Association.

ways to measure reading skills are best constructed with help from a reading specialist. Unfortunately, very few already-constructed informal or standardized tests of reading and study skills for content teachers are available. Textbook authors are becoming more sensitive to the need for such measures, however, and are beginning to include inventories of study skills, such as proficiency in using textbook aids, in their textbooks.

The Content Inventories (McWilliams & Rakes, 1979) is a collection of group inventories already constructed for English, social studies, and science at grades 7 through 12. Students read selected passages and answer questions, and the teacher scores their responses. In addition, several study skills tests are provided. Although *The Content Inventories* covers only the secondary grade levels and the subjects listed, it provides a model other teachers may use to construct a similar set of informal tests.

The Wiebe-Cox Mathematical Reading Inventory provides another model for an informal test of reading skills specific to a content area. Words important to math computations as well as word problems are included in this inventory. In their 1984 article, Cox and Wiebe explain the inventory and include the complete battery of tests. A sample of items in the inventory is reproduced in Activity 4.20.

Teacher-Constructed Textbook Inventories

At the beginning of a school year, content teachers might use a textbook inventory as a class activity to help them learn about their students' proficiency in using textbooks. The inventories illustrated in Activities 4.21, 4.22, and 4.23 were

A C T I V I T Y   4 . 2 1   **TEXTBOOK TREASURE HUNT**

There are many hidden treasures in your grammar book. After you have completed the path below, you will have discovered some interesting facts! Write your answers and the page number(s) on which you found the information on a clean sheet of notebook paper.

1. Give the complete name of the author. How many years did he teach?

2. How many chapters are in your text?

3. Name the publishing company.

6. Give the title of the book from the sample title card.

5. Give the principal parts of the verbs *sit* and *set*.

4. What is the latest copyright date?

7. What is the first word listed on the page reproduced from the *Random House College Dictionary*?

8. What book other than your text will you need to complete exercise 3 in Chapter 27?

9. List the six items given in the summary of information in the card catalog.

12. What are the three kinds of conjunctions?

11. What is the last verb in the list of the most commonly used linking verbs?

10. Copy one nonsense phrase or sentence that helps develop clear, distinct speech.

13. Find the verb that is conjugated: give *one* of the plural forms of the past perfect tense.

14. Find the list of frequently misused irregular verbs. How many infinitives are there?

15. According to the model outline on Training a Dog, what are the two things to avoid?

18. Only one word begins with the letter *q* in the list of 360 suggested vocabulary words. What is it?

17. List the six parts of a business letter.

16. Only three English words end in *-ceed*: list them.

19. What is the definition of the slang word *cool*?

20. How long should a summary be in relation to the original length of the article?

An inquiring mind is one of our greatest treasures

WOW! All that—and more! Browse through your book; look for interesting activities and topics.

(continued on page 144)

A C T I V I T Y   4 . 2 1   **CONTINUED**

Textbook Treasure Hunt Answers

		page
1.	John E. Warriner: 32 years	ii
2.	30	xvi
3.	Harcourt Brace Jovanovich	i
4.	1982	ii
5.	sit: sit, sitting, sat, (have) sat set: set, setting, set, (have) set	171
6.	*The Complete Book of Sports Medicine*	573
7.	funky	593
8.	dictionary	622
9.	call number, author, title, subject, cross references, publisher	574
10.	The big black bug bit the big black bear.	692
11.	could have been	18
12.	coordinating, correlative, subordinating	31
13.	we (or you or they) had flown	163
14.	27	156
15.	coddling, overfeeding	684
16.	exceed, proceed, succeed	649
17.	heading, inside address, salutation, body, closing, signature	447
18.	quaint	642
19.	having a dispassionate or detached attitude	433
20.	1/4 to 1/3	378

The above activity uses the Third Course of *Warriner's English Grammar and Composition* (New York, NY: Harcourt Brace Jovanovich, 1982).

From JoAnne Bryant, "Open to Suggestion" section, *Journal of Reading*, March 1984. Reprinted with permission of the International Reading Association.

designed by teachers to help them make that assessment. The Textbook Treasure Hunt (Bryant, 1984), shown in Activity 4.21, is used with an English textbook. A fourth-grade social studies teacher devised Activity 4.22 for her students to complete to demonstrate their knowledge of the parts of a chapter. Similarly, a middle-school mathematics teacher devised an inventory of students' knowledge of their math book (Activity 4.23).

Readability in Action

Determining the match between the reader and the text is neither simple nor clear-cut. Yochum (1991) found that prior knowledge and text structure both play a part in the difficulty of the reading task. When tenth-grade students were

A C T I V I T Y   4 . 2 2   PARTS OF A CHAPTER

Reading Text Chapter Sheet — Chapter 3

Book title: _Indians of Virginia_

Chapter title: _Virginia Indian Tribes_

Number of pages in chapter: _7 pages_

List major Indian groups of the Eastern Woodland Indians:

1. _Eastern Woodland Indians_

2. _Algonquian Indians_

3. _Iroquoian Indians_

4. _Siouan Indians_

How many maps are in the chapter? _3_
How many pictures are in this chapter? _5_

Developed by Meg McKenzie.

A C T I V I T Y   4 . 2 3   DO YOU KNOW YOUR MATH BOOK?

1. Who are the authors of your book? Who are the publishers?
2. How many chapters are in your book?
3. How many pages are there in the whole book?
4. What is the title of Chapter 15?
5. What is the title of Chapter 10, section 3?
6. On what page will you find the definition of *complex plane*?
7. By using the glossary, check each word that is a mathematical tool:
   calculator   product   remainder   abacus   center

Developed by Dana Walker.

asked to judge their textbooks, they indicated that teacher instruction was more important with some texts than with others (Sosniak & Perlman, 1990). Following are some brief teacher evaluations of text material. These teachers were asked to consider the backgrounds and interests of their students, compute a formula, and analyze text structure. They then drew conclusions about the match between their students and the text.

EXAMPLE 1: HEALTH TEXT FOR SECOND-GRADERS

The class has 21 children, 13 boys and 8 girls. They are mostly middle-class children of average to above-average ability. Three students participate in a gifted pull-out program, and three others attend remedial reading classes. The school is in a suburban area near an urban center.

The Fry formula computed at second-grade level, which is what the text purports to be. I noticed that the material did not seem to get harder with succeeding chapters, which I had expected it to do. I would rather see a text challenge readers than keep them at the same reading level. The concept development is simple, but interesting and child-oriented, with many questions to stimulate thinking skills and discussions. The pictures lend themselves to initiating discussions.

I anticipate few difficulties teaching the lessons because I think the text is user-friendly. Every child in this class can relate to the subject. The layout and illustrations are stimulating. The readability is appropriate. (Lyle Wieber)

EXAMPLE 2: SCIENCE TEXT FOR FOURTH-GRADERS

These children attend an inner-city school. They are from low-income homes, where reading is often not modeled. On recent standardized tests, their scores were lowest in science. The students' attitudes towards content-area reading are somewhat poor, primarily because they view reading as too hard. Their interest can be sparked in just about any area with the right approach. Their reading proficiency ranges from a little above average to virtual nonreaders.

According to the Fry, the readability level is fourth grade. The text is well written, with good visual appeal. Many activities are suggested. The lessons are highly organized. The text seems to be presented well, but students need some background knowledge, which ours don't have. There are so many new concepts and vocabulary that our students may be overwhelmed. The readability is not appropriate until the teacher builds background. (Barbara McCoy, Carolyn Powell, & Carrie Thompkins)

EXAMPLE 3: SOCIAL STUDIES TEXT AT A SIXTH-GRADE LEVEL

My students live in a rural area. They come from a variety of socioeconomic backgrounds, but most are from middle- to upper-class families. They ride a school bus from 15 to possibly 75 minutes. They participate in many activities, but sometimes have to travel a long way to reach the activity. A majority of the students have parents who help with homework, monitor television, attend PTA meetings, communicate with teachers, and the like.

The students range in abilities. Seven participate in gifted classes, two receive extra reading instruction, one is learning disabled. The reading levels range from third to ninth grade, with the majority at high-fifth/low-sixth. I even call some of my students "readaholics."

The Fry came out at seventh-grade level. The passages contained many proper nouns. I found one compound sentence with 22 words. Some of the sections are more difficult than others. The text is arranged in units that focus on one broad topic. Each chapter contains information that supports and gives background information about that broad topic. The use of time lines, maps, pictures of paintings, illustrations, graphs, charts, and other visuals help the student comprehend. I feel very comfortable using this text. (Wanda Hill)

EXAMPLE 4: MATH TEXT FOR 10TH- AND 11TH-GRADERS

My students are in college-preparatory classes at a rural high school. They are mixed culturally and socially. They are not all college-bound. They have average reading abilities.

The Fry measured readability at eighth grade. Even though this seems low, I believe it should be because of the vast amount of new vocabulary and mathematical concepts for these students. The concepts are carefully developed and well spaced. The pattern is chronological and easy for students to understand. The visual appeal is average — more color and picture clarity is desirable. I think pages would be more pleasing to the eye if they were organized in a different manner.

Even though the text seems easy, it won't be for my students. I will have to build background and help a lot with vocabulary. Although concepts are well presented, text discourse is hard to follow. Combined with my students' disinterest, the text is somewhat inappropriate. (Serena Marshall)

The Bottom Line: Who/What Changes?

To teach the content subjects, teachers are generally assigned one textbook of which all students have a copy. The textbook is the same for each student. However, all students are not the same, even though they may be in the same classroom. The match, then, will not be perfect. What should be done? Some educators advocate that, when a mismatch occurs, teachers should change the textbook. Others advocate changing the readers. Another possibility is for teachers to make changes in instruction.

Change the Text?

First, we have to decide if text-based factors are likely to interfere with student learning. If so, changing the text might be a good idea. Readers deserve good writing. Advocates of changing the text argue that students learn more when they read from a variety of interesting, moderately challenging resources. However, all readers will inevitably encounter text that is poorly written or very difficult for them. If they have not been guided to expect such variations and challenges in text, they will be in a weak position to overcome the hurdle. Many students will give up. Pragmatically, teachers are often not in a position where they can readily change textbooks. They may have to clear such changes with their administration. Other resources may be limited. There may be limited funds to buy other texts.

While changing the textbook is sometimes a viable solution, teachers must first determine if and why the text is unsuitable. Many times, once the reason is known, a solution other than the radical one of changing the text becomes clear. The teacher can prepare instruction that compensates for text-based problems.

Change the Reader?

Next, we have to decide if reader-based factors might interfere. By taking time to determine reader background, teachers will know if readers will have problems with the text. The obvious solution in this case is to "change the reader" by helping students build the requisite background. When we help readers change, we give them reading skills that last far beyond one encounter with text; we create lifelong proficient readers.

Change the Teacher?

Teachers need to select appropriate activities to build the best match possible. This may mean helping teachers to change the way they have instructed in the past. Such change is hard work. The effort, however, is well worth the benefits: more interested students, easier lessons to teach, more enjoyment, and grades that better reflect true student learning.

One-Minute Summary

In this chapter, we have argued for the importance of building reader background before assigning reading materials. We have presented research and practical examples that illustrate why preparation is important. We have described several activities, and we have included versions developed by teachers. We have related these activities to two reader-based situations that can cause readability problems. We have considered some examples of how real teachers match text and readers. We have suggested that changes in text, reader, and teacher may be solutions to consider when making the best match.

We have also demonstrated how preparation activities can promote reading, writing, speaking, and listening and can span all steps of PAR. We have tried to emphasize that the *way* a teacher uses an activity is more important than rigorous adherence to prescribed steps. Finally, we have included variations of activities that demonstrate the creativity of the teachers who constructed them.

End-of-Chapter Activities

Assisting Comprehension

Table 4.1 provides an overview of the activities that have been presented in this chapter. We have rated each activity. Do you agree with us? Fill in your own ratings in the column provided.

TABLE 4.1

Chapter 4 Activities Compared and Rated

ACTIVITY	PROBLEM/ SOLUTION	MATCH DERIVED BY	MATERIALS NEEDED	AUTHORS' RATING*	YOUR RATING?
Cloze	Reader-based: background	Student inserts deleted words in consistent pattern	text, teacher, student	★★★★	
Maze	Reader-based: background	Student selects from 3 choices of consistent deletion pattern	text, teacher, student	★★★★	
Pretest	Reader-based: background	Student selects responses based on prior knowledge	text, teacher, student	★★★★	
Word inventory	Reader-based: background	Student rates own word knowledge	text, teacher, student	★★★★★	
Factstorming/ PreP	Reader-based: background	Student states own prior knowledge	teacher, student	★★★★★	
KWL/What I Know	Reader-based: background	Student writes prior knowledge, states purpose	teacher, student, text	★★★★★	
Anticipation guides	Reader-based: background	Student relates statements to prior knowledge	teacher, student, text	★★★★★	
Analogies	Reader-based: background	Teacher connects student experiences to text material	teacher, student, text	★★★★★	
Standardized test results	Reader-based: skills	Teacher studies student scores for patterns	teacher, student	★★	
Content inventories	Reader-based: skills	Student responses: reading/study skills	teacher, student	★★★	
Textbook inventories	Reader-based: skills	Student responses: parts of book	teacher, student, text	★★★★★	

*Up to five stars, based on value received for time spent.

Reflecting on Your Reading   Select a chapter from a content-area textbook. Using the following questions as a guide, reflect on what your text offers to help you as a teacher build your students' backgrounds for reading the text.

What aids are provided in my text chapter to help the teacher build background? Is there a chapter preview or summary that could be used to build background? Are there any statements, such as those identifying objectives, that could be used in an anticipation guide? Is there a graphic organizer?

Are these aids suitable for my students?

Are these aids sufficient for my students?

As a teacher, should I construct some aids to help me build student background? If so, what will I construct?

PART THREE

ASSISTANCE
AND REFLECTION

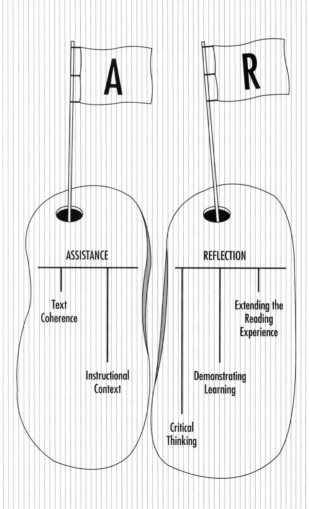

ASSISTANCE

Text
Coherence

Instructional
Context

REFLECTION

Extending the
Reading
Experience

Demonstrating
Learning

Critical
Thinking

CHAPTER 5

Assisting Reading Comprehension

"There are four kinds of readers.

The first is like the hourglass, and their reading being as sand,

it runs in and it runs out, and leaves not a vestige behind.

A second is like the sponge, which imbibes everything,

and returns it in nearly the same state, only a little dirtier.

A third is like a jelly-bag, allowing all that is pure to press away,

and retaining only the refuse and dregs.

And the fourth is like the slaves in the diamond mines of Golcanda, who,

casting aside all that is worthless, retain only pure gems."

Samuel Taylor Coleridge

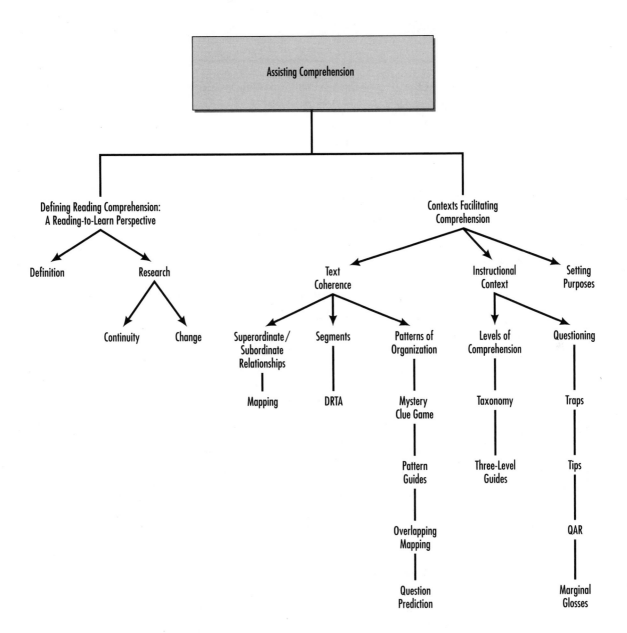

Prepare to Read

1. When you are reading, how do you make sure that you are understanding the material? Do you stop and rephrase? Do you ask yourself questions? Do you take notes?

2. Following is a list of terms used in this chapter. Some of them may be familiar to you in a general context, but in this chapter they may be used in a different way than you are used to. Rate your knowledge by placing a + in front of those you are sure that you know, a √ in front of those you have some knowledge about, and a 0 in front of those you don't know. Be ready to locate and pay special attention to their meanings when they are presented in the chapter.

___ scaffolding
___ product
___ process
___ superordinate
___ subordinate
___ mapping
___ segment
___ chunk
___ DRTA

___ patterns of organization
___ discourse analysis
___ adjunct strategies
___ fact
___ implication
___ application
___ taxonomy
___ metacognition

Objectives

As you read this chapter, focus your attention on the following objectives. You will:

1. be able to define reading comprehension, using both past and present definitions given in the professional literature.

2. understand the difference between process and product as related to reading comprehension.

3. identify three levels of comprehension that will help teachers assist students in comprehension.

4. identify several patterns of organization that are often used in content materials.

5. understand why it is important to set reading purposes and describe several activities that help set purposes.

Reading Comprehension: A Reading-to-Learn Perspective

As a student in an 11th-grade history class, one of the authors had a lesson in what reading comprehension is *not*. The author remembers—painfully—reading each assigned chapter for homework, trying to memorize as much of the content as possible on the first reading because the history teacher always employed the same "instructional strategy." The day after this assigned reading, we

Shoe. Reprinted with permission of Tribune Media Services.

would be told to close our books. The teacher opened his copy and, rocking on his toes, called out the name of a student, then a question from his teacher's manual. He also had the answers, of course. More than once, we didn't have the answers because we could not remember. This lapse on our part caused our embarrassed silence and his consternation, a zero marked in his grading book, and another question. No one in that class liked history that year. Most of us stopped reading the assigned chapters. What was the point?

One parent tells the inspiring story of her daughter who had always received C's and D's in science, but in seventh grade brought home A's all year. Her mother asked her what the secret was. Her daughter explained, "This teacher makes me think, and it's *fun*! I finally understand what science is about."

Reading comprehension is a complex subject, much researched. What is relevant for content teachers to know? We have chosen to concentrate on providing a workable definition and two ways to facilitate comprehension in content subjects.

In Chapters 3 and 4, you discovered ways to *prepare* your students to read in your content area by helping them build a foundation. The reason for preparing them is to enable them to read with greater understanding. The next step in the PAR framework is to *assist* reading by considering the contexts that facilitate comprehension and then providing appropriate activities. To continue the analogy of building a house, as you assist students you are helping them build a house of understanding. Where you see a need to develop comprehension, you will put up **scaffolding**, or ladders, so your students will have help constructing meaning. You will be right there providing assistance until they have their house built.

The concept of scaffolding derives from Vygotsky's (1978a) explanation of how adults help children learn. Adults provide a supportive climate, much like our attention to affect in Chapter 2 and the Preparation step (Chapters 3 and 4); they boost the child beyond the point at which he or she could achieve without assistance (Vygotsky calls this area "the zone of proximal development"); and then adults withdraw to allow the child independence. Principle 9 in Chapter 1 describes this process, using the term *fading*. Strategic scaffolding (Beed,

Hawkins, & Roller, 1991) is the deliberate, conscious teaching of strategies—our Assistance step—which will then enable learners to use these strategies at appropriate times without teacher aid—our Reflection step.

Comprehension is the heart of reading. This analogy works well when one considers the intricate relationship between the human heart and the rest of the body. The heart seems to beat automatically, but unless conditions are favorable, the beating, and life itself, stops. The heart depends on the atria and ventricles for the supply of blood so necessary to life. When arteries become clogged, blood cannot circulate efficiently; the relationship is jeopardized.

Reading may not "beat" automatically either. If readers are not prepared, they may have "clogged" comprehension. The reading heart is more likely to function efficiently when sustained by sensitive teachers, sound instructional practice, well-written texts, a supportive environment, and student interaction with the

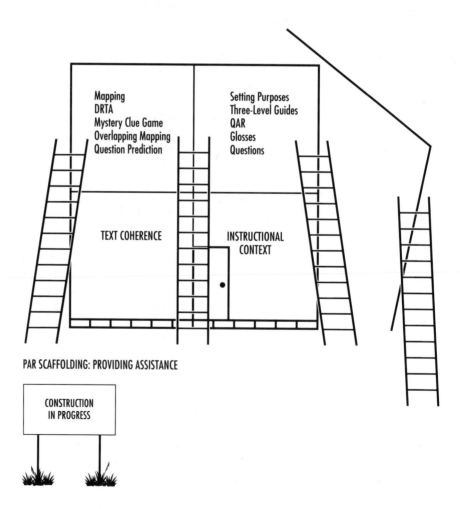

Mapping
DRTA
Mystery Clue Game
Overlapping Mapping
Question Prediction

Setting Purposes
Three-Level Guides
QAR
Glosses
Questions

TEXT COHERENCE

INSTRUCTIONAL CONTEXT

PAR SCAFFOLDING: PROVIDING ASSISTANCE

CONSTRUCTION IN PROGRESS

content. In the 11th-grade history class described earlier, several reading hearts slowed down or stopped beating; in the seventh-grade science class, a reading heart beat to capacity.

Reading Comprehension Defined

William Gray (1941/1984) proposed that comprehension "assumes that the reader not only apprehends the author's meaning but also reflects on the significance of the ideas presented, evaluates them critically, and makes application of them in the solution of problems" (p. 18). Forty-four years later, in *The Reading Report Card* (1985), reading is described as analytic, interactive, constructive, and strategic. This definition implies that apprehension and reflection are requisites of comprehension, as does Gray's definition. A reader must analyze, or think about, the significance of the content; this analysis must be active and interdependent; some positive result will occur that produces a strategy to aid the reader in future reading. The active, integrated thinking that leads to a conclusion as a result of reading *is* comprehension.

Although historically the study of reading comprehension has reflected different schools of thought at different times, the changes in definition over time exhibit more continuity than contrast. Huey (1908/1968) and then Thorndike (1917) defined reading as a thinking process, implying that comprehension is more than recognizing letters and words; it includes thinking about what those symbols mean. Sixty years later, Hillerich (1979) drew the same conclusion when he identified reading comprehension as "nothing more than thinking as applied to reading" (p. 3). A little earlier, Frank Smith (1971), drawing from his study of communication systems, argued for a definition of comprehension as "the reduction of uncertainty" (pp. 17–19). Smith explained that as readers gain information by reading, they rely on what they know to "reduce the number of alternative possibilities" (p. 17). Pearson and Johnson (1978) picture reading comprehension as the building of bridges between the new and the known. The continuity among these definitions, which span 70 years, is apparent.

Process versus Product

Although the definition of comprehension has not changed substantially, the way we study comprehension has changed (Pearson, 1985). New interest in how to teach reading comprehension has been generated by the recognition that comprehension is not a passive, receptive process but an active, constructive, reader-based process. In the past, reading researchers studied measurable results of reading comprehension to help them explain how comprehension occurs. They expected that, after reading, readers would be able to answer questions of varying difficulty, organize information, and explain its implications. The answers, which demonstrate whether the reader has learned the content, are the **products** of comprehension.

The **process** of learning, in contrast, refers to the mental activity that goes on *as* the reader is reading and thinking about the material. While this mental activity is occurring, the reader is seeking assistance in understanding the material. The reader will want to sort facts from implications, identify the organization of the material, and use picture clues and text aids to help with this understanding. The teacher's role is to employ teaching strategies that assist this understanding, including those that integrate listening, speaking, reading, and writing.

The study of comprehension today reflects this emphasis on what occurs as the reader reads to learn. It is process-oriented. By discovering what readers do as they read, we can design strategies for assistance that enhance their learning.

A tape of a child reading a story and reflecting on his reading illustrates this relationship (Goodman & Burke, 1972). The story is about an oxygen failure on a spaceship. A canary is kept on board as a warning device. The child reads aloud but consistently skips the word *oxygen* because, he says, he doesn't know it. At the end of the story, while trying to retell the events to the teacher, he comments that they should have put an oxygen mask on the canary. After this comment, he says with excitement: "Oxygen! That was the word I couldn't get!" This child was thinking as he read, trying to put together the clues. He was assisting his own reading by processing what he thought of as "unknown data." When he reached the stage of retelling the story, he realized that he did know; he had put the clues together. If the teacher had interpreted his failure to pronounce the word while he was reading as a final product, she would have thought he did not know the word. In fact, all along he was still processing the information. Ultimately, this processing led to a correct product. As this experience illustrates, we must give our students every chance to process information, thus discovering meaning as they read, before we measure their understanding.

Most reading professionals today acknowledge that although certain "products" can be expected as a result of reading comprehension, these are not in themselves the act of comprehending. Cooper (1986) explains that "to comprehend the written word, the reader must be able to (1) understand how an author has structured or organized the ideas and information presented in a text, and (2) relate the ideas and information from text to ideas or information stored in his or her mind" (p. 4). Cooper is describing a process that people use while reading. Readers search actively for a pattern of organization and actively relate what they read to what they already know.

It is up to teachers to demonstrate to students *how* to process text so that students can then demonstrate the product—what they have learned. The act leads to the result. The diagram in Figure 5.1 illustrates this distinction between process and product in reading comprehension.

Text Coherence Facilitates Comprehension

In Chapters 3 and 4, we identified three factors that may facilitate or impede reading in content subjects. We showed how the teacher, and ultimately the student, should determine if a problem exists with each, and then how to prepare a reader by building background before reading is assigned. In this chapter, we look at how to help readers during the process of reading. We will focus first on how the text itself can be used to full advantage by the reader.

FIGURE 5.1

Process versus product in reading comprehension.

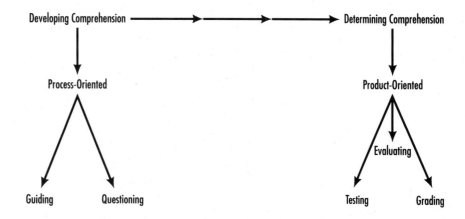

Comprehension is influenced by how a text is organized and by how much teachers help students to understand that organization. Gordon (1990) compared sixth-graders' awareness of text characteristics from the beginning to the end of a school year. She found that one major change was a greater understanding of both narrative and expository text structure. Williams, Taylor, and Ganger (1981) have found that a typical instructional task of "finding the main idea" can be very difficult for students through the middle grade levels, particularly when the text is vague. Brown and Day (1983) found that the ability to construct main idea statements develops later than other summarization skills. Although summarizing is difficult for many poor comprehenders, Hare and Borchardt (1984) trained students to summarize effectively by demonstrating how to use many parts of a text. Finally, Meyer, Brandt, and Bluth (1980) tested children at both the third-grade and ninth-grade levels and found that both groups were deficient in their understanding of superordination and subordination of information.

Superordinate/ Subordinate Relationships

All writing is organized. All writing follows patterns. Good writing will contain a major (**superordinate**) pattern and supporting (**subordinate**) relationships. As Armbruster (1984) has pointed out, expository text should contain major, superordinate ideas that span whole sections of material. Within those sections, subordinate information should clarify the superordinate. Readers need to keep in mind the major thrust of the material in order to understand the relationship between the supporting and the major ideas. For instance, in this textbook, the superordinate theme is PAR, a strategic framework for before, during, and after reading. Subordinate information is introduced in each chapter to explain aspects of PAR.

Mapping is one activity that can assist readers in understanding this relationship. Mapping (Pearson & Johnson, 1978; Heimlich & Pittleman, 1985) has become a popular activity for helping readers develop comprehension. Just as travelers use a map to help them find their way, readers can use a diagram that shows the route to understanding a passage. Mapping is making a map to show understanding. Mapping is not really a new activity, nor is it only a reading activity. Novak and Gowin (1984) refer to *concept mapping* as a good general learning strategy. Researchers also use the terms *mind mapping, webbing,* and *semantic webbing.*

The primary purpose of mapping is to demonstrate the relationship of major and supporting ideas visually by having the readers react and create responses. Because maps encourage students to use prior knowledge and interactive learning, reading educators recognize their value in assisting reader comprehension. Mapping can be used to teach vocabulary, to introduce outlining and note taking, and as a study aid. If mapping is used to introduce a topic before any reading has taken place, it is an excellent activity for preparing the reader. It can also be used to aid reading reflection, especially when it becomes a study aid. (Several of these uses for mapping are discussed in other chapters.)

The following are suggestions for developing a map (based on Santeusanio, 1983):

1. Identify the main idea of the content passage. (Sometimes just the topic or a question may stimulate map generation.) Write it anywhere on the page, leaving room for other information to be written around it.
2. Circle the main idea.
3. Identify secondary categories, which may be chapter subheadings.
4. Connect the secondary categories to the main idea.
5. Find supporting details.
6. Connect supporting details to the idea or category they support.
7. Connect all notes to other notes in a way that makes sense.
8. Mapping a whole chapter may be too time-consuming. Mapping is recommended for portions of a chapter that a teacher identifies as very important, to help a reader understand the superordinate/subordinate relationships.

Maps force students to pay attention as they read, reread, and study; they demonstrate the hierarchical pattern of comprehension. Muth (1987) reports that mapping, because it is a hierarchical strategy, has been found to be a highly successful aid to understanding expository text. Since a map is a diagram of information, it is a visual learning aid. Often, especially for younger readers, drawings added to the map will stimulate learning. Such visual reinforcement capitalizes on visual literacy and right-brain functions. The social studies teacher described in Chapter 1 used mapping extensively in his unit on capital punishment. Activity 5.1 shows how a high school English teacher mapped Act II of *Macbeth.* Activity 5.2 shows how a middle-grades vocational teacher mapped the parts of the Apple IIe computer. Once the teacher has mapped several times with students, students will become proficient at making their own maps.

The integration of all of the communicative arts is apparent when mapping is used. Class discussion must take place for the map to be developed. This requires students to listen to each other and speak on the topic. Reading is the source of the information mapped, and writing can be incorporated if the teacher asks students to use the map as a frame of reference for writing about the topic. For

A C T I V I T Y   5 . 1   **MACBETH, ACT II**

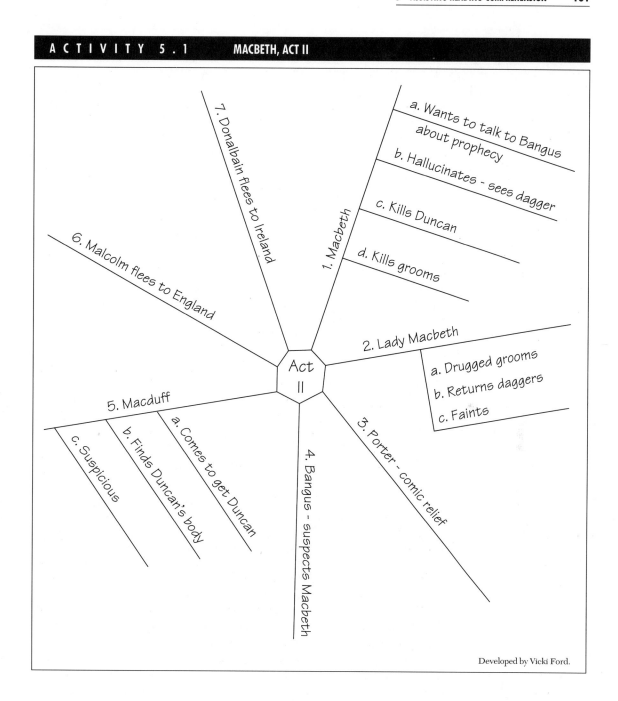

7. Donalbain flees to Ireland

6. Malcolm flees to England

1. Macbeth
a. Wants to talk to Bangus about prophecy
b. Hallucinates - sees dagger
c. Kills Duncan
d. Kills grooms

Act II

2. Lady Macbeth
a. Drugged grooms
b. Returns daggers
c. Faints

3. Porter - comic relief

4. Bangus - suspects Macbeth

5. Macduff
a. Comes to get Duncan
b. Finds Duncan's body
c. Suspicious

Developed by Vicki Ford.

A C T I V I T Y   5 . 2   **MAP OF COMPUTER PARTS**

Developed by Pamela Lundy.

instance, students could be assigned to write a four-paragraph essay about the four parts of the computer, as generated from the map. The details under a statement provide paragraph support. A science teacher who wants students to write reports about planets could have students map the information on a planet provided in an encyclopedia. Next, students might refer to primary sources to find out more about each portion of the map. Finally, the map could be transformed into the table of contents for the report (see Activity 5.3).

Using Segments of Text

Text is usually organized by division into meaningful **segments**, signified by subheadings. Readers must learn to pay attention to these segments as a way to help them focus on important pieces of the material. When readers attend to one segment, or **chunk** of material, at a time, they are making their reading more manageable by "biting off enough to chew on, but not too much." Casteel

A C T I V I T Y   5 . 3   A MAP BECOMES A TABLE OF CONTENTS

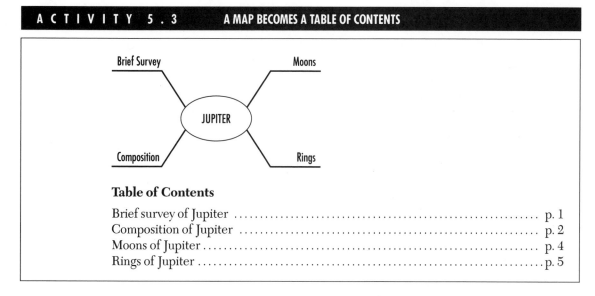

Table of Contents

(1990) found that chunking material helped students in his study, particularly low-ability students, to score higher on tests. Teachers can help students read and understand by encouraging them to turn subheadings into questions or purpose statements, then reading to answer the question or fulfill the purpose.

THE DRTA

The Directed Reading/Thinking Activity (**DRTA**) is one excellent activity that helps students to understand that text is divided into segments, each of which can help them figure out the next. The DRTA, as advocated by Stauffer (1969a), has three basic steps: predicting, reading, proving. Predicting involves asking readers to use what they already know and what they can learn from a quick preview of the material to predict what it will be about. Predicting prepares the reader for comprehension. It is an extremely important step in the DRTA, but it cannot stand alone. Because students are encouraged to predict aloud, and to justify their predictions, this activity offers a lively listening and speaking opportunity. Although an overall prediction may be made, teachers encourage readers to make predictions about specific portions of text, then read the appropriate portion to confirm or alter the predictions. Students reflect aloud on those predictions before going on to read another segment. The teacher guides the DRTA process, making sure that each student is actively involved in understanding each segment before continuing to the next. The DRTA is so versatile that it is difficult to categorize it under any one PAR step. The following examples of DRTAs illustrate their many uses.

Figures 5.2 and 5.3 outline the DRTA steps that might be applied to fiction and nonfiction material, respectively. Note that step 2 in the fiction DRTA requests that readers read to find out if the predictions they made were accurate.

FIGURE 5.2

DRTA, fiction.

1. **Previewing**
   Preread: Title
       Pictures
       Subtitles
       Introduction (if story is long enough)
   Close book and make hypotheses: What do you think will happen?
       Why do you think that? (What gives you the clue?)

2. **Verifying**
   Read: To find whether or not predictions were right

3. **Reflecting on Reading**
   Developing comprehension by:
       Checking on individual and group hypotheses
       Staying with or redefining hypotheses

FIGURE 5.3

DRTA, nonfiction.

1. **Previewing**
   Study: Title
       Introduction
       Subtitles
       Pictures
       Charts
       Maps
       Graphs
       Summary or conclusion
       End-of-chapter questions

2. **Decision Making**
   What is known after previewing?
   What do we need to learn?

3. **Writing**
   Writing specific questions students need to learn

4. **Reading**
   Finding the answers to students' written questions

Step 4 in the nonfiction DRTA requests that readers read to find the answers to questions they have generated. These steps focus on purposeful reading; they are the foundation for a successful DRTA. A teacher must decide in advance how to segment the material for a DRTA. The organization of the material will be the key factor in this segmentation.

The predicting steps of the DRTA build purpose for reading. When readers are asked what they think might happen next and then read to verify their prediction, they are being encouraged to read purposefully. Readers become very excited about this predictive involvement in their own reading. Often they share their predictions orally before the individual reading occurs. This activity incorporates listening and speaking. If students are asked to write down what

ACTIVITY 5.4   DRTA TRANSCRIPT: SEVENTH-GRADE SOCIAL STUDIES

Material Used: "A Coward"
Objective: Students will describe the role of persons or groups in India's society.

Teacher: We have been learning about the caste system in India and how parents arrange their children's marriages. Today we are going to read another story about the caste system and marriages in India. What is the title of this story?
Student: "A Coward."
Teacher: What do you think that has to do with marriage?
Student: He must be afraid to get married.
Teacher: *Read the first paragraph and see if you get any clues.*
Teacher: Was he afraid to get married?
Student: No, SHE's the coward!
Teacher: What do you think will happen?
Student: Maybe he will talk to her parents. He's in a higher caste, so they should like that. He doesn't care about his parents, so he will marry her anyway.
Teacher: *Read the next part and see if he does talk to her parents.*
Teacher: Did he ask her parents?
Student: No, she asked them. So she's gotten braver, but she got into more trouble.
Teacher: How?
Student: They made her quit college.
Teacher: Do you think Reshav will still talk to her parents?
Student: He might. When she doesn't come back to college, he might come to see what is wrong.
Teacher: Do you think Prema's parents will let her marry Reshav if they meet him?
Student: Probably not. They don't want to be disgraced.
Teacher: What do you think will happen next?
Student: I think that Reshav will come to talk to the parents. If they say no, they could run away to another town. If he can talk Prema into leaving her parents.
Teacher: *Read the next section to see if that happens.*
Teacher: Did Reshav come to talk to Prema's parents?
Student: No, her father is going to talk to Reshav. He's afraid that she might kill herself. She's weird!
Teacher: How do you think the meeting with Reshav will go?

(continued on page 166)

they predict during various portions of the reading and then review those written predictions at the end of the DRTA, writing has been used as a way to set purpose within the DRTA. The outline in Figure 5.3 illustrates these relationships.

The dialogue in Activity 5.4, transcribed from a seventh-grade social studies teacher's DRTA lesson on the caste system in India, shows how well PAR is incorporated in a DRTA. The purpose-setting statements, which are based on segments of the material to be read, are italicized.

A C T I V I T Y 5 . 4 **CONTINUED**

Student: They will probably start to like him. He goes to college, so he must be smart. They will probably let him marry her because her father doesn't want her to kill herself.
Teacher: *Read the next section and see what happens.*
Teacher: Did Reshav meet her parents?
Student: No, the two fathers met and Reshav's father got really mad.
Teacher: What about Reshav?
Student: He wants to marry Prema in secret, but he's afraid of his father. Maybe he's going to wait until his father dies, and then marry her.
Teacher: *Finish the story and see if they do get married.*
Teacher: What happened?
Student: Gosh! *He* was the coward! He's going to feel rotten when he finds out what she did. He might even kill himself. Then the parents would really feel bad.

Developed by Faye Freeman.

The next example (Activity 5.5), this one for a middle-grade English class, shows how a teacher used a DRTA to provide for purposeful reading of poetry. Notice how the teacher has divided the reading of the poem by stanzas.

The value of DRTAs is reflected in the many ways they can be used. DRTA lessons help teachers to model the reading process at its best. What good readers do as they read is predict and speculate, read to confirm, stop and carry on a mental discussion of what they understand. Material is divided into manageable units. DRTAs provide a vehicle for figuring out the content as the reading occurs; they emphasize reading as a process rather than a measurement of comprehension. DRTAs also build readers' self-concepts. When readers see that what they predict helps them to understand better, and that everyone's speculations are important whether or not they are proven to be what the author concluded, they feel more confident about their reading. At the elementary level, teachers can encourage readers to become "reading detectives." By playing a game of detection, they are motivated to read, and they are in charge of their own reading. We cannot stress enough the pervasive benefits of using DRTAs to teach content subjects.

THE GUIDED READING PROCEDURE

The guided reading procedure (Manzo, 1975) is an excellent activity for teaching students to gather and organize information around main ideas in the reading. According to researchers Colwell, Mangano, Childs, and Case (1986), this technique is very effective as a way for teachers to direct a lesson. The technique uses brainstorming to collect information as accurately as possible and rereading to correct misinformation and fill in conceptual gaps. This method can be used

A C T I V I T Y   5 . 5   **DRTA TRANSCRIPT: MIDDLE-GRADES ENGLISH**

Goal: The goal of this activity will be to direct students' reading with a purpose and also develop their comprehension. I will teach "Acquainted with the Night" using the DRTA.
Activity: DRTA (directed reading to develop comprehension)

Teacher: Look at the poem by Robert Frost. What do you think the title means? Look first at the word "acquainted." What does that word mean?
Student: To know.
Student: To be familiar with.
Teacher: Those are good answers. Now what do you think the title means?
Student: To know the night?
Teacher: Good. How many times is that word used in the poem?
Student: Three.
Teacher: Why do you think it is used so many times?
Student: It's important to the meaning.
Student: He wants the reader to know why he knows the night.
Teacher: How many of you think you know or understand the night? (A few students raise hands.)
Teacher: What do you know about the night?
Student: It's dark.
Student: Stars come out, and the moon shines.
Student: That's when we sleep.
Student: Crime occurs then.
Teacher: *To find out what Robert Frost knew about the night, read the first stanza. Remember that a stanza in a poem is like a paragraph.* [Students read.]
Teacher: How is the poet "acquainted" with the night?
Student: He is walking at night.
Teacher: What is the weather?
Student: It's raining sometimes.
Teacher: How far does he walk?
Student: He walks past the "furthest city light."
Teacher: Why do you think he walks so far?
Students: Exercise . . . Feels like it . . . Wants to think . . . Enjoys it . . .
Teacher: *Read the next stanza and see if you have correctly predicted why he walks.* [Students read.]
Teacher: Why do you think he walks?
Student: He's depressed, sad. He probably wants to be alone.
Teacher: Which line says that? Read it please.
Student: "I have looked down the saddest city lane."
Teacher: You read that well. Whom does he see while he walks?
Student: A watchman.
Teacher: Why do you think he "drops his eyes, unwilling to explain"?
Student: Watchman wonders why he's there—it's his job—but the walker looks away because he doesn't want to or know how to explain.

(continued on page 168)

A C T I V I T Y   5 . 5   CONTINUED

Teacher: Do you ever look away when you don't want to answer?

Students: Yes. When the teacher is asking for answers . . . When my parents want to know where I've been . . . When my friend wants to know something I don't want to tell her . . .

Teacher: *In the next stanza you are going to read what he hears. Read the next stanza and continue reading until you get through the first line of the next stanza.* [Students read.]

Teacher: What does he hear?

Student: A cry.

Teacher: What does he do?

Student: He stops.

Teacher: Was the crying for him?

Student: No.

Teacher: Read to us the line that says that, please.

Student: "But not to call me back or say good-bye."

Teacher: If you are walking and you hear cries, would you stop to see what was wrong?

Students: Yes . . . Maybe . . . Depends on the situation.

Teacher: How would you feel when you found out that the cries were not for you?

Students: Sad . . . Relieved . . . Lonely . . . Happy . . . Empty . . .

Teacher: These are probably the feelings that the poet felt too. In the next four lines you will read some unusual words. What do you think "unearthly" means?

Student: Doesn't belong to earth.

Teacher: Luminary?

Student: Bright light.

Teacher: Proclaimed?

(continued on page 169)

to aid students in becoming more independent in their thinking and studying. These are the steps teachers follow in using the guided reading procedure:

1. Prepare students for the lesson by clarifying key concepts about the reading; assess students' background knowledge. The teacher may ask students to clarify vocabulary terms or make predictions concerning concepts inherent to the reading.

2. Assign a reading selection of appropriate length and ask students to remember all they can about the reading. Manzo gives these general guidelines for passage length: primary students—90 words, 3 minutes; intermediate students—500 words, 5 minutes; junior-high-school students—900 words, 7 minutes; high-school students—2,000 words, 10 minutes.

3. After the students have completed the assignment, have them close the book and relate everything they know about the material just read. List statements on the board without editing. As a variation, assign two students to act as class recorders. This enables the teacher to do a better job of monitoring and guiding the class discussion.

A C T I V I T Y   5 . 5   **CONTINUED**

Student: Designated, told, pointed out.

Teacher: *Read the rest of the poem. What does the walker decide?* [Students read.]

Teacher: What is the luminary clock?

Student: The moon.

Teacher: What do you think Frost meant by "neither wrong nor right"?

Students: He probably meant no decision was made . . . decided not to commit suicide . . . decided to stop walking . . . the time was sort of in between something. [Discuss all reasoning.]

Teacher: Why are the first and last lines the same?

Students: I don't know . . . Maybe the poet wanted it that way . . . Maybe he wanted to show us that the walks continue . . . Maybe his troubles go on and on . . .

Teacher: Why do the sentences get longer?

Student: The walks get longer.

Teacher: You have done really well interpreting the meaning of this poem. It wasn't too hard, was it? Now I am going to read this poem to you. Note the fact that I do not pause at the end of every line, only at the places where there are punctuation marks. When you read poetry out loud, always read to punctuation marks, so it won't sound sing-songy and will make better sense. [Reads poem.] How many of you think you understand what Frost was saying in this poem? [Hands go up.] Who will volunteer to tell us the meaning of this poem?

Student: Frost knows the night because that is the time he walks and figures out his problems. He walks alone and talks to no one, and he stops when he comes to some conclusion.

Teacher: You expressed that well. To appreciate and understand poetry, you need to read each poem to yourself first and then perhaps again out loud. Few poems can be completely understood after the first reading.

Developed by Frances Lively.

4. Direct students to look for inconsistencies and misinformation, first through discussion and then through rereading the material.

5. Add new information, and help students organize and categorize concepts into a loose outline form. As a variation, students can put information into two, three, or four categories and title each category.

6. Have students reread the selection to determine whether the information they listed was accurate.

7. To strengthen short-term recall, test students on the reading.

Patterns of Organization

At any level, readers need to understand the superordinate and subordinate relationships within the text, identify chunks of text, and identify the significant patterns of organization in the material. This ability takes practice and requires the teacher's assistance.

Although as many as 17 **patterns of organization** have been identified in good writing, some basic patterns predominate in the kind of writing found in textbooks. The study and identification of patterns of organization in written material is called **discourse analysis**. When readers learn to search for the organizational patterns and the relationship between superordinate and subordinate information, they have taken the first steps toward independence in reading.

We have combined lists identifying several basic patterns (Kolzow & Lehmann, 1982; Vacca & Vacca, 1989) to target seven patterns that are often recognizable in content textbooks: simple listing, sequential listing, analysis, cause and effect, compare and contrast, definition, and example. We will briefly describe and illustrate each of these in turn.

Simple Listing A simple listing involves the enumeration of facts or events, in no special order. The superordinate information is the topic or event; the facts or traits that follow are the subordinate or supporting information. Some words that suggest this pattern are *also, another, several*.

Example: "We presented several principles in Chapter 1. For the most part, each can be considered independently of the others. The first one stresses the relationship of the communicative arts to content reading instruction. Another states that reading should be a pleasurable experience."

Sequential Listing In sequential listing, the chronological order of presentation is important. The superordinate information is the topic or event; the facts or traits then presented in order are the subordinate information. Henk and Helfeldt (1987) explain that even capable readers need assistance in applying the sequence patterns used in directions. Some words that suggest this pattern are *first, second, next, before, during, then, finally*.

Example: "Gray's may be the simplest and friendliest of the taxonomies. He said that one must first read the lines and then read between the lines; then one can read beyond the lines."

Analysis Analysis takes an important idea (superordinate information) and investigates the relationships of the parts of that idea (subordinate information) to the whole. Some words and phrases that suggest this pattern are *consider, analyze, investigate, the first part suggests, this element means*.

Example: "Consider how the child concluded that the word he had been unable to pronounce was oxygen. The first portion of his behavior, when he skipped the word, indicated that he did not know the word at all. Yet he was able to recognize it when he had a context for it during the recall stage. This means that he was processing information all along."

Cause and Effect The pattern of cause and effect takes an event or effect (the superordinate information) and presents discourse in terms of the causes (subordinate information) of that event. The effect is thus shown to be a result of causes. Some words and phrases that suggest this pattern are *because, hence, therefore, as a result, this led to*.

Example: "When teachers prepare students to read content material, they help students understand better. Teachers will see, as a result of such preparation, that students are more interested, pay more attention, and comprehend better."

Compare and Contrast Sometimes a writer seeks to highlight similarities and differences between facts, events, or authors. The basic comparison or contrast is the superordinate information, and the specific similarities and differences are the subordinate information. Some words and phrases that suggest this pattern are *in contrast, in the same way, on the other hand, either . . . or, similarly.*
    Example: "A checklist offers less mathematical precision; on the other hand, it provides more qualitative information."

Definition A definition provides an explanation of a concept or topic (superordinate information) by using synonyms to describe it (subordinate information). Some words and phrases that suggest this pattern are *described as, synonymous with, is, equals.*
    Example: "Reading can be described as analytic, interactive, constructive, and strategic. The active, integrated thinking that leads to a conclusion as a result of reading is comprehension."

Example Sometimes a writer uses an example — a specific instance or a similar situation (subordinate information) — to explain a topic or concept (superordinate information). Analogies are a type of example. Some words and phrases that suggest this pattern are *for example, for instance, likened to, analogous to, is like.*
    Example: "Reading is like a game of basketball. To play one's best game, lots of preparation and practice are necessary. In reading, this is analogous to preparing by determining and building background for the material to be read."

    Often, a mixture of these patterns will occur even in one section of text. A writer may analyze by using a compare/contrast pattern. Definition is often presented by example. These patterns and pattern combinations are usually easy to discern in well-written material.
    Some patterns seem to be used more often in particular content subjects. Table 5.1 suggests some possible matchings. It is only a guide, however. Teachers will need to consider the grade level they teach and the specific materials they

TABLE 5.1	SCIENCE	MATH	SOCIAL STUDIES	ENGLISH	HEALTH
Some Patterns of Organization Used in Different Content Textbooks	Sequence Cause/effect Definition	Sequence Listing Analysis Definition	Cause/effect Listing Example Analysis	Cause/effect Compare/contrast Example	Compare/contrast Listing Definition

use, because different patterns may dominate at different grade levels and in different subjects.

When patterns of organization are identified, the possibilities for developing comprehension are greatly enhanced. Just by looking in the table of contents of a textbook, for example, the teacher can help students determine patterns of organization. Groups can also study paragraphs to identify particular patterns. Activities to assist readers can then be devised using identified patterns.

Some Activities to Assist Understanding of Text Organization

Once the teacher—and, ultimately, the student who has become a strategic reader—identifies an organizational pattern, reading to learn is much easier. Teachers will find that certain activities assist students in this process and create an interesting learning environment. We present you with some of our favorite activities.

MYSTERY CLUE GAME

The group mystery clue game is designed to help readers understand sequence. It works very well when it is important for students to understand a sequence of events. The idea for this activity came from *Turn-Ons* (Smuin, 1978), but we have adapted it to fit content materials.

1. To construct a mystery clue game, the teacher first studies the sequence of events in the material and writes clear, specific clue cards for each event. More than one card may be made for each clue.
2. The teacher divides the class into small groups and gives each group member at least one clue card. Each group can have one complete set of cards, but each group member is responsible for his or her own cards within that set.
3. No student may show a card to another in the group, but the card can be read aloud or paraphrased so that all group members know what is on each card. In this way, students who are poorer readers will still be encouraged to try to read and to share in the group process.
4. Each group of students must use the clues the teacher gives them to solve the mystery. For example, they must find the murderer, the weapon, the time and place of murder, the motive, and the victim. Or they must find the equation that will solve a problem, or the formula that will make a chemical.
5. A time limit is usually given.
6. A group scribe reports the group's solution to the whole class.
7. Students are instructed to read the material to find out which group came closest to solving the mystery.

This cooperative activity promotes oral language as well as reading and works equally well in several content areas. For instance, science teachers can write clues to performing an experiment, mathematics teachers can write clues to deriving a formula, and social studies teachers can write clues for sequencing historical events. The goal of the activity is for students to approximate the

A C T I V I T Y   5 . 6   MYSTERY CLUE GAME: MITOSIS

The class will be divided into approximately five groups of 4–5 students each. Each person in the class will be given at least one clue card. The task of the group is to try to answer five questions and record the sequence of events they think is correct. The questions are:

1. What is duplicated during mitosis?
2. What is separated during mitosis?
3. What causes this separation?
4. What is the result of mitosis?
5. What is the best sequence for your cards?

Clues are to be communicated *orally* by *paraphrasing* given clues. Students may not show their clue cards to other group members. They will have approximately 10 minutes to discuss clues in their groups before coming back to the entire class to discuss findings.

Following is the list of statements to appear on the clue cards:

1. Nucleolus begins to disintegrate.
2. Nucleolus disappears completely.
3. Chromosomes become completely visible, and nuclear membrane begins to break down.
4. In animals, centrioles begin to separate and migrate toward opposite poles of the cell.
5. Nuclear membrane disappears completely.
6. Chromosomes become more distinct, and appear as double-stranded structures called sister chromatids.
7. Chromatids become attached to the spindle at their centromeres.
8. Chromosomes are moved toward the center of the spindle.
9. Chromosomes lose their distinct forms to become chromatin.
10. Chromatids begin to separate from one another and are moved to opposite poles of the spindle.
11. One set of single-stranded chromosomes is at each end of the cell.
12. In animals, the cell membrane begins to pinch together at the cell center. In plants, a cell plate begins to appear across the cell center.
13. In animals, the cell membrane pinches in completely. In plants, a cell plate forms completely across the cell center.
14. A nuclear membrane forms around each set of chromosomes. In animals, the centrioles replicate.
15. The nucleolus reappears, and spindle fibers disintegrate.
16. Two daughter cells are formed.

Developed by Greg Perry and Sharon Charles. Based on text material in *Biology: Living Systems*, by R. F. Raymond, Merrill Publishing Company, 1989.

sequence of events before reading, and read with the purpose of checking their predictions. It is not necessary for students to memorize specific details. Activity 5.6 shows how high school science teachers used the mystery clue game to provide a purpose for reading about mitosis. Activity 5.7 shows how a middle-grade social studies teacher used the game to provide a purpose for reading about the Sumerians.

A C T I V I T Y   5 . 7   MYSTERY CLUE GAME: THE SUMERIANS

Directions for the Teacher: Divide the class into small groups, giving each student a clue slip. Explain to the students that they must share their clues with their group members without actually showing their clue slip. They are to work with their group to try and solve the mystery questions. Put these mystery questions on the board or overhead projector. Give the students a time limit to come up with their guesses. After that time has been allowed, ask students to share their responses with the entire class. Next they need to read the assignment to see if their predictions were accurate. These clues were developed from the "Background" information section in the teacher's edition and from the section the students will read, Chapter 1, section 4, "A Line of Conquerors." The teacher should number the clues and mix up the numbers when passing out clues to the students.

1. The Sumerians were constantly threatened with warfare.
2. The first conquerors of Sumer were from the city of Akkad.
3. There were no natural boundaries separating the different cities.
4. The Akkadian Empire lasted from 2400 to 2050 B.C.
5. Sargon of Akkad established an empire around 2300 B.C.
6. The southern Akkadians became the Babylonians.
7. The northwestern Akkadians became the Assyrians.
8. Sargon's empire lasted for about 200 years.
9. About 1800 B.C., Hammurabi conquered and reunited Mesopotamia.
10. Hammurabi developed a code of laws.
11. Babylon was a key city in the Babylonian empire.
12. Hammurabi's law code dealt with subjects like human rights.
13. Hammurabi's code included the "eye for an eye" law.
14. The Assyrian Empire arose after the collapse of Hammurabi's empire.
15. Assyrians lived in the shadow of the Babylonians and of other warlike people to the north of them.

(continued on page 175)

PATTERN GUIDES

Pattern guides (Herber, 1978; Vacca & Vacca, 1989) will be most useful in helping students recognize a predominant pattern, such as cause and effect or compare and contrast, in the text material. To construct them, the teacher locates the pattern, decides on the major ideas to be stressed, and designs the pattern-oriented level. Many workbook exercises are based on a pattern guide.

Pattern guides can help students see causal relationships. Students need to learn to distinguish cause and effect when reading text materials, especially in social studies and science. Simply asking students to search for causes is often not successful; students tend to neglect — or worse, misunderstand and misuse — this pattern without the teacher's intervention, support, and patience. Moreover, finding causal relationships is difficult because the cause of an event or situation may not be known or may not be traceable. Even so, students should endeavor to distinguish cause and effect for the practice in thinking it affords. Such prac-

16. These warriors used chariots — carts drawn by horses.
17. The Assyrians also learned to use chariots and horses.
18. The Assyrians organized armies using chariots, cavalry, and bowmen.
19. The Assyrians used battering rams — heavy beams for breaking down city walls.
20. In 701 B.C., the Assyrian king Sennacherib stormed Palestine, a part of the Fertile Crescent.
21. Sennacherib, the Assyrian king, captured 46 cities.
22. Sennacherib, the Assyrian king, destroyed Babylon in 689 B.C.
23. After destroying Babylon, Sennacherib had canals dug and flooded the city to try and turn it into a meadow.
24. In time the mighty empire of the Assyrians was also overthrown.
25. Free of the Assyrians, Babylon again became the center of Mesopotamian culture.
26. In about 539 B.C., Babylon was conquered by the Persians.
27. The Persians did not adopt the culture of Sumer as had the other conquerors.
28. The Persians developed a system of writing based on their own language.
29. The Mesopotamians invented the wheel and the plow.
30. The Mesopotamians farmed the land and built cities.
31. The Mesopotamians developed mathematics.
32. The Mesopotamians developed laws and recorded them.

Questions for the game:
1. Who were the conquerors?
2. Where did they come from?
3. Why did they do it?
4. What did they accomplish?
5. How did they do it?

Developed by Debra Sims Fleisher. Based on text material in *The World Past and Present*, by Stephen Warshaw, Harcourt Brace Jovanovich, 1965.

tice can be achieved through cause/effect story maps, which depict the interrelationships in a series of unfolding events. Ollmann (1989) describes how she demonstrates cause and effect in the "real world" of her students by taking events in their daily lives, then applying the same process to story maps. Activity 5.8 provides an example of a story map for the elementary level. Cause-and-effect study guides for older students are shown in Activities 5.9 and 5.10.

Pattern guides can also be used to demonstrate the compare/contrast pattern. The example in Activity 5.11 is a compare/contrast pattern guide constructed by an intermediate social studies teacher.

OVERLAPPING MAPPING

Mapping can be a useful aid for comparing and contrasting concepts. We call this "overlapping mapping" because first one map is created, then another. The two maps are overlapped, preferably on overhead transparencies, to demonstrate similarities and differences.

A C T I V I T Y   5 . 8   **CAUSE/EFFECT STORY MAP**

List of events:

1. MaLien is a poor peasant boy who lives in a small village in China.
2. MaLien loves to draw.
3. MaLien is given a magic brush by a wizard.
4. MaLien helps the people of his village.
5. The mandarin sees the power of the brush.
6. The mandarin has MaLien put in prison.
7. MaLien escapes with the help of his brush.
8. MaLien helps more people.
9. The mandarin captures MaLien again.
10. The mandarin forces MaLien to use the magic of his brush for selfish reasons.
11. MaLien tricks the mandarin.

These events are depicted by the following story map:

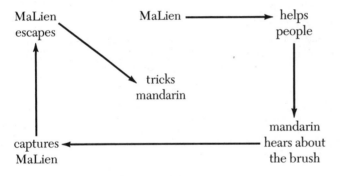

Based on *MaLien and the Magic Brush* by Alvin R. Tresselt.

One of the authors created an overlapping map to assist college freshmen in their understanding of the metaphor in the essay "Pedestrian Students and High-Flying Squirrels." In this essay, Liane Elbison Norman laments the fact that her journalism students are not risk takers, that they are too careful in their actions. She wishes that they were more like squirrels, who take leaps like acrobats. The author followed Pearson and Johnson's (1978) suggestion that vocabulary maps should show the relationship between examples of the word used in the material, properties of the word, and concepts associated with the word. The author drew two maps, in different colors, to show those relationships between the words *squirrels* and *students*. At the bottom of the maps, the author wrote Norman's analogies of students as pedestrians and squirrels as acrobats. The properties or descriptions Norman used were listed to the right of the circled words. The

A C T I V I T Y   5 . 9   CAUSE/EFFECT GUIDE

Below is a list of *effects* of the natural laws discovered by Kepler and Newton. Each was *caused* by one of those laws. Match the causes in the second column to the effects listed in the first column and be prepared to explain your choices.

Effects

_____ 1. Mercury, which is the planet closest to the sun, completes one orbit faster (68 days) than the Earth does (365.24 days).

_____ 2. A car moving 50 mph hits a car stopped on the highway. People not wearing seat belts are thrown forward into the windshield.

_____ 3. A person shoots a shotgun and is knocked backward as the gun fires.

_____ 4. The Earth is closer to the sun during part of its orbit around the sun than at other times.

_____ 5. Halley's comet traveled at a much faster speed as it neared perihelion than when it approached aphelion.

_____ 6. A baseball pitcher throws the ball, the hitter hits it with the bat, and the ball sails over the center-field fence for a home run!

Causes

A. Kepler's first law (all planets travel in elliptical orbits).

B. Kepler's second law (the law of areas).

C. Kepler's third law (the size of the ellipse is related to its period).

D. Newton's first law (law of inertia).

E. Newton's second law (force affects momentum).

F. Newton's third law (action-reaction).

concepts that Norman implied—students are passive, squirrels are active—were written at the top of the maps. When the maps, in two different colors, were overlaid, the comparison became clear to the students.

The mapping of "Pedestrian Students and High-Flying Squirrels" is shown in Activity 5.12. A second example, Activity 5.13, demonstrates how mapped comparisons can be used to teach vocabulary in foreign languages—in this case, Latin.

QUESTION PREDICTION

Using organizational patterns to practice independent questioning strategies is the intent of a procedure known as question prediction. Finley and Seaton (1987) propose the following seven-step procedure to assist reading comprehension:

ACTIVITY 5.10   CAUSE/EFFECT GUIDE

Reading: *The Diary of Anne Frank*, a play by Frances Goodrich and Albert Hackett.
Directions: Match the cause in the first column with the effect or result in the second column.

Causes

_____ 1. Otto Frank is the only survivor of the secret annex.

_____ 2. Miep helps the people in the annex by bringing them food and news from the outside world.

_____ 3. Anne uses her imagination to take a walk in the park.

_____ 4. Mr. Van Daan is caught stealing food.

_____ 5. Anne uses her creativity to make presents for Hanukkah.

_____ 6. Mrs. Van Daan refuses to give up her fur coat.

_____ 7. Peter and Anne grow fond of each other.

_____ 8. Anne is growing up.

_____ 9. Anne is closer to her father than her mother.

_____ 10. The night of Hanukkah, the members of the secret annex hear a thief in the warehouse.

Effects

A. Anne achieves a certain freedom while she is in hiding.

B. The inhabitants experience a moment of escape from the reality of war.

C. The members of the annex were able to survive there for over two years.

D. The members of the annex regard Mrs. Van Daan as materialistic.

E. Otto Frank has Anne's diary published.

F. Tension is created between Mrs. Frank and the Van Daans.

G. Anne is continually discovering things about herself.

H. The mothers become worried that their children are becoming too close.

I. The suspense in the play is increased by a new worry that the Green Police will discover their hiding place.

J. Mrs. Frank is hurt when Anne asks for her father after her nightmare.

Developed by Linda Love.

1. The teacher presents and explains common patterns of organization.
2. The teacher lists common groups (unlabeled) of key words that signal the patterns, such as *first . . . second . . . next* to signal sequence. Then the teacher asks students to scan some paragraphs to find such signal words.
3. The teacher gives students selected topic sentences and asks students to identify the probable pattern from the clue words in the topic sentences.
4. The teacher prepares cloze paragraphs from the content area. The content-specific information is what should be deleted; topic and key pattern words should not be deleted. Students are asked to underline the key words and predict the pattern.

A C T I V I T Y   5 . 1 1   PATTERN GUIDE: COMMUNITIES EVERYWHERE HAVE NEEDS

Thesis: Communities everywhere have needs. Some communities are alike and some are different.

Directions:

1. Read each sentence.
2. Decide if the sentence tells how communities are alike or how they are different.
3. Place an *A* beside the sentence if it shows how communities are *alike*.
4. Place a *D* beside the sentence if it shows how communities are *different*.

When everyone is finished, we will discuss our answers.

_____ 1. Communities everywhere have a need to communicate.
_____ 2. The people of China speak many different dialects.
_____ 3. The people of Africa speak many different dialects. One language spoken is Swahili.
_____ 4. People everywhere live and work together.
_____ 5. People everywhere need food and shelter.
_____ 6. The people of China use chopsticks when eating.
_____ 7. The people of Quebec speak French.
_____ 8. The people in Canada enjoy going to concerts, just like the people in America.
_____ 9. The people of Africa enjoy listening to and watching a storyteller.
_____ 10. The people in Dakar enjoy watching television.
_____ 11. An abacus is used for counting in China.
_____ 12. People everywhere need transportation.
_____ 13. People everywhere need to communicate in writing.
_____ 14. The Chinese language has characters instead of letters.
_____ 15. Rice is an important grain in China.

Developed by Vicki Douglas.

5. The teacher asks students to read several text paragraphs and state the main idea of each paragraph. Then the teacher has students combine the paragraphs' main ideas into an overall main idea.
6. The teacher asks students to translate the main idea statement into a possible question the teacher might ask, particularly on a test.
7. The teacher cautions that students will find several patterns within a text reading, but when students can find the main idea and make questions of it, they will become good pattern detectors.

Instructional Context Facilitates Comprehension

Teachers want their students to learn the content they are teaching. Their instruction should provide the context for this learning. Knowing the organization of the text will help, but comprehension, which is a reader-based factor, will be crucial as well. Teachers will be concerned that their students are able to use

A C T I V I T Y   5 . 1 2   **MAPPING METAPHORS: PEDESTRIAN STUDENTS AND HIGH-FLYING SQUIRRELS**

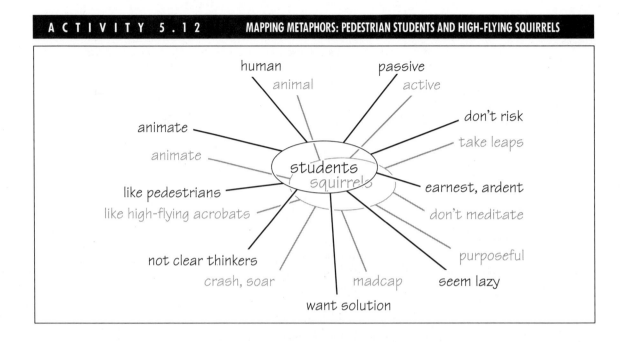

A C T I V I T Y   5 . 1 3   **MAPPING VOCABULARY: LATIN**

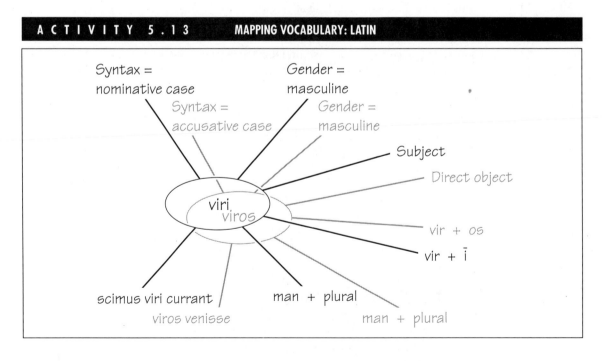

factual information to make inferences and apply what they have learned. What students do as they read is crucial to their comprehension.

Adjunct strategies are used at the Assistance step; they are strategic scaffolding. Such adjunct strategies are used more often than pre- or postreading strategies (Rakes & Chance, 1990). Of the students polled by Rakes and Chance, 78% (of 182) at the secondary level and 59% (of 156) in the elementary grades said that teachers had taught them such strategies.

What do teachers provide in the instructional context? In a recent study of two American history classes, Sturtevant (1992) found that teachers stressed textbook reading and factual information. Another recent study (Hargis, Terhaar-Yonkers, Williams, & Reed, 1988) emphasizes the importance of repetition and practice for reading mastery, especially in the case of learning-disabled and mildly handicapped students.

Reviewing several studies, Garner (1985a) provides evidence that specific instructional assistance can guide students from a stage of strategic deficiency to a stage of strategic efficiency. The sobering news from Garner's review is that teachers too often assume that students automatically comprehend what they read. Comprehension is not that easy. The good news is that with careful and directed instruction, students can acquire effective strategies for reading comprehension. How the teacher presents the content material will make the difference in how well the students learn the material. This section focuses on comprehension activities that foster an optimal instructional context.

Levels of Comprehension

Comprehension occurs at different levels. To simplify, there are three basic levels of comprehension. First, one must understand the **facts**. After one has a basic understanding of the facts, one can begin to see their **implications**. The third level involves the **application** of this understanding to other topics or areas. These three levels—fact, implication, application—are those that classroom content teachers will employ when assisting their students' comprehension. They represent a way to facilitate comprehension, not to simplify or isolate information. Understanding must be connected to be effective. Teachers will want their students to read the material carefully for a literal understanding of the facts, to see the connection between the facts and the entire subject, and to apply what they have learned to other situations.

Consider the following as an example of these three basic levels of comprehension. To understand the significance of the Alamo in this country's history, students would have to comprehend the following: (1) facts—what the Alamo is, where it is located, and what happened there; (2) implication—why the Alamo is considered such an important battle when it involved so few people; (3) application—how phrases such as "Remember the Alamo" might inspire soldiers going to battle.

TAXONOMIES

Mature comprehension demands that readers grasp the facts before they can interpret and apply them. Usually, the literal level must precede the implication level, which must precede the application level. This hierarchical relationship is called a **taxonomy**. Many reading professionals have developed taxonomic views of reading based on these three major levels. Gray's (1960) may be the simplest and friendliest of the taxonomies. He said that one must first read the lines and then read between the lines; then one can read beyond the lines. Herber (1978) described these levels as the literal, interpretive, and applied.

THREE-LEVEL GUIDES

Three-level guides (Herber, 1978) connect and integrate the three levels of comprehension with a series of statements to which students react. Because three-level guides demonstrate the hierarchical relationship of the levels of comprehension and call for student reaction to a series of statements, they provide a comprehensive activity for assisting comprehension. One elementary teacher we have worked with remarked that she would never again teach *Weekly Reader* articles without a three-level guide! Of course, if a teacher used this—or any other—activity that much with the same type of reading material, students would become bored very quickly. But when used occasionally to help readers see the interconnectedness of literal, inferential, and applied learning, the three-level guide is an excellent activity.

Although three-level guides need follow no exact sequence or specific requirements, certain guidelines are helpful in their construction. The following are based on suggestions by Herber (1978) and Vacca and Vacca (1989) and our own trial-and-error experiences:

1. First, determine if the text material requires students to (a) understand a major content concept, (b) identify details that support it, and (c) understand applications of the concept. If so, a three-level guide will be an appropriate activity.

2. Next, determine the content objectives. What specifically do you want the students to know about this material? This specific content should be the major ideas, the implications, or the interpretation that you want students to learn.

3. Take these content ideas and create a series of statements from them. (Some teachers find it easier to write the main ideas as questions, then rephrase them as statements, until they are comfortable with the generation of statements. Other teachers like to insert a mental "The author means . . ." in front of each statement to ensure that the statements match the interpretation level.) An ideal number of statements is about five or six. Edit them for clarity. You have now designed the second level of your guide.

4. By studying these statements and referring to the passage, identify the major facts that support the main ideas contained in your level-two statements. Write these major facts down, either as paraphrases or as exact replications. (Some teachers like to insert a mental "The author says . . ." in front of these statements to ensure that the statements match the literal level.) You should have about two literal statements to support each major inference. These statements are level one of the guide.

5. Now you are ready to design the third level. Statements at this level should apply the major ideas but should also capitalize on students' previous knowledge. These statements often look like those developed for an anticipation guide; the difference is that the statements constructed for a three-level guide are directly connected to the passage content. (Some teachers like to insert a mental "We can use. . ." in front of these statements to ensure that the statements match the applied level.) Probably four or more of these statements will round out the guide.

6. Last, devise your directions and decide if you want to add some distractors, particularly at levels one and two. Both of these tasks will depend very much on your students' ages, abilities, and appreciation of the content. Make sure that directions are complete and clear. If distractors are added, make sure that your students are ready for them.

When introducing three-level guides for the first several times, teachers should use them as a whole class activity. All students should have individual copies or be able to view the guide on a chalkboard or overhead projector. In this way, the new activity is experienced by all students at once. Discussion is promoted in a nonthreatening environment, and students become acclimated to the new activity. Since the value of three-level guides lies in understanding at three levels and in articulating that understanding, oral communication is a very important part of the activity. By discussing reactions with each other, students begin to realize the interdependence of facts, implications, and applications in understanding a topic. The teacher's problem will be to cut off the discussion at an appropriate time. What a wonderful problem to have!

After some experience with guides, students can use them in small groups or independently with homework assignments. Distractors seem to us to be a desirable addition at this point if students are sophisticated enough to be discerning. If distractors are used right away, they can give a hidden message to students that there really are right and wrong responses to these statements. Used later, they can give the message that it is important to be a discriminating reader.

Like anticipation guides, three-level guides offer plentiful writing opportunities. Since the statements require students to connect their former knowledge with new information, particularly at the third level, teachers can ask students to write explanations of why they responded in a certain way to a statement. To encourage reflection, teachers might ask students to write their own statements for each level.

Three-level guides are not necessarily easy to construct. Teachers need to practice making and using them. It might be wise to ask a teacher who is familiar with guides to look at yours before you try it in a class. Once you have tried three-level guides, you'll receive student feedback about your construction efforts. Since the assistance three-level guides provide to readers is immediately discernible, you will probably be as enthusiastic about them as most teachers are.

Because three-level guides are so popular with teachers, we had a difficult time selecting from the many examples developed by teachers we know. The five

ACTIVITY 5.14   A THREE-LEVEL GUIDE FOR MATH

I. Below are eight sentences. Read each one and check the ones that you think say what your author says on pages 1–3. If you have trouble, read the section referred to in parentheses.

_____ Statements made in mathematics have to be true or false. (page 1, paragraph 1)
_____ Statements made in mathematics have to be true. (p. 1, par. 1)
_____ It is possible to make false statements true by using negation. (p. 3)
_____ A value can have more than one expression. (p. 1, par. 2)
_____ A value is defined as a numerical expression. (p. 1, par. 2)
_____ Equations indicate that a numerical expression either equals or does not equal a specified value. (p. 2)
_____ Equations have to contain two expressions of equal value. (p. 2)
_____ Conjunctions and disjunctions are statements using *and, but*, or *or* to link numerical expressions about a value. (p. 2)

II. Place the following number sentences under the correct column. Sentences may be used more than once or not at all! Portions of sentences can be used in some columns.

$4 + 3 \neq 7$ $6 + 1 = 8$
$2 + 2 = 4$ or $2/2 = 4$ Divide 9 by 3.
$4 + 1$ and $3 + 2$ and $5 = 5$ It is not true that $6 + 1 = 8$.

Numerical Expression	Statement	Value	Equation	Conjunction	Disjunction	Negation

III. Consider each assertion below. Check it if you agree with it. Star it if you think it can be supported by information on pages 1–4, and tell why.

_____ Statements are more than assertions.
_____ Values can be expressed in different ways but still be the same values.
_____ Symbols often convey meaning more efficiently than words.
_____ It is important to think carefully about what a statement means.

Developed from information on pages 1–4 of Chapter 1, "Mathematical Statements and Proofs," of *Modern School Mathematics*, Houghton Mifflin, 1971.

we have selected, shown in Activities 5.14–5.18, demonstrate variety in the use of directions and distractors and in considerations of age and content. Note that Activity 5.18 also includes a pattern guide for compare and contrast.

Questioning for Comprehension

The traditional method of developing comprehension is questioning. Durkin (1979) found that teachers use questioning more than any other comprehension technique. When it works, it works very well. Questions can help teachers to know if students are understanding text and can guide readers to consider many aspects of material. Questions are excellent probes.

ACTIVITY 5.15 THREE-LEVEL GUIDE FOR INFORMATION ABOUT STARS

I. Check the items you believe say what the authors said. Sometimes the exact words will be used; other times other words may be used.

_____ **1.** It takes four hydrogen nuclei to convert into one helium nucleus.

_____ **2.** The helium nucleus formed by fusion contains less mass than the four hydrogen nuclei that created it.

_____ **3.** A star that is far away will not appear as bright as a similar star that is closer.

_____ **4.** More massive stars look brighter than other stars at the same distance.

_____ **5.** Fusion takes place faster in stars with more mass than the sun.

_____ **6.** Stars that have less mass than the sun will live longer than the sun.

_____ **7.** The mass of a star determines how long it will live.

_____ **8.** Stars with more mass than the sun will become giants, supergiants, and supernovae.

_____ **9.** A black hole can occur when the mass that remains after a supernova is at least 5 times greater than that of the sun.

_____ **10.** Some astronomers believe small black holes were caused by explosions in space.

II. Put a check on the line beside any of the statements below that you think are reasonable interpretations of the authors' meaning.

_____ **1.** Large amounts of energy can be created when a particular mass becomes smaller through fusion.

_____ **2.** The brightness of a star can be determined by its distance and mass.

_____ **3.** More massive stars live longer than smaller ones.

_____ **4.** Some stars are going to explode.

_____ **5.** There may be several reasons for the existence of black holes in space.

III. Using information you have read or already knew, place a check in the blank beside any statements below with which you and the authors would agree.

_____ **1.** Bigger is not always better.

_____ **2.** Mergers don't always produce more than there was to begin with.

_____ **3.** All living things go through the same life stages and meet the same end.

_____ **4.** It is impossible to be moved by an invisible force.

Developed by Holly Corbett.

Often, however, questioning does not work very well because teachers have fallen into some common "traps." As we pointed out earlier, a major reason that questioning is not successful is that teachers confuse the *product* with the *process* when they question. When a teacher requires students to close their books and recite information before they have had a chance to assimilate that information, that teacher is really testing a product rather than assisting a process.

A second trap is that teachers' questions tend to focus on literal comprehension. This is the conclusion of several reading professionals who have learned a good deal about teachers' questioning habits through classroom observation. For

A C T I V I T Y   5 . 1 6   A GUIDE TO READING "PROFESSIONS FOR WOMEN"

I. Check the items you believe say what the author says. Sometimes the exact words will be used; other times other words may be used. Be able to locate the statement in the essay to support your response.

_____ **1.** Ms. Woolf's profession is literature.

_____ **2.** Other women have paved the way to making her career easier.

_____ **3.** Ms. Woolf sold an article and bought a Persian cat.

_____ **4.** Ms. Woolf had difficulty writing because of the Angel in the House.

_____ **5.** No one has yet adequately described what *woman* is.

_____ **6.** Her imagination left her when she thought her passions were unconventional.

_____ **7.** Ms. Woolf describes two experiences she has had in her professional life.

_____ **8.** For the first time, women are able to ask questions and decide on answers.

II. Put a check on the lines beside any statements that are reasonable interpretations of the author's meaning.

_____ **1.** Women often have to overcome cultural expectations in order to succeed in a challenging career.

_____ **2.** When one is successful, one will often succumb to frivolity.

_____ **3.** Writing fully and honestly, especially when you are a woman, is very difficult to do.

_____ **4.** Although being a female journalist leaves a woman prey to many phantoms, other professions may be much worse.

_____ **5.** Women are often censored for the same things a man could do and be accepted for.

III. To apply what you read means to take information and ideas from what you have read and connect them to what you already know. Place a check beside any statements that are supported in II and by your previous experiences.

_____ **1.** Everyone has a ghost in his or her closet.

_____ **2.** Knowing oneself is a lifetime endeavor.

_____ **3.** Some problems never have solutions.

_____ **4.** Winning the battle does not mean the war is won.

_____ **5.** What appears simple is often complex.

Based on "Professions for Women" by Virginia Woolf, *Collected Essays* (Vol. 2, pp. 284–289), Harcourt Brace & World, 1950.

example, Gusak (1967) reported that in second grade, 78% of the questions asked were literal; in fourth grade, 65% were still literal; in sixth grade, 58% were literal. And the emphasis hasn't changed since 1967. Armbruster et al. (1991) studied science and social studies lessons for fourth-graders and found that 90% of the questions were teacher-generated and explicit. Durkin (1979), observing at the upper elementary level, found that most questions that teachers asked were literal, with only one correct response expected. Durkin (1981) then studied teachers' manuals for basal reading instruction and discovered that low-level literal questions with one correct response were the major instructional strategy provided for teachers. Reutzel and Daines (1987) reached the same conclusion after a study of seven major basal readers.

A C T I V I T Y   5 . 1 7   **THREE-LEVEL GUIDE TO FOLLOWING A PATTERN IN HOME ECONOMICS**

I. Place a check (√) before the statements that are correct based on the information in the guide sheet.

_____ **1.** The first step in making this skirt is gathering the upper edge of the front between large ●'s.

_____ **2.** Pockets are sewn in place after the skirt front is sewn to the back.

_____ **3.** The zipper is placed in the center back seam.

_____ **4.** The zipper is applied after the waistband is sewn to the skirt.

_____ **5.** The waistband is interfaced before it is sewn to the skirt.

_____ **6.** Seams that will be inside the waistband (when it is finished) are trimmed.

_____ **7.** The pictures show that the center back seam and the side seams are pressed open.

_____ **8.** A narrow hem is used to finish the lower edge of the skirt.

II. Place a check (√) before each statement that you think is reasonable based on the information in the guide sheet. Be prepared to support your answer with statements from the guide sheet.

_____ **1.** Sewing a skirt begins with sewing on the skirt front.

_____ **2.** To prevent confusion and error, complete one step before going to another.

_____ **3.** Finish completely (by removing basting, trimming, and pressing) one line of sewing before crossing it with another.

_____ **4.** Trimming and clipping may be needed to keep a seam from being too bulky.

_____ **5.** Pressing is an important part of sewing.

III. To apply what you read means to take information from what you have read and connect it to what you already know. Place a check (√) before any statements that are supported by statements in II and by previous experiences or study. Be sure that you have a reason for your answers.

_____ **1.** A stitch in proper sequence (order) saves time.

_____ **2.** The order in which something is done does make a difference.

_____ **3.** If it's worth doing, it's worth doing well.

_____ **4.** A picture is worth a thousand words.

_____ **5.** A little time well used is better than much time ill used.

Developed by Ava Brendle.

With little practice in answering higher-level questions, students are ill equipped to think critically. Elementary students are trapped into expecting only literal questions; secondary students will remain in the trap because the literal question has been their previous experience. However, research also shows that when instructional strategies are altered so that the focus is on inferences and main ideas, students respond with improved recall and greater understanding (Hansen, 1981; Hansen & Pearson, 1983; Raphael, 1984). Cooter, Joseph, and Flynt (1986) were able to show that third- and fourth-graders who were asked no literal questions in a five-month period performed significantly better than a control group on inferential comprehension and just as well on literal comprehension.

In addition, teachers sometimes misjudge the difficulty of questions they are asking or fail to match the questions to the students' ability. Generally, questions

---

A C T I V I T Y   5 . 1 8   CHANGE AND CONTINUITY IN THE LIVES OF AMERICAN WOMEN

Three-Level Guide

I. Which statements are facts in this essay? Check them.

_____ **1.** Women today live to be about 75.

_____ **2.** After 1850, immigrant families took farm girls' places in factories.

_____ **3.** American women in the work force are usually considered as temporary workers.

_____ **4.** Although many factors have influenced women's lives, three stand out as the most important: industrialization, contraception, and economic instability.

_____ **5.** In the colonial period, a woman's obligations to her children and her household tasks often conflicted with one another.

II. Which statements are major ideas of this essay? Check them.

_____ **1.** Tradition in the manner of gender roles is very strong.

_____ **2.** The patterns of women's lives have shifted dramatically during the past two centuries.

_____ **3.** More women are entering careers every day.

_____ **4.** Women are having fewer children today than in the 1800s.

_____ **5.** The definition of a woman's role has not changed.

III. With which statements would you and the author agree? Check them.

_____ **1.** You've come a long way, baby.

_____ **2.** Physical changes occur more easily and faster than mental changes.

_____ **3.** A woman should be barefoot, pregnant, and in the kitchen.

_____ **4.** It takes a lot to get a little.

_____ **5.** A woman's place is in the home.

Thesis: Women's positions in society have changed dramatically since 1800, yet society has not been willing to accept the change as quickly as it has occurred.

Compare and Contrast

Subject	Yesterday's Women	Today's Women
1. Children	More than seven	Two or fewer
2. Life expectancy	55 years	75 years
3. Independence	After widowed	Before marriage
4. Work force	In home	In and out of home
5. Education	Only men	Advanced education

Based on *Critical Thinking Reading and Writing Across the Curriculum* (pp. 204–210), edited by A.B. Grinols, Wadsworth, 1988.

are simpler when students are able to recognize and locate answers in the text rather than closing books and trying to recall the same information. Easier questions also include those asked during reading or shortly after reading, questions that have only one or two parts, oral questions rather than written ones, and those that allow students to choose an answer from among several alternatives. We are not suggesting that all questions should be asked in the simplest manner;

we are cautioning that many times teachers have not considered the difficulty of their questions and their students' ability to answer them.

Another trap that teachers often fall into is focusing more on the question asked and the response expected than on the student's actual response. As Dillon (1983) remarks, we should "stress the nature of questions rather than their frequency and pace, and the type of student response rather than the type of teacher question" (p. 8). Students' answers can tell a lot about their understanding of the topic. We need to listen for answers that let us know how well we are assisting the development of comprehension.

TIPS FOR CONSTRUCTING GOOD QUESTIONS

We have learned much about how to question from the extensive studies of reading comprehension conducted over the past few decades. Although much of this research has been conducted with elementary students, the implications are relevant for secondary instruction as well. Students who have not received a firm foundation in reading comprehension in elementary school will not be well equipped in secondary school. To help teachers construct good questions, we have tried to summarize what we consider the most important research considerations in the following tips.

1. Simplify your questions! Although teachers want to challenge their students, they should challenge within a range that allows students to succeed. Consider using the following guidelines.

    a. Identify the purpose of the question. (Will it measure fact, implication, or applied levels of comprehension? a particular organizational pattern? a superordinate or subordinate idea?) Is this purpose justified? Does it contribute to a balance of comprehension levels within the lesson?

    b. Identify the type of response demanded by the question (recognition, recall, production, or generation of a new idea from the information). Is this expectation justified, given the age and ability of the group? Have you provided an example of what you want? If you wish students to produce a modern dialogue for a character in *Hamlet*, can you give them an example first?

    c. Might the question elicit more than one reasonable response? If this is a possibility, will you be able to accept different responses and use them to assist instruction?

    d. Does this question contain several parts? Will these parts be clear to the students, and can they remember all of the parts as they respond?

    e. Write the question clearly and concisely. Then decide whether to pose it orally or in writing.

2. Share with students the reasons for your questions. Let them know the process you use to develop questions and the process you would use in answering them. This knowledge helps them to see what types of questions are important to you in this area (Pearson, 1985). It also helps them to understand how they should be thinking when they respond and what you are thinking when

you question. This process — thinking about thinking — is called **metacognition** (Babbs & Moe, 1983). Helping students think about your reasoning and about their own reading processes will eventually produce independent readers.

3. Encourage students to ask questions about your questions and to ask their own questions. Goodlad (1984) suggests that students will thrive when they can participate in classroom questioning more directly than they do in most classrooms today. Beyer (1984) says that teacher-dominated questioning inhibits student independence and limits thinking. "Instruction that leads to systematic question-asking by students would be more appropriate, but such an approach is rare indeed" (p. 489).

4. Provide plenty of practice in answering questions at different levels of comprehension. Check yourself occasionally to make sure that you are not leaning on the literal level too heavily. Training and practice result in learning the material (Brown, Campione, & Day, 1981; Paris, Cross, & Lipson, 1984) and in learning how to understand material in sophisticated ways. Wassermann (1987) argues that students' depth and breadth of understanding improve when they are asked challenging questions. Also, students who learn to take another's perspective may become better readers as a result (Gardner & Smith, 1987). But students must have opportunities for practice to master this ability.

5. Allow discussions, which give students practice in asking and answering questions (Perez & Strickland, 1987; Alvermann, 1987a). Chapter 6 contains many suggestions for generating student discussions to facilitate critical thinking.

6. Ask students the types of questions you know they are able to answer. Try not to expect too much too soon, but do expect as much as students can do. For example, recent research indicates that students can identify main idea statements earlier than they can make such statements (Afflerbach, 1987). If students seem consistently unable to answer a certain type of comprehension question, even after you have followed these suggestions, we suggest that you review the most recent findings in the research literature for clues.

QAR

The question/answer relationship (QAR) has been studied and applied by Raphael (1984, 1986). QAR is a taxonomy with four levels: right there, think and search, the author and you, and on your own. When QAR is introduced to and practiced with students for as little as eight weeks, reading comprehension improves greatly. Teachers should introduce QAR with a visual aid to show the QAR relationship. Figure 5.4 shows one teacher's illustrated introduction to QAR.

After introducing QAR, the teacher should use a short passage to demonstrate how QAR is applied. To model the use of QAR, the teacher should provide, label, and answer at least one question at each QAR level. The teacher should then move gradually to having students answer questions and identifying the QAR for themselves. The teacher should refer to QAR throughout the year of

FIGURE 5.4

Illustrated introduction to QAR (developed by Rebecca McSweeney).

Q A R

I. Where is the answer?

Right there!
_____

Words are right there
in the text.

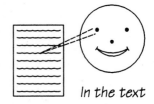

In the text

II. Where is the answer?

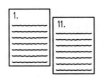

Think and search!
_____

Words are in the text but not
spelled out for you. Think about
what the author is saying.

*Hmm! Gotta
think about this.*

III. Where is the answer?

What I know

You and the author!
_____

Think about what you have learned
and what is in the text.

*What the
author says*

IV. Where is the answer?

On your own!
_____

Answer is in your head!

content instruction. These steps will saturate students with a way of thinking about questions and answers that will help them read with better comprehension. Activity 5.19 demonstrates this procedure as a sixth-grade mathematics teacher used it.

Because QAR is a straightforward procedure, easily implemented, quickly beneficial to students, and useful at any grade and in any content area, we hope that many content teachers will start using it in their instruction. QAR has been proven to increase students' comprehension more than several other questioning strategies (Jenkins & Lawler, 1990). It fosters listening, speaking, and reading, and if students write their own QARs, it also offers opportunities for writing.

ReQUEST

Students should be encouraged to ask informed questions. Manzo's (1969) ReQuest procedure encourages students to think carefully before and during their reading by formulating questions based on the text. Since Manzo had remedial readers and small groups in mind when he designed ReQuest, we have chosen to explain this procedure in depth in Chapter 11. The reader may want to look ahead to find out more about it.

GUIDE-O-RAMAS AND MARGINAL GLOSSES

Another activity that assists readers is the "guide-o-rama" (Cunningham & Shablak, 1975), which signals the reader to note certain information in a reading passage. The teacher creates directions for these reading passages and encourages the students to use the directions as they read. For instance, if the teacher can see that the word *perverse* is used in an unusual way, he might write this: "On page 13, second paragraph, third line, the word *perverse* is used a little differently from what you'd expect. Pay attention to the meaning." When a teacher prepares several directions such as these and gives them to readers to refer to while reading, they have a panoramic view of the reading—hence the name guide-o-rama.

A marginal gloss (Singer & Donlan, 1985) can often be found in content textbooks. Glosses are the comments that authors make to their readers as "asides" or marginal notations. The comments are intended to help the reader understand the passage content; thus, they assist the reader in developing comprehension. Teachers can make their own marginal glosses if their texts do not include them or if they are dissatisfied with those already included. A guide-o-rama can be designed as a gloss also. The point of these activities is similar: they both are like having the teacher go home with the students and look over their shoulders as they read, guiding their reading attention. Singer and Donlan suggest that teachers make marginal glosses as follows:

1. Fold a ditto master against the margin of a text.
2. Identify the book page at the top of the master and line up numbers beside teacher directives.

ACTIVITY 5.19   **QAR PROCEDURE APPLIED TO MATHEMATICS**

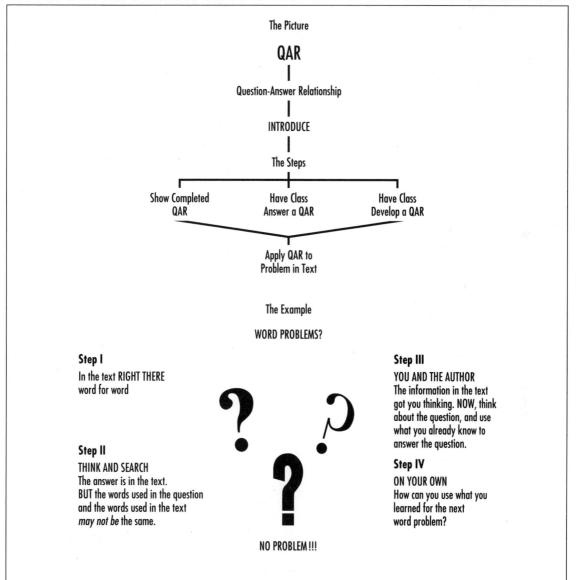

The Picture

QAR

Question-Answer Relationship

INTRODUCE

The Steps

Show Completed QAR   Have Class Answer a QAR   Have Class Develop a QAR

Apply QAR to Problem in Text

The Example

WORD PROBLEMS?

Step I
In the text RIGHT THERE
word for word

Step II
THINK AND SEARCH
The answer is in the text.
BUT the words used in the question
and the words used in the text
may not be the same.

Step III
YOU AND THE AUTHOR
The information in the text
got you thinking. NOW, think
about the question, and use
what you already know to
answer the question.

Step IV
ON YOUR OWN
How can you use what you
learned for the next
word problem?

NO PROBLEM!!!

Laura set a goal to run five miles a day. On Friday she ran one mile before breakfast. Then she went to school. In P.E. class she ran two miles around the school track. After dinner that night, Laura and her dad won first place in the "Run for Your Life" event at the country fair. Laura went home that night tired, but satisfied.

(continued on page 194)

A C T I V I T Y 5 . 1 9   CONTINUED

1. QUESTION: What was Laura's goal?
   ANSWER: to run 5 miles a day
   QAR: RIGHT THERE

2. QUESTION: How far did Laura run before dinner?
   ANSWER: 3 miles
   QAR: THINK AND SEARCH

3. QUESTION: What was the length of the "Run for Your Life" event?
   ANSWER: The race was at least 2 miles long.
   QAR: YOU AND THE AUTHOR

4. QUESTION: What benefits can result from running 5 miles a day?
   ANSWER: You will be a healthier person.
   QAR: ON YOUR OWN

Bill needed to lose some weight. He decided to eat only apples for three days. He should have listened to his mom. On the third day he didn't feel very well.

1. QUESTION: What did Bill need to do?
   ANSWER: _____
   QAR: RIGHT THERE

2. QUESTION: What did Bill's mother tell him?
   ANSWER: _____
   QAR: THINK AND SEARCH

3. QUESTION: Why did Bill get sick?
   ANSWER: _____
   QAR: YOU AND THE AUTHOR

4. QUESTION: How many apples would it take to make you sick?
   ANSWER: _____
   QAR: ON YOUR OWN

Using problem number 6 on page 45 of your *Addison-Wesley Mathematics* book, answer these questions.

1. QUESTION: How much did the uncut stone weigh?
   ANSWER: _____
   QAR: _____

2. QUESTION: How big were the largest and smallest diamonds?
   ANSWER: _____
   QAR: _____

3. QUESTION: How many carats were lost during the cutting process?
   ANSWER: _____
   QAR: _____

4. QUESTION: What is the biggest diamond in the world?
   ANSWER: _____
   QAR: _____

Developed by Mary Frances Siewert.

A C T I V I T Y   5 . 2 0   **ANTICIPATION GUIDE FOR PURPOSE SETTING: FRACTIONS**

Read each of the statements below, and put a check in the appropriate blank space to indicate whether you agree or disagree with the statement. *After reading the text, you will see if your answers are correct.*

Agree   Disagree

_____   _____   When dividing fractions, you take the reciprocal of the first number, then multiply.

_____   _____   For every decimal name there is a fraction name, and vice versa.

_____   _____   Sometimes you can use a shortcut for multiplying fractions.

_____   _____   You always need to get an exact answer when multiplying fractions.

_____   _____   To multiply fractions, you take the reciprocal of the second number.

Developed by Dawn Marie Watson.

3. Write the marginal notes on the ditto master.
4. Duplicate and give students copies of these notes to match to text pages and lines as they read.

For these activities, we suggest that the teacher select either very difficult portions of text to gloss or beginning portions, when the reading may be tougher. Making guide-o-ramas or glosses for use throughout a text would be very time-consuming. However, to provide assistance in developing comprehension with challenging reading, they are worth the time.

Assisting by Setting Purposes for Reading

In optimal circumstances, readers will realize what they already know about a topic and will have the background to continue studying it. However, their *need* to read about the topic is contingent on their purpose for reading. Having a purpose provides basic motivation for accomplishing any task: if one has no particular reason to do something, it probably won't get done.

Setting meaningful purposes for students to read content material is crucial to their comprehension. Telling students to read Chapter 14 or pages 20–50 is usually not very inspiring. Students *might* read that text; they might not. If they do, and the teacher has provided no more purpose than this, students have had very little assistance in knowing why they're reading. Whether or not they discover the organizational pattern and the major ideas will be pretty much a hit-or-miss proposition. The best reason, then, to assist reading by setting purposes is to make sure that the reading gets completed and understood. How many teachers would argue that this is not a goal of their instruction? Yet Durkin (1984) found that elementary teachers instructing from reading materials rarely provided purpose-setting questions for their students.

In the instructional setting, purposes can be set using any of several activities already introduced in this book. In Activity 5.20, for example, an anticipation guide developed by a middle-school mathematics teacher includes a purpose-setting statement (italics added). Whereas in most anticipation guides there will be no "right" answers, in this anticipation guide the teacher does expect correct answers, but not necessarily *before* reading occurs.

One-Minute Summary

In this chapter, we have presented the background for comprehension instruction in content areas. Definitions of comprehension from 1908 to 1985 show that professionals' views of reading have changed little, although the emphasis has shifted from the *product* to the *process* of comprehension. We have also reviewed recent studies of comprehension and what they indicate for reading-to-learn instruction.

We have considered two contexts that facilitate comprehension: text coherence and levels of understanding. Assisting readers to understand text organization includes helping them recognize superordinate and subordinate patterns, chunk large units of text, and identify patterns of organization. To assist readers in levels of understanding, we have focused on a three-level taxonomy and discussed the role of questioning in facilitating comprehension. We introduced several activities to show how text and instructional contexts can be taught. Finally, we have discussed the role of purpose setting in assisting reading instruction.

End-of-Chapter Activities

Assisting Comprehension

Select a textbook from which you teach or might teach in the future. As you peruse a chapter, can you identify a predominant pattern of organization? Do you see what information is superordinate? Can you "chunk" the chapter into definable segments for students? When you review the questions for the chapter, do you find a balance across all three levels? If not, what level of questioning is predominant?

After answering these questions, do you have ideas for appropriate activities you might design to assist your students' comprehension?

Reflecting on Your Reading

What changes can you make in your instruction to provide your students with more "ladders" to assist their understanding? Would you feel more comfortable with questioning activities or with guiding activities? Why?

CHAPTER 6

Reflecting on Reading

*"Teach a child what to think and you make him your slave. Teach a child how to think
and you make all knowledge his slave."*

Henry A. Taitt

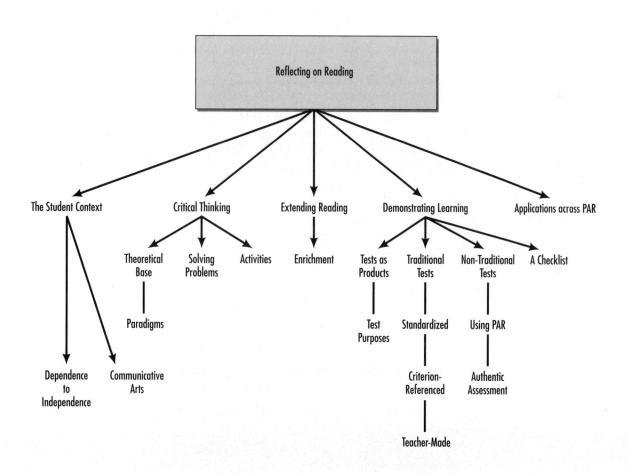

Prepare to Read

1. These questions can help you clarify your previous knowledge about critical thinking:

   a. What is your definition of critical thinking?
   b. List reasons why there could be no agreement on the exact nature of critical thinking.
   c. What systematic steps does a person have to take to solve a problem?
   d. What propaganda techniques do authors often use to get their ideas across?

2. What procedures do you follow when you design classroom tests? Do you write the test before you teach the content? Jot down possible questions as you are teaching the content? Make up the test the night before you administer it?

3. Following is a list of terms used in this chapter. Some of them may be familiar to you in a general context, but in this chapter they may be used in a different way than you are used to. Rate your knowledge by placing a + in front of those you are sure that you know, a √ in front of those you have some knowledge about, and a 0 in front of those you don't know. Be ready to locate and pay special attention to their meanings when they are presented in the chapter.

   ___ fading
   ___ comprehension monitoring
   ___ free ride
   ___ informative communication
   ___ effective thinking
   ___ paradigm
   ___ propaganda

   ___ brainstorming
   ___ I-charts
   ___ nontraditional test
   ___ SCORER
   ___ test-wise
   ___ authentic assessment

Objectives

As you read this chapter, focus your attention on the following objectives. You will:

1. understand the dominant role students must play during reflection.

2. recognize the important part that communicative arts and cooperative learning have in content-area reading instruction.

3. understand the nature of critical thinking, from its narrowest to its broadest sense.

4. be able to use critical thinking games described in the chapter to teach important critical thinking skills.

5. understand how to apply PAR in designing classroom tests.

6. describe traditional tests, including standardized, criterion-referenced, and teacher-made tests.

7. enumerate three problems and several suggestions for improving traditional tests.

8. understand how being test-wise affects student performance on tests.

Reflection

The third step in PAR is Reflection, which takes place after reading has been completed and the student must "put it all together." Both the teacher and the student must make sure that what was read is understood and placed in context. The reader extends the reading experience and thinks critically about the reading material. As we have seen, Gray described this process as "reading beyond the lines." Full understanding cannot be achieved until reflection occurs. Knowledge must be related in a meaningful way to what is already known so that it will be retained and become the base for further learning. Reflection involves three steps: critical thinking, enrichment, and demonstration of learning. Although the teacher may still guide students by providing instructional support, the student's role is crucial at this stage.

From Dependence to Independence

Although teachers must initially prepare and assist readers, readers must take charge of their own learning as soon as possible. Hawkes and Schell (1987) caution that teacher-set reasons to read may encourage dependence and a passive approach to reading. Self-set reasons to read promote reading that is active and ultimately independent.

"By teaching us how to read, they had taught us how to get away" (Robert O'Brien, *Mrs. Frisby and the Rats of NIMH*). In this children's novel, scientists conduct experiments to teach rats to read. Because the rats have been fed a superdrug to make them smart, the scientists anticipate that the rats will learn some letter/sound and word/picture relationships. They do not expect that the rats will actually ever *understand* and *apply* what they read. They underestimate what reading is all about. These rats *want* to escape their lab. Their goal is vital: they are willing to work at reading so they can use this new skill to escape.

The rats use all of their communication skills. They study pictures presented to them, they listen to clues to the meaning of the pictures, and they consult with each other about what they are learning — the connections between letters and sounds, pictures and words. And then they read! Later, in their new home, they even begin to keep a written record of their progress.

The story of the rats of NIMH demonstrates how cooperative study and the communicative arts can produce reflective readers who think critically, enrich their environment, and use reading as a lifelong process. No "test" of their success could demonstrate their learning better than the self-supporting community the rats built.

When the act of reading merges with thinking, reflective comprehension results. The relationship is integral and cannot be separated *if* the conditions for learning are optimal. In this novel, the rats had a great desire to escape NIMH and plenty of opportunities for practice as well as plenty of clues in their environment. The natural result was comprehension and escape. The scientists, to their misfortune, did not realize the important role of the learner in the success of their experiment.

Principle 9 in Chapter 1 states: "Content reading instruction should enable students to become responsible and independent readers." Teachers help students achieve this independence by "**fading** out" of the picture as soon as possible to allow students to take active, responsible roles. When teachers build a strong foundation for reading through appropriate preparation and assist readers with the comprehension process, students should be ready to "fade in" to the picture at the reflection stage. With consistent PAR modeling, students should begin to take the same active role before, during, *and* after reading. As discussed in Chapter 5, this process can be likened to the scaffolding used by builders. When construction is in progress, scaffolding is often erected to support the building. After the structure is completed, the scaffolding is taken down because the building can now stand alone. Students need to stand alone when they reflect.

However, students may be left stranded unless teachers guide them toward independence by showing them how to use their own communication skills. Kletzien (1991) investigated high schoolers' use of strategies for reading. She found that students did use many strategies when they were reading independently, but that poorer comprehenders were less flexible. She recommended that students "need to be given more control over the strategies so that they can use them independently" (p. 83). Olshavsky (1975) and Golinkoff (1976) have described the behavior of good and poor readers in terms of their abilities to use comprehension strategies. Good readers will be able to pause and demonstrate their comprehension by retelling and analyzing what they have read and by using certain strategies consistently. They are practicing **comprehension monitoring**. However, poor readers seem to lose track of their reading and to have no particular strategies for comprehending. In other words, poorer readers do not seem to function independently.

Although teachers can point out what is important about content material, students must ultimately evaluate the worth for themselves (Cioffi, 1992). Thus, for example, Angeletti (1991) used question cards with her second-graders to encourage them to express opinions about content they had read.

Bohan and Bass (1991) helped students in a fourth-grade math class become independent by taking "**free rides**" in solving problems about fractions. "After the teacher covered multiplication of two fractions, the class was told the next type of problem, multiplying mixed numbers, was a free ride—a situation in which they were solving a seemingly new type of problem, but one that was not really new because they had previously acquired the knowledge needed to find the product" (p. 4). The next day, a student volunteered another case where free rides could apply. This situation exemplifies the elements of reflection: the teacher provides a context and encourages students to manage their own learning

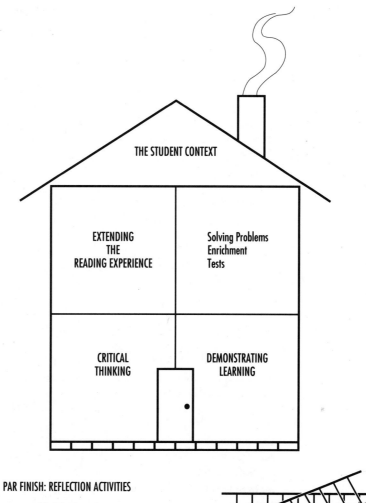

THE STUDENT CONTEXT

EXTENDING
THE
READING EXPERIENCE

Solving Problems
Enrichment
Tests

CRITICAL
THINKING

DEMONSTRATING
LEARNING

PAR FINISH: REFLECTION ACTIVITIES

CONSTRUCTION
COMPLETE

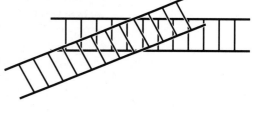

at the application level. Gagne (1974) calls this "self-management that the learner acquires to govern his own process of attending, learning and thinking" (p. 6).

The Role of the Communicative Arts

We believe, as stated in principle 1, that "the communicative arts are tools for thinking and learning in content subjects." As Alvermann (1987b) puts it: "Writers, speakers, readers, and listeners all engage in reciprocal processes aimed at creating understanding through shared responsibilities of communication" (p. 112). Allen, Brown, and Yatvin (1986) use the term **informative communication**. "Through listening, speaking, reading, and writing, children acquire knowledge of the world and learn to use that knowledge productively in their own lives" (p. 204). Just as students read to learn, they listen to learn, speak to learn, and write to learn.

More than at any other stage, reflective learning depends on informative communication. Teachers have to let go, learn *not* to talk, but encourage students to cooperate with each other in their learning. Alvermann (1987b) contends that "one of the simplest things teachers can do to limit the amount of teacher talk and increase the amount of student talk is to stop asking questions" (p. 111). Counselors practice such a philosophy when they avoid too many questions or suggestions and guide their clients by listening attentively.

The *discussion web* (Alvermann, 1991) is an activity in which teachers first prepare students to read, asking them to think of a question they would like to have answered, and then assign the reading. Students then discuss the reading in pairs. Next, two pairs of readers meet together to discuss their information and reach a consensus. A recorder from this group then reports to the whole class. The final step is for each student to write an answer to the question that was asked before the reading began. We presented the discussion web in Chapter 4 as an effective means of confronting misconceptions about prior knowledge. This activity also models the before, during, and after steps (PAR) of reading; puts the student first; employs all of the language arts as well as cooperative grouping; and leads to reflection.

As we present information about critical thinking, enrichment, and ways to determine if learning has occurred, remember that activities that promote a cooperative, communicative-arts approach and place the student in the role of independent learner will work best to promote reflection.

Critical Thinking

Oliver Wendell Holmes once said, "Every now and then a man's mind is stretched by a new idea and never shrinks back to its former dimensions." One of the most important ways to have students reflect on reading is to ask them to think critically about what they read. Postreading activities designed to improve critical thinking are a crucial part of learning in content-area subjects (Clary, 1977). However, recent studies and national reports have indicated that it is also a neglected part of instruction in schools today. Kirsch and Jungeblut (1986) report that today's young adults are literate but have difficulty with the more complex and challenging reading that is required in adult life. The study notes the inability of young people to analyze and understand more complicated material. Sternberg (1985) laments the lack of correspondence between what is required for critical thinking in adulthood and what is being taught in schools today.

By reinforcing the reading experience through critical thinking, teachers can challenge students to think about content material in new ways. Too often, however, classroom teachers, especially at the elementary level, shy away from teaching critical thinking. Among the reasons why teachers do not emphasize critical thinking, we believe, are the following:

1. There is confusion over a clear definition of the construct.
2. Teachers have a misguided notion that "critical" means to find fault and emphasize the negative.
3. It is difficult to measure critical reading and thinking skills through tests.
4. Critical thinking skills often are not mandated for minimum competency in a subject.
5. Teachers have a false notion that slow learners and at-risk students are not capable of thinking critically.
6. Teachers perceive that they do not have adequate time to plan instruction in critical thinking.
7. Teachers lack books, materials, and resources to teach critical thinking.

Despite these perceived obstacles, the teaching of critical thinking should not be neglected at any K–12 grade level. This important ability will lead to greater success in academic subjects and will be of use to students after graduation. In short, critical thinking is a skill that will aid students in all facets of life, during and beyond the school day (Newton, 1978).

Theoretical Base for Critical Thinking

Critical thinking as an important dimension of learning is currently being promoted in textbooks, in the research literature, and in published programs. Interest in the area is underscored by Unks (1985), who states: "The ability to think critically is one of the most agreed upon educational objectives" (p. 240). Even though almost everyone agrees that some elements of critical thinking need to be taught across the curriculum, the concept remains so vague that educators are not certain of its meaning, of the best ways for classroom teachers to teach it, or even whether it can be taught. After examining a textbook on critical thinking, a reviewer once remarked: "It was a good book but it really didn't contain much critical thinking." This comment underscores the subjective nature of the concept, which seems to have no overall, accepted definition.

The literature, in fact, supports two interpretations of critical thinking. The first is a narrow definition of critical thinking as the mastery and use of certain skills necessary for the assessment of statements (Beyer, 1983; Ennis, 1962). These skills take the same form as logic or deduction and may include judging the acceptability of authority statements, judging contradictory statements, and judging whether a conclusion follows necessarily from its premises (Ennis, 1962,

p. 84). A more encompassing definition includes these skills as well as inductive types of skills such as hypothesis testing, proposition generation, and creative argument (Facione, 1984; Ennis, 1981; McPeck, 1981; Sternberg & Baron, 1985). We agree with the latter definition and have emphasized critical thinking in this sense throughout this text.

We can clarify our view of critical thinking by studying what happens when the skill is put to use. McPeck (1981, p. 13) has identified the following features of critical thinking:

1. Critical thinking cannot be taught in the abstract, in isolation. It is not a distinct subject but is taught in content disciplines. It is critical thinking "about something."
2. Although the term may have one correct meaning, the criteria for its correct application vary from discipline to discipline.
3. Critical thinking does not necessarily mean disagreement with, or rejection of, accepted norms.
4. Critical thinking deals with the student's skill to think in such a way as to suspend or temporarily reject evidence from a discipline when the student feels there is insufficient data to establish the truth of some proposition.
5. Critical thinking includes the thought process involved in problem solving and active thinking.
6. Formal and informal logic are not sufficient for thinking critically.
7. Because critical thinking involves knowledge and skill, a critical thinker in one discipline may not be a critical thinker in another discipline.
8. Critical thinking has both a "task" and an "achievement" phase. It does not necessarily imply success.
9. Critical thinking may include the use of methods and strategies as exemplars.
10. Critical thinking does not have the same scope or boundaries as rationality, but it is a dimension of rational thought.

McPeck suggests that at the core of critical thinking is "the propensity and skill to engage in an activity with reflective skepticism" (p. 8). In our complex and rapidly changing society, this ability to be reflective and to be skeptical in weighing evidence before making decisions is of great importance.

More than 60 years ago John Dewey (1933) spoke of the importance of reflective thinking:

> When a situation arises containing a difficulty or perplexity, the person who finds himself in it may take one of a number of courses. He may dodge it, dropping the activity that brought it about, turning to something else. He may indulge in a flight of fancy, imagining himself powerful or wealthy, or in some other way in possession of the means that would enable him to deal with the difficulty. Or, finally, he may face the situation. In this case, he begins to reflect. (p. 102)

Students in kindergarten through 12th grade are seldom taught to reflect, to solve problems by "facing the situation," except in published programs on thinking or in "critical thinking" sections of basal reading materials. The first of

McPeck's features calls into question the effectiveness of any published program that teaches critical thinking as a skill, isolated from content. Reyes (1986), in a review of a social studies series, found that "publishers do not deliver material that develops strong critical thinking, even though they have promised it" (p. 153). In another study, researchers (Woodward, Elliott, & Nagel, 1986) found that the critical thinking skills emphasized in elementary basal materials were those that could be most readily tested, such as map and globe skills.

Evidence indicates that teachers do not need published "thinking" programs and that they cannot depend upon basal reading materials to teach critical thinking skills. However, they do need to integrate their own critical thinking lessons with those of the textbook. For example, to teach critical thinking, teachers might present a paradigm, then have small groups of students practice the steps of the paradigm with carefully chosen textbook lessons and problem-solving exercises. In this manner, students are taught critical thinking in a concrete context of carefully guided thinking. Studies indicate that, especially at early adolescence, formal reasoning and thinking can best be taught through the teacher's use of guided "prompts" such as paradigms, which enable students to structure their thinking more easily (Danner & Day, 1977; Stone & Day, 1978; Karpus, Karpus, Formisano, & Paulsen, 1977; Shayer, Kuchemann, & Wylam, 1976; Arlin, 1984; Martorano, 1977; Strahan, 1983). In addition to asking teachers to emphasize critical thinking, noted educator Art Costa has called for a school environment in which principals and other school leaders encourage teachers "to look carefully at the intelligent behavior of their own students" (Brandt, 1988, p. 13). Further, Costa calls for administrators to model intelligent behavior themselves by:

1. spending time talking about thinking;
2. releasing teachers to engage in critical thinking themselves; and
3. purchasing materials to support critical thinking.

In this text, critical thinking is seen as that multifaceted and complex process alluded to by McPeck that deals with the ability of students to gather data, test hypotheses, and reflect in a skeptical and disciplined manner. The eventual products of this process are life decisions made by persons under pressure to think. Critical thinking, then, is what Moore, McCann, and McCann (1981) call **effective thinking**.

A Paradigm for Teaching Critical Thinking

Students will learn more easily and retain information longer when the teacher uses systematic steps — a **paradigm** — to make the class aware of the skill being emphasized. Any critical thinking topic — relevance, propaganda, propositions, or arguments — can be taught in this manner. Teachers should take the following steps to create awareness in the learner:

1. *Explain the skill to be taught.* Explain to students that they will be asked to think in a certain way, to make judgments, and to practice effective thinking. Define the skill, and give examples of its use. The definition should be on

paper or on the chalkboard so that the skill being taught can be reemphasized at times throughout the lesson.

2. *Introduce the lesson.* When introducing the content lesson, make certain that new information is related to students' prior knowledge.

3. *Develop structured practice using the skill.* Ask students to read the text material or study the problem. Explain how students are to use the critical thinking skill appropriately. Have students practice using the skill for 20 to 30 minutes.

4. *Have students report on their use of the skill.* Students should discuss their observations on how well they acquired the skill or used the skill in a structured practice. They should relate problems and ways to improve in the use of the skill.

5. *Summarize how the skill was used in the content lesson.* Explain again why the skill is important for students to master and how it helped students understand the lesson better.

6. *Review and reinforce the skill.* During the next class period, or certainly within a week, reinforce the skill by asking students to practice using the skill.

7. *Continue practice with the skill.* It is advisable to go through steps 1 through 5 in at least ten additional lessons. For elementary and middle-school students, this practice should be with different content lessons, to ensure transfer of the skill to other disciplines.

Using this paradigm will help students to acquire skills through guided practice and through repeated use of the skill in a structured setting: acquisition of the skill through direct teaching, internalization of the skill through repeated practice, and transfer of the skill to other learning contexts. This type of teacher intervention is a necessary step in improving cognitive ability. Pearson and Tierney (1983) assess the instructional paradigm most used by teachers at present, which features the use of many practice materials, little explanation of cognitive tasks, little interaction with students about the nature of specific tasks, and strong emphasis on one correct answer, to the extent that teachers supply answers if there is any confusion over a task. Not surprisingly, Pearson and Tierney conclude that such a paradigm is ineffective. We think that the paradigm we describe compares favorably.

Activities 6.1 and 6.2 illustrate how our critical thinking paradigm can be used by teachers in different subject areas and at different grade levels. Only the first five steps are included in these examples.

SOLVING PROBLEMS AND MAKING DECISIONS

Probably one of the most important aspects of critical thinking is that it leads to effective decision making. Figure 6.1 presents a model that illustrates steps in problem solving, all of which lead to effective decision making. The most important by-product of having students use such a model is that they will be more effective thinkers; both their creative and contemplative abilities will improve (Parnes & Noller, 1973).

A C T I V I T Y   6 . 1   **CRITICAL THINKING PARADIGM: LANGUAGE ARTS**

Early Elementary

Skill: **Predicting alternatives**

Step 1. Teacher explains that students sometimes need to find alternatives by thinking about possible events.

Step 2. Teacher reads a story aloud, stopping at crucial points of interest.

Step 3. Teacher asks students to predict as many as four outcomes from what has been read to them. Responses are recorded by teacher on the chalkboard.

Step 4. Students are asked why they chose a particular response.

Step 5. Teacher completes story in this manner and summarizes why it is important to practice this skill.

Elementary

Skill: **Fact or opinion**

Step 1. Teacher explains why it is important for students to differentiate fact from opinion, giving examples of each. Teacher tells students that they will be practicing this skill for several weeks.

Step 2. Teacher has students read silently a newspaper editorial on a topic of current interest. Students discuss what they know about the topic.

Step 3. Teacher has all students underline statements in the article. Students form groups to decide which statements are fact and which are opinion.

Step 4. Groups report back to teacher and discuss why they made particular choices.

Step 5. Teacher summarizes both the lesson and the importance of practicing this skill.

A C T I V I T Y   6 . 2   **CRITICAL THINKING PARADIGM: SOCIAL STUDIES**

Early Elementary

Skill: **Detecting propaganda techniques**

Step 1. Teacher gives students worksheet listing propaganda techniques: emotional language, generalities, bandwagon effect, plain-folks approach, overuse of endorsements. Teacher explains that these can influence the reader's judgment of the material and relates these techniques to students' prior knowledge.

Step 2. Teacher introduces lesson on political cartoons of World War I and their effect on U.S. citizens.

Step 3. Students form groups to decide techniques used in the cartoons.

Step 4. Groups report back to teacher and discuss findings.

Step 5. Teacher leads discussion, summarizes lesson, and reemphasizes the importance of the skill learned.

Elementary

Skill: **Evaluating consequences of action**

Step 1. Teacher explains that students need to learn to evaluate consequences of possible courses of action. Teacher hands out worksheet with 1:3 ratio of occurrence to consequence. "If this happens, then these three consequences could occur . . ."

Step 2. Students read to climax or exciting part of story. Together, students list four or five actions protagonist could take.

Step 3. In groups, students list positive and negative consequences that could follow from each action.

Step 4. Groups report back to teacher and discuss findings.

Step 5. Teacher leads discussion, summarizes lesson by reading what protagonist actually does in story, and reemphasizes the importance of the skill learned.

FIGURE 6.1

Model for problem solving.

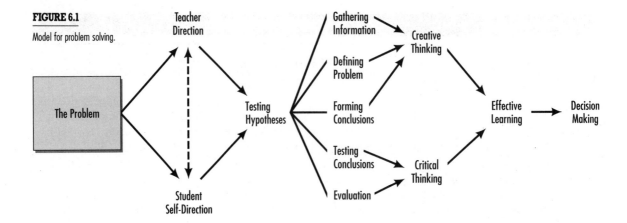

We offer the following stages in problem solving:

1. *Gathering ideas and information.* Students brainstorm to generate enough information to begin defining the problem. They can play the "reading detective" game or do research to gather information from all possible sources.
2. *Defining the problem.* At this stage, students should recognize the need to resolve a situation that has no apparent solution. Students should also be asked to clarify the nature of the task and completely describe the situation in writing.
3. *Forming tentative conclusions.* This is a creative phase in which possible solutions are suggested from available data.
4. *Testing conclusions.* Students discuss in groups which conclusions work best as solutions to the problem. Poor choices are eliminated until workable solutions remain. Students may also establish criteria for evaluating outcomes.
5. *Making a decision.* Students select one of the remaining solutions and give reasons for their choice.

Study guides, such as the one in Activity 6.3, can be constructed by teachers as cognitive maps to assist students in using the problem-solving steps detailed in Figure 6.1. Activity 6.4 contains a guide that can be completed by students to discover the analogies between two stories. It is especially important to start this type of activity in early elementary classrooms because unsophisticated learners seldom let their minds journey *across* stories to think about possible similarities. Activity 6.5 shows how the decision-making model can be used in mathematics.

Group decision making can also be taught through the use of a *group-and-label* technique. The teacher begins by writing the topic on the board and telling students that they will be reviewing important terminology. Then students volunteer any terms they can think of that fall under the topic heading. The teacher may ask leading questions or even eliminate this step by preparing the list in advance on the board or on a worksheet. Students reorganize the list into smaller

A C T I V I T Y   6 . 3   CRITICAL THINKING GUIDE: PROBLEM SOLVING

Problem	
Why do we need to solve problem?	
Ways to Solving Problem	**Reasons for Choosing Method**
Method 1	Positive outcomes
	Negative outcomes
Method 2	Positive outcomes
	Negative outcomes
Method 3	Positive outcomes
	Negative outcomes
Best Way to Solve Problem	Reasons for Choosing to Solve Problem in this Manner

Adapted from a decision-making model by J. McTighe and F. T. Ryman, Jr. (1988), Cueing Thinking in the Classroom: The Promise of Theory-Embedded Tools, *Educational Leadership, 45* (7), 18–24.

A C T I V I T Y   6 . 4   CRITICAL THINKING GUIDE: SIMILARITY IN THEMES OF TWO STORIES

Story Reflection		
Story 1		**Story 2**
Theme:		Theme:
Event		Event
Event	How themes are similar	Event
Event		Event

lists of items that have something in common. Each of these sublists should then be given a label. Students may work individually or in small groups to reorganize and label the words. Activity 6.6 provides an example of a group-and-label technique for consumer mathematics. Activity 6.7 shows how group-and-label might work for a first-grade social studies unit on communities.

A C T I V I T Y   6 . 5   DECISION-MAKING MODEL FOR MATHEMATICS

Mr. and Mrs. Smith wanted to go to Walt Disney World for a week's vacation. They estimated the cost of hotels at $75 a night and meals at $50 a day. Plane tickets were $350, round-trip, for each of them. However, through an enterprising travel agent they found a super-saver package for a week's stay at Disney World that included meals, round-trip fare, and lodging for both of them for $210 a day. Which was the less expensive way for the Smiths to take their vacation?

1. *Defining the problem*
   A couple wishes to travel to Walt Disney World in the least expensive way.

2. *Gathering ideas and information*
   First plan: Hotels — $75 a night for 7 nights
                  Meals — $50 a day for 7 days
                  Plane tickets–$350 each for 2 people
   Second plan: Total cost — $210 a day for 7 days

3. *Forming tentative conclusions*
   Determine cost of first plan by multiplying to find total costs for room, food, and airfare.
   Determine super-saver cost by multiplying per diem cost by 7 days.

4. *Testing conclusions*
   Compare costs of first and second plan.

5. *Making a decision*
   First vacation = $1,575
   Second vacation = $1,470
   Super-saver makes sense!

ANALYZING AUTHORS' TECHNIQUES

Rarely are students asked to examine an author's background to determine whether the author is noted for a particular bias. However, as students evaluate textbook information, they should note the source of that information. Most important, they should ask who the writer is and what his or her qualifications are. Baumann and Johnson (1984, p. 78) ask that students read with these questions in mind:

1. What is the source? Is anything known about the author's qualifications, the reputation of the publisher, and the date of publication?
2. What is the author's primary aim — information, instruction, or persuasion?
3. Are the statements primarily facts, inferences, or opinions?
4. Does the author rely heavily on connotative words that may indicate a bias?
5. Does the author use negative propaganda techniques?

Students can be given these questions to think about and discuss in groups after they read a narrative or expository selection. Also, students can be supplied with multiple-choice items, such as those in Activity 6.8, to assist them in learning

A C T I V I T Y   6 . 6   GROUP AND LABEL: CONSUMER MATHEMATICS

unit price
sales slip
regular time
cash
checking account
straight time
estimate
overtime
FICA
outstanding check
reconciliation statement
income
wage

check stub
deposit slip
gross pay
sales tax
time card
withdraw
net pay
average price
canceled check
piece rate
endorsed
withholding tax

take-home pay
balance
checkbook
fractional price
social security
commission
bank statement
overdrawn
salary plus commission
certified check
deposit

Product Purchasing
unit price
sales slip
estimate
sales tax
average price
fractional price

Money Records/Banking
cash
reconciliation statement
outstanding check
certified check
endorsed
checking account
checkbook
deposit slip
deposit
withdraw
check stub
balance
bank statement
overdrawn
canceled check

Wages
regular time
straight time
overtime
income
wage
gross pay
net pay
take-home pay
withholding tax
FICA
social security
piece rate
commission
salary plus commission
time card

to determine an author's qualifications for writing accurate and unbiased statements on a subject. Such an activity can be used to begin class discussion on a reading or to initiate debate after reading.

DISTINGUISHING FACT AND OPINION
Separating fact from opinion is another higher-level thinking skill that can be taught to students starting in the early elementary years. To do so, teachers must train students to see relationships between and among facts, to distinguish fact from opinion, to grasp subtle implications, and to interpret the deeper meanings

A C T I V I T Y 6 . 7   GROUP AND LABEL: FIRST-GRADE SOCIAL STUDIES

From a jumbled list of words, the students will be asked to divide the words into four groups, according to their similarities. The teacher will write these four groups of words on the chalkboard. The students will label these groups. These labels will be written by the teacher on the board as titles for the groups of words.

Getting to School
>   school bus "The bus driver brings me to school."
>   walking "I walk to school with my sister."
>   Mom's station wagon "My mom drives me to school in her station wagon."
>   Daddy's pickup truck "My daddy drives me to school in his pickup truck."
>   Bicycle "I ride my bicycle to school."

Things Used at School
>   ruler
>   books "I learn to read in first grade."
>   writing tablet "I write in my tablet."
>   pencils "My teacher sharpens my pencil every day."
>   crayons "I like to color pictures with my crayons."
>   glue
>   scissors "I cut the paper with my scissors."

Rooms at School
>   office "I'm scared to go to the principal's office."
>   classroom
>   library "I like to check out books at the library."
>   cafeteria "We eat in the cafeteria."
>   nurse's clinic
>   auditorium
>   gymnasium "I play in the gym."

People at School
>   teacher "My teacher helps me to read."
>   coach "The coach is my friend."
>   librarian "The librarian always reads us a story."
>   principal
>   secretary
>   nurse "The nurse is nice."
>   bus driver
>   cafeteria workers
>   janitors and cleaning workers
>   guidance counselor

Developed by Gail Perrer.

A C T I V I T Y 6 . 8   **RELIABILITY OF SOURCES**

Supply students with multiple-choice items like the following. The student checks the source that is most reliable of the three suggested.

1. Japan has the highest per capita income of any country in the world.
    ____ a. Joan Armentrag, salesperson at Bloomingdale's
    ____ b. Bob Hoskins, star golfer
    ____ c. Dr. Alice MacKenzie, economic analyst, the Ford Foundation
2. Mathematics is of no use to anyone.
    ____ a. Bob Brotig, high school dropout
    ____ b. Bill Johnson, editor, *The Mathematics Teacher*
    ____ c. Susan Winnifred, personnel, the Rand Corporation
3. We have proved that honey bees communicate with each other.
    ____ a. John Bowyer, salesman, Sue Ann Honey Co.
    ____ b. Jane Maupin, high school biology teacher
    ____ c. Martha Daughtry, bank teller
4. Forty-six percent of all married women with children now work outside the home.
    ____ a. Sue Ann Begley, electrician
    ____ b. Carol Radziwell, professional pollster
    ____ c. Joe Blotnik, marriage counselor
5. We must stop polluting our bays and oceans.
    ____ a. Clinton Weststock, president, Save the Bay Foundation
    ____ b. Marjorie Seldon, engineer, Olin Oil Refinery, Gulfport, MI
    ____ c. Carl Kanipe, free-lance writer of human-interest stories

an author has in mind. Often the reader must bring to bear past experiences and background to derive accurate interpretations. With frequent practice, students can become adept at interpreting an author's point of view and detecting biases. Activities 6.9, 6.10, and 6.11 present ideas for constructing guides and worksheets to illustrate fact and opinion, to help students distinguish one from the other, and to give students practice in writing facts and opinions.

DETECTING PROPAGANDA TECHNIQUES

Skilled readers know how to absorb important information and throw away what is of no use. They are especially adept at recognizing **propaganda** — persuasive, one-sided statements used to change beliefs or sway opinion. Propaganda can be glaring or extremely subtle, and students need to be made aware, even in the elementary years, of the effects propaganda can have, particularly in the marketplace.

The following are the most often used forms of propaganda:

1. *Appeal to bandwagon* — aimed at the "masses" to join a large group that is satisfied with an idea or product. Readers of this kind of propaganda are made to feel left out if they don't go along with the crowd.

A C T I V I T Y   6 . 9   **WORKSHEET: FACT AND OPINION**

Place a check by the sentences that state opinions.

_____ 1. Let me tell you about the wild parade.
_____ 2. Young children participating in parades usually look foolish.
_____ 3. Doctors are certified every five years.
_____ 4. According to a recent poll, four out of five doctors feel that their insurance rates are too high.
_____ 5. The sunrise turned the snowy peak a pastel pink.
_____ 6. Van Gogh painted *Starry Night*.
_____ 7. Certain details in *Starry Night* indicate Van Gogh's emotional disturbance.
_____ 8. Last night every time I bowled the first ball of a frame, I left one pin standing.
_____ 9. The disorder in my room is depressing.
_____ 10. After I drop my books on my desk and throw my clothes on the floor, my room is a mess.

A C T I V I T Y   6 . 1 0   **WORKSHEET: STATING OPINIONS**

Directions: Limit the general subjects below and then state a precise opinion about each limited
          subject.

Example:
     General Subject: Traveling

     _____hitchhiking_____   is/are   _____dangerous_____
          (limited subject)   (precise opinion)

  1. General Subject: Politics

     _____   is/are   _____
          (limited subject)   (precise opinion)

  2. General Subject: Medicine

     _____   is/are   _____
          (limited subject)   (precise opinion)

  3. General Subject: Television

     _____   is/are   _____
          (limited subject)   (precise opinion)

  4. General Subject: Sports

     _____   is/are   _____
          (limited subject)   (precise opinion)

  5. General Subject: Education

     _____   is/are   _____
          (limited subject)   (precise opinion)

A C T I V I T Y   6 . 1 1   ENERGY: FACT OR OPINION?

Directions: Place an *F* by the statements that state facts and an *O* by the statements that state opinions.

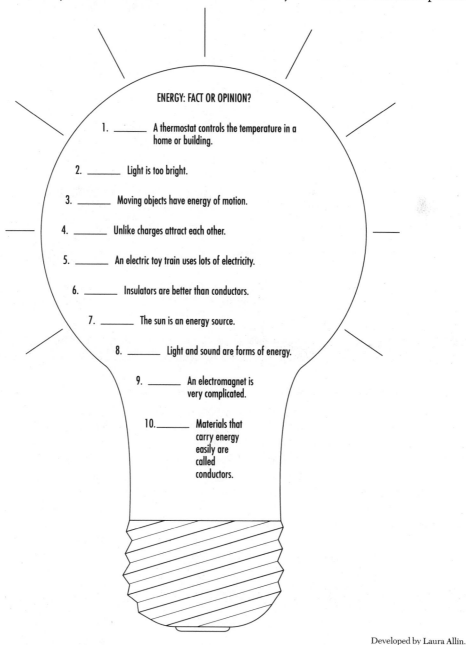

ENERGY: FACT OR OPINION?

1. _____ A thermostat controls the temperature in a home or building.

2. _____ Light is too bright.

3. _____ Moving objects have energy of motion.

4. _____ Unlike charges attract each other.

5. _____ An electric toy train uses lots of electricity.

6. _____ Insulators are better than conductors.

7. _____ The sun is an energy source.

8. _____ Light and sound are forms of energy.

9. _____ An electromagnet is very complicated.

10. _____ Materials that carry energy easily are called conductors.

Developed by Laura Allin.

2. *Emotional language*—plays on the subtle connotations of words, which are carefully chosen to evoke strong feelings in the reader.
3. *Appeal to prestige*—a person, product, or concept is associated with something deemed to be important or prestigious by the reader or viewer.
4. *Plain-folks appeal*—the use of persons in an advertisement who seem typical, average, or ordinary (sometimes even dull). The idea is to make readers or viewers feel that the people depicted are "regular" folks like themselves, thereby building trust.
5. *Testimonial*—use of a famous person to give heightened credibility to a concept, idea, or product.

Teachers at all grade levels need to prepare students through "awareness" sessions to recognize propaganda techniques. After the basic techniques have been explained, students can be asked to bring in examples of advertisements from newspapers and magazines. In literature classes, students can be asked to discover examples in plays, short stories, and novels. *A Tale of Two Cities*, for example, contains examples of each of these propaganda techniques. Master storytellers like Charles Dickens know how to use such techniques deftly to develop complicated plots. When discussing environmental issues in a science class, would proponents of industry be likely to take a different position than Greenpeace? How might this difference be manifested in propaganda techniques?

Activity 6.12 provides a sample activity for teaching students to recognize propaganda. Students are asked to match statements to the propaganda technique they employ.

ACTIVITY 6.12   SPOTTING PROPAGANDA

Match each statement with the propaganda technique used.

_____   1. Come on down to Charlie Winkler's Auto before every one of these beauties is sold.
_____   2. Michael Jordan, former Chicago Bulls star, thinks Nike shoes are the best.
_____   3. You'll be glowing all over in your new Evening Time gown.
_____   4. Why, people in every walk of life buy our product.
_____   5. Join the American Dining Club today, a way of life for those who enjoy the good life.
_____   6. Already, over 85% of our workers have given to this worthy cause.
_____   7. I'll stack our doughnut makers up against any others, as the best in the business!
_____   8. Even butcher Fred Jones likes our new frozen yogurt coolers.
_____   9. One must drink our wine to appreciate the truly fine things in life.
_____ 10. Lift the weights that Arnold Schwartzenegger lifts—a sure way to a better body.
   a. appeal to bandwagon
   b. emotional language
   c. appeal to prestige
   d. plain-folks appeal
   e. testimonial

Activities That Foster Critical Thinking

An activity appropriate to any grade level is **brainstorming**. Brainstorming is reflective and creative in nature; it differs from factstorming, introduced in Chapter 4, which seeks to elicit prior factual knowledge. Brainstorming sessions can last from ten minutes to an hour and can be designed to teach any of the techniques discussed in this chapter. An especially productive brainstorming session is one in which small groups of students list as many possible alternative solutions to a problem as they can. Group captains are chosen to report findings to the entire class. The teacher lists on the chalkboard alternatives deemed worthy by the class. Discussion then centers on how choices can be narrowed to one or two and why the final choices are the best ones. The critical thinking paradigm can be emphasized as the framework for the lesson. An important consideration in these sessions is the size of the brainstorming group. Five-person groups seem to work best; however, three- and four-person groups are also suitable. With groups of six students or more, the more vocal students tend to dominate.

The "ready reading reference bookmark" (Figure 6.2) developed by Kapinus (1986) can be used to get students ready to brainstorm after reading a passage. In the section "After you read," students can use brainstorming to perform the

FIGURE 6.2

Ready reading reference bookmark (reprinted with permission of Barbara Kapinus, Maryland State Department of Education).

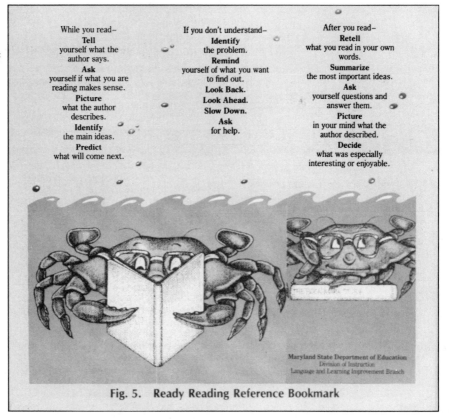

While you read—
Tell yourself what the author says.
Ask yourself if what you are reading makes sense.
Picture what the author describes.
Identify the main ideas.
Predict what will come next.

If you don't understand—
Identify the problem.
Remind yourself of what you want to find out.
Look Back.
Look Ahead.
Slow Down.
Ask for help.

After you read—
Retell what you read in your own words.
Summarize the most important ideas.
Ask yourself questions and answer them.
Picture in your mind what the author described.
Decide what was especially interesting or enjoyable.

Maryland State Department of Education
Division of Instruction
Language and Learning Improvement Branch

Fig. 5.   **Ready Reading Reference Bookmark**

five thinking operations called for: retelling, summarizing, asking, picturing, and deciding. Students can also brainstorm the "While you read" and "If you don't understand" operations at other points in the lesson — before reading, for example, or after reading specific sections.

I-charts support critical thinking, as they encourage students to use communicative-arts skills and take an independent role in learning content material. The *I* stands for *inquiry*. Hoffman (1992) proposes that I-charts offer a way for readers to reflect through reading and writing about their learning. They foster a dynamic, critical thinking process.

The use of I-charts involves three phases:

1. *Planning*. The topic is identified, and a chart is constructed.
2. *Interacting*. Learners think about their prior knowledge of the topic and begin reading and recording.
3. *Integrating/evaluating*. Learners study the information they have recorded on their charts to summarize, compare, research, and report.

The teacher will generally start the I-chart by designing and presenting it to a class, then refer to it as the class reads. The students take over as they fill in the chart and use it to study and learn. "The ultimate goal," writes Hoffman, "would be for students to take a blank I-chart and work through the entire inquiry process independently" (p. 126). One of the authors used a variation called jot charts — because students jotted information down on them — to stimulate fairly passive secondary students to take part in their own learning process. Months after she had left the classroom, one student wrote to her that the students were still creating jot charts and reported that they "dreamed about jot charts almost nightly"!

ACTIVITY 6.13		JOT CHART: NESTING BEHAVIOR OF DINOSAURS			
Dinosaur Species	Description	Method of Birth	Embryo Development at Hatching	Parental Feeding of Newborn	Parental Protection of Newborn
Orodromeus makelai	• Walked on 2 legs • 8 feet high • Embryos 8″–9″	• Hatched from eggs	• Bones developed • Able to walk	• Probably did *not* bring food to nest	• Probably did *not* protect
Maiasaura peeblesorum (duck bills)	• Walked on 2 legs • 30 feet high • Embryos 1″	• Hatched from eggs	• Bones *not* developed • Unable to walk	• Probably did bring food to nest	• Probably did protect

---

A C T I V I T Y 6 . 1 4   **JOT CHART: READING A GUIDE SHEET**

Skim the front of the guide sheet. List six major headings. List three facts about each major point. Find vocabulary words and write them in the last column.

Major Points	Three Facts	Vocabulary Words
Select pattern pieces	The number of pieces given. What the pieces are going to look like. The letter is to tell you what it stands for.	
Cutting and marking	What to do before you cut. What to do after cutting. Shows you some more special cutting notes.	preshrink press
Cutting layouts	Shows sizes. Tell you what pieces to use. Shows inches and centimeters.	nap dots
The pattern	Tells what the symbols mean. How to adjust pattern. Tells you what a normal seam allowance is.	grain line notches cutting line seam line seam allowance selvage
The jumper	Shows sizes. Shows inches and centimeters. Shows the pieces used.	nap selvage
Short overalls	Shows the pieces used. Shows inches and centimeters. Show sizes.	nap selvage

Developed by Frances Lila Mait.

We present four examples of jot charts to demonstrate their diversity in activating reflective readers. The chart in Activity 6.13 was developed for an elementary science unit. Activity 6.14 shows a chart developed for a middle-school home economics class. Activity 6.15 depicts an algebra chart. Activity 6.16 is the "master" handed out by a high school English teacher at the start of a unit; students are expected to fill it in as they reflect on each story.

Another activity that uses cooperative groups and student discussion to build reflection skills is TRIP (Think/Reflect in Pairs). For this activity, the teacher

A C T I V I T Y   6 . 1 5   JOT CHART: ALGEBRA

Shape	Picture	Circumference	Area
Circle		$2\pi r$	πr^2
Triangle		$a + b + c$	$\frac{1}{2}bh$
Square		$4x$	x^2
Rectangle		$2l + 2w$	lw
Cone		——	$\frac{1}{3}\pi r^2 h$
Rectangular Box		——	lwh

Developed by Serena Marshall.

ACTIVITY 6.16   JOT CHART: SHORT STORY PLOTS

Directions: As each story is read, fill in the information about plot development. The events are listed on the board. They are not in the correct order.

	"The Monkey's Paw" (p. 2)	"The Most Dangerous Game" (p. 11)	"Sixteen" (p. 27)
Theme			
Exposition			
Narrative hook			
Rising action			
Climax			
Falling action			
Resolution			

Developed by Linda Cobb.

divides students into pairs. Students share information on TRIP cards, which list propaganda techniques or situational problems. Answers are printed on the back of the cards for immediate reinforcement. Points may be assigned to correct answers, with a designated number of points needed for a good grade in the class. For a different TRIP, students are presented problems from a textbook. They first solve the problem in pairs, then write the problem on the front and the answer on the back of a card. In this manner, students create their own TRIP files for reinforcement or future use. Activity 6.17 shows the front and back of a sample TRIP card. Activity 6.18 shows four TRIP cards made by an eighth-grade civics class.

```
A C T I V I T Y   6 . 1 7          SAMPLE TRIP CARD: PROPAGANDA TECHNIQUES
```

Front	Back
A manufacturer gets a World War II hero to make a statement praising his product. Name the propaganda technique being employed.	testimonial This correct answer worth 5 points.

Extending the Reading Experience

Extensions of the reading experience to include reflection can take many forms: further reading about the topic, additional activities from the teachers' manuals, oral presentations, guest speakers, class reports, or group debates. These activities are valuable and important because they can provide a pleasurable association with the content being studied.

Whenever possible, concrete and entertaining activities will help cement learning for students and leave them with a good feeling about the content. Field trips, videotapes, television programs, and films are examples. Many teachers use writing activities at the extension stage of reading. Chapter 8 presents several such activities. Most teachers are familiar with extension activities because these activities are so often included in teachers' manuals. Therefore, we discuss fewer of them in this chapter.

Emphasis on multitext activities is suggested in many teachers' manuals. Often teachers feel too rushed to cover curriculum and skip this enriching resource. However, research supports the use of many reading materials to solidify learning about a topic. Chapter 3 explains multitext activities in detail, including ways of selecting materials appropriately matched to student needs. In that chapter, the suggested use for multitext is preparation. Using a multitext approach also helps readers reflect by extending their knowledge of a topic after study. Chapter 12 explores in depth the use of literature in content-area study.

Schadt (1989) describes the *literary gift exchange* as a way to enrich readers. Each student brings an object reminiscent of a character or action from literature read in the content area and exchanges it with a designated partner. Students must be able to explain their gifts. Schadt noticed that students began to reread material after he initiated the exchange procedure.

Having students design *post graphic organizers* is an enriching activity that students of all ages enjoy. After reading is completed, students form groups.

ACTIVITY 6.18   FOUR TRIP CARDS: EIGHTH-GRADE CIVICS

Front	**Back**
You must choose between Chic jeans that are priced 50% off and a pair of Levis. What is considered in your decision?	The balance between the cost to you and the benefit you think you will receive from it. This correct answer worth 25 points.
The amounts of a product or service buyers are willing and able to buy at different prices. This defines what term?	Demand This correct answer worth 5 points.
All the farmers have raised the price of strawberries from 50 cents to 90 cents a basket. How will this impact demand?	Demand will decrease. This correct answer worth 5 points.
Your employer must make payments for the capital he uses. What are these payments for the use of capital called?	Interest This correct answer worth 5 points.

Developed by Carol Holmes.

Each group selects a theme for the material studied and designs a way to present the material visually to the rest of the class. A group of secondary social studies students created the post graphic organizer shown in Activity 6.19. It was their representation of an article about prison reform.

Demonstrating Learning

Part of reflection often involves tests of learning. This is the time when the product of comprehension is demonstrated, whether through formal tests or other means of assigning grades that represent a measure of learning. (For an illustration of the relationship between process and product, see Chapter 5, Figure 5.1).

Test Results as Products of Learning

A product results from understanding. Tests are the major way in which this product is derived. There comes a time when the readers have read and thought about the material. The words have been learned, the relationships have been built, patterns of organization have been identified, and activities have facilitated a satisfactory understanding. In short, comprehension has been developed. It is time to measure the learning achieved by determining comprehension.

Tests are the culmination of periods of study about a content topic. Tests come in many forms, from informal observations of student learning to formal final exams. Students' ages and the topics covered will make a difference in the type of assessment to be made. Teachers do need to test in some way; that is part of their instruction.

Tests should match the learning, not vice versa. Beyer (1984) writes: "Much so-called teaching of thinking skills consists largely of giving students practice in answering old test questions, a procedure that probably focuses students' attention more on question-answering techniques than on the specific cognitive skills that are the intended outcomes of such activities" (p. 486). Rather than giving practice with stale questions, teachers will want to discover ways to introduce "zest" into their tests as well as into their teaching strategies, thus eliciting the cognitive skills that are the ultimate goal of instruction.

PURPOSES OF TESTING

The main purpose for giving a test is to determine comprehension by assessing student-generated products that demonstrate learning. The usual format is that teachers ask questions about what they have taught and students answer them. These answers are then evaluated by the teachers to determine how well the material was learned. A secondary reason for testing is that tests provide teachers with grades. Test grades are a form of progress report to students, parents, and administrators.

In addition, test responses give teachers material they can study to evaluate their presentation of material. Although overlooked in the past, this purpose for

ACTIVITY 6.19 POST GRAPHIC ORGANIZER

CRIME AND PUNISHMENT
Corruption of minor offenders and juveniles
Antisocial behavior (juveniles)
1790's
Branding
Abandonment
Embitterment
penitent?
Cruelty
Whippings
Reform!
Pennsylvania
Expensive $
Promotes insanity
Auburn
Not allowed to speak
Solitary confinement allowed for meditation and penitence
Paid for itself
Worked together during the day
More humane (less insanity)
Alone at night

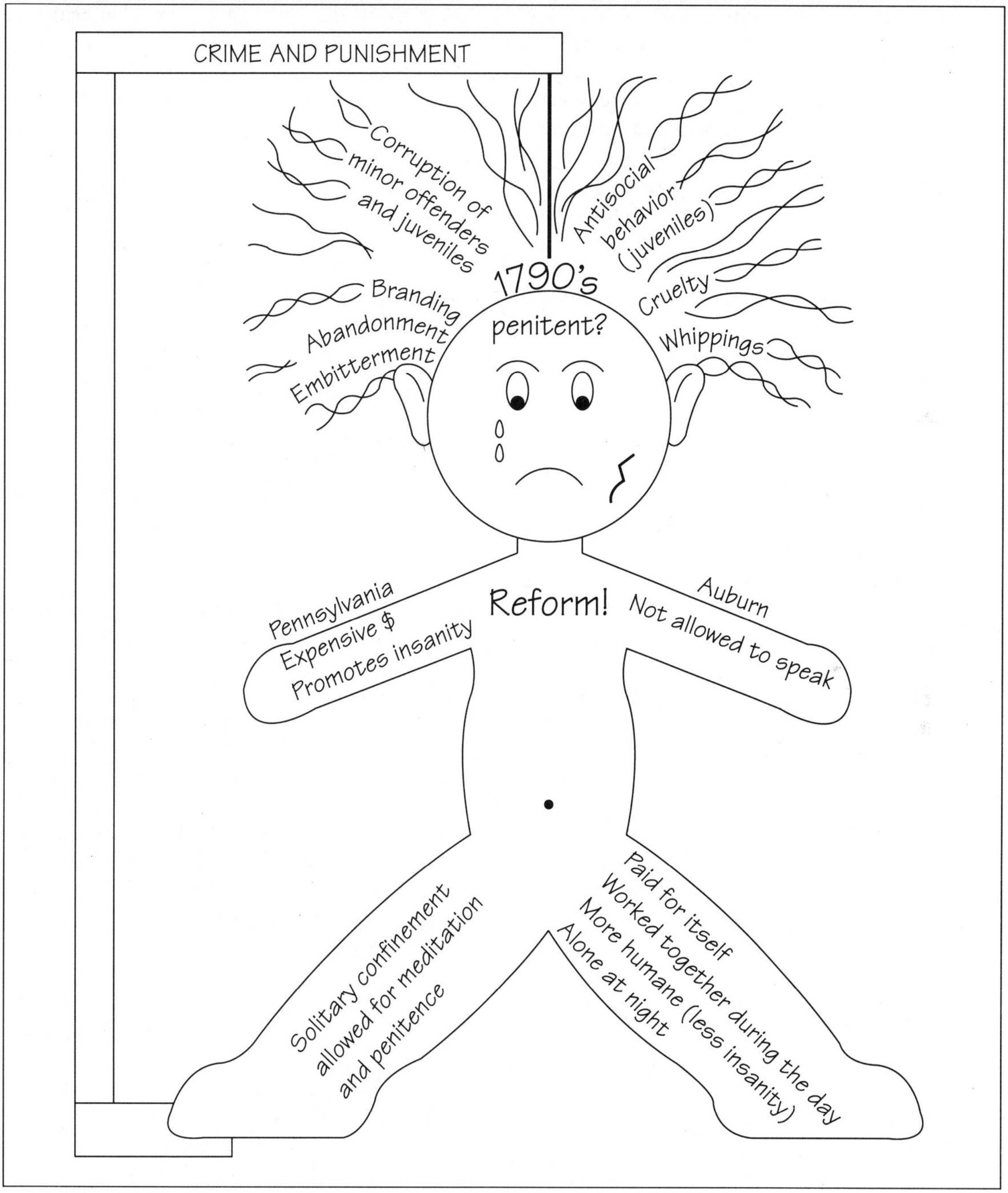

testing has the greatest potential for creating an optimal reading/thinking/learning environment in classrooms. If several students can produce fine responses to questions, teachers may conclude not only that students are confident with the topic but also that they as teachers are presenting the content in ways that assist comprehension effectively. If several students cannot produce satisfactory answers, it is very possible that the material should be retaught using different instructional strategies. When teachers consider tests as a way to evaluate their instruction as well as to determine students' current knowledge levels and to assign grades, they will find that they often alter their instruction and revise their tests. The effect is that both teachers and students begin to improve at their respective jobs.

THE ROLE OF POP QUIZZES IN COMPREHENSION

The use of pop quizzes can confuse the roles of assisting versus measuring comprehension. Teachers probably give pop quizzes to find out if students read the assignment. But suppose students *attempted* to read the assignment and experienced difficulty? In this case, students may be penalized for not understanding rather than not reading the material. They require assistance before they will be able to demonstrate learning.

Nessel (1987) comments that question-and-answer sessions that do not develop understanding "amount to a thinly disguised test, not a true exchange of ideas" (p. 443). When question-and-answer sessions become drills, teachers will not be able to determine whether the question was misunderstood or poorly phrased or whether the student had difficulty constructing a response. Unless teachers use pop quizzes for instruction rather than for grading, they will defeat their own purposes and send an incorrect message to students: it's not important to *understand* the material, just to recount it!

Instead, pop quizzes should be used to test for a product that teachers can be reasonably sure has been achieved. For instance, rather than "popping" at students questions that will be graded, a teacher could check to see if students followed instructions for reading an assignment. A teacher could also use a writing activity such as those described in Chapter 8 to make sure homework was attempted. If understanding the homework was the problem, the students' written comments will show the teacher that an attempt was made. If students do this, they demonstrate that they have tried to read for the assigned purpose. This demonstration will accomplish the same purpose as a pop quiz.

The homework comprehension sheet designed by a middle-school social studies teacher (Activity 6.20) is an example of how a teacher can tell if students attempted their homework. This activity will also help the teacher to focus the lesson. Students surveyed the reading and wrote three questions they expected to answer from it before the reading was assigned as homework. When students arrived in class the following day, the teacher distributed this exercise.

The teacher can rapidly review responses to a homework comprehension sheet to find out who has completed the assignment. Areas of student confusion

---

A C T I V I T Y   6 . 2 0   **HOMEWORK COMPREHENSION SHEET**

On this paper (front and back) I want you to answer the following questions as completely as you can.

1. How did you study pages 192–194 in Social Studies?
2. What did you learn from these pages?
3. Do you see any similarities between your life and the life of the people mentioned?
4. Were there any passages, terms, or concepts you found difficult to understand?
5. What part of this reading did you find most interesting?
6. How do you feel you answered these questions?
7. Why do you feel the way you do?

Developed by Charles Carroll.

---

as well as student interests can be ascertained. This activity serves as a check of homework and also as a way to determine student background for the rest of the lesson.

We encourage teachers to think carefully about why they plan to administer a pop quiz, then design that quiz according to their objectives. If the objective is to promote student independence and responsibility, then the social studies teacher's solution works very well. If it is to "catch" students, we ask teachers to please think again about assisting versus measuring comprehension.

Traditional Tests

Most of us can describe tests. We have taken many of them and, if we are practicing teachers, have administered a few. Test items are usually phrased as objective questions, essay questions, or a combination. Objective tests include multiple-choice, true/false, matching, and completion questions. Teachers find such items easy to grade but more difficult to phrase. Students sometimes label objective items as "tricky," "confusing," or even "too easy." Essay tests require students to write about a given topic. The parameters of the expected response are provided by the teacher within the question. Essay formats are also labeled "subjective" to indicate that teachers must spend time considering responses carefully when grading. Students sometimes label essay questions as "confusing," "too hard," or "not fair." We hope to convince you that essay questions are not subjective when questions are written carefully, nor are they difficult to grade when they are carefully constructed. Furthermore, essay questions are a viable solution to testing critical thinking and the applied level of comprehension.

STANDARDIZED, NORM-REFERENCED TESTS

Standardized, norm-referenced tests were introduced briefly in Chapter 4 as a source of information about students' background knowledge in the content to be studied. Of course, the major purpose of standardized tests is to test information known about a subject; therefore, standardized tests are the ultimate traditional test. They consist usually of multiple-choice or closure questions, which are readily and quickly scored by hand or by computerized scan sheets. One correct answer is expected per item. Many classroom teachers follow standardized test formats as they construct classroom tests.

A major purpose for using standardized tests is to compare the performance of groups, such as the results from one school compared to those of a school system, or a system to the state, or the state to the nation. The test is designed with care by a group of experts and pilot tested on a representative sample of students. The results are studied, the test is modified, and a set of norms is developed. These norms become the basis for comparing results; hence the term *norm-referenced* is often used to describe standardized tests. Scores on a standardized test are rendered according to consistent measures, such as percentiles, stanines, standard score equivalents, grade equivalents, or normal curve equivalents.

Not all standardized tests are equally satisfactory to all users. Perhaps the norming group is not representative of the particular population to be tested. Perhaps the items on the test do not reflect the content taught to the students tested. Perhaps the test purports to test content that, in fact, it does not really test. However, standardized tests are subject to a system of checks that help users make appropriate selections. These measurement concepts include validity and reliability. Validity is the "truthfulness" of the test—a check of whether the standardized test actually measures what it claims to measure. Reliability is the "consistency" of the test—whether it will produce roughly the same results if administered more than once to the same group in the same time period. In other words, reliability is a check of how dependable the test is.

Because the main purpose of a standardized test is to compare the performance of groups rather than to provide a measure of individual student performance and a grade, teachers do not usually rely on these tests in their classroom testing. If such a use were pertinent, the teacher would select the standardized test that was best suited to classroom use by asking:

1. Does this test measure what I have taught?
2. Can I depend on it to give about the same results if I administered it today and tomorrow?
3. Is the norming group similar to my group of students?

Often such questions do not yield satisfactory answers, but standardized tests will be used by the school system as a measure of performance anyhow. In this case, teachers should seek more authentic assessment procedures for their own classrooms in order to supplement the standardized approach.

CRITERION-REFERENCED TESTS

Criterion-referenced tests are less formal than standardized tests. Their format is much like that of standardized tests, usually multiple-choice or closure. In fact, criterion-referenced tests can be standardized, but the results are not meant for comparison, so they are usually not normed. Because they are less formal, short-answer, true/false, and other objective-type items might be included. The purpose of criterion-referenced tests is to measure whether a student can perform a specific task or knows a specific body of knowledge. Thus, their purpose is closer to that of classroom tests.

The criterion is the level of performance necessary to indicate that a student "knows" the task. This criterion is decided by the educators using the test. Thus, two schools could use the same test but set a different criterion. One school might set 85% as a passing score, and the other might set 90% as passing. The level of performance on the task is the score: a score of 85% means that the student responded correctly to 85% of the items. Whether that is acceptable is decided by the test user. No grade-equivalent score, stanines, or other scores are determined.

Because criterion-referenced tests indicate mastery of a task, they should be based on specific objectives. For example, the objective might be stated: "The student will demonstrate mastery by correctly identifying 48 of 50 states and their capitals." If a student has been taught 50 states and capitals and can identify 48 on the test, that student has demonstrated mastery of the criterion.

When criterion-referenced tests are designed by educators to test a general body of content and are disseminated for testing and scoring from a central base, such as a publishing company or a state department of education, they become more like standardized tests in that they are now uniform in item construction, administration, and use. If teachers elect to use a criterion-referenced test developed by an outside source, they should select the best one by asking:

1. Do the objectives and criteria match my objectives in this content?
2. Are there enough items included to give me a good indication that my students have met the criteria?
3. Do the test items reflect the way in which I taught the information?

Again, if answers are not satisfactory to the classroom teacher, then a more authentic means of assessment should also be used before student performance can be thoroughly assessed.

Criterion-referenced tests are not new; only their evolution into more uniform, formalized tests is. In fact, the concept of criterion mastery is what teachers rely on as they design classroom tests. Thus, most of our discussion in this chapter is based on tests that are criterion referenced but designed by individual teachers for individual classroom use.

PROBLEMS WITH TRADITIONAL TESTS

The single greatest problem with traditional tests is that the grades students receive on them are very often disappointing to teachers. We think that the single best solution to this problem is that teachers stop "jumping the gun" by giving tests before students have experienced preparation and assistance. Yet, even allowing for this solution, many other problems with traditional tests have been identified.

Captrends ("Window on the classroom," 1984) reports a study of 342 teacher-made tests in a Cleveland, Ohio, school district. Tests from all grade levels were reviewed by administrators, supervisors, and teachers representing all subject areas. The format these reviewers found throughout the tests was similar to that described by us. Teachers had designed objective, short-answer tests. Only 2% of all items in the 342 tests were essay-type.

The researchers found many problems with the presentation of the test items. Directions were often unclear, sometimes nonexistent. Poor legibility, incorrect grammar, and weak writing skills made some items difficult to read. Point values for test items and sections were noticeably absent. Ambiguity in questions led to the possibility of more than one correct response or student confusion about choices to make in responding to items.

In addition, the types of questions asked were predominantly literal. Almost 80% of all items concentrated on knowledge of facts, terms, and rules. The middle-school tests used literal questions even more than the elementary or high school tests did. Questions at the application level of comprehension accounted for only 3% of all questions asked. (Hathaway, 1983, provides a more complete description of this project.)

After studying content-area reading instruction, many of the authors' students take a hard look at tests they have been giving to their own students. One eighth-grade English teacher found that, on one of her original tests, "the primary comprehension focus was a mixture of all three levels, but more literal and inferential than application . . . comprehension was dependent on recall more than real learning . . . the test was too long and *looked* hard . . . I neglected to give point values or the weight of the test in the final grade" (Baxter, 1985). This teacher revised her test and summarized her satisfaction with the new version in this way:

> All in all, I feel that the best feature of my redesigned test is that it captures many concepts and is in a more appealing form. In relation to the original test, I feel this test allows the student to demonstrate more of his/her knowledge of the material covered in the unit by giving specific responses, especially in the discussion section. I feel this test will net better student response because it appears shorter, looks more appealing, and is different from usual tests I would have given in similar teaching situations before.

A tenth-grade science teacher (Vess, 1985) concluded that her test was cluttered, with 50 objective items crowded on one and one-half pages. In addition, her test was based on literal comprehension, rewarding memory rather than critical thinking. She realized that she had paid little attention to concepts or a progression from the factual to the applied. Another teacher (Givler, 1986) labeled her original test "Exhibit #1 — The Stone Age." Her second attempt became "Exhibit #2 — The Bronze Age," and her third attempt "Exhibit #3 — The Silver Age." She felt that she had not yet progressed to "The Golden Age"!

We see five problems with teacher-designed classroom tests.

First, students today are "overstuffed and undernourished" (Dempster, 1993, p. 434) as they read to learn from textbooks. Textbooks tend to cover a plethora of material, overkilling the learner with an abundance of mentioning but not enough depth of explanation. Students are left with many details but little in-depth understanding of a topic. Tests resulting from such a bombardment of details will of course focus on details rather than major ideas.

Second, teachers seem to rely on the objective format, with factual questions dominating. We infer that teachers find such items easier to construct and more important to test. Certainly, if an excessive amount of detailed material on a topic is presented in a text, teachers would consider such questioning a logical result. Whatever the underlying reasoning, a major problem with this format is that students *will* learn what we model. If we send the message through our tests that the factual level is much more important than the interpretive or applied levels, then that is what students will learn. Even if our instruction emphasizes interpretation and application of content, the message inherent in the test questions will supercede the instructional intent. Students won't learn how to think critically if we don't require that they demonstrate such thinking on tests.

Third, teachers seem to have problems expressing themselves clearly when they write questions and construct tests. This problem may imply that teachers need more practice in writing and in expressing themselves clearly. However, it may indicate more specifically that teachers need practice in constructing good questions.

Fourth, students may not be ready for a test because they have not developed enough understanding of the topic. This problem might occur because teachers need to provide more assistance or because students have not achieved enough responsibility for their own learning.

Fifth, students must be responsible for demonstrating their learning. They need to take an active role in designing assessments that help them demonstrate what they know in relation to real-life situations. If teachers are always the ones designing tests, then students have a very limited role — regurgitating information for the teacher. This is why so many students tend to "give up" rather than study; they don't see any point to a test that doesn't seem "real" to them.

Suggestions for Improving Test Design

In the remainder of this chapter, we will suggest several strategies that can help teachers present improved alternatives to the tests they are now using.

Many teachers prefer the traditional test. There is great value in what is known and experienced. By reviewing the questioning traps and tips presented earlier in this chapter and applying them to constructing test items, teachers can improve traditional tests immensely. In constructing traditional tests, teachers should keep in mind the following general guidelines.

1. Questions on a test should reflect a balance among the three basic comprehension levels.

2. The difficulty of questions should be related to the task required. Recall is harder than recognition; production is harder than recall. Questions with several

parts are more difficult than questions with one part. Selecting is easier than generating. Teachers will want to vary their use of difficult and easier questions within a test.

3. Sometimes the answer a student gives is unanticipated but better than the expected response. Teachers will want to write questions carefully to avoid ambiguity but still encourage spontaneous critical thinking.

4. The best-worded test items do not provide secondary clues to the correct answer. Carter (1986) found that teachers often give inadvertent clues to students, who are very facile at discerning this giveaway. For instance, students learn that correct answers on a multiple-choice test are often keyed to choice C; the longest choice is more likely to be the correct answer; the stem will often have one obvious match among the multiple choices. Students realize that for both multiple-choice and true/false items, positive statements are more likely to be correct choices than negative statements. Teachers sometimes give answers away with grammatical clues. With Carter's study in mind, teachers will want to express themselves very carefully!

5. When wording test items, teachers need to consider their students' language proficiency. A well-worded test that does not match the students' knowledge of language will result in poor comprehension, even though the students' learning may be excellent. Drum, Calfee, and Cook (1981) caution:

> The abilities needed for successful test performance on a comprehension test include the following:
>
> Accurate and fluent word recognition;
>
> Knowledge of specific word meanings;
>
> Knowledge of syntactic/semantic clause and sentence relationships;
>
> Recognition of the superordinate/subordinate idea structure of passages;
>
> Identification of the specific information requested in questions; and
>
> Evaluation of the alternate choices in order to select the one that best fits. (pp. 488–489)

Improvements in Preparing and Assisting Students with Traditional Tests

By using PAR, teachers will have fulfilled much of their instructional role in readying students to take tests. We have found that certain other techniques also prepare and assist students in test performance.

First, teachers who encourage students to use study questions find this technique very helpful. Study questions can be used in a variety of ways. Initially, the teacher might prepare a list of questions to be included on the test. This list could be distributed at the beginning of a unit, for handy reference throughout the unit. Or the teacher could suggest possible questions while the information is being presented, and then collate all of the questions after the unit is completed. With essay questions, this list can become the pool for test items. The teacher might tell students that only questions from this list will be found on the test. Such a technique has merit for two reasons: a test bank is acquired as the unit progresses, thus eliminating last-minute test construction; and students have a study guide that is familiar and nonthreatening but very thorough. If the teacher has created questions that follow the question-construction guidelines and has covered representative content with these questions, the technique works well.

Some teachers advise students before testing what the specific test questions will be. This technique works better with essay questions than with objective questions. Although many teachers are hesitant about providing questions in advance, fearing that students will then not study everything, this can be a wise way to prepare and assist students. The fact is that students cannot study everything anyhow, and they certainly cannot remember everything for a long period of time. If the essential information is covered in the proposed questions, then a question list can be very effective.

Having students create the questions for a test is sometimes a good technique. This option requires that students understand the content thoroughly and also understand how to write good questions. An alternative for younger students and those not as proficient at question construction is to have students use brainstorming to predict possible test topics and then informally generate questions. A first-grader could speculate: "I think you might ask me to explain about how fish breathe." Students can construct possible items for an objective as well as an essay test, or they can review items from sample tests the teacher provides. If teachers encourage students to create possible test questions, they should also include some version of the students' questions on the actual test.

Any variation on student construction of the test questions will provide them with practice in the art of questioning and answering, provoke critical thinking, and promote the students' responsibility for their own learning. A further bonus is that when students are familiar with the teacher's way of designing a test, they will be less anxious about being tested. Test anxiety accounts for much poor test response.

Second, teachers have also found that allowing students to use open books or open notes — or both — enables students to concentrate on producing the best responses on a test and assists them in the actual test-taking process. Such a technique encourages good note-taking strategies and clear organization of information by promoting recognition and production rather than recall. All of these practices contribute to the likelihood of a desirable product.

Nontraditional Tests

Everyone appreciates variety. Teachers may be pleasantly surprised that students increase productivity when the measurement device looks more like the strategies that have been used to instruct than the same old test format. "Conventional policy-based testing . . . is the wrong kind of tool for thoughtfulness. It makes people accountable only for the development of very low levels of knowledge and skill" (R. Brown, 1987, p. 5). Although Brown's comments refer specifically to standardized tests, we think they are applicable to teacher-made tests as well. Novak and Gowin (1984) encourage teachers to use new strategies for testing, arguing that even when poorly made objective tests are redesigned, they do not correlate with the type of achievement required in a world where concepts are more important than facts. They contend that we must alter our testing procedures if we want to produce critical, thoughtful readers. They also argue that creative thinkers often perform much better on tests that are nontraditional and reflect nontraditional instructional activities.

By employing some of the strategies presented in this text, teachers can construct tests that contain few traditional items. The most nontraditional test would eliminate questioning altogether. Although teachers may not wish to design an entire test with no questions, some nontraditional items might spark interest. Primary teachers are especially attracted by nontraditional tests, and intermediate and secondary teachers may prefer adding some nontraditional items to a more traditional test. The possibilities are as numerous as the types of activities presented in this text.

The following activities can be used as nontraditional test items. Teachers who have designed tests using such items report that they elicit more critical thinking from their students. Although only two examples can be presented, we are sure that teachers will see the possibilities for designing many activities as nontraditional test items.

GRAPHIC ORGANIZERS

At the beginning of each chapter in this text is a graphic organizer. At the end of some chapters, the organizer is repeated, but with gaps; the reader is asked to try to identify what is missing and recall where it should be placed within the organizer. This activity encourages readers to make sure they understand what they have read. Similarly, a teacher can instruct using a graphic organizer, map, structured overview, jot chart, or any such visual aid and then present this organizer with blanks on a test. It then becomes a nontraditional test item for eliciting responses that demonstrate knowledge of facts. Such is the case with the example in Activity 6.21, designed by an 11th-grade teacher. If the teacher provides a list of terms that could complete the organizer, then recognition of facts is tested. Such is the case in the example in Activity 6.22, designed by a second-grade teacher.

If a teacher asks students to *explain* why they have positioned words at certain points on the organizer, then the interpretive level of comprehension is being tested. If the teacher asks students to *create* an organizer using terms they have learned during the lesson, the applied level of comprehension is demonstrated. No traditional questions have been asked, yet comprehension can be determined and a product can be graded. The test item might read as follows:

> Study the organizer I have drawn for you. It is like the one we studied in class, but in this one there are several blank spaces. Using the list of terms attached, fill in the term that fits best in each space (1 point each). Now, write one sentence beside each term listed; this sentence should explain why you think the term belongs where you put it in the organizer (2 points each). Next, write an essay that includes the information in this organizer. Your first paragraph should talk about the main idea; your second paragraph should provide four (4) details; your third paragraph should summarize by telling what new information you have learned by reading this chapter (25 points).

ACTIVITY 6.21   GEOMETRY ORGANIZER

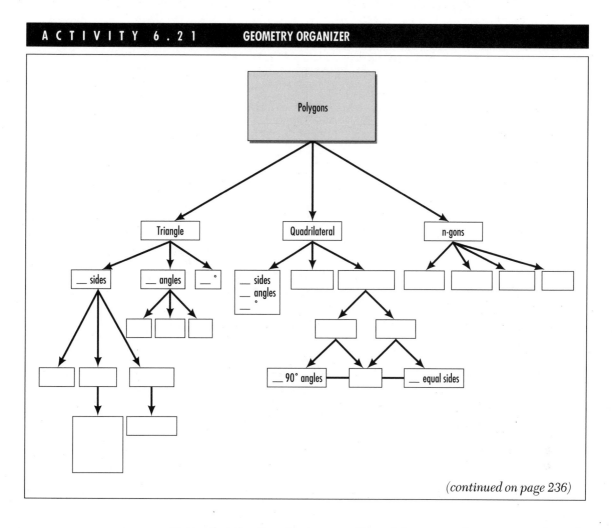

(continued on page 236)

Notice that the directions are specific and that point values are given for each procedure. A visual aid would be provided as well as the list of terms. Factual knowledge is tested, but some interpretation and application are also required. Writing an essay is also a part of this question. Because the components of the essay are defined, grading it should be simplified.

FACTSTORMING

Factstorming is a good preparation activity because students identify familiar terms about a topic before they study further. If a teacher takes a list produced by factstorming and asks students to add to that list *after* the study has been completed, the additions become a measure of new learning. If students are asked to explain each addition, they are demonstrating interpretation of infor-

A C T I V I T Y   6 . 2 1   **CONTINUED**

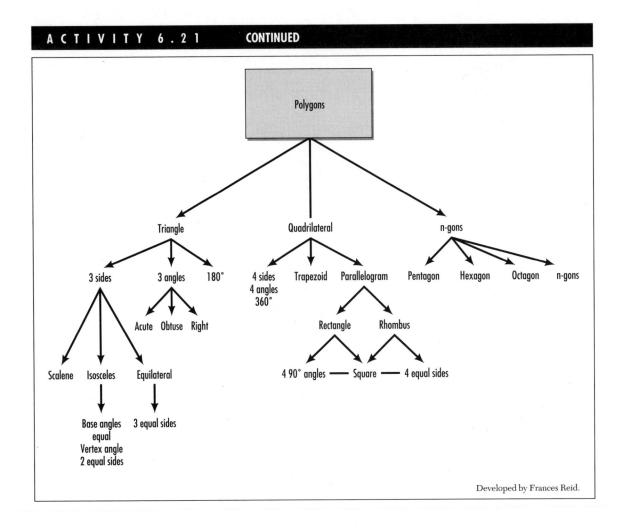

Developed by Frances Reid.

mation. If students categorize the already-known and new information and then write an essay about this categorization, application is demonstrated. Using factstorming as a test item is similar to the last step in either a KWL or a What-I-Know (WIK) activity, but now it is to be graded.

Encouraging Student Responsibility

Assessment can be designed that encourages students to take responsibility for their own learning. Coleman et al. (1969) have stated that students need to perceive themselves as having a significant influence over their own educational destinies. Negative perceptions are often the result of a passive learning situation in which children accept control by others as their fate. Ideally, students should view assessment as an opportunity to express what they have learned rather than as an exercise in futility. How can such an active view of assessment be implemented?

A C T I V I T Y 6 . 2 2   SOCIAL STUDIES ORGANIZER

Description of Activity: The students fill in a graphic organizer to determine comprehension. The overview was previously introduced on an overhead projector to help build background of key concepts in the unit. The students received a copy of the organizer to take home and study. The graphic organizer is presented to the Chapter 1 students as a posttest at the conclusion of the unit. Since Chapter 1 students may have a difficult time remembering the concept names, an answer key has to be included with the organizer.

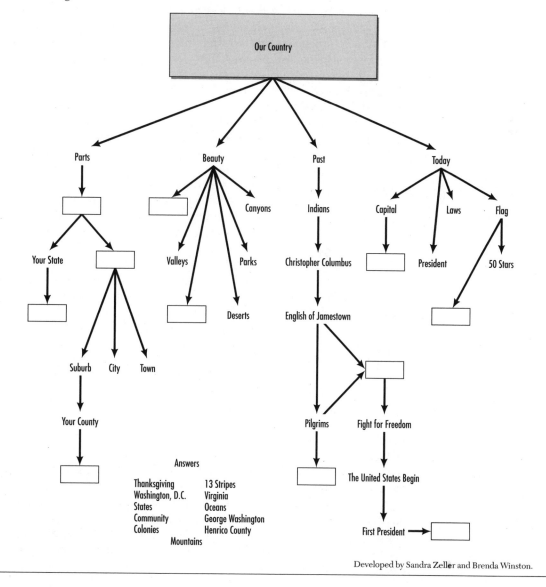

Developed by Sandra Zeller and Brenda Winston.

First, we provide some ideas specific to traditional and nontraditional test formats. Next, we suggest a more encompassing approach to assessment than specific testing.

A TEST PAR

Teachers can design tests with a self-rating included on the test. Hoffman (1983) originated this rating technique to be used in journal entries. Richardson (1992b) has created a version for tests. The first questions on a test might be: How did you study for this test? How much did you study? How well do you think you will do? The answers show how the students prepared. Before the test is returned, a second set of questions should be asked: Now that you have taken the test, and before it is returned, was this test what you expected and prepared for? What grade do you think you will receive? This question can assist the student in taking responsibility for studying and producing a good test response. The third set of questions promotes reflection. It is answered after the teacher has returned and reviewed the test with students: Now that you have gone over your test, would you say that you studied adequately? Was your grade representative of your learning? Why or why not? What have you learned about taking tests?

Such a three-step process built into the testing procedure will send the message that the student is ultimately responsible for producing a demonstration of learning. If teachers use the procedure often on tests, the student should begin to take a more and more active role. Teachers will also be enlightened by students' views of studying and taking tests. This information can aid teachers in instruction and in constructing tests. Student responses to such questions also foster writing opportunities.

For this test PAR to work, teachers should grade and return tests promptly. The answers should be reviewed — through written comments on the tests, in-class discussion, or both — so that students can use the test as a learning experience for the next test. Only under these conditions can an environment for reflection be assured. One of the requirements for designing good tests is to use previous tests as the base for constructing new tests. Students certainly learn how to take an individual teacher's tests by learning that teacher's style. Teachers should learn how to design tests by learning the students' styles as well. Did students need clearer directions? Did they use appropriate study procedures? Do they need reminders about certain test procedures?

SCORER

SCORER (Carmen & Adams, 1972; Lee & Allen, 1981) is a test-taking strategy. High SCORERs **S**chedule their time; identify the **C**lue words to help answer the questions (the directions should contain them); **O**mit the hardest items, at least at first; **R**ead carefully to be sure they understand and fully answer the question; **E**stimate what should be included in the response, perhaps by jotting down some notes or an outline; and **R**eview their responses before turning in the test. Teachers might teach SCORER to students and then insert the acronym into test directions or include it as a reminder on tests. Students could even be asked to account for how they used SCORER while completing the test. This strategy places responsibility on students to take a test wisely, in an organized and comprehensive manner. SCORER can be used as part of any test design.

HELPING STUDENTS BECOME TEST-WISE

Students should be **test-wise**. This does not mean that they should know the test items and answers before a test, although we do advocate that guiding questions and open notes are sometimes very acceptable ways to give tests. Being test-wise means that students have a plan of attack, regardless of the specific test content. They are used to taking tests. They are confident because they understand how tests are designed and can capitalize on that knowledge in demonstrating their learning. Being test-wise is knowing the program, to use Hart's terminology — or, in other words, the system. When they know how to take a test, students can concentrate their energy on answering the items. Being test-wise helps to alleviate test anxiety. Panic — the "blank mind" syndrome — can be avoided. The older mammalian brain can send encouraging messages to the newer mammalian brain, and the student can then apply thinking skills to show knowledge.

Carter's (1986) study indicated that students do discern the inadvertent clues teachers give in designing test items; such students are test-wise. Teachers want to devise clues that are deliberate, not inadvertent. In designing tests, for instance, many teachers will provide a bit of information in one question that can help students answer another question. Students who watch for these clues are SCORERs.

Studies (Scruggs, White, & Bennion, 1986; Ritter & Idol-Mastas, 1986) have indicated that instruction in test-wise skills can help students perform better on tests. An instructional session that reviews a list of test-taking tips is helpful, particularly with older students, in improving results on standardized tests. When a teacher wants students to improve performance on classroom tests, such test-wise instruction is best done in the content teacher's classroom with application to that particular test.

The following list of test-taking tips is representative, but not exhaustive, of the suggestions that teachers can draw upon in helping students become proficient test takers. We encourage teachers to study this list with the goal of designing tests that provide students with intended clues, while avoiding inadvertent ones. Students should be taught to use the intended clues to advantage. Crist and Czarnecki (1979), in *The Care and Feeding of Your Grade Point Average*, provide an entertaining way to learn test-taking tips. Their photographs, quotations, and concise advice can help teachers at any level to teach these skills.

1. Be calm.
2. Read through the entire test before answering any items. Look for questions that might provide clues to other answers.
3. Plan your time. If one question is worth several points and others are worth much less, spend the majority of the time where the greatest number of points can be made.

4. Answer first the questions on which you are most confident of your answers.

5. On objective tests, remember to be logical and reasonable. Consider your possible answers carefully. Look for "giveaway" words that indicate extremes: *all, none, never, always*. They should be avoided in selecting the correct answer. On multiple-choice items, think what the answer should be, then look at the choices. Also, eliminate implausible responses by thinking carefully about each choice.

6. For essays, jot down an outline of what you intend to write before you start writing. Be sure you understand the teacher's terms: *List* means to state a series, but *describe* means to explain the items. *Compare* means to show similarities; *contrast* means to show differences. Make sure you answer all parts of the question.

Parrish (1982) has even developed a test of test-taking ability! Teachers may find such a test to be an effective way to instruct in test-wise skills. Items would be designed to fit the students. A sample item from Parrish's test reads: "In order to read directions effectively, one should: (a) Question as one reads. (b) Read and do one step at a time. (c) Read the directions in their entirety first. (d) Read them aloud" (p. 673).

A Checklist for Designing a Test

The following list of questions summarizes the information presented in this chapter and provides a checklist for test construction. The checklist is useful to teachers who want to review previously designed tests that have produced unsatisfactory results. For further considerations concerning test construction, see Appendix E.

1. How have you prepared students to study for this test? If you suggested certain study strategies, have you asked questions that will capitalize on these strategies? For instance, if you suggested that students study causes and effects by using a pattern guide, are you designing test items that will call for demonstration of causes and effects?

2. Have you included SCORER, a self-assessment of test preparedness, or another way of reminding students about their responsibilities as test takers?

3. Do the items on your test reflect your goals and objectives in teaching this content? Test items should test what was taught. If a major objective is that students be able to name states and their capitals, how can this test measure that objective?

4. What is your primary comprehension focus? Why? If you think that factual knowledge is more important on this test than interpretation or application, can you justify this emphasis? Remember that many tests rely too much on factual questions at the expense of other levels. Be sure that this level is the most important for this test.

5. Do you require comprehension at each taxonomic level? What proportion of your questions addresses each level? What is your reasoning for this division? Remember that tests imply what kind of thinking teachers expect of their students. Have you asked your students to think broadly and deeply?

6. What types of responses are you asking of students? Will they need to recognize, recall, or produce information? A good balance of responses is usually preferable to only recognition, recall, or production. More thinking is required of students when production is requested.

7. Have you phrased your test items so that comprehension is dependent on the learned material rather than on experience or verbatim recall? Remember that although the preparation stage often calls for students to identify what they already know before a topic is taught, your test should find out what they have learned since then.

8. Is the weight of the test in the final grade clear to students? Is the weight of each item on the test clear? Is the weight of parts of an item clear within that item?

9. Did you consider alternatives to traditional test items, such as statements (instead of questions) or organizers? Is writing an important part of your test? Why or why not?

10. For objective tests, what format have you selected and why (multiple-choice, true/false, incomplete sentences, short-answer)? How many of each type did you include? Why?

11. For essay tests, have you carefully asked for all of the aspects of the answer that you are looking for? Are descriptive words (*describe, compare*) clear?

12. Is the wording on this test clear? Is the test uncluttered, with items well spaced? Does the test look appealing?

13. Have you been considerate of the needs of mainstreamed students in your test design?

Authentic Assessment

We have already suggested that students have been stuffed with literal information but often not encouraged to think about how such information can be relevant to them. In fact, traditional tests are an "obstacle to effective educational reform" (Simon, 1993, p. 1) because they do not foster the relevance that reformers advocate. **Authentic assessment**, a current national reform emphasis, is a viable solution. When teachers employ some nontraditional test items, they are moving toward authentic assessment. Authentic assessment has also been called alternative, performance-based, and process assessment.

Tests are specific measures or product samples that occur at a specified time. Authentic assessment is an alternative to the traditional test because student performance is measured or sampled over time to see how student learning develops, matures, and ultimately reflects knowledge of the concepts learned in a real context. Brady (1993) suggests that authentic assessment builds relationships among the physical environment, the people who live in that environment, the reasons for or beliefs about completing activities in that environment, and how these beliefs are manifested in human behavior. In short, authentic assessment is a means of showing students *why* they are learning, as well as a means of showing educators *what* students have learned.

Authentic assessment emphasizes "realistic, challenging, contextualized materials" (Biggs, 1992, p. 626) used over time. It can be a link between previously taught material and current instruction. As Hager and Gable (1993) state, "increased use of observational and performance-based measures, process instruments, as well as content/course specific instruction seem essential" (p. 269) to authentic assessment. Students can help decide what should be assessed, thus gaining an important role in demonstrating their own learning. Contexts include observing a performance or simulation, or completing a task in a real-world situation. Students want to do well because the real-world consequences are clear. For instance, actually driving a car is a more authentic assessment than taking a paper-and-pencil test in a Driver Education course. Or, encouraging the student to show what steps were followed in completing a math problem is a way of demonstrating logical processing of information. The process of completing the task reveals as much about the student's learning — maybe more — than the product recorded as a test grade.

Deciding on Appropriate Measures

What should be observed? How? For how long? Under what conditions? Worthen (1993) suggests that processes, such as learning logs, double-entry journals (both explained in Chapter 8), and observation notes, can reveal much about student performance over time. We know teachers who keep gummed labels on a clipboard; as they traverse the classroom, they make notes on these labels, which they later stick into a student's folder. These notes often reveal important learning patterns. Such notes can be kept in any content classroom; they could be particularly useful during science labs, reading or writing workshops, cooperative group work, or library work. Chapter 8 describes a process activity called C3B4Me which will clearly show how students improve their writing over time. Performance measures might include typing tests, oral debates, post graphic organizers, or driving a car. Wiggins (1990) suggests that a hands-on science test would be more logical than a paper-and-pencil test.

Many educators advocate the use of portfolios, such as an artist might keep to display his or her work, in which students collect representative work over time. Teachers supply each student with a folder. Teacher and students decide what types of work will be kept in the folder. At the end of a specified period of time, students designate which pieces of work in the folder show progress or demonstrate a particular accomplishment. For instance, an attitude survey, pre and post, might be the first and last pieces collected. Some measure of prior knowledge of the topic, such as a prerecognition test or anticipation guide, would provide another baseline measure (see Chapters 3 and 4). Work samples, such as jot charts, notes taken, or post graphic organizers, might be included (see Chapters 5 and 6). Quizzes, tests, and corrections could be kept in the folder. At grading time, the most representative pieces and a "best" piece could be selected. Note that both process activities and products can be collected.

Abruscato (1993) relates how Vermont has adopted writing and math portfolios as a major means of assessment statewide. The assessment includes evidence of problem-solving and communication skills. For the writing portfolio, samples included are a table of contents, a "best piece," a letter, creative writing, a personal response, a prose piece from a content area, and an on-the-spot writing sample. For the math portfolio, samples included are five to seven "best pieces," such as puzzles, a letter to the evaluator, and a collection of math work. So far, results indicate that the students who score highest on their writing read at least once a week for pleasure. The greatest problem discovered by studying the math portfolios is that students have trouble presenting their results clearly and lack variety in their approaches to solving problems. Such findings are very helpful to educators in building a more effective curriculum and enhancing learning.

Getting Started

Statewide efforts with authentic assessment are increasing, but what can an individual teacher in one classroom do? The classroom and school level are really the best places to start because the development, trial and error, dialogue, and self-criticism necessary in any new effort can occur here most readily. Teachers should "start small." It is easier to begin with authentic assessment in just one area. Remember to take samples over time; involve students in designing the assessment and collecting the samples; keep the assessment relevant; make sure that both process and product are measured; and make sure that audiences, such as the students, their parents, and administrators, will be able to understand the samples and how they demonstrate progress in learning. Authentic assessment is the ultimate nontraditional assessment. It is a challenge that can bring new enthusiasm to learning in every content area.

One-Minute Summary

Teachers must understand how to foster learning by developing reading comprehension and providing reflection before assessing. We can summarize what we have covered in this chapter by offering five keys to success.

1. *Use PAR*. By keeping the PAR steps in mind as they teach, teachers will find that students begin to understand and enjoy the content reading. The rewards are almost immediate as students perk up and get involved in their own learning. Assisting comprehension will not work without preparation; reflection will not work without assistance. PAR works when all steps are used in tandem.

2. *Model*. By demonstrating what they do to understand material as they read, teachers help students to learn. Teachers should "talk along" with their students. They need to demonstrate how they would go about learning what they are asking their students to comprehend.

3. *Provide a stimulating environment*. By offering a class where learning is enjoyable and active, teachers can encourage effective content reading. When students get to discuss, write, and help decide how they will be evaluated, they are no longer passive learners. Relevance is clear.

4. *Use reading-to-learn activities as strategic means to an end.* Almost every content reading activity introduced in this textbook has possible applications for almost every PAR step. We have presented activities to illustrate each PAR step, but we realize that these activities are only means to an end: a reader who can use the steps strategically and independently. For instance, we illustrated how the KWL/What-I-Know activity helps readers at the Preparation step. But this same activity can be useful at the Assistance and Reflection steps, as well as encouraging the reader to communicate with others. If the strategy underlying the activity is emphasized foremost, students will understand the place of the activity in helping them become reflective readers.

5. *Direct students to independence.* Adult educators write about lifelong learners. The ultimate goal of content reading is surely to produce lifelong learners. Adults prefer to learn independently. Although they may study in formal courses, they identify their own areas of concentration and structure their learning accordingly. By introducing new activities, allowing plenty of practice, and then directing students to apply the strategies learned from those activities as they read on their own, teachers show students how to become independent learners. This independence goes a long way toward ensuring that students will still be learning about your subject long after they have graduated.

End-of-Chapter Activities

Assisting Comprehension

1. Why is it important that teachers encourage student independence at the Reflection step? How will students achieve this independence while practicing critical thinking, extending their reading, or demonstrating their learning?

2. Using the chart on page 245, analyze the questions that accompany your textbook.

Reflecting on Your Reading

Identify the three most significant things you learned in this chapter. Jot them down and then draft an explanation of why these three items are important to you. Give specific examples of how you can use this new information in your own teaching. Keep this draft for reference in the next few months.

Question	Is it literal/ interpretive/applied?	Is it recall/recognition?	Will it assist/measure?
#1			
#2			
#3			

PART FOUR

HOW PAR WORKS

CHAPTER 7

Teaching Vocabulary through PAR

"Be brief; for it is with words as with sunbeams — the more they are condensed

the deeper they burn."

Robert Southey

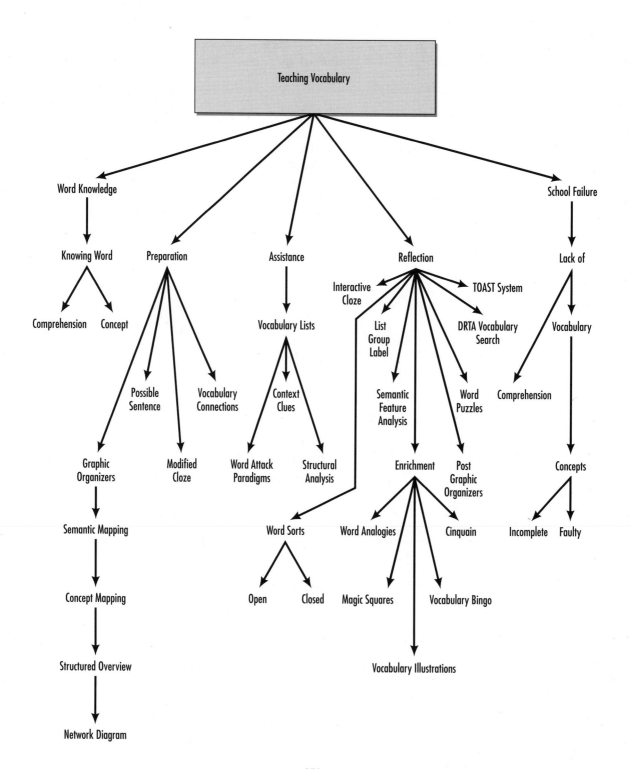

Prepare to Read

1. Are there ways to get students more interested in finding out the meanings of unfamiliar words through the context of passages, the structure of words, or the dictionary? In general, how can content teachers create more enthusiasm for word study?

2. Following is a list of terms used in this chapter. Some of them may be familiar to you in a general context, but in this chapter they may be used in a different way than you are used to. Rate your knowledge by placing a $+$ in front of those you are sure that you know, a $\sqrt{}$ in front of those you have some knowledge about, and a 0 in front of those you don't know. Be ready to locate and pay special attention to their meanings when they are presented in the chapter.

___ misplaced accuracy   ___ contextual knowledge
___ instrumentalist   ___ network diagram
___ aptitude   ___ closed sort
___ general knowledge   ___ open sort

Objectives

As you read this chapter, focus your attention on the following objectives. You will:

1. understand the relationship of vocabulary knowledge to reading comprehension.

2. realize that as students mature, they can add depth to their understanding of words.

3. understand the four types of concepts in teaching vocabulary.

4. realize that a student's lack of understanding of concepts and vocabulary can contribute significantly to school failure.

5. use teaching strategies to increase a student's conceptual understanding of words.

6. identify strategies for teaching vocabulary before, during, and after reading.

The Importance of Vocabulary Instruction

Background knowledge is important to understanding the nuances of meaning of words. Consider these three sentences:

The man stuffed the basket.

The man wove the basket.

The man emptied the basket.

Describe the mental image you have of what is happening in each of the three sentences. Would differences in background experiences create different mental images? Can you describe a second mental image for each sentence?

Vocabulary instruction is an important facet of reading in any discipline. There are times when students need Preparation (P) in vocabulary before reading a chapter or lesson; often students need Assistance (A) with vocabulary during or immediately after the reading; and there are occasions when students need longer periods of Reflection (R) on vocabulary, to determine how terms convey meaning and relationships. Research by Memory (1990) has suggested that vocabulary development can be effective when taught at any of these stages—before, during, or after the reading assignment.

Misplaced accuracy is often a problem in vocabulary knowledge. This situation is analogous to that of car owners who regularly take their cars to the local car wash but forget to take them to a mechanic for important maintenance, such as lubrication, oil and filter changes, and tune-ups. In short, they take more care with the cosmetics than with the substance of the automobile—the engine, drive train, and chassis. Similarly, teachers who always have students read grandly through chapters without concentrating on the vocabulary—especially the vocabulary that carries the major concept load of the chapter—are also guilty of emphasizing form over substance. Meaning in a reading passage is conveyed in words, which are the essence of the chapter, much as the engine and chassis are the underpinnings or the foundation of the automobile. Attention to detail is the foundation of understanding. Words, technical vocabulary, and key concepts are the details of a chapter or passage that must be understood for the "big picture" of the chapter to be brought into focus.

Vocabulary development needs to take place in all classrooms. It has been said that war is too important to leave to the generals. Likewise, vocabulary development is too important to leave to the English and reading teachers. Each content field has unique terms and specialized vocabulary whose meanings, if known, lead the reader to the core of conceptual understanding of the text. For instance, in a mathematics lesson on addition and subtraction of fractions, consider the importance of the term *common denominator.* Little else can make sense to the student who does not know this important concept. If teachers in all content areas concentrate on effectively teaching the understanding of terms and concepts within a unit of instruction, students will develop better speaking, listening, reading, and writing vocabularies.

Vocabulary and Comprehension

Nearly a half-century ago, Davis (1944) and Thurstone (1946) wrote that knowledge of word meanings is one of the most important factors in reading comprehension. Recent research has attested to the correlation between vocabulary knowledge and unit test scores, oral reading rates, and teacher judgment (Lovitt, Horton, & Bergerud, 1987) as well as comprehension (Anderson & Freebody, 1981; Beck & McKeown, 1983). Research has documented the importance of understanding nuances, or shades of meaning. Important concepts are often conveyed through subtle distinctions in meaning. Columnist George Will once wrote that anyone who does not know the difference between *disinterested* (impartial) and *uninterested* (not interested) should be tried in court by an uninterested judge. When students do not understand nuances such as these, they will often have trouble comprehending text. However, when less difficult words are inserted to simplify the readability of a passage, studies show that readers' comprehension of the passage improves (Chall, 1958; Wittrock, Marks, & Doctorow, 1975).

Anderson and Freebody (1981) describe three views regarding the relationship between vocabulary knowledge and reading comprehension. The first, the **instrumentalist** view, assumes that the whole is the sum of its parts; that is, knowing the individual words of a passage is a prerequisite for knowing what the entire passage means. Teachers who follow the instrumentalist view would preteach the vocabulary in the Preparation phase of the PAR framework.

The **aptitude** view assumes that students have different aptitudes for learning vocabulary, and especially for learning new words easily. Teachers who believe in this view will provide Assistance and Reflection on word strategies to help students unlock meanings of language. For instance, a teacher holding such a view might work on word analogies, context clues, and structural word cues.

The third view emphasizes **general knowledge** as the most important aspect of vocabulary and comprehension development. According to this view, readers' background knowledge is very important in determining how much of the vocabulary they will understand and absorb. Those students with broad background and understanding of the world will have an easier time learning vocabulary because of their broader background experience. This view has been substantiated in the research literature for at least two decades (Ausubel, 1968; Henry, 1974; Graves, 1985; Carr & Wixson, 1986). For instance, those students who have toured historic Philadelphia can relate to a passage about the influence of the Constitution more easily than can those who have not had such firsthand experience. Teachers who follow this view would emphasize building on background knowledge in all phases of the PAR framework. For example, a teacher might ask students what they know about small-loan agencies in a business mathematics lesson on small loans. She might carefully present new vocabulary such as *collateral, passbook savings, debt, consolidation loans.* At each phase of the lesson, she would try to identify how much students already know about the topic. In this manner, the teacher would be practicing the general-knowledge view of teaching vocabulary and concepts.

Another aspect of the general-knowledge view is that students can develop a generalized understanding of a word only through seeing words in different contexts (Beck, McCaslin, & McKeown, 1980; Mezynski, 1983; Stahl, 1983). For instance, a student might first encounter the word *metamorphosis* in a geography textbook in a specific reference to the change that occurs when igneous or sedimentary rocks are exposed to intense heat and pressure. Later, the student might encounter the word in a science textbook and in class discussions of the changes that insects pass through from zygote to adult. As a less technical, scientific word for change, *metamorphosis* may also surface in a student's literature textbook to describe the changes in a character's development. This expo-

ACTIVITY 7.1   READING ASSIGNMENT HANDOUT: METAMORPHOSIS

Part I
  A. Check the sentences that the author *said* in your reading. Check 4.
_____ 1. Metamorphosis occurs in four stages.
_____ 2. A caterpillar stores food in its body.
_____ 3. Caterpillars eat pizza.
_____ 4. Butterflies and moths undergo complete metamorphosis.
_____ 5. Butterflies go for walks.
_____ 6. Caterpillars drink milk.
_____ 7. A cocoon is a protective shell around the caterpillar.

  B. Check the sentences that tell what the author *meant*. Check 3.
_____ 1. While in the cocoon, a caterpillar changes into a butterfly or moth.
_____ 2. Butterflies are pretty.
_____ 3. A caterpillar eats the same food as people.
_____ 4. Puppies change into caterpillars.
_____ 5. A caterpillar eats a lot for a small creature.
_____ 6. Metamorphosis means change.

(continued on page 255)

sure to *metamorphosis* in several settings will enable the students to develop a generalized understanding of the word in a variety of contexts. Activity 7.1 illustrates how the concept of metamorphosis in insects might be taught in the early elementary grades.

All three of these views can and should be applied at appropriate times in teaching vocabulary in content subjects. In each phase of the PAR framework, teachers can stress words as concepts necessary for student understanding, teach strategies for learning and enriching language, and develop the background knowledge students need for adequate vocabulary development.

Understanding Words as Concepts

It is generally agreed that readers can "know" a word but that each person may relate it to a different experience. The sentence "John took a *plane*," for example, could be interpreted in different ways. A young child reading it might imagine playing with a toy; a high school student would imagine a scene in an airport; and an adult who is a carpenter might imagine a carpenter's tool. Simpson (1987) notes that "word knowledge is not a static product but a fluid quality that takes on additional characteristics and attributes as the learner experiences more" (p. 21). Dale (1965) has described the following continuum of word knowledge:

A C T I V I T Y   7 . 1   CONTINUED

Part II
Color the stages as directed.

Metamorphosis of a Butterfly

Stage 1—The Egg
The Egg
Color Me Lightly

Stage 2—The Larva
The Caterpillar
Color Me Green

Stage 3—The Pupa
The Cocoon
Color Me Light Brown

Stage 4—The Adult
A Butterfly
Color Me Pretty Colors

1. Student has seen the word.
2. Student has heard the word but doesn't know what it means.
3. Student recognizes the word and knows vaguely what it means.
4. Student knows one or several meanings of the word.

Students can sometimes be successful at stage 2 or 3 of this continuum, but obviously a teacher's goal should be that students learn fully the key words of a discipline of study. Teachers should also remember that "big words" do not always carry as big a conceptual load as smaller ones. Size alone is not always the best criterion for how important a word is. (It is an old saying that *if* is the biggest word in the English language — and it has only two letters.)

Full concept learning of vocabulary, according to Simpson (1987), requires four mental operations: (1) recognizing and generating critical attributes — both examples and nonexamples — of a concept; (2) seeing relationships between the concept to be learned and what is already known; (3) applying the concept to a variety of contexts, and (4) generating new contexts for the learned concept.

A C T I V I T Y   7 . 2   **CONCEPT LEARNING: ELEMENTARY MATHEMATICS**

Exclude the concept that does not belong in this list. Tell the relationship of the concepts that remain.

1. order
2. grouping
3. fraction
4. properties

Concepts excluded: <u>fraction</u>

Relationship of remaining concepts: <u>have to do with categories</u>

A C T I V I T Y   7 . 3   **CONCEPT LEARNING: WORLD HISTORY**

Use the textbook to brainstorm attributes and nonattributes of *nationalism*.

ATTRIBUTES	NONATTRIBUTES
honor	maturity
pride	democracy
superiority	cooperation
wealth	isolationism
power	equality
imperialism	
prestige	
force	
racism	

The first of these skills can be developed by asking students to exclude a concept from a list in which it does not belong (Activity 7.2) or by brainstorming attributes and nonattributes of a given concept (as in Activity 7.3).

Operation 2 can be implemented by having students brainstorm targeted vocabulary concepts, then write definitions. Also, classification exercises such as the one in Activity 7.4 can be completed by students *prior* to reading to determine their knowledge.

For mental operation 3, students can apply what they know about a vocabulary concept by being exposed to the word in different contexts (as in our earlier example of *metamorphosis*). Stahl (1983) has called this teaching comprehension through developing **contextual knowledge**.

Mental operation 4—generating new contexts for a learned vocabulary term—can be developed by having students create new sentences using previously learned concepts (Stahl, 1986). Teachers will want to encourage frequent

A C T I V I T Y   7 . 4   CLASSIFICATION EXERCISE (ELEMENTARY LEVEL)

Below are three categories to describe animals — those that have fur, those that have feathers, and those with smooth skin.

Fur	Feathers	Smooth Skin

Place each of the following animal names under the category to which it belongs.

duck	goose	monkey	parrot	horse	seal
tiger	whale	bear	chicken	robin	frog
fox	dolphin	turkey	snake		

practice in this task. To facilitate such thinking, Simpson recommends a technique called paired-word sentence generation: two words are given, and students are asked to write a sentence demonstrating the relationships between them. Possible examples are *method — analysis, genes — environment, graph — plot, juvenile delinquency — recession*. A sentence for *juvenile delinquency — recession* might be "Incidents of juvenile delinquency occur more frequently during a recession."

Concepts, Vocabulary, and School Failure

Many times there is a mismatch between school expectations and students' achievement, especially in the case of "at-risk" students (discussed more fully in Chapter 11). This is true despite a plethora of compensatory educational programs designed to reduce the conceptual and language deficits of culturally disadvantaged and minority children (Lindfors, 1980). These children are often taught vocabulary through rote exercises that require dictionary definitions of extensive numbers of technical and specialized terms. In a typical exercise, the teacher informs students that before reading the chapter they must find, look up in the dictionary, and define 30 words found in the chapter. No wonder reading is often thought of as decidedly dull by students who have to perform such rote experiences. This method of teaching vocabulary and concepts is product-oriented; the rote production of the written word is the product (Abrahams, 1976). Such vocabulary exercises are used despite the fact that most disadvantaged students, at-risk populations, and generally poor readers use action words in

FIGURE 7.1

Dale's cone of experience adapted for vocabulary building. (From Edgar Dale, *Audio Visual Methods in Teaching*, 3rd ed. Copyright ©1969 by Holt, Rinehart and Winston, Inc. Used with permission of the publisher.)

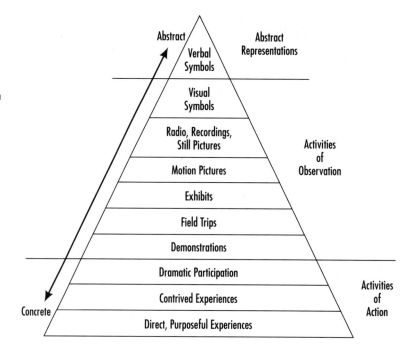

much of their communication ("he gone," for example); they use *process* to facilitate information rather than memorization of an extensive written vocabulary. Because rote vocabulary exercises present words and terms in the abstract, these students seem unable to grasp either their surface or their underlying meaning.

To help these students, who seem to be operating at Piaget's preoperational or early concrete operational level of cognitive functioning (the thinking level of 3- to 7-year olds), teachers need to present concepts in a very concrete manner, through direct and purposeful experiences (Piaget & Inhelder, 1969). Edgar Dale's classic cone of experience (Figure 7.1) demonstrates the importance of what are called "activities of action," through which students learn concepts through direct experience whenever possible. When hands-on experiences are not possible, students need "activities of observation," such as field trips, demonstrations, graphics, and visuals. Dale maintains that learning concepts by starting with written language (the "products" alluded to earlier by Abrahams) is very difficult for poor readers.

Sinatra recommends that teachers structure learning activities to include the physical involvement of students in establishing a "conceptual base" for language development. For example, in a unit on the Old West, the word *pemmican* might be encountered. Teachers might bring beef jerky for students to feel, touch, discuss, and taste. Later, students could study the meaning of *pemmican* within the context of the unit. To check retention, Sinatra recommends cloze passages.

(The interactive cloze procedure will be described later in this chapter.) Sinatra cites his own work with 1,000 black students in grades 1 through 8 in an outdoor camping program. Those students were highly successful at learning vocabulary words associated with the camping experience (Sinatra, 1975). Sinatra's interpretation (1977) of the relationship between the visual and the verbal in learning vocabulary and comprehension is depicted in Figure 7.2. It involves first providing the student with a concrete example of the term. Then the student uses the word in a sentence to increase language facility. Finally, cloze passages are provided to increase reading comprehension and vocabulary knowledge.

In the remainder of this chapter, we will describe several strategies for developing vocabulary. They can be used before reading, during reading, or shortly after reading. They can also be used as follow-up activities (usually the next day) to reading. In keeping with the tenets of Dale and Sinatra, we will describe how teachers can use the strategies whenever possible to teach vocabulary in concrete ways.

FIGURE 7.2

Model showing how to increase conceptual understanding through the structuring of experiential activities. (From Richard Sinatra, "The Cloze Technique for Reading Comprehension and Vocabulary Development," *Reading Improvement*, 1977, *14*, 80–92. Courtesy of Project Innovation, Chula Vista, California.)

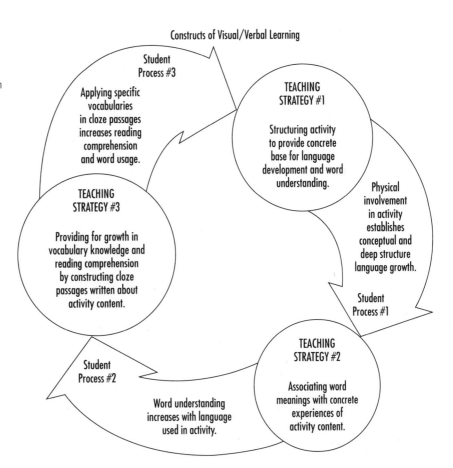

Constructs of Visual/Verbal Learning

Preparing Students to Read through Vocabulary Instruction

Teaching vocabulary *before* reading involves not so much the teacher "teaching" the terms as the student exploring and attempting to make sense of the terms before beginning the reading. Learning is something that must be accomplished by the student; the teacher cannot learn for the student. Remember the scaffolding that must be removed. Therefore, any vocabulary work before reading should be an effort to apply the new terminology to the student's background of experience. Douglas Barnes, in his book *From Communication to Curriculum* (1976), writes:

> Children are not "little vessels . . . ready to have imperial gallons of facts poured into them until they were full to the brim," as Dickens put it. They have a personal history outside the school and its curriculum. In order to arrive at school they have mastered many complex systems of knowledge; otherwise they could not cope with everyday life. School for every child is a confrontation between what he "knows" already and what the school offers; this is true both of social learning and of the kinds of learning which constitute the manifest curriculum. Whenever school learning has gone beyond meaningless rote, we can take it that a child has made some kind of relationship between what he knows already and what the school has presented. (p. 22)

Four strategies — graphic organizers, modified cloze, possible sentences, and vocabulary connections — can be used before reading to solidify, as Barnes put it, the relationship between what the student already knows and what is provided at school.

Graphic Organizers

It has been clear for some time that the use of visuals can enhance learning (Arnheim, 1969; Grady, 1984; Gazzaniga, 1988). The structured overview (Barron, 1969), which was presented as the graphic organizer and described in Chapter 3 primarily as a technique for structuring text, is a visual that has been found to improve comprehension (Williams, 1973). It is also an effective strategy for getting students on the same "wavelength" as the teacher in understanding the direction a lesson is taking. The teacher interacts with students by displaying the diagram and discussing why it is arranged in a particular way. Students can also arrange the graphic organizer into a meaningful pattern, possibly working in small groups.

Activity 7.5 illustrates how graphic organizers can be used to develop vocabulary. The vocabulary terms to be used in the diagram are listed at the bottom. If students have not had practice in this activity, the teacher may wish to place the words next to the part of the diagram where they belong.

A semantic map (Johnson & Pearson, 1984) is a form of graphic organizer depicting the interrelationships and hierarchies of concepts in a lesson. Mapping was introduced in Chapter 5 as a way to develop comprehension. This activity can be used as a prereading or postreading exercise. To use semantic mapping before reading, follow these steps:

A C T I V I T Y   7 . 5   **GRAPHIC ORGANIZER: INTRODUCTORY HORTICULTURE**

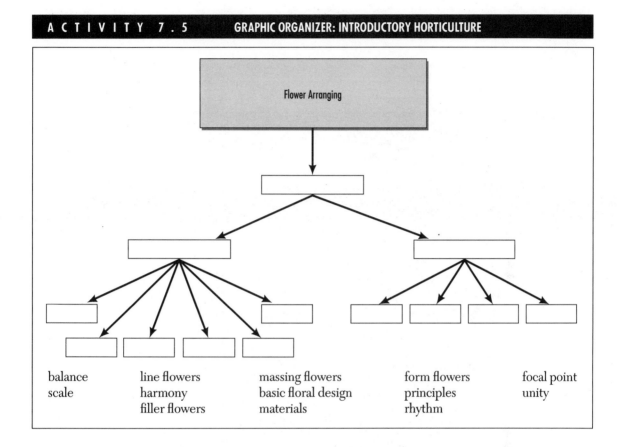

balance   line flowers   massing flowers   form flowers   focal point
scale   harmony   basic floral design   principles   unity
                     filler flowers   materials   rhythm

1. Select an important word from the reading assignment.
2. Ask students to think of as many related words and key concepts as possible that will help in understanding the key word.
3. List these words on the board as they are identified.
4. As an extension of this activity, have students rank the words or categorize them into "most important" and "least important." This activity may help students begin to see that all words in the lesson are not equally important and that information needs to be categorized.
5. Organize the words into a diagram similar to the one in Activity 7.6.

   Novak and Gowin (1984) describe a similar technique they call concept mapping (see Activity 7.7). The biggest difference between their concept map and Johnson and Pearson's semantic map is the former's heavy emphasis on linking words to concepts. Both semantic maps and concept maps are excellent ways of getting students to clarify their thinking before reading the assignment.

   A **network diagram** (see Activity 7.8) is a graphic organizer that can stimulate students to recall what they know about a topic. These diagrams help students

A C T I V I T Y   7 . 6   **SEMANTIC MAP: ANIMALS ARE LIVING THINGS**

organize their thoughts and can involve them in anticipating the reading assignment. The diagram can be constructed either as a handout or on the board. Sometimes students will be able to fill in the diagram only partially before reading; they should be encouraged to return after the reading to finish the diagram or to revise some of their entries.

After students complete the diagram, teachers can discuss new vocabulary terms and explain how they fit into the diagram. In the dinosaur diagram in Activity 7.8, for example, the teacher might ask students what these terms have to do with the diagram: *environment, characteristics, reptile, folklore, physical features, herbivorous.* In this way, teachers ask students to relate new vocabulary to concepts they already know and have recorded in their network diagrams.

Modified Cloze Exercises   Cloze as a means of determining reader background was presented in Chapter 4. Cloze passages can also be constructed to teach technical or general vocabulary. Passages used in this manner are modified for instructional purposes. Instead of deleting words at predetermined intervals, as when measuring reada-

A C T I V I T Y   7 . 7   CONCEPT MAP: RIVERS

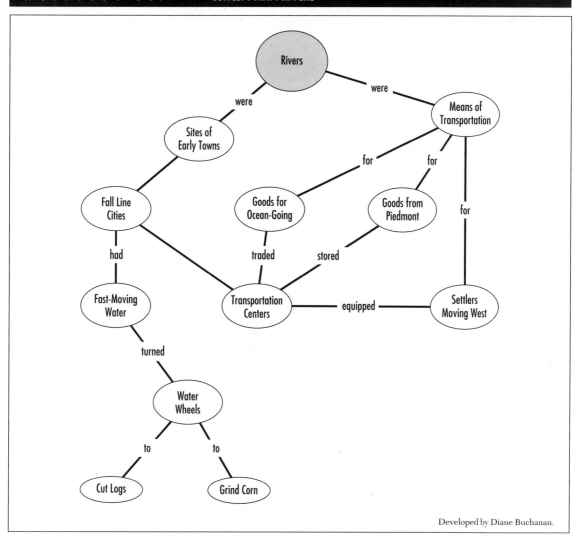

Developed by Diane Buchanan.

bility and checking students' reading ability, teachers select a very important passage from the text and delete key words. Teachers may also create their own cloze passage of 50 to 100 words to assess students' knowledge of vocabulary and concepts on a certain topic. Activity 7.9 presents a passage of approximately 70 words constructed by a teacher to assess students' knowledge of crocodiles. Students can fill in the blanks individually, then discuss their answers in small groups. The best, or most unusual, answers can eventually be shared with the entire class.

A C T I V I T Y   7 . 8   **NETWORK DIAGRAM: DINOSAURS**

(What they are part of)

What they do

What they are like

A C T I V I T Y   7 . 9   **MODIFIED CLOZE EXERCISE: CROCODILES**

This article is about crocodiles, who live mainly in _____ . Crocodiles eat _____ and are ferocious, sometimes reaching a length of over _____ feet and a weight of _____ . A full-grown crocodile can _____ a man while the poor fellow _____ . There are probably about _____ crocodiles alive today. They believe in _____ their young and often have fun _____ with other crocodiles. Crocodiles are known for their _____ and _____ .

Possible Sentences

Possible sentences (Moore & Arthur, 1981) is an activity that combines vocabulary and prediction. It is designed to acquaint students with new vocabulary that they will encounter in their reading and guide them as they attempt to verify the accuracy of the statements they have generated. Additionally, it arouses curiosity concerning the passage to be read. This activity is best used when unfamiliar vocabulary is mixed with familiar terminology. When using this technique, the teacher might give students a worksheet such as the one shown in Activity 7.10.

Students use five to eight terms, such as these from a business class lesson on printing documents: *impact printer, dot matrix, laser, ink-jet, electronic copier, buffer storage, expandable,* and *downtime.* For each term, students write a possible sentence on the left side of the worksheet. Then, during reading, they

A C T I V I T Y   7 . 1 0   POSSIBLE SENTENCES: COMPUTER PRINTING TERMS

Possible Sentences	Real Meaning
1. *Downtime* is when a person is unhappy with what is happening.	1. *Downtime* is time during which production is stopped.
2. He ate so many hamburgers his waistline was *expandable*.	2. A system is *expandable* when it is able to be made larger.

look for the real meaning of the term and write this meaning in a sentence. Students have now created a mnemonic, with the possible sentence cueing them to the real meaning of the word. This is a simple but powerful strategy for learning words. Recent research attests to the advantage of using such mnemonic devices to learn vocabulary (Levin, Levin, Glassman, & Nordwall, 1992; Moore & Surber, 1992; Scruggs, Mastropieri, Brigham, & Sullivan, 1992). Mnemonic devices will be discussed in detail in Chapter 9.

Vocabulary Connections

Iwicki (1992) describes a strategy whereby students use a vocabulary word from a previous book in shared literature study to describe a situation in a book currently being studied. In this way, connections are made between old vocabulary and the new book. For example, the word *pandemonium* found in *Welcome Home, Jelly Bean* (Shyer, 1988) can be related to events in *The Black Stallion* (Farley, 1941). In other content areas, words from a former chapter can be used to see relationships in a new chapter. In occupational mathematics, for example, the term *conversion* may be used with product volumes in one chapter and again in a chapter on use of mathematics in leisure-time activities (converting international track-and-field times from English measurements to metrics). Iwicki reports that vocabulary connections is an activity that retains its appeal to students throughout schooling. It is an excellent way for students to use higher-level thinking skills in comparing vocabulary from one content-area subject to another.

Assisting Students in Vocabulary Development

Students need to have at their disposal, in all content areas and at every grade level, strategies that will provide assistance *as they read* in interpreting unfamiliar words. Teachers cannot "protect" students from words by teaching prior to reading every difficult term they will encounter. McMurray, Laffey, and Morgan (1979) found that students skipped over unfamiliar words when they had no strategy for learning vocabulary. Four excellent techniques for assisting readers are context clue discovery, structural analysis, word attack paradigms, and vocabulary lists.

Context Clue Discovery

To begin to understand the importance of "concepts in context," think of any word in isolation; then try to define it. Take, for example, the word *run*. It is not difficult to give a synonym for the word, but it does not have a clear meaning until it is placed in a context. You may have thought immediately of the most common definition, "to move with haste," but "to be or campaign as a candidate for election," "to publish, print, or make copies," or even "to cause the stitches in a garment to unravel" would have been equally accurate. A precise meaning cannot be determined until the word is seen in context.

Students often use context clues to help determine the meaning of a word (Konopak, 1988; Drum & Konopak, 1987). Sometimes, however, students are not successful at making use of context clues because they lack a systematic strategy for figuring out the unknown word (Hafner, 1967). To help students develop the ability to use context as a way of discovering the meaning of unfamiliar words, teachers can discuss some specific clues they should look for in the text.

Definitions Authors often define a word in the same sentence in which it appears. This technique is used frequently in textbooks when an author introduces terminology. Note the following examples:

> The *marginal revenue product* of the input is the change in total revenue associated with using one more unit of the variable input.

> The *peltier effect* is the production of heat at the junction of two metals on the passage of a current.

Signal Words Certain words or phrases may be used to signal the reader that a word or term is about to be explained or that an example will be presented. Some of the most frequently used signal words are listed below, followed by two sentences using signal words.

the way	especially	such
this	in that	in the way that
for example	these (synonym)	like
such as		

> Americans do need to fear *hyperinflation*, especially as it involves prices rising at a very rapid rate.

> There was a large *extended family*, in that many relatives were living in close proximity.

Direct Explanations Often authors provide an explanation of an unfamiliar term that is being introduced. This is a technique used frequently in difficult technical writing.

> Joe was a *social being*, whose thoughts and behaviors were strongly influenced by the people and things around him and whose thoughts and behaviors strongly influenced the people he was around.

> Mead emphasized that the mind is a social product; indeed, one of the most important achievements of socialization is the development of *cognitive abilities* — intellectual capacities such as perceiving, remembering, reasoning, calculating, believing.

Synonyms A complex term may be followed by a simpler, more commonly understood word, even though the words may not be perfect synonyms. Again, the author is attempting to provide the reader with an explanation or definition, in this instance by using a comparison. In the following example, *obscure* is explained by comparison to the word *unintelligible*. In the second sentence, *attacks* helps explain *audacious comments*.

> The lecture was so *obscure* that the students labeled it unintelligible.

> There were *audacious comments* and attacks on prominent leaders of the opposition.

Antonyms Conversely, an author may define or explain a term by contrasting it with its opposite.

> The young swimmer did not have the *perseverance* of her older teammates and quit at the halfway point in the race.

> All this is rather *optimistic*, though it is better to err on the side of hope than in favor of despair.

Inferences Students can often infer the meaning of an unfamiliar word from the mood and tone of the selection. In this case, meaning must be deduced through a combination of the author's use of mood, tone, and imagery and the reader's background knowledge and experience. The author thus paints a picture of meaning rather than concretely defining or explaining the word within the text.

In the passage that follows, the meaning of *opaque* is not made clear. The reader must infer the meaning from the mood and tone of the paragraph and from personal experience with a substance such as black asphalt.

> This is it, this is it, right now, the present, this empty gas station, here, this western wind, this tang of coffee on the tongue, and I am patting the puppy, I am watching the mountain. And the second I verbalize this awareness in my brain, I cease to see the mountain or feel the puppy. I am *opaque*, so much black asphalt. But at the same second, the second I know I've lost it, I also realize that the puppy is still squirming on his back under my hand. Nothing has changed for him. He draws his legs down to stretch the skin out so he feels every fingertip's stroke along his furred and arching side, his flank, his flung-back throat. (From *Pilgrim at Tinker Creek*, by Annie Dillard, New York: Harper's Magazine Press, 1975.)

Research suggests that students can use context clue strategies to unlock the meaning of unfamiliar terms (Quealy, 1969; Stahl, 1986). Therefore, it is a good idea to have these six clues (with explanations and sample sentences) posted at points around the classroom or on a handout to be kept in the student's work folder.

Structural Analysis

Even if students practice and remember the strategy, there are times when context clues are not going to be of much help in decoding unfamiliar words (Schatz, 1984). For example, readers would probably have trouble guessing the meaning of the following italicized terms from clues in the context:

> Nations impose burdens that violate the laws of *equity*.

> A very important finding about the effects of mass media relates to *latency*.

> They put a *lien* on our house.

Using context clues in these sentences would probably give readers a vague idea of the meaning or no idea at all. In these cases, it may be faster to use structural analysis to derive the meaning.

Consider the following passage concerning "sexual dimorphism":

> An interesting relationship between sexual dimorphism and domestic duties exists among some species. Consider an example from birds. The sexes of song sparrows look very much alike. The males have no conspicuous qualities which immediately serve to release reproductive behavior in females. Thus courtship in this species may be a rather extended process as pair-bonding (mating) is established. Once a pair has formed, both sexes enter into the nest building, feeding and defense of the young. The male may only mate once in a season but he helps to maximize the number of young which reach adulthood carrying his genes. He is rather inconspicuous, so whereas he doesn't turn on females very easily, he also doesn't attract predators to the nest.
>
> The peacock, on the other hand, is raucous and garish. When he displays to a drab peahen, he must present a veritable barrage of releasers to her reproductive IRMs. In any case, he displays madly and frequently and is successful indeed. Once having seduced an awed peahen, he doesn't stay to help with the mundane chores of child

rearing, but instead disappears into the sunset looking for new conquests. (From R.A. Wallace, *Biology: The World of Life.* Copyright 1975 by Goodyear Publishing Co., Santa Monica, California.)

After reading this passage we know:

A relationship exists between sexual dimorphism and some species.

Sparrows share domestic duties.

Peafowl do not share domestic duties.

Mating and pair-bonding are different for sparrows and peafowl.

What is the cause of the difference? Your response should be "sexual dimorphism." If you know that *di* means "two" and *morph* means "form or shape," then you can figure out the term *sexual dimorphism*. (See Appendix F for a list of prefixes, suffixes, and roots of words with meanings and examples.)

Word Attack Paradigm

Students can be given a card with a word attack paradigm to aid them in deciphering new words when they encounter them in reading. Such a paradigm might look like this:

1. Figure out the word from the meaning of the sentence. The word *must* make sense in the sentence.
2. Take off the ending of the word. Certain endings, such as *s, d, r, es, ed, er, est, al, ing,* may be enough to make the word look "new."
3. Break the word into syllables. Don't be afraid to try two or three ways to break the word. Look for prefixes, suffixes, and root words that are familiar.
4. Sound the word out. Try to break the word into syllables several times, sounding it out each time. Do you know a word that begins with the same letters? Do you know a word that ends the same? Put them together.
5. Look in the glossary in the back, if the book has one.
6. Ask a friend in class, the teacher, or as a last resort, find the definition of the word in the dictionary.

A word attack paradigm gives students a way to attempt newfound words without resorting first to a dictionary.

Vocabulary List

Students can also be encouraged to make vocabulary lists of new terms they have mastered, whether by context clue discovery, structural analysis, or word attack paradigm. Students may keep such lists in notebooks or on file cards. With cards, they can write the word and its dictionary pronunciation on the front side and on the back, the sentence in which it was found and the dictionary definition. Periodically, students can exchange their notebooks or file cards and call vocabulary terms to each other, as they often do with spelling words: one student calls the term, and the other gives the definition and uses the word in a sentence. In this manner, students can make a habit of working daily and weekly with words to expand their content vocabulary.

Reflecting on Vocabulary for Increased Comprehension and Retention

An intriguing finding consistently emerging from reading research is that it can be as beneficial to teach vocabulary after reading, or during reading, as before the reading (Memory, 1990). For years conventional wisdom has been that vocabulary is best taught before the reading. In fact, however, the more students are asked to discuss, brainstorm, and think about what they have learned, the more they comprehend and retain the material. Thus, the reflection phase of vocabulary development holds much promise in helping students thoroughly grasp the meaning of difficult terms in their reading. In this section, we offer a number of strategies for reflection; these are best carried out by students working in small groups.

Interactive Cloze Procedure

Meeks and Morgan (1978) describe a strategy called the interactive cloze procedure, which was designed to encourage students to pay close attention to words in print and to actively seek the meaning of passages by studying vocabulary terms. They offer the following paradigm for using the interactive cloze:

1. Select a passage of 100 to 150 words from a textbook. It should be a passage that students have had difficulty comprehending or one that the instructor feels is important for them to comprehend fully.
2. Make appropriate deletions of nouns, verbs, adjectives, or adverbs. The teacher can vary the form and number of deletions depending on the purpose of the exercise.
3. Have students complete the cloze passage individually, filling in as many blanks as possible. Set a time limit based on the difficulty of the passage.
4. Divide students into small groups, three to four students per group. Instruct them to compare answers and come to a joint decision as to the best response for each blank.
5. Reassemble the class as a whole. Read the selection intact from the text. Give students opportunities to express opinions on the suitability of the author's choice of terms compared to their choices.
6. Strengthen short-term recall by testing using the cloze passage.

Meeks and Morgan described using the technique to teach imagery by omitting words that produce vivid images. Activity 7.11 is such a cloze, based on a passage from H.G. Wells's *The Red Room* (1896). The interactive cloze can also be used to have students reflect on difficult concepts, as illustrated in Activities 7.12 and 7.13.

Semantic Feature Analysis

Semantic feature analysis (Baldwin, Ford, & Readance, 1981; Johnson & Pearson, 1984) is a technique for helping students understand deeper meanings and nuances of language. To accomplish the analysis, first the teacher lists terms vertically on the chalkboard and asks students to help choose the features that will be written across the top of the chalkboard. (Teachers can also choose the

A C T I V I T Y 7 . 1 1   INTERACTIVE CLOZE: H.G. WELLS

I saw the candle in the right sconce of one of the mirrors _____ and go right out, and almost immediately its companion followed it. There was no mistake about it. The flame vanished, as if the wicks had been suddenly _____ between a _____ and a thumb, leaving the wick neither _____ nor smoking, but _____ . While I stood _____ , the candle at the _____ of the bed went out, and the _____ seemed to take another step towards me.

Vocabulary words:

finger	gaping	wink	black
shadows	foot	glowing	nipped

A C T I V I T Y 7 . 1 2   INTERACTIVE CLOZE: NATURE VERSUS NURTURE

Is man's behavior an outgrowth of his _____ , that is, the genetic factors, . . . or is it a result of _____ , that is, the totality of the environmental events that he _____ ? . . . It is in this relatively new field of _____ genetics that we see _____ , the _____ , and the importance of their interaction taken seriously.

Words deleted from passage:

behavior	environment	heredity
nature	nurture	experiences

From G. Kimble, N. Garmezy, & E. Zigler, *Principles of General Psychology* (4th ed.). Copyright 1968 by John Wiley & Sons, Inc., New York, NY.

features beforehand.) Students then complete the matrix by marking a (+) for features that apply to each word. In certain situations, students can be asked to make finer discriminations: always (A), sometimes (S), or never (N). We recommend students do this analysis after having read the lesson using a technique such as the guided reading procedure or the directed reading/thinking activity (Chapter 5). Activity 7.14 shows a semantic feature analysis used in a marketing class on trade and exports.

Word Puzzles

Word puzzles are enjoyed by almost all students, and computer programs now make them easier to construct. The teacher enters the vocabulary terms and definitions, and the computer program constructs the puzzle. If a computer is unavailable, teachers can construct their own puzzles by graphically displaying the terms across and down and drawing boxes around the words. The boxes are numbered both across and down, and definitions are placed beside the grid. Activity 7.15 shows a word puzzle constructed for a social studies class of learning-disabled students.

A C T I V I T Y 7 . 1 3   INTERACTIVE CLOZE: MACBETH

> Wherefore was that cry?
>
> *Seyton:* The queen, my lord, is dead.
>
> *Macbeth:* She should have died _____
>
>   There would have been a time for such a word.
>
>   Tomorrow, and tomorrow, and tomorrow,
>
>   Creeps in this _____ pace from day to day
>
>   To the last syllable of recorded time,
>
>   And all our _____ have lighted fools
>
>   The way to dusty death. Out, out, brief candle!
>
>   Life's but a _____ , a poor player
>
>   That struts and frets his hour upon the stage
>
>   And then is _____ . It is a tale
>
>   Told by an _____ , full of sound and fury,
>
>   Signifying _____ .

From L. Damrosch (Ed.), *Adventures in American Literature*. Orlando, FL: Harcourt Brace Jovanovich, 1985, p. 230.

Post Graphic Organizers

Earlier in this chapter, we discussed how students could construct their own graphic organizers before reading to learn new vocabulary terms and to attempt to construct a hierarchical pattern of organization. To enhance concept development, students can return to the organizers after reading. Post graphic organizers to help students reflect have been described in Chapter 6. Here we present a variation specifically for vocabulary. If the teacher uses a DRTA, students can construct a post graphic organizer (Barron & Stone, 1973) directly after the reading. Activity 7.16 shows a post graphic organizer actually completed by several students on the subject of student engagement and classroom reform.

List–Group–Label

Taba (1967) devised a categorization technique that has withstood the test of time as an excellent reflective activity. This word-relationship activity begins with the teacher's suggesting a topic and asking students to supply words they know that describe the topic. The teacher may supplement the words given by the students or ask students to skim the text to find more words. With students whose abilities or backgrounds are limited, the teacher can provide the list. This list shown in Activity 7.17, from a chapter on the history of India, was developed by a teacher.

Next, students organize the list of words into smaller lists of items that have something in common (see Activity 7.17). It is best during this phase for students to work in small groups to categorize and label the words.

Finally, groups explain their categories and labels to the entire class; then the whole class tries to reach a consensus on what the correct labels are and where the particular words belong. The teacher needs to act as guide during this final phase to make certain that discussion and labeling are being channeled in the

A C T I V I T Y   7 . 1 4   SEMANTIC FEATURE ANALYSIS: TRADE AND EXPORTS

Procedure: 1. Have students check off characteristics (*A* for always, *N* for never, *S* for sometimes).
2. Students will use their text to check and correct their answers.

	impacts on U.S. economy	exchanging goods between nations	widening selection of goods	lower consumer prices	communication difficulties	trade barriers	political problems	promotion of products internationally	countries trading as a bloc	economic interdependence
1. Absolute advantage										
2. Balance of trade										
3. Common markets										
4. Comparative advantage										
5. Duty-free zone										
6. Exports										
7. Imports										
8. International marketing										
9. Joint venture										
10. Trade barriers										

A = Always   N = Never   S = Sometimes

ACTIVITY 7.15 WORD PUZZLE: SOCIAL STUDIES

Across Clues:

4. The way things are
7. The first one or ones
8. Carried off against one's wishes
9. Regions; parts of a country
10. A person who is the property of another
12. Grew or became larger
14. Opposite of low
15. Work; workers as a group
17. ________ and manufacturing were both important in the North.
18. Coin; ten cents
20. If you do not get to class on time, you are ________.
22. Pay; money paid for work done
24. Animal that barks; sometimes chases cats
25. Steamboats and ________ were important means of transportation in the 1830s.
26. Not the South; the ______
27. Opposite of yes
28. Crop grown in the South used in making cigarettes
29. It is dark; turn on a ______.

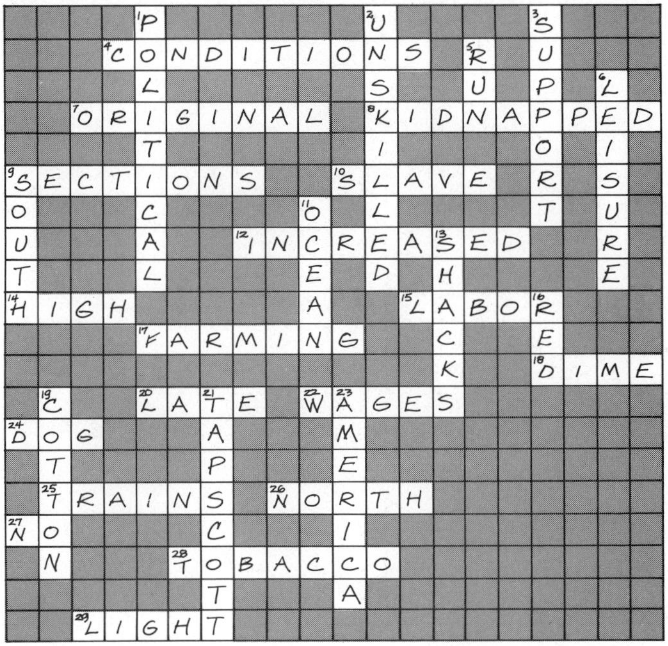

Down Clues:

1. Connected with government
2. Not skilled; not trained in a certain job
3. Get a living for; arrange food, clothing, shelter for
5. Rocky ________ Intermediate School
6. Free time after work is done
9. Not the North but the ______
11. The Atlantic ________
13. Small, poorly built shelters generally made of wood
16. The color of a valentine heart
19. One of the main crops in the South; used to make cloth
21. Teacher of this class: Mrs. ________
23. The United States of ________

Word List:
AMERICA
CONDITIONS
COTTON
DIME
DOG
FARMING
HIGH
INCREASED
KIDNAPPED
LABOR
LATE
LEISURE
LIGHT
NORTH
NO
OCEAN
ORIGINAL
POLITICAL
RED
RUN
SECTIONS
SHACKS
SLAVE
SOUTH
SUPPORT
TAPSCOTT
TOBACCO
TRAINS
UNSKILLED
WAGES

proper direction. It is also essential that students be allowed to provide a rationale for their decisions. The focus on explanation and discussion in this activity makes it an excellent strategy for teaching difficult vocabulary, concept development, and critical thinking, especially since all learning depends on students' ability to create meaningful categories of information. This activity, practiced in a relaxed and purposeful atmosphere, can be a powerful tool for helping students develop concepts, improve comprehension, and retain information.

ACTIVITY 7.16   POST GRAPHIC ORGANIZER: STUDENT ENGAGEMENT AND CLASSROOM REFORM

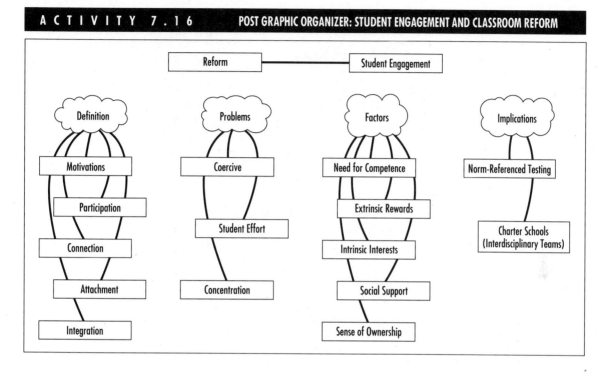

Word Sorts

Very similar to the Taba idea is a word sort as described by Gillett and Temple (1983). In this activity, students individually or in small groups sort out technical terms that are written on cards, on the chalkboard, or on a worksheet. They categorize like words and title the categories. In a **closed sort**, students are given the categories in advance. This teaches classification and deductive reasoning. In an **open sort**, students have to group words as concepts and title the relationship. This teaches inference, or reading between the lines, as discussed in Chapter 5.

DRTA Vocabulary Search

When doing a Directed Reading/Thinking Activity in a content-area classroom, the teacher can ask students to jot down difficult vocabulary terms encountered. The student lists are given to the teacher *without student names*, and these terms become the cadre of words to be studied after the DRTA or at the beginning of the next class period.

The teacher first teaches word recognition by using a "word families" phonics approach to sound out the word. If the word is *fertile*, for example, the teacher asks for other words in the same word family:

fertile   fertility   fertilizer   fertilization

Students work through the word family to sound out the word, thereby achieving word recognition.

ACTIVITY 7.17   LIST–GROUP–LABEL: HISTORY OF INDIA

People of India: Past and Present

Dravidians	Marco Polo	Buddhists
Mauruas	British East India Company	Jawaharlal Nehru
French	Siddhartha Gautama	Vasco da Gama
Hindus	Buddha	Mohandas K. Gandhi
rajah	Mongols	British government
Akbar	Vedas	Alexander the Great
Aryans	Guptas	English
Ashka		

Religion	*Invaders*	*Explorers*
Siddhartha Gautama	Dravidians	Marco Polo
Buddha	Aryans	Vasco da Gama
Hindus	Alexander the Great	English
Buddhists	Mauruas	French
Vedas	Mongols	

Ruled India

rajah
Ashka
Guptas
Akbar
British East India Company
British government
Jawaharlal Nehru

Worked for India's Freedom

Mohandas K. Gandhi

Next comes a skimming and scanning exercise. The teacher begins by asking "Who can find *fertile* first in the story? Give me the page, column, and paragraph number, and then read *the paragraph* the word is found in." After the word search, the paragraph is read, and students with the aid of the teacher try to figure out the meaning of the word in the context of the story or chapter. Here the teacher can ask students to use the context clue discovery strategy explained earlier in this chapter. This word search approach teaches word recognition, speed reading, and comprehension through using context clues. Keep in mind that the words to be studied are the ones with which students are actually having difficulty, not the ones a manual says are going to give them difficulty.

TOAST Vocabulary Study System

Dana and Rodriguez (1992) have proposed a vocabulary study system using the acronym TOAST. In a study they found the system to be more effective for learning vocabulary than other selected study methods. The steps in this vocabulary study technique are as follows:

T	Test	Students self-test to determine which vocabulary terms they cannot spell, define, or use in sentences.
O	Organize	Students organize these words into semantically related groups; arrange words into categories by structure or function, such as those that sound alike or are the same part of speech; categorize words as somewhat familiar or completely unfamiliar.
A	Anchor	Students "anchor" the words in memory by using a keyword method (assigning a picture and caption to a vocabulary term), tape-recording definitions, creating a mnemonic device, or mixing the words on cards and ordering them from difficult to easy.
S	Say	Students review the words by calling the spellings, definitions, and uses in sentences to another student. The first review session begins 5 to 10 minutes after initial study and is followed at intervals by several more.
T	Test	Immediately after each review, students self-administer a posttest in which they spell, define, and use in context all the vocabulary terms with which they originally had difficulty. The response mode may be oral, written, or silent thought.

We recommend this vocabulary study system from early elementary grades through high school as a good method for getting students actively involved in the study of words. Keep in mind that TOAST encompasses all aspects of PAR.

Reflection through Language Enrichment

Many of the activities described in this chapter are so enjoyable for students that interest in words will be heightened. This section, emphasizing word play, offers additional techniques that will help students experience the pleasure of working with words. Specifically, we will present five techniques: word analogies, magic squares, cinquains, vocabulary illustrations, and vocabulary bingo.

Word Analogies

Word analogies are enjoyable activities that are excellent for teaching higher-level thinking. To do word analogies, students must be able to perceive relationships between what amounts to two sides of an equation. This may be critical thinking at its best, in that the student is often forced to attempt various combinations of possible answers in solving the problem. Students may have difficulty initially with this concept; therefore, the teacher should practice with students and explain the equation used in analogies:

_____ is to _____ as _____ is to _____ .

or _____ : _____ :: _____ : _____ .

For elementary students, teachers initially would spell out "is to . . . as" rather than use symbols. In addition, students say that analogies are easier when the blank is in the fourth position, as in items 1–5 of Activity 7.18. More difficult analogies can be constructed by varying the position of the blank, as in items 6–10. Analogies can also present a very sophisticated challenge for older students, as illustrated in Activity 7.19.

Magic Squares

Any vocabulary activity can come alive through the use of magic squares, a technique that can be used at all levels—elementary, junior high, and high school. Magic squares are special arrangements of numbers that when added across, down, or diagonally always equal the same sum. The following example from China is several thousand years old:

4	9	2
3	5	7
8	1	6

magic number = 15

Teachers can construct vocabulary exercises by having students match a lettered column of words to a numbered column of definitions. Letters on each square of the grid match the lettered words. Students try to find the magic number by matching the correct word and definition and entering the number in the appropriate square on the grid. Activity 7.20 illustrates this activity for a French lesson. Activity 7.21 gives several other magic square combinations; note that simply rearranging rows or columns can generate many more combinations from those given here.

Cinquains

A cinquain (pronounced sĭn-kān) is a five-line poem with the following pattern: the first line is a noun or the subject of the poem; the second line consists of two words that describe the first line (adjectives); the third line is three action words (verbs); the fourth line contains four words that convey a feeling; and the fifth line is a single word that refers back to the first line. Students at all educational levels will be pleased to participate in this language-enrichment activity. Cinquains require thought and concentration and can be tried in any content area. Activities 7.22–7.24 contain examples written by students in elementary, junior high, and high school.

Vocabulary Illustrations

Joe Antinarella, an English teacher at Tidewater Community College in Chesapeake, Virginia, has developed a creative way to enrich students' study of vocabulary that he calls vocabulary illustrations. He has students first define a word on a piece of drawing paper, then find a picture or make an original drawing that illustrates the concept. Below the picture, students use the term in a sentence

A C T I V I T Y   7 . 1 8   **WORD ANALOGIES: ELEMENTARY LEVEL**

1. Colt is to horse as child is to _____ .
   brother   mother   sister
2. Chick is to hatched as cub is to _____ .
   born   old   young
3. Animal is to living as chair is to _____ .
   nonliving   moving   running
4. Young is to cub as old is to _____ .
   puppy   chick   bear
5. Hot is to cold as day is to _____ .
   up   night   long
6. _____ is to pretty as like is to different.
   handsome   ugly   cute
7. Day is to night as _____ is to city.
   suburbs   trash   country
8. Puppy is to _____ as young is to old.
   playful   dog   kitten
9. Tadpole is to frog as _____ is to butterfly.
   caterpillar   cocoon   moth
10. _____ is to little as cow is to calf.
    long   wet   big

A C T I V I T Y   7 . 1 9   **WORD ANALOGIES: HIGH SCHOOL BIOLOGY**

1. _____ : tissue :: organ : system
   arm   *cell*   chlorophyll   nucleus
2. _____ : photosynthesis :: root : absorption
   vein   plant   *leaf*   flower
3. photosynthesis : glucose :: respiration : _____
   lungs   pollution   breath   *energy*
4. reptiles : _____:: mammals : hair
   gills   claws   skin   *scales*
5. gymnosperm : cone :: angiosperm : _____
   mosses   ferns   *flowers*   liverworts
6. pseudopod : _____:: cilia : paramecium
   euglena   bacteria   *ameba*   fungi
7. spicules : sponges :: exoskeleton : _____
   cockroach   jelly fish   tapeworm   human

A C T I V I T Y   7 . 2 0   **MAGIC SQUARE: UNE ÎLE MAGIQUE**

Select from the numbered responses the answer that best completes the sentence. Put the number in the proper space in the *île magique* box. The total of the numbers will be the same across each row and down each column.

A. La Martinique est située dans l'océan _____ .
B. Les gens qui habitent la Martinique sont _____ .
C. Les Martiniquais parlent _____ .
D. Le climat de la Martinique est _____ .
E. La Martinique est dans la mer _____ .
F. _____ sont des produits importants de la Martinique.
G. La Martinique et la Guadeloupe sont des _____ d'outre-mer.
H. Beaucoup de Martiniquais sont d'origine _____ .
I. La ville principale de la Martinique est _____ .

1. colonie française
2. tropical
3. le tourisme
4. 1946
5. Fort-de-France
6. français
7. africaine
8. des Martiniquais
9. des Caraïbes
10. Atlantique
11. Joséphine de Beauharnais
12. départements
13. le café, le sucre

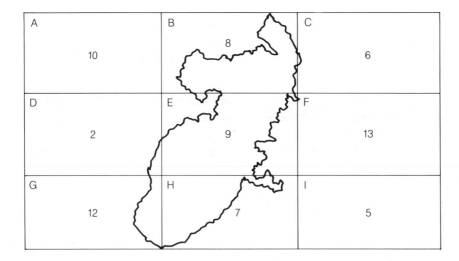

Using what you already know about Martinique and the information you have put together from *un île magique*, write a paragraph of at least seven sentences. Include in your paragraph the answers to the following questions: Qu'est-ce que c'est que la Martinique? Où est la Martinique? Qui sont les habitants de la Martinique? Quelle langue parlent-ils? Quel est le climat de la Martinique? Quels sont des produits importants de la Martinique?

Developed by Billie Anne Baker.

A C T I V I T Y   7 . 2 1   **MAGIC SQUARE COMBINATIONS**

7	3	5
2	4	9
6	8	1

15

9	2	7
4	6	8
5	10	3

18

10	8	6
2	9	13
12	7	5

24

7	11	8
10	12	4
9	3	14

26

16	2	3	13
5	11	10	8
9	7	6	12
4	14	15	1

34

A C T I V I T Y   7 . 2 2   **CINQUAINS: ELEMENTARY SCHOOL**

clouds
dark, heavy
billowing, gliding, creeping
soft pillows of rain
thunderheads

Jon
happy, aware
jumping, darting, asking
has to be challenged
creative

that clarifies or goes along with what is happening in the picture or drawing. Activity 7.25 shows two actual examples created by students in a seventh-grade class.

Vocabulary Bingo

Bingo is one of the most popular of all games. Playing vocabulary bingo lets teachers work with words in a relaxed atmosphere. Steps in playing vocabulary bingo are as follows:

1. Students make a "bingo" card from a list of vocabulary words. (The game works best with at least 20 words.) They should be encouraged to select words at random to fill each square.

A C T I V I T Y   7 . 2 3   **CINQUAINS: JUNIOR HIGH SCHOOL**

(After reading *Johnny Tremain*)

The Sons of Liberty
brave, aggressive
daring, risk-taking, rebelling
they detested British taxes
Whigs

Johnny Tremain
apprentice, brave
hardworking, riding, daring
true to the Whigs
silversmith

Developed in Anne Forrester's class.

A C T I V I T Y   7 . 2 4   **CINQUAINS: HIGH SCHOOL**

viruses
subcellular, deadly
invading, threatening, killing
can attack almost anybody
poison

(On composer Richard Wagner)

monster
conceited, talented
haranguing, groveling, unloving
unscrupulous in every way
genius

Developed in Sharon Gray's class.

2. The teacher (or student reader) reads definitions of the words aloud, and the students cover the word that they believe matches the definition. (It's handy to have the definitions on 3″ × 5″ cards and to shuffle them between games.) The winner is the first to cover a vertical, horizontal, or diagonal row.

3. Check the winner by rereading the definitions used. This step not only keeps everyone honest but serves as reinforcement and provides an opportunity for students to ask questions.

A sample bingo game is shown in Activity 7.26.

A C T I V I T Y   7 . 2 5   VOCABULARY ILLUSTRATIONS

Opulence

Definition - excessive wealth, grandeur)

These four pictures are a good example of opulence because these things are things people with excessive wealth could afford to have.

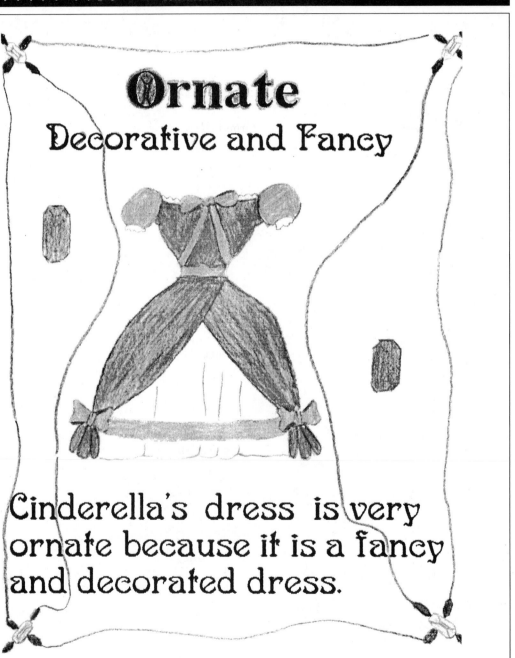

Ornate

Decorative and Fancy

Cinderella's dress is very ornate because it is a fancy and decorated dress.

ACTIVITY 7.26   **VOCABULARY BINGO: GLACIERS**

Words	Definitions
glacier	A moving river of ice
meltwater	Water flowing from melting glacier
esker	Ridge or hill of sand and gravel deposited within a stream channel of a decaying glacier
valley	Type of glacier that forms in high mountains
ice age	A period of colder than normal weather when a continental glacier covered most of North America
kettle lakes	Depressions gouged out by receding continental glaciers and filled by the meltwater of those glaciers
abrade	To rub or wear away by friction
continental	Glacier covering large areas of flat land
Cape Cod	An area of Massachusetts deposited by the last continental glacier
snow line	The point on a glacier where melting matches snowfall
cirque	Bowl-shaped recess or hollow in a mountain caused by glacial erosion
piedmont	Glaciers that form at the foot of mountains where valley glaciers extend onto plains
iceberg	A large chunk of a continental glacier that has broken off and floated out to sea
drift	Pile of boulders, sand, and clay left by a melting glacier
Greenland	An island in the North Atlantic covered by a continental glacier
Alps	Mountains in Switzerland with many horned peaks
plucking	The combination of freezing and pulling that is a major force of erosion by valley glaciers
horn	A three-sided peak eroded by glacier action
moraine	Deposit of unlayered gravel, sand, clay, and boulders left by the melting of a glacier

Bingo card:

meltwater	esker	piedmont	abrade
continental	Cape Cod	snow line	cirque
iceberg	(free)	drift	Greenland
plucking	horn	moraine	ice age
kettle lakes	Alps	valley	glacier

Developed by Patricia Russell.

Bingo is an excellent game to play as a review. Most students enjoy the competition and participate enthusiastically. The constant repetition of the definitions is a good reinforcer for the aural learner. Following are two suggestions for variations on vocabulary bingo:

1. *Periodic table.* Students make bingo cards with symbols of elements, and the names of the elements are called out. For a higher level of difficulty, the caller could use other characteristics of elements such as atomic number or a description—for example, "a silvery liquid at room temperature," or "used to fill balloons."
2. *Math: geometric shapes.* Student bingo cards contain the names of shapes—triangle, octagon, trapezoid, and so on—and the caller uses definitions of those shapes.

One-Minute Summary

This chapter has emphasized that concept development—the main reason for vocabulary study—is enhanced when teachers (1) take more time to prepare carefully for the reading lesson by having students study difficult vocabulary terms, (2) assist students with certain long-term aids and strategies to figure out unfamiliar words, and (3) ask students to reflect on concepts they have learned and had clarified. Numerous vocabulary strategies have been presented with the idea that students will learn and grow intellectually when teachers spend time carrying out these three operations. Research has been cited throughout the chapter in support of the idea that increasing vocabulary knowledge is central to producing richer, deeper reading experiences for students.

End-of-Chapter Activities

Assisting Comprehension

See how well you remember the following specific techniques by recalling what they are and how you would use them. If the activity is done in stages or steps, jot down what you remember about these stages.

structured overview	semantic feature analysis	concept mapping
word analogies	context clue teaching	network diagrams
interactive cloze		

Reflecting on Your Reading

Has reading this chapter changed your thinking in any way on the importance of teaching vocabulary and concepts to your students?

CHAPTER 8

Writing and Reading to Learn

"I never know what I think until I see what I say."

Charlie Citrine in Saul Bellow's *Humboldt's Gift*

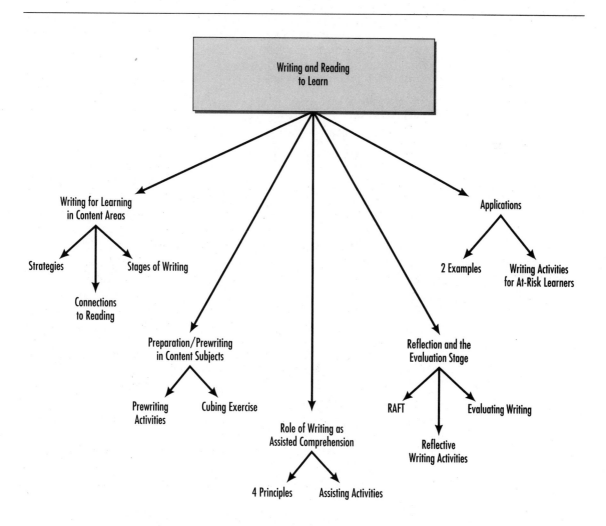

Prepare to Read

1. Before reading this chapter, ask yourself the following questions:

   Why should a content-area teacher use writing activities in the classroom?

   How can writing activities help students learn about my subject?

   How can I fit writing into my already overloaded curriculum?

   How can I teach writing when I'm not trained to do it?

   How can I grade all that writing fairly and efficiently?

2. Following is a list of terms used in this chapter. Some of them may be familiar to you in a general context, but in this chapter they may be used in a different way than you are used to. Rate your knowledge by placing a + in front of those you are sure that you know, a √ in front of those you have some knowledge about, and a 0 in front of those you don't know. Be ready to locate and pay special attention to their meanings when they are presented in the chapter.

   ___ emergent literacy   ___ double-entry journal
   ___ process writing approach   ___ REAP
   ___ zero draft   ___ RAFT
   ___ cubing   ___ collaborative writing
   ___ brainwriting   ___ C3B4Me
   ___ learning log   ___ rubric
   ___ free writing   ___ summary writing

Objectives

As you read this chapter, focus your attention on the following objectives. You will:

1. learn about writing to learn as a link to reading to learn.

2. identify the different stages of writing, from prewriting through revision and publishing activities.

3. discover writing-to-learn activities to help readers with preparation, assistance, and reflection.

4. see how writing can be useful both as a tool for learning and as a means of grading students.

Writing for Learning in Content Areas

Listening, speaking, reading, and writing are integrally connected. Writing may be the most complex of these communication processes (Wolfe & Reising, 1983). Writing challenges the learner to communicate not only with others, but also with oneself. One can progress from a blank sheet to a page filled with statements about content learned, revelations about thoughts, discoveries about self. Writing is active involvement. Writing allows students to explore subject matter. Writing can bring the reader closer to thinking than any of the other language arts *if* it is viewed as a way of discovering, rather than solely as a means of testing knowledge.

What do we know about writing as a tool for learning in the content areas?

Learners remember what they write about content material (Speaker & Grubaugh, 1992).

Writing helps readers increase their metacognitive skills (French, 1991; Murnane, 1990).

Writers become facile at recognizing text coherence by writing summaries of what they have read (Murnane, 1990).

Writing improves thinking (Angeletti, 1991).

Writing can be used in *every* content area as an effective means of learning (Brown, Phillips, & Stephens, 1992; Wolfe & Reising, 1983).

Unfortunately, writing is not used often enough as a way of learning in the content areas. The *National Assessment of Educational Progress* (1980) reported that teachers do not provide enough writing opportunities for students. Probably as a direct result, students' writing skills have been declining for several years. We have been missing out on a valuable way to teach students in content areas.

When one stops to consider ways that writing can be used for learning in the content areas, the list of ideas can grow pretty quickly. Self (1987) has suggested a number of writing-to-learn strategies; they are listed in Table 8.1. These are excellent general writing strategies for all content students.

Connections between Reading and Writing to Learn

EMERGENT LITERACY

Just as students can use reading to learn even in the primary grades, students can become writers at a younger age than was previously thought. Recent research on writing has indicated that very young children create forms of reading and writing that they can explain to adults (Teale & Sulzby, 1986). This writing includes pictures, which Vygotsky (1978b) describes as gestures to represent the child's thought. Children in the early grades are capable of writing reports about content subjects (Calkins, 1986). Although these reports may contain inventive spellings and pictures one might not expect to find in an older student's report, they reflect learning through language. Teachers are now encouraged to recognize this early reading and writing as **emergent literacy** and to foster children's use of all of the communicative arts as early as possible in content subjects.

TABLE 8.1	WRITING TO:	SUGGESTED TEACHER INSTRUCTIONS
Some Writing-to-Learn Strategies	1. Discover what one does or doesn't already know	Write down what you already know about the process of photosynthesis.
	2. Assemble information by taking notes and making notes about subject matter	Draw a line down the center of your paper. On the left side, take notes on the important concepts you read in Chapter 12. On the right side, make a personal note about each recorded note. (React to, rephrase, respond to, question, or associate the ideas with something you know.)
	3. Predict what will happen next in the text	Now that you have read about lungs, what do you need to know next? What do you think will come next in the chapter?
	4. Paraphase, translate, or rephrase the text	There are ten sections in Chapter 12. After receiving a number from one to ten, rephrase your respective section in your own words. Tomorrow we will read our own version of Chapter 12.
	5. Associate images, events, ideas, or personal experiences with subject matter	When you think about the Declaration of Independence, what do you see (images, events, ideas, or even a personal experience that reminds you of that time in our history)?
	6. Define concepts or ideas about subject matter	In your own words, define the terms in bold print found in the second section of Chapter 12.
	7. React or respond to texts or discussions	Take the last five minutes of class to write down the most important ideas for you in our discussion.
	8. Create problems to be solved with subject matter	Make up a word problem that reflects a real-life situation in which the solver would have to use the formula for finding the area of a rectangle.
	9. Apply the subject matter to one's own life	After reading about the concept of supply and demand, choose one product that you frequently use and tell how your life would change if its balance of supply and demand were interrupted.
	10. Sketch or narrate observations and/ or one's responses or reactions to them	Sketch out or tell in story form what happened on your field trip. For some of the events, give your personal reactions to what happened.

TABLE 8.1	**WRITING TO:**	**SUGGESTED TEACHER INSTRUCTIONS**
continued	11. Summarize concepts and ideas from texts or discussions	Write a summary of Chapter 12. *Or* summarize the ideas we discussed in class today.
	12. Question what the text or lecture means or how the parts of the topic relate	List at least three things in Chapter 12 that aren't clear to you. *Or* write down two questions you would like to ask the author of this.
	13. Talk on paper with the teacher or another student about a topic or idea	Choose a friend and write your understanding of and your questions about photosynthesis.
	14. Invent a role or language that characterizes the subject matter or person under study	Having now studied the Middle East, write a statement you think our State Department might release about the recent kidnappings of Americans in Beirut.
	15. Analyze a topic, or one's reactions to it	List the images you see in this poem and try to figure out how they relate to one another or to the message of the poem.
	16. Solve problems with the subject matter	How and where in this story is Hemingway's philosophy of death apparent?

Reprinted from Judy Self (1987), "The Picture of Writing to Learn" in *Plain Talk About Learning and Writing Across the Curriculum*, Virginia Department of Education. Used with permission.

Figure 8.1 contains two writing samples from a first-grader. Both demonstrate learning about science through writing. The teacher made comments about the content of the writing, not about the invented spellings.

WRITING AS A TOOL

The same principle applies with writing to learn as with reading to learn: writing is a tool for learning the content; learning the content is the goal, which writing can facilitate. Content teachers should emphasize writing as a way to learn, just as reading is a way to learn. Content teachers are not expected to teach students to read, or to write, but to use these processes as ways to learn. Figure 8.2 illustrates the place of content writing in the overall learning process.

PROCESS AND PRODUCT RELATIONSHIP IN WRITING

Readers process information and think it through while reading to learn, developing ideas and relying on assistance from teachers or their own metacognitive resources to understand. In the same way, writers think, prewrite, and draft while in the process of writing. The products of reading can be evaluated, perhaps as test responses or completed experiments. The products of writing can also be evaluated, perhaps as test essays or research reports. In both reading

FIGURE 8.1

Writing to learn
in first grade.

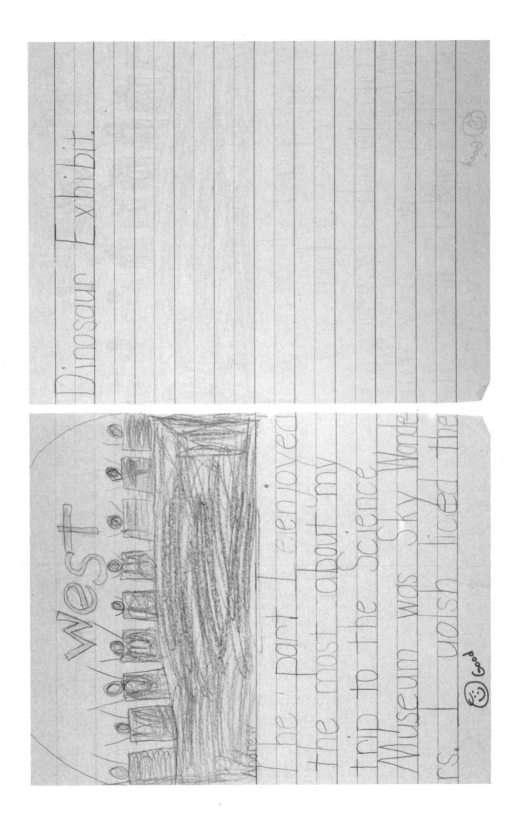

FIGURE 8.1

continued

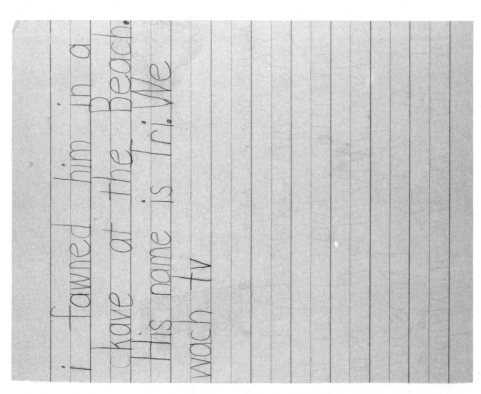

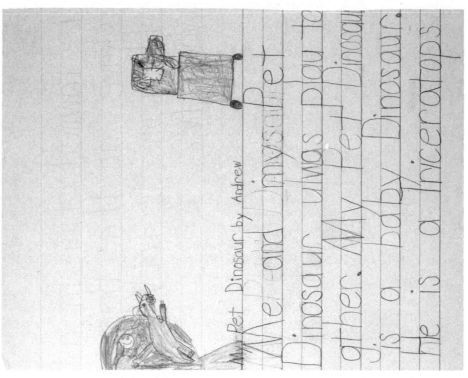

FIGURE 8.2

Content learning through writing (Brown, Phillips, & Stephens, 1992).

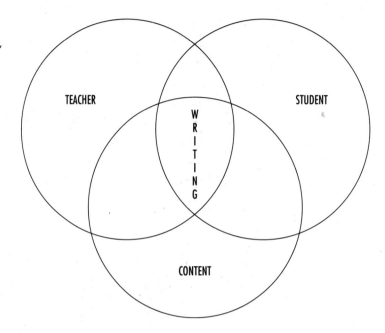

and writing, processing occurs as learning occurs, but a specific product does not have to be generated for comprehension to occur.

Writing is a means of developing comprehension. Many fiction writers confess that they did not know what a particular fictional character was going to do until they started writing. Their preparation gave them direction for writing but not exact knowledge of how the writing would turn out. Only by creating did they discover. The same held true for us as textbook writers. We have learned more about what we know as we have written this book. We have *discovered* ways to express the information we have to share with readers; we did not *know* all that we would write before we drafted this text. In a similar way, readers will learn as they read. Since both reading and writing can assist comprehension, it seems logical to use both in tandem when assisting readers.

Unfortunately, writing is not used very often as an activity to help students understand content material (Pearce & Bader, 1984; Bader & Pearce, 1983). Teachers like Miss K, in *Ralph S. Mouse* by Beverly Cleary, are rare. Miss K would turn anything into a writing project. For example, when she and the class discover that Ralph the mouse has come to school with Ryan, she inspires the students to write about mice and, later, to write rejoinders to a newspaper article that included misinformation about their projects. Most teachers, in contrast, seem to use writing activities that are mainly product-oriented and graded. However, as research has shown, writing can be a powerful tool to assist comprehension. According to Jacobs (1987):

Writing . . . is the ordering of thought. It is the formation of an idea, or a cluster of ideas, from a child's experiences and imagination. It is a conscious shaping of the materials selected by the writer to be included in the composition. In selecting what to put in and leave out, the child is using those elements of writing craftsmanship that he or she can manage. (p. 38)

Self's (1987) diagram (see Figure 8.3) shows the relationship between the process of writing and the products of writing. Much process-oriented writing results in a formal product. The best products will be generated when students are given opportunities for prewriting, writing, and revising. Not all writing does lead to a formal product, but all writing can lead to writing as a means to learning.

The Stages of Writing

Teachers need to be aware that the writing process occurs in stages. Researchers generally agree that the writing process includes at least three stages: prewriting, drafting, and revising. Some authors describe more stages. Table 8.2 compares two such frameworks, each of which will be discussed in turn.

Brown, Phillips, and Stephens (1992) suggest five basic stages in the writing process. In the *prewriting* stage, writers prepare by identifying what they already know about the topic, selecting ideas to write about, and establishing a purpose for their writing. This stage, which might include getting rough thoughts on paper, focusing on one idea, or deciding on a certain approach to the topic, is very much like determining and building background and then setting a purpose for reading. In the *drafting* and *revising* stages, writers create a draft by writing to get the ideas down and to carry out their purposes. During this stage, writers are thinking, changing direction, organizing, and reorganizing. They are writing toward a finished product but, at this stage, are not focusing on functional writing concerns. In the *evaluating* and *publishing* stages, writers reflect on what they have written and rewrite for some form of publication. This step can include major reorganization of the material, additions and deletions, and editorial changes.

FIGURE 8.3

Product and process in writing (reprinted from Self (1987) with permission of the Virginia Department of Education).

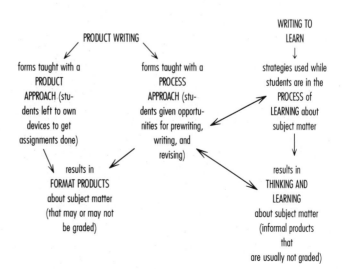

TABLE 8.2

PAR FRAMEWORK	CAW* FRAMEWORK	CAW* FRAMEWORK
(Richardson & Morgan)	(Brown, Phillips, & Stephens)	(Wolfe & Reising)
Preparation Before	Prewriting	Prevision Reflection Selection
Assistance During	Drafting Revising	Zero draft First draft Peer inquiry Revision
Reflection After	Evaluating Publishing	Teacher inquiry Revision Evaluation/ Publication

*Content Area Writing.

Only at this third stage do writers pay a lot of attention to the format of the writing. Up to this point, they are more concerned with writing to get down the content. Writing at the first and second stages is a way of thinking. The last stage of writing is the culmination of that thinking in a product to be shared with a particular audience. It is important to understand that some writing never reaches this last stage because the writer never intended to share it with an audience.

The prewriting stage matches well what happens before reading, which we call Preparation. The drafting and revising stages match what happens during reading, which we call Assistance. The evaluating and publishing stages can be likened to our Reflection, which happens after reading.

Breaking down the writing process into several phases is advisable, because this process is new to many students. Wolfe and Reising, in their book *Writing for Learning in the Content Areas* (1983), describe a ten-stage **process writing approach**.

1. *Prevision experience.* This is the struggling initial stage when students are formulating thoughts about some experience they have had or thinking about a stimulus the teacher has shared with them. Students cannot simply sit down and write without careful thought about the sense of the piece of writing to be crafted.
2. *Reflection.* Here students should begin to focus their thinking about a topic by utilizing individual "think time" or discussing the topic in a small-group brainstorming session.
3. *Selection.* In this phase, the topic or topics and subtopics begin to emerge. Students choose the topic after careful study throughout phases 1 and 2.
4. *Zero draft.* Through free writing, games, or graphic visuals, student(s) begin to build a conceptual framework, which the authors call a **zero draft** or "bank." The bank provides a collection of raw data for the first draft.

5. *First draft*. The student completes a first rendering, with little editing or revising.

6. *Peer inquiry*. The teacher divides students into groups of two to five to exchange ideas about first drafts and deal with student perceptions about the topic. Each student should get at least one response to his or her own writing. If time permits, all papers are read and critiqued by all students.

7. *Revision*. Using the results of phase 6, the student begins to make changes, to revise, and to edit. Here the student is truly becoming a writer, growing and learning through crafting the piece of writing.

8. *Teacher inquiry*. Here the teacher reads not as a grader but as a reviewer of the student's work. The teacher gives as much feedback as possible about ways to further improve the draft.

9. *Revision*. The student makes another revision based on the teacher's comments. The student is asked to reconsider every phase, possibly going back to the prevision stage.

10. *Evaluation/Publication*. The student's writing is evaluated by the teacher and "published," in the sense that the teacher, other students, family, and friends read the work. In special cases, writing may be published outside the classroom, perhaps as letters to the editor or articles in the school newspaper.

Preparation/Prewriting in Content Subjects

Prewriting is seldom used in content classrooms, although its possibilities for preparing content readers are powerful. As Davis and Winek (1989) note, "students who know little about a topic may have difficulty even beginning to write" (p. 178). By providing their students with carefully directed lessons with plenty of opportunities to read, think, and prewrite, these authors found that their seventh-grade social studies students produced some publishable articles.

Cubing

Cubing is an activity that can prepare students as both writers *and* readers. Before we discuss this activity and its applications, try the sample exercise in Activity 8.1.

Cubing was originated by Cowan and Cowan (1980) as a way to stimulate writing, especially when writers have a "block" and can't think of what to write. The writer is encouraged to imagine a cube, put one of the six tasks on each of the six sides, and consider each one for no more than five minutes. All six sides are to be considered, and quickly, forcing the writer to look at a subject from a number of perspectives.

In 1986, Vaughan and Estes applied cubing to reading comprehension. Cubing can be used to provide purposeful reading and to develop reading comprehension. Notice that in Activity 8.1 the directive was to "respond," but we did not indicate whether that response was to be in oral or written form. The response could be either. Activity 8.2 shows how cubing can be used in both ways, while capitalizing on many other aspects of content-area reading that have been stressed in this textbook.

A C T I V I T Y   8 . 1   CUBING

Please read the following paragraphs:

> The wild African elephant faces extinction in the near future. Only 20,000 elephants of the 165,000 that were counted in Kenya fifteen years ago are still alive; 50,000 elephants in Tanzania have been killed within the past ten years. In Uganda, 90% of the elephants have been killed by poachers.
>
> Why is this destruction occurring? Because poachers are killing elephants for their ivory tusks. The ivory is made into jewelry, which is sold all over the world. Would people buy this jewelry if they knew that elephants were a dying race? (facts from The African Wildlife Association, 1988)

Now, show your comprehension of what you read through the following exercise. Take no more than one minute to respond to each of the six tasks.

1. *Describe it.* What is the issue?
2. *Compare it.* Does this issue remind you of any similar example of animal extinction?
3. *Associate it.* What does it make you think of? Is there an incident you recall, or a feeling you get?
4. *Analyze it.* Are there two sides to this issue?
5. *Apply it.* What might be done to solve this problem?
6. *Argue for or against it.* Take a stand. What are your opinions and the reasons for your stand?

A C T I V I T Y   8 . 2   CUBING: TENTH-GRADE ENGLISH

The teacher started the academic year by cubing during the first week of class. Her objectives were:

  To set the "tone" of the class by demonstrating to students that their attitudes and opinions matter

  To determine student attitudes and opinions about the subject matter, for more relevant instruction

  To use discussion to facilitate writing

  To demonstrate the stages of writing, from prewriting to drafting to finished product

  To model the use of preparation

The steps in her lesson were:

1. She made a cube and talked about each direction on it with the class: describe, compare, associate, analyze, apply, argue for or against.
2. She asked, in a whole group setting, for oral responses to the topic "English," using each directive on the cube in turn. Any honest response was acceptable.
3. She told students to jot down in their notebooks their personal responses to each directive. The personal responses could be similar to those from the group, or different.
4. She assigned each student to write a rough draft of an essay on the topic "What I think about English."
5. She collected and responded to each essay, using a checklist format to provide feedback (see Reflection section of this chapter).

(continued on page 299)

6. She assigned a final essay due date and evaluated the essays, which had been revised according to the feedback given.

Here is one student's cubed responses, as she wrote them—errors included, because this is *not* a product to be graded:

1. I would describe English as difficult and sometimes hard.
2. Compared to Gym, gym is more fun and interesting.
3. English makes me think of school even when at home.
4. The parts of English includes how to use good speech, good handwriting, and reading stories.
5. We need English because we need to go out in the real world and know what were doing.
6. I would argue against it because it's very confusing and boring.

Here is another student's essay *draft*, which is presented as written, mistakes included, because it is still a paper in *process*:

> English is a language that at least everyone needs to know. It is hard and easy to certain people. Some people thinks its stupid and the only reason is they haven't learned it well. English is like another language to someone else, its easy for them and harder for us. In this language our words mostly come from latin and Greek origins and they are converted into what we read today. We associate with it everyday of our lives and it is like a little kid learning his alphabet until he learns to read. it is an intelligent language and some words are too advance for people to read it. English has many parts such as grammar which you learn what the pats of speech are and literature has stories which develop your reading skills and learning english you can write effectively and speak clearly. I am for English and any other language because you need to know how to talk to elder people or how to talk when you get a job interview. So that is why I think that English or any other language is very important to learn. It is very useful to use and you need to know how to use it well.

By the time this student wrote his final essay, using class discussions, his own thoughts, his drafted response, and teacher comments, he produced a more polished essay. Although his draft contains several grammatical errors, his final, graded version was much improved because he had the opportunity to draft his thoughts and process his writing first.

Students in this teacher's class began to realize their own roles and responsibilities. The teacher had established the prewriting, drafting, revising, and evaluating steps as a part of her expectations for her students' writing. She also understood quite a bit about her students' attitudes and concepts about her subject.

Students kept their notes, draft with teacher comments, and final graded essay in a folder. Over the semester, they collected other "cubed essays" in the folder. The folder contents then became a means for authentic assessment (see Chapter 6).

When a teacher actually constructs a cube and uses it as a visual prop for students, they can gain a rapid understanding of the reading material. Making a cube is simple. Cover a square tissue box with construction paper, and label each side; or use the outline provided in Figure 8.4 to construct a cube from a strong material, such as cardboard. Activity 8.3 shows the results of a cubing exercise completed by third-graders who were reading about triangles.

FIGURE 8.4

Cubing: making the cube (Brown, Phillips, & Stephens, 1992).

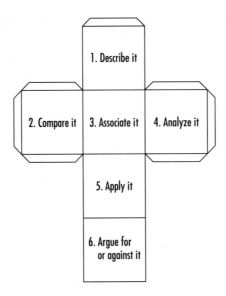

Most teachers, whatever grade level they teach, will find that the cube is an enticing prop for their students to manipulate. One teacher brought a cube to the classroom, but did not have time to cube for several days. The cube, left casually on her desk, generated much student curiosity. One high school teacher, concerned that her students would not be receptive to using a "prop," adapted a "flat cube." Instead of using a cube, she drew a circular diagram labeled with the cubing steps. Students wrote notes in the "flat cube" (see Activity 8.4).

Other Prewriting Activities

The prewriting stage calls for students to determine what the topic will be and what they know about that topic. Students may need to build background through activities such as cubing, to find out what they know. Several other activities discussed in this textbook also provide a writing connection: written responses to anticipation guides, the notations accompanying factstorming and PreP, and What-I-Know sheets are all forms of prewriting. **Brainwriting** (Brown, Phillips, & Stephens, 1992), a variation of factstorming, can help students generate ideas. Small groups of students respond to a topic, write down their ideas, and then exchange and add to each other's lists.

Pearce and Davison (1988) conducted a study to see how often junior high school mathematics teachers used writing activities with their students. They found that writing was seldom used to guide thinking and learning, prewriting least of all. In a follow-up study, Davison and Pearce (1988b) looked at five mathematics textbook series to determine if these texts included suggestions for writing activities. Not surprisingly, they found few suggestions, and almost none were suggestions for prewriting. Teachers in various content areas confirm that they find few suggestions in their textbooks for using writing as a preparation activity. Because teachers rely on textbooks and teachers' manuals for the

ACTIVITY 8.3   CUBING: TRIANGLES

1. Describe it: "It looks like a teepee or a rocket."
2. Compare it: "It is not round like a circle."
3. Associate it (the teacher asked, "What does it make you think of?"): "A fingernail, an arrowhead, a piece of pizza."
4. Analyze it (the teacher asked, "Tell how it is made."): "Three lines, three points, three sharp ends, three flat sides tied together."
5. Apply it (the teacher asked, "How can it be used?"): "As a trowel, as a weapon, to rake stuff up."
6. Argue for or against it (the teacher asked, "Why is it important?"): "We need it so we can dig a hole."

Developed by Debbie Prout.

ACTIVITY 8.4   A "FLAT CUBE": WORLD WAR I

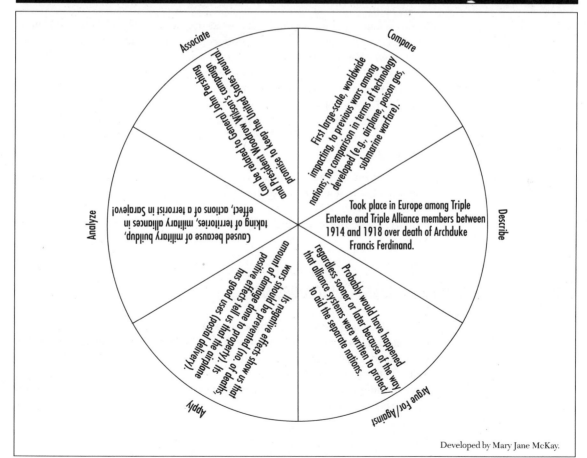

Developed by Mary Jane McKay.

majority of their instruction, they may thus be missing a rich source of preparation through writing activities.

Following are some specific ideas for content teachers to encourage prewriting.

1. Have students predict and write down the definition of a new word in the chapter.
2. Have students write what they think a visual aid is illustrating or could have to do with the topic.
3. Have students write how the new topic might fit with the previous topics studied.
4. For mathematics, students could write out what they think a particular symbol might mean, what the possible steps for solving a problem could be, or why a particular unit of study is presented at a particular place in the text. For example, a fourth-grade mathematics textbook starts the chapter on fractions with a picture of a sectioned pizza, but no explanation is given. Elementary students could be asked to write why they think this illustration has been selected.
5. For science, students could write what they anticipate to be the steps in an experiment, what a formula will produce, what the composition of a substance is, or why certain conditions facilitate certain results.
6. For social studies, students could write about problems people might face when they move from one place to another or after they have settled in a new place (Pearce, 1987).
7. For English, students could write why they think a particular punctuation rule might be necessary: what would happen if we didn't use commas in our writing?

It is important to make sure that students understand clearly what the writing assignment is, that it is not to be graded, and that it will be useful in guiding their reading. Prewriting is clearly a major emphasis in Activity 8.5, developed by a primary science teacher to direct her students through the various stages of writing.

The Role of Writing as Assisted Comprehension

The drafting stage of writing is much like the assisting step in reading. Process is emphasized, and writers begin to realize what they have to say and what they understand about a topic. The flow of thought is represented in the writer's draft, as it is in the reader's discussion.

According to Self (1987), using writing to assist in teaching content material fulfills the following purposes:

1. Focusing students' attention
2. Engaging students actively

A C T I V I T Y 8 . 5   **STAGES IN THE WRITING PROCESS: PRIMARY SCIENCE**

I. Prewriting

The teacher will show the book, *Desert Voices*, written by Byrd Baylor and Peter Parnall, to the class, and she will mention that these authors have worked together on three Caldecott Honor Books. (It may be necessary to refresh their minds about the annual Caldecott and Newbery Awards.)

"Byrd Baylor, who writes the words of the book, lives in the Southwest. I don't know which *particular* state in the southwestern portion of the United States. The title of this book has the word *desert* in it, and she has written another book called *The Desert Is Theirs.* If she lives in the Southwest and likes to write about deserts, could you guess a state where she *might* live?" (The students will remember, hopefully, that Arizona has desert land.)

"Peter Parnall illustrates the book. He lives on a farm in Maine with his wife and two children."

"If the title of the book is *Desert Voices*, who might be speaking? Who are the voices in the desert?" (Wait for responses.) "Byrd Baylor has written the words for ten desert creatures as they tell us what it is like for the desert to be their home. I will read you what the jackrabbit and the rattlesnake have to say." (Teacher reads aloud.)

A. *Factstorming*

The teacher will divide the class into small groups of four or five students. She lists on the chalkboard the names of the other creatures who "speak" in *Desert Voices*: pack rat, spadefoot toad, cactus wren, desert tortoise, buzzard, lizard, coyote. (The tenth voice is entitled "Desert Person.")

B. *The assignment*

"Each group must select one of these creatures or any other desert animal or plant that has been mentioned in our unit. Each group member should jot down on a piece of paper any ideas he has about this creature's feelings relating to living in the desert. You may want to think about the appearance of this creature or thing. Does it have any body parts or habitat specifically suited to the desert's environment? After you jot down your ideas, place your paper in the center of the table and choose another member's paper. Add some of your ideas to his paper. After you have written something on every other group member's page, your group as a whole should compile the *best* list of ideas. Then we will begin to write our individual drafts."

II. Writing

III. Rewriting

Students may work in pairs to edit and proofread each other's work. The child's partner would be from another "creature's" group.

IV. Postwriting

Oral presentations

Room displays

Compilation of compositions dealing with the same "voice" into book form

Note: Naturally this project would continue for several days. Even the group factstorming might require more than one day, especially if some reference work were necessary.

Developed by Kathryn Davis.

3. Arousing students' curiosity
4. Helping students discover disparate elements in the material
5. Helping students make connections between the material and themselves
6. Helping students "make their own meaning" from the material
7. Helping students think out loud
8. Helping students find out what they do and do not know
9. Helping teachers diagnose the students' successes and problems
10. Preparing students to discuss material

Gebhard (1983) suggests four principles for developing writing activities that assist in comprehension. First, students need an audience other than the teacher. Peers are a fine resource because they can provide supportive comments and suggestions. Often, students become much more active and committed to writing when the audience is someone other than the teacher. Using peers as an audience conveys the message that the process of writing is more important than the final product, which is the case when writing is an activity to assist comprehension. Writing for peers may alleviate the teacher's need to "grade" the writing at all. If the teacher does decide to grade, then the peer revision and editing will mean that the teacher will see a more polished product. Correction will take second place to content.

Second, the writing tasks should be "consequential." Just because the teacher may grade a piece of writing does not mean the student is motivated. Students need to be able to write about topics that interest them. The *Foxfire* books illustrate this principle of consequential writing very well. Eliot Wigginton (1986) inspired his English students in Raburn Gap, Georgia, to write about the crafts and habits of their own community. Thus, Wigginton combined the subjects of English and social studies using writing as the medium. The assignment itself was much more inspiring to students than receiving a grade. The audience was their fellow students and their community. The work was collaborative, with many students planning and writing together. The collaboration assisted students in creating a cultural history of their community. The result of their writing is the *Foxfire* books, the success of which has been phenomenal — not an inconsequential task, by any means!

Third, writing assignments should be varied. No one wants to do the same old thing again and again. Copying definitions gets pretty old pretty fast. In this section, we provide several teacher-tried ideas to vary writing assignments. Several recent publications also help content teachers find innovative and varied ways to introduce writing across the curriculum. Some are suggested at the end of this chapter.

Fourth, writing activities should connect prior knowledge to new information, providing students with a creative challenge. As we have shown, cubing does this well. Another excellent activity to encourage this connection is the jot chart, introduced in Chapter 6 as a way to promote critical thinking. As we have pointed out, writing also stimulates critical thinking, so jot charts certainly can have more than one purpose. Jot charts provide a matrix for learning, by providing students with an organizational guide, a series of boxes in which they can enter their "jottings" about the content as they read along, and thereby see the connections between what they already knew, what they need to find out, and—when completed—what they have learned.

Davison and Pearce (1988a), by modifying Applebee's (1981) classification system, divide writing activities into five types:

1. Direct use of language—copying and transcribing information, such as copying from the board or glossary.
2. Linguistic translation—translation of words or other symbols, such as writing the meaning of a formula.
3. Summarizing/interpreting—paraphrasing, making notes about material, such as explaining in one's own words or keeping a journal.
4. Applied use of language—a new idea is applied to the information in written form, such as writing possible test questions.
5. Creative use of language—using writing to explore and convey related information, such as writing a report. (pp. 10–11)

Davison and Pearce found that the copying tasks were those predominantly used by the junior high school mathematics teachers in their study. Creative activities were seldom used, group writing opportunities were scarce, and the audience for the writing was usually the teacher. In practice, then, teachers do not seem to be following the suggestions that Gebhard has made, probably because they do not realize how helpful writing activities can be to assist students' comprehension. Yet, the possibilities are great. Following are a number of ideas for content teachers, beginning with learning logs and annotations.

Learning Logs

Request that students write regularly in the form of a journal called a **learning log**, under such headings as "The two new ideas I learned this week in science and how I can apply them to my life" or "How I felt about my progress in math class this week." These entries can be read by other students or by the teacher, but should be valued for their introspective qualities and not graded. Richardson (1992a) has found that such journal writing helps students to work through problems they are having learning material and to verbalize concerns that the reader can respond to individually, also in written form.

One vocational education teacher discovered that journal writing enabled her to better monitor the progress her co-op students were making as they worked in their placements. "Since I have 13 students in five different concentration areas, it is not always easy to deal with all of their problems at once. For me as the teacher, I can focus on each student's problems or successes one at a time; no one gets left out. For the students it's a catharsis" (Sheryl Lam).

Learning logs are a relatively simple yet always effective way to get all students to write in content-area classes. Logs are used to stimulate thinking. Normally students write in their logs every day, either as an in-class activity or an out-of-class assignment. Students can be asked to write entries that persuade, that tell

A C T I V I T Y 8 . 6   LEARNING LOG IDEAS

Read _____ , and in your learning log write: (teacher chooses one from below)

1. any passage or item that puzzles you.
2. any items that intrigue you.
3. three things you agree (disagree) with.
4. how it makes you feel.
5. what you think will happen next.
6. three new concepts and your definition of them.
7. how this reading relates to your life.
8. two things this reading has in common with _____ .
9. what you think the author was like.
10. why you think _____ acted like (he/she) did.
11. what you think it would be like to live in <u>(setting)</u> .
12. a summary of this <u>(chapter, section, book)</u> .
13. your reaction to _____ .
14. three things you'd like the class to discuss.
15. a cause-effect flowchart.
16. how you can use this knowledge in your own life.
17. something the reading reminds you of.
18. what you think it means, and why you think that.
19. what you would do if you were <u>(character)</u> .
20. Why _____ is important.

From B. Glaze, "Learning Logs," in *Plain Talk About Learning and Writing Across the Curriculum*, 1987.
Richmond: Virginia Department of Education, p. 151. Used with permission.

of personal experiences and responses to stimuli, that give information or that are creative and spontaneous. Activity 8.6 shows how teachers can motivate students by providing a number of learning-log assignments. Activity 8.7 gives an example of how a content area learning log might look if the teacher structures columns to get students thinking and reacting to what is being learned. This structure especially helps the reluctant student to focus on a task and come to closure.

Once students have practiced keeping a log, the teacher can ask them to respond in a more open-ended, less structured fashion. For instance, Page (1987) got the following response from a student, Carla, in exploring *Antigone* in a high school English class:

I get Sophocles and Socrates mixed up. Socrates is a philosopher. Athens is talked about a great deal in mythology. Wow, they had dramatic competitions. I wonder if he had the record for the most wins at the competition. I bet if Polyneices were alive, he would be very proud of his sister. I would! The chorus seems similar to today's narrator.

A C T I V I T Y   8 . 7   **LEARNING LOG FORM**

Date	Prediction: What's going to happen?	Facts: What have I learned?	Question: What don't I understand yet?	My Opinion: How do I feel about this reading?

Name _____ Class (Subject) _____

Page notes also that students are more motivated to learn when they keep a journal or log. She cites positive comments of three students about such writing:

> I love the writing journals. Having to keep a writing journal is the extra push I need to expand my ideas, when otherwise I would not. My journal has brought to life many ideas that may have died if I had not been required to keep a journal. I am somewhat proud of it. — *Carla*

> Writing journals are my favorite. I like having a place to write down important events in my life and literary ideas, poems, stories, etc. — *Allison*

> I feel that the writing journal by far is the most expressive and open writing that we have done in class. I always try to come up with original and creative entries. I feel that the journal has sparked some new creativity in me — and my essays (product paper) reflect it. They seem to be more imaginative than before. — *Betsy*
> (1987, pp. 39–40)

Learning-log entries like those quoted here are examples of what is sometimes called **free writing** — an attempt to motivate students by getting them to write of their perceptions of certain events or classroom operations. Students are encouraged to think and write without the encumbrance of worry over mechanics and correctness. It may be just the prescription for students, at all grade levels, who are "turned off" to learning.

A class log, or class notebook (Richardson, 1992a), is a combined writing and note-taking activity that encourages students to take responsibility for writing about class content. Walpole (1987) describes this strategy as she used it:

> I first heard about class logs during a summer spent with the Northern Virginia Writing Project. The class log is a notebook maintained by a different student each day; the student simply takes his notes for the day in the class log instead of in his own notebook. Though there are many uses for the class log, its primary use is as a reference for students who are absent. Never again will I have to listen to someone ask, "Did we do anything in here yesterday?" The class log is my proof. Since people generally take unusually good notes when writing in the log (because they feel their notes are "on display"), absent students find the log convenient to learn from; this saves both them and me hours of individual catch-up sessions after school.
>
> As a side benefit, the log often builds class spirit. I encourage students to take notes on everything going on, as long as the academics aren't slighted ("Oh, yay — it's snowing!!!! OK, back to radicals . . . math is the 'root' of civilization . . . boo!"). Students delight in finding themselves quoted, and will flip through the log looking for gossip or doodles, as well as for explanations of new material. When this kind of spirit erupts in a class, I find that it rather surprisingly contributes to the educational value of the log. Students don't just read the funny comments; they also find themselves noticing note-taking styles, and they begin competing informally to be the clearest and the best at taking notes. This increases their awareness of the importance of note-taking in general. Of course, some classes will maintain their log simply because I tell them they must and therefore never really benefit from it as they could. But the classes that make it into a gossipy game also end up creating an extremely valuable learning tool. (pp. 56–57)

The **double-entry journal** (Vaughan, 1990) is a pre/post learning log. Students write on the left side of a page about their prior knowledge of a topic. After reading, they enter comments about what they learned on the right side of the page. These comments might also include drawings or questions.

Annotations

Students need frequent chances to practice critical thinking in their reading and writing. One way of providing these opportunities for older students — middle and secondary level — is through a system of annotation. Annotating what they read will help students think about their understanding of the material and enable them to get their reflections down in writing.

One such system is **REAP** (read, encode, annotate, ponder), developed by Eanet and Manzo (1976). This procedure is designed to improve comprehension skills by helping students summarize material in their own words and develop writing as well as reading ability. The four steps in REAP are as follows:

R — Reading to discover the author's ideas

E — Encoding into your own language

A — Annotating your interpretation of the author's ideas

P — Pondering whether the text information is significant

Creating annotations will help students increase their maturity and independence in reading. Although annotations may be submitted for grading — perhaps as homework or class grades — they are probably more valuable as written notes to facilitate understanding. We will describe seven different annotation styles, which students can use singly or in combination.

1. The *heuristic annotation* is a statement, usually in the author's words, that has two purposes: to suggest the idea of the selection and to provoke a response. To write it, the annotator needs to find the essence of the selection and then select a quotation that hints at this essence in a stimulating manner. The quote selected must represent the theme or main idea of the selection.

2. The *summary annotation* condenses the selection into a concise form. It should be brief, clear, and to the point. It includes no more or less than is necessary to convey adequately the development and relationship of the author's main ideas. In the case of a story, the summary annotation is a synopsis — the main events of the plot.

3. The *thesis annotation* is an incisive statement of the author's proposition. As the word *incisive* implies, it cuts directly to the heart of the matter. With fiction, it can substitute for a statement of theme. One approach is to ask oneself, "What is the author saying? What one idea or point is being made?" The thesis annotation is best written in precise wording; unnecessary connectives are removed to produce a telegram-like, but unambiguous, statement.

4. The *question annotation* directs attention to the ideas that the annotator thinks most germane; it may or may not be the same as the author's thesis. The annotator must first determine the most significant issue at hand and then express this notation in question form. This annotation answers the question, "What question(s) is the author answering with the narrative?"

5. The *critical annotation* is the annotator's response to the author's thesis. In general, a reader may have one of three responses: agreement, disagreement, or a combination of the two. The first sentence in the annotation should state the author's thesis. The next sentence should state a position. The remaining sentences are devoted to defending this position.

6. The *intention annotation* is a statement of the author's intention, plan, or purpose — as is perceived by the student — in writing the selection. This type of annotation is particularly useful with material of a persuasive, ironic, or satirical nature. Determining intention requires that the annotator bring to bear all available clues — both intrinsic, such as tone and use of language, and extrinsic, such as background knowledge about the author.

7. The *motivation annotation* is a statement that attempts to speculate about the probable motive behind the author's writing. It is an attempt to find the source of the author's belief system and perceptions. The motivation annotation is a high form of criticism, often requiring penetrating psychological insight.

Activity 8.8 uses a single passage to demonstrate each type of annotation. In fact, no one would write each type for every material; writing different annotations for different content materials promotes reflective study.

A C T I V I T Y   8 . 8   ANNOTATIONS

Some time ago, while watching a TV program called "The Vidal Sassoon Show," I came across the quintessential example of what I am talking about. Vidal Sassoon is a famous hairdresser whose TV show is a mixture of beauty hints, diet information, health suggestions, and popular psychology. As he came to the end of one segment of the show in which an attractive woman had demonstrated how to cook vegetables, the theme music came up and Sassoon just had time enough to say, "Don't go away. We'll be back with a marvelous new diet and, then, a quick look at incest." Now, this is more — much more — than demystification. It is even more than revelation of secrets. It is the ultimate trivialization of culture. Television is relentless in both revealing and trivializing all things private and shameful, and therefore it undermines the moral basis of culture. The subject matter of the confessional box and the psychiatrist's office is now in the public domain. I have it on good authority that, shortly, we and our children will have the opportunity to see commercial TV's first experiments with presenting nudity, which will probably not be shocking to anyone, since TV commercials have been offering a form of soft-core pornography for years. And on the subject of commercials — the 700,000 of them that American youths will see in the first 18 years of their lives — they too contribute to opening to youth all the secrets that once were the province of adults — everything from vaginal sprays to life insurance to the causes of marital conflict. And we must not omit the contributions of news shows, those curious entertainments that daily provide the young with vivid images of adult failure and even madness. (From Neil Postman, "The Day Our Children Disappear: Predictions of a Media Ecologist." *Phi Delta Kappan.* Bloomington, Indiana: Phi Delta Kappa, 1981. Used with permission of Neil Postman and the *Phi Delta Kappan.*)

Heuristic annotation: Television represents the ultimate in trivializing all things private and shameful. This trivialization undermines the moral basis of culture.

Summary annotation: Postman describes a Vidal Sassoon television show to demonstrate television's propensity to trivialize all subjects. He says that commercials offer soft-core pornography and news shows show vivid images of adults as failures.

Thesis annotation: Television trivializes the culture. It brings everything — the profound, the ordinary, the mundane — to the same level.

Question annotation: What makes television viewing so bad, anyway? Postman thinks he knows, and he explains why in this article.

Critical annotation: Postman uses emotional language to describe the total destruction that he sees television wreaking on our society; this language is intended to ignite sparks in the reader. His biased thinking ignores the good television does through informational, documentary, and educational programs.

Intention annotation: The author intends to strip the mystique of television and expose the negative influences of the medium.

Motivation annotation: The author is trying to protect children who are subjected to a steady bombardment of harmful television programs.

Other Assisting Activities   **1.** Have students write out the steps they would follow in solving a math problem or completing an experiment. Ask them to speculate on what would happen if they altered one step.

2. Bachman (1989) suggests "Top it off!" for practice in writing about mathematics problems. For instance, in the intermediate-level examples shown in Activity 8.9, students are given numerical or algebraic expressions and are asked

ACTIVITY 8.9	WRITING MATHEMATICS QUESTIONS

The following examples are missing directions that tell you what to do. You are to write two different questions pertaining to each example.

24 and 36

1. (What is the sum of 24 and 36?)
2. (What is the name of the sign that will precede the sum?)

$7^2 + 90 \div 3$

1. (What are the operations involved in the expression?)
2. (Simplify the expression.)

to write questions about them. The questions must reflect students' knowledge of the vocabulary and the correct operations.

3. Ask students to rewrite an historic event by altering one cause or one effect. Then have them compare the way it really happened to their invented way.

4. Ask students to take the perspective of a topic being studied and write from this perspective. In English, one might become an author and, through the author's words, explain word choice or style or plot choices. In science, one might become a blood cell and describe a journey throughout the body. Activity 8.10 presents a story written by a child who has become a blood cell.

5. Have students write modified "biopoems," poems whose subject is the writer himself or herself. Gere (1985, p. 222) provides a pattern for writing biopoems, shown in Activity 8.11. A biopoem can also be adapted to different subject matter, as illustrated in Activity 8.12. In this modified version, written by an elementary social studies teacher, the subject is the state of Virginia, and the poem is condensed to only seven lines.

6. Encourage students to write information they discover on a jot chart, then to use the jotted information to write essays. For examples of jot charts, see Activities 6.12–6.15 in Chapter 6.

7. Cinquains, discussed in Chapter 7 as a way to learn content vocabulary, are an excellent and readily implemented writing activity.

8. Have students rewrite a passage they have read, using guidelines explained in Chapter 3. If students can rewrite material, they are showing understanding.

9. As a way to demonstrate understanding of newly learned vocabulary, the teacher can guide writing using a "What I Learned" activity (A. Miller, 1989), as outlined in Activity 8.13.

10. Two-column responses help students understand what their text material means. In the first column, students are directed to write the phrase in the text that causes them difficulty. In the second column, they should write their own interpretation of the phrase. This written response helps students think out loud. It also provides the teacher with a specific response to check and gain insight about where a student may have gotten off track. Ollmann (1992) describes how

A C T I V I T Y   8 . 1 0   A DAY IN THE LIFE OF A BLOOD CELL

There I was, stuck on a boring day doing absolutely nothing. It was 1:32 in the afternoon. Agent 002 was in hot pursuit of the gangster known as Ned the Nucleus. Agent 0012 called me for backup because there was a shootout at the Cell Bank on 112 Membrane Street. I rode out there, but there was a backup in the bloodstream so I rode down the back way. Ned the Nucleus was threatening to blow the cell bank sky high. I snuck up and over the cell wall. I climbed up the cell bank with the help of Don the DNA. I went in and brought out Bob the Brain Cell. How could I be that stupid; now Ned the Nucleus had a gun. He was shooting at the cops. What could we do?

I went back to the station and figured out a plan. I'd go in the bank disguised as a customer! He'd hold me hostage, then I'd hit him with my elbow and put him under arrest! I got into the building okay. Then I went up to the top floor. He had two other hostages. Their names were Rick the Red Blood Cell and Wally the White Blood Cell. He was arrested on the spot. I got promoted to Chief Lieutenant. Ned the Nucleus got 15–20 years and $500,000 cell bail. A very good lesson was learned today. Killing cells doesn't pay.

Headlines!
Ned the Nucleus Breaks Out of Jail!!

So now I had to get him back in jail. I went to headquarters so I could get all of the information. Then it hit me like a Mike Tyson jab. Where else would he be than Ned's Night Club in downtown Los Nucleus? So I took the bloodstream down there. He wasn't there, but I got some useful information. They told me he was at the dock. On San Fran Cellular's finest dock, Cells Wharf. I pulled up in the bad neighborhood. I wasn't alone, though. I had the help of Carl the Blood Clot, and Priscilla the Spore. Ned the Nucleus was not alone; in fact, he had his whole gang there! I recognized some of their faces; they were Beau the Bruise, Cad the Cut, Rick the Red Blood Cell, and Wally the White Blood Cell, who had faked being a hostage at the bank. We called for backup and got out of there.

We missed the bullets shot at us and met the other cops at my house, where we had told them to go. We went back to the wharf with the SWAT team and the rest of the police squad. We had a stakeout. People shot at us from the water with their stun guns. Our snipers from the roof shot them. Then we had a shootout. But we had them surrounded, so they just gave up. I got a medal of honor and became head of the SWAT team and the police. But to me it was just another day in the life of a detective.

Written by Jon Morgan.

she used this procedure in response to literature. Teachers can dictate the phrases to be written in the first column ("In the Text"), but students must write their own responses in the second column ("In My Head").

Reflection and the Evaluation Stage of Writing

When writing is to be published or finished as a product, writers should be concerned not only with the content of the writing but also with the form. After the writing is revised, an audience will read it and react in a formal way. During revision, writers are still learning to express what they understand about the

ACTIVITY 8.11   PATTERN OF A BIOPOEM

Line 1: First name
Line 2: Four traits that describe the author
Line 3: Relative ("brother," "sister," "daughter," etc.) of
Line 4: Lover of (list three things or people)
Line 5: Who feels (three items)
Line 6: Who needs (three items)
Line 7: Who fears (three items)
Line 8: Who gives (three items)
Line 9: Who would like to see (three items)
Line 10: Resident of
Line 11: Last name

ACTIVITY 8.12   MODIFIED BIOPOEM

Virginia
Coastal, warm, fertile
Land, missionary, adventure
Planter, slave, farmer
First, tobacco, General Assembly
Smith, Rolfe, Pocahontas
Southern Colony

Written by M. J. Weatherford. Used with permission.

ACTIVITY 8.13   "WHAT I LEARNED" ACTIVITY

1. List several fact words (the teacher sets the number) learned about a content subject.
2. Write a sentence about one of those words. (sentence one)
3. Underline a noun or pronoun in sentence one, and write a second sentence explaining it.
4. Underline the most important noun in the second sentence, and write a third sentence explaining that noun.
5. Repeat steps 1–4; use all of your words.

Sample sentences (Melvin Harris, seventh grade):

1. I have learned that a science experiment sometimes has a *control group*.
2. The control group does not receive any testing, treatment, or all of the things an *experimental group* receives.

information, but they are also learning to be considerate of their audience by putting the writing in a consistent, organized format. It is during revision that writers should be concerned with correct spelling, grammar, and organization. Often, teachers confuse the evaluation stage with the drafting stage and expect students to produce writing that meets format considerations before or while they are writing to express content. This is a difficult chore for the most polished writers.

RAFT (Vanderventer, 1979) is one way for writers and their teachers to keep the appropriate audience in focus. *R* stands for the *role* of the writer: what is the writer's role — reporter, observer, eyewitness? *A* stands for *audience:* who will be reading this writing — the teacher, other students, a parent, people in the community, an editor? *F* stands for *format:* what is the best way to present this writing — in a letter, an article, a report, a poem? *T* stands for the *topic:* what is the subject of this writing — a famous mathematician, prehistoric cavedwellers, a reaction to a specific event? When teachers are clear about the purpose of the writing and students keep RAFT in mind, the product will be clearer and more focused.

Much of the writing that students complete for a grade in school is research-type writing, in which students report on assigned topics they have researched using many resources. Calkins (1986) suggests the following cycle for content-area research writing:

1. Choose the research area, and focus on a specific writing topic.
2. Take notes to learn about the topic.
3. Focus in depth on the topic by analyzing information.
4. Do more research on the topic.
5. Get ready to write by rehearsing for writing.
6. Write drafts, revise, have teacher/student conferences.
7. Edit and publish the material.
8. Cycle back for more research, perhaps with a new focus.

Calkins's point 7 is very important in getting students to write with attention to the finished product. Whenever possible, students should write for an audience, even if "publishing" means merely taking completed writing products home to parents or other family. Note that Calkins's steps include prewriting, drafting and revising, and evaluation steps.

Activities for Reflective Writing

A number of activities are well suited to helping students write reflectively, toward building a product.

GUIDED WRITING PROCEDURE

The guided writing procedure (Smith & Bean, 1980) is a strategy that uses writing specifically to enhance comprehension. Smith and Bean give seven steps for its implementation, to be completed in two days. Because guided writing leads to a graded product, we have classified it as a reflection activity; however, guided writing also involves preparation and assistance steps.

On the first day, the teacher should (1) activate students' prior knowledge to facilitate prewriting, (2) have students factstorm and categorize their facts, (3) have students write two paragraphs using this organized list, and (4) have students read about the topic. On the second day, the teacher should (5) have students check their drafts for functional writing concerns, (6) assign rewriting based on functional needs and revision to incorporate the information from the reading, and (7) give a quiz. Although Smith and Bean recommend giving a quiz, we suggest that other alternatives, such as submitting the rewritten paragraphs, are just as appropriate.

Activity 8.14 is an example of a modified guided writing procedure, used by a middle-school English teacher to help her students write limericks.

REACTION GUIDE

A reaction guide (Bean & Peterson, 1981; Herber, 1978), somewhat like an anticipation guide, asks students to consider several statements about a content topic. Some statements on the guide may be incorrect, to stimulate more critical thinking. Students must support their reactions with evidence from text. Wood (1992) has added the component of writing to the reaction guide: students must write their reactions next to each statement. Because written reactions cannot be completed until after reading, this activity seems to fit best at the reflection stage. It could be a homework assignment or end-of-classtime assignment for small groups. The reaction guide could be submitted for a grade.

BOOK DIARY

A book diary (Steen, 1991) is an exercise in which students respond in writing to the supplementary reading they have done. The teacher designs a form on which students write responses to specific questions about the material. For example: "This is what I already know about _____ "; "I liked this part of the book best because _____"; "The most important facts I learned were _____ ." Steen saw much progress in students' maturity as writers as a result of using book diaries. Teachers will be able to see immediately the learning that is taking place about the content. Depending on how the teacher phrases the questions and designs the format, book diaries could be used equally well for younger students, as were Steen's, or older students. At-risk learners may find them less threatening than assignments that start with a blank page.

COLLABORATIVE WRITING

Collaborative writing was mentioned in connection with the *Foxfire* books, cited earlier as an example of making writing relevant and relating it to students' backgrounds. Collaborative writing is most effective in demonstrating to students the necessity of finished products that reflect consideration for the intended reader. When students work together, they are less intimidated by what they see as the immensity of the tasks involved in thinking, drafting, revising, and evaluating.

ACTIVITY 8.14   GUIDED WRITING: LIMERICKS

Strategy: The purpose of this activity is to extend the students' abilities to compose a poem. They will achieve this purpose in a guided writing exercise. I have students write poetry because they will understand poetry better after they have become poets. The exercise will begin with clustering, and from there the students will be guided through their first and final drafts. Because this is a guided exercise, I will first determine the students' background, build on that background, direct the study, and finally determine their comprehension. The final extension of this activity is publishing these poems.

First step: prewriting (determining background)

The teacher writes the word *limerick* on the board and then draws a circle around it. He/She then asks the students to think about the characteristics of that word. As they give answers, the teacher writes them on lines extended from the main word. Then the teacher directs them to look at some limericks in the text.

Second step: prewriting (building background)

The limericks are read and studied for rhyme scheme and rhythm. The characteristics are listed as further subtopics of the main topic limericks.

Third step: guiding the first draft (developing comprehension)

1. Tell the students that instead of writing limericks, they will be writing pigericks.
2. Pigericks are like limericks, except they are always about pigs. They are short, have lines that rhyme, and contain a definite rhythm. Furthermore, they are humorous.
3. Pass out handouts on pigericks and show Arnold Lobel's book titled *The Book of Pigericks.* Go over the poems, noticing the similarities between limericks and pigericks.
4. On the board or overhead, begin a line for a pigerick. Have the students continue brainstorming the remainder of the poem.
5. Assign the writing of a pigerick. Monitor.

Fourth step: revising (reflection)

6. Have students exchange their poems and share suggestions.
7. Students then revise and rewrite onto large index cards. Next, they illustrate.
8. Post the finished products on the bulletin board.

(continued on page 317)

Brunwin (1989) organized the students in an entire elementary school to produce an historical account of their neighborhood. They developed questions, targeted the best persons to ask, conducted and transcribed interviews, organized their material, and wrote a book to report their findings.

Collaborative writing need not involve such large groups. One teacher divided her class into several groups. Each individual read an article and reacted to it independently. Then individuals brought their reactions to their assigned group. Within the group, a common draft was produced, using the individual reactions.

A C T I V I T Y   8 . 1 4   CONTINUED

Clustering

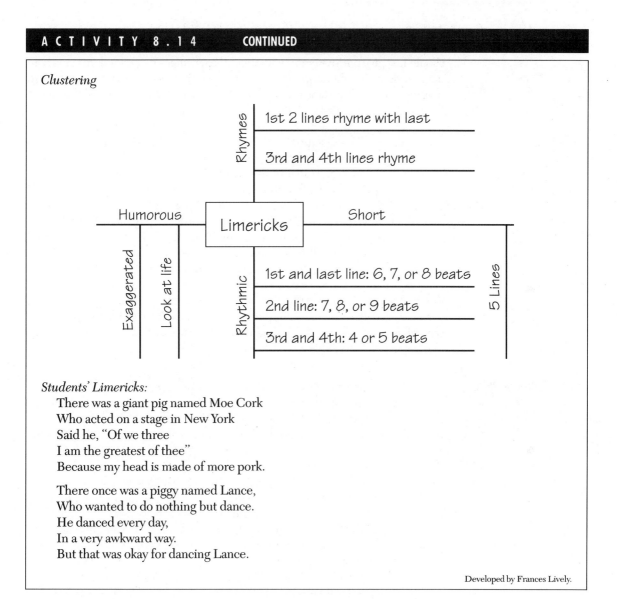

Students' Limericks:

There was a giant pig named Moe Cork
Who acted on a stage in New York
Said he, "Of we three
I am the greatest of thee"
Because my head is made of more pork.

There once was a piggy named Lance,
Who wanted to do nothing but dance.
He danced every day,
In a very awkward way.
But that was okay for dancing Lance.

Developed by Frances Lively.

Each group member then revised the draft and brought suggestions back to the group. Last, the group evaluated and rewrote the paper, which the teacher then graded. She discovered that students were able to demonstrate their knowledge of the content very well while practicing good writing skills — and, as an added bonus, she received fewer papers to be graded!

In an elementary math setting, small groups of students collaborated to write problems such as this one: "Mrs. Carter had 23 roses. She gave away 18. How many does she have left?"

PQP (Praise–Question–Polish) PQP (Lyons, 1981) helps writers working cooperatively to evaluate one another's writing. The first *P* stands for *praise:* students should first give positive comments about the writing. The *Q* stands for *question:* next, students should ask questions about the writing to guide the writer toward revision. The final *P* stands for *polish:* the students should now tell the writer their suggestions to polish the writing before it is ready for publication.

C3B4Me (See Three Before Me) **C3B4Me** was introduced by Yeager (1991) to remind students that writing that is to be turned in for a grade must be carefully reviewed and revised. Students should remember to see three other helpers before submitting the work to the teacher. First, the writer should confer with oneself. Next, the writer should confer with a peer, asking for specific advice about designated portions of the writing — not just, "Do you like my work?" but "Do you think I have been clear enough in this section?" Last, the writer should be able to consult a "reading associate." Teachers can facilitate the revising/ evaluating process by organizing the class into three types of associates. The first consists of students who have volunteered to be editors for other class members; they and the teacher agree that they have this skill. The writer might also consult a reading associate who has volunteered to illustrate others' written work. A third type of associate can be designated to help a writer find an available editor or illustrator.

Grading Reflective Writing

Teachers sometimes question whether they should accept writing from students when it contains grammatical errors, misspellings, and other errors. "Surely seventh-graders can write better than this!" they admonish. However, teachers must allow students to start where they are and to focus on one stage of writing at a time.

Errors are a normal part of learning, and they will occur in student writing. The amount and types of writing practice students have had will determine their level of sophistication. If the pressure to focus on errors is eliminated during the prewriting and drafting stages, when the focus should be on content, then attention to errors can be greater during the revision stage. If students have had prewriting and drafting opportunities, their revised writing will reflect both improved content and improved form.

Teachers can guide students in their writing activities by making clear their expectations for the final product. When the students' writing is evaluated — after prewriting, drafting, and revision — students should understand exactly what will be evaluated. Of course, the content of the writing is most important. But "content" is a vague criterion. To clarify expectations and grading criteria for students, Pearce (1983) suggests that teachers use a checklist or a rubric. A **rubric** is an expectation guide that lists the qualities of the papers — from the strongest to the weakest (see Activity 8.15). A rubric aids the students, who can refer to it as they revise, and the teacher, who can refer to it during grading. Similarly, checklists are useful because they list the features the teacher expects

ACTIVITY 8.15   A RUBRIC FOR GRADING

Paper topic: 1960s approaches to civil rights in the U.S.

High-quality papers contain:
An overview of civil rights or their lack during the 1960s, with 3 specific examples.
A statement defining civil disobedience, with 3 examples of how it was used and Martin Luther King's role.
At least one other approach to civil rights, with specific examples, and a comparison of this approach with King's civil disobedience that illustrates differences or similarities in at least 2 ways.
Good organization, well-developed arguments, few mechanical errors (sentence fragments, grammatical errors, spelling errors).

Medium-quality papers contain:
An overview of civil rights during the 1960s, with 2 specific examples.
A statement defining civil disobedience, with 2 examples of its use and Martin Luther King's involvement.
One other approach to civil rights, with examples, and a comparison of it with King's civil disobedience by their differences.
Good organization, few mechanical errors, moderately developed arguments.

Lower-quality papers contain:
A general statement defining civil disobedience with reference to Martin Luther King's involvement and at least 1 example.
One other approach to civil rights and how it differed from civil disobedience.
Fair organization, some mechanical errors.

Lowest-quality papers contain:
A general statement on who Martin Luther King was or a general statement on civil disobedience.
A general statement that not all Blacks agreed with civil disobedience.
A list of points, poor organization, many mechanical errors.

From D. L. Pearce, "Guidelines for the Use and Evaluation of Writing in Content Classrooms," *Journal of Reading*, December 1983. Reprinted with permission of D. L. Pearce and the International Reading Association.

in the writing (see Activity 8.16). Teachers can use a checklist to quickly rate the features of a written assignment, and students can check their papers against this list during revision.

Teachers might even provide their point scale for checklists and hand out the rubric or checklist when the assignment is given. In this way, students know in advance what factors will be considered in their grade and have a chance to organize their writing accordingly. Activity 8.17 shows the checklist an eighth-grade teacher used for a social studies writing assignment.

As with reflective reading, students should be very involved at the evaluation and publishing stage of writing. Even if the teacher gives the final grade — as the teacher does if students take a test to demonstrate learning after reading —

| **A C T I V I T Y   8 . 1 6** | **A GENERAL CHECKLIST OF WRITING QUALITY** |

	Poor	Fair	Good	Outstanding	Superior
1. Definition of topic					
2. Exploration of topic (covered main points)					
3. Evidence to support generalizations					
4. Understanding beyond that of class and text					
5. Logical development of ideas					
6. Writing clarity					
7. Personal interpretation or reaction					
8. Summation of findings					
9. Correct spelling, diction, and grammatical usage					

Comments:

From D. L. Pearce, "Guidelines for the Use and Evaluation of Writing in Content Classrooms," *Journal of Reading*, December 1983. Reprinted with permission of D. L. Pearce and the International Reading Association.

students should have every opportunity to evaluate their own writing before giving it to the teacher. Only when students know that their own analysis is a crucial part of the process will they take responsibility for that process.

Another way to facilitate such realization and responsibility is to allow prevision and revision opportunities. Teachers can give students the option of turning in drafts of assigned writing early, for prevision review at "no cost" to the grade. After receiving a graded writing assignment, students can be encouraged to rewrite the paper and receive an average of the first grade and a second grade. Using a computer and word processing program helps students become more

Content	Weak	Average	Strong
1. Clear and interesting topic or main idea.			
2. Topic appropriate to the assignment.			
3. Ideas and details support and develop the topic.			
4. Ideas stated clearly and developed fully.			
5. Good use of language.			

Form

6. Introduction, body, and conclusion.			
7. Details arranged logically; appropriate to the topic.			
8. Coherent; paragraphs constructed well.			

Mechanics

9. Grammar and usage.			
10. Spelling, capitalization, punctuation.			

Comments:

Key:
Strong — 10 points
Average/Strong — 7 points
Average — 5 points
Weak — 3 points

Developed by Dianne Duncan.

receptive to polishing their writing (Brown, Phillips, & Stephens, 1992). Writing a draft, then returning to it with a critical eye is much easier when the major work does not have to be recopied. Cronin, Meadows, and Sinatra (1990) found that secondary students who used the computer for writing assignments across the curriculum increased in writing ability, attaining 100% success on a standard written essay test.

Writing Activities for At-Risk Learners

Motivating poor readers and those students at risk of failure requires techniques to engage them in both practical writing and creative writing. First of all, students need to be given adequate time to write. A homework assignment in writing is usually not successful with at-risk students. In the primary and intermediate grades, students will be motivated by pictures that the class can discuss and then use as a basis for a story. The class can discuss characters in a picture, and students can be asked what is happening in the picture, what may be about to happen, and what may have happened in the past. To accompany the picture, the teacher may construct partial sentences for the students to complete. For example, for a picture showing the signing of the Declaration of Independence:

1. The man in the picture is _____ .
2. He is signing _____ .
3. If I were at the signing, I would _____ .
4. The men in the picture look _____ .
5. There are no women in the picture because _____ .
6. The men will soon be _____ .

In addition to practicing with closure, students can be motivated to write by being given a beginning to a story, such as the following:

> The man knew it was not wise to refuse the "mugger," who was young and strong and mean looking. But he wanted to save his pocket watch. That watch was so special; it had a long history in his family. Should he refuse to give it to the thief?

By explaining why they would or would not surrender their pocket watch, students practice composing their own paragraphs.

For exceptionally reluctant learners, the teacher might scramble sentences and ask students to reassemble them into a coherent paragraph. An example from high school business math is shown in Activity 8.18.

The purpose of using writing as a means of learning is to help at-risk students read and think better through awareness of their own ability to write. From an emphasis on paragraphs, teachers can eventually move to research and writing about ever-bigger amounts of information. The most important factor in motivating the writing of slow learners, perhaps, is making certain not to emphasize mechanics too early in learning the writing process. Such students have been discouraged by teachers who find fault and dwell on their inadequacies.

A C T I V I T Y   8 . 1 8   **UNSCRAMBLING A PARAGRAPH**

Directions: Put these sentences in the proper order, making a coherent paragraph. Use these transition words: also, unfortunately, however (if you wish to use another, please justify).

_____ State laws governing unemployment insurance differ widely.
_____ People are afraid of being unemployed.
_____ There is no uniform method by which benefits are computed.
_____ People are scared of having no income to support their families.
_____ Every state has some form of unemployment insurance.

Many failing students have poor handwriting skills and are often weak in spelling and grammar. In grading, teachers should inform students that they will be graded on the sincerity and fluency of their efforts. Later, teachers can ask for more clarity in student writing. Finally, the goal is to produce students who write correctly and with some style. Remember that motivation comes from following this progression in grading student writing:

Fluency → Clarity → Correctness → Eloquence & Style

Also, research suggests that semiliterate students may have a vocabulary not exceeding 500 words (Pei, 1965; Tonjes & Zintz, 1981). Patience is the key when teaching students with these limitations.

At-risk students are generally characterized as passive learners who lack the ability to produce and monitor adequate reading behaviors (Harris & Graham, 1985; Torgensen & Licht, 1983). Yet, as Adler (1982) points out, "genuine learning is active, not passive. It involves the use of mind, not just the memory. It is a process of discovery, in which the student is the main agent, not the teacher" (p. 50). Writing that stresses discovery and active learning represents an excellent way for passive students to become active learners who are responsible for "building" their own concepts as they write. Such techniques can aid even children with severely limited capacity to learn. More than four decades ago, Strauss and Lehtinen (1947) successfully used writing in helping to teach brain-injured children to read. They saw writing as valuable in developing the visual-motor perception and the kinesthetic abilities of these children. Researchers since that time, including Myklebust (1965), Chomsky (1971), Graves (1983), and Moffett (1979), have advocated that writing programs be adopted in the schools. Recent research has also documented the benefits of teaching the writing process to learning-disabled students and other students with special needs (Barenbaum, 1983; Douglass, 1984; Kerchner & Kistinger, 1984; Harris & Graham, 1985; Radencich, 1985; Roit & McKenzie, 1985).

In this section, we describe some writing activities that are excellent for at-risk learners. These strategies act as catalysts to help learning-disabled and at-risk children gain control and become much more active and involved in their

A C T I V I T Y   8 . 1 9   PROMPTS FOR STORY WRITING

Character	Trait	Problem	Location
cannibals	mean	shipwrecked	in a tent
coward	nasty	horrified	in a spaceship
champion	miserable	no way to leave cave	at a movie
hero	elegant	scared by a ghost	at school
giant	impudent	soaked with rain	on a deserted island
soldier	nice	lights went out	in a crowded city
prince	ungrateful	car was out of control	on a boat
baby	lonely	teetering on the brink	on Mars

learning. Zaragoza (1987) lists several fundamental elements that differ from those of Wolfe and Reising. In the "time to write" stage, she describes how students need a 30-minute block of time each day devoted expressly to writing so that they will acquire the habit of writing. Zaragoza also calls for children to have considerable freedom in choosing the topic, in order to build the self-confidence that what they say is important. The entire idea of process writing is to establish a feeling of control by the student, to "learn that the influence of their choices extends beyond their work to the larger classroom environment" (p. 292). She also recommends that after the first draft a revision be done and that teachers edit this version. Later, children "publish" their work in the form of student-made books.

The critical element in the writing process, according to Zaragoza, is the teacher/student conference. These conferences, which can take place during any phase of the program, allow for one-on-one advising, editing, and sharing. The researcher feels that emphasizing the writing process can help develop in children "traits that will perhaps save them from being labeled LD" (p. 298).

Children who are very reluctant can be taught to write stories through "prompter" cards that name characters, traits, problems to write about, and locations for the story. These attributes can be changed to encourage the child to write fresh stories. Some sample prompts are listed in Activity 8.19.

Research shows that poor readers have trouble identifying important ideas in a passage and have trouble using the rules for summarizing (Winograd, 1984). **Summary writing** can help at-risk students by allowing them to reduce their thinking about the reading passage. That is, the teacher can get these students to concentrate on the "big picture," or gist of the reading, instead of getting caught up in minutiae. Zakaluk and Klassen (1992) report that Dan, a remedial ninth-grader labeled as learning disabled, was taught to use check marks while reading so he could identify important points. Then he used the check marks to write headings for an outline. By going back to the text, he found supporting details. Then he was able to write summary paragraphs about what he had learned.

Another practical way to get students to concentrate on the gist of the reading is to start them with the ABOUT/POINT technique, discussed in Chapter 10: "This article on cumulus clouds is about _____ and the points are _____ and _____ ."

A number of reading professionals and researchers have formulated rules for condensing major ideas in a text (Kintch & Van Dijk, 1978; Brown, Campione, & Day, 1981). Here are the rules students should generally follow:

1. *Delete unnecessary detail.* With practice, students will become adept at separating important text information from minor facts and trivial statements.
2. *Delete redundant information.* Students make lists and collapse information into broader categories of information as they notice redundancies occurring.
3. *Use blanket terms.* Students should replace lists of smaller items of information with more encompassing terms.
4. *Select topic sentences; summarize paragraphs.* Often paragraphs have easily identifiable topic sentences. Sometimes there is no discernible topic sentence, however, and students have to create their own topic sentence for the summary. This can be very difficult for poor readers. Much practice is needed for these students to feel successful at this difficult stage.
5. *Write first draft of summary.* Here students need to integrate information by making more general certain topic sentences, key words, and phrases already compiled in steps 1–4. The first four stages prepare students to write the first draft of the summary.
6. *Revise summary.* With the help of other students or the teacher, students rework the summary to make it more readable. By doing so, students will get a clearer idea of the major points covered in the material.

Hare and Borchardt (1984) used similar rules in an experimental study with minority high school students. Compared to a control group, which made little progress, the experimental group improved in summary-writing ability as well as the ability to use the rules to write summaries. It would appear from the results of this study and from our observation in the classroom that summary writing can be used to help the at-risk student. A number of practical applications of writing to learn for at-risk students are presented in Activities 8.20 and 8.21.

One-Minute Summary

In this chapter, we have described writing for learning in content areas, with examples of how writing can be applied across the content areas and at different grade levels. Connections are drawn between reading to learn and writing to learn, including the emerging nature of both forms of literacy, reading and writing as tools for content learning, the similarities in stages between reading and writing to learn, and the relationship between process and product in both communicative arts.

A C T I V I T Y   8 . 2 0   WRITING TO LEARN: FIRST-GRADE SCIENCE

Ms. Bynum-Saunders, a first-grade teacher, wondered if writing to learn was a possibility for her young, inner-city students. She tried a project with them to determine the worth of content writing. In her science lessons, she identified difficult vocabulary and designed graphic organizers. She presented one before each lesson, encouraging discussion as she highlighted each word and its contribution to the content. During the same time period, she assigned each student to keep a journal. Journal writing was part of a school goal. If students could not yet express themselves in writing, they were to draw pictures. The journal was a type of learning log, wherein students were encouraged to make comments about content they were studying.

After a few weeks, this teacher began to read the same words discussed on the graphic organizers in her students' journals. Student drawings were replaced by phrases, then by sentences. After two months, this teacher compared the journals her students were writing to those of another first grade. She discovered that her students were writing with more knowledge and sophistication about science, and their writing was more mature in expression, length, and form.

Following is a journal entry written toward the end of first grade by Nakeisha Briley, which demonstrates the substantial progress these children made. Note that this was not an essay to be graded, but a spontaneous journal entry in which spelling was not a factor.

The Earth

THE EARTH IS ROUND LIKE A BALL.
THE EARTH HAS LAND, WATER AND SKY.
THE EARTH IS OLD.
THE EARTH GOES ARONUD THE SUN 365
DAYS.
THE EARTH HAS ONE MOON. IT HAS COLOS
ON IT TOO. THE EARTH COLOS ARE
BLUE, GREEN AND WHITE. THE EARTH HAS
POPLE AND ANIMULS. THE EARTH HAS
TREES AND PLANTS. THE EARTH IS
BUTFEU. WE ALL LOVE THE EARTH. WE
ALL SHUD BE GLAED WE ARE ON THE
EARTH. I AM GLAED I AM ON THE EARTH.
WE ARE ON THE EARTH TO LIVE AND TO
HAVE FUN.MISS.SANDERS SAID SHE IS
HAPPY FOR THE EARTH AND I AM HAPPY
FOR IT TOO. THE END

Research, considerations for the teacher, and suggestions are presented at each stage, using the categories of preparation/prewriting, writing as assisted comprehension, and reflection and evaluation. Activities to promote the use of writing to learn are explained at each stage to demonstrate how easily writing to learn can be incorporated into content instruction. Some real classroom applications are included to show teachers how content writing works in action.

A C T I V I T Y   8 . 2 1   **WRITING TO LEARN: USING CARTOONS**

Although the types of stimuli from which teachers can select for student writing assignment is almost endless, we have picked one simple resource readily available to all teachers — a cartoon. Although teachers at different grade levels might need to adapt the activities we suggest for each content area, the basic activity shows how writing to learn in content areas can be applied very simply. The task and outcomes, with the exception of mathematics, are taken from Wolfe and Reising's text *Writing for Learning in the Content Areas*.

CONTENT	TASK	OUTCOME
English	In small groups, students invent a cartoon character and write a five-frame cartoon each week to share with other groups.	Students learn about humor and types of invention.
Social Studies	Using editorial cartoons from local newspapers, students write interpretations of them.	Students learn about current events, types of humor, and invention.
Science	Using the Sunday comics in a local newspaper, students locate a cartoon or comic strip that deals with some scientific concept; they write a report that defines and describes the cartoon or comic strip and the scientific concept.	Students practice research skills, develop inference-making abilities, and apply scientific knowledge in report writing.
Mathematics	Using the Sunday comics in a local newspaper, students locate a cartoon or comic strip that deals with some statement about math; they analyze whether the statement implies a positive or negative attitude about math.	Students practice research skills, develop analysis and application abilities, and recognize negative and positive associations people have with math.
Business	In small groups, students invent a cartoon called "The Boss" and write a five-frame cartoon each week to share with other groups.	Students learn about the possibilities of humor in communications, as well as explore various types of confrontations.
Vocational Ed	In small groups, students invent a cartoon character (such as "Sally the Seamstress") or a family of cartoon characters (such as "Family Patterns") and write a five-frame cartoon each week to share with other groups.	Students learn to bring both authenticity and humor to their thinking about a subject of interest.

End-of-Chapter Activities

Assisting Comprehension   Select one or more activities discussed in Chapters 3–7. Does the activity foster writing opportunities for students? Are students actively involved in their learning while using this activity? Is cooperative learning featured? Could this activity be used for prewriting, drafting and revising, evaluation and publication, or any combination of these processes?

Reflecting on Your Reading   The following textbooks are excellent extension reading resources for finding out more about writing to learn in content classrooms:

> *Toward Literacy: Theory and Applications for Teaching Writing in the Content Areas,* by J. Brown, L. Phillips, and E. Stephens. Belmont, CA: Wadsworth, 1992.

> *Writing for Learning in the Content Areas,* by D. Wolfe and R. Reising. Portland, ME: J. Weston Walch, 1983.

CHAPTER 9

Study Strategies and Systems of Study

"Cultivation to the mind is as necessary as food is to the body."

Cicero

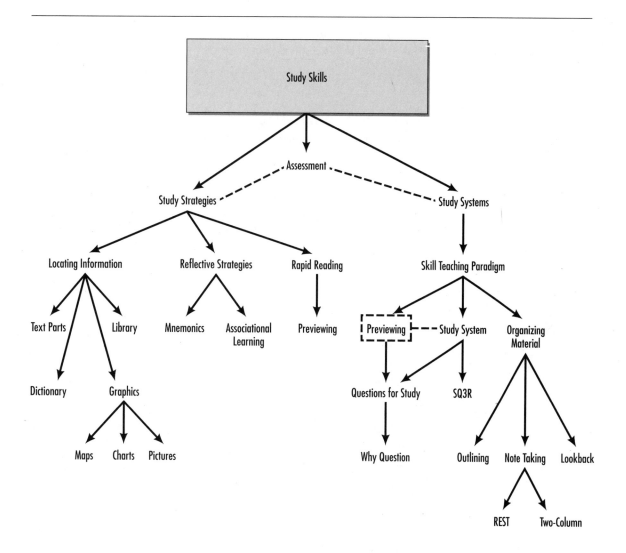

Prepare to Read

1. Assess yourself by checking whether you perform these skills when study-reading:

____ previewing   ____ using table of contents
____ skimming   ____ using glossary
____ using a system for study   ____ using index
____ outlining   ____ studying charts and graphs
____ taking notes while reading   ____ studying maps and pictures

How many skills did you check? How often do you share your study strategies with students? Remember that teachers are more willing to teach what they believe in and practice themselves.

2. Following is a list of terms used in this chapter. Some of them may be familiar to you in a general context, but in this chapter they may be used in a different way than you are used to. Rate your knowledge by placing a + in front of those you are sure that you know, a √ in front of those you have some knowledge about, and a 0 in front of those you don't know. Be ready to locate and pay special attention to their meanings when they are presented in the chapter.

____ massed study   ____ rauding
____ visual aids   ____ mental push-ups
____ mnemonics   ____ rapid-reading drill
____ associational learning   ____ previewing
____ acronym   ____ study system
____ acrostic   ____ text lookback
____ skimming

Objectives

As you read this chapter, focus your attention on the following objectives. You will:

1. understand the importance of assessing students' ability to use study skills at all grade levels.

2. be able to assess students at all grade levels in their use of study skills.

3. understand reflective study strategies such as mnemonics and associational learning.

4. understand and be able to use speed reading and previewing.

5. understand systems of study described in this chapter and be able to use them in your own classroom.

6. be able to instruct students in how to organize materials through underlining, note taking, and outlining.

7. be able to teach students how to locate information in textbooks and in the library.

Study as Hard Work

The National Bureau of Standards suggests this formula for calculating the temperature of a house's basement:

$$t_b = \frac{A_f U_f t_i - t_o(A_G U_G - A_{w1} U_{w1}) + t_g(A_b U_b + A_{w2} U_{w2})}{A_f U_f + A_g U_g + A_{w1} U_{w1} + A_b U_b - A_{w2} U_{w2}}$$

The world we live in is often complex and genuinely confusing (though not, one hopes, as confusing as this formula). Alfred North Whitehead may have pinpointed the problem when he said, "We think in generalities, we live in detail." Many K–12 students are not good at the detailed thinking Whitehead alluded to. Study and disciplined inquiry of all kinds are, in actuality, attention to detail. Many students refuse to study when the details seem, to them, overwhelming and confusing. For example, a student once said, "My teachers pressure me to study. My parents pressure me to study. You've got to be strong. I just say no to studying." This speaks to how ineffective our posturing, lecturing, and badgering is in getting children to enjoy learning and to study efficiently.

The techniques described in the present chapter emphasize the importance of the Reflection phase of the PAR framework. The postreading activities bring greater retention of the reading matter. The best place to teach students how to be reflective in studying is in the classroom. Because teachers have little control over study behaviors outside of class, they must provide careful guidance and practice which will then carry over to independent study.

The teaching of reflective study can begin when teachers are honest with students, letting them know that learning can sometimes be difficult but that it is always rewarding. Sternberg (1991) has noted that learning and retention are enhanced when students study in fairly equal distributions over time rather than what he calls **massed study** — cramming study in at the last minute before a test or exam. Many students study in this manner because it is human nature to put off study to the last minute. Also students form this habit because teachers do not explain to them how retention is enhanced through distributed study. The famous Ebbinghaus (1908) studies around the turn of the century described the difficulty of learning. Ebbinghaus postulated that tremendous amounts of information are forgotten in a short period of time — up to 60% or 70% in only a few days (see Figure 9.1). He also made these important discoveries, which still seem to hold true today:

1. Fatigue is a factor in one's ability to remember.
2. Earlier study and learning tends to get buried by later learning.
3. Learned images may decay over time and end up changed in meaning from what was originally perceived.
4. Memories erode, and most information (an estimated 90%) is forgotten over prolonged periods of time.

In short, forgetting is natural and remembering is difficult.

FIGURE 9.1

Ebbinghaus curve of forgetting.

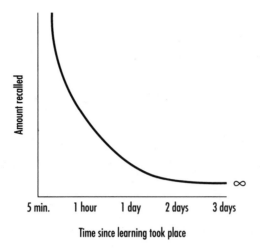

Many students seem to think that remembering is natural and forgetting is difficult, except in their *own* case! Students often assume that everyone else in the class is absorbing and remembering material—that everyone is better at retaining information than they are. Teachers need to allay students' fears by explaining that learning how to study and how to retain information is difficult. These are skills that require the development and practice of prescribed techniques.

In this chapter, we describe study strategies that both enhance retention and make the arduous task of study more fun and rewarding for students. We will be describing techniques such as note taking, mnemonic and associational learning aids, and rapid reading with previewing, along with how to locate and organize information in studying.

Reading and Study Skills

In 1917 Thorndike described the process of reading a paragraph. Educators today can still profit from studying his interpretation for its remarkable clarity about the nature of the reading process.

> Understanding a paragraph is like solving a problem in mathematics. It consists in selecting the right elements of the situation and putting them together in the right relations, and also with the right amount of weight or influence or force for each. The mind is assailed as it were by every word in the paragraph. It must select, repress, soften, emphasize, correlate and organize, all under the influence of the right mental set or purpose or demand. (p. 329)

As Thorndike suggests, reading can be seen as a problem-solving task. This task can be difficult because it requires that readers have a positive attitude toward the purpose for reading, the demands of the text, and their own background experience. Most important, the reader must be in a good frame of mind — have a good mental set — and must have clarity of thought before beginning to read. Reading for study cannot occur unless these conditions are met. In short, the combination of reading and study is a disciplined inquiry that demands much training over many years of schooling.

Although children are taught to read at an early age, often there is no concomitant emphasis on study or study skills (Durkin, 1979; Wertsch, 1978; Schallert & Kleiman, 1979). In middle school — or even high school — a teacher may announce that for a period of time students will be trained in how to study and better retain information they have read. We find two problems with this approach: it is isolated from the reading process and transmits the message that study isn't really connected to reading; and this focus on study skills in middle school or high school transmits the message that study skills are pertinent and applicable only late in one's education.

It is because of this hit-or-miss approach toward teaching study and retention strategies, we believe, that so many studies and reports suggest that training in these skills does not guarantee a high level of comprehension (Armbruster & Anderson, 1981; J. Britton et al., 1975). This is particularly unfortunate since Elliott and Wendling (1966) substantiated over two decades ago that 75% of academic failure is caused by poor study and examination strategies, and Brown and Peterson (1969) found that dropouts often are unable to memorize and retain information. A number of researchers (Elliott & Wendling, 1966; Weinstein & Mayer, 1986; Borkowski, Johnston, & Reid, 1987; Borkowski, Estrada, Milstead, & Hale, 1989) have reported that these are teachable skills that enhance achievement and performance and by means of which a high percentage of high school students could learn and do passing work. There is also growing evidence (Schunk & Rice, 1992; Borkowski, Weyhing, & Carr, 1988) that convincing students of the value of study strategies will both promote student achievement and ensure that their use of such strategies is maintained.

Study Skills Assessment

Most standardized achievement tests include subtests of study skills. However, these subtests are usually limited in scope, measuring the students' knowledge of such "standard" items as reference skills, alphabetization, and the ability to read maps, charts, and graphs. Often neglected are such important skills as following directions, presenting a report, test taking, note taking, and memory training. To address the need for a broader assessment of study skills, Rogers (1984) divides them into three broad categories: special study/reading comprehension skills, information-location skills, and study and retention strategies. His "study/reading skills checklist," reproduced as Activity 9.1, is thorough. Content-area teachers can design tests for each of the areas on this checklist or have a

ACTIVITY 9.1 **STUDY/READING SKILLS CHECKLIST**

	Degree of skill		
	Absent	Low	High
I. Special study-reading comprehension skills			
A. Ability to interpret graphic aids			
Can the student interpret these graphic aids?			
1. maps			
2. globes			
3. graphs			
4. charts			
5. tables			
6. cartoons			
7. pictures			
8. diagrams			
9. other organizing or iconic aids			
B. Ability to follow directions			
Can the student follow . . .			
1. simple directions?			
2. a more complex set of directions?			
II. Information location skills			
A. Ability to vary rate of reading			
Can the student do the following?			
1. scan			
2. skim			
3. read at slow rate for difficult materials			
4. read at average rate for reading level			
B. Ability to locate information by use of book parts			
Can the student use book parts to identify the			
following information?			
1. title			
2. author or editor			
3. publisher			
4. city of publication			
5. name of series			
6. edition			
7. copyright date			
8. date of publication			

(continued on page 335)

	Degree of skill		
	Absent	Low	High
Can the student quickly locate and understand the function of the following parts of a book?			
1. preface			
2. foreward			
3. introduction			
4. table of contents			
5. list of figures			
6. chapter headings			
7. subtitles			
8. footnotes			
9. bibliography			
10. glossary			
11. index			
12. appendix			
C. Ability to locate information in reference works Can the student do the following?			
1. locate information in a dictionary			
a. using the guide words			
b. using a thumb index			
c. locating root word			
d. locating derivations of root word			
e. using the pronunciation key			
f. selecting word meaning appropriate to passage under study			
g. noting word origin			
2. locate information in an encyclopedia			
a. using information on spine to locate appropriate volume			
b. using guide words to locate section			
c. using index volume			
3. use other reference works such as:			
a. telephone directory			
b. newspapers			
c. magazines			
d. atlases			

(continued on page 336)

	Degree of skill		
	Absent	Low	High
3. use other reference works such as:			
a. telephone directory			
b. newspapers			
c. magazines			
d. atlases			
e. television listings			
f. schedules			
g. various periodical literature indices			
h. others ( )			
D. Ability to locate information in the library Can the student do the following?			
1. locate material by using the card catalog			
a. by subject			
b. by author			
c. by title			
2. find the materials organized in the library			
a. fiction section			
b. reference section			
c. periodical section			
d. vertical file			
e. others ( )			
III. Study and retention strategies			
A. Ability to study information and remember it Can the student do the following?			
1. highlight important information			
2. underline important information			
3. use oral repetition to increase retention			
4. ask and answer questions to increase retention			
5. employ a systematic study procedure (such as SQ3R)			
6. demonstrate effective study habits			
a. set a regular study time			
b. leave adequate time for test or project preparation			
c. recognize importance of self-motivation in learning			

(continued on page 337)

	Degree of skill		
	Absent	Low	High
B. Ability to organize information Can the student do the following?			
1. take notes			
2. note source of information			
3. write a summary for a paragraph			
4. write a summary for a short selection			
5. write a summary integrating information from more than one source			
6. write a summary for a longer selection			
7. make graphic aids to summarize information			
8. write an outline of a paragraph			
9. write an outline of a short selection			
10. write an outline for longer selections			
11. write an outline integrating information from more than one source			
12. use the outline to write a report or to make an oral report			

Source: "Assessing Study Skills," by D. B. Rogers, *Journal of Reading*, January 1984. Reprinted with permission of Douglas B. Rogers and the International Reading Association.

reading specialist help question children, individually or in small groups, on how often and how well they use the skills listed. Teachers may also want to design an assessment of what parents do to help students study and how students evaluate their own study habits. Activity 9.2 provides examples of these kinds of assessment.

Locating Information

Eighteenth-century chronicler James Boswell, in his *Life of Johnson*, wrote, "Knowledge is of two kinds. We know a subject ourselves, or we know where we can find information upon it." As students progress in school, this second kind of knowledge becomes more important. They need to know how to find information in textbooks, dictionaries, encyclopedias, and trade books. Therefore, instruction in locating information should begin as soon as reading instruction starts. Picture dictionaries, such as *My Little Dictionary* (Scott, Foresman, 1964) and the *Story-book Dictionary* (Golden Press, 1966), can provide an introduction to this reference skill. In addition, teachers can create their own picture dictionaries from

A C T I V I T Y   9 . 2   STUDY SKILLS FOR KINDERGARTEN AND FIRST-GRADE STUDENTS

SURVEY OF PARENTS

Please circle YES or NO in front of each statement.

YES	NO	1. My child has a special place to study. Where? _____
YES	NO	2. My child has an independent reading time each night. When? _____
YES	NO	3. My child watches television while completing homework.
YES	NO	4. I always supervise my child's homework period.
YES	NO	5. I sometimes help my child with homework.
YES	NO	6. I listen to my child read.
YES	NO	7. My child has a set bedtime. When? _____
YES	NO	8. I check over my child's homework.
YES	NO	9. My child has a place to put materials that must be returned to school.
YES	NO	10. My child eats breakfast daily.
YES	NO	11. I discuss with my child how he or she does in school each day.
YES	NO	12. I read to my child often.

SURVEY OF STUDENTS

Circle the true sentences as I read them.

1. I bring my books to school each day.
2. I listen in class.
3. I read the directions when I begin my work.
4. I ask questions when I don't know what to do.
5. I do my homework every night.
6. I have a special place to do my homework.
7. No one helps me with my homework.
8. I watch TV when I do my homework.
9. I bring my homework to school.
10. I am a good student.

These two surveys were adapted with permission from surveys done by Cornelia Hill.

file cards of words and pictures that students match to each other. As children mature, teachers can introduce alphabetizing through these handmade picture books or they can emphasize alphabetizing more in the published picture dictionaries.

In the intermediate grades, students read well enough to gain from systematic instruction in how to locate information in an encyclopedia. However, even in primary grades students can be taught how to file pictures and materials alphabetically according to key index words, such as *farm, city, animal, house,* and so on. In this unobtrusive manner, students can be introduced to the telephone book, almanacs, and *Readers' Guide to Periodical Literature.*

A C T I V I T Y   9 . 3   LIBRARY LEARNER

1. Find a book on a famous American president.
   Book name: _____
2. Tell how you found it in the card catalog.
   _____
   _____
3. Information given in card catalog: _____
   _____
   _____
   _____

Children in the primary grades can also be shown how to use tables of contents and how to scan a textbook for its overall organization. In content reading classes, teachers can discuss tables of contents, glossaries, indexes, headings, picture clues, charts, maps, and graphs. The teacher can introduce all of these skills by asking children first to find the reference (glossary, table of contents) and then to locate particular information (a definition in the glossary, a section in the table of contents). Teachers should train students to locate information as they complete daily lessons in their basal readers and content textbooks. In this manner, students at an early age will see the usefulness of this skill.

Another effective strategy is for students to visit the library in a group or with the whole class. To test students' knowledge of the library, have them fill out "library learner" tickets, which are 3" x 5" cards with specific questions to answer. Activity 9.3 provides an example.

Another technique for locating information is the "library search and seizure" (Smuin, 1978), which helps students become acquainted with reference sources in the school library. In the activity, students locate and record information on a specific subject. Activity 9.4 presents a sample set of questions for a high school English class.

Reading Visual Aids

Visual aids are graphic cues designed to help readers comprehend a content textbook. Yet one of the most common responses of students when questioned about such aids is that they "skip over them." Worse yet, the only time many students get instruction in how to read charts, maps, and graphs is during the infamous "chart, map, and graph week" instituted by many well-meaning but misdirected schools and school systems. Because these skills are taught in isolation, there is little transfer by students into everyday instruction. Teachers need to teach these specialized reading procedures during day-to-day instruction, not just during special weeks.

Find the answers to the following questions in our school library. You may ask the teacher or the librarian for help, but remember, you must do the work! All of the answers are in the school library. Happy searching!

1. How many different encyclopedia sets does our library contain?
2. What is the difference between *Dictionary of American Biography* and *Contemporary Authors*?
3. Find a book about Edgar Allen Poe written by Frances Winwar.
   a. What is the title of the book?
   b. How long is it?
   c. Who published it?
4. Find an article about capital punishment written in 1981.
   a. What magazine published it?
   b. What is the title of the article?
   c. How long is it?
   d. What is the publication month?
   e. Do we have this magazine in our library?
5. Find a book about *Macbeth* published by Ginn in 1908.
   a. Who wrote this book?
   b. What is the title?
6. Find *Reader's Guide to Periodical Literature.* In volume 40, find a reference of interest to you and complete the following:
   Author _____ Title _____ Journal _____ Date _____ Pages _____ Vol. _____ No. _____
7. Find a resource that will tell you the following facts about Nathaniel Hawthorne on one page.
   a. What is the resource?
   b. When did Hawthorne live?
   c. What novels did he write?
   d. What was the name of his home in Concord, Massachusetts?

Charts and Graphs

If students are having particular difficulty reading graphic information, teachers can use a modified cloze procedure to teach the skill. Activity 9.5 shows how a modified cloze procedure can be used to help students read an air-pressure map. Activity 9.6 shows how questioning can help students read a chart detailing the frequency with which members of the House of Representatives use their franking privileges (sending mail to constituents without paying postage). Although it may seem evident to teachers why the privilege is used by legislators more in election years than in other years, this is an inference many poor readers may not make without explanation or questioning from the teacher. The point is that students need much interpretive skill to read charts and graphs. This skill is improved only through frequent guided practice.

A C T I V I T Y   9 . 5   **READING AN AIR-PRESSURE MAP**

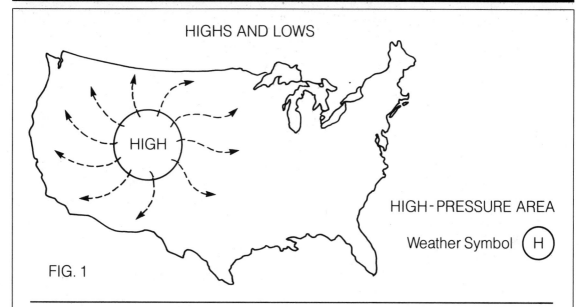

HIGHS AND LOWS

HIGH

HIGH-PRESSURE AREA

Weather Symbol (H)

FIG. 1

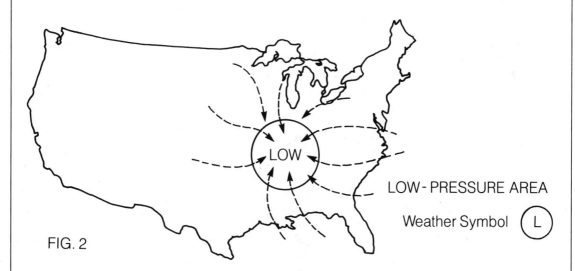

LOW

LOW-PRESSURE AREA

Weather Symbol (L)

FIG. 2

Directions: In Fig. 1, draw and label a low-pressure area and show its air direction. In Fig. 2, draw and label a high-pressure area and show its air direction. Answer the following on the back of the paper: The air in a high-pressure area is spiraling _____ in a _____ direction, with the highest pressure at its _____ . The air in a low-pressure area is spiraling _____ in a _____ direction, with the lowest air pressure at its _____ .

ACTIVITY 9.6   READING A CHART

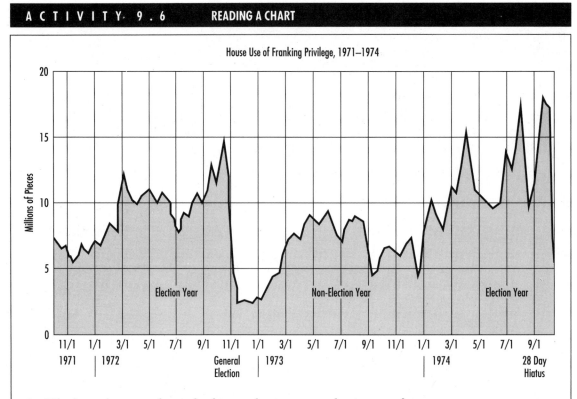

House Use of Franking Privilege, 1971–1974

1. Which are the years of most franking — election or nonelection years?
2. Which are the months of most franking activity?
3. Is there a clue as to why legislators might be using their franking privileges more at these times?

From *American Government Today*, by M. Lewinski, 1982. Glenview, IL: Scott, Foresman, p. 262. Used with permission.
Copyright © 1982, 1980 by Scott, Foresman and Company.

Pictures and Maps

Pictures make a textbook interesting and vital. Teachers should frequently ask students to "read" the picture in an effort to clarify thinking about a concept in the chapter. Cartoons are specialized pictures that carry significant messages or propaganda, as our use of cartoons in this text demonstrates. However, students sometimes need considerable background experience to understand cartoons. Therefore, teachers need to question students about the perceptual content of cartoons, as demonstrated in Activity 9.7.

Activity 9.8 demonstrates how teachers can teach students to label maps. Labeling may be done either after students memorize a map or as they consult maps in their textbook. We recommend map labeling as the primary way to get students to learn to use maps and to better remember certain important locations on a map.

ACTIVITY 9.7   INTERPRETING A CARTOON

1. Describe what is happening in this cartoon.
2. Explain the meaning of each of the three figures.
3. Explain the significance of the decoy, labeled "INF." What is the INF treaty?
4. From your reading of this cartoon, do you feel we should trust the Russians and enter into more and bigger disarmament treaties with them? Why or why not?

Cartoon by Roberto Lianez, Norview High School, Norfolk. Used with permission.

A C T I V I T Y   9 . 8   **DEVELOPING MAP SKILLS**

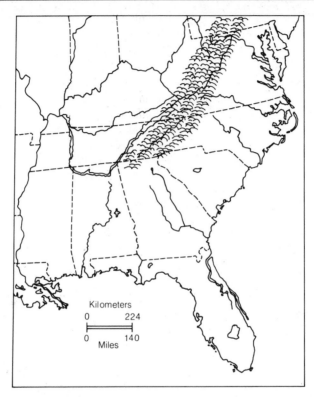

Complete this map. Use the map of the Colonial Southeast on page 210 to help you complete this activity.

1. Color the water area BLUE.

2. Color the area covered by the eleven states of the Southeast LIGHT YELLOW.

3. Print the names of the states in the proper places on the map.

4. Print these names in the proper places:
   Mountains: Appalachians, Blue Ridge
   Plains: Atlantic Coastal, Gulf Coastal
   River: Potomac, James, Savannah, Mississippi, St. Johns
   Bays: Chesapeake, Delaware

5. Print these names of early settlements in the proper places on the map:
   Jamestown   St. Mary's
   Charleston   Williamsburg
   Savannah

6. With a BLUE crayon trace over each of the rivers listed above.

Mnemonic and Associational Learning

Probably no technique for enhancing memory has been around longer than **mnemonics**, or **associational learning**. Long before the advent of written symbols, people used rather complex forms of associations in recounting lengthy stories in the oral tradition. It is also known that in 19th-century Europe, serious scholarly thought was given to mnemonics. One of the earliest references to the term *mnemonics* is found in an obscure book entitled *A View of the Elementary Principles of Education, Founded on the Study of the Nature of Man*, written in 1833 by a Viennese medical doctor, G. Spurzheim. It seems there is a lengthy history of teacher apathy toward memory training, for even then the author spent most of his chapter entitled "Mnemonics" trying to convince teachers to use some system for better memory.

> The mutual influence of the faculties is the basis of what is called Mnemonics, or of the art of strengthening memory. This art is very ancient, but in consequence of its principles not being sufficiently understood, it has been rejected by some, and extolled to excess by others. (p. 135)

More than 150 years ago Spurzheim described problems that still exist today concerning how we get students to remember better. The simple fact remains that students have difficulty remembering material for any length of time, as Ebbinghaus found at the turn of the century.

Benefits of Mnemonics

In his new book *Horace's School* (1992), Theodore Sizer writes eloquently of "the importance of knowing some things well enough to commit them to memory, and the joy of reciting them. It provides students with the confidence that arises from memorizing something of consequence" (p. 66). This is a salient point often lost in the constant push to teach "higher-level thinking skills." When students commit information to memory, the very act of knowing something increases their confidence, and often their self-image. This is especially important for students who may have gotten the idea that they do not know anything and that what they say has no value. The chief benefit of mnemonics and memory training is that, by making difficult study easier, they can kindle in the student a desire to learn.

A recent study by Peters and Levin (1986) found that mnemonics benefited both above- and below-average readers when they read short fictional passages as well as longer content passages. Students instructed in mnemonic strategies remembered significantly more information on names and accomplishments than did those in the control group. Similarly, Levin, Morrison, and McGivern (1986) found that students given instruction in mnemonic techniques scored significantly higher on tests of immediate recall and on recall tests administered three days later than did either a group taught to memorize material or a group that was given motivation talks and then used their usual methods of study. Mnemonics instruction has also been found to be effective for learning new

A C T I V I T Y   9 . 9   **MNEMONICS**

MNEMONIC	TYPE	LEARNED MATERIAL
MEAL REPS	acronym	Areas flourishing from 1865–1915: Mass Entertainment, Architecture, Literature, Religion, Education, Painting, Sports (grade 11, history)
All Eager Children Must Play Yet Always Be Happy.	acrostic	Standard United States time zones: Atlantic, Eastern, Central, Mountain, Pacific, Yukon, Alaska, Bering, Hawaii (grade 7, social studies)
Ocie and Alfe Canak in their MG (two French-Canadian brothers riding in their sports car)	acrostic	Elements of the earth's crust, in order of natural abundance: O (oxygen), Si (silicon), Al (aluminum), Fe (iron), Ca (calcium), Na (sodium), K (potassium), Mg (magnesium)

words in foreign-language classes (Cohen, 1987). Recent studies (Levin, Levin, Glassman, & Nordwall, 1992; Scruggs, Mastropier, Brigham, & Sullivan, 1992) have found that key-word mnemonics significantly affected retention of text material, attesting to the benefits of mnemonic techniques.

Despite these favorable studies, we have observed that teachers still do little memory training with their students, even though it takes only a small effort to get students to try mnemonics. For example, a teacher can give vocabulary or chapter terms that need to be memorized and ask students to form groups in which they create their own mnemonics and share them with the class. The teacher can give rewards for the one judged to be the best. Through such practice, students form the habit of creating mnemonics for themselves. Activity 9.9 lists some actual mnemonics generated and used by students in a number of content areas.

Memory-Enhancing Techniques

CHUNKING

Chunking, mentioned briefly in Chapter 5, refers to grouping large amounts of material into two or three categories to help students remember material more readily and retrieve information more quickly. The following social studies concepts can be hard to remember separately:

labor	machines	drills
trees	computers	water
power plants	wildlife	soil
trucks	oil	buildings
union workers	sunlight	airports

A C T I V I T Y   9 . 1 0   **CHUNKING CONCEPTS: HICCUP**

H	I	C	C	U	P
Human relations training	Instruction	Classroom management	Content	Use of materials	Preparation
C Caring	C Clear	F Flexible grouping	F Fast-paced	C Current	C Content
E Enthusiasm	A Active for students	A Ability grouping	O On grade level	O Other cultures	A Avoid assumptive teaching
L Laughter	T Tactile	S Systematic	R Reliable	M Main text	P Process
L Love	S Sound pedagogically	T Time-oriented	T Trade books	E Experiment	R Research
O Other-oriented				S Supplement	

However, chunking information into these categories makes learning the 15 items much easier:

NATURAL RESOURCES	CAPITAL RESOURCES	HUMAN RESOURCES
sunlight	airports	union workers
wildlife	buildings	labor
oil	drills	
water	machines	
soil	computers	
trees	trucks	
	power plants	

Chunking information through categorization exercises (which can be used to review for tests) is an excellent way to help poor readers better understand text material. Chunking capitalizes on connecting prior knowledge to new knowledge, thus enhancing learning. Once students become more practiced at chunking, they can construct hierarchies of mnemonics to learn 30 to 60 items. Activity 9.10 provides an example on the subject of what makes for good teaching. By memorizing the acronyms CELLO, CATS, FAST, FORT, COMES, and CAPeR,

ACTIVITY 9.11	BEING A SUCCESSFUL BABYSITTER

Acronym = JOG

(J)ob acceptance	(O)n the job	(G)etting started
P — parents' permission	N — No TV	P — Prompt for arrival
A — Address of family	A — Attend to task	A — Address where couple will be
D — Day and time	M — Make file of family after job	R — Reaching doctors, firefighters, etc.
M — Meet children	E — Exploring in house is out	
O — Offer fee	S — Stay awake	
M — Meet family		

all under HICCUP, one could talk on the subject of "good teaching" for a considerable time. The total permutations, or items, learned is 32. Another example, from a "Teen Living" class in home economics, is shown in Activity 9.11.

Remember that such hierarchies of mnemonics are best constructed by middle-school and high school students who have considerable experience with using simple acronyms and acrostics. This level of chunking is the most difficult mnemonic to construct, but it is a way to allow students considerable leeway in memorizing prodigious amounts of information.

ASSOCIATIONS

Students can be taught to memorize words by associating the words with outrageous images. For instance, students can imagine:

dress	. . . dress
car	. . . giant car wearing huge dress
piano	. . . a piano flying over a giant car
computer	. . . a computer coming alive to play the piano

In this manner, one word leads to the next to make a long list of associations.

METHOD OF LOCI

This method improves students' ability to remember lists of unrelated objects. It also can be a sequencing task, enabling a student to remember items in a definite order. In this ancient method, used by Roman orators, a person mentally "walks through" a house that has very familiar surroundings. By choosing 15 to 20 distinct loci — familiar places such as a stove or a closet — a student can place objects to be learned in strategic points throughout the house. Figure 9.2 suggests some household places that might be used to remember names.

PEG WORDS

Whereas association involves linking words together through an outrageous image, peg-word systems associate a target word to a fixed numbered word. Listed below are ten peg words that identify familiar places found at many schools:

1.	Computer center	6.	Classroom
2.	Guidance office	7.	Hallway
3.	Cafeteria	8.	Principal's office
4.	Auditorium	9.	Nurse's clinic
5.	Library	10.	Gymnasium

FIGURE 9.2

A loci map. (* = places with which to associate remembrances.)

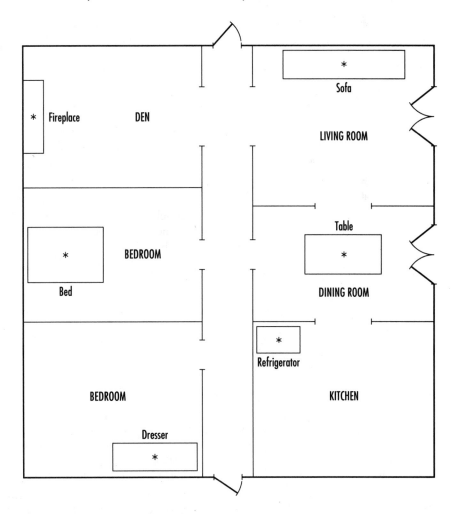

The words to be remembered are linked to the numbered peg word. The peg words do not have to be places. They can also be words that sound similar or rhyme with the word to be learned. An example would be the peg word *commotion* for *commodities* in an economics class or *this criminal* for *discrimination*.

ACRONYMS

The most time-honored mnemonic, an **acronym** is a word or phrase composed entirely of letters that are cues to the words we want to remember. PAR is an acronym for the instructional framework used in this book. Other examples appear in Activities 9.9, 9.10, and 9.11.

Suppose that we are reviewing musculoskeletal systems for a test, and among the things we want to remember are the six boundaries of the axilla: Apex, Base, Anterior wall, Posterior wall, Medial wall, and Lateral wall. The initial letters are *A, B, A, P, M,* and *L.* We could rearrange these letters to form an acronym, such as A.B. PALM. Or take the following list of the six branches of the axillary artery: Supreme thoracic, Thoracromial, Lateral thoracic, Anterior humeral circumflex, Posterior humeral circumflex, and Subscapular. We could use the initial letters *S, T, L, A, P,* and *S* to form the name of a fictitious patron saint of arteries: ST. LAPS. Following are a few more examples of commonly used acronyms:

HOMES	Names of the Great Lakes: Huron, Ontario, Michigan, Erie, Superior
ROY G. BIV	Colors of the spectrum: red, orange, yellow, green, blue, indigo, violet
FACE	The notes represented by the spaces of the G clef

ACROSTICS

An **acrostic** is a sentence or rhyme in which the first letter of each word is a cue. (See Activity 9.9.) Thus, another way of remembering the boundaries of the axilla—initial letters *A, B, A, P, M,* and *L*—would be to create a sentence such as

Above, Below, And Pretty Much Lost.

To help us remember the names of the planets, we might use the following acrostic:

My Very Educated Mother Just Served Us Nine Pizzas.	Mercury, Venus, Earth, Mars, Jupiter, Saturn, Uranus, Neptune, Pluto

MAD TECHNIQUE

One way to familiarize primary and upper elementary children with mnemonics is to go MAD—the Mnemonic-A-Day technique. Have students work in groups to make a mnemonic a day for 30 days. The only stipulation is that each new mnemonic has to be in a different content area than the one created the day before. Children keep MAD logs and periodically refer to the logs to make certain they remember all accumulated mnemonics. By making a game of it, teachers can reward those students or groups of students who can create a MAD example for the most days consecutively. This can be an enjoyable yet purposeful activity.

Mnemonic learning techniques can be a welcome learning aid, especially for poor readers who find that they forget material too quickly (remember Ebbinghaus's studies showing that forgetting is natural). If we could help students to remember 10 to 50 items with ease, think how their self-concepts and self-images might be affected. With practice, there seems to be almost no limit to improvement in long-term memory skill. We recommend familiarizing children in primary grades with these memory-enhancing technqiues. Then they will possess a skill useful for the rest of their education.

Rapid Reading with Previewing

Edmund Burke Huey's 13th tenet in *The Psychology and Pedagogy of Reading* (1908/1968) was that children should be taught, *from the first of reading instruction*, to read as fast as the nature of the reading material and their purpose would allow. He recommended speed drills to help students get information "efficiently and effectively." In 1925, William S. Gray, in a review of the literature on speed of reading, endorsed speed-reading by concluding that such training could result in increased speed without a concurrent drop in comprehension. Many studies followed that addressed the value of speed-reading, yet 80 years after Huey's pronouncement, there is probably no area of reading as controversial as that of speed-reading (Carver, 1992). The very mention of "speed-reading" carries with it a negative connotation for many teachers at all levels of education. In recent studies of adult readers, Carver (1985; 1992) concluded that speed-readers he tested comprehended less than 75% of eighth-grade level material when reading faster than 600 words per minute. He also found that much of what passes as speed-reading is really **skimming** — glossing material at 600 to 1,000 words per minute at fairly low comprehension levels. Other studies have questioned the quality of speed-reading research (Collins, 1979; Fleisher, Jenkins, & Pany, 1979), the limited utility of eye-movement training (McConkie & Rayner, 1976; Rayner, 1978), and the limits to speed in the act of reading (Carver, 1985; Spache, 1976). Yet there is much more research needed on speed-reading, evidenced in a recent study by Just, Carpenter, and Masson (1982) that found fairly positive results for speed-readers when they answered higher-level comprehension questions.

Because of the rather suspect nature of speed-reading, we recommend rapid reading, or speeding up one's reading, along with an emphasis on previewing the material. Previewing brings purpose to the reading by having the reader decide what he or she needs and wants to know. Previewing involves sampling chapter subheadings, pictures, charts, maps, and graphs to formulate questions to be

"I want a book on speed-reading and 85 Westerns."

Herman. Copyright 1981 Universal Press Syndicate. All rights reserved. Reprinted with permission of Universal Press Syndicate.

answered in full reading. We maintain that students can find answers to their questions quickly by reading more rapidly after the previewing stage. We also suggest that it is better to read a chapter several times rapidly than it is to read the chapter one time at a laboriously slow rate. Samuels (1979) found that repeated reading of a material enhanced reader fluency and comprehension, providing verification for several rapid readings. We are not advocating reading at 1,000 words or more a minute, but we do believe that some study reading should be at rates above 300 words per minute.

Shifting Gears

Carver (1992) describes five basic reading processes—scanning, skimming, "rauding," learning, and memorizing—that bring the nature of speed reading into better focus. Table 9.1 summarizes these five processes in terms of their goals and culminating components, with typical reading rates for college students using each process. According to Carver, **rauding** is the bringing together of reading (looking and understanding) and auding (listening and understanding) into "ordinary reading." He states that the typical seventh-grader has a rauding rate of 190 words per minute, but a below-average student may raud at 140 words per minute. The large variability in rauding rates means that poor readers will be left far behind in the volume of reading they can accomplish, unless teachers intervene to show students that they can read at different rates depending on the purpose for reading. Specifically, students can learn to "shift gears" to scan and skim material during the previewing stage. Students may then raud at 200 to 300 words per minute for better comprehension. When studying for a test or attempting to memorize great amounts of material, students may need to shift to gear 2 or 1 and reread material at a much slower rate. A frequent problem is that, without training, students do not change their speed of reading for more difficult or easier material (Carver, 1983; Miller & Coleman, 1971; Zuber & Wetzel, 1981), but use their rauding speed for all reading.

Rapid-Reading Exercises

There are three reasonably easy exercises teachers can ask students to practice in rapid reading. The first of these, called **mental push-ups**, consists of rate and comprehension drills. At the beginning of class, the teacher asks students to use a 3″ x 5″ card to "mentally push" themselves down one page of a content chapter or story so fast that they cannot absorb all the information on the page. (Older students who have had practice at the technique and who have better fine motor control can use a finger to pace themselves.) Then students close the book and write down what they learned. After the first reading, the amount retained is usually two to three words. The students repeat the procedure as many times as needed (usually two to four) until there is a "rush" of information—that is, until they comprehend and can write out or verbalize most of what is on the page.

TABLE 9.1

Summary of the Relationships among Gears, Basic Reading Processes, Goals, Culminating Components, and Rates

READING GEAR	FIVE BASIC READING PROCESSES	GOALS OF MODEL PROCESS	CULMINATING COMPONENT OF THE MODEL PROCESSES	TYPICAL COLLEGE RATES FOR MODEL PROCESSES
5	Scanning	Find target word	Lexical access	600 wpm
4	Skimming	Find transposed words	Semantic encoding	450 wpm
3	Rauding	Comprehend complete thoughts in sentences	Sentential integration	300 wpm
2	Learning	Pass multiple-choice test	Idea remembering	200 wpm
1	Memorizing	Recall, orally or in writing	Fact rehearsal	138 wpm

From "Reading Rate: Theory, Research, and Practical Implications," by R. P. Carver, 1992, *Journal of Reading, 36*(2). Used with permission.

With extended practice, it will take fewer readings for students to comprehend the material. This technique can be used to clarify cognitive structure and increase student attention at the beginning of a class period. With practice, it will help make students more facile and mentally alert in reading short passages.

A second activity in rapid reading is a variation on mental push-ups. **Rapid-reading drills** of three minutes can be conducted by teachers at the beginning of classes. Students are asked to read as fast as possible, in a straightforward, rapid-reading drill. Again, young children can use a 3″ × 5″ card as a pacer; they can later use the finger-pacing technique. The teacher can conduct one or two three-minute drills without taking away too much time from the day's lesson. In rapid-reading drills, students are not asked to write out what they learned. As a variation, however, they could be asked to form groups and discuss what each remembered from the reading.

A third exercise, the preview and rapid-reading drill, can be used when the teacher is directing the reading of a content chapter. Here the teacher monitors the previewing phase, culminating with students' writing specific questions they wish to have answered in the reading. The previewing phase can be done as a whole class, in groups, or individually. Then the teacher asks that students read more rapidly than usual to find the answers to their preview questions. These three activities can be accomplished in any content area and can be started with better readers at a second-grade level.

Previewing: The Foundation of Study

Chapter 5 describes the DRTA (Stauffer, 1969a), which is a technique teachers can use to model correct reading process. Fundamental to the DRTA is the previewing stage, which is important for clarifying "cognitive structure" (Ausubel, 1968), or the clarity of student thinking, before students read textbook material. In the **previewing** stage, students select strategies that will match the depth and duration of study needed. To select proper strategies — whether note taking, underlining, or rapid skimming in reading — students must spend time clarifying their thinking about the topic to be read. Students need to ask themselves questions such as the following:

How interested am I in this section?

How much do I already know about this topic?

How deeply do I need to think and concentrate to learn this material?

How fast can I read this material?

What do I still need to learn about this topic?

After this previewing stage, students may alter their plan for reading. Teachers might take students step-by-step through the previewing phase, then ask them to write down how they will study the material.

Just as you might size up a piece of clothing and decide it is too big and needs altering, you can size up a reading selection and realize that you need to make "mental alterations." This assessment is the purpose of previewing. Sometimes the preview will yield all the information the reader needs, so that the material need not be read. In many instances, however, the preview will build anticipation for material that is not familiar to the reader. Chapter 4, on building the reader's background, provides many activities to enhance previewing, which both develops comprehension and encourages good study habits.

During a recent informal study with a group of adults taking a reading improvement course, one randomly selected group of students was asked by one of the authors to read a selection without using a preview strategy and to answer ten questions after reading the selection. Another group was shown a previewing strategy and asked to use the techniques in reading a selection similar in readability and interest to the first selection. The second group was asked to answer ten comprehension questions after the reading. The group without the preview strategy correctly answered 64% of the comprehension questions; the group using the preview strategy correctly answered 86% of the comprehension questions. Thus, the preview strategy appeared to aid readers in comprehending the selection. Moreover, the 22% difference in comprehension scores between the two groups is significant; it can mean the difference between understanding and not understanding the material. A strategy such as previewing, then, if modeled and practiced by teachers from elementary school onward, can enhance students' comprehension of expository and narrative material.

How to Preview

Previewing in order to clarify thinking reduces uncertainty about the reading assignment, allowing students to gain confidence, read in a more relaxed manner, gain interest, and improve attitude toward the material. In addition, previewing strategies enable students to decide how much of the material is in their own background of experience. The result of the previewing strategy is that learners are clearer about what they know and what they need to know. In effect, they have set a purpose for reading before they begin.

When previewing a technical chapter or a report, students should examine and think about the following:

1. Title and subtitle — to discover the overall topic of the chapter or article.
2. Author's name — to see if it is a recognized authority.
3. Copyright — to see if the material is current.
4. Introduction — to learn what the author intends to talk about.
5. Headings and subheadings — to identify the topic for the sections to follow. (Forming these headings into questions gives purpose to the reading.)
6. Graphs, charts, maps, tables, pictures — to aid in understanding specific aspects of the chapter or article.
7. Summary — to get an overview of the reading.
8. Questions — to review important topics covered in the chapter.

In practicing with a group or class, the teacher assists students in deciding what they already know about the material and what they need to learn. The reader turns those things that are not known into questions, which provide a purpose for reading.

Students reading fiction need to preview the title, illustrations, and introduction in order to make hypotheses about the outcome of the story. This preview heightens suspense and aids in maintaining interest throughout the story. Most important, predicting story structure gives the reader a purpose for reading — namely, to find out if the predictions are correct. Whether reading fiction, expository, or informational material, a very important reason for previewing is that it forces a student to do the more sophisticated kind of thinking required for drawing inferences and developing interpretations. Thus, the student thinks critically about the chapter or story before the reading, operating at times on those higher levels of cognition described by Adler and Van Doren (1972), Bloom (1956), Herber (1978), and Barrett (1972).

We have found that, generally, students on any level will not preview material on their own unless teachers model and provide practice in this important skill. Teachers should first make students aware that both content and the strategy of previewing are being taught. Second, teachers need to review with students the table of contents of a textbook to aid them in discovering the theme or structure of the course material. In this way, students will get the "gist" or overall idea of what the author is attempting to teach in the textbook. The teacher might ask, for example, why the authors chose to organize a table of contents in a particular manner.

For each new reading or unit of instruction, the teacher can ask students to return to the table of contents to see how this particular segment of learning fits into the overall textbook scheme or pattern. Teachers with a class of poor readers can model the previewing strategy by using preview questions they have constructed and annotated.

Skimming and Scanning

Researchers have reported on the importance of skimming content materials for organizing details and making inferences (Sherer, 1975). Carver, as noted earlier, talks of the importance of scanning to find particular target words in the text. It is these skills that allow students to preview information. However, students need much practice (beginning at an early age) to acquire these skills. We recommend skimming-rate drills, in which teachers ask students to skim rapidly looking for answers to *who, what, when,* and *where* questions in the chapter. Students need to be reminded to skim one or two sentences in each paragraph in addition to scanning the title, author, headings, and so on, as described earlier. Also, students need to be assured that they need not worry about what they missed during the preview and skimming phase. They need to be reminded that previewing helps to clarify thinking and set a purpose for reading and that they will learn further details in the full reading.

Developing Study System Strategies throughout the Grades

Children in first grade, as soon as they are ready, should begin reading stories under the teacher's direction using the DRTA technique (Stauffer, 1969a). If such guided practice continues, teachers gradually give more and more responsibility for learning to students, as illustrated in Pearson's (1985) model (see Figure 9.3).

If practice using the DRTA is schoolwide and responsibility is taught, students will receive a firm foundation in study-reading. By fifth or sixth grade, students can be taught a systematic way of studying text, called a **study system**, such as the SQ3R (Robinson, 1961). In effect, this system is a natural outgrowth of previewing, skimming, and teacher-modeled reading lessons such as the DRTA. SQ3R — which stands for Survey, Question, Read, Recite, Review — should be the first *individual* practice in those concepts already taught in groups and with the entire class. Table 9.2 summarizes the steps in SQ3R.

Tadlock's (1978) explanation of the success of SQ3R is based on information-processing theory (Neisser, 1967; Hunt, 1971; Newell & Simon, 1972). According to Tadlock, we naturally try to reduce uncertainty by (1) processing information through sensory organs; (2) sending information through memory systems; (3) structuring and categorizing information in the most meaningful manner, in order to see conceptual relationships; and (4) storing information for recall at a future time (p. 111). She postulates that SQ3R compensates for any deficiencies

FIGURE 9.3

The gradual release of responsibility of instruction.

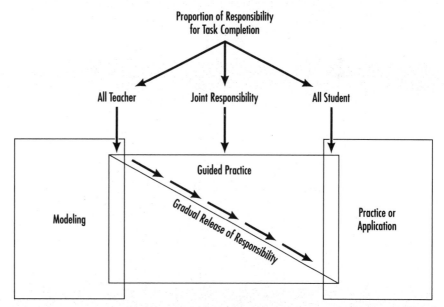

From "Changing the Face of Reading Instruction," by P.D. Pearson, *Journal of Reading*, April 1985. Reprinted with permission of P.D. Pearson and the International Reading Association.

	TECHNIQUE	PROCEDURE	VALUE
TABLE 9.2 SQ3R	Survey	Read questions and summary at end of the chapter. Skim-read divisions of material, which are usually in boldface type. Read captions under pictures and graphs.	Highlights major ideas and emphases of chapter; helps organize ideas for better understanding later.
	Question	Turn each heading into a question. (Practice will make this skill automatic.) Write questions in outline form.	Arouses curiosity; increases comprehension; recalls information already known; highlights major points; forces conscious effort in applying the reading process.
	Read	Read each section of the material to answer questions from headings.	Promotes active search for answers to specific questions; forces concentration for better comprehension; improves memory; aids in lengthening attention span.
	Recite	After reading entire section, close book and write the answer to your question plus any significant cues; use *own* words; write key examples; make notes brief.	Encourages students to use their own words and not simply copy from book; improves memory and assures greater understanding.
	Review	Study the topical outline and notes; try to see relationships; check memory by trying to recall main points; cover subpoints and try to recall them from seeing main points.	Clarifies relationships; checks short-term recall; prepares students for class.

in our information-processing system through the use of a highly structured study and memory technique. It is important to note that other study systems similar to SQ3R, such as PQ4R (Preview, Question, Read, Recite, Review, Rewrite), SQ4R (Survey, Question, Read, Recite, Review, Rewrite), and SRR (Survey, Read, Review), can work equally well because all are based on the same premise. Students should be encouraged to try a study system and adapt it to their own needs. Strict adherence to the steps is not as important as applying a study strategy that is based on the four criteria described by Tadlock.

An alternative to the SQ3R is REAP, described in Chapter 8 as a writing-to-learn activity. REAP is also useful for improving study skills because when students annotate, they pay attention and reinforce their reading by writing.

Study systems such as these have not really permeated schools across the country. There are probably two reasons for this. First, teachers themselves did not learn through such a study system; hence, they often give only lip service to the techniques described. Teachers need to practice previewing and study systems themselves before they can believe in and teach the system to others. Second, study strategies are not systematically introduced throughout educational systems from the early elementary years.

Organizing Information

Students need to understand how reading material is organized and patterned and be able to organize and outline it and take useful notes. The next sections deal with these very important skills.

Outlining

Outlining and note taking are the two most frequently used study strategies (Annis & Davis, 1978, 1982). There is no agreement, however, on the best way to teach these study skills. Underlining is often cited in the literature as a way to help students organize their thinking enough to begin an outline. Underlining, then, can be a first step to outlining. McAndrew (1983), in a review of the literature on underlining, made several suggestions for teaching this skill.

To begin with, teachers should use "preunderlining" reading assignments through handout materials that coincide with the text. Have students mark the text if possible. Teachers need to show students how to underline relevant material. They need to learn how to underline higher-level general statements rather than details. Students will be underlining less, but what is underlined will be more important. McAndrew notes that teachers should remind students that with underlining, less is more. And, he notes, any time saved by underlining can be put to good use in further study of the material. Teachers also need to teach students when to use techniques other than underlining. McAndrew cites research (Fowler & Baker, 1974; Rickards & August, 1975; Cashen & Leicht, 1970) showing that when these suggestions are followed, significant learning occurs. Even when underlining in textbooks is not possible, preunderlining is an important study strategy for students to learn.

Outlining is an organizational tool, a graphic representation of the chapter that a student wants to understand. Outlines should show the relationship of main ideas, supporting details, definitions of terms, and other data to the overall topic. Outlines are valuable because they help students understand difficult texts, take notes, write papers, and give oral presentations.

A C T I V I T Y 9 . 1 2 **OUTLINING**

A TIME OF WARS

I. Charlemagne
   A. King of the _____
   B. Crowned head of the _____ Empire
   C. Set up _____
   D. Ruled fairly
II. Vikings
   A. Fierce warriors interested in _____
   B. Traders
III. Crusaders
   A. Pope wanted to free _____ from the Moslem Turks
   B. _____ took the cross as their sign
   C. _____ major crusades
   D. Trade developed
      1. Spices
      2. _____ clothing

When students first begin to practice outlining, they should not concentrate on form (no need for a B for every A). Teachers can help students learn to outline by preparing outlines with key words missing. By replacing the missing words or terms, even younger children can begin to learn outlining. An example of such an outline used in middle school is shown in Activity 9.12.

The following are some features of successful outlines:

1. The number of headings and subheadings in an outline is determined by the material.
2. Each heading contains one main idea.
3. Ideas are parallel. All ideas recorded with Roman numerals are equally important.
4. All subheadings relate to the major headings.
5. In a formal outline, each category has more than one heading.
6. Each level of heading is indented under the one above it.
7. The first letter of the first word in each heading and subheading is capitalized.

An outline is a type of note taking that enables students to organize material in a hierarchical fashion. This can be accomplished in a graphic pattern as well as in traditional ways. Activity 9.13 shows a graphic representation of material that follows a cause-and-effect pattern of organization.

Note Taking

Note taking, the second most often used study skill, has been found to produce good study results. Research that focused on the time students spent on study procedures (isolated from actual study time) showed that note taking is more

ACTIVITY 9.13   **NOTE TAKING: CAUSE/EFFECT PATTERN GUIDE**

After the Industrial Revolution, the United States emerged
as the world's greatest industrial power.

CAUSE   U.S.   EFFECT

8. _____   8. The U.S. became a major world military power.

7. Businesses grew to become large corporations.   7. _____

6. The U.S. had a wealth of natural resources.   6. _____

5. _____   5. The U.S. had an abundant supply of labor.

4. A large number of goods were produced in factories during the Civil War.   4. _____

3. The railroads were the largest employer in the U.S.   3. _____

2. _____   2. The West was settled rapidly during the second half of the 1900s.

1. A. Carnegie rose to become the greatest steelmaker.   1. _____

Industrialization

Adapted for classroom use by Patricia Mays Mulherin.

effective than underlining (McAndrew, 1983). McAndrew offers teachers the following suggestions to help their students become effective note takers (p. 107):

1. Be sure students realize that the use of notes to store information is more important than the act of taking the notes.
2. Try to use a spaced lecture format.
3. Insert questions, verbal cues, and nonverbal cues into lectures to highlight structure.
4. Write material on the board to be sure students will record it.
5. When using transparencies or slides, compensate for possible overload of information.

6. Tell students what type of test to expect.
7. Use handouts, especially with poor note takers.
8. Give students handouts that provide space for student notes.

To the students who are taking notes, Morgan, Meeks, Schollaert, and Paul (1986) offer some practical advice. First, note taking is a personal matter; students should develop their own style. To facilitate note taking, students should use a two- or three-ringed notebook with loose-leaf paper to arrange handout material and notes. They should write on every other line whenever possible or when it seems logical to separate lines. There will then be room to correct errors or go back and add points that might have been missed. In addition, every-other-line note taking makes for easier reading when reviewing or studying for an exam.

Older students should develop their own shorthand system. Abbreviate frequently used words. Morgan et al. offer examples of such abbreviations:

compare	comp.	data bank	d.b.
important	imp.	evaluation	eval.
advantage	advan.	developed	dev.
introduction	intro.	literature	lit.
continued	cont.	definition	def.
organization	org.	individual	ind.
information	info.	psychology	psych.
example	ex.		

Content words should be written in full and spellings checked with a dictionary or textbook.

Another good technique is for students to record the next assignment for class as a reminder of where the note taking is heading. Also, students should ask questions for better understanding, especially when confused by a concept or when a point has been missed in the lecture. Recognizing what we don't know leads to learning. No one should be embarrassed to ask for clarification; others may need it, too.

Review your notes often and with different purposes in mind. When rereading text assignments, coordinate the chapter with your notes. Be sure to incorporate main ideas from the chapter directly into your lecture notes. For some, rewriting notes is a helpful memory aid. Even though this process is time-consuming, it may well be worth the effort.

REST SYSTEM OF NOTE TAKING

The REST system of note taking (Morgan et al., 1986) has been proposed as a way to prepare for note taking before a lecture. This system takes into account the importance of note taking to help integrate the lecture with the textbook. In using the REST system, students should follow these four steps:

1. *Record.* Write down as much of what the teacher says as possible, excluding repetitions and digressions.

A C T I V I T Y   9 . 1 4   **NOTE TAKING: LECTURE ON CHINESE HISTORY**

Topics and notes to yourself	Lecture notes
Check on meaning of term "accoutrements" in Chinese society. Egocentric—country means "at center of earth." Imp. → know all "barriers" to other civilizations for test.	1. Isolated development of Chinese civilization. 2. China's attitude negative toward other areas & civilizations. 3. Early relations with Western Europe not positive. 4. Cut off physically (barriers) from Europe. 5. Chinese very aware of past.

Summarization and main ideas

China has to be studied through viewing its history.
Cycles of Chinese history show "up & down" periods.

2. *Edit.* Condense notes, editing out irrelevant material.
3. *Synthesize.* Compare condensed notes with related material in text, and jot down important points stressed in the lecture and the text.
4. *Think.* Think and study to ensure retention.

To help students practice REST, teachers should distribute handouts for note taking that include spaces for recording notes on the lecture, for making notes to oneself, and for summarizing main ideas. An example of such a handout, filled out by a middle-school student, is shown in Activity 9.14.

TWO-COLUMN NOTE-TAKING SYSTEM

The Cornell system (Pauk, 1974), a practical approach to taking notes, is an alternative to the REST system. Pauk's two-column note-taking system, as it is sometimes called, has an advantage over REST in that it can be used with younger children. To use this system of note taking, students divide the page in the following way:

1/3 page	2/3 page
Headings Notes to oneself Key words	Lecture notes

Table 9.3 describes the two-column note-taking system and summarizes its rationale and function (Aaronson, 1975). Activity 9.15 is an example of a note-taking handout teachers can prepare and give to students before a lecture so that they can practice using the Pauk method. This handout employs a modified cloze procedure; students fill in gaps as they listen to the lecture. More and more notes are omitted in subsequent lessons, until eventually students complete all the note taking themselves.

The authors have seen students' grades improve markedly when they use the Pauk two-column note-taking system. We believe that the reason for such improvement is that students using this system of study are practicing "getting the big picture" of what is being learned in the class. Just as much discussion today centers around giving students "physical space," here students are being given

TABLE 9.3 Two-Column Note-Taking System	How to organize	Use 8½ × 11 loose-leaf paper, sectioned in 2 columns — wide column (⅔ of page) for actual notes — narrow column for headings
	Input from lecturer	Right side (record column) (1) main points, flow of ideas (2) use of indentations and numbers or letters for subordinate ideas (3) use of common abbreviations to simplify note taking
	Input from student	Left side (recall column) (1) topics, questions, key phrases, definitions, comments, summarized ideas (2) headings act as recall cues to corresponding information on right side

	Rationale for two columns:
	    Psychological
		Use of insights from psychology of learning and memory
		(1) process of involvement strengthened:
		       student makes notes, revises, organizes
		(2) use of meaningful association:
		       mass of information consolidated and organized under headings
		(3) emphasis on immediate review: slows forgetting process

	Functional	Compartmentalization of functions and goals (1) input from lecturer: lecture, received (2) input from student: lecture, edited and revised Use of headings (1) helps label and identify notes for easy access (2) can be used to set up possible test questions Sectioning — helps study: input from lecturer covered to test recall

From "Notetaking Improvement: A Combined Auditory, Functional and Psychological Approach," Shirley Aaronson, *Journal of Reading*, October 1975. Reprinted with permission of Shirley Aaronson and the International Reading Association.

A C T I V I T Y   9 . 1 5   **TWO-COLUMN NOTE TAKING: ENGLISH**

WILLIAM SHAKESPEARE
ELIZABETHAN THEATRE
NOTES

I. Shakespeare
  1. Born
  2. Died
  3. Family
  4. Career

April _____ in Stratford-upon-Avon, England
April _____
Wife _____ and three children
Wrote _____ plays, _____ narrative poems, and _
sonnets

II. The Globe Theatre
  1. Built in
  2. Construction

  3. Staging of plays

_____ in London
wooden, many sided with galleries on _____ levels. Also
had a _____ roof.
A. No _____ . Audience knew by _____ and
_____ what the setting was.
B. _____ were cheap. The best seats were in the _____
of the _____ .
C. Actors spoke their lines _____ .

  4. Destroyed

During a performance of <u>Henry VIII</u>, on July _____ a
cannon was fired from the roof, accidentally caught it on fire, and the
theatre was burned to the ground.

III. Elizabethan Theatre
  1. The first English
    playhouse
  2. Shape of theatre

Called _____ built in _____ by James Burbage

A. Round or _____
B. _____ tiers of _____
C. _____ area surrounding the _____
D. _____ , also known as cutpurses, wandered through the
crowd.
E. The more _____ audience members occupied the
_____ .
F. The most expensive seats were on the _____ .
G. Over the _____ was the _____ , a roof
supported by two three-story columns and painted with _____
and _____ .
H. The _____ wall of the stage looked like the _____
of a _____ building.
I. The back _____ area was called the _____
house.

(continued on page 366)

3. Audience	J. _____ acting areas consisted of a _____ balcony. K. The _____ was separated by a curtain. A. _____ stood in _____ , paid the lowest price, were tradesmen, _____ , sailors, and _____ . B. The _____ reeked of _____ , body odor, ate and drank during the _____ , and reacted verbally to what was happening on _____ . They threw rotten _____ and _____ if they didn't like what was happening on stage.

"intellectual space"—literally, space in the left-hand column for determining major goals and aspirations in a given class. This gives students another method of clarifying cognitive structure on an ongoing basis—individually, with classmates, and with the teacher. As a result, students are better able to "chunk" bits of information from the right side and create their own categories of learning.

Lookbacks

Garner (1985b) also discusses the importance of reexamination of text, called "backtracking" or **text lookback**, in overcoming memory difficulties. There is evidence that both children and adults fail to use such strategies (Garner, Macready, & Wagoner, 1985; Alexander, Hare, & Garner, 1984), even though recent research (Amlund, Kardash, & Kulhavy, 1986), as well as earlier research (Samuels, 1979), has shown that repeated readings and reinspection of text make a significant difference in recall. Ruth Strang, the great reading educator, once remarked that she was disappointed when she entered a school library and found students reading for long periods of time without looking up to reflect on what they were reading and not glancing back over material during their study.

We recommend that teachers ask students to use the lookback strategy after a reading by working in groups to clarify confusing points. For instance, students in a social studies class can be asked to reinspect a chapter on economic interdependence to find why credit and credit buying are so important to the American economy and to economic growth. Students can then be asked to write a group summary of what the text says about the important concept of credit. For both summaries and text lookback, Garner (1985b) stresses the following:

1. Some ideas are more important than others.
2. Some ideas can (and must) be ignored.
3. Students need to be taught how to use titles and topic sentences.
4. Students need to learn that ideas cross boundaries of sentences.
5. "Piecemeal" reading that focuses on comprehending one sentence at a time is not conducive to summarizing or gaining ideas from text.

6. Rules of summarization need to be learned and practiced.
7. Students must be taught how and when to apply both the summarization and lookback strategies.
8. These strategies cannot be adequately accomplished in a hurried classroom atmosphere and environment.
9. Students need to practice these strategies in a number of content areas to effect transfer.

Garner and associates (Garner, Hare, Alexander, Haynes, & Winograd, 1984) also maintain that readers should be taught the following: *why* to use lookbacks (because readers can't remember everything); *when* to use them (when the question calls for information from the text); and *where* to use them (where skimming or scanning will help one to find the portion of the text that should be read carefully). Next, readers should practice looking back for answers to questions asked after the reading is completed. Lookbacks are necessary when readers realize that they didn't understand all of what was read. Good readers evaluate their reading and make decisions on whether to look back. But poorer readers rarely have this skill, so text lookbacks will give them much-needed practice in this aspect of critical thinking.

The Great Why Question: Assessing Students' WhyQ

As a final reminder in this chapter on reading and study skills, we would like to point out the benefits of the Great Why Question. You have heard that teachers should ask *who? what? when? where?* and *why?* throughout their instruction, but comparing the first four types of questions to the *why* question is like comparing tapioca to chocolate mousse. The first four require factual recall, which students certainly need to have during study periods. The *why* question, however, is much more powerful, because it forces students to use a higher awareness level, another dimension of thought. This type of question literally takes more thought and energy to answer; it takes students from the *how* of an event or circumstance to crucial inferences about its significance and deeper meaning.

Through repeated modeling of the question, teachers can aid in making it a habit for students to ask *why?* as they study. Entire homework assignments can be centered around the question "Why do you think _____ did that in the story (chapter)?" Group study sessions can be focused on students' writing four reasons why _____ happened in a story or chapter. Finally, teachers can ask, "Why are you feeling that way after reading the story?" or "Why do you think the stock market declined so much yesterday?" or "Why do we need to know about cross-fertilization of plants?" The Great Why Question, if internalized and properly practiced by teachers and students alike, can be a great source of thinking power in reading and study.

One-Minute Summary

Study skills need to be taught systematically, and they need to be emphasized in early elementary grades through high school. As students mature and progress through school, the skills taught may include locating information, previewing material, organizing material for study, and using systems of study (REST, two-column note taking, SQ3R). In this chapter, we have also described assessment techniques designed to find out whether students use adequate study skills. The teaching of study skills cannot be left to chance. Students need to be made aware of good study practices at all levels of their schooling and at each step of PAR. Table 9.4 summarizes the strategies discussed in this chapter and where each can be introduced in the school continuum.

TABLE 9.4

Introducing and Teaching Reading-Study Skills: A K–12 Timetable

	K	1	2	3	4	5	6	7	8	9	10	11	12
Analyzing pictures													
Formulating the WHY question													
Previewing													
Lookbacks													
Mnemonics													
Skimming													
Locating information													
Interpreting charts and graphs													
Reading maps													
Rapid reading													
System for study													
SQ3R													
Two-column note taking													
Associational learning													
Outlining													
Note taking													
REST note taking													

Now make a note of how many of these study skills you teach in your particular subject. Does this lead you to thoughts about how you could improve instruction?

End-of-Chapter Activities

Assisting Comprehension

Either use the two-column note-taking system to take notes in a class you are presently attending, or practice the REST system described in this chapter. If you feel these were good aids to learning, use one with your students in a forthcoming lesson. Ask students whether they enjoyed the activity.

Reflecting on Your Reading

Without returning to the chapter, categorize the following terms under the three headings provided. Use a separate sheet of paper.

previewing	table of contents	rapid reading
glossary	maps	SQ3R
index	setting purpose	mnemonics
skimming	study-skills assessment	acrostics
REST system	graphs	acronyms
outlining	cartoons	hierarchies of mnemonics
note taking	pictures	method of loci
REFLECTIVE STUDY STRATEGIES	USING A STUDY SYSTEM	ORGANIZING FOR STUDY

After completing the exercise, check your work by skimming the chapter again to determine the suitability of your answers.

CHAPTER 10

Cooperative Study for Reflection and Retention

"No entertainment is so cheap as reading, nor any pleasure so lasting."

Lady Montagu

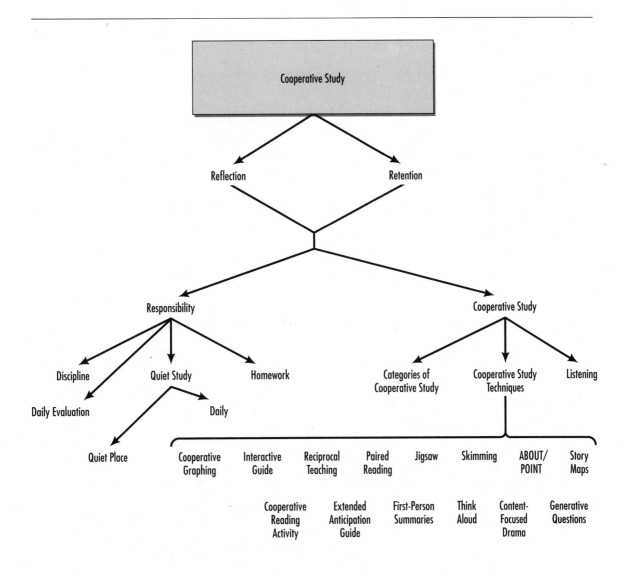

Prepare to Read

1. Following is a list of terms used in this chapter. Some of them may be familiar to you in a general context, but in this chapter they may be used in a different way than you are used to. Rate your knowledge by placing a + in front of those you are sure that you know, a √ in front of those you have some knowledge about, and a 0 in front of those you don't know. Be ready to locate and pay special attention to their meanings when they are presented in the chapter:

   ___ cooperative study   ___ paired reading
   ___ individual phase   ___ student-generated questions
   ___ narrative story guide   ___ summarization
   ___ extended anticipation guide   ___ reciprocal teaching
   ___ ABOUT/POINT   ___ think aloud

2. Do you like to study alone or in cooperative study groups? Think about whether you are a "loner" in your study habits or whether you are a "groupie." If you like to study alone, reflect on and list some benefits you might derive from working cooperatively in a study group. If you enjoy cooperative study, reflect on and list the benefits of "going it alone" in studying text material. Whatever your preference, as you read this chapter keep an open mind concerning the flexibility of using both types of study behaviors — quiet, individual study and group study.

Objectives

As you read this chapter, focus your attention on the following objectives. You will:

1. understand the term *cooperative study.*

2. understand the various categories of cooperative study.

3. be able to use cooperative study techniques such as anticipation guides and story guides.

4. understand the importance of cooperative learning through writing.

5. understand the importance of teacher-monitored listening strategies to student achievement in all content classes.

What Is Cooperative Study?

Almost three decades ago, William Perry (1959) warned of an overemphasis on teaching study skills at the expense of teaching why the skills should be used and when they should be used. He stated that "the mechanics of reading skill are inseparable . . . from the individual's purpose as he reads" (p. 198). Thus, it is as important for teachers to set a purposeful tone and atmosphere for classroom study as it is for them to teach a particular study technique or skill.

There is a growing body of research to indicate that giving students opportunities to study cooperatively in the classroom can enhance learning (Larson & Dansereau, 1986; Leal, Crays, & Moetz, 1985; Palincsar & Brown, 1984; Johnson & Johnson, 1987; Abrami, Chambers, d'Apollonia, Farrell, & DeSimone, 1992). **Cooperative study** will also aid young children in maintaining and generalizing study skills. Studies show that without continued practice in a relaxed atmosphere, students discontinue the use of a skill or forget it (Brown & Barclay, 1976; Hagen, Hargrave, & Ross, 1973). One by-product of cooperative learning is that it may lessen stress reactions such as self-deprecation, lack of clear goals, disparagement, immature relationships with teachers, or pervasive depression (Gentile & McMillan, 1987). Most important, students learn the skill of working together as they discuss what and how material can best be learned. Students who work together also appear to have a higher regard for school and for the subjects they are studying and are more confident and self-assured. Rasinski and Nathenson-Mejia (1987) note that the cooperative classroom environment teaches social development, social responsibility, and concern for one another. Vaughan and Estes (1986), in discussing cooperative learning, observed that

> an advantage is an increase in the amount of understanding of ideas; with two people studying a text, the chances are that one of them will understand something that confuses the other. Hence, we find again . . . that the object of study is understanding. Rarely, outside of school settings, does one find solitary attempts at understanding; usually people invite others to share in their discoveries and to engage in cooperative learning activities. This is true for erudite scientists and casual readers alike. (p. 147)

Slavin (1991) conducted a review of the literature on 60 studies that contrasted the achievement outcomes of cooperative learning and traditional methods in elementary and secondary schools. His conclusions were as follows:

1. Cooperative learning has positive effects on student achievement. The groups must have two important features: group goals and individual accountability.
2. When students of different racial or ethnic backgrounds work together toward a common goal, they gain liking and respect for one another. Cooperative learning improves social acceptance of mainstreamed students by their classmates as well as increasing friendships among students in general.
3. Other outcomes include gains in self-esteem, time on task, attendance, and increased ability to work effectively with others.

Ninety years earlier, in 1900, Dewey recognized the worth of cooperative learning with this observation:

> When the school introduces and trains each child of society into membership within such a little community, saturating him with the spirit of service and providing him with the instruments of effective self-direction, we shall have the deepest and best guaranty of a larger society which is worthy, lovely, and harmonious. (pp. 27–28)

Cooperative study means more than telling students to get together in groups and work. Rather, it is a structured experience in which students, preferably in groups of two, three, or four, practice learning content by using study skills emphasized by the teacher for a particular lesson. Glasser (1986, p. 75) gives eight reasons why "small learning teams" will motivate almost all students. According to Glasser, these teams do the following:

1. Create a sense of belonging.
2. Provide initial motivation for students who have not worked previously.
3. Provide ego-fulfillment for stronger students to help weaker ones.
4. Provide continued motivation for weaker students, who see that team effort brings rewards, whereas their individual efforts were usually not good enough to get rewarded.
5. Free students from dependence on the teacher.
6. Enable students to get past superficiality to learn in-depth and vital knowledge.
7. Teach students how to convince others that they have learned the material (communication skills).
8. Keep students interested and achieving by having teachers change the teams on a regular basis. There is always the chance a student, if not doing well with one team, will be more successful as a member of another cooperative learning team.

At this point, we suggest that you review Chapter 2 on affective teaching, rereading the section entitled "Strengthening Affective Bonds through Group Process and Decision Making." To review, we said that cooperative study takes place most effectively when an **individual phase** precedes the group learning phase. This individual phase brings *commitment* to the task, which is often missing in today's classroom. In the group phase, *consensus* can be reached more easily and discussion is more meaningful when students are committed to their own thoughts or ideas. Finally, in the third phase, the whole class achieves *arbitration* through further discussion of those areas in which students could not reach consensus.

Another reason for the use of cooperative study is that it helps students set purposes for their reading and monitor whether those purposes are being met. Although teachers must help readers set purposes initially, readers must begin to set their own purposes for reading as soon as possible. Hawkes and Schell (1987) caution that teacher-set reasons to read may encourage dependence and a passive approach to reading. Self-set reasons to read promote the development of readers who are active and ultimately independent. To wean readers from dependence, teachers could use many of the activities mentioned in this chapter until students are familiar with them and understand what purpose setting involves. That is, what students can initially accomplish only with the aid of the teacher, they are eventually able to perform alone (Gavelek, 1986). The goal is that the teacher gradually releases purpose-setting responsibility to the students, enabling them to become independent learners. This goal is especially difficult to meet with at-risk students, but it is just as important.

Developing Responsibility

We have suggested previously that the reason for the failure of training in study skills and retention skills is that these skills are not assessed and taught early in the elementary years and that little systematic training takes place from kindergarten through the middle-school years. When a child gets to high school, or even college, it is often too late to break old habits and learn the type of disciplined thinking needed for concentration and study. As we emphasize throughout this text, we believe that study skills need to be taught from kindergarten on, in a systematic program that is understood and practiced by teachers schoolwide.

Teaching responsibility from the early elementary grades will aid students in overcoming two negative factors described by Vaughan and Estes (1986): compulsiveness and distractability. Students will attend to tasks better if they are taught at an early age to concentrate and think about what they are learning, to be responsible for their own learning, to listen carefully to directions, and to have a quiet place and time to study, even if it is for only a short time.

Stanton (1986) lists the following basic elements to be considered in teaching discipline and responsibility:

1. *Won't power.* Discipline means having to make choices. Letting students know what they *won't do* is as important as deciding what they will do. For instance, students can be told they will have to be able to tell how a graph provides important information but they won't have to reproduce it.
2. *Delayed gratification.* Teachers need to help students in deciding to delay immediate gratification in order to realize long-term or medium-term goals. For instance, students need to be told that they may not have time to watch television before a test so that they can spend time on study. After the test, watching television could be a bonus.
3. *Self-development.* Young children can evaluate their own progress in classes and use this self-evaluation to improve. Self-improvement can be a part of each student's grade.

Responsibility can be fostered through daily work routines in the early elementary grades. For example, after students complete assigned seat work, they can be offered a choice of activities. Students whose names are written on a card in green can be allowed to pick from four choices of follow-up activities that the teacher has labeled on charts in the room. Students whose names are written in yellow can select from three choices. Figure 10.1 illustrates this method of allowing students to monitor their own learning and free time.

Homework activities can also be structured to foster responsibility. For example, teachers can send progress reports home with students once a week (see Activity 10.1). Students in kindergarten and first grade can be asked to keep a "home reader" report to record how often they read stories to their parents (see Activity 10.2); students are asked to read the same book to the teacher after completing the home assignment. Our most important message is that students

FIGURE 10.1   Room chart for student activities.

can be responsible, even in kindergarten, for monitoring their own homework assignments and completing assignments at home with their parents (see Activity 10.3). In early elementary school, students can monitor themselves on self-evaluation logs (see Activity 10.4).

By using these suggestions and aids, teachers can begin early in the elementary grades to teach responsibility and discipline. The sense of accomplishment and self-development students feel as a result will be beneficial in helping them establish lasting study and learning patterns.

Types of Cooperative Study

Oral Cooperative Study

Wood (1987), in a comprehensive review of cooperative learning approaches, maintains that verbalizing newly acquired information is the most powerful study technique. Following are some of Wood's suggestions for combining oral and cooperative study.

Group retelling. Content teachers provide groups of two or three students with different reading material about the same topic. Students read material silently and retell, in their own words, what they have learned to their group.

A C T I V I T Y   1 0 . 1   WEEKLY PROGRESS REPORT

Name: _____   Date: _____

		Needs	
Outstanding	Satisfactory	Improvement	
_____	_____	_____	Pays attention
_____	_____	_____	Follows directions
_____	_____	_____	Participates in class discussions
_____	_____	_____	Cooperates with teacher
_____	_____	_____	Exhibits good behavior
_____	_____	_____	Controls talking

Your child needs the circled supplies replaced as soon as possible.

Glue   Crayons   Scissors   Pencils   Notebook

_____ Your child needs to turn in his/her homework.

Developed by Georgette Kavanaugh.

A C T I V I T Y   1 0 . 2   HOME READER REPORT

Name of Book	Date	Parent's Initial
Farmer in the Dell	9/14	
Run to the Rainbow	9/16	
City Fun	9/21	
Let's Go, Dear Dragon	10/3	
All Upon a Stone	10/10	
Now I Know About Dinosaurs	10/17	

Developed by Georgette Kavanaugh.

Group members may add to any retelling by sharing similar information from their reading or from their own experiences.

Associational dialogue. Students work in pairs from an assigned vocabulary list to discuss each word on the list. In this manner, students learn by interacting with others.

Needs grouping. To determine students' conceptual knowledge of a subject, teachers give pretests. Students who did not do well on particular areas of the pretest can be grouped together for reflective study over that part of the unit.

ACTIVITY 10.3 **HOMEWORK ASSIGNMENT SHEET: KINDERGARTEN**

HOMEWORK: OCTOBER 5–8

Monday	Tuesday	Wednesday	Thursday
Write your name five times on the first page of your notebook.	Think about the things in your classroom. Tell your parent at least 8 things and ask him or her to write them in your book.	Look in a magazine or newspaper. Find a picture that reminds you of fall. Cut it out and paste it in your book.	This week was fire prevention week. Draw a picture of yourself in your notebook. Tell your parent what you would do if there were a fire in your house. Ask your parent to write down what you said beside your picture.
Remember, only the first letter is capitalized. Write your real name, not your nickname.	Can you name more?		

Parents: Notebook should *not* be returned until Friday. All completed assignments will be checked at one time.

Developed by Georgette Kavanaugh.

Buddy system. Teachers pair weaker students with stronger ones. In this ability grouping, each is asked to take responsibility for the other's learning. Daniel Fader also describes this process in *Hooked on Books* (1966).

Cybernetic sessions. Wood cites Masztal's (1986) work in describing a technique to summarize lessons through group interaction. After reading a selection, groups brainstorm answers to thought-provoking questions posed by the teacher. Answers are shared in the group and with the whole class.

Research grouping. During a unit of study, students work in groups to research a topic in the classroom or in the library.

Written Cooperative Study

Writing can be incorporated into cooperative study in several ways. Davey (1987), for example, recommends the following steps as effective in guiding students' writing of research reports:

1. *Topic selection.* Students use factstorming to select a topic or subtopic. (See Chapter 4 for examples of factstorming.)
2. *Planning.* Teams meet to establish a research plan. They generate questions to be answered and a schedule for study.
3. *Researching the topic.* Teams divide questions to be answered and begin taking notes, working in class and in the library. The teacher may help with a library search guide (explained in Chapter 9).
4. *Organizing.* Teams meet to share information, organize material in outline form, and decide what information to delete and which questions to research further.

ACTIVITY 10.4   STUDENT LOG: LIFE IN THE OCEAN

Directions: At the end of each lesson, rate yourself using the number from the code below that best describes how you think you did on that lesson.

Date	Skill	Student Evaluation	Student Comment	Teacher Comment

#5
S.O.S

#3
storm
brewing

#2
calm
seas

#1
smooth
sailing

#4
rough
seas

ACTIVITY 10.5   **NARRATIVE STORY GUIDE**

_____
(title)

Once upon a time in _____ , there lived
            (setting)

_____ and _____
            (character)   (character)

They had a problem. The problem was that _____

_____
(problem)

So their goal, or what they wanted to do, was _____

_____
(goal)

In order to accomplish this goal, they did four different things.

They _____

They _____

They _____

And they _____

When they had finished doing these things (episodes) they had solved their problem. So the resolution
was that _____

_____
(resolution)

This story was created by _____
                                        (author)

_____

From "The Missing Link in Narrative Story Mapping," by M. Dianne Bergenske, 1987, _The Reading Teacher, 41_ (3), pp. 333–335.
Reprinted with permission of M. Dianne Bergenske and the International Reading Association.

5. _Writing._ Team members work individually or in pairs to write first draft, check initial drafts, and revise and edit the final report.

For early elementary students, Bergenske (1987) suggests using a **narrative story guide** as a cooperative learning technique. Such activity guides readers to learn the narrative sequence. She recommends that guides be made before story maps or post graphic organizers. At first, children can work with the teacher to complete a narrative story guide such as the one shown in Activity 10.5. Narrative or general story maps, such as the one in Activity 10.6, may be used by children to create stories in pairs or in groups of three or more.

Visual Cooperative Study

Bergenske maintains that after completing narrative story guides, students in early elementary grades will be better able to make and produce postreading concept maps and post graphic organizers, both valuable aids for cooperative study and learning. A recent study (Bean, Singer, Sorter, & Frazee, 1986) found

ACTIVITY 10.6 **GENERAL STORY MAP**

Name: _____

1. Title: _____
2. Setting: _____
3. Characters: _____
   _____
4. Problem: _____
5. Goal: _____
6. Episodes: _____
   _____
7. Resolution: _____
   _____

From "The Missing Link in Narrative Story Mapping," by M. Dianne Bergenske, 1987, *The Reading Teacher, 41* (3), pp. 333–335. Reprinted with permission of M. Dianne Bergenske and the International Reading Asociation.

that a group given instruction in summarizing, generating questions, and creating graphic organizers scored significantly better on text recall than did either a group instructed in graphic organizers only or a group instructed in outlining.

Graphic organizers allow students to display graphically and visually what they comprehend in a particular reading selection. They also encourage class participation and enable students to interact with each other while involved in the learning process. Students can take part in a group process to create graphic organizers such as the one in Activity 10.7, which is the product of students' brainstorming after reading a rule book on volleyball in physical education class.

Why Cooperative Study Works

Weinstein (1987) has suggested that cooperative study and learning strategies are successful in aiding student comprehension and retention because they fall into one or more of what she calls "categories of learning strategies" — processes and methods useful in acquiring and retrieving information. Weinstein proposes five categories of learning strategies, as follows:

1. *Rehearsal strategies.* Techniques discussed in this chapter include cooperative reading activity, content-focused drama, and think-alouds.
2. *Elaboration strategies.* Techniques discussed in this chapter include jigsaw, group retelling, cybernetic sessions, paired reading, student-generated questions, and listening strategies.
3. *Organizational strategies.* Techniques discussed in this chapter include summarizing, narrative story guides, ABOUT/POINT, mapping, and cooperative graphing.

A C T I V I T Y   1 0 . 7   POST GRAPHIC ORGANIZER: RULES OF VOLLEYBALL

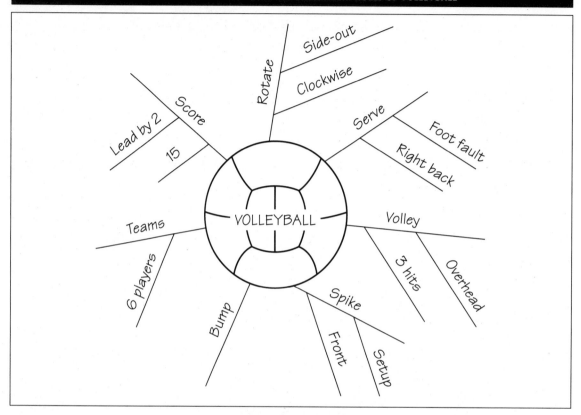

4. *Comprehension-monitoring strategies.* Techniques discussed in this chapter include extended anticipation guides, reciprocal teaching, and think-alouds.

5. *Affective strategies.* Techniques discussed in this chapter include paired reading, positive rewards for learning in groups, buddy system, and first-person summaries.

In underscoring the importance of cooperative study, we wish to reemphasize a point made frequently throughout this book: learning is difficult in a hurried, pressured classroom environment. A first-grader recently complained, "The teacher never lets me finish. I never have enough time to finish." This is a lament that holds true in all too many classrooms. Jeremy Rifkin, in his book *Time Wars* (1987), argues that we appear to be trapped in our own technology. Rifkin maintains that the constant pressure to become more efficient causes Americans to feel that they do not have enough time to get things done. This pressure, which has permeated today's classroom, is detrimental because all types of classroom effort succeed best in a calm, unhurried atmosphere in which students have freedom to explore ideas, develop creativity, solve problems, and be thoughtful and reflective.

A C T I V I T Y   1 0 . 8   ANTICIPATION GUIDE AND EXTENDED ANTICIPATION GUIDE: *THE JUNGLE*

PART I: ANTICIPATION GUIDE

Instructions: Before you begin reading *The Jungle*, read the statements below. If you agree with a statement, place a check in the Agree column. If you disagree with the statement, place a check in the Disagree column. Be ready to explain or defend your choices in class discussion.

Agree	Disagree	Statement
		1. Anyone who works hard can get ahead.
		2. An employer has a responsibility for his employees' safety and welfare.
		3. Companies that process packaged food should be responsible for policing themselves for health violations.
		4. Immigrants were readily accepted into the American system at the turn of the century.
		5. Unions can remedy all labor grievances.

PART II: EXTENDED ANTICIPATION GUIDE

Instructions: Now that you have read *The Jungle* and information related to the statements in Part I, get into groups to complete this section. If you feel that what you read supports your choices in Part I, place a check in the Support column below. If the information read does NOT support your choice in Part I, check the No Support column and write a reason why the statement cannot be supported in the third column. Keep your reasons brief and in your own words.

Support	No Support	Reason for No Support (in your own words)
1.		
2.		
3.		
4.		
5.		

Activities for Cooperative Study

Extended Anticipation Guides

Another technique that can be adapted to cooperative learning is the **extended anticipation guide** (Dufflemeyer, Baum, & Merkley, 1987; Dufflemeyer & Baum, 1992). As noted in Chapter 4, anticipation guides can aid students in predicting outcomes. The extended guides can spark discussion and reinforce or verify information that students have learned and can enable them to modify predictions to take into account new insights and information. Activity 10.8 includes both an anticipation guide for high school students to complete individually before reading *The Jungle* and an extended anticipation guide to be completed by students working in groups after reading *The Jungle*.

ABOUT/POINT

The **ABOUT/POINT** study strategy is a versatile aid for cooperative study (Morgan et al., 1986). In kindergarten and first grade, teachers can use it as a listening and speaking aid after reading a story aloud to students. In upper elementary and junior high school, students can work in groups to recall information from content material. To use the ABOUT/POINT strategy, teachers ask students to reread a passage, then to decide in groups what the passage is "about" and what details — "points" — support their response. Teachers can provide study sheets such as the one in Activity 10.9.

Paired Reading

Another strategy that works with middle and secondary students is **paired reading**, developed by Larson and Dansereau (1986). Students begin by reading a short assignment. Then, working in pairs, one partner is designated "recaller" and the other is designated "listener." The recaller retells the passage from memory; the listener interrupts only to ask for clarification. Then the listener corrects ideas summarized incorrectly and adds important ideas from the text material that were not mentioned in the retelling. During the time the listener is clarifying, the recaller can also add clarification. In this manner, the pair works together to reconstruct as much as possible of what they read. The pair can use drawings, pictures, and diagrams to facilitate further understanding of the material. Students alternate roles of reteller and listener after each reading segment, which may number four or five over the course of one class period. Wood notes that paired reading is successful because it is "based on recent research in metacognition which suggests that without sufficient reinforcement and practice, some students have difficulty monitoring their own comprehension" (1987, p. 13). Paired reading is also based on elaboration strategy which, according to Weinstein (1987), helps students learn new concepts by drawing on their prior experiences.

Self-Generated Questions for Cooperative Study

Recent studies have centered on **student-generated questions**. Davey and McBride (1986) found that children who were trained to develop probing questions after the reading, either individually or in small groups, scored better on a test of comprehension of the material. A similar study by MacDonald (1986) found that groups instructed in methods for asking questions had higher comprehension scores than those groups without this training.

Summarizing in Groups

A number of researchers have addressed the importance of **summarization** to the study and retention of reading material (Scardamalia & Bereiter, 1984; Garner, 1985b). Garner notes that summarization involves (1) judging ideas deemed important, (2) applying rules for condensing text, and (3) producing a shortened text in oral or written form. Studies consistently show that skilled readers have the ability to summarize, whereas unskilled readers almost always lack this ability (Scardamalia & Bereiter, 1984; Garner, 1985b; Brown & Smiley, 1977).

A C T I V I T Y   1 0 . 9   **ABOUT/POINT STUDY SHEET: CONSUMER MATHEMATICS**

This reading is ABOUT:

The high cost, including hidden costs, of automobile ownership.

And the POINTS are:

Few people have cash enough to buy a car outright.

Therefore, they borrow from banks, auto dealers, or small loan agencies.

Costs are affected by the state and region in which the borrower lives.

Few institutions will lend money unless the borrower purchases life insurance.

To learn to write effective summaries, students can be asked to work in groups and use the following six rules, suggested by Brown and Day (1983), to write a summary of a text:

1. Delete all unnecessary material.
2. Delete redundancies.
3. Substitute a superordinate term for a list of items.
4. Use a superordinate term for a list of actions.
5. Select topic sentences from ones provided in the text.
6. Construct topic sentences when not provided explicitly in the text.

One way to have students summarize in groups is for the group to develop a concept map around the ideas they believe to be important in a chapter or a portion of a chapter. Groups can share their mapping exercises on the board, and discussion can center on why groups chose different concepts to be mapped. An example of a group-made concept map is shown in Activity 10.10. Mapping can be an excellent cooperatively generated activity for small-group interaction. Davidson (1982) suggests that such concept maps are "low-risk" activities for even the most limited students and can be an unobtrusive way for students to summarize what they learned in the reading.

First-Person Summaries   Students can write first-person summaries and then share them in cooperative learning groups. Often students read an assignment or memorize information without a true understanding of the material. First-person summaries allow students to process information by writing in their own words about a topic. Using the first person forces students to become personally involved in the material. Teachers may be able to recognize and correct any deficiencies in students' understanding by reading their summaries. For instance, when studying photosynthesis in science, students might write a first-person essay in which they take the part of a water molecule. They must explain how they get into a plant, where they journey in the plant, what happens once they reach the chloroplast, and so on. In this way, students gain a deeper understanding of the

ACTIVITY 10.10 CONCEPT MAP: OFFICE TECHNOLOGY

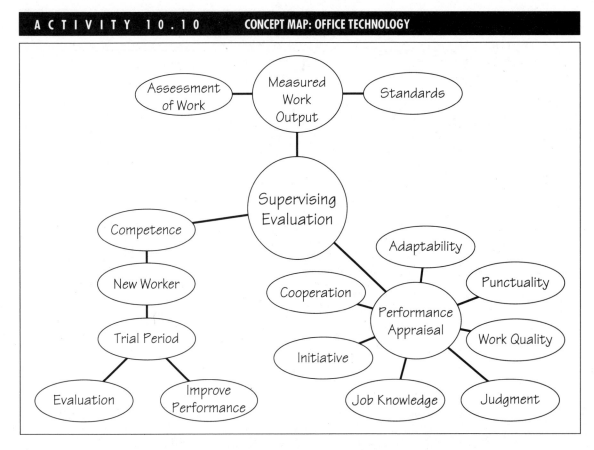

process, and teachers can identify problems in student understanding. This type of assignment also works well with topics such as "A Day in the Life of a New Irish Immigrant in 1835" or "My Life as a Red Blood Cell."

Reciprocal Teaching

Palincsar and Brown (1986) have described a strategy to promote independent learning from a text. In this strategy, called **reciprocal teaching**, students and teachers establish a dialogue and work together in comprehending text. At the heart of reciprocal teaching are four shared goals: prediction, summarization, questioning, and clarification. First, the teacher assigns a paragraph. Next, the teacher summarizes the paragraph and asks students several questions about the paragraph. The teacher then clarifies any misconceptions or difficult concepts. Finally, the students predict in writing what will be discussed in the next paragraph or segment. When the next cycle begins, roles are reversed and students become the modelers.

We recommend this strategy because reciprocal teaching uses small segments of reading; thus, the poor reader is not overwhelmed by too much reading. It is a highly structured method that incorporates all of the language arts — listening, writing, reading, and speaking. According to Palincsar and Brown (1986), this technique has been proven successful with small and large groups, in peer tutoring, in science instruction, and in teaching listening comprehension.

Jigsaw

Aronson (1978) describes a cooperative learning strategy called *jigsaw*, named for the jigsaw puzzle. In this strategy, each student in a five- to six-member group is given unique information on a topic that the group is studying. After reading their material, the students meet in "expert groups" with their counterparts from other teams to discuss and master the information. In a variation called Jigsaw II (Slavin, 1980), all students are first given common information. Then student "experts" teach more specific topics to the group. Students take tests individually, and team scores are publicized in a class newsletter.

Jigsaw uses two distinct grouping patterns for the students in the classroom. *Study groups* are arranged heterogeneously by ability or age level to learn about subtopics of the main topic. The purpose of the study group is to allow each member to become expert in a particular topic in common with other group members. *Discussion groups* are arranged homogeneously by ability or age level to discuss the different subtopics that members have studied in their study groups. The purpose of the discussion group is to allow each member to share his or her expertise with others who share a common perspective.

The number of members in each discussion group must equal or exceed the number of study groups. This is to ensure that at least one discussion group member is in each study group. For example, a class of 22 students might be divided into three groups by reading ability — say, one group of 9 advanced readers, one group of 7 grade-level readers, and one group of 6 low-level readers. These could be the homogeneous discussion groups of jigsaw. Discussion groups would then count off by fours to establish the heterogeneous study groups, thus ensuring equal representation of the reading groups in each study group.

Suppose the topic under discussion were "The Life of the Native American." The subtopics might be "Traditional Myths and Legends," "Occupations and Products," "Lifestyles," and "Origin and History." Each study group would be assigned one of the subtopics to research, dividing the available materials and informational resources among its members. After each member completed his or her assignment, the study group would meet for a sharing session. Each member of the study group would teach the other members what he or she had learned about the subtopic, so that all members of the group would become experts on the subtopic.

When study group members are experts on their assigned subtopic, they bring the results of their study back to the discussion group for sharing with students who have become experts on other subtopics. In this way, all students have the opportunity to do a small amount of research, to present their findings about what they have learned, and to listen to and learn from other students.

Another technique very similar to jigsaw is called group investigation, developed as a small-group activity for critical thinking (Sharan & Sharan, 1976). In this strategy, students work in small groups, but each group takes on a different task. Within groups, students decide what information to gather, how to organize it, and how to present what they have learned as a group project to classmates. In evaluation, higher-level thinking is emphasized.

Think Aloud

Think Aloud, developed by Davey (1983), uses a modeling technique to help students improve their comprehension. Teachers verbalize their thoughts as they read aloud — modeling the kinds of strategies a skilled reader uses during reading and pointing out specifically how they are coping with a particular comprehension problem.

The teacher models five reading comprehension techniques:

1. Form hypotheses about text's meaning before beginning to read.
2. Produce mental images (spontaneously organize information).
3. Link prior knowledge with new topic.
4. Monitor comprehension.
5. Identify active ways to "fix" comprehension problems.

Using a difficult text, the teacher talks it through out loud while students follow the text silently. This training helps poor students realize that text should make sense and that readers use both information from text and prior knowledge to construct meaning.

To demonstrate the five techniques, teachers can make predictions and show how to develop a hypothesis; describe visual images being formed; share analogies and otherwise link new knowledge to prior knowledge; verbalize a confusing point or problem; and demonstrate such "fix-up" strategies as rereading, reading ahead to clarify a confusing point, and figuring out meanings of words from context.

After the teacher has modeled think-alouds a few times, students can work with partners to practice the strategy, taking turns reading orally and sharing thoughts. This strategy can become an excellent cooperative study technique. Teachers can also provide students in the twosomes with a checklist to self-evaluate their progress (see Activity 10.11).

A recent study by Baumann, Seifert-Kessell, and Jones (1992) found that think-alouds were as effective as Directed Reading/Thinking Activities (DRTA) at teaching the skill of comprehension monitoring. In addition, students who performed the think-aloud strategy demonstrated more depth of comprehension-monitoring abilities. This research suggests that think-alouds are an important cooperative study strategy for teaching metacognition.

Cooperative Reading Activity

Opitz (1992) describes a new strategy for emphasizing cooperative study called cooperative reading activity (CRA), which he offers as an alternative to ability grouping. It entails locating a reading selection and breaking it into sections, having students individually read and identify important points of a particular

ACTIVITY 10.11	THINK-ALOUD CHECKLIST

How Am I Doing on Think-Alouds?

	Not Often	Sometimes	Often	Always
Made predictions				
Formed mind pictures				
Used comparisons (this is like that)				
Found problems				
Used fix-ups				

section, and forming groups in which students who have read the same section come to an agreement on essential points. Each group, in turn, is expected to share its findings with the rest of the class. Opitz suggests the following steps for constructing a CRA:

1. Choose selections that are already divided by headings into sections roughly equal in length. A selection with an interesting introduction is helpful.
2. Count the sections of the selection and determine the number of students in each group. Generally, groups of four are ideal.
3. Prepare copies of the text you will use for the CRA. Prepare enough copies so that each group member will have a cut-and-paste version of the proper section and a card with the section heading, which will be used to assign students to groups.
4. Design a form readers can use to record important information gleaned from the reading (see Activity 10.12).

To carry out a CRA, the research suggests that students first read their section and record important concepts. When students finish reading and completing their record sheets, they get into groups and each person reads the important points out loud from his or her record sheet. After everyone has had a turn, each group makes a list of important details, using a marker on a piece of chart paper. If details are similar, students still write them on the group list. Then other details are added that students feel are important. Students must come to an agreement *before* a detail goes on the list.

When the work is completed, each group in turn reads its list to the class. Students are held accountable for all the information presented. Lists are then posted for all to see. In this manner, the groups construct cooperatively the essential meanings of the textbook.

Interactive Guide   Wood (Wood, Lapp, & Flood, 1992; Wood, 1992) offers the interactive guide as an effective solution for teachers who find that groups of students within a class

ACTIVITY 10.12   **COOPERATIVE READING ACTIVITY: RECORD SHEET**

My name: _Brian_

My section: _Sizing things up_

Most important information:

1. The Empire State Building is in New York. 2. The largest Ocean is Pacific.
3. Measurement is used to answer questions like: How long? How short? How high? How wide? How heavy? How hot? How fast?

Used with permission of the International Reading Association and Michael Opitz.

need additional help with a difficult reading passage. The interactive reading guide allows for a combination of individual, paired, and small-group activity throughout a learning task. According to Wood, such a guide is based upon two assumptions: (1) students need differing amounts of time to complete a task, and (2) sometimes the best way for students to learn a subject is through interacting with other students.

After teachers "walk step by step" through the use of the guide, students are given group assignments and asked to work portions of the guide individually, in pairs, in small groups, and with the class as a whole. The teacher may use the guide with the whole class or with a portion of the class that needs a slower pace of instruction. This allows groups to move ahead or spend more time working on a particular phase of the lesson. Activity 10.13 provides an example of an interactive reading guide used in mathematics.

Content-Focused Drama

Cooter and Chilcoat (1991) describe how content-focused melodramas can be cooperatively studied and performed by high school students to stimulate connections between what students know and what is described in historical texts. Students pick a topic of interest within a unit of study and, in groups of five or six, develop a melodrama by writing the plot, developing characters, and making scenery. Students draft the writing in several stages: (1) prewriting stage, in which the topic is researched, facts are organized, and characters are developed; (2) initial draft of the script; and (3) conferencing with teacher to revise, edit, and polish the final script. Cooter and Chilcoat advise that the teacher work with students on grasping the elements of melodrama: stereotyped characters, super-heroes, archvillains as ruffians and cads, romantic loves, excessive acting, over-blown conflict, plenty of action. The authors list a number of benefits of such drama: development of cultural literacy, student collaboration and responsibility training, teacher support, teaching of creativity, and the teaching of reading/writing connections.

Such theater productions can be carried out in any content-area subject. Mark Forget, a communication-skills teacher at Green Run High School in Virginia Beach, Virginia, has developed a similar activity he calls math theater. The method is used to help readers improve their reading fluency through the use of expressive reading of scripts they make from text. No set or props are necessary for this activity, and students benefit from the rereading in preparation of scripts as well as the dramatic oral reading in which it culminates.

Math theater provides the opportunity for students to manipulate mathematical concepts in a tactual, kinesthetic mode by acting out certain problems in the classroom. Students experiencing difficulty understanding the concept of subtracting negative numbers in simplifying algebraic expressions, for example, are encouraged to play the roles of positive and negative numbers in expressions or equations. Students, working cooperatively, create their own scripts from the written problems. They might elect to show negative numbers or positive numbers by the expressions on the faces of the actors, the directions they face, or some other means. Variables may be represented in various ways, such as colored-paper

ACTIVITY 10.13   **INTERACTIVE READING GUIDE: MATHEMATICS**

△ Work individually

⊠ Work in groups

△△ Work in pairs

☐ Work as a whole class

Factoring

☐   1. Discuss instructions for each set of problems pp. 179–180.

☐   2. Review important vocabulary; check for inclusion in notes.

△   3. Work problems 9 & 10, p. 179.

△   4. Work problems 21 & 22, p. 180.

⊠   5. Complete problems 1–4. Discuss which factor is needed.

△△   6. Complete problems 5–8. Compare with group and discuss results.

△△⊠   7. Continue working problems 11–20. Check with other group members for accuracy.

⊠   8. Work even problems 24–42. If disagreement occurs, first check g.c.f., then verify by distribution.

☐   9. Question-and-answer time for general concerns. Time for extension problems.

Developed by Cheryl Haley; adapted from Wood (1992).

renderings. The teacher provides direction and assistance at the initial stage of planning. By manipulating the variable indicators, division and multiplication can be carried out; movement of the actors themselves, at the direction of a narrator, portrays addition and subtraction. The cooperative planning, teacher assistance, and kinesthetic manipulation of mathematical concepts all provide students with opportunities to reflect in a concrete way on meanings of expressions that otherwise may seem very abstract to students.

Cooperative Graphing

Another excellent activity for teaching cooperative study can be termed cooperative graphing. Students work in groups to rate the importance of concepts in a chapter; the ratings appear in the form of a graph. In the second part of the lesson, students work cooperatively to justify their ratings. Teachers can construct study guides for this cooperative graphing exercise such as the one shown in Activity 10.14. The activity can be modified for English classes or whenever story structure is being studied by changing the "most important–least important" continuum of the graph to "most liked–least liked" to enable students to rate how they empathized with characters in the story. This activity is an excellent one for teaching both cooperative study and graphing ability.

Listening

Listening is a study skill that can enhance learning in any classroom. Gold (1981) describes the directed listening technique as a strategy for motivating and guiding students to improve listening. Teachers motivate students before the lesson by asking them to listen for certain information in the lecture or in the oral reading. In this prelistening discussion phase, students brainstorm areas of interest and questions to be answered. Teachers then deliver a lecture or read to the students portions of a chapter from a textbook. Thus, students are trained to know why they must listen and what they are expected to learn from listening.

As a variation, listening guides, similar to the extended anticipation guides explained earlier in this chapter, can be constructed to point to parts of the lecture or oral reading that need to be emphasized. In this manner, students are taught to listen more carefully for details and key points. Through such an *active listening* strategy, even primary students can be trained to be better listeners.

Alvermann (1987a) has developed a strategy called listen-read-discuss, or LRD. With this technique, the teacher first lectures on a selected portion of material. Students then read that portion with the purpose of comparing lecture and written content. Afterwards, students and teacher discuss the lecture and reading. LRD works best to promote discussion if the material is well organized.

The student listening activity, or SLA (Choate & Rakes, 1987), is another technique for improving listening skills. In using this strategy, the teacher first discusses concepts in the material and sets a clear purpose for listening, then reads aloud, interspersing several prediction cues with the reading. Finally, the

A C T I V I T Y   1 0 . 1 4   COOPERATIVE GRAPHING GUIDE: ACCOUNTING

Cost Factors That Influence Decisions

Part I. Make a graph of how important the following concepts are, from most important to least important. An example is done for you.

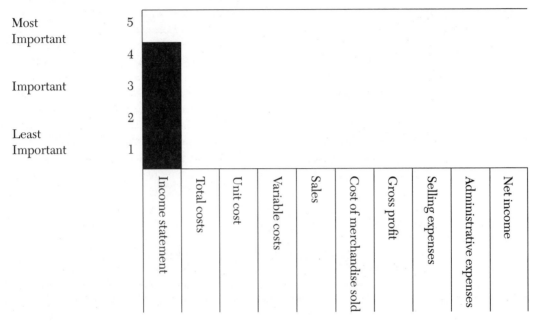

Most Important	5
	4
Important	3
	2
Least Important	1

Income statement · Total costs · Unit cost · Variable costs · Sales · Cost of merchandise sold · Gross profit · Selling expenses · Administrative expenses · Net income

Part II. Please work in small groups to justify your answers.

I gave _____ an importance of 5 (most important) because

_____ .

I gave _____ an importance of ____ because

_____ .

I gave _____ an importance of ____ because

_____ .

I gave _____ an importance of ____ because

_____ .

(continued on page 395)

A C T I V I T Y   1 0 . 1 4   CONTINUED

I gave _____ an importance of _____ because
_____ .

I gave _____ an importance of _____ because
_____ .

I gave _____ an importance of _____ because
_____ .

I gave _____ an importance of _____ because
_____ .

I gave _____ an importance of _____ because
_____ .

I gave _____ an importance of _____ because
_____ .

teacher questions students about what they heard, using three levels of questions: factual, inferential, and applied.

Another technique, called First Step to Note Taking, also promotes listening and purpose setting. One incidental result of this technique is that it offers practice in group note-taking strategies. The activity can be modified for teacher-based instruction or for an independent student learning experience, depending on the ages of students. First Step to Note Taking actually includes five steps:

1. A listening purpose is set by either the teacher or a student. If, for instance, the student is completing the activity for independent practice, perhaps he or she will listen to the evening news with the purpose of identifying the major news stories and two significant details of each story.
2. Listening with a purpose commences. Students might listen to the teacher read, listen to the news on television, or listen to a tape recording, for example. No writing is allowed during the listening.
3. The students react by listing what they heard in relationship to the stated purpose. Responses are now recorded, but no modifications are made.
4. Students listen to the material again, with the list in sight. No writing is allowed during the listening. (If students listened to the evening news, then either a recording of that news broadcast or a late evening news show would provide an appropriate second listening.)

A C T I V I T Y   1 0 . 1 5   LISTENING ACTIVITY: ALL UPON A STONE

Listening purpose: Listen to identify all of the creatures you hear about.

Directions: Listen once, then list as many creatures as you can in column 1. Listen a second time, and list any additional creatures in column 2.

shrimp	*fairy* shrimp
salamander	wood beetle
mole cricket	*other* mole crickets
sow bug	spider
lizard	sponge
ants	lichens
fireflies	
centipede	
snail	
mosquito	
butterfly	
jellyfish	

After you edit these lists, creatures can be grouped by similar characteristics, or put into sequence as they are mentioned in the story.

5. Individually or in small groups, students now edit the list — adding, deleting, or modifying information — and organize it into information — a logical pattern. They have now generated notes for study.

Activity 10.15 shows a list generated by students after listening a first and second time to *All Upon a Stone*, by Jean Craighead George.

One-Minute Summary

In Chapters 9 and 10, we have explained study skills, study systems, and cooperative learning strategies that will enhance students' ability to think and learn. By explaining and modeling study methods, teachers can show students how to obtain the most from their study. In addition, cooperative learning and listening have been identified as strategies that enhance retention of content because they provide an opportunity for students to practice, under a teacher's guidance, five important categories of learning: rehearsal, elaboration, organizational thinking, comprehension monitoring, and affective thinking. Specific techniques and when each can be introduced are summarized in Table 9.4 (page 368) and Activity 10.16.

Techniques described in this chapter work best when students have learned to be relaxed and to incorporate the PAR framework described in Chapter 1.

ACTIVITY 10.16   INTRODUCING AND TEACHING COOPERATIVE STUDY FOR REFLECTION AND RETENTION

Skill	Grade Level												
	K	1	2	3	4	5	6	7	8	9	10	11	12
needs grouping													
narrative story guides													
general story maps													
student-generated questions													
group retellings													
associational dialogue													
research grouping													
summarizations													
buddy system													
cybernetic sessions													
extended anticipation guides													
content-focused drama													
cooperative graphing													
paired readings													
ABOUT/POINT													
first-person summaries													
think aloud													
cooperative reading activity													
jigsaw													
reciprocal teaching													

Cooperative study requires an atmosphere of seriousness of purpose, confidence, assistance, and above all, commitment to disciplined inquiry and study. Jacob Bronowski (1973), one of the great thinkers of the 20th century, wrote concerning the importance of commitment in human endeavor:

> We are all afraid — for our confidence, for the future, for the world. That is the nature of human imagination. Yet every man, every civilization, has gone forward because of its engagement with what it has set itself to do. The personal commitment of a man to his skill, the intellectual commitment and the emotional commitment working together as one, has made the Ascent of Man. (p. 438)

End-of-Chapter Activities

Assisting Comprehension   What does the Bronowski quotation that ended this chapter mean to you? What relevance does it have to this chapter?

Reflecting on Your Reading   Think about and list ways you might change the day-to-day operations of your class to incorporate some or all of the techniques described in this chapter.

PART FIVE

SPECIAL APPLICATIONS

CHAPTER 11

Reading for At-Risk Students

A MAJOR PORTION OF THIS CHAPTER WAS WRITTEN BY DR. LINDA GAMBRELL OF THE UNIVERSITY OF MARYLAND

"When I get a little money, I buy books: and if any is left, I buy food and clothes."

Desiderius Erasmus

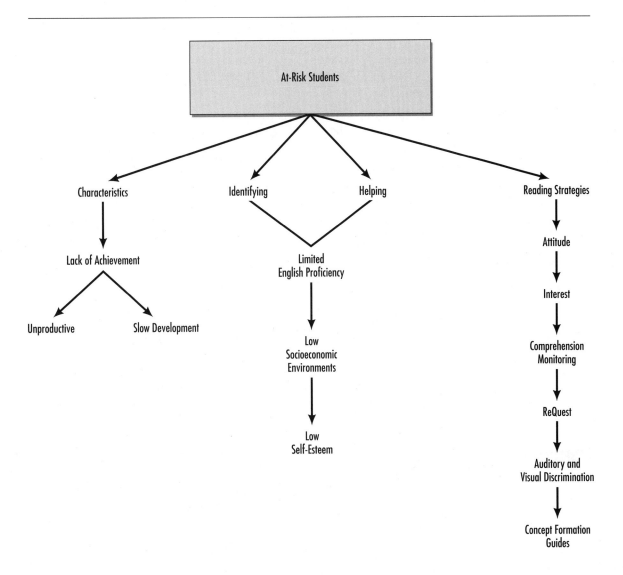

Prepare to Read

1. Here are some thoughts that at-risk students have expressed:

   I was in line at Hardee's today with my friend Jim, and he yelled that he deserved to go first because he was five levels higher in reading than I was. Everybody heard it.

   The teacher talked to the whole class on "present participles" — I'm still not sure what they mean.

   I gave the teacher a poem I made up just for her, and she told me it was nice but I needed to work harder on my handwriting. My printing wasn't neat enough.

   I'm never going to get anywhere in school. I'm a failure. I know I'll never be what my parents want me to be. Maybe I should just give up.

   With the help of these examples, practice an imaging exercise in which you try to think as a poor reader or failing student might. The idea is to try to experience in some small way the frustrations felt every day by children who are bewildered by constant failure and lack of respect. Try imagining how these students would feel in the following circumstances:

   a. Being berated by a teacher.
   b. Getting a fifth consecutive failing grade on the weekly spelling test.
   c. Being threatened by a parent after receiving a poor report card.

2. Following is a list of terms used in this chapter. Some of them may be familiar to you in a general context, but in this chapter they may be used in a different way than you are used to. Rate your knowledge by placing a + in front of those you are sure that you know, a √ in front of those you have some knowledge about, and a 0 in front of those you don't know. Be ready to locate and pay special attention to their meanings when they are presented in the chapter:

   ___ limited English proficiency
   ___ transitional bilingual education
   ___ cultural discontinuity
   ___ group frame
   ___ motivation
   ___ self-efficacy
   ___ attribution theory
   ___ crisis opportunity interview
   ___ comprehension monitoring
   ___ fix-up strategies
   ___ ReQuest
   ___ auditory discrimination
   ___ visual discrimination

Objectives

As you read this chapter, focus your attention on the following objectives. You will:

1. understand and identify characteristics of "at-risk" students.

2. understand why teachers have to discourage passive approaches to reading.

3. identify a number of teacher-directed strategies for aiding at-risk learners in reading.

Shoe. Reprinted with permission of Tribune Media Services.

Every classroom is made up of students who are diverse in terms of intellectual ability, social and emotional background, language proficiency, racial background, cultural background, and physical attributes. As teachers, we must be prepared to deal effectively with our students' individual differences (Au, 1992; Heilman, Blair, & Rupley, 1986). Secretary of Education William Bennett has spoken of the need to reach all children:

> All, regardless of race or class or economic status, are entitled to a fair chance and to the tools for developing their individual powers of mind and spirit to the utmost. This promise means that all children by virtue of their own efforts, competently guided, can hope to attain the mature and informed judgment needed to secure gainful employment and to manage their own lives, thereby serving not only their own interest but also the progress of society itself. (National Commission on Excellence in Education, 1983, p. 8)

Many students in our classrooms are at risk of school failure, for a wide variety of reasons — among them, poverty, drug and alcohol abuse, crime, teen pregnancy, low self-esteem, ill health, poor school attendance, and welfare dependence. Current statistics should give us pause: real wages are down, the incidence of poverty is up, the youthful population is declining, and the proportion of minorities and those for whom English is not the first language is growing. In addition, minorities and those with limited English proficiency are disproportionately represented among the poor and among those who are failed by our school system. Many of these students, failed in many ways by society, will face a lifetime of debilitating poverty unless we, as educators, generate the imagination, will, and resources necessary to educate these at-risk students for independent, productive, and effective lives (Hornbeck, 1988).

In 1987, David W. Hornbeck, as president of the Council of Chief State School Officers, declared that the focus of the council would be on the "children and youth of the nation with whom we have historically failed." As a result of the council's work, an important volume was published which drew national attention to the plight of at-risk youth, *School Success for At-Risk Youth*. In the introduction to this volume, Hornbeck writes:

In our grand experiment in universal free public education in America, we have fashioned a system that works relatively well, especially for those who are white, well-motivated, and from stable middle- to upper-middle-class families. But as students have deviated more and more from that norm, the system has served them less and less well. We sometimes seem to say to them, "We've provided the system. It's not our fault if you don't succeed." Whether that attitude is right or wrong, the critical mass of at-risk youth has grown proportionately so large that we are in some danger of being toppled by our sense of rightness and righteousness. Instead of blaming the students for failing to fit the system, we must design and implement a new structure that provides appropriate educational and related services to those most at risk. (Hornbeck, 1988, p. 5)

Characteristics of At-Risk Students

In Chapter 2 we discussed the four psychological needs of power, love, freedom, and fun described by Glasser (1986) in *Control Theory in the Classroom*. At-risk learners are desperate, yet unfulfilled, in search of these four important affective needs. Often their lives are governed by fear, threat, and negative thinking. They feel helpless and powerless and exhibit an external locus of control (discussed in Chapter 2), feeling out of control of their own destiny.

Pellicano (1987) defines at-risk students as "uncommitted to deferred gratification and to school training that correlates with competition, and its reward, achieved status (p. 47)." Thus Pellicano sees at-risk students as "becoming unproductive, underdeveloped, and noncompetitive" (p. 47) in our necessarily technological and complex world. He sees at-risk youngsters as not so much "socially disadvantaged" (the label of the 1960s) but, rather, economically disadvantaged. Pellicano cites a litany of dropouts, school failures, alcohol and drug abusers, handicapped and poverty-stricken children—all putting the United States "at risk" of becoming a third-rate world power unable to respond to economic world market forces. He calls for a national policy agenda that "legitimates the school as a mediating structure for those who are powerless to develop their own potential" (p. 49).

Zaragoza (1987) has defined at-risk first-graders as children from a low socio-economic background who often do not speak English, have poor standardized test scores, and perform unsatisfactorily on reading and writing exercises. Many of these students come from the inner city. The students alluded to by Pellicano and Zaragoza manifest the poorest reading behaviors and are so fearful and negative that they often cannot be motivated, especially by threats (see Chapter 2). Psychologists tell us that when an organism is threatened, its perception narrows to the source of the threat. This may be why so many poor students "take it out" on the teacher. Feeling threatened, they don't pay attention to coursework, to commands, to anything but how to repay the teacher for all the failure and frustration they feel. Like children who have not matured, at-risk students tend to focus entirely too much on the teacher, thus developing an external locus of control. Remember that in Chapter 2 we stated that students are more likely to read because of feelings they have for a teacher than because of a specific reading activity. Therefore, a teacher's attitude toward students and learning can be powerful; in fact, it appears to be a major factor in promoting interested readers (Wigfield & Asher, 1984).

Identifying and Helping the At-Risk Student

The current attention on at-risk students can serve a useful purpose by helping educators focus on the importance of identifying and helping these students so that they become successful learners. Care must be taken, however, that the term *at risk* is not used as a prediction of failure, resulting in a negative label that perpetuates a self-fulfilling prophecy (Gambrell, 1990).

How do we develop the potential of this type of student? First and foremost, teachers need to be positive and caring enough to realize that these students are not going to change overnight. They have acquired bad study habits and negative thinking over an entire lifetime. As Mark Twain once said, "A habit cannot be tossed out the window. It must be coaxed down the stairs a step at a time." Bad behavior and poor reading habits are difficult to break. However, through modeling and guided practice in using techniques such as those listed for good readers in Table 11.1, even the poorest students can change their reading patterns.

We know that virtually all students can learn to read. We also know a great deal about how to succeed with students who are at risk of reading failure. To succeed with these students is not always easy; in some cases, it is extremely difficult. The routes to success for at-risk students, however, are not mysterious (Allington, 1991; Au, 1992; Gambrell, 1990). The work of Allington (1991) and Pallas, Natriello, and McDill (1989) suggests that improvement in the teaching and learning of at-risk students does not lie in special remedial programs. Rather, we need to make changes in the approaches we use with these students in the regular classroom (Au, 1992).

Hilliard (1988) contends that we already have the knowledge needed to help at-risk students. Hilliard draws the following conclusions from research on programs for at-risk students:

- At-risk students can be taught to perform successfully at demanding academic levels.
- Dramatic positive changes in the academic achievement of at-risk students are possible within a short period of time.
- There is no one way to achieve success with at-risk students.
- There are no absolute critical periods with human beings; it is never too late to learn.
- At-risk students thrive on intellectual challenge, not on low-level remedial work.
- There is no special pedagogy for at-risk students; the pedagogy that works for them is good for all students.

TABLE 11.1

Contrasting Good and Poor Readers

GOOD READERS	POOR READERS
Before Reading	
Build up their background knowledge on the subject.	Start reading without thinking about the subject.
Know their purpose for reading.	Do not know why they are reading.
Focus their complete attention on reading.	
During Reading	
Give their complete attention to the reading task.	Do not know whether they understand or do not understand.
Keep a constant check on their own understanding.	Do not monitor their own comprehension.
Monitor their reading comprehension and do it so often that it becomes automatic.	Seldom use any of the fix-up strategies.
Stop only to use a fix-up strategy when they do not understand.	
After Reading	
Decide if they have achieved their goal for reading.	Do not know what they have read.
Evaluate comprehension of what was read.	Do not follow reading with comprehension self-check.
Summarize the major ideas in a graphic organizer.	
Seek additional information from outside sources.	

A dramatic improvement for poor readers results when they are taught to apply intervention strategies to content text.

Orange County, California, Public Schools, 1986. Used with permission.

All the characteristics associated with at-risk youth cannot be adequately dealt with in a chapter such as this one. Physical and mental disabilities, substance abuse, and many other issues are beyond the scope of this chapter. What will be covered in this chapter are some of the characteristics associated with at-risk youth and school failure that are critically linked to reading achievement: limited English proficiency, low socioeconomic environments, and low self-esteem. It is worth noting that these factors are not independent of one another. An at-risk student with limited English proficiency may also come from a low socioeconomic environment or suffer from low self-esteem. Rarely is a student at risk of school failure as a result of only one of these characteristics.

We do not claim that simply using the strategies described in this chapter will solve our nation's problem with at-risk students. The task is arduous and often frustrating for teachers, and no one set of strategies will solve such an overwhelming problem. We do suggest, however, that using the PAR system and the strategies explained in this text, along with much attention to the affective domain of teaching, will be a step in the right direction. We must begin now to enable this sizable group of failing students to become successful participants in the educational process.

Students with Limited English Proficiency

Public Law 93-380, enacted in 1974, stipulates that there be provisions for bilingual education in virtually every aspect of the educational process. This law recognizes that students with **limited English proficiency** have special educational needs that must take into account the cultural heritage into which the student was born (Harris & Smith, 1986).

Teachers are being called on to work with increasing numbers of students whose first language is not English. These students may experience a language and cultural environment in the home that differs significantly from the language and culture of the school. These differences may be so pronounced that, for some students, there is serious conflict. The student may be placed in the position of having to choose between the school or home language and culture. According to Reyhner and Garcia (1989), such a choice is counterproductive to the educational development of the student. Rejection of the home background may result in a serious loss of self-esteem, while rejection of the language and culture of the school may result in a serious loss of educational opportunities. With demographers continuing to predict increasing numbers of immigrant students from Central and South America and Asia in our classrooms, teachers must consider how their instruction can be modified to meet the special needs of those with limited English proficiency.

School Programs

Currently, three types of programs are prevalent in American schools for students with limited English proficiency (SLEP) — pupils for whom English is not the first language but who have some degree of proficiency in spoken English so that they can receive reading and writing instruction in English. These programs are usually conducted by an ESL specialist outside the classroom. When students receive language instruction in special programs, it is important that classroom teachers monitor student progress and make sure that they receive adequate classroom opportunities to develop English reading and writing skills (Mason & Au, 1990).

1. *English as a Second Language (ESL),* or *Teaching English to Speakers of Other Languages (TESOL),* emphasizes the learning of English exclusively. In this approach, instruction in English progresses from oral skills (listening and speaking) to written skills (reading and writing). The methodology emphasizes "whole-language skills and learner-centered activities stressing the communication of meaning" (Chamot & McKeon, 1984). The ESL/TESOL approach is similar to that of secondary-school programs for teaching students a second language.

2. *Bilingual education* provides instruction in both English and the native language. Separate instructional periods are provided, one in English and one in the students' native language. A variation of this approach is called the **transitional bilingual education**. In this program, bilingual teachers begin instruction in the students' native language and gradually introduce English.

3. *Education of the Bilingual Program (EBP)* provides instruction in English but takes into account the linguistic and cultural features of the native language (Chamot & Stewner-Manzanares, 1985).

Bilingual programs reflect differences in the value attached to the first language. In some programs, the use of the native language is encouraged as a means of helping the student make the transition to English; in other programs, the objective is to have the student develop and maintain skill in both languages. In short, instructional programs for students with limited English proficiency may emphasize English, may emphasize the students' first language, or may give equal attention to both languages.

Mason and Au (1990) caution that teachers should realize that bilingual education is a controversial topic. Teachers must be aware of the view of the community and school system concerning bilingual education. In some communities, parents may feel strongly that their children's education should emphasize bilingual competence; in other communities, parents want their children to speak and read only in English.

Cultural Discontinuity

Cultural discontinuity is a term used by Reyhner and Garcia (1989) to describe the serious internal conflict brought about by a disparity between the language and culture of the home and the language and culture of the school. Unfortunately, students for whom English is a second language may feel that they have to choose between the language and culture of the home and that of the school. It is important that teachers learn about the different cultures represented in their classrooms and provide instruction that encourages acceptance of the native language and culture while facilitating the learning of English.

From the research of the past decade we know that culture shapes a student's view of the world, behavior, and interpretation of events. More specifically, culture shapes students' assumptions about the reading process and the value of reading (Field & Aebersold, 1990). Culture also influences a student's approach to cognitive tasks, social style, and attitudes. Fillmore (1981) has identified and described five categories of cognitive activities that appear to vary substantially in different cultures:

1. *Task attention* — students' willingness to attend to a task over a period of time and their attitude toward the activity.
2. *Verbal memory* — students' ability to memorize, recite, or repeat text or narration.
3. *Analytical ability* — students' ability to recognize patterns and generate new material using them.

4. *Playfulness* — students' willingness to experiment with and manipulate ideas and materials.

5. *Mental flexibility* — students' ability to generate guesses and predictions, consider alternatives, and hypothesize.

Teachers need to be aware of cultural differences that may affect a student's approach to cognitive tasks and, in particular, may influence second language acquisition.

Social Style and Attitudes

Differences among cultures with respect to social style and attitudes also have implications for reading instruction. A number of studies (Downing, 1973; Downing, Ollila, & Oliver, 1975; Heath, 1986; Schieffelin & Cochran-Smith, 1984) confirm that students from non-school-oriented cultures do not have the same literacy skills as students from school-oriented cultures. The value and utility of literacy in the culture, and particularly in the home environment, influence the development of literacy skills. A study by Lee, Stigler, and Stevenson (1986) found that the superior reading performance of Chinese students in Taiwan, as compared to their American counterparts, was related to social/cultural variables such as time spent in class, amount of homework, and parental attitudes. This study suggests that the Chinese students were better readers because they worked harder and were encouraged and supervised more frequently by parents and teachers.

Instructional Guidelines for Working with Students with Limited English Proficiency

In working with students with limited English proficiency, teachers should keep the following guidelines in mind.

1. *Identify and assess the language proficiency of students who speak English as a second language.* Students should have their level of English language proficiency determined so that they can be placed in an appropriate program, where available. Specialists should be available in school districts to perform this kind of assessment.

2. *Identify available programs designed to help the student develop proficiency in English.* Students with limited English proficiency should, whenever possible, be placed in appropriate programs where instruction can be provided in the student's native language to the extent that it will allow the student to achieve competence in English. Most school districts have ESL/TESOL programs and bilingual programs designed specifically for students who are not fluent in English. In addition, care should be taken to provide students with access to support services such as those provided by counselors, school psychologists, and social workers if needed.

3. *Learn as much as possible about the students' language and culture.* There is ample evidence that background knowledge is a significant factor in reading comprehension (Anderson & Barnitz, 1984; Hittleman, 1988). Teachers should therefore become knowledgeable about the native culture of students from other cultures. Field and Aebersold (1990) suggest that the teacher determine answers to the following questions: Is their native culture literate? What is the common method of instruction in their native culture? Are the relatives living in the present home literate in English? Is English spoken in the home? Is reading (in any language) a part of their home activities? It is relatively easy for a teacher to determine answers to these questions by interviewing the student, parents, relatives, or other members of the culture. Using local reference sources such as community groups, libraries, and knowledgeable professionals can also provide insights about other cultures.

4. *Teaching practices should reflect the knowledge that oral language ability precedes reading.* Students can read what they can say and understand. Accordingly, students should either begin reading instruction in their native language, or they should receive instruction that focuses on language development prior to formal reading instruction.

5. *Whenever possible, reading materials used for instruction should reflect the background and culture of the student.* According to Cooter (1990), students must receive instruction using books that are meaningful to them. Materials used for reading instruction contain relatively few stories from any single minority group (Reyhner, 1986). Teachers can supplement the existing reading materials with literature representative of the native cultures represented in the classroom. Teachers can implement daily teacher read-aloud sessions using trade books that feature minority cultures. Students can be encouraged to contribute proverbs, recipes, and stories from parents and grandparents that can be used as the basis for experience stories (Reyhner & Garcia, 1989).

6. *Create learning situations in which students with limited English proficiency can develop a sense of security and acceptance.* Language proficiency is developed through oral and written activities that direct the students' attention to significant features of English. Students can gain fluency in English through working with proficient English-speaking peers, learning key phrases for school tasks, and reading predictable texts.

7. *Determine the students' concepts related to reading and the reading process.* Johns (1986) suggests the following activities to help determine cultural differences in cognitive, social, and attitudinal factors related to reading:

- Provide opportunities for students to share their perceptions about reading. Interview the students to determine what they think about reading and what they view as relevant and useful.
- Think about and list the assumptions you make while teaching that students from different cultures might not share or understand.
- Think about and list specific terminology you use during teaching that students from different cultures might not understand.
- Audiotape or videotape several of your lessons. Note terms or assumptions that were not on your original lists.
- Plan instructional strategies to help students from different cultures develop or refine their perceptions of reading and your instructional language.

8. *Be conscious of the issues related to working successfully with students from other cultures, without feeling restricted by them.* Teachers are in a unique position to positively affect the attitudes of children from differing cultures by adopting methods, materials, and ideals that are linguistically and culturally sympathetic to the students' backgrounds (Cooter, 1990). Field and Aebersold (1990) suggest, "What is most important is that we remain aware of how culture functions as a cognitive filter for all of us, shaping our values and assumptions, the ways we think about reading, and the ways we teach reading" (p. 410).

Approaches That Work Well with Limited English Proficiency Students

Since 1989 several approaches have been published that have been targeted mainly for use with limited English proficiency students. Approaches such as Freeman and Freeman (1989), the Cognitive Academic Language Learning Approach (Chamot & O'Malley, 1989), and Guided Language Experience (Brechtel, 1992) make use of the principles of whole-language learning defined by Goodman and Goodman (1981) and others. These approaches also make use of some of the strategies stressed in this text, such as cooperative learning, response journals, higher-level thinking skills, use of visuals to teach vocabulary and concepts, directed readings, and use of predictions in reading.

One strategy from the Guided Language Experience model that is recommended for reading and writing, and is directly applicable to content-area material, is the **group frame** (Brechtel, 1992). In this method, the teacher takes dictation (pertaining to the content area) from the class and records the information on a chart. This information is used to model revising and editing for the group. The revised dictation is reproduced and used for the reading lesson. Activity 11.1 shows a group frame from an elementary mathematics lesson on flowcharts and algorithms. In this example, the teacher can either begin with the child's native language (in this case, Spanish) or start with English and dictate later in the second language.

Students from Low Socioeconomic Environments

By all accounts there are far too many students in classrooms today who suffer from the effects of living in poverty. In the 1980s, the proportion of children living in poverty in the United States was one out of five (Neckerman & Wilson, 1988). The impact of poverty on students' lives is profound, and the consequences are complex. Hornbeck (1988) contends that schools have persistently failed to serve students of poverty adequately.

Heilman, Blair, and Rupley (1986) list the following characteristics of the lifestyle of poverty in which these students live:

• Housing is usually substandard, crowded, and in unattractive surroundings. Some students may even be homeless, living in shelters or even less desirable circumstances.

A C T I V I T Y 1 1 . 1   **GROUP FRAME: ELEMENTARY MATHEMATICS**

Dictation from Students	*Dictation from Students*
We use a series of steps to solve a problem.	Usamos una a serie de pasos para resolver un problema.
We can make a chart showing how we solved the problem.	Podemos hacer un esquema que nos muestra cómo resolveríamos el problema.
The answer to the problem should be at the end of the chart.	La solución del problema debería estar al final del esquema.
Revised Dictation	*Revised Dictation*
A series of steps to solve a problem is called an *algorithm.*	Una serie de pasos para resolver un problema se llama un "algorithm."
The picture of this is called a *flowchart.*	El diagrama se llama un "flowchart."
Shapes of things in the flowchart tell you something.	Las formas de los pasos en el esquema te indican algo.

- Food and clothing are often inadequate to meet nutritional and health standards.
- Family units are often unstable because of the restrictions imposed by the environment, poor economic conditions, and the psychological factors associated with these conditions.
- Jobs are usually at the lower end of the continuum in terms of pay, prestige, and security — if jobs are held at all.
- The educational level of the parents seldom exceeds junior high school.
- Exposure to crime, violence, and immorality is early and continuous.

Poverty and School Achievement

The conditions that exist in the environment of these students puts them at serious risk of school failure. Poverty is particularly associated with low achievement and school dropout, for reasons that include the following (Neckerman & Wilson, 1988):

- Poorly educated parents spend less time reading to their children.
- Class or ethnic differences in patterns of language acquisition contribute to difficulties in the early years of schooling.
- As poor children get older, they are much more likely to become teenage parents.
- As poor children get older, they are much more likely to get into trouble with the law or have disciplinary problems in school.
- The preconceived notions some teachers hold about poor students' capacity to learn may result in less effective instruction for them.

Low-Literacy Home Environment

Many students from low socioeconomic families come from homes characterized by "oral literacy" rather than books, magazines, and adults who read. In an oral environment, children are socialized through the use of stories, parables, proverbs, and legends that are committed to memory (Egan, 1987). According to Reyhner and Garcia (1989), schools often fail to recognize the cultural and linguistic strengths of students from an oral literacy environment.

Goal Orientation and Low Socioeconomic Environments

Many students come to school with a future orientation — able to set goals, and to set smaller subgoals in order to reach the larger goals. Some students from low socioeconomic environments, however, have not been exposed to and have not developed the traditional goal orientation that typifies school achievement. These students have had little experience with the type of success in which most teachers believe. According to May (1990), it is important for teachers to be aware that lack of goal orientation does not necessarily mean that these students are lazy. It may simply mean that the teacher must try a variety of means for motivating them. Behavior-management techniques that require the teacher and student to establish short-range goals may help these students develop the skills necessary for successful school learning.

Instructional Guidelines for Working with Students from Low Socioeconomic Environments

Surveys have shown that even those at the poverty level in American society see education as the key to a better life (Orfield, 1988). The teacher should keep in mind the following guidelines for working with students from low socioeconomic environments.

1. *Teachers must be sensitive to the environmental conditions of the home and community that may influence the students' behavior and achievement.* Students from deprived environments tend to have a poor self-concept and low aspirational levels, to be tardy and absent frequently, to be poorly oriented to school tasks, to display hostility toward school and authorities, and to resist or reject values that are foreign to them (Heilman, Blair, & Rupley, 1986).

2. *Teachers should be aware of the impact of poor nutrition and health on learning.* The capacity to learn is obviously influenced by nutrition and health. Students without sound diets and with health problems are not likely to be able to concentrate and will lack the feeling of well-being that is essential to learning. Teachers must work with families and social-service agencies in the community to diagnose and address the diet and health-care needs of students to improve their capacity to learn (Levin, 1988).

3. *Teachers should take action to change students' lives for the better.* Rhodes' (1990) admonition, "Don't be a bystander," should be taken to heart by every teacher who works with students who live in a culture of poverty. Richard Rhodes, recipient of the Pulitzer Prize and the National Book Award for his 1987 book *The Making of the Atomic Bomb*, suffered the effects of physical abuse and poverty during early adolescence. In contemplating why he survived with his capacity to love intact, Rhodes comes to the conclusion that he did so because others not only cared, they acted. He cites several teachers who took action to

help him—in particular, one teacher who saw that he was undernourished and managed to supplement his meager lunch, and another who saw that he was poorly clothed and provided clothing.

Teachers should not be bystanders when they see students who suffer from the consequences of poverty. Many resources are available to the teacher to help these students: social-service agencies that can address basic needs of families, including health care, shelter, nutrition, and counseling; youth agencies, such as Big Brothers and Big Sisters, that can offer enrichment programs after school, on weekends, and during summers; adult tutors, particularly senior citizens who can work with individual students. Teachers should not be passive bystanders in the lives of children of poverty; timely intervention can make a decisive difference in the lives of these students.

Students with Low Self-Esteem

During adolescence, students are in a state of flux, constantly searching, focusing, and reevaluating themselves. It is during adolescence that students are trying to find a stable image of themselves (Kerr, Nelson, & Lambert, 1987). Unfortunately, by the time some students enter middle school they have developed a negative self-image, viewing themselves as helpless and without control over their level of achievement. They behave in ways that cause teachers to label them as unmotivated, immature, uncooperative, and even hostile. Although the behavior of these students may be inappropriate, it is most likely a reflection of their distress at facing failure in the classroom day after day.

The relationship between self-esteem and learning is stressed continually throughout the current literature on at-risk students. According to Coopersmith (1967), the four basic components of self-esteem are significance, competence, power, and virtue.

Significance is found in the acceptance, attention, and affection of others, particularly significant others. At-risk students may feel rejected, ignored, and that they do not belong.

Competence is developed as one masters his or her environment. For the student, the school environment is of particular concern. Success in school tasks generates feelings of competence. The at-risk student may experience failure in school tasks, which in turn stifles motivation and promotes feelings of incompetence.

Power resides in the ability to control one's behavior and gain the respect of others. At-risk students may feel helpless and powerless, particularly with respect to school learning, and may feel that their failure cannot be overcome (Dweck, 1975).

Virtue is worthiness, as judged by the values of one's culture and of significant others. Feelings of being worthy and valued are necessary in order for life to be fulfilling. The at-risk student may feel worthless and valueless as a result of school failure. Appearing and behaving somewhat differently from their peers may also make some students feel less worthy or acceptable (Harris & Smith, 1986).

Motivation and Self-Esteem

Motivation has been defined as the process of initiating, directing, and sustaining behavior. Motivation is viewed as a drive toward competence that is sustained and augmented by the feelings of efficacy that accompany competent interaction with the environment (Connell & Ryan, 1984). Bandura (1977) popularized the term **self-efficacy** — the belief in our own effectiveness to cope with given situations. Self-efficacy determines the degree and quality of effort and the limits of persistence of which an individual is capable.

Self-efficacy is related to a more specific form of motivation: achievement motivation. Achievement motivation is the need to try to reach a goal that is determined by expecting and valuing successful completion of the task (Wigfield & Asher, 1986). According to Dweck (1985), two kinds of goals are important to achievement motivation: learning goals and performance goals. Learning goals help students strive toward increased competence; performance goals lead students to gain positive and avoid negative judgment.

Attribution theory posits that motivation results from an individual's beliefs regarding the cause or reasons for success and failure. Weiner (1979) identified four categories of attributions: ability, effort, luck, and task difficulty. The principal hypothesis of attribution theorists is that students will be motivated when they attribute their successes and failures to effort rather than ability. With an effort attribution, the student is in control. If students attribute failure to ability or luck, factors over which they have no control, motivation decreases over time.

At-risk students need a great deal of support as they work toward becoming self-regulated learners. Attribution retraining programs have been developed (McCombs, 1986) that focus on increasing the learner's self-control and competence in learning situations. These training programs focus on the selection of appropriate strategies, knowledge of when and how to use them, monitoring of comprehension, and time and stress management.

Building Positive Relationships

Brendtro, Brokenleg, and Bockern (1990) stress the importance of teachers' building positive relationships with at-risk students. They offer the following guidelines for building relationships that promote self-esteem (adapted from Brendtro, Brokenleg, & Bockern, 1990, pp. 62–63).

Building Relationships as a Process Building a positive relationship is a process of giving that is typified by caring, knowledge, respect, and responsibility (Fromm, 1956). *Caring* is real concern for the life and growth of the student. *Knowledge* is genuine understanding of the students' feelings, even if they are not readily apparent. *Respect* is the ability to see and appreciate students as they are. *Responsibility* means being ready to act to meet the needs of the student.

Crisis as Opportunity The at-risk students who are most difficult to work with are those who create trouble rather than friendships. These students are often labeled "hard to reach": if one were to wait for them to warm up to the adult, it might never happen. Many effective teachers have long recognized the great hidden potential of turning crisis into opportunity, as in the following story shared by a high school teacher:

> Rob entered first period class ten minutes after the bell, looking disheveled and agitated. I asked for his late pass and he swore and stormed from the room. I stepped into the hall to confront him about his behavior but recalled our discussion of "crisis as opportunity." I called him back and asked simply, "What's wrong, Rob?" "What's wrong!" he exclaimed. "I'm driving to school and my car gets hit. After I get through with the police, I'm late into the building and get stopped by the principal. When I tell him what happened he tells me to get to class. Now you send me out of class!" He whirled around starting down to the office. "Where are you going?" I asked. "To get a pass!" he replied. "That's OK, Rob, enough has gone wrong for one day; you're welcome in class." His hostility melted in tears. After a moment he regained his composure, thanked me and we went back in the room. (Brendtro, Brokenleg, & Bockern, 1990, p. 62)

The teacher in this example could easily have responded in a manner that would have alienated this student. Instead, the teacher used this crisis situation as an opportunity for relationship building. When a teacher manages a crisis with sensitivity, the relationship bonds become more secure.

Redl (1952) developed a strategy that uses crisis opportunities for building positive relationships between teachers and students. Known as the **crisis opportunity interview**, this practical approach to communication and problem solving includes the following steps:

1. *Select an incident.* Select an incident or situation that lends itself to discussion. For example, Jamie, a high school junior, announces that she hates school and is going to drop out.
2. *Gain the student's perception.* Talk with the student to discover his or her view of the situation. Jamie, the student in our example, may perceive that her teachers do not like her and that school is worthless. The teacher encourages the expression of the student's view, however distorted and inaccurate, while not agreeing or disagreeing. This nonadversarial communication lowers the defenses of the student and allows the student to verbalize concerns freely.
3. *Develop a plan of action.* Once the problem has been clarified, the teacher and the student examine alternative solutions. The student must feel ownership of the final plan of action. For example, Jamie might decide that having a conference with her teachers may help to develop a better working relationship.

This procedure can be used by teachers to interact more effectively with at-risk students and to put the student in an active decision-making role. When using the crisis opportunity interview procedure, teachers must be receptive to the student's point of view, present alternative views in a nonmoralistic manner, and support the students as they make decisions. Students are more motivated and have increased self-esteem when they feel they have some control over their environment.

Loving the Unlovable At-risk students — students who suffer from low self-esteem, those who are withdrawn, or those from a different economic or cultural background — may not find others lining up to build relationships with them. These are the students who are sometimes ignored or rejected. These students often believe that teachers are uncaring, unfair, and ineffective (Wehlange & Rutter, 1986). Teachers need to take affirmative action to enhance the standing of these students with their peers. This will require that teachers actively focus on identifying the strengths of these at-risk students (Gambrell & Wilson, 1973).

Earning Trust Perhaps the central ingredient in building positive and effective relationships is trust. According to Brendtro, Brokenleg, and Bockern (1990), trust between the student and the teacher develops over a period of time in a series of predictable stages.

1. *Casing.* In this stage, the student has a need to "check out" the teacher. The student is involved in observing how the teacher behaves, how much power the teacher wields, and how others respond to this adult. All these observations are crucial data to students who may view virtually all teachers and adults as threatening.

2. *Limit testing.* During this stage, the student will "test out" interactions with the teacher. A student who is distrustful of the teacher's friendly manner may misbehave or provoke the teacher in order to determine if this person is really different. In this situation, it is important for the teacher to take a calm but firm approach in order to avoid either "giving in" or confirming the student's view that this adult is really just like all the others and not to be trusted.

3. *Predictability.* The previous two stages, casing and limit testing, provide a foundation for developing a more secure relationship between the student and the teacher. Consistency is important to building a trusting relationship. In such a relationship, each party — the student and the teacher — knows what to expect from the other. In some situations where trust building is difficult, it may be better for the teacher to simply acknowledge "I know you don't feel you can trust me yet, and that's all right." It takes patience and persistence to build trust, and it is important to remember that trust begets trust.

Guidelines for Working with Students with Low Self-Esteem

Intuition tells us that when students feel better about themselves, they do better in school. Improving the self-esteem of students is a major concern of most teachers, but especially for teachers of at-risk students.

1. *Focus on the strengths of students with low self-esteem.* At-risk students typically have low self-esteem because they have not been successful in school. These students, however, may have had many successful experiences outside the classroom. With some discussion and probing, students often identify successful aspects of their lives that they have not recognized before. Spend time having students recall, write about, draw, and share their past achievements. Teachers must plan instruction that allows students with low self-esteem to demonstrate their strengths.

2. *Make sure these students are given opportunities to read from materials that are within their reading proficiency level.* Students need to be successful in their reading in order to build positive self-concepts as readers. This means that the material should be familiar enough so that the student can engage in using sense-making strategies. When readers continually have to deal with text that is too difficult, they expend their energy constructing a hazy model of meaning and do not have the opportunity to elaborate on the content or strategies needed to enhance comprehension (Walker, 1990).

3. *Provide opportunities for students to engage in cooperative learning.* Research conducted by Johnson and Johnson (1987) and Slavin (1983) and his associates provides evidence that cooperative learning promotes higher self-esteem, greater social acceptance, more friendships, and higher achievement than competitive or individual learning activities. Cooperative learning experiences such as those described in Chapter 10 are beneficial for all students, but especially for those with low self-esteem. Students can be organized into small groups that are monitored and rewarded for both individual and group accomplishments. Cooperative learning can be used in any content area, as well as for reading and writing lessons and activities. The major principle of cooperative learning is that members of a team can only succeed if all members of the group are successful. Students have a vested interest in assuring that the other group members learn.

Reading Instruction for At-Risk Students

The preceding sections of this chapter have focused primarily on what it means to be at risk in our society, particularly within the school setting. This section will address more specifically what it means to be at risk in reading.

Proficiency in reading stands at the center of academic learning. The student who is at risk in reading avoids reading at all costs. Such students will read when instructed to do so, but only to "get through" the assignment. Their view of themselves as helpless and unable to overcome failure results in lack of participation and passive reading at best. In short, these students have not learned how to read to learn.

Factors in Learned Helplessness

Vacca and Padak (1990) have identified a number of factors associated with the learned helplessness that typifies many at-risk students.

Knowledge of the Reading Process At-risk students may lack knowledge of the reading process and, as a result, may have trouble identifying appropriate purposes for reading and resolving comprehension failure. At-risk readers who experience reading difficulty must learn to be *aware* of the demands of the reading task and learn *how* to handle these demands. This awareness is important in order for the reader to make decisions about the strategies needed either to meet their purposes or to resolve their comprehension difficulties.

Self-Image as a Reader At-risk readers typically view themselves as poor, ineffective readers. They do not see themselves as competent, proficient readers. This self-view may manifest itself in avoidance behaviors related to reading. These students don't read because they don't believe they will be successful.

Reading Attitude and Interest When students fail to value reading as a source of information and enjoyment, they are at risk of reading failure. Motivation is a central component of the reading comprehension process (Mathewson, 1976). When students are motivated, they will *want* to pick up materials to read. Encouraging students to *choose* reading as an activity should be a primary goal of reading instruction. The teacher plays a critical role in motivating students to read. One of the keys to motivating a student to read is a teacher who values reading and is enthusiastic about sharing a love of reading with the students. If a teacher associates reading with enjoyment, pleasure, and learning, students will be more likely to become voluntary lifelong readers (Wilson & Gambrell, 1988).

Comprehension Monitoring At-risk readers may lack the ability to monitor their own comprehension. Because they lack experience in constructing meaning, they read words passively instead of actively questioning their understanding (Walker, 1990). **Comprehension monitoring** is the conscious control of one's own level of reading comprehension (Brown, 1980). Comprehension monitoring occurs when readers begin to scrutinize their comprehension processes and actively evaluate and regulate them. In short, comprehension monitoring occurs when readers think about their own comprehension. This awareness of processing allows the reader to take remedial action to rectify comprehension failure. Before readers can independently employ specific strategies to enhance comprehension, they must first be aware that their comprehension is less than adequate.

Strategy Repertoire At-risk readers have access to a limited number of strategies for enhancing their comprehension of text (Olshavsky, 1975; Paris, 1986). Proficient readers use such strategies deliberately and flexibly, adapting them to fit a variety of reading situations (Duffy & Roehler, 1987). When used for resolving comprehension difficulties, these are often referred to as **fix-up strategies**. When at-risk readers encounter difficulty with text, their response may be to "shut down," to stop, to give up because the text is too difficult. The proficient reader, on the other hand, is aware of specific strategies — such as visual imagery, self-questioning, and rereading—that can be used to "fix up" or resolve the comprehension difficulty (see Activity 11.2).

The research suggests that proficient readers spontaneously use fix-up strategies, whereas at-risk readers do not—even though they can and do use fix-up strategies under teacher direction (Gambrell & Bales, 1986). In fact, the most

A C T I V I T Y   1 1 . 2   **FIX-UP STRATEGIES: ELEMENTARY MATHEMATICS**

Visualization:

Visualize a tree house that you and your friends would like to build in your backyard or in a nearby woods.

How would you measure it? In yards? In feet? In inches?

Visualize how big it would be and your measuring of it.

Visualize some objects that are one inch long.

Visualize some objects that are one foot long.

Visualize some objects that are one yard long.

Visualize something that is one mile long.

Self-Questioning:

What are the standard units of length?

Why do I need to know them?

Why do we measure in fractions?

What if we couldn't measure in fractions?

important goal of reading instruction for the at-risk reader may be to develop the ability to use strategies to enhance comprehension (Winograd & Paris, 1988).

ReQuest

Manzo (1969) describes a questioning strategy called **ReQuest** that encourages students to ask informed questions. This procedure was referred to in Chapter 5 (on comprehension), but is described here because it seems to work especially well in a remedial situation or with very poor readers. The key to this technique is that it requires students to "open up" their thinking, to question and think critically. Also, a very short selection is involved, usually a paragraph, which doesn't overwhelm the slow reader.

With this technique, the teacher and students first read silently a selected portion of the text (usually one or two paragraphs). The students then ask the teacher questions about what they read. The teacher must keep the book closed during this phase. When the students exhaust their questions, the teacher begins asking questions. During this phase, the students must also keep their books closed. The activity can be repeated with other paragraphs, as time allows. The teacher then sets purposes for reading the remainder of the lesson, referring to the questions asked and information received during the ReQuest.

Since Manzo had remedial readers and small groups in mind when designing ReQuest, some modifications for the content class are in order. The teacher should probably select a small but representative portion of text and not try to use ReQuest for a long period of time. The teacher might also want to limit the questioning time. It is likely that students' questions will be mainly literal; the teacher can then concentrate on inferences and applications. If ReQuest is used often, students will readily adapt to asking more sophisticated questions. After focusing on listening, speaking, and reading in this activity, teachers can follow the same steps using written rather than oral questions. Written questions tend to be more intricate than oral questions and will thus enhance students' levels of sophistication with writing as well.

Additional Strategies for Very Poor Readers and Nonreaders

What can the content-area teacher do with the student who can barely read or who is a nonreader? The teacher can (1) pretend such a student is really not that bad a reader and do nothing, (2) get help from a reading specialist, or (3) assign extra work to help students in this situation. Ideally, content area teachers will do both (2) and (3). The reading specialist can help with basic skills while aiding the content teacher in adapting assignments for this type of student. While most of the techniques described in this book will help the very poor reader or nonreader, two techniques that are especially important for the success of such students are presented here. They are auditory and visual discrimination exercises, and concept-formation study guides.

AUDITORY AND VISUAL DISCRIMINATION GUIDES

As children mature and develop, they usually master basic auditory and visual discrimination abilities. However, auditory and visual discrimination problems may continue for many children into middle school and even high school. Weaknesses in these two important areas may mean that students will be severely hindered in learning to read. **Auditory discrimination** can be defined as a student's ability to differentiate between sounds, including differences in rhythm, volume, and tone. **Visual discrimination** is the student's ability to perceive similarities and differences in letter-like forms, letters, and words. We suggest that content-area teachers ask reading specialists to evaluate nonreaders on these two important factors. Nonreaders weak in these areas can be helped through auditory and visual discrimination games and activities. For instance, words similar or alike in beginning, middle, and ending sounds to selected words in the unit can be called to the nonreader by the teacher or by another student. It can be done in this manner:

> Are the beginning (middle, ending) sounds of these two words alike or different?
> zygoma [word in unit] xylophone

Teachers can also construct auditory discrimination games in which students get points for correct answers or move a space across a racetrack for each correct answer.

To develop students' visual discrimination, Herber (1978) proposed what he called "word recognition exercises." These are lists, 25 lines long, of words of similar configuration. Students are asked to pick the word that is the same as the first word or to find two words anywhere on the line that are the same (see Activity 11.3). Herber recommended that students in need of visual discrimination training keep records of their speed and accuracy.

A C T I V I T Y   1 1 . 3   WORD RECOGNITION EXERCISE: HIGH SCHOOL SCIENCE

1. weather   wealthy   weapon   weather   whether
2. atmosphere   atmospheric   atmosphere   atomic   almost
3. temperature   temperament   temperance   tepid   temperature
4. meteorologists   meteor   meteorologists   metallic   meteorological
5. humidity   humility   humidity   humorous   humanity
6. predict   predict   predestined   predicament   predicate
7. observation   observe   preservation   observation   obtain
8. hygrometer   hydrogen   hygrometer   hyperactivity   hibiscus
9. dew   due   dues   dew   do
10. frost   foster   frown   fawn   forest   frost
11. clouds   clouds   clout   closure   clown
12. cirrus   circus   serious   cirrus   circumference
13. cumulus   accumulate   calcium   cumulative   cumulus
14. stratum   stride   status   stratum   straight
15. precipitation   prescription   precipitous   precipitation   precipitate
16. forecast   forecast   overcast   forehead   forewarn
17. barometer   bargain   barometer   bartender   baron
18. mercury   merchant   merry   mercury   mercurial
19. anemometer   anemone   anemometer   meter   antimatter
20. front   fond   frown   front   from
21. tornado   torrent   tornado   torture   torn
22. radar   raiding   radiant   radar   radio
23. satellites   satiate   satisfy   static   satellites
24. hurricane   hurry   hurricane   hurried   hamper
25. wind   wand   wind   wane   windy

With much practice in auditory and visual discrimination over one semester, the very poor reader or nonreader should master these skills and begin to make real progress in reading. Once these readiness skills have been mastered by students in upper elementary grades and above, these students can often "hurdle" a number of grade levels in reading because of their age and prior knowledge.

CONCEPT-FORMATION STUDY GUIDES

Concept-formation study guides (Thompson & Morgan, 1976) are excellent motivational tools for reluctant readers. Such guides make use of a fundamental learning operation: the categorization of facts (lower-order concepts) under more inclusive, higher-order concepts. Thompson and Morgan note that "once a key concept has been acquired, we use it at different levels of abstraction, complexity, and generality, depending upon our stage of motivation" (p. 132). It

A C T I V I T Y 1 1 . 4   **CONCEPT-FORMATION STUDY GUIDE: ELEMENTARY**

I. Read the story. Put an X before each statement you think is true.
_____ 1. A person should find out how the neighborhood feels about pets.
_____ 2. Some small pets grow into large pets.
_____ 3. Someone must care for your pet if you are sick.
_____ 4. A kangaroo will not make a good pet.
_____ 5. Do not read about a pet before you buy it.
_____ 6. It is hard to keep a pet in a small apartment in the city.

II. Put true statements from Part I where they fit below.

Choosing a pet depends on:
Size   Care   Space

III. When you are finished, get together with a classmate and discuss your answers.

is the function of this type of study guide to teach the key concepts of a passage and to provide practice in applying those concepts to more complex and more general situations. Again, creating higher-level generalities of concepts is a skill often completely lacking in reluctant readers and at-risk learners. Activities 11.4 and 11.5 present two examples of concept-formation study guides, the first for elementary students and the second for high school social studies.

One-Minute Summary

There is an old saying in education that we, as teachers, must work with the haves, the halves, and the have-nots. The reader would probably agree that one does not have to be a great teacher to teach the "haves" — those with the motivation to learn and the skills to do work above their grade level. The true art of teaching is in relating to the "halves" and the "have-nots." The "halves" are those who have marginal skills to learn a subject but are not motivated to do so. The "have-nots" are usually not motivated to learn, and they do not have the necessary thinking, reading, and study skills to be successful. This chapter has presented unique strategies for unique individuals — those at-risk students who, more than ever in our nation's history, need teacher assistance and empathy to help them become productive citizens in a technological society. With such students, the challenge for teachers is great, and the rewards may be few. But these special students can and must be reached if our society is to prosper.

A C T I V I T Y   1 1 . 5   **CONCEPT-FORMATION STUDY GUIDE: HIGH SCHOOL SOCIAL STUDIES**

The Move to Winter Grasslands

Key Concept: Social transience

Main Idea: Interaction between a people and the physical and social environment that surrounds them influences the way the basic needs of life are met.

PART I

Directions: Think of a family that you know who recently moved. What reasons did this family have for moving? In the chart below, complete a listing of reasons American families and Al'Azab families have for moving from one place to another.

Reasons for Moving

American Families	Bedouin Al'Azab Clan
1. Dad's new job	1. Good grasslands
2.	2.
3.	3.
4.	4.
5.	5.
6.	6.
7.	7.
8.	8.
9.	9.
10.	10.

PART II

From your list in Part I, answer the following questions:

1. Select those items under the "American" list that are related to making a living. Do the same thing for the Al'Azabs. How are the reasons different? Alike?

2. Based on the information you have organized above, make a list of the Al'Azab basic needs of life. Are they different from the American family's basic needs?

3. Based on the information you have organized above, define in your own words what you think *social transience* is.

End-of-Chapter Activities

Assisting Comprehension   Discuss ways we can identify and help at-risk students in content-area classrooms.

Reflecting on Your Reading   Write specific plans you have for improving instruction for at-risk students in your classes.

CHAPTER 12

Supporting the Textbook with Literature

"Through literature I become a thousand [people] and yet remain myself."

C. S. Lewis

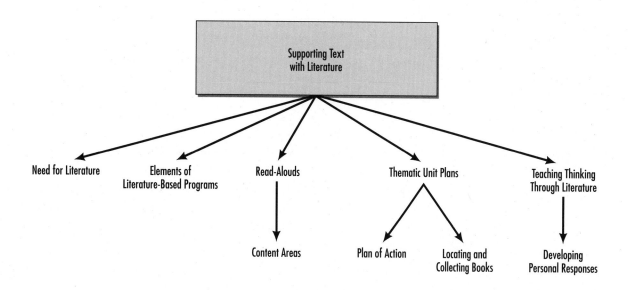

Prepare to Read

1. Review Chapter 3 on text-based problems and Chapter 5 on text coherence. Think of several reasons why supplementing your textbook with literature could enhance the study of your content area.

2. Following is a list of terms used in this chapter. Some of them may be familiar to you in a general context, but in this chapter they may be used in a different way than you are used to. Rate your knowledge by placing a + in front of those you are sure that you know, a √ in front of those you have some knowledge about, and a 0 in front of those you don't know. Be ready to locate and pay special attention to their meanings when they are presented in the chapter.

___ psychosocial
___ sense of identity
___ conflict resolution
___ reading/writing connection
___ literature-rich environment

___ read-alouds
___ thematic units
    of instruction
___ webbing approach

Objectives

As you read this chapter, focus your attention on the following objectives. You will:

1. understand the need for supplementing content-area instruction with literature.

2. identify the elements that comprise literature-based classrooms.

3. understand how to plan for thematic units using both textbooks and literature as a basis for instruction.

4. identify ways to teach thinking through literature by having students respond to literature selections.

The American student population is growing ever more diverse. It is not unusual for a classroom to include a half-dozen nationalities and cultures or for students to speak several languages. There is growing concern that teachers in all content subjects must be adept at offering reading choices that reflect students' interests, cultures, and customs. In the past decade, the use of trade books has increased dramatically, especially in elementary and middle schools. Since familiarity with a book influences whether a teacher will use it in the classroom, teachers need to familiarize themselves with a wide variety of literature that reflects the diverse population they serve. The importance of the literature component of a classroom is summed up this way by Sloan (1984):

> The literate person . . . is not one who knows how to read, but one who reads: fluently, responsively, critically, and because he wants to. . . . Children will become readers only if their emotions have been engaged, their imaginations stirred and stretched by what they find on printed pages. One way—a sure way—to make this happen is through literature.

Why Textbooks Need Supplementing

The traditional notion of using one textbook for all classroom assignments is being questioned because of what we know about the limitations of such an approach. Textbooks have been criticized for their density of concepts (Hurd, 1970) and for their overly factual presentation of material (Calfee, 1987). They have also been characterized as difficult for students to read and comprehend, primarily because of text-coherence issues (Armbruster & Anderson, 1984). Textbooks are often bland collections of facts with not enough emphasis on showing students the relationships among facts or concepts. They often have uneven readability, with some sections that are more difficult to read than others. Furthermore, the expository writing found in textbooks is simply more difficult — and usually less interesting — for readers than is the narrative or journalistic style. At times teachers use textbooks that are old and outdated, with numerous errors in light of factual and conceptual changes within a field of study. The textbook used may not even be the one a teacher wants or needs for that particular class, but one that was chosen by a textbook adoption committee or by a teacher who formerly taught the class. These factors were discussed in depth in Chapter 3.

Because of these limitations, researchers are calling for the use of "real" literature in all content-area subjects (Wilson, 1988). Calfee (1987) has noted that trade books offer causal relationships between concepts and provide a better framework for students to answer their own questions about the reading. Although trade books may also have uneven readability, they possess several advantages over textbooks. Guzzetti, Kowalinski, and McGowan (1992) have confirmed that using trade books improves the affective domain of learning for students; the researchers were impressed "with students' enthusiasm for self-selection of 'real books'" (p. 115). Textbooks can be supplemented by fiction — novels and short stories — and nonfiction trade books in psychology, philosophy, religion, technology, history, biography, and autobiography. Also useful in a broad-based literature approach are reference books, magazines, and teacher-created materials from outside sources such as newspapers.

When teachers become interested in bringing supplementary reading selections to their students, they can help revitalize instruction by opening new avenues for student and teacher alike. A number of recent research reports have called for the use of Asian-American literature (Pang, Colvin, Tran, & Barba, 1992), literature that focuses on minority groups (Bealor, 1992), literature in content areas such as social studies (Guzzetti et al., 1992), and literature for special populations such as deaf teenagers (Hartman & Kretschner, 1992). The authors know of a vocational-education teacher in a shipbuilding class who regularly reads to his students from books about ships (such as "Getting It Right at Swan Hunter," from *The Naval Architect*) and books about the sea (such as *World Beneath the Sea*, National Geographic Society, 1967). He also provides reading lists to supplement each unit of study about shipbuilding. Such a class is intellectually stimulating, and the teacher is constantly modeling his positive feelings for reading with his use of literature.

Another reason to supplement the textbook with literature is that it offers an opportunity to teach important **psychosocial** themes—themes dealing with social and psychological aspects of life—to children of all ages. Templeton (1991) has stated that "in a psychological and social sense, children need narratives for the same reasons we adults do: to make sense of their lives and to give meaning to them" (p. 342). Developmental psychologist Erik Erikson (1963) describes eight stages of conflict or opposition that people must pass through to reach maturity. The resolution of each of the eight social crises must be accomplished by most children and adults if they are to be well adjusted in society. Erikson's five stages most important to elementary and secondary education are as follows: trust versus mistrust (birth to 18 months of age), autonomy versus shame and doubt (18 to 36 months), initiative versus guilt (4 to 5 years), industry versus inferiority (6 to 11 years), and identity versus role confusion (12 to 18 years).

Teachers deal mostly with students in the last three stages of conflict, although teachers also encounter students who have deep-seated mistrust and feelings of shame. Most students in elementary school are at the initiative-versus-guilt or industry-versus-inferiority stage. Older students are trying to establish a **sense of identity** as to who they are and how they fit into society. Jones, Morgan, and Tonelson (1992) note that "adolescents try out many roles as they grope with vocational choices, choose physical relationships, and ponder their status relative to the adult world. A core identity, which, according to Erikson, includes acceptance of a value system and commitment to work, is essential, for otherwise a negative identity or self-confusion is likely to occur" (pp. 15–16).

Another developmental psychologist, Jane Loevinger (1976), has postulated that one can judge developmental level by the defense mechanism a person uses, particularly in junior and senior high school, when life changes come rapidly. Literature of various kinds—historical, biographical, novels, short stories—suggests appropriate ways of reacting to problems, disappointments, and frustrations, giving youth an insight into appropriate ways to react to life circumstances.

Literature can facilitate an understanding of self. Through characters in stories, students can learn more about themselves and ways of overcoming guilt and inferiority and establishing a strong positive identity. **Conflict resolution** in literature can help students come to terms with the underlying conflicts and self-confusion that they are experiencing. Reading of events in the lives of their peers may help them resolve their own anxieties. The use of imagination related to the themes in literature also provides a way to embellish their future outlook and prospects. Finally, as Lynch-Brown and Tomlinson (1993) point out, "with this approach to teaching, children investigate content more deeply than in non-integrated approaches and begin to see that their learning to read and write has practical, worthwhile uses" (p. 210).

Elements of Effective Literature-Based Classrooms

When content-area teachers wish to supplement textbooks with literature-based materials and trade books, a number of elements must be present both in the classroom curriculum and throughout the school.

1. *Teachers must be flexible in their work habits.* To incorporate literature from outside sources in the classroom, teachers must be willing to rearrange topics in the curriculum to take advantage of current articles or stories about a particular topic. Teachers must also be prepared to abandon lesson plans on occasion to follow a gripping news or personal-interest story. Interest in these stories is fleeting and usually cannot wait until some other unit is finished. In other words, teachers must be able to adapt the curriculum to fit the materials available, not vice versa. In addition, teachers need to become adept at saving interesting articles. Students — the teacher's greatest resource — can help as researchers, finding new material. Students need to be challenged from the beginning of the school year to bring in items of interest or items related to what is being studied. These items can be shared with other classes in an effort to convince others that they should bring in new materials, too!

2. *Books and resource materials must be everywhere throughout the school.* It is essential that students have access to many books in the classroom, in the school library or media center, and in a nearby public library. Teachers and librarians/media-center specialists need to work together to find informational books at a wide range of readability levels and interest levels related to content-area units in both academic and vocational subjects. Teachers in all disciplines within the school need to make up reading lists of acceptable literature and other supplemental books. Reading specialists and librarians/media-center specialists can help compile as many books as possible or borrow ones not easily located from nearby public libraries.

3. *Teachers plan how to use literature.* Teachers need to develop the philosophy that literature is an integral part of any content-area curriculum and, as such, is an important resource for studying any discipline. In literature-based classrooms, teachers actively plan to use literature and make this aspect *as important* as the textbook in their teaching. Activity 12.1 presents a semantic map or web adapted from Huck (1979) on exploring the theme of alienation and loneliness in the intermediate grades. Teachers plan their instruction to get children interested in these books and in researching the topics in small groups. Teachers also provide time for students, after they become accustomed to a literature-based environment, to brainstorm and explore their own ideas about topics and how they would like to research them. All of this does not just happen; careful planning by teachers is needed to make such explorative classes work.

4. *Students are given numerous ways to respond to literature.* Students become personally involved in reacting cognitively and affectively to literature. There is additional emphasis on the reflective (R) part of the PAR lesson frame-

A C T I V I T Y   1 2 . 1   LITERATURE-BASED EXPLORATION OF A THEME: A WEB OF POSSIBLE ACTIVITIES (INTERMEDIATE GRADES)

Art Interpretation

Make a model of Mafatu's boat.
Create a diorama of the Marse or
    Sacred place.
Symbolize Mafatu's seven tests.
Create a mural of the story.

Drama

Dramatize the different groups talking
    about Mafatu.
Select a character of today.
    Dramatize what his peers think about
        him.
    Dramatize how his family sees him.
    Dramatize how his teachers see him.

Developing Characterization

The first chapter describes how various
    people of the tribe "saw" Mafatu:
        His father.
        The older people.
        Kana, his friend.
        The other boys.
        Mafatu, himself.

Values Clarification

What takes the greatest courage?
    Admit a wrong.
    Take a stand against a popular
        belief.
    Stand up for your rights.
Which would you rather be and
    why?
        A mountain climber.
        A police officer.
        A surgeon.
What if Mafatu had decided not
    to go?

**CALL IT COURAGE
BY
ARMSTRONG SPERRY**

**Developing
Literary Awareness**

Plot Development

Meaning of Mafatu's various tests:
    Decision to leave.
    Swamping of boat.
    Stealing the spear.
    Killing the shark.
    Killing the wild pig.
    Diving for his knife.
    Final escape.
Rising climax.
Similarity of beginning and
    ending paragraphs.

Use of Symbols

Uri, the Dog = love and faithfulness.
Kivi, the crippled Albatross = hope.
Others?

Personal Response

Do you have any hidden fears?
Have you ever felt as rejected
    as Mafatu?
        When?
What tests of physical courage are
    available to children of today?

Related Literature

Tests of Courage Today

The Bear's House by Sachs
Rosa Parks by Greenfield
Mustang, Wild Spirit of the West
    by Henry
Dag Hammarskjöld by Simon
Profiles in Courage by Kennedy

Incredible Journeys

James and the Giant Peach
    by Dahl
A Wrinkle in Time by L'Engle
A Wind in the Door by L'Engle
North to Freedom by Holm
Journey Outside by Steele
The Farthest Shore by LeGuin

Kinds of Courage

Carolina's Courage by Yates
Sounder by Armstrong
Julie of the Wolves by George
Where the Lilies Bloom
    by the Cleavers
Shadow of a Bull
    by Wojciechowska
One Is One by Picard

Other Survival Stories

The Silent Storm
    by Brown and Crone
Island of the Blue Dolphins
    by O'Dell
Walkabout by Marshall
Whichaway by the Swarthouts
The Endless Steppe by Hautzig
Hey, I'm Alive
    by Klaben and Day

work to allow students, both orally and in writing, individually and in groups, to respond to the meaning they have derived from the reading. Guzzetti (1990) reports on the importance of students responding visually through cognitive maps, charts of character traits (visual illustrations), and written paradigms (creation of a new product based on the author's ideas and students' experiences) to historical fiction and novels. According to Guzzetti, such visual responses help students clarify their thinking and help motivate them through creative activity related to the interpretation of meaning from text.

5. *The reading/writing connection is emphasized in each content-area classroom.* Students learn to write to get ready to read, to read, and then to write about the meaning they derived from reading. This is the **reading/writing connection**, and in this atmosphere writing ability improves dramatically as students read varied literature. Students become used to combining reading and writing in this manner; it happens naturally in the literature-based classroom.

6. *The media center is a hub of learning for the school.* Literature-based programs rely on close cooperation among administrators, teachers, and reading and media specialists to make books a central focus for the school. One vocational-education school we know about utilizes a research-based curriculum in which the media specialist plays a central role in helping students do research. Teachers in the school stress the use of Directed Reading/Thinking Activities (DRTAs) in each vocational and academic class. When students have unanswered questions remaining on their What-I-Know sheets, teachers create a committee and give students on the research committee a number of days to find the answers. The teacher and students sign a special form (see Activity 12.2) and take it to the media specialist. The media specialist, in turn, signs the form to acknowledge the research question and helps the student committee find reference and other material sufficient to answer the students' questions. In this manner the media specialist, teacher, and students have teamed to find answers to research questions emanating from student inquiry in reading.

7. *Reading is perceived as important.* In many schools, reading is offered as a carrot to those students who finish their regular classroom assignments. This places a lower value on reading. Consider the lament of a content-area teacher who said, "You would ask me to have students read in class? My students don't read in class, they go home and read!" When reading is done only as homework, it is assigned a lesser value by students who often do not even bother to do the homework assignment because it has such little value to them. In a **literature-rich environment**, students are read to daily by the teacher, they are allowed to read silently on a subject or story of interest, and they read and do research in groups on topics assigned by the teacher or self-selected by the group. Students also keep records and daily logs of reading and writing abilities so that a portfolio is built of their successes in the class.

8. *Teachers model good reading process.* Teachers in literature-based classrooms read orally to students to motivate them to read further on a topic or to complete a story. Teachers also direct students to maturity in reading by model-

---

A C T I V I T Y   1 2 . 2   **RESEARCH FORM**

Class: ___Ship Construction___

Research topic: ___What is the difference between a brittle fracture of a ship's hull and a ductile failure of the hull?___

Teacher's signature: ___Mr. Applegate___

Student committee's signatures:
___Fred Bovine___
___Susan Henley___
___Ray Birdsong___

Media specialist's signature: ___Dorothy Sabotka___

Beginning date of search: ___January 3___

Search to be completed by: ___January 10___

---

ing correct reading process using many of the techniques mentioned in this text, such as DRTAs or QARs. When students are reading silently, the teacher reads silently also to model good reading behavior and show interest in the lesson. Teachers also share what they are reading and writing with the students and generally provide an intellectually stimulating environment.

9. *Teachers stress the affective domain in reading.* Through reading aloud and encouraging the sharing and discussion of books, teachers emphasize the affective domain of reading—how students feel about what they are doing. In our study skills chapter (Chapter 9), we presented a study log to be kept so that students can self-evaluate how they are doing in the classroom. Through such a device, teachers can allow students to become more internally motivated and to move toward internal locus of control (discussed in Chapter 2). If students enjoy what they are doing, they tend to feel more "in control" of what is happening in the class. This emphasis on the affective domain is especially evident in the reflective (R) phase of the PAR lesson framework. If students are given real opportunities, in an unhurried environment, to think critically and share their thoughts on reading material, their attitude toward a class will improve. Allowing more time for sharing and reflection can be done in any grade and in any subject, from kindergarten to the most abstract and difficult 12th-grade subject.

10. *Intellectual curiosity is encouraged.* In literature-based classrooms, teachers always encourage questions from students about topics related to the subject being studied. Teachers point students in directions to find their own answers rather than simply telling students what they need to know. Teachers also try to get parents involved in stimulating their children's intellectual curiosity. Activity 12.3 shows a letter that a second-grade teacher sent to parents, along

A C T I V I T Y   1 2 . 3   ENCOURAGE READING AT HOME

Dear Parents:

Enclosed is a supplementary reading list for our science textbook, *Discover Science*. Many of your children have expressed an interest in science this year. So, I have created a list of books that can be found at the public library. Our Henrico County Student Outcomes, by which I teach, are divided into headings. These headings are the subjects your children learn about in second-grade science. These subjects include the human body, physical science, earth and space, plants, animals, and dinosaurs. Please encourage your child to read some of these books. With the holidays approaching, they would make great gifts as well as enhance your child's understanding of various science topics.

Sincerely,

Kelly Taylor

Title Author Publisher Date	Summary of Book	Reading Rating	Related Science Content	Nonfiction/ Fiction
Shooting Stars Franklyn M. Branley Thomas Y. Crowell 1989	Through beautiful illustrations, this book explains what shooting stars are, what they are made of, and what happens when they land on Earth.	Average	Earth and Space (Stars)	Nonfiction
Under the Sun Ellen Kandoian Dodd, Mead 1987	Molly's mother answers her questions about where the sun goes each night by taking her on a visual journey around the world.	Easy	Earth and Space (Sun)	Nonfiction
The Magic School Bus Inside the Earth Joanna Cole Scholastic, Inc. 1987	On a special field trip in the magic school bus, Ms. Frizzle's class learns firsthand about different kinds of rocks and the formation of the earth.	Average	Earth	Nonfiction °A combination of fact and fancy
The Magic School Bus Lost in the Solar System Joanna Cole Scholastic, Inc. 1990	The magic school bus turns into a spaceship and takes the students on an exploration of the solar system.	Average	Space	Nonfiction °A combination of fact and fancy

(continued on page 436)

Title Author Publisher Date	Summary of Book	Reading Rating	Related Science Content	Nonfiction/ Fiction
The Sun, Our Nearest Star Franklyn M. Branley Harper & Row 1988	This book describes the sun and how it provides the light and energy that allow plant and animal life to exist on Earth.	Average	Earth and Space (Sun)	Nonfiction
My First Book About Space Dinah L. Moche Western Publishing 1982	This is an entertaining question-and-answer book about space. It includes interesting facts and illustrations.	Average	Earth and Space	Nonfiction
The Planets in Our Solar System Franklyn M. Branley Thomas Y. Crowell 1981	This book introduces the solar system and its nine planets. It includes directions for making two models, one showing relative sizes of the planets and the other their relative distances from the sun.	Average	Earth and Space	Nonfiction
Comets Franklyn M. Branley Harper & Row 1984	This book explains what comets are, how they are formed, and how their unusual orbits bring them into earth's view at predictable intervals, with a special focus on Halley's comet.	Average	Space (Comets)	Nonfiction
The Pumpkin Patch Elizabeth King Dutton 1990	The text and photographs describe the activities in a pumpkin patch as pink-colored seeds become fat pumpkins, ready to be carved into jack-o-lanterns.	Average	Plants	Nonfiction
The Berenstain Bears in The Bears' Nature Guide Stan and Jan Berenstain Random House 1975	On a nature walk, Papa Bear introduces animals, plants, and other beauties and wonders of the earth.	Average	Nature	Nonfiction

(continued on page 437)

A C T I V I T Y   1 2 . 3   CONTINUED

Title Author Publisher Date	Summary of Book	Reading Rating	Related Science Content	Nonfiction/ Fiction
The Story of Johnny Appleseed Aliki Prentice-Hall 1963	This book tells the story of Johnny Appleseed and how he became a legend. His love of people and nature shines through in the rich, warm colors and lively drawings.	Average	Nature and trees	Nonfiction
The Biggest Living Thing Caroline Arnold CarolRhoda Books 1983	This book presents facts about giant sequoia trees, including how they grow, the circumstances of their discovery, how their age is determined, and how forest fires actually help them grow.	Average	Trees	Nonfiction
Trees George Sullivan Follett 1970	This book examines the parts of a tree and contains a lot of information about trees. It also includes various projects the reader can do — for example, make a leaf collection, find out the age of a tree.	Average	Trees	Nonfiction
The Tremendous Tree Book May Garelick and Barbara Brenner Four Winds Press 1979	This book contains the history of trees as well as interesting information about trees, with cut-and-paste illustrations.	Average	Trees	Nonfiction
Discovering Trees Douglas Florian Scribner 1986	This book includes an introduction to trees, their growth, reproduction, usefulness, and facts about specific kinds of trees.	Difficult	Trees	Nonfiction
A Kid's First Book of Gardening Derek Fell Running Press 1989	This book presents information on soil, seeds, easy-to-grow flowers, flowers that keep blooming, bulbs, vegetables, fruits, trees, shrubs, houseplants, gardening in containers, and unusual plants.	Difficult	Plants (Gardening)	Nonfiction

Developed by Kelly Taylor.

with a book list, in an attempt to stimulate reading. The book list includes a brief description of each book, its level of difficulty, topics covered, and whether it is fiction or nonfiction. This is an excellent way to encourage the natural curiosity of the child.

The Importance of Read-Alouds

Read-alouds occur when one person shares reading material with another by reading that material, or a portion of it, aloud. Read-alouds take place often: in many families, parents read nightly to their children; or one person says, "Listen to this!" and then proceeds to read a portion of a newspaper article to another person. Content and context shift, but the practice has been a favorite for as long as there have been readers.

A social studies teacher tried read-alouds as an assisting activity to help her students understand myths, legends, and fairy tales of different cultures. After listening to read-alouds, students were expected to read stories from Eastern and Western cultures, then write their own myths. These students were ninth-grade honors level, resistant to "baby" activities.

Every day during the first unit, on India, and every other day during the second and third units, on China and Japan, the teacher read a myth, a legend, or a fairy tale during the last 5–10 minutes of class. The class then discussed the characteristics of these stories, as well as their historical merit. Next came the study of ancient Greece, after which students were to write their own myth, legend, or fairy tale from one of the civilizations studied.

Students were given two weeks to complete their writing assignment, which was worth a test grade; students could also present their stories orally, for a quiz grade. The products generated were of high quality. Although this is to be expected from honors students, the enthusiasm with which the students participated was greater than usual for this unit. Students began to remind the teacher when to start the daily read-aloud time.

When this teacher asked her students to evaluate the read-alouds, 63% responded that they would like them to continue for other units — and this was probably an understatement. "I really believe more students enjoyed this than even said they did, because they kept looking at each other's papers. . . . I've had several students talk with me about the survey after we had completed it. The comments orally were much more positive."

In science, read-alouds at the secondary level might include brief articles from local newspapers. A recent article in a Food section, entitled "Lost in the Sauce," relates a food editor's experiences with readers who complain because they followed a recipe *exactly*, but the product flopped. The editor then gives some examples of readers' "exact adaptations"! For instance, one erstwhile cook left the cake batter — a mixture of flour, baking powder, and liquid — for 45 minutes before putting it into the oven. Of course, the baking powder begins to give off a gas as soon as it is mixed with liquid; thus the cake batter had no bubbles left to make the cake rise by the time it met the oven! This read-aloud could be chemistry in practice. Often, newspapers include a Science section at least once weekly. The features included can become short, relevant read-alouds.

Mrs. Frisby and the Rats of NIMH, a novel mentioned earlier in this text, is an example of a science experiment that worked better than expected. The scientists divide rats and mice into three groups — control, experimental A, and experimental B — and then inject serums and conduct experiments. The serum works so well for group A that those rats and mice escape and set up their own society. The example of infinity in *The Phantom Tollbooth* has captivated mathematics teachers in middle and high schools. The beaver with a 30-foot tail who could build Boulder Dam, also in this novel, provides a humorous look at word problems.

Dorothy Giroux, of Loyola University of Chicago, has compiled a comprehensive list of science and mathematics children's trade books, as well as professional teacher resources, for science and mathematics. This list is included as part of Appendix G.

The Unit Plan of Action

Content-area teachers who wish to try literature-based reading and writing, including read-alouds, or who wish to supplement their instruction with fiction and informational books need to organize their classroom around units that address particular topics or themes. Activity 12.1, presented earlier in this chapter, demonstrated the organization of a unit, with related literature, around the theme of courage. Appendix H provides two more fully elaborated examples of **thematic units of instruction**. The authors have seen teachers construct many thematic units with titles such as "The Vietnam Era," "Survival in the World in the 1990s," and "Welcome to Planet Earth."

Units can be very large and encompassing, such as the one in Activity 12.1, or they can be on a smaller scale, such as the nine-step unit plan developed for a middle-school English class around *The Call of the Wild*, shown in Activity 12.4. On a larger scale, middle-school and high school teachers should be encouraged by administrators to meet in teams to plan activities across the curriculum for interdisciplinary units. Such "breaking down" of the traditional disciplines into more favorable climates for interdisciplinary study is a trend that gained momentum in the 1980s and may well become a major aspect of all instruction in middle and secondary schools by the turn of the century.

For instance, in the thematic unit centered around *The Call of the Wild*, the English teacher could work with the social studies/geography teacher to develop collateral activities such as tracing the route followed in the novel on a map of Alaska, identifying landmarks, and discussing Alaska's statehood history. In science, the biology teacher could explain Darwinism and how Buck regresses,

A C T I V I T Y   1 2 . 4   UNIT PLAN: THE CALL OF THE WILD

1. Read the novel during the time of the Ididerod Races in Alaska. One will be able to find current pieces on climate, geography, living conditions, and the history of dog races. Use these to compare and contrast with the novel.

2. Read books or articles about gold mining. Help the students identify the physical hardships and dangers of this occupation.

3. Read poetry by Robert Service ("The Cremation of Sam McGee") about Alaska.

4. Read Jack London's short stories about Alaska. Identify and explain the similarities and differences.

5. Discuss types of conflict (man vs. man, man vs. nature, etc.). Read newspaper and magazine articles and ask students to identify the type of conflict; then ask them to do it for key scenes in the novel.

6. Study articles on modern-day sled dogs and their mushers. How are things different today?

7. Write to Alaska's tourist bureau (at least a month before you read the novel) and ask them to send all their brochures. You can also ask for information about a specific topic.

8. Compare the personalities of the main characters (including the dogs) to people prominent in the news. Students will have to read the newspaper and news magazines to make informed comparisons.

9. When bringing outside sources into the classroom, remember to bring ones that are topical and current. A book about a dog written 70 years ago suddenly becomes a modern adventure story if it is coupled with events taking place today. The students instantly see how the novel can relate to their lives. It ceases to be another old and boring book.

Developed by Beth Pallister, Bayside Middle School, Virginia Beach, Virginia.

break down the steps of hypothermia, and identify how the dogs were able to adapt physically to the harsh Alaskan environment. Even in situations where departmentalized classes contribute to a lack of communication between teachers, coordination can take place if teachers can meet long enough to decide on some books that can be used in common for a particular unit. For instance, high school history and language arts teachers could coordinate the study of the American Civil War by mutually deciding to read and discuss such books as *Voices from the Civil War* (Metzger, 1989), *Civil War Trivia and Fact Book* (Garrison, 1992), *Touched by Fire: A Photographic Portrait of the Civil War* (W. C. Davis, 1985), *The Long Surrender* (B. Davis, 1985), *A Separate Battle: Women and the Civil War* (Chang, 1991), *Crowns of Thorns and Glory: Mary Todd Lincoln and Varina Howell Davis, The Two First Ladies of the Civil War* (Vander Heuvel, 1988), *Civil War: America Becomes One Nation* (Robertson, 1992), *Blood Brothers: A Short History of the Civil War* (Vandiver, 1992), *Forged in Battle: The Civil War Alliance of Black Soldiers and White Officers* (Glatthaar, 1990), and *Diary of a Confederate Soldier* (W. C. Davis, 1990).

Activity 12.5 presents cross-disciplinary thematic unit activities developed by a team of teachers working together in staff development sessions on "Cleaning

A C T I V I T Y   1 2 . 5   THEMATIC PLANNING ACROSS THE CURRICULUM: CLEANING UP THE CHESAPEAKE BAY

Goals: Students will research causes of pollution and develop a plan of action to improve
environmental characteristics of the Chesapeake Bay.

Process Objective: Students will integrate information and process skills across the curriculum to
produce a plan of action to improve the Chesapeake Bay.

Content Areas:

Math	Earth Science	History/Geography	Art

metric system
making graphs
study wave functions
finding parts per
   million
finding rate of increase
   or decrease of water
   level, living
   creatures, area of
   bay, temperature of
   water, etc.
calculating distance,
   depth
	weather
	rocks, soil
	rivers
	quantitative
	   measurement
	% of pH
	phosphates, etc.
	volume of water
	   transport
	estuary
		laws enacted—federal,
		   state
		map reading
		newspaper, magazine
		   articles
		historical development
		cultural development
		time line of
		   development
		map making
			research artwork done
			   in the past: drawings,
			   pictures/photos,
			   sculpture/clay
			music
			Indian arts/crafts,
			   tradition
			produce art of the past:
			   drawing, photo,
			   sculpture, clay
			interpreting art:
			   practice futuristic art
			   on the bay: paint,
			   sketch, sculpt, music
			create a model of the
			   bay

English	Vocational	Business

research techniques
proofread, polish final proposal
evaluate controversial issues
interviews
appreciate life on the bay
analyze conflict related to life
   on Chesapeake in the novel
create poems relevant to
   subject
	take pictures, identify industry
	   on the bay
	identify new jobs that may be
	   created
	determine how ships dispose of
	   waste
	identify manufacturers and
	   their processes that produce
	   waste in or near the bay
	research OSHA laws
	research EPA guidelines
	how waste is presently treated
		develop an ad campaign
		develop a budget on clean-up
		   costs—what factors should
		   be in a budget?
		what are factory cost and
		   consumer cost?
		projection
		type proposal

(continued on page 442)

Notes: 9-week unit

Kids selected to participate in program are average/below-average ability.

Math and science team teach.

English and history team teach (research causes).

Two-day field trip at the beginning to Tangier Island
  1. Photos
  2. Samples (physical and bio)
  3. Inteviews, etc.

Take the proposal to an appropriate audience at the end of this project (for example, the General Assembly in Richmond to a committee on environmental protection, to a congressional committee in Washington, DC).

Divide the units so that all areas have the same focus — e.g., Unit 1: Documenting the Problem.

English and history — research background causes and moral dilemma.

Developed by teachers at Norview High School, Norfolk, Virginia.

Up the Chesapeake Bay." This nine-week unit was developed in Norfolk, Virginia, by Norview High School teachers of math, science, social studies, art, English, business, and vocational education working together over shared planning periods. Activity 12.6 presents another thematic plan across the curriculum, this time on "The Journey of Lewis and Clark." Planning such units can be time-consuming and sometimes difficult, but the benefits in adding new dimensions and vigor to the curricular offerings are certainly worth the effort.

When developing a unit plan, teachers may need to construct the unit in distinct phases. Moss (1990) lists four main phases in constructing a literature unit:

1. determining unit objectives and goals;
2. determining the theme or focus of the unit;
3. gathering books to be used in the unit; and
4. deciding student activities for the unit and the sequence of the activities.

In determining unit goals, it is important to examine both the curriculum to be taught and the backgrounds and abilities of students. If this unit is to be taught well into the school year, the teacher should know what the students can absorb emotionally and socially, as well as their reading abilities for reading supplemental literature. If the unit is taught at the beginning of the year, the teacher may need to carry out considerable assessment using strategies presented in Chapter 4. Templeton (1991) advises teachers to wait several weeks to start a unit at the beginning of the school year so that students can learn classroom procedures and the teacher can assess student abilities and characteristics.

To begin determining the activities, teachers (either alone or with other teachers) can use the **webbing approach** depicted earlier in Activity 12.1 to brainstorm ideas. In this method (Cullinan, Karrer, & Pillar, 1981; Huck, 1979; Huck, Hepler, & Hickman, 1987), the teacher first identifies large categories of information based on unit objectives and continues until smaller concepts are represented by numerous activities. The teacher does not have to use all the activities that are brainstormed, but this brainstorming process provides a springboard to determining how the final unit plan will appear. The teacher can choose themes and activities based on students' needs and interests, current events, and activities that were successful in other thematic units.

A C T I V I T Y   1 2 . 6   THEMATIC PLANNING ACROSS THE CURRICULUM: THE JOURNEY OF LEWIS AND CLARK

Goals: Students will write a 14-day journal describing the experiences of accompanying Lewis and Clark on their expedition.

Process Objective: Students will integrate information and process skills across the curriculum to produce a mock journal of the expedition of Lewis and Clark.

Content Areas:

Math	Earth Science	History/ Geography	Art	English	Vocational	Business
compass direction	latitude and longitude	geography of route	research picture of expedition	journal writing and reading	transportation of the time	cost of trip
provisions, physical requirements	crude measurements	cartography	Ansel Adams' photography	story of Sacajawea	time spent cooking	original budget of President Jefferson
calculating mileage	weather	regions and climate	*National Geographic*	Excerpts of Lewis & Clark's diary	building tools for trip	your budget: differences beween today and the past
computing time/distance/ mileage	map reading	landforms	student projects: clay, sketching, beadwork, tatting, quilting	other fiction	survival guide/ kit	obtaining financial backers
reading map scales	rocks, soil	research resources: books, films		poetry	load plans	
averaging	rivers	Indian tribes: customs and cultures	Indian arts/ crafts and traditions	other literature and authors of the time	surveying	marketing the expedition
	altitudes and seasons	events of time		newspapers of the time	making clothes	advertising campaign
	physics of transportation	dioramas				bartering
	identification of plants/animals along route	purpose of journey				
	physical and survival needs	*National Geographic*				
	food: identify new food/ preservation					
	herbal medicine					

(continued on page 444)

A C T I V I T Y   1 2 . 6   CONTINUED

Math	Earth Science	History/ Geography	Art	English	Vocational	Business
compass: concept mapping cooperative learning map reading: paired reading on aspects of math provisioning: brainstorm concept mapping	physical and survival needs: brainstorm concept mapping anticipation guide identify plants and animals: anticipation guide post graphic organizer	natural features: what-I-know sheets modified cloze flip-a-coin quiz period history and political events: structured overview post graphic organizer	student projects: imaging physical features of uninhabited west: linking what-I-know sheets anticipation guide	writing: imaging paired reading of stories paired summarizing journal writing: cinquains post graphic organizers modeling imaging	Export: concept map what I know survival guide: structured overview concept mapping surveying: paired reading hands-on cooking: time spent concept mapping paired hands-on	advertising structured overview cooperative learning post graphic organizer cost of trip: anticipation guide marketing the expedition: cooperative learning

Developed by Elise Harrison and Ray Morgan.

Concerning the collection of books, Lynch-Brown and Tomlinson (1993) advise that teachers should let the curriculum drive what books are used, not vice versa. That is, teachers should not include books that are not very relevant simply because they have collected the books over the years, or decide on the theme or focus based on one or two books that they have recently found or have collected in the past. Teachers need to be constantly watching for books and materials that might be used in a particular unit of instruction. Also, whenever possible, teachers should ask students to help find books about certain subjects of interest to the class and of importance to class objectives. To find sources of interest, teachers can start with the card catalog and the periodical indexes in the school library. If resources there are scanty, teachers should check the local public library for availability of resources on a desired topic.

In any search, the school media specialist and reading specialist (if available) should be called upon for valuable assistance. The media specialist may show a teacher how to borrow materials from libraries elsewhere in the state or from the state library. In choosing materials, teachers may wish to use the SMOG readability formula (explained in Chapter 3) to give them a quick estimate of how readable a book may be for students. Teachers may use any or all of the following supplementary materials in a unit: magazine articles, audiovisuals, artifacts, large-print books, taped books, videotapes, Braille materials, and computer programs. Appendix G includes a compilation of bibliographic sources and indexes that can help teachers find traditional literature and other supplementary information, as well as selected listings of traditional literature, historical fiction, and informational books that may be of help in teaching units for various content areas.

Teaching Thinking through Personal Responses to Literature

Teachers need to know ways of having students respond to supplemental literature through writing, discussions in response groups, and even art and drama renderings. Earlier chapters have described cooperative learning response groups (Chapter 10), writing activities and learning logs (Chapter 8), post graphic organizers and other visuals (Chapter 7), and cooperative drama (Chapter 10), as well as ways to guide students to respond through directed readings (Directed Reading/Thinking Activities, guided reading procedure, question/answer relationships).

Teachers can have students in small groups respond to every phase of the PAR lesson framework when reading a piece of literature. For example, high school students in a group can first be asked to respond to a prediction guide, such as the one in Activity 12.7 for "The Sniper," by Liam O'Flaherty. Then the group can be asked to read to the point in the story where the sniper says he has a plan to kill the other sniper on the roof across the street. Students can respond by making their own plans in writing; these can then be shared with plans developed by other small groups. Finally, students can be asked to read nearly to the end of the story and discuss, in the group, what the surprise ending might be. In this manner, the students in the group are responding to each phase of PAR in sharing their reactions to an exciting story. The key to sharing literature responses in the reflection (R) phase is having students revisit predictions they made in a study guide or informally in the group and in having them share, often in writing, what they learned in reading the piece and how they feel after completing the assignment. In using PAR with literature across the curriculum:

P = multitext to prepare readers for forthcoming text content

A = multitext to assist readers in understanding the topic under discussion

R = multitext to reinforce knowledge of a topic or find out more about a topic just studied in the textbook

One-Minute Summary

With the ever-expanding amount of content to be digested and learned in every content-area subject, teachers increasingly realize that no one textbook can deliver all the concepts and do justice to the differing viewpoints involved in any unit of study. Therefore, many content-area teachers are turning to supplementary fiction and nonfiction to enhance instruction. This chapter has explored the numerous reasons why textbooks need supplementing, the elements of effective

A C T I V I T Y   1 2 . 7   PREDICTION GUIDE: "THE SNIPER"

Before you read Liam O'Flaherty's "The Sniper," answer the statements below by writing Agree or Disagree next to each one.

Premise: You are a highly trained sniper during a civil war in your own country.

_____ 1. In a war, a "kill or be killed" attitude is necessary for survival.

_____ 2. A sniper's primary job is to kill as many of his enemies as possible.

_____ 3. Innocent people are often the necessary casualties of war.

_____ 4. A sniper's survival depends on his ability to make split-second decisions.

_____ 5. In many ways, war is like a game with a series of moves between opponents with serious consequences.

_____ 6. Once a target is identified, a sniper must shoot to kill above all other considerations.

_____ 7. A person who is independent, resourceful, and able to solve problems under pressure would make the best sniper.

_____ 8. An effective sniper must not let emotions influence his decisions.

_____ 9. A sniper's enemy is anyone who shoots at him.

Developed by Joe Antinarella.

literature-based instruction, and a plan of action for creating thematic units of instruction. We have also described how to locate and collect appropriate literature and discussed ways to get students to make personal responses to literature they have read. Appendixes G and H list relevant biographical indexes and fictional, nonfictional, and informational materials for use in content-area classrooms.

End-of-Chapter Activities

Assisting Comprehension

Why is there a need to supplement literature in teaching a thematic unit of instruction in a content-area classroom? What elements need to be present for a school or a class to be successful with literature-based instruction?

Reflecting on Your Reading

Choose a topic that you wish to focus on in a future unit of instruction and make a web of possible activities, as described in this chapter. Share your rendering with other content-area teachers to get their ideas. Practice at constructing such a web will definitely help you with new topics that you will be teaching.

Reading Across the Curriculum Conference

VCU, APRIL 3, 1984, BY BRIAN KANE

Introduction

Several years ago I was jolted by a *National Geographic* article on attempts to teach language to a chimpanzee. Having spent twenty years teaching in public high school, I felt threatened by this prospect. Fortunately, in spite of some premature claims of success, it is generally accepted that the monkey has not really assimilated language.

I, however, am of the opinion that a high school student *can* assimilate language. This has led me to the conclusion that the way to improve the reading and writing skills of human beings is by requiring that they read and write. Allow me to repeat. I believe that if you require students to read and write, they will improve in their ability to read and write.

This startling observation is the apex of my comments. However, I do want to comment on four additional areas:

   I. Reading and the content areas
  II. High school as a place where students avoid responsibility
 III. Practice and reality
  IV. Real reading

I. Reading and the Content Areas

Education is premised upon language. Language involves reading, writing and speaking. You cannot separate language from education. Language not only conveys, it shapes. If you increase or refine the ability of a human being to use language, you literally affect his mind. You cannot deal with any subject on any level without language. Indeed, how you use language affects the subject matter. Subject matter and language are fused. They cannot be separated.

The bulk of what we know as education is built upon the ability to read. Reading has different levels. Skimming the phone book, reading *People* magazine, or a poem, or *Moby Dick*, or a tax book are all forms of reading but they are all different. To assume that students who read a paragraph out loud in class understand or can learn that material can be fallacious.

It is easier to explain to students than it is to require that they read, understand and assume responsibility for what they have read. It may be easier to explain, *but it is not as effective in terms of what the student learns*. The proper type of reading is, at its best, individualized instruction. It is one-on-one: the student's intellect attempts to decipher the meaning of printed symbols. Confronting, deciphering, understanding the information contained in the written word is, in the jargon of our trade, a learning experience. Having deciphered and understood the written word, the student is then in a position, with additional effort, to learn.

It is important to note that I am speaking of learning and not "covering the material." In my judgment, if you are serious about having students learn, you have to be serious about reading and writing. A student who can read, understand and explain the *Declaration of Independence* has learned.

II. High School as a Place Where Students Avoid Responsibility

The game. The basis for the game is that the school is responsible for the student. Somehow the student never becomes responsible for himself. As students move through the grades they become more adult, more aware, and more cynical about the system that treats them as children and they respond in kind. "I can't, I don't have a pencil." "My book is in my locker." "I did my homework, but my dog ate it." "I had to work last night." "My sister didn't bring my textbook home." The school perpetuates the idea that the student isn't responsible for himself with passes, excused absences, make-up policies, notes from parents that are often forged or lies. When a student asks a teacher, "May I be excused from class?" he is asking for the teacher to accept responsibility for the student's absence.

Learning, however, *is* a student's responsibility. You can't push a string, and if a student doesn't or won't accept responsibility for learning, he won't learn. The student must at some point, for some reason, elect to learn.

In the same manner, a student must elect to read in an attempt to understand. He must engage the printed symbols on the page in an attempt to fathom the intent. As a teacher, I can prepare, or assist, or clarify, or answer questions, but I cannot read for the student. Nor can I, in the last analysis, make him read. Therefore, teachers must conduct their classes such that the student *elects* to read and attempts to understand in lieu of a slow and painful death. Not only is it okay to give the student unfair choices, I urge you to do so, just so long as he reads.

III. Practice and Reality

Too often we engage in practices that promote the avoidance of the responsibility for reading and learning while at the same time reward the student for *not* reading and learning. Students know that in spite of all the talk, they are in school to get grades, earn credits, move on to graduation. Learning is not an important consideration. This has been described as the vaccination theory of education: a course is something you take and having taken it, you have had it. Having had it, you need not take it again. Thus my government students cry out "but this is government class and we shouldn't be graded on English." What they mean is they passed English, and therefore it is unfair of me to expect them to use English. I try to point out that it is difficult to explain what you know about "how a bill becomes a law" in an essay without using English. But logic never convinces them.

Book reports, "read chapter 23," "read chapter 23 and do the questions at the end" are examples of practices that allow the student to avoid the responsibility of reading while earning grades.

Book reports are a time-honored tradition in school. Everyone has made book reports, and a few have even read the books. Students don't read books because they get graded on the *report*, not on reading books. (Am I telling anybody anything new?) Yet, year in and year out, we require, with full knowledge that books are not being read, that book reports be done. Book reports are assigned, generated, grades are produced, recorded and averaged. Students then graduate reading on an eighth-grade level having made twelve book reports.

Teacher assigns chapter 23 to be read for homework. While students avoid learning whatever it is we are teaching, they do learn. They know that the day chapter 23 is due, the teacher will explain chapter 23 and therefore they don't read chapter 23. It is my guess that most of the chapters assigned for reading in American public high schools are not read; don't have to be read; all you have to do is pass the unit test.

"Read chapter 23 and do the questions at the end." Provided the student does his own work and doesn't copy the homework in homeroom, he will more than likely first turn to the end of the chapter and read the first question. Then he will turn to the start of the chapter and skim until he finds the answer, which is often in italics. Having recorded the correct answer, he moves on to the second question and will complete the assignment and again receive a grade which will be averaged with his book report grade. Thus the assignment is completed, grades are obtained, and reading is avoided.

IV. Real Reading

Real reading, or reading as a means to understanding and learning, is a relatively slow and often ponderous chore. Real reading involves encountering new words, information, concepts or views. It requires that I utilize my intellect, that I have a dialogue with the printed symbols. The words must talk to me, and I must respond. Real reading can be trying to understand an IRS tax book, or *Moby Dick*, or a poem, or the Gettysburg Address, or a theorem in geometry. It is *not* reading a Harlequin romance, or the comics, or *Hot Rod* magazine. This process of attempting to understand or learn by reading is hard work and is thus avoided by most human beings, including students. Thus we, as teachers, *must* require it if it is to be utilized and developed. And if we are successful and students do this sort of reading, then two things occur: first, students learn and second, students learn *how* to learn so that they gain the potential of controlling their education and can elect to learn what is important or interesting to them in the course of their life.

Thank you. — *Brian Kane, Teacher*

Reprinted with permission of Brian Kane.

Assessing Attitudes toward Reading

Elementary Reading Attitude Survey

Directions for Use

The Elementary Reading Attitude Survey provides a quick indication of student attitudes toward reading. It consists of 20 items and can be administered to an entire classroom in about 10 minutes. Each item presents a brief, simply worded statement about reading, followed by four pictures of Garfield. Each pose is designed to depict a different emotional state, ranging from very positive to very negative.

ADMINISTRATION

Begin by telling students that you wish to find out how they feel about reading. Emphasize that this is *not* a test and that there are no "right" answers. Encourage sincerity.

Distribute the survey forms and, if you wish to monitor the attitudes of specific students, ask them to write their names in the space at the top. Hold up a copy of the survey so that the students can see the first page. Point to the picture of Garfield at the far left of the first item. Ask the students to look at this same picture on their own survey form. Discuss with them the mood Garfield seems to be in (very happy). Then move to the next picture and again discuss Garfield's mood (this time, a *little* happy). In the same way, move to the third and fourth pictures and talk about Garfield's moods — a little upset and very upset. It is helpful to point out the position of Garfield's *mouth*, especially in the middle two figures.

Explain that together you will read some statements about reading and that the students should think about how they feel about each statement. They should then circle the picture of Garfield that is closest to their own feelings. (Emphasize that the students should respond according to their own feelings, not as Garfield might respond!) Read each item aloud slowly and distinctly; then read it a second time while students are thinking. Be sure to read the item *number* and to remind students of page numbers when new pages are reached.

SCORING

To score the survey, count four points for each leftmost (happiest) Garfield circled, three for each slightly smiling Garfield, two for each mildly upset Garfield, and one point for each very upset (rightmost) Garfield. Three scores for

Scoring Sheet

Student name _____

Teacher _____

Grade _____ Administration date _____

Scoring guide

4 points	Happiest Garfield
3 points	Slightly smiling Garfield
2 points	Mildly upset Garfield
1 point	Very upset Garfield

Recreational reading

1. _____
2. _____
3. _____
4. _____
5. _____
6. _____
7. _____
8. _____
9. _____
10. _____

Raw score: _____

Academic reading

11. _____
12. _____
13. _____
14. _____
15. _____
16. _____
17. _____
18. _____
19. _____
20. _____

Raw score: _____

Full scale raw score (Recreational + Academic): _____

Percentile ranks   Recreational

Academic

Full scale

each student can be obtained: the total for the first 10 items, the total for the second 10, and a composite total. The first half of the survey relates to attitude toward recreational reading; the second half relates to attitude toward academic aspects of reading.

INTERPRETATION

You can interpret scores in two ways. One is to note informally where the score falls in regard to the four nodes of the scale. A total score of 50, for example, would fall about midway on the scale, between the slightly happy and slightly upset figures, therefore indicating a relatively indifferent overall attitude toward reading. The other approach is more formal. It involves converting the raw scores into percentile ranks by means of Table B.1. Be sure to use the norms for the right grade level and to note the column headings (Rec = recreational reading, Aca = academic reading, Tot = total score). If you wish to determine the average percentile rank for your class, average the raw scores first; then use the table to locate the percentile rank corresponding to the raw score mean. Percentile ranks cannot be averaged directly.

Technical Aspects

THE NORMING PROJECT

To create norms for the interpretation of scores, a large-scale study was conducted in late January, 1989, at which time the survey was administered to 18,138 students in Grades 1–6. A number of steps were taken to achieve a sample that was sufficiently stratified (i.e., reflective of the American population) to allow confident generalizations. Children were drawn from 95 school districts in 38 U.S. states. The number of girls exceeded by only 5 the number of boys. Ethnic distribution of the sample was also close to that of the U.S. population (*Statistical Abstract of the United States*, 1989). The proportion of Blacks (9.5%) was within 3% of the national proportion, while the proportion of Hispanics (6.2%) was within 2%.

Percentile ranks at each grade for both subscales and the full scale are presented in Table B.1. These data can be used to compare individual students' scores with the national sample and they can be interpreted like achievement-test percentile ranks.

RELIABILITY

Cronbach's alpha, a statistic developed primarily to measure the internal consistency of attitude scales (Cronbach, 1951), was calculated at each grade level for both subscales and for the composite score. These coefficients ranged from .74 to .89 and are presented in Table B.2.

It is interesting that with only two exceptions, coefficients were .80 or higher. These were for the recreational subscale at grades 1 and 2. It is possible that the stability of young children's attitudes toward leisure reading grows with their decoding ability and familiarity with reading as a pastime.

TABLE B.1   Mid-Year Percentile Ranks by Grade and Scale

RAW SCR	GRADE 1			GRADE 2			GRADE 3			GRADE 4			GRADE 5			GRADE 6		
	REC	ACA	TOT	REC	ACA	TOT	REC	ACA	TOT	REC	ACA	TOT	REC	ACA	TOT	REC	ACA	TOT
80			99			99			99			99			99			99
79			95			96			98			99			99			99
78			93			95			97			98			99			99
77			92			94			97			98			99			99
76			90			93			96			97			98			99
75			88			92			95			96			98			99
74			86			90			94			95			97			99
73			84			88			92			94			97			98
72			82			86			91			93			96			98
71			80			84			89			91			95			97
70			78			82			86			89			94			96
69			75			79			84			88			92			95
68			72			77			81			86			91			93
67			69			74			79			83			89			92
66			66			71			76			80			87			90
65			62			69			73			78			84			88
64			59			66			70			75			82			86
63			55			63			67			72			79			84
62			52			60			64			69			76			82
61			49			57			61			66			73			79
60			46			54			58			62			70			76
59			43			51			55			59			67			73
58			40			47			51			56			64			69
57			37			45			48			53			61			66
56			34			41			44			48			57			62
55			31			38			41			45			53			58
54			28			35			38			41			50			55
53			25			32			34			38			46			52
52			22			29			31			35			42			48
51			20			26			28			32			39			44
50			18			23			25			28			36			40
49			15			20			23			26			33			37
48			13			18			20			23			29			33
47			12			15			17			20			26			30
46			10			13			15			18			23			27
45			8			11			13			16			20			25
44			7			9			11			13			17			22
43			6			8			9			12			15			20
42			5			7			8			10			13			17
41			5			6			7			9			12			15
40	99	99	4	99	99	5	99	99	6	99	99	7	99	99	10	99	99	13
39	92	91	3	94	94	4	96	97	5	97	98	6	98	99	9	99	99	13
38	89	88	3	92	92	3	94	95	4	95	97	5	96	98	8	97	99	10

(continued on page 455)

TABLE B.1   Continued

RAW SCR	GRADE 1 REC	ACA	TOT	GRADE 2 REC	ACA	TOT	GRADE 3 REC	ACA	TOT	GRADE 4 REC	ACA	TOT	GRADE 5 REC	ACA	TOT	GRADE 6 REC	ACA	TOT
37	86	85	2	88	89	2	90	93	3	92	95	4	94	98	7	95	99	8
36	81	79	2	84	85	2	87	91	2	88	93	3	91	96	6	92	98	7
35	77	75	1	79	81	1	81	88	2	84	90	3	87	95	4	88	97	6
34	72	69	1	74	78	1	75	83	2	78	87	2	82	93	4	83	95	5
33	65	63	1	68	73	1	69	79	1	72	83	2	77	90	3	79	93	4
32	58	58	1	62	67	1	63	74	1	66	79	1	71	86	3	74	91	3
31	52	53	1	56	62	1	57	69	0	60	75	1	65	82	2	69	87	2
30	44	49	1	50	57	0	51	63	0	54	70	1	59	77	1	63	82	2
29	38	44	0	44	51	0	45	58	0	47	64	1	53	71	1	58	78	1
28	32	39	0	37	46	0	38	52	0	41	58	1	48	66	1	51	73	1
27	26	34	0	31	41	0	33	47	0	35	52	1	42	60	1	46	67	1
26	21	30	0	25	37	0	26	41	0	29	46	0	36	54	0	39	60	1
25	17	25	0	20	32	0	21	36	0	23	40	0	30	49	0	34	54	0
24	12	21	0	15	27	0	17	31	0	19	35	0	25	42	0	29	49	0
23	9	18	0	11	23	0	13	26	0	14	29	0	20	37	0	24	42	0
22	7	14	0	8	18	0	9	22	0	11	25	0	16	31	0	19	36	0
21	5	11	0	6	15	0	6	18	0	9	20	0	13	26	0	15	30	0
20	4	9	0	4	11	0	5	14	0	6	16	0	10	21	0	12	24	0
19	2	7		2	8		3	11		5	13		7	17		10	20	
18	2	5		2	6		2	8		3	9		6	13		8	15	
17	1	4		1	5		1	5		2	7		4	9		6	11	
16	1	3		1	3		1	4		2	5		3	6		4	8	
15	0	2		0	2		0	3		1	3		2	4		3	8	
14	0	2		0	1		0	1		1	2		1	2		1	3	
13	0	1		0	1		0	1		0	1		1	2		1	2	
12	0	1		0	0		0	0		0	1		0	1		0	1	
11	0	0		0	0		0	0		0	0		0	0		0	0	
10	0	0		0	0		0	0		0	0		0	0		0	0	

TABLE B.2   Descriptive Statistics and Internal Consistency Measures

Grade	N	RECREATIONAL SUBSCALE M	SD	S_eM	Alpha[a]	ACADEMIC SUBSCALE M	SD	S_eM	Alpha	FULL SCALE (TOTAL) M	SD	SeM	Alpha
1	2,518	31.0	5.7	2.9	.74	30.1	6.8	3.0	.81	61.0	11.4	4.1	.87
2	2,974	30.3	5.7	2.7	.78	28.8	6.7	2.9	.81	59.1	11.4	3.9	.88
3	3,151	30.0	5.6	2.5	.80	27.8	6.4	2.8	.81	57.8	10.9	3.8	.88
4	3,679	29.5	5.8	2.4	.83	26.9	6.3	2.6	.83	56.5	11.0	3.6	.89
5	3,374	28.5	6.1	2.3	.86	25.6	6.0	2.5	.82	54.1	10.8	3.6	.89
6	2,442	27.9	6.2	2.2	.87	24.7	5.8	2.5	.81	52.5	10.6	3.5	.89
All	18,138	29.5	5.9	2.5	.82	27.3	6.6	2.7	.83	56.8	11.3	3.7	.89

[a]Cronbach's alpha (Cronbach, 1951).

VALIDITY

Evidence of construct validity was gathered by several means. For the recreational subscale, students in the national norming group were asked (a) whether a public library was available to them and (b) whether they currently had a library card. Those to whom libraries were available were separated into two groups (those with and without cards) and their recreational scores were compared. Cardholders had significantly higher ($p < .001$) recreational scores ($M = 30.0$) than noncardholders ($M = 28.9$), evidence of the subscale's validity in that scores varied predictably with an outside criterion.

A second test compared students who presently had books checked out from their school library versus students who did not. The comparison was limited to children whose teachers reported not requiring them to check out books. The means of the two groups varied significantly ($p < .001$), and children with books checked out scored higher ($M = 29.2$) than those who had no books checked out ($M = 27.3$).

A further test of the recreational subscale compared students who reported watching an average of less than 1 hour of television per night with students who reported watching more than 2 hours per night. The recreational mean for the low televiewing group (31.5) significantly exceeded ($p < .001$) the mean of the heavy televiewing group (28.6). Thus, the amount of television watched varied inversely with children's attitudes toward recreational reading.

The validity of the academic subscale was tested by examining the relationship of scores to reading ability. Teachers categorized norm-group children as having low, average, or high overall reading ability. Mean subscale scores of the high-ability readers ($M = 27.7$) significantly exceeded the mean of low-ability readers ($M = 27.0$, $p < .001$), evidence that scores were reflective of how the students truly felt about reading for academic purposes.

The relationship between the subscales was also investigated. It was hypothesized that children's attitudes toward recreational and academic reading would be moderately but not highly correlated. Facility with reading is likely to affect these two areas similarly, resulting in similar attitude scores. Nevertheless, it is easy to imagine children prone to read for pleasure but disenchanted with assigned reading and children academically engaged but without interest in reading outside of school. The intersubscale correlation coefficient was .64, which meant that just 41% of the variance in one set of scores could be accounted for by the other. It is reasonable to suggest that the two subscales, while related, also reflect dissimilar factors — a desired outcome.

To tell more precisely whether the traits measured by the survey corresponded to the two subscales, factor analyses were conducted. Both used the unweighted least squares method of extraction and a varimax rotation. The first analysis permitted factors to be identified liberally (using a limit equal to the smallest eigenvalue greater than 1). Three factors were identified. Of the 10 items comprising the academic subscale, 9 loaded predominantly on a single factor while the 10th (item 13) loaded nearly equally on all three factors. A second factor was dominated by 7 items of the recreational subscale, while 3 of the recreational items (6, 9, and 10) loaded principally on a third factor. These items did, however, load more heavily on the second (recreational) factor than on the first (academic). A second analysis constrained the identification of factors to two. This time, with one exception, all items loaded cleanly on factors associated with the two sub-scales. The exception was item 13, which could have been interpreted as a recreational item and thus apparently involved a slight ambiguity. Taken together, the factor analyses produced evidence extremely supportive of the claim that the survey's two subscales reflect discrete aspects of reading attitude.

Norming and Validation Information[*]

The *Mikulecky Behavioral Reading Attitude Measure* was developed to be a sound reading-attitudes measure appropriate for use with mature readers. To establish the instrument on sound theoretical foundations, all items were written with direct reference to the Hovland-Rosenberg tricomponent model of attitude and to the stages of Krathwohl's *Taxonomy of the Affective Domain*. A pool of 40 items, each of which was designed to reflect a specific Krathwohl substage, was reduced to 20 items after considering the evaluations of a panel of judges familiar with Krathwohl's Taxonomy and after an item analysis which eliminated all items that correlated at $r = .600$ or less with the sum of items reflecting the Krathwohl stage appropriate to each item. The hierarchical framework hypoth-esized by Krathwohl was supported by an analysis of subjects' item responses using a method for Scaling a Simplex developed by Henry Kaiser (*Psychome-trika*, 1962). The MBRAM Hierarchy gave evidence of a .933 out of a possible 1.000 goodness-of-fit to an ideal hierarchy. This was interpreted as empirical support for the Krathwohl theoretical foundation of the MBRAM.

A graduate-level seminar on Affective Domain Measurement helped survey and refine all items to reflect everyday reading-related behaviors, thereby estab-lishing *face validity*. Correlations of *concurrent validity* ranging from .446 to .770 were established with such formal reading-attitude measures as the Estes Scale, the Dulin-Chester Scale, and the Kennedy-Halinski Reading Attitude Measure. The MBRAM correlated more highly with the Estes Scale and the Dulin-Chester Scale than either of those measures did with the other.

To establish *construct validity*, five informal criteria for reading-attitude (self-reported Liking and Amount of reading, Teacher and Classmate judgment of reading attitude, and Number of books read in 6 months) were administered along with the MBRAM. All MBRAM correlations with these informal criteria were significant to the $p < .001$ level, and the majority of correlations ranged from .500 to .791. The MBRAM correlated significantly more highly with these informal measures than did the other, formal reading-attitude measures used in the study. Analysis of variance statistically demonstrated the ability of the MBRAM to discriminate subjects of high, average, and low reading-attitude as measured by the informal criteria.

[*] Mikulecky, L. J. *The developing, field testing, and initial norming of a secondary/adult level reading attitude measure that is behaviorally oriented and based on Krathwohl's Taxonomy of the Affective Domain.* Unpublished doctoral dissertation, University of Wisconsin–Madison, 1976.

Mikulecky Behavioral Reading Attitude Measure

Name _____ Instructor's Name _____

Age _____ Sex _____ School _____

Example
> You receive a book for a Christmas present. You start the book, but decide to stop halfway through.
> VERY UNLIKE ME   1   2   3   ④   5   VERY LIKE ME

1. You walk into the office of a doctor or dentist and notice that there are magazines set out.
   VERY UNLIKE ME   1   2   3   4   5   VERY LIKE ME

2. People have made jokes about your reading in unusual circumstances or situations.
   VERY UNLIKE ME   1   2   3   4   5   VERY LIKE ME

3. You are in a shopping center you've been to several times when someone asks where books and magazines are sold. You are able to tell the person.
   VERY UNLIKE ME   1   2   3   4   5   VERY LIKE ME

4. You feel very uncomfortable because emergencies have kept you away from reading for a couple of days.
   VERY UNLIKE ME   1   2   3   4   5   VERY LIKE ME

5. You are waiting for a friend in an airport or supermarket and find yourself leafing through the magazines and paperback books.
   VERY UNLIKE ME   1   2   3   4   5   VERY LIKE ME

6. If a group of acquaintances would laugh at you for always being buried in a book, you'd know it's true and wouldn't mind much at all.
   VERY UNLIKE ME   1   2   3   4   5   VERY LIKE ME

7. You are tired of waiting for the dentist, so you start to page through a magazine.
   VERY UNLIKE ME   1   2   3   4   5   VERY LIKE ME

8. People who are regular readers often ask your opinion about new books.
   VERY UNLIKE ME   1   2   3   4   5   VERY LIKE ME

9. One of your first impulses is to "look it up" whenever there is something you don't know or whenever you are going to start something new.
   VERY UNLIKE ME   1   2   3   4   5   VERY LIKE ME

10. Even though you are a very busy person, there is somehow always time for reading.
    VERY UNLIKE ME   1   2   3   4   5   VERY LIKE ME

11. You've finally got some time alone in your favorite chair on a Sunday afternoon. You see something to read and decide to spend a few minutes reading just because you feel like it.
    VERY UNLIKE ME   1   2   3   4   5   VERY LIKE ME

(continued on page 459)

12. You tend to disbelieve and be a little disgusted by people who repeatedly say they don't have time to read.
VERY UNLIKE ME   1   2   3   4   5   VERY LIKE ME

13. You find yourself giving special books to friends or relatives as gifts.
VERY UNLIKE ME   1   2   3   4   5   VERY LIKE ME

14. At Christmas time, you look in the display window of a bookstore and find yourself interested in some books and uninterested in others.
VERY UNLIKE ME   1   2   3   4   5   VERY LIKE ME

15. Sometimes you find yourself so excited by a book you try to get friends to read it.
VERY UNLIKE ME   1   2   3   4   5   VERY LIKE ME

16. You've just finished reading a story and settle back for a moment to enjoy and remember what you've just read.
VERY UNLIKE ME   1   2   3   4   5   VERY LIKE ME

17. You *choose* to read nonrequired books and articles fairly regularly (a few times a week).
VERY UNLIKE ME   1   2   3   4   5   VERY LIKE ME

18. Your friends would not be at all surprised to see you buying or borrowing a book.
VERY UNLIKE ME   1   2   3   4   5   VERY LIKE ME

19. You have just gotten comfortably settled in a new city. Among the things you plan to do is check out the library and book stores.
VERY UNLIKE ME   1   2   3   4   5   VERY LIKE ME

20. You've just heard about a good book but haven't been able to find it. Even though you're tired, you look for it in one more book store.
VERY UNLIKE ME   1   2   3   4   5   VERY LIKE ME

The MBRAM demonstrated a test-retest reliability of .9116.

The MBRAM was administered to 1,750 subjects ranging from 7th grade through college-adult. 1,343 of the subjects were public school students selected from urban, suburban, and rural populations. These subjects were randomly sampled to create a composite, stratified Wisconsin Population Model. Norms for the MBRAM are reported for each grade level in terms of this model and also in terms of urban, suburban, and rural populations. For ease of interpretation of scores, attitude-level scoring bands are provided. No significant differences in scores of urban, suburban, or rural subjects were found from 7th–10th grade, but rural subjects exhibited slightly higher MBRAM mean scores in the upper grades. Reading-attitude scores decreased slightly in all locations with each year in school.

Summary Statistics: Junior High School (7–9 Grades) and Senior High School (10–12 Grades); Urban, Suburban, and Rural Subjects, MBRAM Scores

Level	URBAN				SUBURBAN				RURAL			
	N	Mean	Range	S.D.	N	Mean	Range	S.D.	N	Mean	Range	S.D.
Jr	127	55.93	27–90(63)	12.11	276	59.60	25–98(73)	14.33	182	60.81	22–92(70)	13.91
Sr	332	55.24	20–90(70)	12.51	144	58.29	24–95(71)	15.55	190	59.28	29–97(68)	15.17

Attitude Bands for Junior and Senior High School by Location

Attitude Level	URBAN		SUBURBAN		RURAL	
	Jr. High	Sr. High	Jr. High	Sr. High	Jr. High	Sr. High
Above Average	66–100	62–100	68–100	67–100	69–100	68–100
Average	53–65	49–61	52–67	59–66	54–68	52–67
Below Average	20–52	20–48	20–51	20–49	20–53	20–51

Adult Norms: Results of Analyses of Variance and *post hoc* Scheffe Tests of Attitude Toward Reading (MBRAM Score) by Each Demographic Variable

All Cases	N	Mean	S.D.	F-Ratio	*Post Hoc* Test of Significance
Sex					
M	118	65.02	14.15	33.58	° ° °
F	166	74.47	13.10		
Race					
W	262	70.78	14.36	.43	Not Significant
B	20	67.90	14.22		
O	2	65.50	0		
Education					
Less Than High School	40	66.87	12.13	2.48	°
High School	88	68.69	15.79		
Post High School	93	71.07	14.19		
College	42	73.71	13.34		
Graduate Work	22	77.09	11.13		
Family Income					
Less Than 3,000–	13	69.38	12.72	2.79	°
3–5,000	17	70.12	13.37		
5–10,000	39	71.69	10.76		
10–20,000	112	69.26	15.23		
Greater Than 20,000	86	73.85	12.89		
No Response	17	60.94	19.46		
Employment					
Full Time	141	68.38	15.75	3.008	° °
Part Time	20	75.45	11.80		
Housewife	49	74.96	11.45		
Unemployed	9	78.67	17.33		
Student	36	67.81	11.57		
Retired	29	71.10	12.26		

°$p<.05$
°°$p<.01$
°°°$p<.001$

From Mikulecky, Shanklin, & Caverly (1979).

Stages of Krathwohl's Taxonomy as Reflected by Mikulecky Behavioral Reading Attitude Measure Items

Stage 1 (Attending) of the taxonomy is reflected by items 1,3,5,7. Each item provides from 1 to 5 points. A perfect score at this stage would be 4 items × 5 points — 20 points. A student can be said to have attained a stage if he/she has 75 percent of the possible points at that stage. By interpreting items and stages, a deeper understanding of a student's reading attitude is possible.

KRATHWOHL STAGES	ITEMS (1–5 POINTS POSSIBLE EACH ITEM)	CRITERION SCORE (75 PERCENT OF POSSIBLE POINTS)
I. Attending: The individual is generally aware of reading and tolerant of it.	1,3,5,7	15 pts.
II. Responding: The individual is willing to read under certain circumstances. He or she begins to choose and occasionally enjoy reading.	11,14,16	11 pts.
III. Valuing: The individual begins to accept the worth of reading as a value to be preferred and even to extend to others.	13,15,17 18,19,20	23 pts.
IV. Organization: For the individual, reading is part of an organized value system and is so habitual that it is almost "instinctive."	9,10,12	11 pts.
V. Characterization: For the individual, reading is so much a part of life that both the reader and others see reading as crucial to this person.	2,4,6,8	15 pts.

Text Analysis Charts

TEXT BOOK ANALYSIS CHART

Book Title *Centennial Edition Silver Burdett Music*

Publisher *Silver Burdett*

Grade Level *2*

Content Area *Music*

+ Excellent/ Evident Throughout	✓ Average/ Somewhat Evident	− Poor/ Not Evident	Checklist	Comments
			LINGUISTIC FACTORS:	
		✓	Generally appropriate to intended grade level(s) according to _modified Fry_ formula	According to Fry, the text was too easy. I have taught from it for 3 yrs. and I disagree. I find it very appropriate.
✓			Linguistic patterns suitable to most populations and fit intended level(s)	Suitable to all population. I have taught.
	✓		Vocabulary choice and control suitable	Sometimes hard for slow readers.
✓			New vocabulary highlighted, italicized, in boldface or underlined	Italicised in boldface or colored
	✓		New vocabulary, defined in context	New vocabulary introduced + defined + illustrated w/ songs.
		✓	New vocabulary defined in margin guides, glossary, beginning or end of chapter	Book is not organized by chapters. No margin guides. or glossary. New vocab. defined in ton xt.
			CONCEPTUAL FACTORS:	
✓			Conceptual level generally appropriate to intended grade level(s)	All musical concepts are appropriate for 2nd grade introduction and paced well
	✓		Concepts presented deductively	Presented this way a sufficient no. of times
✓			Concepts presented inductively	Major way concepts are presented.
✓			Major ideas are highlighted, italicized, in boldface type or underlined	Italicized in boldface or colored.
✓			Appropriate assumptions made regarding prior level of concepts	For use by K-9, but can stand alone, so concepts are appropriately introduced.
	✓		Sufficient development of new concepts through examples, illustrations, analogies, redundancy	Book cannot stand alone. Student needs teacher guidance trecards Concepts repeated
✓			No evidence of sexual, racial, economic, cultural, or political bias	Pictures include children of many races + cultures and both sexes.
			ORGANIZATIONAL FACTORS:	
✓			Units, chapters, table of contents, index present clear, logical development of subject	Organized into units built around concepts. Clearly presented with an index + table of contents.
		✓	Chapters of instructional segments contain headings and sub-headings that aid comprehension of subject	No chapters.
✓			Introductory, definitional, illustrative, summary paragraphs/sections used as necessary	Few paragraphs, mostly songs. Illustrative sections used as needed.
	✓		Topic sentences of paragraphs clearly identifiable or easily inferred	Few paragraphs; many single sentences, but topics are clear.
		✓	Each chapter/section/unit contains a well-written summary and/or overview	Presented in teacher's guide.
			WRITING STYLE:	
✓			Ideas are expressed clearly and directly	Text is brief and clear.
✓			Word choice is appropriate	Readable for majority of 2nd graders
✓			Tone and manner of expression are appealing to intended readers	Direct "no frills" expression.
✓			Mechanics are correct	Did not find any incorrectness.

+ Excellent/ Evident Throughout	✓ Average/ Somewhat Evident	– Poor/ Not Evident	Checklist	Comments
			LEARNING AIDS:	Most 2nd level students will have developed necessary coordination + concepts
✓			Questions/tasks appropriate to conceptual development of intended age/grade level(s)	
	✓		Questions/tasks span levels of reasoning: literal, interpretive, critical, values clarification, problem-solving	Seem to center most often on literal interpretive + critical
	✓		Questions/tasks can be used as reading guides	Questions are guides for songs
		✓	Suitable supplementary readings suggested	None mentioned but supplementary listening material is suggested in teacher's edition.
			TEACHING AIDS:	
✓			Clear, convenient to use	Very helpful, easy to use.
✓			Helpful ideas for conceptual development	Many suggestions in teacher's ed
✓			Alternative instructional suggestions given for poor readers, slow learning students, advanced students	Instructions for phys. handicapped in teacher's edition
✓			Contains objectives, management plans, evaluation guidelines, tests of satisfactory quality	Listed in teacher's edition.
✓			Supplementary aids available	Spirit masters, records, instruments, competency tests, teachers guide.
			BINDING/PRINTING/FORMAT/ILLUSTRATIONS:	
✓			Size of book is appropriate	Easy to hold for second grade.
✓			Cover, binding, and paper are appropriate	Durable and eye-catching.
✓			Type-face is appropriate	Large and easy to read
✓			Format is appropriate	Easy to follow and appealing.
✓			Pictures, charts, graphs are appealing	Colorful varied, clear
✓			Illustrations aid comprehension of text	Very much interrelated.
✓			Illustrations are free of sexual, social, cultural bias	Show many cultures + both sexes

SUMMARY:

26	7	4	Totals	This book seems very strong, and I agree, after teaching it

The strengths are: Eye catching illustrations, easy-to-read print, clear concept organization, and clear directions for students. The book provides for gradual, consistent progress and may be complete in itself or used as a part of the 9-year program.

The weaknesses are: ① In a few songs, all verses are used on the record, but only two are printed in the student text. ② Text not organized into clear chapters.

As a teacher, I will need to: give a large amount of help and reinforcement to slow readers as they try to keep up with the words on fast songs. The teaching pace may need to be slower and charts, etc., may need to be used. I will also need to give much guidance on instrument-playing activities and demonstrations to reinforce directions given in their book.

*Original TEXT ANALYSIS CHART by: Dr. Lois Bader, Michigan State University

+ Excellent/ Evident Throughout	✓ Average/ Somewhat Evident	— Poor/ Not Evident	TEXT BOOK ANALYSIS CHART

This text is used as a primary source in independent study course for high school students who have previously failed this course. Teacher is primarily a tutor.

Book Title _Rise of the American Nation_

Publisher _Harcourt Brace Jovanovich_

Grade Level _11_

Content Area _U.S. History_

LINGUISTIC FACTORS:

+	✓	—	Checklist	Comments
		—	Generally appropriate to intended grade level(s) according to ___SMOG___ formula	Readability is inappropriate for independent study by weak students
	✓		Linguistic patterns suitable to most populations and fit intended level(s)	Reasonable sentence length + frequency of subordination.
+			Vocabulary choice and control suitable	Not dumbed down nor intellectual.
+			New vocabulary highlighted, italicized, in boldface or underlined	Use of italics good to bring words to students attention
+			New vocabulary, defined in context	
		—	New vocabulary defined in margin guides, glossary, beginning or end of chapter	No margin guides - no glossary. Definite weakness for students reviewing for tests.

CONCEPTUAL FACTORS:

+	✓	—	Checklist	Comments
	✓		Conceptual level generally appropriate to intended grade level(s)	Without teacher explanation, concepts not evident.-
		—	Concepts presented deductively	Concepts drawn for students little student critical thinking.
	✓		Concepts presented inductively	Weakness in study situation
+			Major ideas are highlighted, italicized, in boldface type or underlined	Boldface headings assist pre-reading
	✓		Appropriate assumptions made regarding prior level of concepts	Text for stronger students Not for independent study
	✓		Sufficient development of new concepts through examples, illustrations, analogies, redundancy	Accomplished by accompanying independent study syllabus
+			No evidence of sexual, racial, economic, cultural, or political bias	Effort made to include minorities who played a part in U.S. History

ORGANIZATIONAL FACTORS:

+	✓	—	Checklist	Comments
+			Units, chapters, table of contents, index present clear, logical development of subject	Overall time order, subdivided into thematic subject areas using cause-effect or problem-solution.
+			Chapters of instructional segments contain headings and sub-headings that aid comprehension of subject	Boldface and brightly colored - helpful for pre-reading + review
	✓		Introductory, definitional, illustrative, summary paragraphs/sections used as necessary	No summary sections a weakness. All others included.
+			Topic sentences of paragraphs clearly identifiable or easily inferred	Many inferred easily by teacher, but not by students.
+			Each chapter/section/unit contains a well-written summary and/or overview	Each chapter has overview and outline, but no summary.

WRITING STYLE:

+	✓	—	Checklist	Comments
+			Ideas are expressed clearly and directly	Text is well written.
+			Word choice is appropriate	Not dumbed down; not too intellectual
	✓		Tone and manner of expression are appealing to intended readers	Factual, not involving.
+			Mechanics are correct	No problem; well written.

+ Excellent/ Evident Throughout	✓ Average/ Somewhat Evident	− Poor/ Not Evident	Checklist	Comments

LEARNING AIDS:

Few very challenging questions
Focus on recall of interrelationships

	✓		Questions/tasks appropriate to conceptual development of intended age/grade level(s)	
	✓		Questions/tasks span levels of reasoning: literal, interpretive, critical, values clarification, problem-solving	Almost totally literal and inferential questions in syllabus
+			Questions/tasks can be used as reading guides	Accompanying syllabus questions very good for this purpose.
		−	Suitable supplementary readings suggested	None suggested.

TEACHING AIDS: None available

		−	Clear, convenient to use	Teacher uses independent study
		−	Helpful ideas for conceptual development	syllabus as study guide for
		−	Alternative instructional suggestions given for poor readers, slow learning students, advanced students	students by using end of chapter questions for pre-reading activities and student
		−	Contains objectives, management plans, evaluation guidelines, tests of satisfactory quality	self-monitoring of comprehension.
		−	Supplementary aids available	Course not designed to be teacher assisted.

BINDING/PRINTING/FORMAT/ILLUSTRATIONS:

	✓		Size of book is appropriate	Too much text to cover independently
+			Cover, binding, and paper are appropriate	Sturdy; good quality.
+	✓		Type-face is appropriate	Type style alternates every
+			Format is appropriate	few units, I don't know why
+			Pictures, charts, graphs are appealing	Colorful maps, period photos
	✓		Illustrations aid comprehension of text	Few needed because many photos
+			Illustrations are free of sexual, social, cultural bias	Accurate to historical period.

SUMMARY:

Appropriate in classroom, lacks learning aids for independent study.

| 17 | 12 | 9 | Totals |

The strengths are: This text is well organized, has a clear writing style, and is accompanied by excellent illustrations and maps. New vocabulary is defined in context, which is helpful to weaker readers who do not use glossaries. Accompanying course syllabus for independent study complements text by providing learning objectives, discussion (overview) and review.

The weaknesses are: Lack of teaching aids make adaptation of this course to individual differences difficult. Syllabus questions do not challenge higher level thinking skills (even though end-of-chapter questions in text do, they are not assigned as part of course.) Text may be too difficult for independent reading. Text long and too detailed.

As a teacher, I will need to:
continue to adapt the activities in the accompanying syllabus to individual student needs. Students need a lot of help with reading comprehension strategies since the majority of learning relies on each student's reading ability. Addition or substitution of more questions at the evaluative or critical thinking levels.

*Original TEXT ANALYSIS CHART by: Dr. Lois Bader, Michigan State University

Using the Fry Graph for Short Selections

The Procedure

The Fry graph can be used with selections of less than 100 words if some conversions are made (Forgan & Mangrum, 1985). This technique will be useful to teachers of primary grades where material is partly visual and partly verbal, or for teachers using newspaper or magazine articles to supplement instruction. It can also help teachers measure the difficulty of word problems in math or of essay questions on tests. The material should contain fewer than 100 words; if the material contains at least 100 words, then the Fry graph can be applied. To use this short-selection version, a teacher should

1. count the total number of words.
2. round *down* to the nearest ten.
3. refer to the conversion chart (Figure D.1), and identify the conversion number corresponding to the rounded number.
4. count the number of syllables and sentences in the rounded-down number of words (see steps 1 and 2).
5. multiply the number of syllables by the number on the conversion chart; multiply the number of sentences by the number on the conversion chart.
6. plot the final numbers on the regular Fry graph.

FIGURE D.1

Conversion chart for Fry's graph for selections with fewer than 100 words. (From *Teaching Content Area Reading Skills*, 3rd edition, by Harry W. Forgan and Charles T. Mangrum II, copyright © 1985. Merrill Publishing Co., Columbus, OH. Used with permission.)

If the number of words in the selection is:	Multiply the number of syllables and sentences by:
30	3.3
40	2.5
50	2.0
60	1.67
70	1.43
80	1.25
90	1.1

An Example

The following two essay questions have been assessed using this procedure.

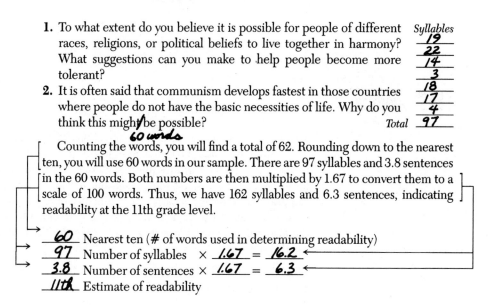

1. To what extent do you believe it is possible for people of different races, religions, or political beliefs to live together in harmony? What suggestions can you make to help people become more tolerant?

2. It is often said that communism develops fastest in those countries where people do not have the basic necessities of life. Why do you think this might be possible?

	Syllables
	19
	22
	14
	3
	18
	17
	4
Total	97

60 words

Counting the words, you will find a total of 62. Rounding down to the nearest ten, you will use 60 words in our sample. There are 97 syllables and 3.8 sentences in the 60 words. Both numbers are then multiplied by 1.67 to convert them to a scale of 100 words. Thus, we have 162 syllables and 6.3 sentences, indicating readability at the 11th grade level.

__60__ Nearest ten (# of words used in determining readability)
__97__ Number of syllables × __1.67__ = __16.2__
__3.8__ Number of sentences × __1.67__ = __6.3__
__11th__ Estimate of readability

A MODEL FOR
Constructing Tests
WITH MAINSTREAMED STUDENTS IN MIND

Wood and Miederhoff (1988) point out that if tests are a "necessary nuisance" for the majority of students, they are a symbol of failure for mildly handicapped students, who are often provided with some special instruction but spend much of their time in the regular classroom. They are expected to perform in the "main stream" academically but usually encounter more learning problems than the average learner. They suggest that minor changes in test construction can "mean the difference between success and failure for mainstreamed students" (p. 2). In most cases, the adaptations will be minor, and they will often be useful for all the students. Figure E.1 shows their model for adapting a teacher-made test. Using Wood's (1987) model, Wood and Miederhoff present the following suggestions for constructing tests for students in general, and for mainstreamed students in particular.

Test Directions

SUGGESTIONS FOR ALL STUDENTS

1. Keep directions simple; avoid unnecessary words.
2. State directions in sequential order or place them at the beginning of each separate test section.
3. State only one direction in each sentence.

FIGURE E.1

Model for adaptations when constructing the teacher-made test. (From "A Model for Adapting the Teacher-Made Test," by J. W. Wood (1987). *Statewide Institutes for Adapting Instruction for Regular Educators (Project TRAIN).* Richmond: Virginia Commonwealth University. Reprinted with permission.)

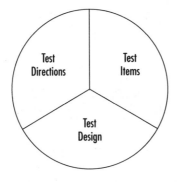

4. Underline the word *Directions* to focus the students' attention.
5. Avoid using words such as *never, not, always*. If you must use these, underline and capitalize.
6. List directions vertically if there is more than one statement. (pp. 4–5)

SUGGESTIONS FOR MAINSTREAMED STUDENTS

1. Define any unfamiliar or abstract words.
2. Provide an example of how the student is to respond. (This suggestion, and others that involve giving visual prompts, is to be used at the discretion of the teacher. Some educators feel that providing an example invalidates a test designed to measure memory of specific facts or processes. However, some handicapped students may never be able to remember material without visual prompts. For them failure is an almost certainty without modifications.)
3. Avoid oral direction as the only means of making the purpose of the test known to students. Read directions orally as well as having them clearly written on the test. (p. 5)

Multiple-Choice

SUGGESTIONS FOR ALL STUDENTS

1. Avoid using unnecessary words that do not help the student in selecting the correct answer.
2. State the question and the responses for the item simply.
3. Be sure that all choices are grammatically correct. (p. 6)

SUGGESTIONS FOR MAINSTREAMED STUDENTS

1. Avoid frequent use of choice responses that may distract from the actual question, such as *either . . . or, all of the above, none of the above*.
2. Let the student circle the correct answer rather than select a letter from a group of possible responses. This reduces the possibility of copying errors when transferring letters to the blanks.
3. Arrange answers and distractors vertically on the page. (pp. 6–7)

Matching

SUGGESTIONS FOR ALL STUDENTS

1. Place all matching items and choice selections on the same page.
2. Place a blank next to each item for the letter of the correct answer. Blanks should all be arranged on the same side of the questions. (p. 7)

SUGGESTIONS FOR MAINSTREAMED STUDENTS

1. Use no more than ten items in the matching lists. If you have more than ten items, group them by concepts in clusters of ten.
2. Have only one correct answer for each item.

3. Avoid having students draw lines to the correct answer. This is visually confusing.
4. Keep all matching items brief. The student who has comprehension and/or reading problems may not be able to process long, wordy items.
5. Keep items in a logical order. Alphabetize one column of matching items and/ or place numbers in sequence. (pp. 7–8)

True/False

SUGGESTIONS FOR ALL STUDENTS

1. Avoid stating questions in the negative.
2. Avoid tricky items.
3. Avoid long, wordy sentences.
4. Avoid trivial statements or ones that do not assess student knowledge. (p. 8)

SUGGESTIONS FOR MAINSTREAMED STUDENTS

1. Avoid using *never, not, always* in statements. If you must use them, underline and capitalize.
2. Be specific and give examples for answering.
3. Avoid using too many true/false questions at one time. No more than ten per test is suggested. (p. 9)

Completion

SUGGESTIONS FOR ALL STUDENTS

1. Write simple and clear test items.
2. Avoid the use of statements taken directly from the textbook. Taken out of context, these are frequently too general and ambiguous to be used as questions. (p. 9)

SUGGESTIONS FOR MAINSTREAMED STUDENTS

1. Provide large blanks for students with handwriting and/or motor control problems.
2. Place possible answers immediately under the blank to reduce memory load. (pp. 9–10)

Essay

SUGGESTIONS FOR ALL STUDENTS

1. Define any unclear terms.
2. Select questions that correspond to the domain level of the student. For example, *define* is on the knowledge level, *predict* is on the interpretive level. (p. 10)

SUGGESTIONS FOR MAINSTREAMED STUDENTS

1. Use items that can be answered briefly.
2. Be sure students know the meaning of clue words, such as *discuss, contrast, compare, criticize, define, describe, list*. Underline clue words.
3. Provide an answer check sheet that lists the components expected in the response.
4. Allow students to outline answers, or provide an outline for them.
5. Make sure the question is written at the students' reading level.
6. Use a limited number of essay questions on each test. Allow students extra time to write the answers.
7. Allow students to record answers orally rather than writing them. (p. 11)

Test Design

SUGGESTIONS FOR ALL STUDENTS

1. If possible, test, teach, and retest for a final grade.
2. Construct the test in logical, sequential order, from simple to complex items.
3. Use test items that reflect the technique used to teach.
4. Type or print legibly. Use large print when available. If hand-writing the test, be sure items are listed clearly, concisely, and neatly.
5. Prepare a study guide for the test that matches the design of the actual test. (p. 12)

SUGGESTIONS FOR MAINSTREAMED STUDENTS

1. Design the test to reflect the students' knowledge rather than elements such as the ability to follow complicated directions, use of elaborate vocabulary, or ability to work under time constraints.
2. Adjust readability level of the test to meet the students' needs.
3. Prepare the test in short sections that can be administered individually if necessary.
4. Place only one type of question on a page: one page for multiple-choice questions, one page for essays.
5. Review individually with the student, or allow a peer tutor or the resource teacher to review with the student prior to the test.
6. After consulting the student privately concerning personal testing preferences, design the test to meet those needs.
7. If using the chalkboard for tests, clear other material from the board, then print or write in large, legible letters. Avoid lengthy tests for students with copying difficulties.
8. Avoid oral tests and quizzes.
9. Plan to allow handicapped students to take tests in the special classroom if time, reading ability, or embarrassment are problems.

10. Duplicate clearly, using *black ink* if available. Avoid using faded purple dittos with all students, but especially for those students with visual-acuity and visual-perception difficulties.

11. Use a large sheet of dark construction paper under the test to act as a border. Provide a sheet of paper with a "window frame" cut in it to help the student read the test. This helps those students with visual-acuity and visual-perception problems.

12. If the student has difficulty finishing on time, administer an adapted, shortened version of the test. Another option is "split-halves" testing, with one section of the test administered one day and one section the next day.

Vocabulary Building: Prefixes, Suffixes, and Roots

Common Prefixes

PREFIX	EXAMPLE	MEANING
a-, an-	amoral	not, without, lacking
ab-, a-, abs-	abhor	away from
ad-, ac-, af-, ag-, al-, an-, ap-, ar-, as-, at-	adhere	toward
ambi-	ambivalence	both
amphi-	amphitheater	on both sides, around
ante-	antebellum	before
anti-	antibiotic	against
auto-	automatic	self
bi-	bisect	two
centi-	century	hundred
circum-	circumstance	around
con-, com-, co-, col-, cor-	correlate	with, in association, together
contra-	contradiction	against
de-	descend	away from, out of, separation
dec-, deca-	decade	ten
di-	dicotyledon	two, twice, double
dia-	diameter	through, between, across
dis-	dissatisfied	not
ex-, e-, ef-	evict	out of, from
for-	forehand	away, off, wrong
fore-	forefront	before, front, superior
hemi-	hemisphere	half
hepta-	heptagon	seven
hexa-	hexagon	six
hyper-	hypersensitive	over, above
in-, il-, ir-, im-	invisible, invade	not, also means in and is used as an intensifier

PREFIX	EXAMPLE	MEANING
inter-	interact	between, among
intra-, intro-	introvert	within
kilo-	kilocycle	thousand
milli-	millennium	thousand
mis-	misspell	wrong, not
mono-	monopoly	one
multi-	multitude	many
non-	nonsense	not
nona-	nonagon	nine
ob-, oc-, of-	obstruct	toward, to, on, over, against
oct-	octagon	eight
omni-	omnipotent	all
pan-	pantheist	all
per-	perceive	through, thoroughly, very
pro-	promote	in favor of, advancing
quadr-	quadrupled	four
quin-	quintuplet	five
re-	reorganize	backward, again
retro-	retrograde	backward
se-	select	apart
semi-	semiannual	half
sept-	September	seven
sex-	sextant	six
sub-, suc-, suf-, sur-, sug-, sus-	supplant	under, below, slightly
super-	supercede	above, beyond
syn-, sym-	synchronize	with, together
tele-	telegraph	distance
tetra-	tetrameter	four
trans-, tra-	traverse	across, beyond, through
tri-	triple	three
ultra-	ultramodern	beyond, farther
un-	unnatural	not
uni-	unilateral	one

Common Suffixes

SUFFIX	EXAMPLE	MEANING
-able, -ible	durable, visible	able
-acy	piracy, privacy	quality, state, office

SUFFIX	EXAMPLE	MEANING
-age	breakage, orphanage	pertaining to; also, a noun-forming suffix
-al	rental, abdominal	adjective- or noun-forming suffix
-ance, -ence	insurance, competence	adjective- or noun-forming suffix
-ant	reliant, servant	adjective- or noun-forming suffix
-arium, -orium	aquarium, auditorium	place, instrument
-ary	dictionary, elementary	pertaining to, connected with
-ate	activate, animate	verb-forming suffix used with English nouns
-ation, -ition	creation, condition	combination of -ate, and -ion used for forming nouns
-cle, -icle	corpuscle, denticle	small, diminutive
-esque	picturesque	style, manner, distinctive character
-ferous	coniferous	bearing
-ful	colorful	full of
-fy, -ify	fortify, magnify	to make, to cause to be
-hood	childhood, statehood	station, condition, nature
-ic	democratic, phonic	suffix forming adjectives from nouns
-ism	conservatism, Marxism	used to form nouns denoting action, practice, principles, doctrines
-itis	appendicitis	inflammation, abnormal state or condition
-ity	acidity, familiarity	used to form nouns expressing state or condition
-ive	creative, suggestive	suffix of adjectives expressing tendency, disposition, function
-ize	memorize, modernize	verb suffix
-ment	statement	denotes an action, resulting state, product

SUFFIX	EXAMPLE	MEANING
-mony	testimony, parsimony	result or condition, denotes action or condition
-oid	avoid, ellipsoid	resembling, like
-or	conqueror, generator	one who does something
-ose, -ous	verbose, porous	full of
-osis	hypnosis	denotes action, state, process, or condition
-tude	solitude, altitude	indicates nouns formed from adjectives

Common Roots

ROOT	EXAMPLE	MEANING
ag, act	activate, enact, agile, agency	to do
anthrop	anthropology, anthropomorphic, misanthrope	man
aqua	aquifer, aquatic, aqueous	water
aud	audible, audition, auditorium, audience	hear
auto	automatic, automation, automaton	self
bene	benefit, benevolent, benign	good
cap, capt, chap	decapitate, capture, captain, chapter	head
ceed, cede, cess	proceed, precedent, cease	go, yield
chrom	chromatic, chromosome	color
chron	synchronize, chronology, chronic	time
cogn	cognition, recognize, cognitive	know
corp	corporate, corpulent, corporation	body

ROOT	EXAMPLE	MEANING
cred	credit, incredible, credulous	belief
dent, dont	orthodontist, dental, dentifrice	tooth
derm	dermatology, epidermis, dermatitis	skin
dic, dict	dictionary, dictate, predict, indict	say
don, donat	donate, donor, condone, pardon	to give
dox	doxology, paradox	belief
duc	duct, reduce, produce, conduct	lead in
fac, fic, fy	manufacture, factory, verify	make, do
fer	transfer, ferry, confer, defer, suffer	bear
fie	confident, infidel, confide	faith
fluc, flux	fluxtuate, fluxion	flow
graph	graphite, telegraph, phonograph	write
gress	transgress, congress, egress	step
ject	deject, rejection, conjecture, trajectory	throw
loc	local, locate, location, dislocate	place
loq, loc	eloquent, elocution, interlocutor	speak
mal	malevolent, malapropism, malefactor	bad
manu	manufacture, manuscript, manacle, manual	hand
miso, misa	misanthrope, misogamy	bad
mit, mis	emit, permit, dismissal, omit, missile	send

ROOT	EXAMPLE	MEANING
morph	morphology, endomorph, metamorphosis	shape
mort	mortician, mortuary, mortify	dead
mov, mot, mob	motivate, motion, motile, remove	move
neb	nebulous, nebula	cloudy
omni	omnipresent, omniscient, omnipotent	all
path	sympathy, empathic, pathetic	suffering, disease, feeling
ped	pedestrian, pedometer, pedicure	foot
phil	philosophy, philanthropy, philharmonic	love
pod	podiatrist, pseudopod	foot
scrib, script	transcript, prescribe, description	write

Bibliographies

Literature in the Content Curriculum

Books for Children on African-American History

Angelou, Maya. *I Know Why the Caged Bird Sings*. New York: Random House, 1972.

Angelou, Maya. *Gather Together in My Name*. New York: Random House, 1974.

Angelou, Maya. *Singin' and Swingin' and Gettin' Merry Like Christmas*. New York: Random House, 1976.

Bernard, Jaqueline. *Journey Toward Freedom: The Story of Sojourner Truth*. New York: Grosset & Dunlap, 1967.

Brownmiller, Susan. *Shirley Chisholm*. New York: Archway Books, 1968.

Bryan, Ashley (selected and illustrated). *I'm Going to Sing*. New York: Atheneum, 1982.

Felton, Harold William. *James Weldon Johnson*. New York: Dodd, Mead, 1971.

Fox, P. *Slave Dancer*. Scarsdale, NY: Bradley Press, 1973.

Gilroy, Tom. *In Bikole*. Westminster, ME: Alfred A. Knopf, 1978.

Goodman, Walter. *Black Bondage: The Life of Slaves in the South*. New York: Farrar, Strauss & Giroux, 1969.

Greenfield, Eloise. *Childtimes: A Three-Generation Memoir*. New York: Thomas Y. Crowell, 1979.

Hamilton, Virginia. Illustrator Eros Keith. *The House of Dies Drear*. New York: Macmillan, 1968.

Hamilton, Virginia. *Junius Over Far*. New York: Harper & Row, 1985.

Hamilton, Virginia. *Zeely*. New York: Macmillan, 1967.

Hermence, Belina. *Tancy*. Boston: Houghton Mifflin, 1984.

Hotchkiss, J. *African-Asian Reading Guide for Children and Young Adults*. Metuchen, NJ: Scarecrow Press, 1976.

Kaufman, Mervyn D. *Jesse Owens*. New York: Thomas Y. Crowell, 1973.

Meltzer, Milton. *The Black Americans: A History in Their Own Words*. New York: Thomas Y. Crowell, 1982.

Ojigbo, A. Okion (compiler and editor). *Young and Black in Africa*. New York: Random House, 1965.

Robeson, Susan. *The Whole World in His Hands: A Pictorial History of Paul Robeson*. Secaucus, NJ: Citadel Press, 1981.

Sterling, Dorothy. *Freedom Train*. New York: Scholastic Book Services, 1971.

Taylor, Mildred. *Roll of Thunder Hear My Cry*. New York: Bantam Books, 1984.

Vlakos, Olivia. Illustrator George Ford. *African Beginnings*. New York: Viking Press, 1967.

Webb, Sheyann, and Rachel West Nelson. *Selma, Lord, Selma*. Tuscaloosa, AL: University of Alabama Press, 1980.

Books for Teachers on African-American History

Berlin, Ira, and Ronald Hoffman. *Slavery and Freedom in the Age of the American Revolution*. Charlottesville, VA: University of Virginia Press, 1984.

Blassingame, John (editor). *Slave Testimony*. Baton Rouge, LA: Louisiana State University Press, 1977.

Brodie, Fawn. *Thomas Jefferson: An Intimate History*. New York: Bantam Books, 1974.

Buckley, Gail Lumet. *The Hornes: An American Family*. Westminster, MD: Alfred A. Knopf, 1986.

Chase-Riboud, Barbara. *Sally Hemmings*. New York: Viking Press, 1979.

Clark, Barbara Smith. *After the Revolution*. Westminster, MD: Pantheon Books, 1982.

Dixon, Melvin. *Change of Territory*. Charlottesville, VA: University of Virginia Press, 1983.

Farish, Hunter. *Journal and Letters of Phillip Vickers Fithian 1773–1774: A Plantation Tutor of the Old Dominion*. Charlottesville, VA: University of Virginia Press, 1984.

Maddex, Jack P., Jr. *The Virginia Conservatives*. Chapel Hill, NC: University of North Carolina Press, 1970.

Mallial, William. *Slave*. New York: W. W. Norton, 1986.

Martin, Waldo E. *The Mind of Frederick Douglass*. Chapel Hill, NC: University of North Carolina Press, 1982.

Morgan, Edward S. *American Slavery–American Freedom: The Ordeal of Colonial Virginia*. New York: W. W. Norton, 1984.

Roark, James L. *Masters Without Slaves*. New York: W. W. Norton, 1977.

Rosengarten, Thomas. *Tombee: Portrait of a Cotton Planter*. West Caldwell, NJ: William Morrow, 1985.

Sims, R. *Shadow and Substance: Afro-American Experience in Contemporary Children's Fiction*. Urbana, IL: National Council of Teachers of English, 1982.

Smith, Page. *Trial by Fire*. New York: McGraw-Hill, 1982.

Sweet, Leonard. *Black Images of America*. New York: W. W. Norton, 1984.

Tate, Thad W. *The Negro in 18th Century Williamsburg*. Charlottesville, VA: University of Virginia Press, 1984.

Williamson, Joel. *After Slavery*. Chapel Hill, NC: University of North Carolina Press, 1970.

Woodward, C. Van (editor). *Mary Chestnut's Civil War*. New Haven, CT: Yale University Press, 1981.

Books for Teachers and Children on Native Americans

Aliki. *Corn is Maize: The Gift of the Indians*. New York: Crowell, 1976.

Anderson, Bernice. *Indian Sleepman Tales*. New York: Bromhall House, 1940.

Baker, Olaf. Illustrator Stephen Gammell. *Where the Buffaloes Begin*. New York: Frederick Warne, 1981.

Balch, Glenn. *Brave Riders*. New York: Thomas Y. Crowell, 1959.

Baylor, B. *And It Is Still That Way: Legends Told by Arizona Indian Children*. New York: Scribner's, 1976.

Bierhorst, John (editor). *Indian Poetry: The Sacred Path*. New York: William Morrow, 1983.

Bonham, Frank. *Chief*. New York: E. P. Dutton, 1971.

Brain, Jeffrey. "Eyewitness Documents Gain New Authority from Records of Archaeology." *Clues to America's Past*. Washington, DC: National Geographic Society, 1976.

Brink, Carol Ryrie. *Caddie Woodlawn: A Frontier Story*. New York: Macmillan, 1935.

Clifford, Ethel Rosenberg. Illustrator Richard Cuffari. *The Year of the Three-Legged Deer*. Boston: Houghton Mifflin, 1972.

Corcoran, Barbara. Illustrator Richard Cuffari. *This Is a Recording*. New York: Atheneum, 1971.

Crompton, Anne Eliot. *The Ice Trail*. New York: Methuen, 1980.

Distad, Audree. Illustrator Tony Chen. *Dakota Sons*. New York: Harper & Row, 1972.

Farquhar, Margaret C. Illustrator Brinton Turkle. *Indian Children of America*. New York: Holt, Rinehart & Winston, 1964.

Flores, Dan L. (editor and introduction by). *Jefferson and Southwest Exploration: The Freeman and Curtis Accounts of the Red River Expedition of 1806*. Oklahoma City: University of Oklahoma Press, 1984.

Hilton, Suzanne. *Getting There: Frontier Travel Without Power*. Philadelphia: Westminster Press, 1980.

Hofsinde, Robert. *Indian Medicine Man*. New York: William Morrow, 1966.

Jones, Weyman B. *Edge of Two Worlds*. New York: Dial Press, 1968.

Lampman, Evelyn Sibley. *Half-Breed*. Garden City, NY: Doubleday, 1967.

Lee, B. *Charles Eastman: The Story of an American Indian*. Minneapolis, MN: Dillon, 1979.

Lyback, Johanna R. M. Illustrator Dick West. *Indian Legends of Eastern America*. Chicago: Lyons & Carnahan, 1963.

Manjo, F. N. Illustrator Anita Lobel. *Indian Summer*. New York: Harper & Row, 1968.

McDermott, G. *Arrow to the Sun, a Pueblo Indian Tale*. New York: Viking, 1974.

Miles, Miska. Illustrator Peter Parnall. *Annie and the Old One*. Boston: Little, Brown, 1971.

Moulton, Gary. *John Ross, Cherokee Chief*. Athens, GA: University of Georgia Press, 1986.

National Geographic. *Trails West*. Washington, DC: National Geographic Society, 1974.

National Geographic. *The World of the American Indian*. Washington, DC: National Geographic Society, 1974.

O'Dell, Scott. *Sing Down the Moon*. Boston: Houghton Mifflin, 1970.

Patent, Dorothy Hinshaw. *Buffalo*. Holiday House, 1986.

Raskin, Joseph. *Indian Tales*. New York: Random House, 1969.

Richter, Daniel K. *Rediscovered Links in the Covenant Chain*. Charlottesville, VA: University of Virginia Press, 1984.

Steele, William O. *Flaming Arrows*. New York: Harcourt Brace Jovanovich, 1957.

Steptoe, J. *The Story of Jumping Mouse, a Native American Legend*. New York: Lothrop, Lee, and Shephard, 1984.

Tamany, Irene R. Illustrator L. F. Cary. *Indian Tales*. Columbus, OH: C. E. Merrill, 1968.

Tobias, T. *Maria Tallchief*. New York: Thomas Y. Crowell, 1970.

Books for Children on Immigration and Settlement of the Western United States

Friedman, Russell. *Immigrant Kids*. New York: E. P. Dutton, 1980.

Gay, Kathryn. *The Germans Helped Build America*. New York: Messner, 1971.

Hautzig, Esther. *The Endless Steppe: A Girl in Exile*. New York: Scholastic Book Services, 1974.

Haviland, Virginia (editor). Illustrator Ann Strugnell. *North American Legends*. New York: Philomel Books, 1979.

Holland, Ruth. Pictures by H. B. Vestal. *The German Immigrants in America*. New York: Grosset & Dunlap, 1969.

Johnson, James. *The Irish in America*. Minneapolis, MN: Lerner Publications, 1966.

Kunz, Virginia. *The Germans in America*. Minneapolis, MN: Lerner Publications, 1966.

Lasky, Kathryn. *Irish Immigrants*. New York: Macmillan, 1984.

Madison, Winifred. *Maria Luisa*. Philadelphia: J. B., Lippincott, 1971.

Marzollo, Jean. *Half Way Down Paddy Lane*. New York: Dial Press, 1981.

Norris, Gunilla Brodde. *A Feast of Light*. Westminster, MD: Alfred A. Knopf, 1967.

Robins, Albert. *Coming to America: Immigrants from Northern Europe*. New York: Dell, 1981.

Trapp, Maria Augusta. *The Sound of Music*. New York: Dell, 1969.

Books for Teachers on Immigrants

Barringer, Felicity. *Flight from Sorrow*. New York: Atheneum, 1984.

Catton, Bruce, and William C. Catton. *The Bold and Magnificent Dream: America's Founding Years, 1842–1915*. Garden City, NY: Doubleday, 1978.

Flexnor, James Thomas. *An American Saga*. New York: Little, Brown, 1984.

Gilbert, Martin. *Scharansky: Hero of Our Time*. New York: Viking Press, 1986.

Ivinskaya, Olga. *A Captive of My Time: My Years With Pasternak*. Garden City, NY: Doubleday, 1978.

Jordan, Terry. *German Seed in Texas Soil*. Austin, TX: University of Texas Press, 1966.

Riley, Edward. *The Journal of John Harrower: An Indentured Servant in the Colony of Virginia, 1773–1776*. Charlottesville, VA: University of Virginia Press, 1984.

Rosenfeld, Harvey. *Raoul Wallenberg: Angel of Rescue*. Buffalo, NY: Prometheus Books, 1982.

Rugoff, Milton. *The Beechers: An American Family in the 19th Century*. New York: Harper & Row, 1981.

Schector, Leona and Jerrold. *An American Family in Moscow*. Boston: Little, Brown, 1975.

Shevchenko, Arkady. *Breaking with Moscow*. Westminster, MD: Alfred A. Knopf, 1985.

Singer, Isaac Bashevis. *A Man in Search of Love*. Garden City, NY: Doubleday, 1985.

Smith, Hedrick. *The Russians*. New York: Ballentine Books, 1976.

Stratton, Joanna L. *Pioneer Women: Voices from the Kansas Frontier*. New York: Simon and Schuster, 1981.

Wallace, Amy. *Genius, The Prodigy: A Biography of William James Sides, America's Greatest Child Prodigy*. New York: E. M. Dutton, 1986.

Books for Teachers and Children on Math

Adler, Irving and Ruth. *Directions and Angles: The Reason Why Books*. New York: John Day, 1969.

Bendick, Jeanne. *Science Experience: Shapes*. New York: Franklin Watts, 1968.

Burns, Marilyn. *Math for Smarty Pants*. Boston: Little, Brown, 1982.

Charosh, Mannis. *Straight Lines, Parallel Lines, Perpendicular Lines*. New York: Thomas Y. Crowell, 1970.

Diggins, Julia E. *String, Straight Edge, and Shadow: The Story of Geometry*. New York: Viking Press, 1965.

Fekete, Irene, and Jasmine Denyer. *Mathematics: The World of Science*. New York: Facts on File Publications, 1984.

Foster, Leslie. *Mathematics Encyclopedia*. New York: Rand-McNally, 1986.

Freeman, Mae and Ira. *Fun with Figures*. New York: Random House, 1946.

Froman, Robert. *Angles Are Easy as Pie*. New York: Thomas Y. Crowell, 1975.

Hogben, Lancelot. *The Wonderful World of Mathematics*. New York: Doubleday, 1968.

Phillips, Jo. *Exploring Triangles: Paper Folding Geometry*. New York: Thomas Y. Crowell, 1975.

Phillips, Jo. *Right Angles: Paper Folding Geometry*. New York: Thomas Y. Crowell, 1972.

Sitomer, Mindel and Harry. *Circles*. New York: Thomas Y. Crowell, 1971.

**Books for Teachers
and Children in Science**

Aliki. *Digging Up Dinosaurs*. New York: Thomas Y. Crowell, 1981.

Amos, William H. *Life in Ponds and Streams*. Washington, DC: National Geographic Society, 1982.

Berman, Sam. *Dinosaur Joke Book*. New York: Grosset & Dunlap, 1969.

Branley, F. *Experiments in the Principles of Space Travel*. New York: Crowell, 1973.

Brown, Marc, and Krensky, S. *Dinosaurs, Beware! A Safety Guide*. Boston: Little, Brown, 1982.

Clark, Ann Nolan. *Along Sandy Trails*. New York: Viking Press, 1969.

Cortesi, Wendy. *Explore a Spooky Swamp*. Washington, DC: National Geographic Society, 1978.

Ipcar, Dahlov. *The Wonderful Egg*. New York: Doubleday, 1958.

Children's Trade Books in Math*

**Counting and Number
Books**

Aker, Suzanne. *What Comes in 2's, 3's and 4's?* New York: Simon & Schuster, 1990. (ISBN 0-671-79247-4)

Anno, Mitsumasa. *Anno's Counting Book*. New York: Thomas Y. Crowell, 1975. (ISBN 0-690-01288-8)

Aylesworth, Jim. *One Crow: A Counting Rhyme*. New York: J. B. Lippincott, 1988. (ISBN 0-397-32175-9)

Bang, Molly. *Ten, Nine, Eight*. New York: Greenwillow. (ISBN 0-688-00906-9) Also available in paperback.

Carter, David A. *How Many Bugs in a Box?* New York: Simon & Schuster, 1988. (ISBN 0-671-64965-5)

Demi. *Demi's Count the Animals 1-2-3*. New York: Grossett & Dunlap, 1986. (ISBN 0-448-18980-1)

Haskins, Jim. *Count Your Way Through India*. Minneapolis: Carolrhoda Books, 1991. (ISBN 0-87614-414-8)

Haskins, Jim. *Count Your Way Through Israel*. Minneapolis: Carolrhoda Books, 1991. (ISBN 0-87614-415-6)

Additional *Count Your Way . . .* titles include:

. . . *Through Africa* (ISBN 0-87614-514-4)

. . . *Through the Arab World* (ISBN 0-87614-487-3)

. . . *Through Canada* (ISBN 0-87614-515-2)

. . . *Through China* (ISBN 0-87614-486-5)

. . . *Through Germany* (ISBN 0-87614-407-5)

. . . *Through Italy* (ISBN 0-87614-406-7)

. . . *Through Japan* (ISBN 0-87614-485-7)

. . . *Through Korea* (ISBN 0-87614-516-0)

. . . *Through Mexico* (ISBN 0-87614-517-9)

. . . *Through Russia* (ISBN 0-87614-488-1)

Hellen, Nancy. *The Bus Stop*. Shapleigh, ME: Orchard Books, 1988. (ISBN 0-531-05765-8)

Hoban, Tana. *Count and See*. New York: Macmillan, 1974. (ISBN 0-02-744800-2)

*Compiled by Dorothy Giroux, Ph.D.

Kitamura, Satoshi. *When Sheep Cannot Sleep; The Counting Book*. Farrar, Straus, & Giroux, 1986.

Maestro, Betsy. *Harriet Goes to the Circus: A Number Concept Book*. New York: Crown, 1977. (ISBN 0-517-55303-1)

McMillan, Bruce. *Counting Wildflowers*. New York: Lothrop, Lee & Shepard, 1986. (ISBN 0-688-02859-4)

Moerbeek, Kees, and Carla Dijs. *Six Brave Explorers*. Los Angeles: Prince Stern Sloan, 1988. (ISBN 0-8431-2253-6)

Pluckrose, Henry. *Numbers*. New York: Franklin Watts, 1988. (ISBN 0-531-10453-2)

Trinca, Rod, and Kerry Argent. *One Woolly Wombat*. New York: Kane/Miller, 1985. (ISBN 0-916291-00-6)

Number Operations

Anno, Mitsumasa. *Anno's Counting House*. New York: Philomel Books, 1982. (ISBN 0-399-20896-8)

Anno, Mitsumasa. *Anno's Mysterious Multiplying Jar*. New York: Philomel Books, 1983. (ISBN 0-399-20951-4) Introduces factorials.

Dee, Ruby. *Two Ways to Count to Ten*. New York: Henry Holt, 1988. (ISBN 0-8050-1314-8)

Ehlert, Lois. *Fish Eyes: A Book You Can Count On*. Orlando, FL: Harcourt Brace Jovanovich, 1990. (ISBN 0-15-228050-2) Reinforces addition.

Gerstein, Mordicai. *Roll Over!* New York: Crown, 1984. (ISBN 0-517-55209-4) Reinforces subtraction.

Giganti, Paul, Jr. *Each Orange Had 8 Slices*. New York: Greenwillow, 1992. (ISBN 0-688-10428-2) Reinforces multiplication.

Hutchins, Pat. *The Doorbell Rang*. New York: Greenwillow, 1986. (ISBN 0-688-05251-7) Reinforces division.

Mathews, Louise. *Bunches and Bunches of Bunnies*. New York: Scholastic, 1978. (ISBN 0-590-41880-7) Reinforces multiplication.

Owen, Annie. *Annie's One to Ten*. New York: Alfred A. Knopf, 1988. (ISBN 0-394-82791-0)

Zaslavsky, Claudia, *Zero: Is It Something? Is It Nothing?* New York: Franklin Watts, 1989. (ISBN 0-531-10693-4)

Geometry

Emberley, Ed. *The Wing of a Flea: A Book About Shapes*. Boston: Little, Brown, 1988. (ISBN 0-316-23600-4)

Froman, Robert. *Angles Are as Easy as Pie*. New York: Thomas Y. Crowell, 1975. (ISBN 0-690-00916-X)

Hoban, Tana. *Circles, Triangles and Squares*. New York: Macmillan, 1974. (ISBN 0-02744830-4)

Hoban, Tana. *Is It Larger? Is It Smaller?* New York: Greenwillow, 1985. (ISBN 0-688-04028-4)

Hoban, Tana. *Shapes, Shapes, Shapes*. New York: Greenwillow, 1986. (ISBN 0-688-05833-7)

Pluckrose, Henry. *Big & Little*. New York: Franklin Watts, 1987. (ISBN 0-531-10373-9)

Pluckrose, Henry. *Capacity*. New York: Franklin Watts, 1988. (ISBN 0-531-10547-4)

Pluckrose, Henry. *Length*. New York: Franklin Watts, 1988. (ISBN 0-531-10618-7)

Pluckrose, Henry. *Pattern*. New York: Franklin Watts, 1988. (ISBN 0-531-10619-5)

Pluckrose, Henry. *Sorting*. New York: Franklin Watts, 1988. (ISBN 0-531-10548-2)

Pluckrose, Henry. *Weight*. New York: Franklin Watts, 1988. (ISBN 0-531-10525-3)

Walter, Marion. *Look at Annette*. M. Evans & Company, 1977. (ISBN 0-87131-071-6)

Walter, Marion. *Make a Bigger Puddle, Make a Smaller Worm*. M. Evans & Company, 1971. (ISBN 0-87131-073-2)

Walter, Marion. *The Mirror Puzzle Book*. Parkwest Publications, 1985. (ISBN 0-906212-39-1)

Money

Hoban, Tana. *Twenty-Six Letters and Ninety-Nine Cents*. New York: Greenwillow, 1987. (ISBN 0-688-06362-4)

Schwartz, David. *If You Made a Million*. New York: Lothrop, Lee & Shepard, 1989. (ISBN 0-688-07017-5) Also available in paperback from Scholastic Inc. (ISBN 0-590-43608-2)

Viorst, Judith. *Alexander Who Used to Be Rich Last Sunday*. New York: Macmillan, 1980. (ISBN 0-689-71199-9)

Large Numbers

Myers, Bernice. *The Millionth Egg*. New York: Lothrop, Lee & Shepard, 1991. (ISBN 0-688-09886-X)

Schwartz, David. *How Much Is a Million?* New York: Lothrop, Lee & Shepard, 1985. (ISBN 0-688-04049-7) Also available in paperback from Scholastic Inc. (ISBN 0-590-33966-4)

Miscellaneous Math Topics

Abbott, Edwin A. *Flatland: A Romance of Many Dimensions*. Dover. (ISBN 0-486-20001-9)

Adler, David A. *Roman Numerals*. New York: Thomas Y. Crowell, 1977. (ISBN 0-690-01302-7)

Anno, Mitsumasa. *Anno's Math Games*. New York: Philomel Books, 1987. (ISBN 0-399-21151-9)

Anno, Mitsumasa. *Anno's Math Games II*. New York: Philomel Books, 1989. (ISBN 0-399-21615-4)

Anno, Mitsumasa. *Anno's Math Games III*. New York: Philomel Books, 1991. (ISBN 0-399-22274-X)

Birch, David. *The King's Chessboard*. New York: Dial Books for Young Readers, 1988. (ISBN 0-8037-0365-1)

Burns, Marilyn. *The I Hate Mathematics Book*. Little, Brown, 1975. (ISBN 0-316-11741-1)

Burns, Marilyn. *Math for Smarty Pants*. Little, Brown, 1982. (ISBN 0-316-11739-0)

Dennis, J. Richard. *Fractions Are Parts of Things*. New York: Thomas Y. Crowell, 1971. (ISBN 0-690-31521-X)

Gamow, George. *One, Two, Three . . . Infinity: Facts and Speculations of Science*. Dover. (ISBN 0-486-25664-2)

Greene, Carol. *The Thirteen Days of Halloween*. Chicago: Children's Press (ISBN 0-516-48231-9)

Jonas, A. *Round Trip*. New York: Scholastic, 1983. (ISBN 0-590-40956-5)

Juster, Norton. *The Dot and the Line: A Romance in Lower Mathematics*. New York: Random House, 1977. (ISBN 0-394-73352-5)

Juster, Norton. *The Phantom Tollbooth*. New York: Random House, 1972. (ISBN 0-394-82199-8)

Kaye, Marilyn. *A Day with No Math*. Orlando, FL: Harcourt Brace Jovanovich, 1992. (ISBN 0-15-301037-1)

McMillan, Bruce. *Eating Fractions*. New York: Scholastic, 1991. (ISBN 0-590-43770-4)

Munsch, Robert. *Moira's Birthday*. Annick, 1987. (ISBN 0-920303-85-4) Reinforces estimation.

Nesbit, E. *Melisande*. Orlando, FL: Harcourt Brace Jovanovich, 1989. (ISBN 0-15-253164-5) Exponents and measurement.

Nozaki, Akihiro, and Anno, Mitsumasa. *Anno's Hat Tricks*. New York: Philomel Books, 1985. (ISBN 0-399-21212-4)

Phillips, Louis. *263 Brain Busters: Just How Smart Are You Anyway?* Viking, 1985. (ISBN 0-670-80412-6)

Pittman, Helen Clare. *A Grain of Rice*. Mamaroneck, NY: Hastings House, 1986. (ISBN 0-8038-2728-8) Also available in paperback as a Bantam Skylark Book. (ISBN 0-533-15986-0)

Tompert, Ann. *Grandfather Tang's Story*. New York: Crown, 1990. (ISBN 0-517-57272-9)

Children's Trade Books in Science*

"Science trade books, unlike textbooks, begin not with a scope and sequence chart but with a passion or a curiosity or an interest. The best science books are personal books, not personal in the sense of self-indulgent, but personally exciting."

—Wendy Saul and Sybille A. Jagusch, *Vital Connections: Children, Science, and Books*, p. 8

Scientific Method

Brown, Ruth. *If At First You Do Not See*. New York: Henry Holt, 1982.
Caney, Steven. *Steven Caney's Invention Book*. New York: Workman, 1985.
Cobb, Vicki. *Science Experiments You Can Eat*. New York: Harper Trophy, 1972.
Cobb, Vicki. *More Science Experiments You Can Eat*. New York: Harper Trophy, 1979.
Demi. *The Empty Pot*. New York: Henry Holt, 1990.
Kramer, Stephen B. *How to Think Like a Scientist*. New York: Thomas Y. Crowell, 1987.

Environment

Butterfield, Moira. *Amazon Rainforest*. Nashville, TN: Ideals, 1992.
Cooney, Barbara. *Miss Rumphius*. New York: Puffin Books, 1982.
Jeffers, Susan. *Brother Eagle, Sister Sky*. New York: Dial Books, 1991.
Savan, Beth. *Earthwatch*. Reading, MA: Addison-Wesley, 1991.
Suess, Dr. *The Lorax*. New York: Random House, 1971.

Weather

Allison, Linda. *The Reason for Seasons*. Boston: Little, Brown, 1975.
Barrett, Judi. *Cloudy With a Chance of Meatballs*. New York: Macmillan, 1978.
dePaola, Tomie. *The Cloud Book*. New York: Holiday House, 1975.
Dickinson, Terence. *Exploring the Sky by Day*. Ontario: Camden House, 1988.
Wyatt, Valerie. *Weatherwatch*. Reading, PA: Addison-Wesley, 1990.

Rocks

Baylor, Byrd. *Everybody Needs a Rock*. New York: Aladdin Books, 1974.
Gans, Roma. *Rock Collecting*. New York: Harper Trophy, 1984.
Lauber, Patricia. *Dinosaurs Walked Here and Other Stories Fossils Tell*. New York: Aladdin Books, 1992.

The Human Body

Allison, Linda. *Blood and Guts*. Boston: Little, Brown, 1976.
Cole, Joanna. *The Magic School Bus Inside the Human Body*. Illustrated by Bruce Degen. New York: Scholastic, 1989.

*Compiled by Dorothy Giroux, Ph.D.

Professional Teacher Resources

Butzow, Carol M., and Butzow, John W. *Science Through Children's Literature: An Integrated Approach*. Englewood, CO: Teacher Ideas Press, 1989.

Galda, Lee, and DeGroff, Linda. "Exploration and Discovery: Books for a Science Curriculum." *The Reading Teacher, 44*(4), December 1990.

Moir, Hughes (ed.). *Collected Perspectives: Choosing and Using Books for the Classroom*. Boston: Christopher Gordon, 1992.

Saul, Wendy, and Jagusch, Sybille A. (eds.). *Vital Connections: Children, Science, and Books*. Portsmouth, NH: Heineman, 1991.

———. "Outstanding Science Trade Books for Children in 1991." *Science and Children, 29*(6), March 1992.

Resources on Critical Thinking

Adams, Dennis. "Teaching Students Critical Viewing Skills." *Curriculum Review*, Vol. 26, no. 3 (January–February 1987), pp. 29–31.

Brown, Jerry. "On Teaching Thinking Skills in the Elementary and Middle School." *Phi Delta Kappan*, Vol. 64 (June 1983), pp. 707–714.

De Bono, Edward. "The Direct Teaching of Thinking as a Skill." *Phi Delta Kappan*, Vol. 64 (June 1983), pp. 703–08.

"Direct Instruction" and "Teaching for Thinking." *Educational Leadership*, Vol. 42 (May 1985), entire issue.

Duffy, G., Roehler, L., and Hermann, B. (1988). Modeling mental processes helps poor readers become strategic readers." *The Reading Teacher*, Vol. 41. (1988), pp. 762–767.

Ennis, Robert. "A Logical Basis for Measuring Critical Thinking Skills." *Educational Leadership*, Vol. 43, no. 44 (October 1985), pp. 44–48.

Erickson, Bonnie. "Increasing Critical Reading in Junior High Classrooms." *Journal of Reading*, Vol. 30, no. 5 (February 1987), pp. 430–439.

"Framework for Teaching Thinking." *Educational Leadership*, Vol. 43 (May 1986), entire issue.

Graham, K. G., and Robinson, H. A. (1984) *Study Skills Handbook: A Guide for All Teachers*. Newark, DE: International Reading Association.

Haggard, M. R. "Developing Critical Thinking with the Directed Reading-Thinking Activity." *The Reading Teacher*, Vol. 41 (1988), pp. 526–533.

Hughes, Carolyn. "Teaching Strategies for Developing Student Thinking." *School Library Media Quarterly*, Vol. 15, no. 1 (Fall 1986), pp. 33–36.

Jay, Ellen. "The Elementary School Media Teacher's Role in Educating Teachers to Think." *School Library Media Quarterly*, Vol. 15, no. 1 (Fall 1986) pp. 28–32.

Jones, B. F., Palincsar, A., et al. (1987). *Strategic Teaching and Learning: Cognitive Instruction in the Content Areas*. Alexandria, VA: Association for Supervision and Curriculum Development.

Karras, Ray. "A Realistic Approach to Thinking Skills: Reform Multiple Choice Questions." *Social Science Record*, Vol. 22, no. 1 (Fall 1985), pp. 38–43.

Klein, M., Peterson, S., and Simington, L. (1991), *Teaching Reading in the Elementary Grades*. Needham Heights, MA: Allyn and Bacon.

Langer, J. A. "From Theory to Practice: A Prereading Plan." *Journal of Reading*, Vol. 25 (1981), pp. 152–156.

Mancall, Jacqueline. "Educating Students to Think. The Role of the School Library Media Program." *School Library Media Quarterly*, Vol. 15, no. 1 (Fall 1986), pp. 18–27.

Moses, Monti. "Teaching Students to Think: What Can Principals Do?" *NASSP Bulletin*, Vol. 70, no. 488 (March 1986), pp. 16–20.

Murray, Ann. "A Collaborative Approach to the Teaching of Thinking." *Journal of Staff Development*, Vol. 6, no. 2 (October 1985), pp. 133–137.

Ogle, D. "K-W-L: A Teaching Model That Develops Active Reading of Expository Text." *The Reading Teacher*, Vol. 39 (1983), pp. 564–570.

Palincsar, A. S., & Brown, A. L. "Reciprocal Teaching of Comprehension Fostering and Comprehension Monitoring." *Cognition and Instruction*, Vol. 1 (1984), pp. 117–175.

Patching, W., Kameenui, E., Gersten, R., Carnine, D., and Colvin, G. "Direct Instruction in Critical Reading Skills." *Reading Research Quarterly*, Vol. 18 (1983), pp. 406–418.

Reahm, Douglas. "Developing Critical Thinking Through Rehearsal Techniques." *Music Educators Journal*, Vol. 72, no. 7 (March 1986), pp. 29–31.

Reyes, Donald. "Critical Thinking in Elementary Social Studies Text Series." *Social Studies*, Vol. 77, no. 4 (July–August 1986), pp. 151–154.

Rhoades, Lynn. "Using the Daily Newspaper to Teach Cognitive and Affective Skills." *Clearing House*, Vol. 59, no. 4 (December 1985), pp. 162–164.

Rosenbaum, Roberta. "Teaching Critical Thinking in the Business Mathematics Course." *Journal of Education for Business*, Vol. 62, no. 2 (November 1986), pp. 66–69.

Rothen, Kathleen. "Hazel, Fiver, Odysseus, and You: An Odyssey into Critical Thinking." *English Journal*, Vol. 76, no. 3 (March 1987), pp. 56–59.

Sadler, William. "A Holistic Approach to Improving Thinking Skills." *Phi Delta Kappan*, Vol. 67, no. 3 (March 1987), pp. 56–59.

Scenters-Zapica. "From Oral Communication Skills to Research Skills." *English Journal*, Vol. 76, no. 1 (January 1987), pp. 69–70.

Sternburg, Robert. "Teaching Critical Thinking, Part 1: Are We Making Critical Mistakes?" *Phi Delta Kappan*, Vol. 67, no. 3 (November 1985), pp. 194–198.

———. "Teaching Critical Thinking, Part 2: Possible Solutions." *Phi Delta Kappan*, Vol. 67, no. 4 (December 1985), pp. 277–280.

Stoodt, Barbara D. *Teaching Language Arts*. New York: Harper & Row, 1988.

Strahan, David. "Guided Thinking: A Strategy for Encouraging Excellence at the Middle Level." *NASSP Bulletin*, Vol. 70, no. 487 (February 1986), pp. 75–80.

Sullivan, David. "Using a Textbook for Critical Thinking: An Introductory Lesson for Identifying Point of View." *New England Social Studies Bulletin*, Vol. 43, no. 2 (Winter 1985–86), pp. 31–33.

"Teaching Thinking Skills." *Educational Leadership*, Vol. 39 (October 1981), entire issue.

Templeton, Shane. *Teaching the Integrated Language Arts*. Boston: Houghton Mifflin, 1991.

"Thinking Skills in the Curriculum." *Educational Leadership*, Vol. 42 (September 1984), entire issue.

Thurmond, Vera. "Analytical Reading: A Course That Stresses Thinking Aloud." *Journal of Reading*, Vol. 29, no. 8 (May 1986), pp. 729–732.

Tralter, Gwendolyn. "I Thought What?" *Clearing House*, Vol. 60, no. 2 (October 1986), pp. 76–78.

Vandergrift, Kay. "Critical Thinking Misfired: The Implications of Student Responses to 'The Shooting Gallery'." *School Library Media Quarterly*, Vol. 15, no. 2 (Winter 1987), pp. 86–91.

"When Teachers Tackle Thinking Skills." *Educational Leadership*, Vol. 42 (November 1984), entire issue.

Annotated Bibliography: Books about the Middle Ages for Use with Sixth-Graders*

This annotated bibliography provides a list of trade books about Europe during the Middle Ages. The books are suitable for use with sixth-grade students. The teacher will be able to use the books to help build the students' background knowledge of life in Europe from about 500 A.D. to 1500 A.D. The teacher will also be able to use the books to help provide enrichment activities for the students.

SPECIFIC USES AND ACTIVITIES:

(P) = Preparation Stage   The activity is provided to build the students' background knowledge of life in Europe during the Middle Ages.

(R) = Reflection Stage   The activity is provided to enrich the students' knowledge of some particular topic related to the Middle Ages.

TITLE/AUTHOR/ PUBLISHER/ COPYRIGHT	SUMMARY	READ- ABILITY (SMOG) GRADE LEVEL	REASON FOR BOOK SELECTION	SPECIFIC USES AND ACTIVITIES
Adam of the Road Elizabeth Janet Gray Viking Press New York, 1942	Adam is an 11-year-old boy who lives in 13th-century England. His dog, Nick, disappears, and he suspects his father has taken the dog. So Adam takes to the road and travels to find his dog and minstrel father. He travels along many roads and encounters many different situations. (317 pages)	7	— Middle Ages background — Newbery Award winner — Illustrations	1. Read aloud the whole book during the time the students are involved in studying the Middle Ages. (P)(R) 2. Develop a vocabulary list. (P)(R)
Age of Discovery, 1450–1600 Pierre Miquel Silver Burdett Morristown, NJ, 1981	This book is one in the Silver Burdett History Series. The growth of the middle class, the changes in medicine and scientific thinking, the growth of religious conflicts, the invention of many new machines, and the development of industries and new jobs are all discussed. (64 pages)	6.5	— Colorful illustra- tions to accompany the text — Vocabulary list — Sequential list of important dates	1. Read aloud; show illustra- tions; discuss facts remem- bered while listening. (P) 2. Use as a resource for re- search. (R)

*Compiled by Wanda Hill.

TITLE/AUTHOR/ PUBLISHER/ COPYRIGHT	SUMMARY	READ-ABILITY (SMOG) GRADE LEVEL	REASON FOR BOOK SELECTION	SPECIFIC USES AND ACTIVITIES
Art of the Early Middle Ages François Souchal Abrams New York, 1968	There are 242 pictures of Romanesque to early Gothic art of the Middle Ages in this book. The book shows how religion and political aspects influenced the art forms during this period of time. (263 pages)	Adult	—Colorful pictures showing the architecture of castles, towers, churches, and cathedrals	1. Find 5 examples of a religious influence on art. (R) 2. Find 5 examples of a political influence on art. (R) 3. Show illustrations; discuss. (P)
Castle David Macaulay Houghton-Mifflin Boston, 1977	This is the story of King Kevin le Strange, who lives in the imaginary town of Aberwyvern. The text and detailed drawings present the planning and construction of a castle and adjoining town in 13th-century Wales. (80 pages)	7.8	—Detailed illustrations of castle construction	1. Read aloud; discuss construction of a castle. (P) 2. Use for supplemental reading. (P)(R) 3. Use as a source of drawing activities. (R)
The Castle Book Michael Berenstain McKay New York, 1977	This book tells about a tour through a typical medieval castle. The tour starts in the underground tunnel and dungeons and ends in the watchtowers. As you go through each section of the castle, various events and actions are described. (28 pages)	3	—Colorful illustrations —Large print —Low-level reader —Art activities	1. Show illustrations; discuss. (P) 2. Assign book to low-level reader; student makes list of sections of the castle; makes list of events that happen in each section. (P)(R)
The Castle Book Aldred Duggan Pantheon Books New York, 1961	The castle is described in relation to how it protects people from the enemy. Various battles are used as examples, and the book tells how enemies have disguised themselves and gotten into the castle. Types of armory are also discussed. (96 pages)	7	—Simple illustrations —Detailed information about the castle as protection	1. Use as supplemental reading for advanced readers. (P)(R) 2. Use as listening activity; list 5 questions on the board; read aloud; discuss answers. (P)
Days of Knights and Castles, 1066–1485 Pierre Miquel Silver Burdett Morristown, NJ, 1981	This book is one in the Silver Burdett Picture History Series. The life of people in a village and in a castle is discussed and represented in colorful illustrations. Population problems, famines, plagues, jousting tournaments, fashions, and currency are only some of the topics also discussed. (64 pages)	6.5	—Colorful illustrations to accompany the text —Vocabulary list —Sequential list of important events	1. Assign one student to read a specific section; share information with the class. (P)(R) 2. Read aloud; students create fact list. (P) 3. Discuss specific vocabulary that is listed and related to topic. (P)(R)

TITLE/AUTHOR/ PUBLISHER/ COPYRIGHT	SUMMARY	READ-ABILITY (SMOG) GRADE LEVEL	REASON FOR BOOK SELECTION	SPECIFIC USES AND ACTIVITIES
History of Art: An Introduction to Paintings and Sculpture Norton Lynton Warwick Press New York, 1981	Individual works of art from the time of Giotto to the 20th century are shown and discussed. The history of art is presented in short sections. There are segments on Medieval art, Romanesque art, Gothic art, Donatello, van Eyck, Botticelli, Michelangelo, Raphael, and Leonardo da Vinci. (179 pages)	7	— Artworks of famous artists of the Renaissance — Colorful illustrations	1. Research the life of an artist of the Renaissance; tell some characteristics of the art produced by that person. (R) 2. Show illustrations; discuss style of art; compare/ contrast specific art. (P)(R)
Illustrated Minute Biographies William A. DeWitt Grosset & Dunlap New York, 1964	This book contains 150 life stories of famous people. It includes many people who lived during the Middle Ages: Christopher Columbus, Erasmus, Galileo, Johann Gutenberg, Joan of Arc, Michelangelo, Marco Polo, Shakespeare, and many others. (160 pages)	6.5	— Short biographies in one book	1. Read aloud; discuss. (P) 2. Research source. (R) 3. Create a Fact Find based on information in selected biographies. (R)
Joan of Arc Joanna Johnston Doubleday New York, 1961	Joan was born in Domremy, France, and was the daughter of a common laborer. A strong interest in religion and superstitious tales led to many unusual happenings for Joan during her childhood. The book tells the story of her life from early childhood to her death and eventual sainthood. (89 pages)	6	— Biographical information — Illustrations of life in France in the 1400s and during battles	1. Read aloud a specific part of her life; discuss how she lived as compared to how the students of today live. (R) 2. Show illustrations; discuss what each represents. (P)(R) 3. Use as supplemental reading for students. (R)
Kings, Bishops, Knights, and Pawns: Life in a Feudal Society Ralph Arnold Grosset & Dunlap New York, 1964	The chapters at the beginning of this book describe how the feudal system began, how the lords and vassals shared responsibilities, and how a knight did his job. The middle chapters discuss the life of farmers, life around the castle, monastery life, and actions during a famous battle. The last chapters tell about the medieval town and the townspeople. (95 pages)	8.5	— Source of in-depth information — Detailed sketches and illustrations of castles, knights, and armor	1. Read aloud specific sections of facts; make fact sheet; discuss. (P) 2. Use as source of information for doing visual projects on castles, knights, armor. (R)

TITLE/AUTHOR/ PUBLISHER/ COPYRIGHT	SUMMARY	READ-ABILITY (SMOG) GRADE LEVEL	REASON FOR BOOK SELECTION	SPECIFIC USES AND ACTIVITIES
Knights in Armor Shirley Glubok Harper & Row New York, 1969	The Metropolitan Museum of Art (New York City) and the Kunsthisto-rishches Museum (Vienna, Austria) were the sources of many pictures of the knight's armor and weaponry. The text explains the various styles of armor and weapons, the rules of chivalry, and the steps for becoming a knight. (48 pages)	6.5	— Photographs of armor and weaponry used by knights during the Middle Ages — Diagrams of armor	1. Show photographs; discuss. (P) 2. Use as source of art projects concerning armor and weaponry for knights. (R) 3. Use as research source (R)
Knights of the Crusades Editors of *Horizon Magazine* and Jay Williams Harper & Row (American Publishing) New York, 1962	This book provides a historical account of feudalism and of the role of the knights. Paintings and sculptures help to describe battles, the Crusades, and castle life. (152 pages)	7.5	— Pictures of Middle Ages artworks — Detailed information	1. Read aloud specific section; discuss ideas and facts. (P) 2. Use as research source for art projects (R) 3. Show pictures; ask questions. (P)
Leonardo Jack Wasserman Doubleday New York, 1980	The 139 illustrations show the full range of Leonardo da Vinci's abilities as a painter, sculptor, and architectural theorist. His contributions to the fields of engineering, military science, anatomy, and music are also discussed. The book tells how he wrote using his left hand, but from right to left — like a mirror image. (179 pages)	Adult	— Illustrations showing the scope of Leonardo da Vinci's abilities — Biographical information	1. Read aloud interesting facts about his life; take notes; study skill (P) 2. Show illustrations; note the different media used. (P) 3. Discuss his advanced scientific theories on flying; show helicopter drawing. (P)(R)
Living in Castle Times Robyn Gee Usborne London, 1982	Thomas Middleton, his parents, and his sister live in a town during the Middle Ages. Home life, town life, shopping opportunities, school days, and a trip to a monastery are discussed. The roles of a man, woman, and child during the Middle Ages are compared and contrasted with those of modern day. (29 pages)	4.5	— Low-level reader — Colorful illustrations to accompany short paragraphs	1. Assign book to be read by a low-level reader; student does oral report. (P)(R) 2. Use as resource for artwork. (R)

TITLE/AUTHOR/ PUBLISHER/ COPYRIGHT	SUMMARY	READ-ABILITY (SMOG) GRADE LEVEL	REASON FOR BOOK SELECTION	SPECIFIC USES AND ACTIVITIES
Ferdinand Magellan Alan Blackwood Wayland East Sussex, England, 1985	This book tells about Magellan's life during the Renaissance. It describes his job as a page to King John of Portugal. King John had a love of the sea, and Magellan learned from him. Eventually, Magellan became a skilled and fearless sailor. The days of his explorations and the events leading up to his death are described. (32 pages)	5.5	—Colorful illustrations —Biographical information —Glossary of terms —List of main events in Magellan's life —Large print	1. Use as supplemental reading material. (P)(R) 2. Use as research source. (R) 3. Read aloud last voyage; discuss why Magellan did not make it around the world. (P)(R)
The Normans Anne & Barry Steel Rourke Vero Beach, FL, 1986	This book explains who the Normans were, how they took over England in 1066, and how they lived in villages, towns, and castles. At the back of the book are hints for making a castle and a shield. (24 pages)	4.5	—Low-level reader —Boldfaced vocabulary —Glossary —Large print —Colorful illustrations —Detailed information	1. Assign book to be read by a low-level reader; student creates poster listing important facts about the Normans. (P)(R) 2. Use as research source. (R)
Pantheon Story of Art for Young People Ariane Ruskin Batterberry Pantheon Books New York, 1975	This book tells the history of art and describes how the beliefs of the people of a period of time will influence art. There are several chapters that focus on Medieval times and the Renaissance. (160 pages)	6.8	—Colorful illustrations —Large print —Simple explanations	1. Show illustrations; discuss how the period could have influenced the art. (P)(R) 2. Use as research source. (R)
Marco Polo Gian Paolo Ceserani Putnam's New York, 1982	The story starts with a description of Marco's life in Venice while his father and uncle are in China. When they return to sell their goods, Marco is fascinated. When his father and uncle leave again, Marco goes with them. He spends years and years in and around China learning about the customs and new inventions. When he returns to Venice, he decides to write a book. (39 pages)	5.5	—Biographical information —Simple illustrations that dominate each page and depict life in Venice and China	1. Read aloud; list details about Marco Polo's life; discuss concerns that he had about China. (P)(R) 2. List new things he saw in China. (P) 3. Use as supplemental reader. (P)(R)

TITLE/AUTHOR/ PUBLISHER/ COPYRIGHT	SUMMARY	READ-ABILITY (SMOG) GRADE LEVEL	REASON FOR BOOK SELECTION	SPECIFIC USES AND ACTIVITIES
William Shakespeare Dorothy Turner Wayland East Sussex, England, 1985	This book tells about Shakespeare's life and his writing of poems and plays—comedies, tragedies, and histories. Information is also given concerning the presentation of his plays in modern times.	5.5	—Colorful illustrations —Biographical information —Glossary —List of Shakespeare's plays —Large print	1. Read aloud; list details about Shakespeare's early life. (P) 2. Discuss effect of his writings on people of his time. (P)(R)
Stories of Shakespeare Retold by Marchette Chute World New York, 1956	In this book are 36 of Shakespeare's comedies, tragedies, and histories retold in 20th-century language. Some of the narratives contain quotations from the original works. (351 pages)	Adult	—Sample of Shakespeare's writing —Stories in modern language	1. Read aloud some shorter works; discuss how they compare to stories of today. (P)(R) 2. Duplicate some quotations; discuss sentence structure, vocabulary. (P)(R)
Story of a Castle John S. Goodall Margaret K. McElderry Books New York, 1986	The book starts with a list of what Medieval events are going to be depicted in the pictures. Then the rest of the book is a series of pictures in two-page layouts. The pictures illustrate life in a typical English castle from the 1170s to the 1970s. (29 pages)	3	—Colorful watercolor pictures —No text for the student	1. Discuss each picture in small-group activity; assign writing activity as follow-up. (P) 2. Assign various low-level readers to write about what is happening in specific pictures. (P)(R) 3. Compare/contrast castle activities of the past and present. (R)

Annotated Bibliography of Multicultural Literature*

Multicultural literature is the current trend. With the influx of non-English-speaking children in our schools, the issue is obviously topical. Multicultural literature also acknowledges our nation's largest minority population, Afro-Americans, as well as the culture of Native Americans.

The purpose of this specific bibliography is to identify resources that expose students to cultures around the world and within our country's boundaries. Another objective is to sensitize and educate students to the similarities and differences that exist among these cultures.

This bibliography is organized according to the PAR learning framework. The first three books prepare readers by triggering prior knowledge and establishing purpose for the topic of multicultural issues. The next seven books assist the reader in the comprehension of existing issues surrounding the topic:

1. Students will understand the fears associated with experiencing or adjusting to a new culture.
2. Students will interpret the feelings and struggles of a child immigrating from a non-English-speaking country to the United States.
3. Students will gain an appreciation for the oral tradition of Native Americans as recorded in songs, myths, prayers, and chants.
4. Students will recreate historical moments in the life of Martin Luther King, Jr., as a crusader for the civil-rights movement.
5. Students will experience Chinese culture through the words of a boy of their own age.
6. Students will acquire an understanding of the hardships of refugees immigrating to our country for economic or political reasons.
7. Students will be able to compare and contrast two or more cultures.

The remaining books in this bibliography will enable students to reflect on their newly acquired information. The accompanying activities will provide for enrichment of the topic. Students will complete a comparative study of international folktales, sing Black spirituals, participate in cultural games, and hear the eloquence of an opera set in Ethiopia.

This bibliography was intended for students in second and third grades. Each book chosen for the bibliography should be of interest to a child in the targeted grades. The readability of each book was determined by using the Fry Readability Graph. A few of the books, designated for the preparation and reflection stages, may require teacher-guided reading due to their readability rating. The books that assist comprehension, however, should be easily read and eventually comprehended by students.

*Compiled by Mary Driebe.

	TITLE OF BOOK: *People*	TITLE OF BOOK: *Nine O'Clock Lullaby*
Bibliographic Information	*Author:* Peter Spier *Copyright:* 1980 *Publisher:* Delacorte	*Author:* Marilyn Singer *Copyright:* 1991 *Publisher:* HarperCollins
Readability Estimate	Fifth-grade readability	Fifth-grade readability
Annotation	The author highlights a plethora of world cultures in his book. The emphasis is on the vast differences and yet subtle similarities that exist among world cultures. Spier leads his audience to the conclusion that these existing differences contribute to the beauty of our world.	While a child is read a bedtime story in Brooklyn, morning music is heard in India and a grandfather rests in a Japanese garden. Readers are transported across time zones to distant lands, catching a quick glimpse of other world cultures.
Reason for Selection	—large print —records the script of 40 languages; depicts the international foods, holidays, homes, games, and clothing representative of a variety of cultures —appealing to children due to *busy* illustrations [similar to a *Where's Waldo?* book]	—provides an illustrated explanation of time zones —colorful illustrations demonstrate the culture, shelter, food, and clothing of the chosen country
PAR Placement and Activities	This book would entice readers to the topic of multicultural issues. The book would be used at the preparation stage to set purpose for the unit. The activity, What-I-Know, would stimulate prior knowledge and then continually monitor comprehension of the book.	This book would be instrumental at the preparation stage of presenting our topic. A graphic organizer would organize the information and illustrations offered to the reader.

	TITLE OF BOOK: *African Journey*	TITLE OF BOOK: *How My Parents Learned to Eat*
Bibliographic Information	*Author:* John Chiasson *Copyright:* 1987 *Publisher:* Bradbury Press	*Author:* Ina R. Friedman *Copyright:* 1984 *Publisher:* Houghton Mifflin
Readability Estimate	Eighth-grade readability	Second-grade readability
Annotation	John Chiasson, a photojournalist, traveled through Africa capturing its beauty, people, wildlife, and ever-existing poverty. Chiasson takes the reader from rural scenery to the city of Dakar and then the squalor of Ethiopia.	A sailor stationed in Yokohama, Japan, courts a schoolgirl. Before sharing a meal, they each feel anxiety in regard to the other's cultural table rituals (chopsticks vs. silverware).
Reason for Selection	—photography is vivid —includes maps, captions, and chapter titles —provides a visual resource	—can be read individually by the majority of the targeted audience —exposes fears that even adults have when adjusting to or experiencing a new culture
PAR Placement and Activities	*African Journey* will prepare students for multicultural issues by creating a visual image. Students will explore the book using the previewing activity. Cooperative groups will be established. Due to the readability estimate, each group would be provided with a teacher rewrite of the introduction.	I would use this book to assist comprehension of our topic. Prior to reading, I would provide students with the opportunity to use chopsticks and compare their experience to using silverware. After reading, I would use the QAR example to generate discussion at all levels of thought.

	TITLE OF BOOK: *I Hate English*	**TITLE OF BOOK:** *Dancing Teepees*
Bibliographic Information	*Author:* Ellen Levine *Copyright:* 1989 *Publisher:* Scholastic Inc.	*Author:* Virginia Driving Hawk Sneve *Copyright:* 1989 *Publisher:* Holiday House
Readability Estimate	Third-grade readability	Fourth-grade readability
Annotation	A young girl and her family immigrate to the United States and settle in New York's Chinatown. Mei Mei has a difficult time adjusting to the language until a sympathetic American teacher is able to win her trust and love.	The author has selected a variety of stories, chants, songs, prayers, and poems that have been passed through generations of Native American cultures.
Reason for Selection	—addresses a current issue of the multicultural topic —involves the reader in Mei Mei's struggle as well as providing a glimpse of the Chinese culture.	—illustrations depict a variety of paintings, beading, and designs representative of many of the Indian tribes, including Navaho and Sioux —presents an oral tradition preserved by the first culture inhabiting America
PAR Placement and Activities	This book will assist comprehension. The three-level guide would assist my readers to *interpret* Mei Mei's feelings as a new immigrant from a foreign country and to understand the concepts presented by the author.	*Dancing Teepees* would further assist students' comprehension of the cultures existing in our country. The use of marginal glosses for various selections might explain some of the imagery or provide additional background.

	TITLE OF BOOK: *Martin Luther King, Jr.: The Story of a Dream*	**TITLE OF BOOK:** *Our Home Is the Sea*
Bibliographic Information	*Author:* June Behrens *Copyright:* 1979 *Publisher:* Regensteiner	*Author:* Riki Levinson *Copyright:* 1988 *Publisher:* E. P. Dutton
Readability Estimate	Fourth-grade readability	Second-grade readability
Annotation	This play is set in a classroom, as a group of students begin to learn about Martin Luther King and his civil-rights accomplishments that won him much acclaim and respect. Every other scene is a flashback to a historical moment in the civil-rights movement.	Against the backdrop of the cosmopolitan city of Hong Kong, a small boy leaves school to meet his father at the wharves. The love and pride a small boy has for his home and culture are portrayed in this book.
Reason for Selection	—biography of an Afro-American who contributed positively to the multicultural issues of his time —the format of the biography is a play	—conveys the perspective of a family from another culture content and satisfied with their home —oil-painting illustrations are powerful —recreates a child's life in Hong Kong
PAR Placement and Activities	This play would be produced to assist comprehension of the issues. Prior to reading and performing the play, I would use the factstorming activity to identify the prior knowledge of my students in regard to King.	I would use this book to assist comprehension of our topic. Prior to reading, I would distribute a self-inventory to trigger prior knowledge and have students gain familiarity with the vocabulary of the book.

	TITLE OF BOOK: *How Many Days to America?*	TITLE OF BOOK: *Jafta and the Wedding*
Bibliographic Information	*Author:* Eve Bunting　*Copyright:* 1988 *Publisher:* Clarion Books	*Author:* Hugh Lewin *Illustrator:* Lisa Kopper *Publisher:* Carolrhoda Books　*Copyright:* 1981
Readability Estimate	Second-grade readability	Fifth-grade readability
Annotation	A family departs a Caribbean island in the hope of reaching America and its many freedoms. They must leave their possessions and relatives and then encounter many obstacles on their journey. When they do reach the United States, they are eventually met with a welcome and a meal of celebration.	Jafta, a South African boy, recounts the daily preparations of the week prior to his sister's wedding.
Reason for Selection	—realistic depiction of the plight of refugees —current Thanksgiving story motif	—large print —description of a South African wedding is ideal to be used in a comparative study with American weddings —South African vocabulary used throughout the book is explained on the concluding page of the book
PAR Placement and Activities	This book will assist comprehension of the feelings and emotions experienced by ethnic groups as they leave their home for the United States. The DRTA would guide the reading of the book, monitoring students' comprehension of the story line.	*Jafta and the Wedding* will be used to assist the reader in comprehending the topic. Overlap mapping will be a well-matched activity for the comparison/contrast study of weddings in both cultures.

	TITLE OF BOOK: *Children's Games from Many Lands*	TITLE OF BOOK: *Walk Together Children*
Bibliographic Information	*Author:* Nina Millen　*Copyright:* 1965 *Publisher:* Friendship Press	*Author:* Ashley Bryan　*Copyright:* 1974 *Publisher:* Atheneum
Readability Estimate	Sixth-grade readability	Fourth-grade readability
Annotation	A complete collection of 258 games played by children of 64 different countries. The games vary in activity level, but each game aims for a cooperative exchange between players.	Bryan has included 24 spirituals of a variety of rhythm, subjects, and moods.
Reason for Selection	—extremely thorough collection of games —includes games from Indian tribes —organized format and directions	—book of spirituals; very authentic written portrayal of the Black American heritage —illustrations accompany each spiritual —music and lyrics are published
PAR Placement and Activities	Teaching students games from various countries would be a reinforcement exercise. I would like to use a variation on the Mystery Clue Game to capitalize on sequential order of the international games. The class would be divided into teams and each team given a game to put in sequence.	This book would be used in the reflection stage. A cloze activity would be a beneficial activity in that it would emphasize the rhythm and repetition characteristic of black spirituals. The introduction should be rewritten to a manageable readability so that students could learn from it.

	TITLE OF BOOK: *The Two Stonecutters*	TITLE OF BOOK: *Ashanti to Zulu*
Bibliographic Information	*Author:* Eve Titus *Copyright:* 1967 *Publisher:* Doubleday	*Author:* Margaret Musgrove *Copyright:* 1976 *Publisher:* Dial Books for Young Readers
Readability Estimate	Sixth-grade readability	Sixth-grade readability
Annotation	In this Japanese folktale, an elderly stonecutter foolishly uses six wishes granted to him by the Goddess of the Forest. He is continuously discontent with his position in life, desiring to be more powerful and more rich. He is finally rescued from the consequences by his brother, who held the seventh and last wish. A lesson on the misfortunes of greed is learned.	Musgrove uses the 26 letters of the alphabet as a guide through the traditions of 26 African peoples. Musgrove conveys the great diversity among the African population and their unyielding loyalty to their customs.
Reason for Selection	—a folktale —sequential rhythm —repetitious —exceptional storyline	—Caldecott Award winner —pronunciation key to each vocabulary word provided —each word is defined and then used in the contextual setting of the culture —map of Africa marking the location of each identified people
PAR Placement and Activities	This book will encourage reflection on multicultural issues when combined with a jot chart activity. A comparison study of three international folktales will be constructed. The two other titles include *The Treasure* and *Mufaro's Beautiful Daughters*.	This book will be read to reflect on our topic. Capitalizing on the format of the book, a vocabulary activity could be used following the reading. A word puzzle could be developed by the teacher.

	TITLE OF BOOK: *The Treasure*	TITLE OF BOOK: *Mufaro's Beautiful Daughters*
Bibliographic Information	*Author:* Uri Shulevitz *Copyright:* 1978 *Publisher:* Farrar, Straus & Giroux	*Author:* John Steptoe *Copyright:* 1987 *Publisher:* Lothrop, Lee and Shepard Books
Readability Estimate	Third-grade readability	Fifth-grade readability
Annotation	The timeless cliché "Sometimes one must travel far to discover what is near" is taught to the audience through an elderly man's search for a treasure.	When the king decides to marry, the two most beautiful daughters in the land are sent for. Although both daughters have outward beauty, there is a vast difference in their spirits. On the journey the king disguises himself as an old woman, a hungry boy, and a small garden snake. Each time he is met with kindness by only one daughter: the daughter he intends to marry.
Reason for Selection	—winner of the Caldecott Award —one of the few books located depicting life and culture in an Eastern European city	—winner of the Caldecott Award —an authentic folktale collected from the Zimbabwe heritage —the illustrations were inspired from an archeological dig in Zimbabwe
PAR Placement and Activities	This book will encourage reflection on multicultural issues when combined with a jot chart activity. A comparison study of three international folktales will be constructed. The two other titles include *The Two Stonecutters* and *Mufaro's Beautiful Daughters*.	This book will encourage reflection on multicultural issues when combined with a jot chart activity. A comparison study of three international folktales will be constructed. The two other titles include *The Two Stonecutters* and *The Treasure*.

	TITLE OF BOOK: *Aida*	TITLE OF BOOK: *Jambo Means Hello: Swahili Alphabet Book*
Bibliographic Information	*Author:* Leontyne Price *Copyright:* 1990 *Publisher:* Culliver Books, Harcourt Brace Jovanovich	*Author:* Muriel Feelings *Copyright:* 1974 *Publisher:* Dial Press
Readability Estimate	Sixth-grade readability	Fifth-grade readability
Annotation	A beautiful fairy tale set in the country of Ethiopia. A princess named Aida is captured by the Egyptians during a struggle between the two countries. Aida's growing love for the leader of the Egyptian army tests her loyalty to her country and her family.	Twenty-four Swahili words have been selected to correspond to the 24 Swahili letters of the alphabet. Each word chosen by the author is explained in context with the culture of East Africa.
Reason for Selection	—illustrations are created by a Caldecott medalist —based on an opera by Giuseppi Verdi —retold by a premier opera vocalist	—pronunciation key provided for each vocabulary word —map of Africa locating areas where the Swahili language is spoken —definition of each word is provided —words are placed in the contextual setting of the culture —an explanation of the art medium used for the illustrations
PAR Placement and Activities	*Aida* would be read to reinforce our topic. In light of the drama and the climactic plot, I would use the book to motivate students to write their own story. The activity I would enlist therefore would be guided writing with a process approach.	The book would serve as a reflection story. I would use a postreading exercise, monopolizing on the vocabulary presented to the reader. I would construct a magic square activity.

Children's Periodicals Featuring Nonfiction Articles

Boy's Life
Chickadee
Classical Calliope
Cobblestone
Cricket
Current Events
Current Science
Dynamath
The Electric Company
Faces
Highlights for Children
Junior Scholastic

The Mini Page
National Geographic World
Odyssey
Owl
Ranger Rick
Science World
Sesame Street
Stone Soup
3-2-1 Contact
Turtle
Your Big Back Yard
Zillions

Periodicals That Review Children's Literature*

Appraisal: Science Books for Young People.
Bookbird: International Periodical on Literature for Children and Young People.
Booklist. American Library Association.
Book Links: Connecting Books, Libraries, and Classrooms. American Library Association.
Bulletin of the Center for Children's Books.
CBC Features. Children's Book Council.
Children's Literature Association Quarterly. Children's Literature Association, University of Calgary.
Children's Literature in Education. Agathon Press.
The Horn Book Magazine. Anita Silvey, editor. Horn Book Pub.
Journal of Youth Services in Libraries (formerly Top of the News). Association of Library Services to Children and Young Adult Services Division.
The Kobrin Letter.
Language Arts. National Council of Teachers of English.
The Lion and the Unicorn. Department of English, Brooklyn College.
The New Advocate. Joel Taxel, editor; Christopher Gordon, publisher.
The New York Times Book Review. Weekly column in the New York Times.
Phaedrus: An International Journal of Children's Literature Research. Fairleigh Dickinson University.
Publisher's Weekly. Bowker, publisher.
The Reading Teacher. International Reading Association.
School Library Journal. Bowker, publisher.
School Library Media Quarterly. American Library Association.
Science and Children. National Science Teachers Association.
Scientific American.
The Web: Wonderfully Exciting Books. Ohio State University.
Wilson Library Bulletin. Wilson Publishers.

*Compiled by Linda Baughman.

Additional Resources for Finding Literature

Association for Supervision and Curriculum Development
1250 N. Pitt Street
Alexandria, VA 22314
Telephone (703) 549-9110

California State Department of Education, Sacramento, CA

Center for Education Statistics, U.S. Department of Education, Washington, DC

ERIC Clearinghouse, Urbana, IL

Evaluation, Dissemination, and Assessment Center, University of California, Los Angeles

Georgetown Center for Applied Linguistics, Washington, DC

International Reading Association
800 Barksdale Road
PO Box 8139
Newark, DE 19714-8139

National Clearinghouse for Bilingual Education, Rosslyn, VA

National Council of Teachers of English
1111 Kenyon Road
Urbana, IL 61801

National Institute of Education, Washington, DC

TESOL (Teachers of English to Speakers of Other Languages), Washington, DC

U.S. Department of Education, Washington, DC

Virginia Beach in a Box: A Social Studies Unit for Third-Graders*

Diagnostic Instruments

Interest Inventory

Name of student: _____

1. After school I usually like to _____
2. In the evening I usually like to _____
3. On the weekends I like to _____
4. I like to play _____
5. My family and I like to _____
6. I belong to _____
7. When I am grown _____
8. I think my father and mother want me _____
9. I think museums are _____
10. I enjoy school most _____

Attitude Inventory

Directions: Write 1 — I agree. 2 — I disagree. 3 — I am undecided.

_____ 1. Virginia Beach is a great place for a vacation.
_____ 2. There is a lot to do in Virginia Beach.
_____ 3. It would be more fun to live in the mountains than in Virginia Beach.
_____ 4. Virginia Beach is a safe city in which to live.
_____ 5. Museums are boring.
_____ 6. It would be interesting to learn about Virginia Beach.
_____ 7. Citizens should know about the city in which they live.
_____ 8. It would be more fun to live on a farm than in Virginia Beach.
_____ 9. Virginia Beach is unattractive.
_____ 10. Cities should have lots of parks for families.

A Cloze Passage: Christmas at Adam Thoroughgood's House

It was the night before Christmas at Capt. Adam Thoroughgood's plantation on the Lynnhaven River. Great logs burned in the _____ and bread baked in _____ brick oven which got _____ warmth from the fire. _____ and his wife Frances _____ talking together in their _____ story-and-a-half _____ house. The busy mother

*Developed by Barbara Teuscher.

504

_____ the family had worked _____ weeks cooking and preparing _____ the great Christmas party _____ take place next day. _____ year was 1675.

Upstairs, _____ in their trundle beds _____ deep feather mattresses, were _____ sons: Argoll, John, Adam, Francis, _____ Robert. Baby Rose slumbered _____ a wooden cradle which _____ Thoroughgood now and then _____ with her foot.

"Adam," _____ Frances Thoroughgood. "The ship _____ England is overdue. I _____ worried about the young _____, Master Lovitt, whom we _____ to educate the boys. _____ also long for the _____ we have ordered from _____. I had so hoped _____ would be here in _____ for the children's Christmas.

"_____ bother your pretty head," _____ comforted his wife. "Didn't _____ old carol you were _____ to baby Rose have _____ about 'I saw three _____ come sailing in, on _____ Day, on Christmas Day'?"

"_____ have hummed for _____, and prayed too," replied _____, "and looked long down _____ river, but never a _____ in sight.

"Well, _____ time for you to _____. I have told young Moses _____ can wake the boys _____ soon as it is _____. Caleb will build the _____ up and Sukey has _____ breakfast started. Merry Christmas, _____ Thoroughgood. The clock points _____ twelve."

The winter sunrise colored the eastern sky and was reflected in the waters of the Lynnhaven.

Answer sheet for cloze test:

1. fireplace	18. Madam	35. ships
2. the	19. rocked	36. Christmas
3. its	20. said	37. I
4. Adam	21. from	38. weeks
5. sat	22. am	39. Frances
6. snug	23. teacher	40. the
7. brick	24. engaged	41. sail
8. of	25. I	42. it's
9. for	26. things	43. dream
10. for	27. London	44. he
11. to	28. they	45. as
12. The	29. time	46. light
13. asleep	30. Don't	47. fire
14. on	31. Adam	48. the
15. five	32. the	49. Madam
16. and	33. humming	50. to
17. in	34. words	

Philosophy

It is the responsibility of today's schools to educate our students to be active thinkers and problem solvers. We cannot accomplish this goal if we continue to have teacher-directed instructional strategies. Progressive theorists have suggested that the role of teachers will have to change dramatically. Teachers would not teach; they would become facilitators. The goal of teaching in the content area would be to encourage the students to be active in discovering and structuring reality for themselves, to become assertive inquirers and managers of their environment, and to encourage students to develop their own understanding and to draw inferences, rather than be given information. These rather lofty goals can be accomplished through such student-oriented strategies as this unit plan.

Concepts to Be Taught

1. To have students acquire some knowledge of the historical background of Virginia Beach.
2. To have students acquire some knowledge of the geography of Virginia Beach.
3. To have students acquire some understanding of how the city government operates.
4. To have students develop skills in collecting, evaluating, and organizing information from a variety of sources.
5. To have students develop skills in interpreting data from maps, charts, and graphs.
6. To encourage inductive thinking.

Materials

Maps

1. Bicentennial Map
2. Chamber of Commerce, Ocean Front
3. Historical Map of Virginia Beach
4. 1930 Map at Princess Anne Court House
5. Planning Dept. Map of Virginia Beach
6. Revolutionary War Map
7. Virginia Beach

Miscellaneous

8. Flow Chart — Government
9. Virginia Seal

Pamphlets and Brochures

10. The Battle of the Virginia Capes
11. Council-Manager Plan — Answers to Your Questions
12. Virginia Beach, Va., Municipal Government: An Outline
13. Virginia Beach — A Self-Guided Motor Tour
14. Annotated Pictures of Historical Sites in Virginia Beach
15. Brochures of Francis Land House, Lynnhaven House, and Rose Hall

A-V Materials

16. Virginia Beach, An Emerging City (Film)
17. Videotape of Virginia Beach

Books

18. Kyle, L. V. *The Witch of Pungo*. 1973. JCP Corp. of Virginia Beach
19. *A Country Woman's Scrapbook*. 1980. JCP Corp. of Virginia Beach
20. *Virginia Beach: A Pictorial History*. 1974. Richmond, Va.: Hale Publishing Co.

Concept Key for Materials

MATERIALS	\	CONCEPTS					
		1	2	3	4	5	6
1.		x	x			x	x
2.			x			x	x
3.		x	x			x	x
4.		x	x			x	x
5.				x	x	x	x
6.		x				x	x
7.			x			x	x
8.			x		x	x	x
9.					x		
10.		x	x				
11.				x	x		
12.				x	x		
13.						x	
14.		x			x		
15.		x			x		
16.		x	x	x	x		
17.		x	x	x	x		
18.		x	x				
19.		x	x				
20.		x	x		x		

Activities

1. Show film, *Virginia Beach: An Emerging City*.
2. Play tape, *Virginia Beach*.
3. Administer interest inventory.
4. Administer attitude scale.
5. Begin reading *The Witch of Pungo* aloud to the class.
6. Visit City Hall chambers.
7. Assign individuals or groups to visit places of interest and report to class-room—either oral or written, with displays and posters. Places might be Lynnhaven House, Mt. Trashmore, Seashore State Park, Back Bay, Fort Story.
8. Take field trip to Cape Henry Lighthouse and Cross.
9. Take walking field trip to old Coast Guard Station and the Norwegian Lady.
10. Construct a lighthouse using pattern.
11. Interview a longtime resident of the city concerning changes that have taken place and the city's history.
12. Structured overview of Virginia Beach
13. Cloze procedure
14. DRTA
15. Three-level study guide
16. Concept guide
17. Make a time line of events in the city.
18. Locate on the outline map the community in which they live.
19. Identify a problem in the city. Research the problem and detail some possible solutions.
20. Identify the characteristics of a good leader.
21. Design a mural showing the most important events in the development of the city.
22. Plan a model city.
23. Design a bumper sticker.
24. Make charts showing the amount of local tax money spent for various services in the community.
25. Make a graph showing the number of qualified voters in the city and the percentage who voted in the last five elections.
26. Maintain bulletin board of current Virginia Beach news.
27. Have a Virginia Beach Historic Fair as a culminating activity. Students wear old costumes, cook old-style food, display homemade crafts, play old games, hold contests, etc.
28. End-of-unit evaluation

Concept Key for Activities

ACTIVITIES	CONCEPTS					
	1	2	3	4	5	6
1.	x	x	x	x		
2.	x	x	x	x		
3.	–	–	–	–	–	–
4.	–	–	–	–	–	–
5.	x	x	x	x	x	x
6.			x	x		x
7.	x	x	x	x		x
8.	x			x		
9.	x			x		
10.				x	x	x
11.	x	x	x	x		x
12.	x	x	x	x	x	x
13.						x
14.						x
15.	x	x			x	
16.	x	x				
17.	x	x	x	x	x	x
18.		x			x	x
19.				x		x
20.				x		x
21.	x			x		x
22.				x		x
23.						x
24.				x	x	x
25.				x	x	x
26.	x	x	x	x	x	x
27.	x	x	x	x	x	x
28.	x	x	x	x	x	x

Fry's Readability Formula for *The Witch of Pungo*. Kyle, L. V., 1973, JCP Corp. of Virginia Beach.

    Paragraph I
        Sentences: 6.50
        Syllables: 129
    Paragraph II
        Sentences: 6.25
        Syllables: 123
    Paragraph II
        Sentences: 6
        Syllables: 128
    Grade level: 6th grade

DRTA Synopsis

Title: *The Witch of Pungo*. Kyle, L. V. 1973, JCP Corp. Virginia Beach.

Discussion: Joey looked at the title and the few pictures. He said he had been to Pungo. He described it as being neat, pretty, and having lots of farms. Then we discussed witches—his perception was the stereotyped appearance of a tall black hat, black dress, red eyes, wart on the end of her nose, and long fingers with warts on her hands. They did evil magic on people. They don't live today, but did long ago.

Prediction: The story is about a witch that lived in Pungo a long time ago who did evil things to people.

Evaluation: I fully endorse this teaching technique as a guided reading process. It teaches the correct reading process, develops self-worth in the students, and provides a vehicle for students to go from the concrete level of thinking to the more formal and abstract.

Structured Overview

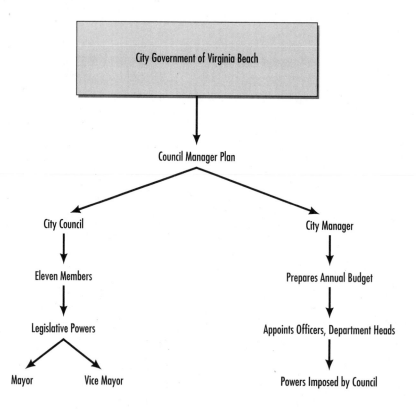

Three-Level Study Guide: *Blackbeard's Treasure*

Part I: Getting the facts.

Directions: Read each statement below. Check each true statement about the story.

_____ 1. While boating, Lem discovered a trunk buried in the sand.
_____ 2. Lem built a lookout where Blackbeard was supposed to have his.
_____ 3. Blackbeard was a famous pirate operating off Cape Henry.
_____ 4. Blackbeard's lookout was in Chesapeake Bay.
_____ 5. Edward Teach was Blackbeard's real name.
_____ 6. Blackbeard's head was cut off and placed on the bowsprit of a ship.
_____ 7. It is said that Blackbeard's headless body swam seven times around his ship and then sank from sight.
_____ 8. The chest that Lem found was about 300 years old.
_____ 9. The buried gold allowed Lem to go to college in England.
_____ 10. There was not enough gold to take care of Lem's family and plantation.

Part II: What did the author mean? (Check three statements.)

_____ 1. Everyone liked Blackbeard.
_____ 2. Pirates were thieves and murderers.
_____ 3. Lem actually found a buried treasure.
_____ 4. Lem liked learning and school.
_____ 5. Lem was just a pleasure seeker.

Part III: How can we use these meanings? Check those that apply.

_____ 1. Where there's smoke, there's fire.
_____ 2. Silence is golden.
_____ 3. You can't judge a book by its cover.
_____ 4. The early bird catches the worm.
_____ 5. Every cloud has a silver lining.
_____ 6. Leave no stone unturned.

Concept Guide: *The Witch of Pungo*

Check the following statements if they are true from your reading.

_____ 1. Women who sold their souls to the Devil were witches.
_____ 2. In return they received magical powers from the evil spirit.
_____ 3. In some parts of the world there are people who practice witchcraft.
_____ 4. If her neighbors did not like her, they could say a woman was a witch.

_____ 5. If a witch was ducked and drowned, she was innocent.

_____ 6. If she untied herself, and was able to swim, she was called a witch.

_____ 7. Grace Sherwood was an ugly woman with long black hair and a wart on the end of her nose.

_____ 8. It was said Grace Sherwood had come through the keyhole into a lady's bedroom and changed her into a big black cat and rode away on her.

_____ 9. Grace Sherwood danced around cows in the pasture and made them give sour milk.

_____ 10. Grace Sherwood drowned; therefore she was not a witch.

Place the above sentences under the correct categories.

DO WITCHES EXIST?   **TRAITS OF WITCHES**   **FATE OF WITCHES**

Virginia Beach in a Box: Unit Test

Answer these items True or False. 2 points each.

_____ 1. Two council members are elected from each borough.

_____ 2. Virginia Beach ranks third in population in comparison with other cities in Virginia.

_____ 3. The Mennonites are leaving Virginia Beach because it is becoming too heavily populated.

_____ 4. Agriculture and tourism are two industries in Virginia Beach.

_____ 5. Oceana is one of the largest submarine bases in the world.

_____ 6. Camp Pendleton is located at Cape Henry.

_____ 7. Tunis was the first name of Oceana.

_____ 8. Virginia Beach ranks third in land size in comparison with other cities in Virginia.

_____ 9. Four council members are elected at-large.

_____ 10. Walking was the main way of travel in early Princess Anne County.

Fill in the blank with the correct answer. 20 points.

1. We have _____ council members in Virginia Beach.

2. The _____ connects Virginia Beach with the Eastern shore.

3. The _____ and the _____ are two historic houses in Virginia Beach.

4. The president of the city council is called the _____ .

5. Chesapeake Bay means "_____ ."

6. _____ and _____ are two churches of early Princess Anne County that are still in use today.

7. _____ and _____ are two colleges in Virginia Beach.

Match Section A to Section B. 20 points.

SECTION A

a. Adam Thoroughgood
b. fishermen
c. council-manager
d. Kempsville
e. Neptune

f. a witch
g. Norwegian Lady
h. George Washington
i. city manager
j. Cape Henry

SECTION B

_____ **1.** He was responsible for the first lighthouse at Cape Henry.
_____ **2.** The form of government we have in Virginia Beach.
_____ **3.** The name of the festival held in the fall in Virginia Beach.
_____ **4.** He renamed the Chesopean River the Lynnhaven River.
_____ **5.** The place where the first permanent settler set foot.
_____ **6.** Grace Sherwood was one of these.
_____ **7.** Title of the head of the city government.
_____ **8.** Erected to the memory of people lost in a shipwreck off the beach.
_____ **9.** The first settlers in Virginia Beach after the Indians.
_____ **10.** The name of the town at Kemps Landing.

Identify. 16 points.

1. Name two capes at the entrance to the Chesapeake Bay.
2. Name two military bases located in Virginia Beach.
3. Name the four boundaries of Virginia Beach.

Answer the following questions in one to two sentences. 7 points each.

1. Early Indians used the area around present-day Pungo for what reason?
2. In 1824 the Court House was built at Princess Anne. Why was it felt this was a good location?
3. Name four of the seven boroughs in Virginia Beach.
4. Describe early schools in Virginia Beach.

You may use the back of your test to complete these answers.

Answer Sheet to Unit Test   **TRUE/FALSE**

1. False   **6.** False
2. True   **7.** True
3. True   **8.** True
4. True   **9.** True
5. False   **10.** False

FILL-IN-THE-BLANK

1. Eleven
2. Chesapeake Bay Bridge Tunnel
3. Adam Thoroughgood House, John B. Dey Home, the Huggins House, the Hermitage
4. Mayor
5. Mother of waters
6. Old Donation, Eastern Shore Chapel, Nimmo Church, and Oak Grove Church
7. Tidewater Community College, Virginia Wesleyan College

MATCHING

1. h
2. c
3. e
4. a
5. j
6. f
7. i
8. g
9. b
10. d

IDENTIFY

1. Cape Henry and Cape Charles
2. Fort Story, Little Creek, Oceana
3. North — Chesapeake Bay
   East — Atlantic Ocean
   South — North Carolina
   West — Norfolk

SHORT-ANSWER ESSAY

1. Hunting
2. Well-populated area
3. Kempsville, Pungo, Blackwater, Virginia Beach, Lynnhaven, Princess Anne, and Bayside
4. Small one-room schoolhouses

Student Daily Log Sheet

Name _____

ACTIVITY	I LEARNED A LOT	I LEARNED SOME	I DIDN'T LEARN	I LIKED IT	I DIDN'T LIKE IT	I NEEDED HELP
1.	x			x		x
2.	x			x		
26.	x			x		
23.		x		x		x
11.	x			x		
10.			x			x

Teacher's Activity Roll

NAME	DAY 1	DAY 2	DAY 3	DAY 4	DAY 5	DAY 6	DAY 7
John	1,2	26,4,15	10	16	18,25	11,23	5,7
Nan	1,2	26,4,15	10	16	18,25	11,23	5,7
Joe	1,2	26,4,15	10	16	18,25	11,23	5,7
Tom	1,2	25,4	15	10	18,16	11,23	5,7
Sue	1,2	25,4	15	10	18,16	11,23	5,7
Sally	1,2	25,4	15	10	18,16	11,23	5,7

References

Aaronson, S. (1975). Note taking improvement: A combined auditory, functional and psychological approach. *Journal of Reading. 19* (1), 8–12.

Abrahams, R. D. (1976). *Talking black.* Rowley, MA: Newbury House.

Abrami, P. C., Chambers, B., d'Apollonia, S., Farrell, M., & DeSimone, C. (1992). "Group outcome: The relationship between group learning outcome, attributional style, academic achievement, and self-concept." *Contemporary Educational Psychology, 17,* 201–210.

Abruscato, J. (1993). Early results and tentative implications from the Vermont portfolio project. *Phi Delta Kappan, 74,* 474–477.

Adler, A. (1931). *What life should mean to you.* New York: Capricorn.

Adler, M. J. (1982). *The Paideia proposal.* New York: Macmillan.

Adler, M. J., & Van Doren, C. (1972). *How to read a book.* New York: Simon & Schuster.

Afflerbach, P. (1987). How are main idea statements constructed? Watch the experts. *Journal of Reading, 30,* 512–518.

Alexander, P. A., Hare, V. C., & Garner, R. (1984). The effects of time, access, and question type on response accuracy and frequency of lookbacks in older, proficient readers. *Journal of Reading Behavior, 16,* 119–130.

Allen, R., Brown, K., & Yatvin, J. (1986). *Learning language through communication: A functional approach.* Belmont, CA: Wadsworth.

Allington, R. L. (1991). How policy and regulation influence instruction for at-risk learners: Or why poor readers rarely comprehend well and probably never will. In L. Idol & B. F. Jones (Eds.), *Educational values and cognitive instruction: Implications for reform* (pp. 277–299). Hillsdale, NJ: Erlbaum.

Alvermann, D. (1987a). Discussion strategies for content area reading. In D. Alvermann, D. R. Dillon, & D. G. O'Brien (Eds.), *Using discussion to promote reading comprehension* (pp. 34–42). Newark, DE: International Reading Association.

Alvermann, D. (1987b). Integrating oral and written language. In D. Alvermann, D. Moore, & M. Conley (Eds.), *Research within reach: Secondary school reading* (pp. 109–129). Newark, DE: International Reading Association.

Alvermann, D. (1991). The discussion web: A graphic aid for learning across the curriculum. *The Reading Teacher, 44,* 92–98.

Amlund, J. T., Kardash, C. A. M., & Kulhavy, R. W. (1986). Repetitive reading and recall of expository text. *Reading Research Quarterly, 21,* 49–53.

Ammons, R. I. (1987). Trade books in the content areas. Tempe, AZ: Jan V.

Anderson, B. V., & Barnitz, J. G. (1984). Cross-cultural schemata and reading comprehension instruction. *Journal of Reading, 29,* 610–616.

Anderson, R. C. (1985). The role of the reader's schema in comprehension, learning and memory. In H. Singer & R. B. Ruddell (Eds.), *Theoretical models and processes of reading* (3rd ed.) (372–384). Newark, DE: International Reading Association.

Anderson, R. C., & Freebody, P. (1981). Vocabulary knowledge. In J. T. Guthrie (Ed.), *Comprehension and teaching: Research perspectives* (pp. 80–82). Newark, DE: International Reading Association.

Anderson, R. C., Hiebert, E., Scott, J., & Wilkinson, I. (1984). *Becoming a nation of readers*. Washington, DC: The National Institute of Education.

Anderson, R. C., & Pearson, P. D. (1984). A schema-theoretic view of basic processes in reading comprehension. In P. D. Pearson (Ed.), *Handbook of reading research* (255–291). New York: Longman.

Anderson, T., & Armbruster, B. (1984). Content area textbooks. In R. C. Anderson, J. Osborn, & R. J. Tierney (Eds.), *Learning to read in American schools: Basal readers and content texts* (pp. 193–226). Hillsdale, NJ: Erlbaum.

Angeletti, S. (1991). Encouraging students to think about what they read. *The Reading Teacher, 45,* 288–296.

Annis, L., & Davis, J. K. (1978, February). Study techniques — Comparing their effectiveness. *The American Biology Teacher,* pp. 106–110.

Annis, L., & Davis, J. K. (1982). A normative study of students' reported preferred study techniques. *Reading World, 21,* 201–207.

Applebee, A. N. (1981). *Writing in the secondary school.* Urbana, IL: National Council of Teachers of English.

Applebee, A. N., Langer, J., & Mullis, I. (1987). *Learning to be literate in America: Reading, writing and reasoning.* Princeton, NJ: Educational Testing Service.

Arlin, P. K. (1984). *Arlin test of formal reasoning.* East Aurora, NY: Slosson Educational Publications.

Armbruster, B. (1984). The problem of inconsiderate text. In G. Duffy, L. Roehler, & J. Mason (Eds.), *Comprehension instruction* (pp. 128–143). New York, NY: Longman.

Armbruster, B. (1992). Content reading in RT: The last two decades. *The Reading Teacher, 46,* 166–167.

Armbruster, B., & Anderson, T. (1981). *Content area textbooks* (Reading Education Report Number 23). Urbana: University of Illinois, Center for the Study of Reading.

Armbruster, B., & Anderson, T. (1984). *Producing "considerate" expository text: Or easy reading is damned hard writing* (Reading Education Report No. 36). Champaign: University of Illinois, Center for the Study of Reading.

Armbruster, B., Anderson, T., Armstrong, J., Wise, M., Janisch, C., & Meyer, L. (1991). Reading and questioning in content areas. *Journal of Reading Behavior, 23,* 35–59.

Arnheim, Rudolf. (1969). *Visual Thinking.* Los Angeles: University of California Press.

Aronson, E. (1978). *The jigsaw classroom.* Beverly Hills, CA: Sage.

Ashby-Davis, C. (1985). Cloze and comprehension: A qualitative analysis and critique. *Journal of Reading, 28,* 585–593.

Au, K. H. (1992). *Literary instruction in multicultural settings.* Fort Worth, TX: Harcourt Brace Jovanovich.

Ausubel, D. (1960). The use of advance organizers in learning and retention of meaningful verbal material. *Journal of Educational Psychology, 51,* 267–272.

Ausubel, D. (1963). *The psychology of meaningful learning.* New York: Grune & Stratton.

Ausubel, D. (1968). *Educational psychology: A cognitive view.* New York: Holt, Rinehart & Winston.

Babbs, P., & Moe, A. (1983). Metacognition: A key for independent learning from text. *The Reading Teacher, 36,* 422–426.

Bachman, C. (1989, April). *Reading, writing and thinking math activities.* Paper presented at the Capital Consortium Reading to Learn Conference, Richmond, VA.

Bader, L. (1987). Textbook analysis chart. *Reading, writing, speaking, listening and critical thinking in content area subjects.* Unpublished manuscript, Michigan State University.

Bader, L., & Pearce, D. (1983). Writing across the curriculum, 7–12. *English Education, 15,* 97–106.

Baldwin, R. S., Ford, J. C., & Readance, J. E. (1981). Teaching word connotations: An alternative strategy. *Reading World, 21,* 103–108.

Bandura, A. (1977). Self-efficacy: Toward a unifying theory of behavioral change. *Psychological Review, 84,* 191–215.

Barenbaum, E. (1983). Writing in the special class. *Topics in Learning and Learning Disabilities, 3,* 12–20.

Barnes, D. (1976). *From communication to curriculum.* New York: Penguin Books.

Barrett, T. (1972). A taxonomy of reading comprehension. *Reading 360 Monograph.* Lexington, MA: Ginn.

Barron, R. (1969). The use of vocabulary as an advance organizer. In H. L. Herber & P. L. Sanders (Eds.), *Research in reading in the content areas: First year report.* Syracuse, NY: Syracuse University, Reading and Language Arts Center.

Barron, R., & Stone, F. (1973). *The effect of student constructed graphic post organizers upon learning of vocabulary relationships from a passage of social studies content.* Paper presented at the meeting of the National Reading Conference, Houston.

Bartlett, F. C. (1932). *Remembering.* Cambridge: Cambridge University Press.

Baumann, J. F., & Johnson, D. D. (1984). *Reading instruction and the beginning teacher: A practical guide.* Minneapolis: Burgess.

Baumann, J. F., Seifert-Kessell, N., & Jones, L. A. (1992). Effect of think-aloud instruction on elementary students' comprehension monitoring abilities. *Journal of Reading Behavior, 24,* pp. 143–172.

Baxter, J. (1985). *Designing a test.* Unpublished paper from a course assignment: Reading in the content areas. Richmond: Virginia Commonwealth University.

Bealor, S. (1992). Minority literature book groups for teachers. *Reading in Virginia, 17*(1), 17–22.

Bean, T. W. (1988). Organizing and retaining information by thinking like an author. In S. Glazer, L. Searfoss, & L. Gentile (Eds.), *Reexamining reading diagnosis* (pp. 103–127). Newark, DE: International Reading Association.

Bean, T. W., & Peterson, J. (1981). Reasoning guides: Fostering readiness in content areas. *Reading Horizons, 21,* 196–199.

Bean, T. W., Singer, H., Sorter, J., & Frazee, C. (1986). The effect of metacognitive instruction in outlining and graphic organizer construction on students' comprehension in a tenth-grade world history class. *Journal of Reading Behavior, 18,* 153–169.

Beck, I. L., McCaslin, E., & McKeown, M. (1980). *The rationale and design of a program to teach vocabulary to fourth-grade students.* Pittsburgh: University of Pittsburgh, Learning Research and Development Center.

Beck, I. L., & McKeown, M. G. (1983). Learning words well: A program to enhance vocabulary and comprehension. *The Reading Teacher, 36,* 622–625.

Beck, I. L., McKeown, M., Omanson, R. C., & Pople, M. (1984). Improving comprehensibility of stories: The effects of revisions that improve coherence. *Reading Research Quarterly, 19,* 263–277.

Beck, I. L., McKeown, M. G., Sinatra, G. M., & Loxterman, J. A. (1991). Revising social studies text from a text-processing perspective: Evidence of improved comprehensibility. *Reading Research Quarterly, 26,* 251–276.

Beed, P., Hawkins, E., & Roller, C. (1991). Moving learners toward independence: The power of scaffolded instruction. *The Reading Teacher, 9,* 648–655.

Beil, D. (1977). The emperor's new cloze. *Journal of Reading, 20,* 601–604.

Bellow, S. (1987). Foreword. In Allan Bloom, *The closing of the American mind* (pp. 11–18). New York: Simon & Schuster.

Bergenske, M. D. (1987). The missing link in narrative story mapping. *The Reading Teacher, 41,* 333–335.

Berry, M. (1969). *Language disorders of children: The bases and diagnoses.* New York: Appleton-Century-Crofts.

Beyer, B. K. (1983). Common sense about teaching thinking skills. *Educational Leadership, 41,* 44–49.

Beyer, B. K. (1984). Improving thinking skills: Defining the problem. *Phi Delta Kappan, 65,* 486–490.

Biber, D. (1991). Oral and literate characteristics of selected primary school reading materials. *Text, 11,* 73–96.

Biggs, S. A. (1992). Building on strengths: Closing the literacy gap for African-American students. *Journal of Reading, 35,* 624–628.

Bloom, A. (1987). *The closing of the American mind.* New York: Simon & Schuster.

Bloom, B. C. (1956). *Taxonomy of educational objectives: Cognitive domain.* New York: David McKay.

Bohan, H., & Bass, J. (1991, Fall). Teaching thinking in elementary mathematics and science. *Educator's Forum,* pp. 1, 4–5, 10.

Borkowski, J. G., Carr, M., Rellinger, E., & Pressley, M. (1990). Self-regulated cognition: Interdependence of metacognition, attributions, and self-esteem. In B. F. Jones & L. Idol (Eds.), *Dimensions of thinking and cognitive instruction* (pp. 53–92). Hillsdale, NJ: Erlbaum.

Borkowski, J. G., Estrada, M. T., Milstead, M., & Hale, C. A. (1989). General problem-solving skills: Relations between metacognition and strategic processing. *Learning Disability Quarterly, 12,* 57–70.

Borkowski, J. G., Johnston, M. B., & Reid, M. K. (1987). Metacognition, motivation, and controlled performance. In S. J. Ceci (Ed.), *Handbook of cognitive, social, and neuropsychological aspects of learning disabilities* (Vol. 2, pp. 147–173). Hillsdale, NJ: Erlbaum.

Borkowski, J. G., Weyhing, R. S., & Carr, M. (1988). Effects of attributional retraining on strategy-based reading comprehension in learning-disabled students. *Journal of Educational Psychology, 80,* 46–53.

Bormouth, J. R. (1969). *Development of a readability analysis.* Final Report, Project No. 7-0052, Contract No. OEC-3-7-070052-0326. USOE, Bureau of Research, U.S. Department of Health, Education and Welfare.

Bormouth, J. R. (1975). Literacy in the classroom. In W. D. Page (Ed.), *Help for the reading teacher: New directions in research* (pp. 60–90). Urbana, IL: National Conference on Research in English and ERIC/RCS Clearinghouse.

Bracey, G. (1991). Why can't they be like we were? *Phi Delta Kappan, 73,* 104–120.

Bracey, G. (1992). The condition of public education. *Phi Delta Kappan, 74*, 104–117.

Brady, M. (1993). Critical issues that will determine the future of alternative assessment. *Phi Delta Kappan, 74*, 444–456.

Brandt, R. (1988). On teaching thinking: A conversation with Art Costa. *Educational Leadership, 45*, 10–13.

Branscomb, L., et al. (1986). *A nation prepared.* New York: Carnegie Forum on Education and the Economy.

Bransford, J., & Johnson, M. (1973). Considerations of some problems of comprehension. In W. Chase (Ed.), *Visual information processing* (pp. 383–438). New York, NY: Academic Press.

Brechtel, M. (1992). *Bringing the whole together: An integrated whole-language approach for the multilingual classroom.* San Diego: Dominie Press.

Brendtro, L. K., Brokenleg, M., & Bockern, S. V. (1990). *Reclaiming youth at risk: Our hope for the future.* Bloomington, IN: National Educational Service.

Britton, B. K., Van Dusen, L., Gulgog, S., Glynn, S. M., & Sharp, L. (1991). Accuracy of learnability judgments for instructional texts. *Journal of Educational Psychology, 83*, 43–47.

Britton, J., et al. (1975). *The development of writing abilities.* London: Methuen/School Council.

Bronowski, J. (1973). *The ascent of man.* Boston: Little, Brown.

Brooks, M., Fusco, E., & Grennon, J. (1983). Cognitive levels matching. *Educational Leadership, 40*, 4–8.

Brophy, J. (1982). *Classroom organization and management.* Washington, DC: National Institute of Education.

Brown, A. L. (1980). Metacognitive development and reading. In R. J. Spiro, B. Bruce, & W. F. Brewer (Eds.), *Theoretical issues in reading comprehension* (pp. 453–481). Hillsdale, NJ: Erlbaum.

Brown, A. L., & Barclay, C. R. (1976). The effects of training specific mnemonics on the meta mnemonic efficiency of retarded children. *Child Development, 47*, 71–80.

Brown, A. L., Campione, J. C., & Day, J. D. (1981). Learning to learn: On training students to learn from texts. *Educational Researcher, 10*, 14–21.

Brown, A. L., & Day, J. D. (1983). Macrorules for summarizing texts: The development of expertise. *Journal of Verbal Learning and Verbal Behavior, 22*, 1–5.

Brown, A. L., & Smiley, S. S. (1977). Rating the importance of structural units of prose passages: A problem of metacognitive development. *Child Development, 48*, 1–8.

Brown, J., Phillips, L., & Stephens, E. (1992). *Toward literacy: Theory and applications for teaching writing in the content areas.* Belmont, CA: Wadsworth.

Brown, R. (1987). Who is accountable for thoughtfulness? *Phi Delta Kappan, 69*, 49–52.

Brown, S. B., & Peterson, T. T. (1969). The rebellious school dropout. *School and Society, 97*, 437–439.

Brunwin, B. (Ed.). (1989). *The Bucktrout swamp.* Written by first- to sixth-grade students at Greenbriar Elementary School, Chesapeake, Virginia.

Bryant, J. A. R. (1984). Textbook treasure hunt. *Journal of Reading, 27*, 547–548.

Byrd, H. (1987). Paper submitted in partial fulfillment of course requirements for Reading in the Content Areas. Virginia Commonwealth University, Richmond.

Cadenhead, K. (1987). Reading level: A metaphor that shapes practice. *Phi Delta Kappan, 68*, 436–441.

Calfee, R. C. (1987). *The role of text structure in acquiring knowledge: Final report to the*

U.S. Department of Education (Federal Program No. 122B). Palo Alto, CA: Stanford University, Text Analysis Project.

Calkins, L. (1986). *The art of teaching writing.* Portsmouth, NH: Heineman.

Callan, P. M. (1990). An interview with John Goodlad. Denver: Education Commission of the States.

Carmen, R., & Adams, W. (1972). *Study skills: A student's guide to survival.* New York: Wiley.

Carnes, E. J. (1988). Teaching content area reading through nonfiction book writing. *Journal of Reading, 31,* 354–360.

Carr, E., & Ogle, D. (1987). KWL plus: A strategy for comprehension and summarization. *Journal of Reading, 30,* 626–631.

Carr, E., & Wixson, K. K. (1986). Guidelines for evaluating vocabulary instruction. *Journal of Reading, 29,* 588–595.

Carson, J., Chase, N., Gibson, S., & Hargrove, M. (1992). Literacy demands of the undergraduate curriculum. *Reading Research and Instruction, 31,* 25–50.

Carter, K. (1986). Test-wiseness for teachers and students. *Educational Measurement: Issues and Practices, 5,* 20–23.

Carver, R. P. (1983). Is reading rate constant or flexible? *Reading Research Quarterly, 18,* 190–215.

Carver, R. P. (1985). How good are some of the world's best readers? *Reading Research Quarterly, 20,* 389–419.

Carver, R. P. (1990). *Reading rate: A review of research and theory.* New York: Academic Press.

Carver, R. P. (1992). Reading rate: Theory, research, and practical applications. *Journal of Reading, 36*(2), 84–95.

Cashen, V. J., & Leicht, K. L. (1970). Role of the isolation effect in a formal educational setting. *Journal of Educational Psychology, 61,* 900–904.

Casteel, C. (1990). Effects of chunked text-material on reading comprehension of high and low ability readers. *Reading Improvement, 27,* 269–275.

Chall, J. (1947). The influence of previous knowledge on reading ability. *Educational Research Bulletin, 26,* 225–230.

Chall, J. (1958). *Readability: An appraisal of research and application.* Columbus: Ohio State University, Bureau of Educational Research.

Chall, J. (1983). *Stages of reading development.* New York: McGraw-Hill.

Chamot, A. U., & McKeon, D. (1984). ESL teaching methodologies. In A. U. Chamot & D. McKeon (Eds.), *Educating the minority student: Classroom and administrative issues* (pp. 1–5). Rosslyn, VA: National Clearinghouse for Bilingual Education. (ERIC Document Reproduction Service No. ED 260 600)

Chamot, A. U., & O'Malley, J. M. (1989). The cognitive academic language learning approach. In P. Rigg (Ed.), *When they don't all speak English: Integrating the ESL student into the regular classroom* (pp. 108–125). Urbana, IL: National Council of Teachers of English.

Chamot, A. U., & Stewner-Manzanares, G. (1985). *A synthesis of current literature on English as a second language: Issues for education policy: C. Research agenda.* Rosslyn, VA: National Clearinghouse for Bilingual Education. (ERIC Document Reproduction Service No. ED 261 537)

Chandler, T. A. (1975). Locus of control: A proposal for change. *Psychology in Schools, 12,* 334–339.

Choate, J. S., & Rakes, T. A. (1987). The structured listening activity: A model for improving listening comprehension. *The Reading Teacher, 41*, 194–200.

Chomsky, C. (1971). Write first, read later. *Childhood Education, 47*, 296–299.

Cioffi, G. (1992). Perspective and experience: Developing critical reading abilities. *Journal of Reading, 36*, 48–52.

Clark, B. (1983). *Growing up gifted: Developing the potential of children at home and at school* (2nd ed.). Columbus, OH: Charles Merrill.

Clary, L. M. (1977). How well do you teach critical thinking? *Reading Teacher, 31*, 142–147.

Cohen, A. D. (1987). The use of verbal and imagery mnemonics in second-language vocabulary learning. *Studies in Second Language Acquisition, 9*, 43–61.

Cohen, M. R., Cooney, T. M., Hawthorne, C., McCormack, A. J., Pasachoff, J. M., Pasachoff, N., Rhines, K. L., & Siesnick, I. L. (1991). *Discover science*. Glenview, IL: Scott, Foresman.

Coleman, J. C., et al. (1969). *Equality of educational opportunity*. Washington, DC: Superintendent of Documents.

College Board, Touchtone Applied Science Associates. (1986). *Degrees of reading power*. New York: College Board.

Collins, C. (1979). Speedway: The action way to speed read to increase reading rate for adults. *Reading Improvement, 16*, 225–229.

Collins, M. L. (1977). *The effects of training for enthusiasm on the enthusiasm displayed by pre-service elementary teachers*. Unpublished doctoral dissertation, Syracuse University, Syracuse, NY.

Colwell, C. G., Mangano, N. G., Childs, D., & Case, D. (1986). Cognitive, affective, and behavioral differences between students receiving instruction using alternative lesson formats. *Proceedings of the National Reading and Language Arts Conference*.

Combs, A. W., & Snygg, D. (1959). *Individual behavior*. New York: Harper & Row.

Conley, M. (1985). Promoting cross-cultural understanding through content area reading strategies. *Journal of Reading, 28*, 600–605.

Connell, J. P., & Ryan, R. M. (1984). A developmental theory of motivation in the classroom. *Teacher Education Quarterly, 11*, 64–77.

Cooper, J. D. (1986). *Improving reading comprehension*. Boston: Houghton Mifflin.

Coopersmith, S. (1967). *The antecedents of self-esteem*. San Francisco: W. H. Freeman.

Cooter, R. B. (1990, October/November). Learners with special needs. *Reading Today*, p. 28.

Cooter, R. B., & Alexander, J. E. (1984). Interest and attitude: Affective connections for gifted and talented readers. *Reading World, 24*, 97–102.

Cooter, R. B., & Chilcoat, G. W. (1991). Content-focused melodrama: Dramatic renderings of historical text. *Journal of Reading, 34*, 274–277.

Cooter, R. B., Joseph, D., & Flynt, E. (1986). Eliminating the literal pursuit in reading comprehension. *Journal of Clinical Reading, 2*, 9–11.

Cowan, G., & Cowan, E. (1980). *Writing*. New York: Wiley.

Cox, J., & Wiebe, J. (1984). Measuring reading vocabulary and concepts in mathematics in the primary grades. *Reading Teacher, 37*, 402–410.

Craig, L. (1977). If it's difficult to read, rewrite it! *The Reading Teacher, 21*, 212–214.

Creek, R. J., McDonald, W. C., & Ganley, M. A. (1991). *Internality and achievement in the intermediate grades*. (ERIC Document No. ED 330 656)

Crist, B., & Czarnecki, L. (1978). Your study skills, or the care and feeding of your grade point average. Shippensburg, PA: Shippensburg State Press.

Cronin, H., Meadows, D., & Sinatra, R. (1990). Integrating computers, reading, and writing across the curriculum. *Educational Leadership, 48*, 57–62.

Cullinan, B. E., Karrer, M. K., & Pillar, A. M. (1981). *Literature and the child.* New York: Harcourt Brace Jovanovich.

Culver, V. I., & Morgan, R. F. (1977). *The relationship of locus of control to reading achievement.* Unpublished manuscript, Old Dominion University, Norfolk, VA.

Cunningham, R., & Shablak, S. (1975). Selective reading guide-o-rama: The content teacher's best friend. *Journal of Reading, 18,* 380–382.

Currie, H. (1990). Making texts more readable. *British Journal of Special Education, 17,* 137–139.

Curry, B. A. (1990). *The impact of the Nicholls State Youth Opportunities Unlimited Program as related to academic achievement, self-esteem, and locus of control.* Master's thesis, Nicholls State University, Thibodaux, LA. ERIC Document.

Dale, E. (1965). Vocabulary measurement: Techniques and major findings. *Elementary English, 42,* 895–901.

Dale, E., & Chall, J. (1948). A formula for predicting readability. *Educational Research Bulletin, 27,* 11–20, 37–54.

Dale, E., & O'Rourke, J. (1976). *The living word vocabulary.* Elgin, IL: Dome.

Dale, E., O'Rourke, J., & Bamman, H. (1971). *Techniques of teaching vocabulary.* Palo Alto, CA: Field Educational Publications.

Dana, C., & Rodriguez, M. (1992). "TOAST: A System to Study Vocabulary." *Reading Research and Instruction, 31* (4), 78–84.

Danielson, K. E. (1987). Readability formulas: A necessary evil? *Reading Horizons, 27,* 178–188.

Danner, F. W., & Day, M. C. (1977). Eliciting formal operations. *Child Development, 48,* 1600–1606.

Davey, B. (1983). Think aloud: Modeling the cognitive processes of reading comprehension. *Journal of Reading, 27,* 44–47.

Davey, B. (1987). Team for success: Guided practice in study skills through cooperative research reports. *Journal of Reading, 30,* 701–705.

Davey, B. (1988). How do classroom teachers use their textbooks? *Journal of Reading, 31,* 340–345.

Davey, B., & McBride, S. (1986). Effects of question-generation training on reading comprehension. *Journal of Educational Psychology, 78,* 256–262.

Davidson, J. L. (1982). The group mapping activity for instruction in reading and thinking. *Journal of Reading, 26,* 52–56.

Davis, F. B. (1944). Fundamental factors of comprehension in reading. *Psychometrika, 9,* 185–197.

Davis, S., & Winek, J. (1989). Improving expository writing by increasing background knowledge. *Journal of Reading, 33,* 178–181.

Davison, A. (1984). Readability formulas and comprehension. In G. Duffy, L. Roehler, & J. Mason (Eds.), *Comprehension instruction* (pp. 128–143). New York, NY: Longman.

Davison, D., & Pearce, D. (1988a). Using writing activities to reinforce mathematics instruction. *Arithmetic Teacher, 35,* 42–45.

Davison, D., & Pearce, D. (1988b). Writing activities in junior high mathematics texts. *School Science and Mathematics, 88,* 493–499.

Day, B., & Anderson, J. (1992). Assessing the challenges ahead. *The Delta Kappa Gamma Bulletin, 58*(4), 5–10.

de Bono, E. (1976). *Teaching thinking.* London: Temple Smith.

Dechant, E. (1970). *Improving the teaching of reading.* Englewood Cliffs, NJ: Prentice-Hall.

Dempster, F. N. (1993). Exposing our students to less should help them learn more. *Phi Delta Kappan, 74,* 433–437.

Derby, T. (1987). Reading instruction and course-related materials for vocational high school students. *Journal of Reading, 30,* 308–316.

DeSanti, R. J., & Alexander, D. H. (1986). Locus of control and reading achievement: Increasing the responsibility and performance of remedial readers. *Journal of Clinical Reading, 2,* 12–14.

Dewey, J. (1900). *The school and society.* Chicago: University of Chicago Press.

Dewey, J. (1933). *How we think.* Boston: Heath.

Dillon, J. T. (1983). *Teaching and the art of questioning.* Bloomington, IN: Phi Beta Kappa Educational Foundation. Fastback # 194.

Dole, J. A., Valencia, S. W., Greer, E. A., & Wardrop, J. L. (1991). Effects of two types of prereading instruction on the comprehension of narrative and expository text. *Reading Research Quarterly, 26,* 142–159.

Douglass, B. (1984). Variations on a theme: Writing with the LD adolescent. *Academic Therapy, 19,* 361–362.

Downing, J. (1973). *Comparative reading.* New York: Macmillan.

Downing, J., Ollila, L., & Oliver, P. (1975). Cultural differences in children's concepts of reading and writing. *British Journal of Educational Psychology, 45,* 312–316.

Dreikurs, R., Grunwald, B., & Pepper, F. (1971). *Maintaining sanity in the classroom: Illustrated teaching techniques.* New York: Harper & Row.

Dreyer, L. G. (1984). Readability and responsibility. *Journal of Reading, 27,* 334–338.

Drum, P. (1985). Retention of text information by grade, ability, and study. *Discourse Processes, 8,* 21–51.

Drum, P., Calfee, R., & Cook, L. (1981). The effects of surface structure variables on reading comprehension tests. *Reading Research Quarterly, 16,* 486–514.

Drum, P., & Konopak, B. (1987). Learning word meanings from written context. In M. McKeown & M. Curtis (Eds.), *The nature of vocabulary development.* Hillsdale, NJ: Erlbaum.

Drummond, R. J., Smith, R. K., & Pinette, C. A. (1975). Internal-external control construct and performance in an individualized community college reading course. *Reading Improvement, 12,* 34–38.

Dufflemeyer, F. A., & Baum, D. D. (1992). The extended anticipation guide revisited. *Journal of Reading, 35,* 654–656.

Dufflemeyer, F. A., Baum, D. D., & Merkley, D. J. (1987). Maximizing reader-text confrontation with an extended anticipation guide. *Journal of Reading, 31,* 146–149.

Duffy, G. G., & Roehler, L. R., (1987). Teaching reading skills as strategies. *The Reading Teacher, 40,* 414–418.

Durkin, D. (1979). What classroom observations reveal about reading comprehension. *Reading Research Quarterly, 14,* 481–533.

Durkin, D. (1981). Reading comprehension instruction in five basal reading series. *Reading Research Quarterly, 16,* 515–544.

Durkin, D. (1984). Is there a match between what elementary teachers do and what basal reader manuals recommend? *The Reading Teacher, 37,* 734–744.

Dweck, C. S. (1975). The role of expectations and attribution in the alleviation of learned helplessness. *Journal of Personality and Social Psychology, 41,* 1041–1048.

Dweck, C. S. (1985). Intrinsic motivation, perceived control, and self-evaluation maintenance: An achievement goal analysis. In C. Ames & R. Ames (Eds.), *Research on motivation in education* (Vol. 2, pp. 289–305). Orlando, FL: Academic Press.

Eanet, M., & Manzo, A. V. (1976). REAP—A strategy for improving reading/writing/study skills. *Journal of Reading, 19,* 647–652.

Earle, R., & Barron, R. F. (1973). An approach for teaching vocabulary in content subjects. In H. L. Herber & R. F. Barron (Eds.), *Research in reading in the content areas: Second year report* (84–100). Syracuse, NY: Syracuse University, Reading and Language Arts Center.

Ebbinghaus, H. (1908). *Abriss der Psychologie* (M. Meyer, Trans. and Ed.). New York: Arno Press, 1973.

Egan, K. (1987). Literacy and the oral foundations of education. *Harvard Educational Review, 57,* 445–472.

Elliott, D., & Wendling, A. (1966). Capable dropouts and the social milieu of the high school. *Journal of Educational Research, 60,* 180–186.

Ennis, R. (1962). A concept of critical thinking. *Harvard Educational Review, 30,* 81–111.

Ennis, R. (1981). Rational thinking and educational practice. In J. Soltis (Ed.), *The philosophy of education* (pp. 143–183). Chicago: University of Chicago Press.

Erickson, B., Huber, M., Bea, T., Smith, C., & McKenzie, V. (1987). Increasing critical reading in junior high classes. *Journal of Reading, 30,* 430–439.

Erikson, E. (1963). *Childhood and society.* New York: Norton.

Erwin, B. (1991). The relationship between background experience and students' comprehension: A cross-cultural study. *Reading Psychology, 12,* 43–61.

Facione, P. A. (1984). Toward a theory of critical thinking. *Liberal Education, 30,* 253–261.

Fader, D. (1966). *Hooked on books.* New York: Berkley.

Farley, W. (1941). *The black stallion.* New York: Random House.

Feathers, K., & Smith, F. (1987). Meeting the reading demands of the real world: Literacy-based content instruction. *Journal of Reading, 30,* 506–511.

Field, M. L., & Aebersold, J. A. (1990). Cultural attitudes toward reading: Implications for teachers of ESL/bilingual readers. *Journal of Reading, 33,* 406–410.

Fillmore, L. W. (1981). Cultural perspectives on second language learning. *TESL Reporter, 14,* 23–31.

Finley, C. D., & Seaton, M. N. (1987). Using text patterns and question prediction to study for tests. *Journal of Reading, 31,* 124–132.

Fisher, C. W., & Berliner, D. (Eds.). (1985). *Perspectives on instructional time.* New York: Longman.

Fleisher, L. S., Jenkins, J. R., & Pany, D. (1979). Effects on poor readers' comprehension of training in rapid decoding. *Reading Research Quarterly, 15,* 30–48.

Forgan, H. W., & Mangrum, C. T. (1985). *Teaching content area reading skills.* Columbus, OH: Merrill.

Fowler, R. L., & Baker, A. S. (1974). Effectiveness of highlighting for retention of text material. *Journal of Applied Psychology, 59,* 358–364.

Fredericks, A. (1992). Magic bullets or empty blanks? *Reading Today, 9*(4), 30.

Freeman, D., & Freeman, Y. S. (1989). A road to success for language-minority high school students. In P. Rigg (Ed.), *When they don't all speak English: Integrating the ESL student into the regular classroom* (pp. 126–138). Urbana, IL: National Council of Teachers of English.

French, M. (1991). Increasing metacognitive awareness through reflective reading. *Journal of Reading Education, 16,* 33–42.

Fromm, E. (1956). *The art of loving.* New York: Harper & Row.

Fry, E. (1968). The readability graph validated at primary levels. *The Reading Teacher, 3,* 534–538.

Fry, E. (1977). Fry's readability graph: Clarifications, validity, and extension to level 17. *Journal of Reading, 21,* 242–252.

Fry, E. (1987). The varied uses of readability measurement today. *Journal of Reading, 30,* 338–343.

Fry, E. (1989). Reading formulas — maligned but valid. *Journal of Reading, 32,* 292–297.

Fry, E. (1990). A readability formula for short passages. *Journal of Reading, 33,* 594–597.

Gage, N. L. (1979). The generality of dimensions of teaching. In P. I. Peterson & H. J. Walberg (Eds.), *Research on teaching* (pp. 264–288). Berkeley, CA: McCutchan.

Gagne, R. (1965). *The conditions of learning.* New York: Holt, Rinehart & Winston.

Gagne, R. (1974). Educational technology and the learning process. *Educational Researcher, 3,* 3–8.

Gambrell, L. B. (1990). Introduction: A themed issue on reading instruction for at-risk students. *Journal of Reading, 33,* 485–488.

Gambrell, L. B., & Bales, R. J. (1986). Mental imagery and the comprehension-monitoring performance of fourth- and fifth-grade poor readers. *Reading Research Quarterly, 21,* 454–464.

Gambrell, L. B., & Wilson, R. M. (1973). *Focusing on the strengths of children.* Belmont, CA: Fearon.

Gardner, M. K., & Smith, M. M. (1987). Does perspective-taking ability contribute to reading comprehension? *Journal of Reading, 30,* 333–336.

Garner, R. (1985a). *Strategies for reading and studying expository text.* Unpublished paper, University of Maryland.

Garner, R. (1985b). Text summarization deficiencies among older students: Awareness or production ability? *American Educational Research Journal, 22,* 549–560.

Garner, R., Alexander, P., Slater, W., Hare, V. C., Smith, J., & Reis, R. (1986, April). *Children's knowledge of structural properties of text.* Paper presented at the meeting of the American Educational Research Association, San Francisco.

Garner, R., Hare, V. C., Alexander, P., Haynes, J., & Winograd, P. (1984). Inducing use of a text lookback strategy among unsuccessful readers. *American Educational Research Journal, 21,* 789–798.

Garner, R., Macready, G. B., & Wagoner, S. (1985). Reader's acquisition of the components of the text-lookback strategy. *Journal of Educational Psychology, 76,* 300–309.

Gavelek, J. R. (1986). The social contexts of literacy and schooling: A developmental perspective. In T. Raphael (Ed.), *The contexts of school-based literacy* (pp. 3–26). New York: Random House.

Gazzaniga, M. S. (1988). *Mind matters.* Boston: Houghton Mifflin.

Gebhard, A. (1983). Teaching writing in reading and the content areas. *Journal of Reading, 27,* 207–211.

Gentile, L., & McMillan, M. (1987). Stress and reading difficulties: Teaching students self-regulating skills. *The Reading Teacher, 41,* 170–178.

Georgia Department of Education. (1975). *Reading mathematics.* Atlanta: Author.

Gere, A. (1985). *Roots in the sawdust: Writing to learn across the disciplines.* Urbana, IL: National Council of Teachers of English.

Gervitz, H. (Ed.). (1963). *Contemporary moral issues.* Belmont, CA: Wadsworth.

Gillett, J. W., & Temple, C. (1983). *Understanding reading problems: Assessment and instruction.* Boston: Little, Brown.

Givler, J. (1986). *Designing a test*. Unpublished paper from a course assignment: Reading in the content areas. Richmond: Virginia Commonwealth University.

Glasser, W. (1986). *Control theory in the classroom*. New York: Harper & Row.

Glaze, B. (1987). Learning logs. In J. Self (Ed.), *Plain talk about learning and writing across the curriculum* (pp. 149–154). Richmond: Virginia State Department of Education.

Gold, P. C. (1981). The directed listening–language experience approach. *Journal of Reading, 25*, 138–141.

Goldman, W. (1973). Preface. In J. Morgenstern, *The princess bride*. New York: Ballantine Books.

Golinkoff, R. (1976). A comparison of reading comprehension processes in good and poor comprehenders. *Reading Research Quarterly, 11*, 623–659.

Goodacre, E. J. (1968). Teachers and their pupils' home background. Slough, England: National Foundation for Educational Research.

Goodlad, J. (1984). *A place called school*. New York: McGraw-Hill.

Goodman, K. S., & Goodman, Y. (1981). Twenty questions about teaching language. *Educational Leadership, 38*, 437–442.

Goodman, Y. M., & Burke, C. L. (1972). *Reading miscue inventory kit: Procedure for diagnosis and correction*. New York: Macmillan.

Gordon, C. (1990). Changes in readers' and writers' metacognitive knowledge: Some observations. *Reading Research and Instruction, 30*, 1–14.

Gough, P. B. (1987, May). The key to improving schools: An interview with William Glasser. *Phi Delta Kappan*, pp. 656–662.

Grady, M. P. (1984). *Teaching and brain research: Guidelines for the classroom*. New York: Longman.

Grady, M. P. (1990). *Whole brain education*. Bloomington, IN: Phi Delta Kappa Educational Foundation.

Graves, D. (1983). *Writing: Teachers and children at work*. Portsmouth, NH: Heinemann.

Graves, D., Prenn, M., & Cooke, C. (1985). The coming attraction: Previewing short stories. *Journal of Reading, 28*, 594–598.

Graves, M. F. (1985). *A word is a word . . . or is it?* New York: Scholastic.

Gray, W. (1925). *Summary of investigations related to reading* (Supplementary Educational Monographs No. 28). Chicago: The University of Chicago Press.

Gray, W. (1960). The major aspects of reading. In H. Robinson (Ed.), *Development of reading abilities* (Supplementary Educational Monographs #90). Chicago: University of Chicago Press.

Gray, W. (1984). *Reading*. Newark, DE: International Reading Association. (Originally published 1941)

Gusak, F. J. (1967). Teacher questioning and reading. *The Reading Teacher, 21*, 227–234.

Guthrie, J. T., Burnam, N., Caplan, R. I., & Seifert, M. (1974). The maze technique to assess and monitor reading comprehension. *The Reading Teacher, 28*, 161–168.

Guzzetti, B. (1990). Enhancing comprehension through trade books in high school English classes. *Journal of Reading, 33*, 411–413.

Guzzetti, B., Kowalinski, B. J., & McGowan, T. (1992). Using a literature-based approach to teaching social studies. *Journal of Reading, 36*, 114–122.

Guzzetti, B., Snyder, T., & Glass, G. (1992). Promoting conceptual change in science: Can texts be used effectively? *Journal of Reading, 35*, 642–649.

Haas, M. E. (1991). An analysis of the social science and history concepts in elementary social studies textbooks grades 1–4. *Theory and Research in Social Education*, *19*, 211–220.

Hafner, L. (1967). Using context to determine meanings in high school and college. *Journal of Reading*, *10*, 491–498.

Hagen, J. W., Hargrave, S., & Ross, W. (1973). Prompting and rehearsal in short-term memory. *Child Development*, *44*, 201–204.

Hager, J. M., & Gable, R. A. (1993). Content reading assessment: A rethinking of methodology. *The Clearing House*, *66*, 269–272.

Hamachek, D. E. (1975). *Behavior dynamics in teaching, learning and growth.* Boston: Allyn & Bacon.

Hansen, J. (1981). The effects of inference training and practice on young children's comprehension. *Reading Research Quarterly*, *16*, 391–417.

Hansen, J., & Pearson, D. (1983). An instructional study: Improving the inferential comprehension of fourth grade good and poor readers. *Journal of Educational Psychology*, *75*, 821–829.

Hare, V. C., & Borchardt, K. M. (1984). Direct instruction of summarization skills. *Reading Research Quarterly*, *20*, 62–78.

Hargis, C. H., Terhaar-Yonkers, M., Williams, P. C., & Reed, M. T. (1988). Repetition requirements for word recognition. *Journal of Reading*, *31*, 320–327.

Harris, K., & Graham, S. (1985). Improving learning disabled students' composition skills: Self-control strategy training. *Learning Disability Quarterly*, *8*, 27–36.

Harris, L. A., & Smith, C. B. (1986). *Reading instruction: Diagnostic teaching in the classroom.* New York: Macmillan.

Harris, T., & Hodges, R. (1981). *A dictionary of reading.* Newark, DE: International Reading Association.

Hart, L. (1975). *How the brain works.* New York: Basic Books.

Hart, L. (1983). Programs, patterns and downshifting in learning to read. *The Reading Teacher*, *37*, 5–11.

Hartman, M., & Kretschner, R. E. (1992). Talking and writing: Deaf teenagers reading *Sarah, Plain and Tall. Journal of Reading*, *36*, 174–180.

Hathaway, W. (Ed.). (1983). *Testing in the schools.* San Francisco: Jossey-Bass.

Hawkes, K. S., & Schell, L. M. (1987). Teacher-set prereading purposes and comprehension. *Reading Horizons*, *27*, 164–169.

Hayes, H., Stahl, N., & Simpson, M. (1991). Language, meaning, and knowledge: Empowering developmental students to participate in the academic community. *Reading Research and Instruction*, *30*(3), 89–100.

Heath, S. B. (1986). Critical factors in literacy development. In S. de Castell, A. Luke, & K. Egan (Eds.), *Literacy, society and schooling: A reader* (pp. 209–229). New York: Cambridge University Press.

Heathington, B., & Alexander, J. (1984). Do classroom teachers emphasize attitudes toward reading? *The Reading Teacher*, *37*, 484–488.

Heilman, A. W., Blair, T. R., & Rupley, W. H. (1986). *Principles and practices of teaching reading.* Columbus, OH: Merrill.

Heimlich, J. E., & Pittleman, S. D. (1985). *Semantic mapping: Classroom applications.* Newark, DE: International Reading Association.

Heller, M. (1986). How do you know what you know? Metacognitive modeling in the content areas. *Journal of Reading*, *29*, 415–422.

Henk, W. A., & Helfeldt, J. P. (1987). How to develop independence in following written directions. *Journal of Reading, 30,* 602–607.

Henry, G. H. (1974). *Teach reading as concept development: Emphasis on affective thinking.* Newark, DE: International Reading Association.

Herber, H. (1978). *Teaching reading in the content areas* (2nd ed.). Englewood Cliffs, NJ: Prentice-Hall.

Herber, H. (1987). Foreword. In D. Alvermann, D. Moore, & M. Conley (Eds.), *Research wtihin reach: Secondary school reading.* Newark, DE: International Reading Association.

Herber, H., & Nelson-Herber, J. (1987). Developing independent readers. *Journal of Reading, 30,* 584–588.

Hill, W., & Erwin, R. (1984). The readability of content textbooks used in middle and junior high schools. *Reading Psychology, 5,* 105–117.

Hillerich, R. L. (1979). Reading comprehension. *Reporting on Reading, 5,* 1–3.

Hilliard, A. G. (1988). Public support for successful instructional practices for at-risk students. In D. W. Hornbeck (Ed.), *School success for at-risk youth: Analysis and recommendations of the Council of Chief State School Officers* (pp. 195–208). Orlando, FL: Harcourt Brace Jovanovich.

Hinchman, R. (1987). The textbook and three content area teachers. *Reading Research and Instruction, 26,* 247–263.

Hirsch, E. D. (1987). *Cultural literacy.* Boston: Houghton Mifflin.

Hittleman, D. R. (1978). Readability, readability formulas, and cloze: Selecting instructional materials. *Journal of Reading, 22,* 117–122.

Hittleman, D. R. (1988). *Developmental reading, K–8.* Columbus, OH: Merrill.

Hoffman, J. (1992). Critical reading/thinking across the curriculum: Using I-charts to support learning. *Language Arts, 69,* 121–127.

Hoffman, S. (1983). Using student journals to teach study skills. *Journal of Reading, 26,* 344–347.

Holdzkom, D. (1987). Readability. In D. Alvermann, D. Moore, & M. Conley (Eds.), *Research within reach: Secondary school reading* (pp. 80–92). Newark, DE: International Reading Association.

Holmes, B., & Roser, N. (1987). Five ways to assess readers' prior knowledge. *Reading Teacher, 40,* 646–649.

Hornbeck, D. W. (1988). All our children: An introduction. In D. W. Hornbeck (Ed.), *School success for at-risk youth: Analysis and recommendations of the Council of Chief State School Officers* (pp. 3–9). Orlando, FL: Harcourt Brace Jovanovich.

Houseman, M. (1987). Textbook-related methods in social studies. *The Reading Teacher, 40,* 820–822.

Huck, C. (1979). *Children's literature in the elementary school.* New York: Holt, Rinehart & Winston.

Huck, C., Hepler, S., & Hickman, J. (1987). *Children's Literature in the Elementary School.* Fort Worth, TX: Holt, Rinehart, & Winston.

Huey, E. (1968). *The psychology and pedagogy of reading.* Cambridge, MA: MIT Press. (Originally published 1908)

Hunt, E. B. (1971). What kind of computer is man? *Cognitive Psychology, 2,* 57–98.

Hunt, K. (1965). *Grammatical structures written at three grade levels.* Champaign, IL: National Council of Teachers of English.

Hurd, P. (1970). *New directions in teaching secondary school science.* Chicago: Rand-McNally.

International Reading Association. (1988). *New directions in reading instruction.* Newark, DE: Author.

Iwicki, A. L. (1992). Vocabulary connections. *The Reading Teacher, 45,* 736.

Jacobs, L. (1987). Reading, writing, remembering. *Teaching Pre K–8, 18,* 38.

Jenkins, C., & Lawler, D. (1990). Questioning strategies in content area reading: One teacher's example. *Reading Improvement, 27,* 133–138.

Johns, J. L. (1986). Students' perceptions of reading: Thirty years of inquiry. In D. B. Yaden, Jr., & S. Templeton (Eds.), *Metalinguistic awareness and beginning literacy* (pp. 31–40). Portsmouth, NH: Heinemann.

Johnson, D. W., & Johnson, R. T. (1987). *Learning together and alone: Cooperative, conjunctive, and individualistic learning.* Englewood Cliffs, NJ: Prentice-Hall.

Johnson, D., & Pearson, P. D. (1984). *Teaching reading vocabulary* (2nd ed.). New York: Holt, Rinehart & Winston.

Jones, F. R., Morgan, R. F., & Tonelson, S. W. (1992). *The psychology of human development* (3rd ed.). Dubuque, IA: Kendall-Hunt.

Jongsma, E. (1980). *Cloze instruction research: A second look.* Newark, DE: International Reading Association.

Just, M. A., Carpenter, P. A., & Masson, M. E. J. (1982). *What eye fixations tell us about speed reading and skimming* (Technical report). Pittsburgh: Carnegie-Mellon University.

Kaestle, C. F., Damon-Moore, H., Stedman, K. T., Tinsley, K., & Tollinger, W. V. (1991). *Literacy in the United States: Readers and reading since 1880.* New Haven, CT: Yale University Press.

Kane, B. (1984). *Remarks made at the regional meeting on reading across the curriculum.* Reading to Learn in Virginia, Capital Consortium.

Kapinus, B. (1986). *Ready reading readiness.* Baltimore: Maryland State Department of Education.

Karpus, R., Karpus, E., Formisano, M., & Paulsen, A. (1977). A survey of proportional reasoning and control of variables in seven countries. *Journal of Research in Science Teaching, 14,* 411–417.

Kellogg, R. (1972). Listening. In P. Lamb (Ed.), *Guiding children's language learning* (pp. 141–170). Dubuque, IA: William C. Brown.

Kerchner, L., & Kistinger, B. (1984). Language processing/word processing: Written expression, computers and learning disabled students. *Learning Disability Quarterly, 7,* 329–335.

Kerr, M. M., Nelson, C. M., & Lambert, D. L. (1987). *Helping adolescents with learning and behavior problems.* Columbus, OH: Merrill.

Kinder, D., Bursuck, B., & Epstein, M. (1992). An evaluation of history textbooks. *The Journal of Special Education, 25,* 472–491.

Kintch, W., & Van Dijk, T. (1978). Toward a model of text comprehension and production. *Psychological Review, 85,* 363–394.

Kirsch, I. S., & Jungeblut, A. (1986). *Literacy: Profiles of America's young adults.* Princeton, NJ: National Assessment of Educational Progress.

Klare, G. (1974/75). Assessing readability. *Reading Research Quarterly, 10,* 62–102.

Kletzien, S. (1991). Strategy use by good and poor comprehenders reading expository text of differing levels. *Reading Research Quarterly, 26,* 67–86.

Kohl, H. (1973). *Reading, how to.* New York: Bantam Books.

Kolb, B., & Whishaw, I. Q. (1985). *Fundamentals of human neuropsychology* (2nd ed.). New York: Freeman.

Kolzow, L. V., & Lehmann, J. (1982). *College reading strategies for success.* Englewood Cliffs, NJ: Prentice-Hall.

Konopak, B. C. (1988). Using contextual information for word learning. *Journal of Reading, 31,* 334–338.

Krathwohl, D., Bloom, B., & Masia, B. (1964). *Taxonomy of educational objectives: Handbook 2. Affective domain.* New York: McKay.

Laffey, J., & Morgan, R. (1983). *Successful interactions in reading and language: A practical handbook for subject matter teachers.* Harrisonburg, VA: Feygan.

Lange, K. (1902). Apperception. In C. de Garma (Ed.), *A monograph on psychology and pedagogy.* Boston: Heath.

Langer, J. (1981). From theory to practice: A prereading plan. *Journal of Reading, 25,* 152–156.

Larson, C., & Dansereau, D. (1986). Cooperative learning in dyads. *Journal of Reading, 29,* 516–520.

Leal, L., Crays, N., & Moetz, B. (1985). Training children to use a self-monitoring study strategy in preparation for recall: Maintenance and generalization effects. *Child Development, 56,* 643–653.

Lee, P., & Allen, G. (1981). Training junior high LD students to use a test-taking strategy. ED 217 649.

Lee, S., Stigler, J. W., & Stevenson, H. W. (1986). Beginning reading in Chinese and English. In B. Foorman & A. W. Siegel (Eds.), *Acquisition of reading skills* (pp. 123–149). Hillsdale, NJ: Erlbaum.

Lefcourt, H. M., Gronnerud, P., & MacDonald, P. (1972). *Cognitive activity and hypotheses formation during a double entendre word association test as a function of locus of control and field dependence.* Unpublished educational document, Ontario Mental Health Foundation, Toronto.

Levin, H. M. (1988). Accelerating elementary education for disadvantaged students. In D. W. Hornbeck (Ed.), *School success for at-risk youth: Analysis and recommendations of the Council of Chief State School Officers* (pp. 209–226). Orlando, FL: Harcourt Brace Jovanovich.

Levin, J. R., Levin, M. E., Glassman, L. D., & Nordwall, M. B. (1992). Mnemonic vocabulary instruction: Additional effectiveness evidence. *Contemporary Educational Psychology, 17,* 156–174.

Levin, J. R., Morrison, C. R., & McGivern, J. E. (1986). Mnemonic facilitation of text-embedded science facts. *American Educational Research Journal, 23,* 489–506.

Lindfors, J. W. (1980). *Children's language and learning.* Englewood Cliffs, NJ: Prentice-Hall.

Loevinger, J. (1976). *Ego development: Conceptions and theories.* San Francisco: Jossey-Bass.

Lovitt, T. C., Horton, S. V., & Bergerud, D. (1987). Matching students with textbooks: An alternative to readability formulas and standard tests. *B.C. Journal of Special Education, 11,* 49–55.

Lubarsky, N. (1987). A glance at the past, a glimpse of the future. *Journal of Reading, 30,* 520–529.

Lynch-Brown, C., & Tomlinson, C. M. (1993). *Essentials of children's literature.* Boston: Allyn and Bacon.

Lyons, B. (1981). The PQP method of responding to writing. *English Journal, 70,* 47–52.

MacDonald, J. (1986). Self-generated questions and reading recall: Does training help? *Contemporary Educational Psychology, 11,* 290–304.

MacLean, P. (1978). A mind of three minds: Educating the triune brain. In J. Chall & A. Mirsley (Eds.), *Education and the brain* (pp. 308–342). Chicago: University of Chicago Press.

Manzo, A. V. (1969). The ReQuest procedure. *Journal of Reading,, 11,* 123–126.

Manzo, A. V. (1975). The guided reading procedure. *Journal of Reading, 18,* 287–291.

Maria, K., & MacGinitie, W. (1987). Learning from texts that refute the readers' prior knowledge. *Reading Research and Instruction, 26,* 222–238.

Martorano, S. (1977). A development analysis of performance on Piaget's formal operations tasks. *Developmental Psychology, 13,* 66–72.

Mason, J. M., & Au, K. H. (1990). *Reading instruction for today.* Glenview, IL: Scott, Foresman.

Masztal, N. B. (1986). Cybernetic sessions: A high involvement teaching technique. *Reading Research and Instruction, 25,* 131–138.

Mathewson, G. (1976). The function of attitudes in the reading process. In H. Singer & R. Ruddell (Eds.), *Theoretical models and processes of reading* (pp. 908–919). Newark, DE: International Reading Association.

May, F. B. (1990). *Reading as communication: An interactive approach.* Columbus, OH: Merrill.

McAndrew, D. A. (1983). Underlining and note taking: Some suggestions from research. *Journal of Reading, 27,* 103–108.

McCombs, B. L. (1986). The role of the self-system in self-regulated learning. *Contemporary Educational Psychology, 11,* 314–332.

McConkie, G. W., & Rayner, K. (1976). Asymmetry of the perceptual span in reading. *Bulletin of the Psychometric Society, 8,* 365–368.

McDermott, R. P. (1978). Some reasons for focusing on classrooms in reading research. *Reading: Disciplined inquiry in process and practice.* Clemson, SC: 27th Yearbook of the National Reading Conference.

McKenna, M. C., & Kear, D. J. (1990). Measuring attitude toward reading: A new tool for teachers. *The Reading Teacher, 43,* 626–639.

McLaughlin, H. (1969). SMOG grading—a new readability formula. *Journal of Reading, 12,* 639–646.

McMurray, M., Laffey, J., & Morgan, R. (1979). College students' word identification strategies. *Twenty-eighth Yearbook of the National Reading Conference.*

McPeck, J. (1981). *Critical thinking and education.* New York: St. Martin's Press.

McTighe, J., & Lyman, F. T., Jr. (1988). Cueing thinking in the classroom: The promise of theory-embedded tools. *Educational Leadership, 45*(7), 18–24.

McWilliams, L., & Rakes, T. (1979). *The content inventories.* Dubuque, IA: Kendall/Hunt.

Meeks, J. (1987, May). *Toward defining affective metacognition.* Paper presented at the meeting of the International Reading Association, Anaheim, CA.

Meeks, J., & Morgan, R. (1978). New use for the cloze procedure: Interaction in imagery. *Reading Horizons, 18,* 261–264.

Meloth, M. S., & Deering, P. D. (1992). Effects of two cooperative conditions on peer-group discussions, reading comprehension, and metacognition. *Contemporary Educational Psychology, 17,* 175–193.

Memory, D. M. (1990). Teaching technical vocabulary: Before, during, or after reading assignment? *Journal of Reading Behavior, 22,* 39–53.

Meyer, B. J. F., Brandt, D. M., & Bluth, G. J. (1980). Use of top-level structure in text: Key for reading comprehension of ninth grade students. *Reading Research Quarterly, 16,* 72–103.

Mezynski, K. (1983). Issues concerning the acquisition of knowledge: Effects of vocabulary training on reading comprehension. *Review of Educational Research, 53,* 253–279.

Miklos, J. (1982). A look at reading achievement in the United States. *Journal of Reading, 25,* 760–762.

Mikulecky, L., Shanklin, N., & Caverly, D. (1979). Mikulecky behavioral reading attitude measure. In *Adult reading habits, attitudes and motivations: A cross-sectional study.* Bloomington, IN: Indiana University, School of Education.

Miller, A. (1989, April). *Writing to learn in science.* Paper presented at the Capital Consortium Reading to Learn Conference, Richmond, VA.

Miller, G. (1956). The magical number seven, plus or minus two. *Psychological Review, 63,* 81–97.

Miller, G. R., & Coleman, E. B. (1971). The measurement of reading speed and the obligation to generalize to a population of reading materials. *Journal of Reading Behavior, 4*(3), 48–56.

Moffett, J. (1979). Integrity in the teaching of writing. *Phi Delta Kappan, 61,* 276–279.

Moore, D., & Arthur, S. V. (1981). Possible sentences. In E. K. Dishner, T. W. Bean, & J. E. Readance (Eds.), *Reading in the content areas: Improving classroom instruction.* Dubuque: Kendall/Hunt.

Moore, D., Moore, S. A., Cunningham, P., & Cunningham, J. (1986). *Developing readers and writers in the content areas.* New York: Longman.

Moore, D., & Murphy, A. (1987). Selection of materials. In D. Alvermann, D. Moore, & M. Conley (Eds.), *Research within reach: Secondary school reading* (pp. 94–108). Newark, DE: International Reading Association.

Moore, J. C., & Surber, J. R. (1992). Effects of context and keyword methods on second language vocabulary acquisition. *Contemporary Educational Psychology, 17,* 286–292.

Moore, W., E., McCann, H., & McCann, J. (1981). *Creative and critical thinking* (2nd ed.). Boston: Houghton Mifflin.

Morgan, R., & Culver, V. (1978). Locus of control and reading achievement: Applications for the classroom. *Journal of Reading, 21,* 403–408.

Morgan, R. F., Meeks, J. W., Schollaert, A., & Paul, J. (1986). *Critical reading/thinking skills for the college student.* Dubuque, IA: Kendall/Hunt.

Morgan, R., Otto, A., & Thompson, G. (1976). A study of the readability and comprehension of selected eighth grade social studies textbooks. *Perceptual and Motor Skills, 43,* 594.

Moss, J. (1990). *Focus units in literature: A handbook for elementary school teachers* (2nd ed.). Urbana, IL: National Council of Teachers of English.

Murnane, Y. (1990). Writing as a thinking tool: How writing can foster metacognition. In B. Anderson (Ed.), *Teacher education for literacy around the world* (pp. 61–64). St. Cloud, MN: Organization of Teacher Educators in Reading.

Muth, K. D. (1987). Structure strategies for comprehending expository text. *Reading Research and Instruction, 27,* 66–72.

Myklebust, H. (1965). *Development and disorders of written language.* New York: Grune & Stratton.

National assessment of educational progress (Report No. 10-W-01). (1980, December). Education Commission of the States, Suite 700, 1960 Lincoln Street, Denver, CO 80295.

National Commission on Excellence in Education. (1983). *A nation at risk: The imperative report to the nation and the secretary of education.* Washington, DC: U.S. Government Printing Office.

Neckerman, K. M., & Wilson, W. J. (1988). In D. W. Hornbeck (Ed.), *School success for at-risk youth: Analysis and recommendations of the Council of Chief State School Officers* (pp. 25–44). Orlando, FL: Harcourt Brace Jovanovich.

Neisser, V. (1967). *Cognitive psychology.* New York: Appleton-Century-Crofts.

Nessel, D. (1987). Reading comprehension: Asking the right questions. *Phi Delta Kappan, 68,* 442–445.

Newell, A., & Simon, H. A. (1972). *Human problem solving.* New York: Prentice-Hall.

Newton, B. T. (1978). Higher cognitive questioning and critical thinking. *Reading Improvement, 15,* 26–27.

Novak, J. D., & Gowin, D. B. (1984). *Learning how to learn.* Cambridge: Cambridge University Press.

O'Brien, R. (1971). *Mrs. Frisby and the rats of NIMH.* New York: Atheneum.

Ogle, D. (1986). KWL: A teaching model that develops active reading of expository text. *The Reading Teacher, 39,* 564–570.

Ogle, D. (1992). KWL in action: Secondary teachers find applications that work. In E. K. Dishner, T. W. Bean, J. E. Readance, & D. W. Moore (Eds.), *Reading in the content areas: Improving classroom instruction* (3rd ed.) (pp. 270–281). Dubuque, IA: Kendall/Hunt.

Ollmann, H. (1989). Cause and effect in the real world. *Journal of Reading, 33,* 224–225.

Ollmann, H. (1992). Two-column response to literature. *Journal of Reading, 36,* 58–59.

Olshavsky, J. (1975). Reading as problem solving: An investigation of strategies. *Reading Research Quarterly, 12,* 654–674.

Olson, M. W., & Gee, T. (1991). Content reading instruction in the primary grades: Perceptions and strategies. *The Reading Teacher, 45,* 298–307.

Opitz, M. (1992). The cooperative reading activity: An alternative to ability grouping. *The Reading Teacher, 45,* 736–738.

Orfield, A. (1988). Race, income, and educational inequity. In *School success for at-risk youth: Analysis and recommendations of the Council of Chief State School Officers* (pp. 45–71). Orlando, FL: Harcourt Brace Jovanovich.

Page, B. (1987). From passive receivers to active learners in English. In J. Self (Ed.), *Plain talk about learning and writing across the curriculum* (pp. 37–50). Richmond: Virginia Department of Education.

Palincsar, A. S., & Brown, A. L. (1984). Reciprocal teaching of comprehension-fostering and comprehension-monitoring activities. *Cognition and Instruction, 1,* 117–175.

Palincsar, A. S., & Brown, A. L. (1986). Interactive teaching to promote independent learning from text. *The Reading Teacher, 39,* 771–777.

Pallas, A. M., Natriello, G., & McDill, E. L. (1989). Changing nature of the disadvantaged population: Current dimensions and future trends. *Educational Researcher, 18,* 16–22.

Pang, V. O., Colvin, C., Tran, M. Y., & Barba, R. H. (1992). Beyond chopsticks and dragons: Selecting Asian-American literature for children. *Journal of Reading, 46,* 216–223.

Paris, S. G. (1986). Teaching children to guide their reading and learning. In T. E. Raphael & R. Reynolds (Eds.), *Context of literacy* (pp. 115–130). New York: Longman.

Paris, S. G., Cross, D. R., & Lipson, M. Y. (1984). Informal strategies for learning: A program to improve children's reading awareness and comprehension. *Journal of Educational Psychology, 76,* 1239–1252.

Paris, S. G., Lipson, M. Y., & Wixson, K. K. (1983). Becoming a strategic reader. *Contemporary Educational Psychology*, *8*, 393–396.

Paris, S. G., & Winograd, P. (1990). How metacognition can promote academic learning and instruction. In B. Jones & L. Idol (Eds.), *Dimensions of thinking and cognitive instruction* (pp. 15–52). Hillsdale, NJ: Erlbaum.

Parnes, S. J., & Noller, R. B. (1973). *Toward supersanity: Channeled freedom*. East Aurora, NY: D.O.K.

Parrish, B. (1982). A test to test test-wiseness. *Journal of Reading*, *25*, 672–675.

Pauk, W. (1974). *How to study in college*. Boston: Houghton Mifflin.

Pearce, D. (1983). Guidelines for the use and evaluation of writing in content classrooms. *Journal of Reading*, *17*, 212–218.

Pearce, D. (1987). Group writing activities: A useful strategy for content teachers. *Middle School Journal*, *18*, 24–25.

Pearce, D., & Bader, L. (1984). Writing in content area classrooms. *Reading World*, *23*, 234–241.

Pearce, D., & Davison, D. (1988). Teacher use of writing in the junior high mathematics classroom. *School Science and Mathematics*, *88*, 6–15.

Pearson, P. D. (1985). Changing the face of reading comprehension. *The Reading Teacher*, *38*, 724–738.

Pearson, P. D., & Johnson, D. (1978). *Teaching reading comprehension*. New York: Holt, Rinehart & Winston.

Pearson, P. D., & Spiro, R. (1982, May). The new buzz word in reading is schema. *Instructor*, pp. 46–48.

Pearson, P. D., & Tierney, R. (1983). In search of a model of instructional research in reading. In S. Parris, G. Okon, & H. Stevenson (Eds.), *Learning and motivation in the classroom*. Hillsdale, NJ: Erlbaum.

Pei, M. (1965). *The story of language* (rev. ed.). New York: Mentor Books.

Pellicano, R. (1987). At-risk: A view of "social advantage." *Educational Leadership*, *44*, 47–50.

Penfield, W. (1975). *The mystery of the mind: A critical study of consciousness and the human brain*. Princeton, NJ: Princeton University Press.

Perez, S. A., & Strickland, D. (1987). Teaching children how to discuss what they read. *Reading Horizons*, *27*, 89–94.

Perry, W. (1959). Students' use and misuse of reading skills. *Harvard Educational Review*, *29*, 193–200.

Peters, E. E., & Levin, J. R. (1986). Effects of a mnemonic imagery strategy on good and poor readers' prose recall. *Reading Research Quarterly*, *21*, 179–192.

Phelps, S. (1984). A first step in content area reading instruction. *Reading World*, *23*, 265–269.

Piaget, J. (1952). *The language and thought of the child*. London: Routledge & Kegan Paul.

Piaget, J. (1963). *The origin of intelligence in children*. New York: Norton.

Piaget, J., & Inhelder, B. (1969). *The psychology of the child*. New York: Basic Books.

Purves, A. C., & Bech, R. (1972). *Literature and the reader: Research in response to literature, reading interests, and the teaching of literature*. Urbana, IL: National Council of Teachers of English.

Quealy, R. (1969). Senior high schools students' use of contextual aids in reading. *Reading Research Quarterly*, *4*, 512–533.

Radencich, M. (1985). Writing a class novel: A strategy for LD students? *Academic Therapy, 20*, 599–603.

Rakes, T., & Chance, L. (1990). A survey of how subjects remember what they read. *Reading Improvement, 27*, 122–128.

Raphael, T. (1984). Teaching learners about sources of information for answering comprehension questions. *Journal of Reading, 27*, 303–311.

Raphael, T. (1986). Teaching question/answer relationships, revisited. *The Reading Teacher, 39*, 516–522.

Rasinski, T., & Nathenson-Mejia, S. (1987). Learning to read, learning community: Consideration of the social contexts for literacy instruction. *The Reading Teacher, 41*, 260–265.

Raths, L., Wassermann, S., Jones, A., & Rothstein, A. (1986). *Teaching for thinking: Theories, strategies and activities for the classroom.* New York: Teachers College Press.

Rayner, K. (1978). Eye movements in reading and information processing. *Psychological Bulletin, 85*, 616–660.

Readance, J. E., & Baldwin, R. S. (1979). Independence in critical reading: An instructional strategy. *Educational Considerations, 6*, 15–16.

Readance, J. E., Bean, T. W., & Baldwin, R. S. (1981). *Content area reading: An integrated approach.* Dubuque, IA: Kendall/Hunt.

The reading report card: Progress toward excellence in our schools: Trends in reading instruction over four national assessments, 1971–1984 (Report #15-R-01). (1985). Princeton, NJ: National Assessment of Educational Progress and Educational Testing Service.

Redl, F. (1952). *Controls from within.* New York: Free Press.

Restak, R. (1979). *The brain: The last frontier.* Garden City, NY: Doubleday.

Restak, R. (1982). The brain. *The Wilson Quarterly, 6*, 89–115.

Restak, R. (1984). *The brain.* New York: Bantam Books.

Reutzel, D. R., & Daines, D. (1987). The text-relatedness of reading lessons in seven basal reading series. *Reading Research and Instruction, 27*, 26–35.

Reyes, D. J. (1986). Critical thinking in elementary social studies text series. *The Social Studies, 77*, 151–157.

Reyhner, J. (1986). Native Americans in basal reading textbooks: Are there enough? *Journal of American Indian Education, 26*, 14–22.

Reyhner, J., & Garcia, R. L. (1989). Helping minorities read better: Problems and promises. *Reading Research and Instruction, 28*, 84–91.

Rhodes, R. (1990, October 14). Don't be a bystander. *Parade*, pp. 4–7.

Richardson, J. (1975). *A study of the syntactic competence of adult beginning readers.* Unpublished doctoral dissertation, University of North Carolina at Chapel Hill.

Richardson, J. (1991). Developing responsibility in English classes: Three activities. *Journal of the Virginia College Reading Educators, 11*, 8–19.

Richardson, J. (1992a). Generating inquiry-oriented projects from teachers. In A. Frager & J. Miller (Eds.), *Using inquiry in reading teacher education* (pp. 24–29). Kent, OH: Kent State University, College Reading Association.

Richardson, J. (1992b). Taking responsibility for taking tests. In N. Padak & T. Rasinski (Eds.), *Literacy research and practice: Foundations for the year 2000* (pp. 209–215). Kent, OH: Kent State University, College Reading Association.

Richardson, J., & Morgan, R. (1991). Crossing bridges by connecting meaning. *TAIR, 34*, 1.

Rickards, J. P., & August, G. J. (1975). Generative underlining strategies in prose recall. *Journal of Educational Psychology*, *67*, 860–865.

Rieck, B. J. (1977). How content teachers telegraph messages against reading. *Journal of Reading*, *20*, 646–648.

Rifkin, J. (1987). *Time wars*. New York: Henry Holt.

Ritter, S., & Idol-Mastas, L. (1986). Teaching middle school students to use a test-taking strategy. *Journal of Educational Research*, *79*, 350–357.

Robinson, F. P. (1961). *Effective study* (rev. ed.). New York: Harper & Row.

Robinson, H. A. (Ed.). (1977). *Reading and writing instruction in the United States: Historical trends*. Newark, DE: International Reading Association.

Rogers, D. B. (1984). Assessing study skills. *Journal of Reading*, *27*, 346–354.

Roit, M., & McKenzie, R. (1985). Disorders of written communication: An instructional priority for LD students. *Journal of Learning Disabilities*, *18*, 258–260.

Rosenshine, B. (1968). Objectively measured behavioral predictors of effectiveness in explaining. In N. L. Gage et al. (Eds.), *Explorations of teachers' effectiveness in explaining* (pp. 36–45). Stanford, CA: Stanford Center for Reading and Development in Teaching, Technical Report No. 4.

Rosenshine, B., & Furst, N. (1971). Research on teacher performance criteria. In O. Smith (Ed.), *Research in teacher education: A symposium*. Englewood Cliffs, NJ: Prentice-Hall.

Rosenshine, B., & Stevens, R. (1984). Classroom instruction in reading. In P. D. Pearson (Ed.), *Handbook of reading research*. New York: Longman.

Rotter, J. B. (1966). Generalized expectancies for internal versus external control of reinforcement. *Psychological Monographs: General and Applied*, *80*(1).

Rumelhart, D. E. (1980). Schemata: The building blocks of cognition. In R. J. Spiro, B. C. Bruce, & W. F. Brewer (Eds.), *Theoretical issues in reading comprehension* (pp. 33–58). Hillsdale, NJ: Erlbaum.

Sachar, E. (1991). *Shut up and let the lady teach: A teacher's year in the public school*. New York: Poseidon Press.

Sagan, C. (1977). *The dragons of Eden*. New York: Random House.

Samuels, S. J. (1979). The method of repeated readings. *The Reading Teacher*, *32*, 403–408.

Santeusanio, R. (1983). *A practical approach to content area reading*. Reading, MA: Addison-Wesley.

Scardamalia, M., & Bereiter, C. (1984). Development of strategies in text processing. In H. Mandl, N. L. Stein, & T. Trabasson (Eds.), *Learning and comprehension of text* (pp. 379–406). Hillsdale, NJ: Erlbaum.

Schadt, W. (1989). Literary gift exchange. *Journal of Reading*, *33*, 223–224.

Schallert, D. L., & Kleiman, G. M. (1979). *Why the teacher is easier to understand than the textbook*. Reading Education Report No. 9. Urbana: University of Illinois, Center for the Study of Reading.

Schatz, E. K. (1984). *The influence of context clues on determining the meaning of low frequency words in naturally occurring prose*. Unpublished doctoral dissertation, University of Miami.

Schieffelin, B. B., & Cochran-Smith, M. (1984). Learning to read culturally: Literacy before schooling. In H. Goelman, A. Oberg, & F. Smith (Eds.), *Awakening to literacy* (pp. 3–23). Portsmouth, NH: Heinemann.

Schumm, J. (1992). Content area textbooks: How tough are they? *Journal of Reading*, *36*, 47.

Schumm, J., Mangrum, C., Gordon, J., & Doucette, M. (1992). The effect of topic knowledge on the predicted test questions of developmental college readers. *Reading Research and Instruction*, *31*, 11–23.

Schunk, D. H., & Rice, J. M. (1992). Influence of reading comprehension strategy information on children's achievement outcomes. *Learning Disabilities Quarterly*, *15*(1), 51–64.

Scruggs, T., Mastropier, M. A., Brigham, F. J., & Sullivan, G. S. (1992). Effects of mnemonic reconstructions on the spatial learning of adolescents with learning disabilities. *Learning Disability Quarterly*, *15*(3), 154–167.

Scruggs, T., White, K., & Bennion, K. (1986). Teaching test-taking skills to elementary students: A meta-analysis. *Elementary School Journal*, *87*, 69–82.

Self, J. (1987). The picture of writing to learn. In J. Self (Ed.), *Plain talk about learning and writing across the curriculum* (pp. 9–20). Richmond: Virginia State Department of Education.

Shanker, A. (1984, September 5). Where we stand: Who should evaluate the textbooks? *Education Week*, p. 69.

Sharan, S., & Sharan, Y. (1976). *Small-group teaching*. Englewood Cliffs, NJ: Educational Technology Publications.

Shayer, M., Kuchemann, D. E., & Wylam, H. (1976). The distribution of Piagetian stages of thinking in British middle and secondary school children. *British Journal of Educational Psychology*, *46*, 164–173.

Sherer, P. (1975). Skimming and scanning: De-mything the process with a college student. *Journal of Reading*, *19*, 24–27.

Shyer, M. F. (1988). *Welcome home, Jelly Bean*. New York: Macmillan.

Siedow, M. D., & Hasselbring, T. S. (1984). Adaptability of text readability to increase comprehension of reading disability students. *Reading Improvement*, *21*, 276–279.

Simon, K. (1993). Alternative assessment: Can real-world skills be tested? *The Link*, *12*, 1–7.

Simpson, M. L. (1987). Alternative formats for evaluating content area vocabulary understanding. *Journal of Reading*, *30*, 20–27.

Sinatra, R. (1975). Language experience in Title I summer camping problems. *Reading Improvement*, *12*, 148–156.

Sinatra, R. (1977). The cloze technique for reading comprehension and vocabulary development. *Reading Improvement*, *14*, 80–92.

Sinatra, R. (1986). *Visual literacy connections to thinking, reading and writing*. Springfield, IL: Thomas.

Singer, H., & Bean, T. (1988). Three models for helping teachers to help students learn from text. In S. J. Samuels & P. D. Pearson (Eds.), *Changing school reading programs* (pp. 161–183). Newark, DE: International Reading Association.

Singer, H., & Donlan, D. (1985). *Reading and learning from text*. Hillsdale, NJ: Erlbaum.

Sizer, T. (1992). *Horace's school: Redesigning the American high school*. New York: Houghton Mifflin.

Slavin, R. E. (1980). Cooperative learning. *Review of Educational Research*, *50*, 315–342.

Slavin, R. E. (1983). *Cooperative learning*. New York: Longman.

Slavin, R. E. (1991). Synthesis of research on cooperative learning. *Educational Leadership*, *48*, 71–82.

Sloan, G. D. (1984). *The child as critic: Teaching literature in elementary and middle schools* (2nd ed.). New York: Teachers College Press.

Smith, D. (1992). Common ground: The connection between reader-response and text-book reading. *Journal of Reading, 35*, 630–635.

Smith, F. (1971). *Understanding reading.* New York: Holt, Rinehart & Winston.

Smith, F. (1973). *Psycholinguistics and reading.* New York: Holt, Rinehart & Winston.

Smith, F. (1988). *Understanding reading: A psycholinguistic analysis of reading and learning to read* (4th ed.). Hillsdale, NJ: Erlbaum.

Smith, F. (1989). Overselling literacy. *Phi Delta Kappan, 70*, 352–359.

Smith, M. C. (1990). A longitudinal investigation of reading attitude development from childhood to adulthood. *Journal of Educational Research, 83*, 215–219.

Smith, N. B. (1965). *American reading instruction.* Newark, DE: International Reading Association.

Smith, S., & Bean, R. (1980). The guided writing procedure: Integrating content reading and writing improvement. *Reading World, 19*, 290–294.

Smuin, S. (1978). *Turn-ons.* Belmont, CA: Fearon Pitman.

Sosniak, L., & Perlman, C. (1990). Secondary education by the book. *Journal of Curriculum Studies, 22*, 427–442.

Spache, G. (1953). A new readability formula for primary grade reading materials. *Elementary School Journal, 53*, 410–413.

Spache, G. (1976). *Investigating the issues of reading disabilities.* Boston: Allyn and Bacon.

Speaker, R., & Grubaugh, S. (1992). The development of memory for writing: Examining cloze performance and meaning changes at four grade levels. *Reading Research and Instruction, 31*, 64–73.

Speigel, D. L., & Wright, J. (1983). Biology teachers' use of readability concepts when selecting texts for students. *Journal of Reading, 27*, 28–34.

Spurzheim, G. (1833). *A view of the elementary principles of education, founded on the study of the nature of man* (2nd ed.). Boston: Capen and Lyon.

Stahl, S. (1983). Differential word knowledge and reading comprehension. *Journal of Reading Behavior, 15*, 33–50.

Stahl, S. (1986). Three principles of effective vocabulary instruction. *Journal of Reading, 29*, 662–668.

Stanton, S. (1986). *The 25 hour woman.* Old Tappan, NJ: F. H. Revell.

Stauffer, R. G. (1969a). *Directing reading maturity as a cognitive process.* New York: Harper & Row.

Stauffer, R. G. (1969b). *Teaching reading as a thinking process.* New York: Harper & Row.

Steen, P. (1991). Book diaries: Connecting free reading with instruction, home and school, and kids with books. *The Reading Teacher, 45*, 330–333.

Steffenson, M. S., Joag-Des, C., & Anderson, R. C. (1979). A cross-cultural perspective on reading comprehension. *Reading Research Quarterly, 15*, 10–29.

Sternberg, R. J. (1985, November). Teaching critical thinking: 1. Are we making critical mistakes? *Phi Delta Kappan*, pp. 194–198.

Sternberg, R. J. (1991). Are we reading too much into reading comprehension tests? *Journal of Reading, 34*, 540–545.

Sternberg, R. J., & Baron, J. B. (1985). A statewide approach to measuring critical thinking skills. *Educational Leadership, 43*, 40–43.

Stetson, E., & Williams, R. (1992). Learning from social studies textbooks: Why some students succeed and others fail. *Journal of Reading, 36*, 22–30.

Stevenson, H. W. (1992). A conversation with Harold Stevenson. *Humanities, 13*, 4–9.

Stone, C., & Day, M. (1978). Levels of ability of a formal operational strategy. *Child Development, 49,* 1054–1065.

Strahan, D. B. (1983). The emergence of formal reasoning during adolescence. *Transescence, 11,* 7–14.

Strauss, A. A., & Lehtinen, L. (1947). *Psychopathology and education in the brain-injured child* (Vol. 1). New York: Grune & Stratton.

Streeter, B. (1986). The effects of training experienced teachers in enthusiasm on students' attitudes toward reading. *Reading Psychology, 7*(4), 249–259.

Sturtevant, E. (1992). *Content literacy in high school social studies: Two case studies in a multicultural setting.* Unpublished doctoral dissertation, Kent State University, Kent, Ohio.

Taba, H. (1967). *Teacher's handbook for elementary social studies.* Reading, MA: Addison-Wesley.

Tadlock, D. R. (1978). SQ3R — Why it works, based on an information processing theory of learning. *Journal of Reading, 22,* 110–112.

Taylor, B. M., Frye, B. J., & Maruyama, G. M. (1990). Time spent reading and reading growth. *American Educational Research Journal, 27,* 351–362.

Taylor, W. (1953). Cloze procedure: A new tool for measuring readability. *Journalism Quarterly, 30,* 415–433.

Teale, W., & Sulzby, E. (1986). *Emergent literacy: Writing and reading.* Norwood, NJ: Albex.

Templeton, S. (1991). *Teaching integrated language arts.* Boston: Houghton Mifflin.

Thompson, G., & Morgan, R. (1976). The use of concept-formation study guides for social studies reading materials. *Reading Horizons, 7,* 132–136.

Thorndike, E. L. (1917). Reading and reasoning. *Journal of Educational Psychology, 8,* 323–332.

Thorndike, E. L. (1932). *Educational psychology.* New York: Columbia University, Teachers College Press.

Thurstone, L. L. (1946). A note on a re-analysis of Davis' reading tests. *Psychometrika, 11,* 185–188.

Toch, T. (1984, March 7). Bell calls on education to push publishers for better materials. *Education Week,* p. 11.

Tonjes, M. J., & Zintz, M. V. (1981). *Teaching reading/thinking study skills in content classrooms.* Dubuque, IA: Brown.

Torgensen, J., & Licht, B. (1983). The learning disabled child as an inactive learner: Retrospect and prospects. In J. McKinney & L. Feagans (Eds.), *Current topics in learning disabilities* (Vol. 1, pp. 3–31). Norwood, NJ: Ablex.

Twenty-fourth yearbook of the national society of the study for education (1925). Bloomington, IL: Public School Publishing Company.

Unks, G. (1985). Critical thinking in the social studies classroom. *Social Education, 44,* 240–246.

Vacca, R., & Vacca, J. (1989). *Content area reading.* Glenview, IL: Scott, Foresman.

Vacca, R. T., & Padak, N. (1990). Who's at risk in reading? *Journal of Reading, 33,* 486–488.

Valeri-Gold, M. (1987). Previewing: A directed reading-thinking activity. *Reading Horizons, 27,* 123–126.

Vanderventer, N. (1979, Winter). RAFT: A process to structure prewriting. *Highway One: A Canadian Journal of Language Experience, 26.*

Vaughan, C. L. (1990). Knitting writing: The double-entry journal. In N. Atwell (Ed.), *Coming to know: Writing to learn in the intermediate grades* (pp. 69–75). Portsmouth, NH: Heinemann.

Vaughan, J., & Estes, T. (1986). *Reading and reasoning beyond the primary grades.* Boston: Allyn and Bacon.

Veatch, J. (1968). *How to teach reading with children's books.* New York: Citation Press.

Vess, L. (1985). *Designing a test.* Unpublished paper from a course assignment on reading in the content areas, Virginia Commonwealth University, Richmond.

Vygotsky, L. (1978a). Interaction between learning and development. In M. Cole, V. John-Steiner, S. Scribner, & E. Souberman (Eds.), *Mind in society: The development of higher psychological process* (pp. 79–91). Cambridge, MA: Harvard University Press.

Vygotsky, L. (1978b). The prehistory of written language. In M. Cole, V. John-Steiner, S. Scribner, & E. Souberman (Eds.), *Mind in society: The development of higher psychological process* (pp. 105–119). Cambridge, MA: Harvard University Press.

Wade, S. E., & Adams, R. B. (1990). Effects of importance and interest on recall of biographical text. *Journal of Reading Behavior, 22,* 331–353.

Walberg, H. J., & Tsai, S. (1985). Correlates of reading achievement and attitude: A national assessment study. *Journal of Educational Research, 78,* 159–167.

Walker, B. J. (1990). *Remedial reading.* Washington, DC: National Education Association.

Walker, J. (1985). Requiem for readability. *Reading Today, 3,* 13.

Walpole, P. (1987). Yes, writing in math. In J. Self (Ed.), *Plain talk about learning and writing across the curriculum* (pp. 51–59). Richmond: Virginia State Department of Education.

Wassermann, S. (1987). Teaching for thinking: Louis E. Raths revisited. *Phi Delta Kappan, 68,* 460–466.

Wehlange, G. G., & Rutter, R. A. (1986). Dropping out: How much do schools contribute to the problem? *Teachers College Record, 87,* 374–392.

Weiner, B. (1979). A theory of motivation for some classroom experiences. *Journal of Educational Psychology, 71,* 3–25.

Weinstein, C. E. (1987). Fostering learning autonomy through the use of learning strategies. *Journal of Reading, 30,* 590–595.

Weinstein, C. E., & Mayer, R. E. (1986). The teaching of learning strategies. In M. C. Wittrock (Ed.), *Handbook of research on teaching* (3rd ed., pp. 315–327). New York: Macmillan.

Wertsch, J. V. (1978). Adult-child interaction and the roots of metacognition. *The Quarterly Newsletter of the Institute of Comparative Human Development, 2,* 15–18.

Westbury, I. (1992). Comparing American and Japanese achievement: Is the United States really a low achiever? *Educational Researcher, 21,* 18–24.

White, E. B. (1951). Calculating machine. In *The second tree from the corner* (pp. 165–167). New York: Harper & Row.

White, E. E. (1886). *The elements of pedagogy.* New York: American Book Company.

Wigfield, A., & Asher, S. R. (1984). Social and motivational influences on reading. In P. D. Pearson (Ed.), *Handbook of reading research.* New York: Longman.

Wigfield, A., & Asher, S. R. (1986). Students' thought processes. In M. C. Wittrock (Ed.), *Handbook of research on teaching.* New York: Macmillan.

Wiggins, G. (1990, August). A conversation with Grant Wiggins. *Instructor,* p. 51.

Wigginton, E. (1986). *Sometimes a shining moment: The Foxfire experience.* New York: Anchor/Doubleday.

Williams, C. K. (1973). *The differential effects of structured overviews, level guides, and organizational pattern guides upon the reading comprehension of twelfth-grade students.* Unpublished doctoral dissertation, State University of New York at Buffalo.

Williams, J., Taylor, M. B., & Ganger, B. (1981). Text variations at the level of the individual sentence and the comprehension of simple expository paragraphs. *Journal of Educational Psychology, 73,* 851–865.

Wilson, M. (1988). How can we teach reading in the content areas? In C. Weaver (Ed.), *Reading process and practice: From sociopsycholinguistics to whole language.* Portsmouth, NH: Heinemann.

Wilson, R. M., & Gambrell, L. B. (1988). *Reading comprehension in the elementary school.* Boston: Allyn and Bacon.

Window on the classroom: A look at teachers' tests (1984). *Captrends, 10,* 1–3.

Winograd, P. (1984). Strategic difficulties in summarizing texts. *Reading Research Quarterly, 19,* 404–425.

Winograd, P., & Paris, S. (1988). A cognitive and motivational agenda for reading instruction. *Educational Leadership, 46,* 30–36.

Wittrock, M. D., Marks, C., & Doctorow, M. (1975). Reading as a generative process. *Journal of Educational Psychology, 67,* 481–489.

Wolfe, D., & Reising, R. (1983). *Writing for learning in the content areas.* Portland, ME: J. Weston Walch.

Wood, J. W. (1987). A model for adapting the teacher-made test. *Statewide Institutes for Adapting Instruction for Regular Teachers* (Project TRAIN). Richmond, VA: Virginia Commonwealth University.

Wood, J. W., & Miederhoff, J. (1988). Adapting test construction for mainstreamed language arts students. Unpublished paper, Virginia Commonwealth University.

Wood, K. D. (1987). Fostering cooperative learning in middle and secondary level classrooms. *Journal of Reading, 31,* 10–18.

Wood, K. D. (1992). Fostering collaborative reading and writing experiences in mathematics. *Journal of Reading, 36,* 96–103.

Wood, K. D., Lapp, D., & Flood, J. (1992). *Guiding readers through text: A review of study guides.* Newark, DE: International Reading Association.

Woodward, A., Elliott, D. L., & Nagel, K. C. (1986). Beyond textbooks in elementary social studies. *Social Education, 50,* 50–53.

Worthen, B. (1993). Critical decisions that will determine the future of alternative assessment. *Phi Delta Kappan, 74,* 444–456.

The writing report card: Writing achievement in American schools. (1987). Princeton, NJ: The National Assessment of Educational Progress and the Educational Testing Center.

Yeager, D. (1991). *The whole language companion.* Glenview, IL: Goodyear.

Yochum, N. (1991). Children's learning from informational text: The relationship between prior knowledge and text structure. *Journal of Reading Behavior, 23,* 87–108.

Zakaluk, B., & Klassen, M. (1992). Enhancing the performance of a high school student labeled learning disabled. *Journal of Reading, 36,* 4–9.

Zaragoza, N. (1987). Process writing for high-risk learning disabled students. *Reading Research and Instruction, 26,* 290–301.

Zuber, B. L., & Wetzel, P. A. (1981). Eye movement determinants of reading rate. In B. L. Zuber (Ed.), *Models of oculomotor behavior and control* (pp. 193–208). Boca Raton, FL: CRC Press.

PAR Diagram, p. 9, Dawn Watson and Walter Richards, Chesterfield County Schools

"1-Meter Fun Run," p. 21, Robert Davis

Biology Interest Inventory, Activity 2.5, p. 54, Terri Kilmer, Henrico County Schools

Bader Textbook Analysis Chart, Figure 3.1, pp. 77–79, Dr. Lois Bader, Michigan State University

Mathematics Multitext Activity 3.1, p. 88; Mathematics Graphic Organizer, Activity 3.5, p. 95; Geometry Organizer, Activity 6.21, pp. 235–236, Frances Reid, King William County Schools

Written Preview, Activity 3.4, p. 93; TRIP Cards, Activity 6.18, p. 223, Carol Homes, Richmond City Schools

English Graphic Organizer, Activity 3.7, p. 97; English Self-Inventory, Activity 4.9, p. 127, Rebecca McSweeney

Science Graphic Organizer, Activity 3.8, p. 98; Stages in the Writing Process/Science, Activity 8.5, p. 303, Kathryn Davis, Edward T. Rabbitt Bookstore

Science Pre-Guiding Questions, Activity 3.9, p. 99, Tom Fleming, King William County Schools

Music Anticipation Guide, Activity 4.1, p. 110; Textbook Analysis Checklist, Appendix C, Todd Barnes, Northumberland County Schools

Prior Knowledge Telegram, p. 113, Grace Hamlin

Science Clozure, Activity 4.2, pp. 118–119, Carol B. Forkey, Goochland County Schools

Science Recognition Pretest, Activity 4.5, p. 123; Science Three-Level Guide, p. 185, Holly Corbett, Henrico County Schools

Keyboarding Recognition Pretest, Activity 4.6, pp. 124–125; Computer Map, Activity 5.2, p. 162, Pamela Lundy, Petersburg City Schools

Mathematics Self-Inventory, Activity 4.7, p. 126, Sherry Gott

Health Self-Inventory, Activity 4.8, p. 126; Health Analogy, Activity 4.18, p. 137, Kathy Feltus, Chesterfield County Schools

Mathematics PreP Example, Activity 4.10, p. 128, Nancy Campbell, Hanover County Schools

Science What-I-Know (WIK), Activity 4.11, p. 130, Marcie Mansfield, Henrico County Schools

English What-I-Know (WIK), Activity 4.12, p. 130, Leslie Tucker

Geography Prediction Guide, Activity 4.14, p. 133; Math Theater, p. 391, Mark Forget

Auto Technology Anticipation Guide, Activity 4.15, p. 134, Steve Boykin, Newport News Schools

Art Anticipation Guide, Activity 4.16, p. 134, Joan Phipps, Richmond City Schools

Anticipation Guide Acrostic, Figure 4.1, p. 135; Story Jot Chart, Activity 6.16, p. 221, Linda Cobb, Richmond City Schools

English Modified Anticipation Guide, Activity 4.17, p. 135, Robert Witherow, Hopewell City Schools

Primary Mathematics Analogy, pp. 136–137; Fact or Opinion: Energy, Activity 6.11, p. 215, Laura Allin, Henrico County Schools

Whale of Tale Mathematics Problems, Activity 4.19, p. 139, Janet Daingerfield, Sandra Davis, and Harriet Glass, Petersburg City Schools

Social Studies Inventory of Skills, Activity 4.22, p. 145, Margaret McKenzie, Hanover County Schools

Mathematics Inventory of Skills, Activity 4.23, p. 145, Dana Walker, Hanover County Schools

Readability in Action: Health Text Example, p. 146, Lyle Wieber, Richmond City Schools

Readability in Action: Science Text Example, p. 146, Barbara McCoy, Carolyn Powell, and Carrie Thompkins, Richmond City Schools

Readability in Action, Social Studies Example, pp. 146–147; Books About the Middle Ages, Appendix G, pp. 490–495, Wanda Hill, Louisa County Schools

Readability in Action, Mathematics Text Example, p. 147; Algebra Jot Chart, Activity 6.15, p. 220, Serena Marshall

Map of MacBeth, Activity 5.1, p. 161, Vicki Ford, Henrico County Schools

DRTA in Social Studies, Activity 5.4, pp. 165–166, Faye Freeman, Virginia Beach Schools

DRTA in English, Activity 5.5, pp. 167–168; Guided Writing: Limericks, Activity 8.14, pp. 316–317, Frances Lively, Henrico County Schools

Mitosis Mystery Clue Game, Activity 5.6, p. 173, Greg Perry, Peace Corps, and Sharon Charles, The Collegiate School

Mystery Clue Game: The Sumerians, Activity 5.7, pp. 174–175, Deborah Fleisher, Henrico County Schools

Cause/Effect Study Guide, Activity 5.10, p. 178, Linda Love, Virginia Beach Schools

Compare/Contrast Guide, Activity 5.11, p. 179, Vicki Douglas, Henrico County Schools

Three Level Guide for Home Economics, Activity 5.17, p. 187, Ava Brendle

QAR for Mathematics, Activity 5.19, pp. 192–193, Mary Frances Siewert, Henrico County Schools

Anticipation Guide for Fractions, Activity 5.19, p. 195, Dawn Watson, Chesterfield County Schools

Group and Label, Activity 6.7, p. 212, Gail Perrer, King William County Schools

Reading a Pattern Guide: Jot Chart, Activity 6.14, p. 219, Frances Lila Mait, Hanover County Schools

Homework Comprehension Sheet, Activity 6.20, p. 227, Charles Carroll, International School, Yan Goon

Example Test Comments: p. 230, Jane Baxter, Chesterfield County Schools; Linda Vess, Chesterfield County Schools; Julie Givler, Hanover County Schools

Social Studies Graphic Organizer, Activity 6.22, p. 237, Sandra Zeller and Brenda Winston, Henrico County Schools

Concept Map: Rivers, Activity 7.7, p. 263, Diane Buchanan, Norfolk City Schools

Magic Squares: French, Activity 7.20, p. 280, Billie Anne Baker, Henrico County Schools (retired)

Cinquain: Social Studies, Activity 7.23, p. 282, Anne Forrester, Chesapeake City Schools

Cinquain: Science, Activity 7.24, p. 282, Sharon Gray, Virginia Beach Schools

Vocabulary Illustrations, Activity 7.25, pp. 283–284; Prediction Guide: The Sniper, Activity 12.7, p. 446, Joe Antinarella, Tidewater Community College

Bingo Game/Science, Activity 7.26, p. 285, Patricia Russell, Department of Defense Schools

Writing Examples, Figure 8.1, pp. 292–293, Andrew Pettit, student at Byrd Middle School, Henrico County

Cubing Mathematics, Activity 8.3, p. 301, Debbie Prout, Henrico County Schools

Flat Cube for Social Studies, Activity 8.4, p. 301, Mary Jane McKay, The Governor's School

Using Journals in Vocational Education, p. 305, Sheryl Lam, Hanover County Schools

Math Top It Off, Activity 8.9, p. 311, Connie Bachman, Henrico County Schools

Story of a Blood Cell, Activity 8.10, p. 312, Jon Morgan, student at Kemps Landing Middle School, Virginia Beach Schools

Biopoem, Activity 8.12, p. 313, M. J. Weatherford, Henrico County Schools

What I Learned, Activity 8. 13, p. 313, Anne Miller, Henrico County Schools, and Melvin Harris, Goochland County Schools

Writing Checklist, Activity 8.17, p. 321, Diane Duncan, Hanover County Schools

The Earth, Activity 8.20, p. 236, Nakeisha Bailey, Richmond City Schools

Writing to Learn Example, Activity 8.20, p. 326, Sharon Bynam-Saunders, Richmond City Schools

Study Skills Surveys, Activity 9.2, p. 338, Cornelia Hill, West Point Schools

Interpreting a Political Cartoon, Activity 9.7, p. 343, Roberto Lianez, student at Norview High School, Norfolk

Notetaking: Cause/Effect Pattern Guide, Activity 9.13, p. 361, Patricia May Mulherin, Chesterfield County Schools

Weekly Progress Report, Activity 10.1, p. 377; Home Reader Report, Activity 10.2, p. 377; Homework Assignment: Kindergarten, Activity 10.3, p. 378, Georgette Kavanaugh, Norfolk City Schools

Interactive Reading Guide: Mathematics, Activity 10.13, p. 392, Cheryl Haley, Norfolk City Schools

Encouraging Home Reading in Science, Activity 12.3, pp. 435–437, Kelly Taylor, Henrico County Schools

Unit Plan: Call of the Wild, Activity 12.4, p. 440, Beth Pallister, Virginia Beach Schools

Unit Plan: Cleaning up the Chesapeake Bay, Activity 12.5, pp. 441–442, teachers at Norview High School, Norfolk City Schools

Unit Plan: The Journey of Lewis & Clark, Activity 12.6, pp. 443–444, Elise Harrison, Hampton City Schools

Remarks, pp. 447–450, Brian Kane, Chesterfield County Schools

Bader Textbook Checklist, Appendix C: English, pp. 463–464, Adrienne Gillis, Hanover County Schools

A Model for Constructing Tests with Mainstreamed Students in Mind, pp. 469–473, Dr. Judy Wood, Virginia Commonwealth University

Counting and Number Books, pp. 484–487; Children's Trade Books in Science, pp. 487–488, Dr. Dorothy Giroux, Loyola University

Annotated Bibliography of Multicultural Literature, pp. 496–501, Mary Driebe, Henrico County Schools

List of Periodicals That Review Children's Literature, p. 502, Linda Baughman

Virginia Beach in a Box, Social Studies Unit, pp. 504–515, Barbara Teuscher, Virginia Beach Schools

GRADE LEVEL	SCIENCE	MATH
Primary	PAR Example 2 (pp. 12–16) Activity 1.4 Graphic Organizer (p. 15) Activity 3.8 Graphic Organizer (p. 98) Activity 4.11 What-I-Know (WIK)/KWL (p. 130) Activity 4.13 Anticipation Guide (p. 132) Activity 8.5 Guided Writing (p. 303) Activity 8.20 Writing Example (p. 326) Activity 10.4 Student Log (p. 379) Activity 10.15 First Step to Notetaking (p. 396) Activity 12.3 Encouraging Home Reading (pp. 435–437) Appendix G List of Tradebooks (pp. 487–488)	Activity 3.3 Preview (p. 92) Activity 4.20 Wiebe-Cox Inventory (p. 142) Analogy Example (pp. 136–137) Activity 8.3 Cubing (p. 301) Appendix G List of Tradebooks (pp. 484–487)
Intermediate	GATOR Example (p. 59) Readability in Action (p. 146) Activity 6.11 Fact-Opinion (p. 215) Activity 6.13 Jot Chart (p. 218) Activity 7.1 Metamorphosis (p. 254) Activity 7.4 Classification Exercise (p. 257) Activity 7.6 Semantic Map (p. 262) Activity 7.8 Network Diagram, Dinosaur (p. 264) Activity 7.18 Word Analogies (p. 279) Activity 8.10 Story about Blood Cells (p. 312) Activity 10.4 Life in the Ocean (p. 379) First Person Summary Example (p. 385) Activity 11.4 Concept Formation Guide (p. 423)	Activity 4.10 PreP (p. 128) Activity 4.19 Whale of a Tale (p. 139) Free Rides (p. 200) Activity 6.3 Decision-Making Model (p. 209) Activity 7.2 Concept Learning (p. 256) Writing Example (p. 302) Activity 10.9 ABOUT/POINT (p. 385) Activity 10.12 Record Sheet (p. 390) Activity 11.1 Group Frame Example (p. 412) Activity 11. 2 Fix-Up Strategy (p. 420)
Middle	Activity 4.2 Cloze (pp. 118–119) Activity 4.5 Recognition Pretest (p. 123) Activity 5.3 Table of Contents Map (p. 163) Activity 5.15 Three-Level Guide (p. 185) Activity 7.9 Cloze (p. 264) Activity 8.13 What I Learned (p. 313) Activity 9.5 Reading Air-Pressure Map (p. 341) Read Aloud Example (pp. 438–439)	Activity 4.7 Self-Inventory (p. 126) Activity 4.23 Math Inventory (p. 145) Activity 5.19 QAR (pp. 191–192) Activity 5.20 Anticipation Guide (p. 195) Activity 6.15 Jot Chart (p. 220) Activity 8.9 Top It Off! (p. 311) Read Aloud Example (p. 439)
Secondary	Activity 2.5 Biology Interest Inventory (p. 54) Activity 3.9 PreGuiding Questions (p. 99) Activity 5.6 Mystery Clue Game (p. 173) Activity 5.9 Cause-Effect Guide (p. 177) Example Test Comments (p. 230) Activity 7.12 Interactive Cloze (p. 271) Activity 7.19 Biology Analogies (p. 279) Activity 7.24 Cinquain (p. 282) Activity 7.24 Bingo (p. 285) Activity 11.3 Word Recognition Exercise (p. 422)	Activity 3.1 Multitext (p. 88) Activity 3.5 Geometry Overview (p. 95) Readability in Action (p. 147) Activity 5.14 Three-Level Guide (p. 184) Activity 6.6 Group and Label (p. 211) Activity 6.21 Graphic Organizer (pp. 235–236) Math Theater (pp. 391–392) Activity 10.13 Interactive Reading Guide (p. 392) Activity 10.14 Cooperative Graphing (p. 394)

SOCIAL STUDIES | ENGLISH/LANGUAGE ARTS | OTHER